Letter to E. Samios (Helen Kazantzakis), Autumn, 1924. See page 117.

NIKOS KAZANTZAKIS

A BIOGRAPHY BASED ON HIS LETTERS

by HELEN KAZANTZAKIS

TRANSLATED BY AMY MIMS

SIMON AND SCHUSTER · NEW YORK

FIRST PRINTING

LIBRARY OF CONGRESS CATALOG CARD NUMBER: 68–14840
DESIGNED BY EDITH FOWLER
MANUFACTURED IN THE UNITED STATES OF AMERICA
BY AMERICAN BOOK–STRATFORD PRESS, INC.

NOTE

Throughout this book Greek names have been transliterated rather than given English equivalents. Hence, Helen Kazantzakis is rendered as Eleni Kazantzaki. Until her marriage with NK she is referred to by her maiden name, Eleni Samios.

ACKNOWLEDGMENTS

I would like, first of all, to thank those friends who were kind enough to let me quote from letters in their possession; together, they have made it possible for me to evoke the memory of Nikos Kazantzakis. Without their help I could not have begun my task.

I would particularly like to thank:
——Mmes. Anestasia Saklabanis and Eleni Theodossiadis (Nikos Kazantzakis' sisters) and their children;
——Rahel Minc, Elsa Lange, Leah Dunkelblum, Edvige Gunalakis, Marguerite Panaït Istrati, Anna Angelos Sikelianos, Téa Anémoyanni and Marika Papaioannou-Hormouziou;
——Iannis Angélakis, Iannis Konstantarakis, Iannis Kakridis, Börje Knös, Stamos Diamantaras, Renaud de Jouvenel and Max Tau;
——Messrs. Papadaki and Tzordzaki, who saved from destruction Nikos Kazantzakis' letters to his childhood friend H. Stephanidis;
——Pandelis Prevelakis, who helped us by editing and annotating the four hundred letters of Nikos Kazantzakis in his possession, and whose chronology of the life of Nikos Kazantzakis is of inestimable value to every scholar.

I would also like to thank the following friends and colleagues for their help:
——Jean Herbert, who was good enough to read my original manuscript and to give me the benefit of his advice;
——Amy Mims, who not only translated my text into English, but helped to check and annotate many hundreds of letters in three languages;
——George Hill, of Bruno Cassirer, Ltd., Oxford, England; Marcel Jullian, of Librairie Plon, Paris; and, most particularly, Michael V. Korda, the young Executive Editor of Simon and Schuster, without whose understanding, patience and confidence I should never have been able to complete this book.

May this work, based on one man's life and death, inspire young people to follow their hopes, even in despair. To them, I dedicate this book.

E. K.

Geneva, 1967

AMITIÉ DU PRINCE

Et je te dis encore ceci: Homme-très-attrayant, o Sans-coutume-parmi-nous, o Dissident! une chose est certaine, que nous portons le sceau de ton regard; et un très grand besoin de toi nous tient aux lieux où tu respires, et de plus grand bien-être qu'avec toi nous n'en connaissons point . . . Tu peux te taire parmi nous, si c'est là ton humeur; ou décider encore que tu vas seul, si c'est là ton humeur; on ne te demande que t'être là! (Et maintenant tu sais quelle est ta race) . . .

FRIENDSHIP OF THE PRINCE

And this also I tell you: Man-who-attracts, O Without-conformity-among-us, O Dissenter! one thing is certain, that we all wear the seal of your gaze; and a very great need of you keeps us in the place where you breathe, and a greater contentment than being with you we do not know . . . You may be silent among us, if that is your humour; or decide to go alone, if that is your humour; we ask nothing but to be there! (And now you know what race is your race) . . .

> —SAINT-JOHN PERSE, *Eloges and Other Poems*,
> translated by Louise Varèse (New York:
> Pantheon Books [Bollingen Series LV],
> 1956)

9

PROLOGUE

BY WAY OF A PREFACE

Bent over your notebooks and your letters, my Nikos, I am struggling to crystallize your many-faceted image—so precise and yet so elusive—for those who love you through your books. From what angle can I evoke you without betraying you? Everything you preached, everything you longed for, everything you were, I rediscover in these papers that have already turned yellow, crackling like a fine film of ice on an autumn pond. Long silences broken only by the rhythmic puffing on your pipe; voluble monologues in the company of those you loved; your extraordinary gift for unlocking the most tightly shut souls, for acting as confessor to friends, to friends of our friends, even to people met by chance in the anonymous streets, even to those village idiots whom no one but you could get to express themselves.

You went out to buy the newspaper or post a letter, and came back to me loaded like a mailman, your sack full of tales. I would take the same path, meet the same faces, but return empty-handed. And when you were riveted to your worktable, your hand poised in the air, still armed with its pencil, it was you who would tell me something to make me laugh.

Unity and clarity in the depths of the waters, remaining always calm, even if the storm ruffled their surface, even if for a passing moment your face might become contorted, your voice hoarse.

How can I manipulate the words, how stretch them, fit them, make them supple and obedient, cram tenderness and harshness into them without their exploding, and so find a way of making them capable of embracing you?

"When I die, you will write a book about me . . ."

"No, no, no! That would require a writer of talent."

"You will write a book about me, Lenotschka! You will do it. For they will say so many inaccurate things. And you are the only person who knows me well!"

How often I swore I would not do it. And then?

And then, I would never have done it—or, to tell the whole truth, I would have abandoned the task halfway through—had I not found one night among the scrap papers a bit of your handwriting, hastily scribbled in pencil. It was the first draft of an outline for my book.

And so here I am, put to the test. Not to construct a novel; that I could do and even with ease. To describe you, to squeeze you and pin you down with a gold needle, as if I were pinning a butterfly. And all the while I am rebelling against it. For I love butterflies, and I like to imagine them fluttering above my head, defying capture.

PART ONE

THE SEED

1883–1923

B ETWEEN two nights, as though between a pair of hooks, hang suspended thirty-three years of light. The first had been a night only in name. The earth reflected the moon and the moon the blueish rose of dawn. We walked over a pewter mirror barely marked by a few age-old symbols: thyme, cypress, masticha trees, thorns.

The last night, the night of death—no man has yet been born who could ever describe it. Death, the dying man, the being at the point of death, immortality of the soul, eternal recurrence—the disheartening litany of dead words fermented by death, whose inviolable secret only death itself possesses.

What exactly did death mean to the heart still beating? What words did the final silence embrace? What was said by the motionless eye refusing pity? Despair? Supreme Felicity? The only one who has a right to answer—our dead one himself—is silent, and we are left to penetrate his silence.

In order to give flesh and blood to the beloved Shade, I must move upstream like a carp. No, not like a carp. Like an old fisherman ascending to the source, leaping from steep rock to steep rock and from stone to stone. He slips, gets up, lingers, bends down, scoops a little water into the palm of his hand, quenches his thirst, departs in silence. The rocks and stones will serve me as calendar and landmarks: Here, in the year nineteen hundred and . . . There, while we were living on top of a mountain . . .

A hard stone, thousands of flames emanating from him. Some people saw him as red in hue; others saw him as white or yellow or violet. They thought him "fluid"; he remained a hard stone. As easy to decipher as an alphabet, provided that the alphabet is an easy book.

A, b, c . . . Once upon a time . . .

Once upon a time, far far away in the north, in a land where the sun is corroded with mold, there was a lonely man of boundless aspirations, who had seen or thought he had seen a burro: "A fellow countryman! Ah for the honey-soaked figs!"

On fire, his glance veiled, this man had been roaming the streets of Berlin, branding on his flesh the demented acts of a people debased by defeat. He heard from afar the call of Lenin. He was hoping to be able to throw his pen into the river after all the mothers who had plunged into it before him. He was hoping to learn some manual trade and run off to join the army of the just. And precisely at this point, a tiny donkey, a four-footed countryman, made him turn in the opposite direction. "And here I am packing my books in my suitcases and shaking the hands of my flabbergasted friends. 'Auf wiedersehen! Auf wiedersehen!' The figs are beckoning me to Greece."

He did not like Athens or its cafés and the interminable chatter that dissipates the spirit and drains one's rightful anger. But thank God, he had "his Crete," and he also had the Greek people, who in his eyes made up for all the rest, and who, despite the pedantic Phanariots* and the emancipated University of Athens, had succeeded in forging a supple tongue, capable of expressing the inexpressible. Even if one already had an aim in life, it was worth sacrificing it for this language. "Ah yes, what was that word I just discovered in a Cypriot song? 'The lady-in-a-long-cloak—makromantóussa . . . ah, makromantóussa kéra.' And that other one in the Cretan song? 'Kroufopahiá'—a lady-who-is-pretty-fleshy-despite-her-deceptive-appearance; a lady pseudo-thin— 'kroufopahiá . . .' How delicious!"

And now my story begins, on the eighteenth of May, 1924, when I met this man who was to give up everything in the name of the modern Greek language and freedom.

Well before Nikos Kazantzakis' return to Greece in the month of May 1924, I had met his wife Galatea. Two years his senior, graced with a beautiful head and the gift of lively repartee, she reigned over a small group of acolytes—writers, literary critics, artists of every kind, who shared her political sympathies and aversions. A writer—she wrote with amazing facility and in several genres—she was much appreciated by

---

* The Phanariots, the erudite Greeks of Constantinople who fabricated a purist language.

the Greek left wing. Separated from Nikos for several years now, independent and proud, she was already living side by side with a fine companion, whom she was to marry after 1926. But—there was an imponderable *but*, which no one has ever elucidated—why did Nikos Kazantzakis keep returning to a roost that only held new troubles in store for him? For what hidden reason was the intelligent Galatea incapable of liberating herself from him? And what complex compelled her up to the end of her life to speak constantly of him, to make him the object of suspicion and antipathy among those who did not know him, and to chide whosoever dared to speak ill of him in her presence?

Having witnessed this game on many occasions, I preferred to decline Galatea's invitation that day to go to the station with their friends and welcome Nikos Kazantzakis back from Germany.

And now he was there. From Dexameni* utterly fantastic rumors spread through the city: "His laugh rings like a bell!" "He has a giant's appetite." "He eats nothing; he's a real ascetic." "He flirts with the ladies." The most contradictory stories were traveling from mouth to mouth. My friends, Ketty and Marika,† left me no peace. To hear them, it was impossible to get along without him. He was tall, handsome, marvelous. And worst of all, he never stayed put. One fine morning he'd just take off. And that would mean losing my one chance of coming face to face with a great man.

That night we were to cross Mount Pendeli, arriving at the seashore at dawn—an organized excursion, twenty enthusiasts, young and old, "nature-lovers." To add zest to our hiking exploits, we used to flourish a shepherd's crook from Parnassus, or a long heavy stick. We all met at the station of the "Monster," as we used to call the miniature steam engine which would land us in Maroussi at the foot of Pendeli.

The moon had just risen when I saw him coming, with his long, slightly skipping stride. Straight as a cypress tree, deep-set eyes looking black beneath shaggy eyebrows, an immense forehead, delicate, well-shaped ears. He wore a wide straw hat and was carrying a pink jar full of sardines floating in vinegar sauce. "There's nothing like them for excursions," explained Galatea, as she followed our amused glance.

I no longer remember his first words. The two deep hollows furrowing his face, however, did impress me.

---

* The fashionable quarter high up over the city, where the reservoir was and the Kazantzakis' home.
† The Papaioannou sisters; both excellent pianists.

Among all the young girls present that day, why did he choose me? Did he himself know why? In the semidarkness of the train, he immediately began plying me with the questions I often used to hear him ask later on:

"What writer do you like best? What has been your greatest joy? What is your favorite color?"

I must have said it was Maeterlinck, for two days later, on the occasion of my name day, he presented me with a little volume of Maeterlinck's, bound in almond-green suede. On the frontispiece he had traced the palm of my hand and its lines, which he had amused himself in reading while we were roasting on the sand at Rafina. He destroyed this page several years afterward, without ever giving me a satisfactory explanation.

The way he appeared to me that first day is the way he remained all through his life. Full of contradictions, yet always moving along the same path, without compromise, humble and demanding, hospitable and solitary; loving luxury because it had enabled great artists to flourish; execrating the rich who yielded nothing to the poor; living like an ascetic because he could not preach one thing and do another.

"Nikosmou, Nikosmou,"* I would sometimes complain. "Won't we two ever be entitled to a bit of comfort—to a trip in first class?"

Laughter in his eyes and his mouth teasing, he used to answer: "Are you forgetting, my love, that we're privileged people? What would Schweitzer do in our place? Wouldn't he choose fourth class? And wouldn't he tell you that the person who seeks comfort is selling his soul to the devil?"

A mystic poet and visionary—"Dreams," he used to say, "have played a great role in my life and work"—he struggled desperately to get out of his own skin and become another being, a political leader. But that other being, in a latent state in his vitals, never reached the point of hatching.

"Thálatta! Thálatta!"

In the twinkling of an eye, the nocturnal rovers were metamorphosed into tritons and naiads. I capered like them, flinging my dusty sandals off.

---

* "My Nikos."

"Are you going bathing with all these people? And suppose you were to stay with me?"

"Once upon a time . . ."

I didn't know either the *Black Decameron* of Frobenius or *The Annunciation Made to Mary* or "The Graveyard by the Sea" or anything at all. I didn't even have much idea of what was going on in the U.S.S.R. One single sentence uttered by my father,* a peace-loving bourgeois, had been engraved in my mind: "My children, I believe that a new Christ has been born in Russia!" Without my knowing it, perhaps a few drops of my maternal grandfather's blood†—he had been a rugged mountaineer, a doctor-poet and active patriot—flowed in my veins.

"The sun will roast us," I countered obstinately. "The sea is so cool."

"The sea demands solitude and withdrawal," he murmured pensively. Then, straightening his chest like a fakir seated on coals, he said: "I'm an African, I love the sun! It's about you, my frail Athenian, we have to think."

He moved slightly, so as to shelter me with his shadow, thereafter stirring only with the sun. "Once upon a time . . ."

His words proved as refreshing as the waves, for they made me forget my wild longing for the sea.

From that time on, he insisted on our meeting every day. When I couldn't go up to dine with him and his friends at the modest *taverna* run by an old Cretan at the foot of Lycabettos, he used to come down to bring me some book or write me to make an appointment for the next day.

On Sundays and public holidays we would visit the Byzantine chapels or some abandoned monastery that he dreamed of acquiring and turning into a coenobium, where he could live with other artists. "We'll work during the day and prattle by night," he used to say dreamily. "That would be marvelous. Provided that the government decides to let

---

* Constantine Samios, a high functionary, specialist in waters and forests; also wrote books.

† Theodore Aphenduli, professor of pharmacological subjects, rector of the University of Athens; he was married to a Cretan woman and participated in the struggles for the liberation of Crete.

21

me have it." Alone or in company with Sikelianos* he had knocked on the doors of the Ministries several times. The governments of Greece all made the same mistake. They were always deaf and blind in the presence of any worthwhile interlocutors.

We would set off empty-handed, lunching on a piece of bread, some fruit and a tomato. I was astonished by such frugality and even suffered from it. But I had to save face. There were compensations.

He had an innate elegance. He wore his badly tailored suits with ease. He had aristocratic ankles, tapering fingers, nails that any beautiful woman might have envied. He no longer wore a necktie, using a gold "Alexander" coin to fasten his shirt. He also wore an enormous Minoan ring and an old silver belt from Georgia. These were all the riches he had. And always in his hands immaculate white gloves and a miniature Dante, his "traveling companion." Toward the end of his life, he gave up gloves and ring. Dante alone remained at his bedside until his last breath.

He did not wear a mask. He practiced what he preached, and he preached what he wanted to do, burning the candle at both ends, excessively indulgent toward others, demanding the impossible from himself. In his letters, in his books, in his intimate life or in the midst of crowds, he remained always his own self, serene and incandescent at the same time, whether serious or laughing, with his weaknesses and his strength, indifferent to what people might say against him. People who approached him either adored or detested him. Some loved him and fled from him at the same time. "I didn't want to come to see you," the journalist G. N. wrote him. "You are my conscience and I prefer not to hear it!"

"Create an idealized image of yourself, and try to resemble it," he had counseled me ever since that first day. That was a fixed idea which he put in the mouth of almost all his heroes and which he himself practiced constantly.

KAPODISTRIAS (alone, knowing that he is about to be killed, looking out to sea):

For shame, my soul! Are you afraid? Rise up! Never forget that in the hidden recesses of your mind you have created a Kapodistrias

* Angelos Sikelianos, one of the greatest contemporary Greek poets. Sik. and N.K., though of utterly different natures, loved each other deeply.

*far better than yourself and you have vowed never to do any act
that might put him to shame.**

Also, Prometheus before the catastrophe.

PROMETHEUS:

*The greatest Prometheus I myself have molded—proud as I want
him; and he rushes forth, and I follow, struggling insofar as I am
able to follow in his tracks. The time will come when both of us
will become one!†*

Nikos Kazantzakis was not an angel, but a profoundly religious
nature, seeking God with determination, demanding that He be a just
and liberating God.

*I could have been a king in art, but I stretch out my hand—as one
might beg for alms—and seek God. Like the salamanders we have seen
in the zoo, I am all sound. Not only sound—I listen so profoundly that
I create the distant voice. Just as the whole body trembles, because it
does not know where the loved one will kiss it, just so my soul trembles
at the invisible kiss.‡*

"You like to travel," he said to me one day. "So why do you stay in
Athens? Here, even the bravest soul is in danger of foundering."

"And go where? What would my guardians say?"

"At the present moment the world is being forged in the U.S.S.R.
You'll have to learn some skill that will enable you to live in Moscow."
It was only a small step from there to imagining that fashion was also
avant-garde in Moscow. He blithely leaped to that conclusion. "I've got
it! You like pretty hats, eh? Well, you'll go to Moscow and learn to
make some!"

---

* Kapodistrias, the first governor of liberated Greece. He was assassinated in
church on the very day when he was about to fulfill his promise of distributing the national lands to the poor. N.K. wrote a tragedy in verse on the
subject.
† *Prometheus Bound*, from the verse trilogy by N.K.
‡ "Conversations with Rahel," Notebook for 1923.

Rarely did he let himself go like that. But when he did, he was the first to make fun of himself, and his laughter would resound like a carillon that could be heard for ten leagues roundabout.

He detested Athens, where there was no harmonious roost for him. After a strange malady in Vienna—described in *The Greek Passion* (Manolios with the "sexual mask") and in his *Report to Greco*—and after two years in Berlin, he now felt able to free himself from his old fetters.

On the fifth of July, 1924, Kazantzakis set off for Crete, having two diametrically opposed plans in mind: to meet the leaders of the Communist Party on his island and help them if possible with his own experience; and at the same time, to isolate himself and open the floodgates and let the waves of his Odyssey flow. Two days later he wrote me:

Heraklion, July 7

Liebe, liebe Genossin,*

The second Odysseus has returned to his fatherland, gazed upon the enormous head of the mountain† over the city where he was born, walked on the ancient road along the coast, and knocked once again upon the door of his paternal home. . . . The courtyard was full of basil, marjoram, and marigolds. Old "Laertes" had aged. His mother was kind, serene, taciturn, staring at the man-of-many-travels. How thin he'd grown, how sunken his temples, how broad and black his sun-baked, snow-blown brow!‡

And the second Odysseus, your companion in your evening strolls, Genossin, the person who took great delight in you, who talked a lot (and kept silence a lot), moved up and down the staircases of his paternal home. . . . Everything was the same—clean, simple, neat. The road seemed narrow to him. Everything seemed smaller and more simple. His father talked about the vineyards and the olive groves, his mother about his life abroad. . . . What sort of time he'd had in foreign lands, among foreign people and foreign women; why he'd grown thin, what were his worries; when would he stop? . . . The relatives began arriving; the fat, fat female cousins (provincially fat);

---

* "Dear, dear Comrade," a form of address used frequently in the letters.
† Mount Youhtas, shaped like a man's head.
‡ The Greek language allows the formation of adjectives composed of several words.

the male cousins, fat millionaires . . . a gulf between us, staring at me as at some strange, incomprehensible fruit off the tree of their kin; my young nephews avaricious, silent, drinking it all in, staring, storing up in order that after decades (perhaps never) they might understand their traveled, black, ascetic uncle.

I come and go inside my father's home, quietly reveling in the bitterness of the things I used to love and which are far removed from me now. I think of Berlin, the fever of human agony there, the terrifying Jewish Analaya Toubari,* my cruel duty to reject my father and mother, to separate from them and take my stand contrary to their morality, religion, social prejudices, economic endeavors. Yesterday evening I talked to my father a little about Bolshevism. He got all heated, then silent, then he got up and went off to his own room. There is no greater expression of his rage.

Liebe, liebe Genossin, God willing, I shall always part from the persons and things I love with difficulty. I wander through Heraklion, gazing on the familiar steel-blue sea, the sun-beaten mountains, the white soil, the stones, the plants, the old familiar doors, the unfamiliar young girls, and the girls who were my friends and have aged; I feel as though I were living in some old dream, as though I were looking through deep, translucent waters at a sunken city I once knew.

My old uncles ask me about England, France, politics; if there's going to be a war; who will win . . . A young cousin asks me in what branch of science he should become enrolled. A girl asks my advice about whether she should go to America, so that she can get married.

"Are you in a hurry?"

"Yes."

"Why?"

"I want to have a child. I'm jealous of the women who have a child to embrace on their bosoms."

And I am calm, sometimes laughing, sometimes suddenly pale from controlled emotion, giving answers about all these human concerns, struggling to love all these uncongenial spirits, to identify myself with them, to become interested in England, to choose a faculty, and to go off to America to find a father for my child. I feel lost, dissolving, here in our little courtyard, Lenotschka. I'm not indifferent to anything. I live, love, suffer with all these people who are coming to my father's home to stare with curiosity and awe at Sindbad-the-Sailor-of-the-Spirit.

---

* Heroine of Frobenius' African tale.

The table on which I'm writing you in the room where I grew up is full of fruit, sweets, bananas, everything I love. I'm in a hurry to set off for the Libyan Sea, to start my agony in solitude . . . and later on, God will decide . . . Russia? God willing! But here too, I'll be happy, because I'll be working.

As soon as I arrive in Leda, I'll write you and I'll wait for you. Be good, serene. Take care of your body. Love, have pity on, be tolerant of human beings. Don't forget our words, walks, the hot rocks where we sat, the pine trees, the mountains, the stars we saw together, despairing and happy . . .

Heraklion, July 15, 1924

. . . I wander through the narrow ancient little streets of this city, looking at the poor trees, the sun-baked men, the unfamiliar warm women. I go to the sea, enjoying the waves, undressing, feeling the whole sea as the flowing of my own blood, breathing in the air, stretching out on the hot sand, knowing that I am the clear voice of all this inarticulate outcry of the elements. And my heart pounds, Genossin, leaps like a living thing, small and ephemeral, patient and omnipotent. I remember you in all the bitter, obdurate moments. I remember your eyes, the silence, the words, our shadows on the stones, all our wanderings along the shores and in the fields and between our souls. Ah, what an awesome mystery is the human heart! How I rejoice when I look behind me and see this "red line" carved by the warm drops of my human heart!

And when I return from the sea in the evening, and my lips and hair and thinking faculties are still full of brine, I meet secretly with the leaders of the Communist movement here in a house, and we work out the plan for the future battle. There are some ten people, simple, uneducated, strong minds; warm, fiery spirits. It is a brilliant mass erotically waiting for the Spirit to descend upon them like a man, and make them fertile. The entire sea, the entire vision of solitude and eternity are still in my eyes, the entire "Cycle." And suddenly, among these poor, simple "fishers of men," among these humble, abused, hungry, contemporary apostles, there wells up inside me the ephemeral, burning love for man. This despairing, frenzied era in which it was my lot to be born and the entire Cycle become contracted into a single incandescent point . . . immediate action.

I say to myself: "These comrades constitute the lowest, the first stage of enlightenment in my religion." They themselves are surging forward to be saved from injustice and poverty. They are, as we used to say, Lenotschka, the insects who believe that the honey of the flowers was created for them to eat and get their fill of.

The second stage (so far, I have three such "brothers" here) is: "We are not struggling for ourselves, but for man. It is man we must save, not our own insignificant selves."

The third and highest stage is: "We are fighting neither for ourselves nor for man. All of us, voluntarily or involuntarily, consciously or unconsciously—plants, animals, human beings and ideas—are struggling for the salvation of God."

. . . I am happy that it has been my lot, here on my ancestral soil, in the sacred, from-time-immemorial-illuminated land of Crete, to cast unconsciously the roots of my God. I must plow this mass well, adapting it to modern needs, making use of the modern world-wide anxiety, here in this tiny fatherland shining in the steel-blue sea, and find the simplest, most gripping expression for today of my own mystic Theogony.

Ah Lenotschka, if only my body as a whole could become worthy of my head! At certain times my eyes are pierced by flashes of African lightning. I shout: "Here! I'm ready!" Then once again they fade away. Fade away, or achieve organization in an unintermittent storm. We shall see. The cell bequeathed to me by my father, Bernardone, is a cruel one; the cell of Pica, my mother, a tender, passive one. May God grant me a little time before I die to achieve the supreme synthesis.

Beloved companion, I kiss your hands. I remember the hot rocks, the two seas opening and closing the first cycle of our contact. I remember St. John the Hunter.* They all glimmer in my mind, serenely in the blue of eternity.†

Heraklion, July 20, 1924

. . . My heart is filled with unbearable bitterness. I have no illusion, and that is why I am struggling untiringly, desperate and free. I know that when this miserable, faded social class falls, the proletariat will come. They will give whatever thought, whatever beauty they are capable of, and then they too will become stingy. They will vent their

---

* An abandoned monastery on Mt. Hymettos which N.K. hoped to acquire in order to found his phalanstery.
† Letter to E. Samios.

27

wrath. The Great Spirit will abandon them and another class will come—and so on incessantly, until the earth fades utterly away, and life like a parasite will vanish from this crust of our insignificant planet.

It is evening, our dangerous hour. Just now I got your letter, and my heart is pounding as though it would burst. Many roads open up before me, all equally exact, sacred, human, enchanting, all leading us to the grave. Why should I choose the most uphill path, the harshest and most laughterless? At this terrifying twilight hour, as I hold your letter, my heart pounds, questioning in agony. Do you remember what I told you about my brothers, the Africans? When a man dies, according to them, his eyes go down to the earth and say, "We have seen nothing!" The ears say, "We have heard nothing!" The lips, "We have kissed nothing!" The hands, "We have touched nothing!" My God, at this moment, as I write you, all my senses in despair are roaring this African cry.

Genossin, I live each moment so intensely that I dissolve and become lost each day . . . The other day I went with Lefteris* to the village of Varvari,† where my grandfather was born. . . . It is on top of a hill. On the hard white earth below, grapevines and cypresses are sown all around. I shall never forget how my heart pitched all the while I was going through the narrow streets, looking through the low open doors into the courtyard, the flowerpots of basil, the water jug covered with thyme, the women sitting at their doorsteps spinning and, inside the house, the young girls at the loom, weaving.

I went to my ancestral village in order to set fire to it . . . to cast a seed of fire, our Idea, that it might burn and be saved. There can be no greater act of gratitude. This was the first village whence I started my march through Crete.

We must rouse and make those who are satisfied unsatisfied. We must show these humbly happy people that they are unhappy. We must cast burning coals in the courtyard of every peaceful home. . . . Here is our difficult, heavy, supreme duty. And why? So that the world will not rot in tranquillity and stagnation; so that our soul will not rot away in comfort and forbearance. . . .

Ah Genossin, how happy I am that God has given me the chance

---

* Lefteris Alexiou, brother of Galatea, professor, writer in his free time, musician.
† Varvari means "Barbarians." Nicephoros Phocas had settled Africans there when he liberated Crete. Hence, the idea of N.K. that he had Arabic blood in his veins.

28

to talk with you and warm the air between our two bodies! This is, as you say, a prologue. May God grant that a whole book be completed, heroic, full of bitterness and love, full of action, patience, kindness . . .

Once again I am joyfully awaiting a letter from you. My hand is always open, like Buddha's begging bowl, begging. It will always remain open, and when I die, not even the earth will be able to close it. At the very moment I conceive the supreme hope, I crush this hope because it cannot be contained inside me.

Liebe Genossin, liebe Genossin, may our God, the cruel, hope-denying, fire-bearing God be with us!*

Heraklion, July 29, 1924

Galatea writes me that you are coming with her to Crete . . . . We'll go together to Leda. We'll make ourselves as comfortable as possible. (I still don't know whether it will be comfortable or uncomfortable. . . . But what does that matter? God will be with us!) The sea is heavenly. We will read and talk in the evening.

I don't want to go to Russia this year. Upon this soil first, we must consolidate the Idea.

Genossin, this life is a miracle. Here you are coming to Crete. Here we are about to see the sacred island together along the Libyan Sea, facing Africa.

Come quickly. The grapes, figs, pears, cantaloupes, Homer, Buddha, our two souls, the first rains coming on . . . Everything is .ripe, ready, good, sacred, Genossin.†

A mineral spring, or—to be more precise—a puddle set in a deep orchard. Lemon trees and citron trees with dark, moist leaves, the way Douanier Rousseau loved them. Flies and ill-tempered ants. A crescent-shaped beach, bounded on both ends by steep rocks. A single roof covering a loft filled with jars and grain. A single inhabitant, a half-deaf, blind old man . . . Leda! This was the "ideal" retreat chosen for the poet-ascetic . . .

At a moment's glance, Kazantzakis sized up the situation: Untenable. All the more reason for persevering.

"A glass of water, please," I requested, my throat parched after so many hours on mule-back through the arid mountains.

---

* Letter to E. Samios.
† Letter to E. Samios.

The old man got up, stroked his beard, wiped his knobby hands on his indigo-blue breeches, groped for his stick and went off toward the spring. He came back with a bowl of lukewarm water, in which some gigantic ants were floating.

"Ants!" I screamed.

"Bah! *Melita-a-a-aki!* They never hurt anybody!"

"Let's leave, this very moment," I begged, turning my gaze toward the mules.

"We'll leave whenever you like," Nikos responded, simultaneously amused and upset. "But first let's go and pay our respects to the spring."

We bent over double to crawl under the dense citron trees. Suddenly for no reason at all, in front of the famous spring, we were seized with a fit of mad laughter. That laugh, I think, did more to bring us together than all the Bergsons, Dantes, Lenins, and Zorbas in creation.

"If we do stay, Galatea will say we wanted to lure her into this trap. And if we go away, she'll say we're refusing to let her share in the enjoyment of this terrestrial paradise. It's up to you to decide," said Nikos in a playful tone.

We stayed on. Without knowing it, we had just signed a contract for life and death.

Held in the hot palm of the night, stretched out on the sand, we followed the three crafty accomplices, Venus, Mars, Jupiter-the-Trickster,* making their rounds punctually, beckoning to us, yet beyond our grasp; like celestial kites on which we strung our wishes in the guise of streamers; wishes and noble aspirations setting forth in the night and losing themselves in the furrow of the universal curve.

All day long, crouched over the sea in a narrow, oyster-shaped grotto, we virtuously read Goethe's *Iphigenia in Tauris*, Aeschylus, and Shestov. Every so often, my companion would toss his head back and, as though sighing, would begin reciting his favorite lines: "*O insensata cura dei mortali* [Oh foolish concern of mortals]."

"*O insensata cura . . .*" Oh foolish man! What were you doing here with a young girl in flower, while the world around you was collapsing, calling for help?

Was the poetry he had so generously lavished on me now retaliating upon him? For all his desperate efforts, it was not politics that won

---

* This is how the Cretan shepherds refer to Jupiter, because they mistake it for Venus and get up ahead of time.

st of us will defend ourselves like men. Do you know how to use this eapon?"

"I know how," murmured the child, who didn't know how to kill a y.

1902–1906.   The years passed quickly. Since Crete did not have a niversity, the young student was forced to exile himself to Athens. An ssiduous correspondence began with his family.

With his mother and his sisters, whom he adored, he adopted a antering tone, speaking to them only about things they could under-tand, teasing them each in turn, paying them compliments, offering hem advice and little gifts, searching for powders and ribbons for them, nd even a corset. Whereas to his Father, whom he addressed in the econd person plural, he assumed a tone of absolute seriousness, express-ng to him only his respect, filial love and gratitude:

Athens, September 21, 1902

Dear and respected Father,

As soon as I arrived here yesterday, I sent you a note to inform you hat I had gotten here in excellent shape. Indeed I have never had a better trip. I was neither seasick nor cold, and my only grief, though a great one, was in having parted from you and gone far from paternal and maternal love. That is why I am very sad now, because I am not near you. . . .

At this moment as I write now, through the window blinds I can hear the noise of this great city . . . The newspaper vendors going to and fro, the shouts, the grocers, the milkmen, the carriages, the tram-ways, rushing incessantly back and forth.

Tomorrow, Sunday, I'll go to visit the professor, Mistriotis. . . . It will take five or six days for one to get used to this new life.

Respected Father, it is indeed very sad for a person to have to go far away from his father, mother, and sisters. But it was necessary, since some day you want me to become a human being and not to be ashamed to call myself your child.

So patience, my dear parents, my love and respect for you is growing here in exile. . . .

34

his soul. "O insensata cura dei mortali . . ." I have seen him sacrifice, in order to create a fine line of verse, one after the other, all the things that human beings most appreciate: honors, travel, comfort, friendships, relatives, music, books—even his most burning aspiration, his other self, the prophet of "Meta-Communism."

While Nikos Kazantzakis was struggling on a twofold front in Crete—trying to give birth to his Ulysses* and at the same time to avoid being harassed by the police—my sisters and I were also waging a battle, this one against death. By surprise, death had robbed us of our tenderest companion, our younger brother. Nikos, who had met him in Berlin, made an effort to find consoling words.

Heraklion, September 29, 1924

At this difficult moment, Comrade, I am with you, struggling to share as much grief as I can. I shall never forget your brother, that twilight over the lake in Berlin—how good he was, calm, not speaking, gazing at the beauty of the evening with understanding and feeling. And in the midst of the aimless hubbub his companions were making, he smiled forbearingly.

And the second time I saw him, in May, at your home, I shall never forget his large eyes and his wordless, serene nobility.

Genossin, all speech is in vain in the presence of this awesome mystery. A beloved form comes, lives, speaks, grows up with us; then suddenly, calmly, without turning around, vanishes. To what purpose all these multifarious daily martyrdoms of the heart? Where do we come from? Where are we going to? What is the meaning of all these dearly beloved shades upon the earth?

At this moment, when my heart is flooded with the shade of your brother, all these eternal, futile questions fill my mind with anguish. Ah, if only I could wring your hand now, it would be some consolation. We know that there is no answer. But there are hands which answer when they clasp each other with warmth. Genossin, liebe Genossin, how good it is to go away; I have felt this most deeply at critical moments . . . to go to the opposite bank, to make an end to this meaningless, badly written tragedy. Only he who loves can resist. . . .†

---

* Which was to become his epic poem, The Odyssey.
† Letter to E. Samios.

31

Heraklion, October 7, 1924

. . . In a few days I am moving to the house near the sea.* I shall work during the winter, but once again the urge for travel is making me giddy. Ah, if only I go to Egypt and fill my eyes with the sight of date trees, bananas and fellahs. Odysseus in his second journey crosses the Nile. I want to go with him.

All day long today I was composing my Apology.† They summoned me to the police station because of a revolutionary article I'd written, and gave me 24 hours to prepare my defense. How miserably petty life in our country is! If it were somewhere else, I'd run the risk—the hope—of having them kill me. Here, they won't even give me a trial, nor will they give me the chance to see whether I am brave. Ah, if only I were a Russian! Ah, if only I could find myself beneath the heavy sword of danger at each and every moment.

Liebe, liebe Genossin, don't ever forget me. Give me your hand. Yesterday evening, as I was rereading some parts of a tragedy of mine, The Christ, I saw the following verses; and just now, as I was writing you those last words, I remembered them:

> all
> the creatures of the earth are good and true.
> And the stones, bread and wine and sea
> are alive, because I hold the beloved hand!‡

Heraklion, December 5, 1924

. . . How well the outlines of our temperaments can be seen in our letters, en relief [in relief]. You . . . measured, disciplinée, froide et serrée [disciplined, cold and closed], and I an Oriental nature, prime-sautière et illogique [impetuous and antirationalistic]. If we were together, I would put up another gigantic struggle to make you transcend the limits of logic and silence. Now you're too far away, in abysmal Athens, where my spirit is incapable of exercising any power, incapable of touching anyone. Every day I am losing you; in everything you write and in the way you write, with lips pursed, joyless, resolute, I sense it. Which way you are going, no one knows. Oh God, how at one

---

* This house belonged to his schoolmate and intimate friend, Manolis Georgiadis, who was shot by the Germans.
† See Appendix.
‡ Letter to E. Samios.

are my memory and my heart! How eternally pre How unending inside me is anything that has once b

I hold you forever, malgré vous. You can no three stars over the Libyan Sea rise forever, and twilight, lying on the sand, and all through the night

Never have I felt you so close. Never has th enfolding me, so warmly, despairingly, ineffably sw am master of my own memory; now that everyday only Essence remains! . . .

At the present moment, I am becoming haun of new travels . . . Will we ever meet outside Gree

1883–1904.   His youth, his adolescence, the bon the liberation, the first soft down shed upon encou and foreign world, the ideas, the women and the influence on his thought or his body—all this we k

"God, make a God of me! God, make a God of m

There we find him, a little fellow with a top-he ing the divine thunderbolts, when he could still barel two feet in his mother's courtyard.

And this same courtyard echoing with his laught imprecations: "Woe! Woe! Woe to him who does days! Mama, did I suckle on Wednesdays and Frida into tears when his mother nodded "Yes" . . .

His first meeting with Death, in the cemetery wl taken him for a walk: Anica, the plump neighbor-lady silky, reduced to a hideous skull which the gravedigg earth with a swing of his shovel. A second and encounter when he was forced to kiss the feet of the the Turks on the plane tree in the public square.

"I can't, Father, I can't . . ."

"You can. You must be able to. . . ."

This mythological father who demanded just two son: not to tell lies and not to allow anyone to beat h prepared even as a small child to kill his mother and l the Turks ever violate the ancestral threshold. "Do you kill them. We cannot allow them to be dragged into

---

* Letter to E. Samios.
† See Report to Greco.

Above all, many hugs and warmest respects to my dear mother; she must not weep. I'm getting along well here, and besides, it won't be long before I see her again. The months pass quickly . . .

As I reread these letters written on both sides, I seem to see his little eyes sparkle with ill-restrained mischief and feeling. Four pages, the first one penned painstakingly, destined for Kapetan Mihalis; the other three addressed to the women of his family, wherein, carried away by his feeling for them, he no longer bothered to control his handwriting. Mother and sisters complained about it, and he promised to be more careful in the future.

Athens, 1904

Dearest Mother, Anestasia and Eleni,

I am very, very happy with our housekeeping.* Day before yesterday we hired a cook. Today we had stuffed eggplant and stuffed squash. Miserable cooking. I came home at noon, and saw some thick eggplant filled with undercooked rice as hard as bones. The squashes had turned to pulp, and there wasn't a sign of them anywhere. So I got furious. "Angeliki," I said, "do you call this food? The next time you must just come and ask my advice, since you don't know. The eggplant should be smooth, and you must put them in the bottom of the pot, and the squashes on top to keep them from getting mushy."

It's really funny, Eleni, to see us in the kitchen. When we get back from the university, we dash right over to the pot. I take the lid off and sniff, while the other two stand over me asking, "Did it turn out all right? How do you find it?"

I taste two or three forkfuls, pretend to think it over, and if I'm hungry I tell them, "Disgusting!" (So I can tell Angeliki to put more on my plate without the others' starting a brawl.)

I've got them on a diet. Every day I want vegetables. "Look here," they say to me, "won't you get some meat just once? We'll forget what it's like."

"Meat?" I ask them. "Meat? You know what illnesses it causes?

---

* With two companions, who remained faithful friends to the end, he had rented an apartment in Athens. A third friend, H. Stephanidis, used to eat his meals there as a boarder.

You know there's no more dangerous food? Meat? So you want us to get sick?" . . .

How I wish it were possible for us all to be in Athens together, and you could stay here ten days or so to see what the world really means.

Perhaps this will happen. For, as I see, progress is being made—since you are learning to dance now. So you know the polka perfectly! Bravo! But don't neglect your French. And I'll go to the best dancing school in Athens. But not now—in December. Now there's no extra money.

He spent his holidays in Crete. He needed to be close to his mother in order to replenish his strength. An idyll was also developing, destined to end in marriage at a later point. But his difficulties, his doubts and his wildest hopes he kept to himself. Heraklion was not the place where he could find some wise man of letters to help him in the early stages of his literary career—when, like the cicada, whose manner of hatching had so impressed him, his spirit was slowly and painfully struggling to wriggle out of its matrix.

His first literary work, *The Serpent and the Lily*, was a long novella that was published under a pen name as legendary as its contents: "Karma Nirvami." Red on the outside as well as the inside and decorated with gold letters, very *fin-de-siècle*. A story much in the manner of D'Annunzio. Kazantzakis later disavowed it, as he did with all his earliest writing. And yet with what feeling and fire he had written it! *The Serpent and the Lily* had hardly been completed when he plunged into a social drama.* He sent it off at once to D. Kalogeropoulo, director of the periodical *Pinakothiki* in Athens, a very cultivated and progressive man, who had shown a lively interest in the author of *The Serpent and the Lily*. In the letter accompanying it, he gave free rein to his feeling:

. . . I've had it [the manuscript] on my desk for ten days already and haven't been able to calm myself. I didn't know whether it was worth reading or not. . . . What encourages me—the only thing, alas!—is the sincerity with which I write. . . . If I told you that I

---

* Daybreak, a play written in 1906.

sometimes weep when I write and suffer and become physically exhausted, *would you believe me?*

I have emphasized the three phrases I consider revealing. From 1906 to 1957—fifty-one years of life as a writer—and the man remains the same. Always the same modesty, the same forthrightness, the same doubts about the perfection of his work.

Without even closing my eyes, I can see him coming into my room, blushing like a schoolboy, the prologue of *Toda Raba* in his hands. "Lenotschka, read it, I beg of you, and tell me if it's any good!"

We had been living for some weeks "at the pinnacle of happiness and of Czechoslovakia," as he had declared in his letters. He had just returned from the U.S.S.R., where he had stayed on alone to complete the trip begun in company with Panaït Istrati, Panaït's companion, Bilili, and me. He was forty-six years old and thought himself capable of bearing on his own shoulders all of human injustice.

So here we were in the Erzgebirge, or more exactly at Försterhäuser, near Gottesgab, in the Sudeten region. In a mammoth house belonging to a diminutive Herr Kraus, who had never in his life seen a Greek or an olive or a date. The first time he saw a candied orange, he shouted exultantly, "What a delicious olive!" On St. Nicholas' Day, he donned his fireman's uniform, helmet and all, and came to offer his most rococo greetings to Nikos, whom he called "Herr Direktor!"

There was also Hilda, as blond as the hay in which she frolicked with her goat. And Hilda's mother, who came to life only when she caught sight of the Gypsies:

"Butter thieves! Butter thieves! For the love of God, bolt the doors!"

A happy time, birth, rebirth of a man and a woman. Solitude. On this snowed-under plateau in the Erzgebirge, I learned, among other things, the meaning of the word *solitude* for my traveling companion. Space, a free area to sit like a shaman under a tree and fit his flute to his lips and begin to sing. To create shadows, shadows which would soon become beings as alive and independent as their creator.

Two years later, we went back to these same Krauses. In the meantime they had contrived a bed the right size for Nikos and installed a stove in his room. And Nikos began writing his third version of *The Odyssey*, this time not in bed and wearing mittens with the thermometer at 20 degrees below zero. We could even have friends come to visit us: G. Nazos,* Prevelakis,† Lefteris, and others.

Nikos skipped lunch in order to avoid interrupting his work. But he was gay and relaxed. Once a week we would go off in the morning for a long ramble in the villages roundabout. Every evening he liked to read me the day's work. This year it was *The Odyssey* and *Kapetan Elias.* And again the same timidity, the same uneasiness—"Read it, Lenotschka, and tell me if it's worth anything."

Thirty years later, the same uneasiness, the same sincere self-doubt. We were in Antibes, Nikos feverishly working on *Report to Greco* at the same time that we were getting ready for our trip to China. He felt certain, he claimed, that nothing bad could happen to us during that trip. The doctors had given us a clean bill of health. But perhaps some alarm bell had been pressed by his subconscious mind. As soon as he had written the prologue, he came down to have me read it.

"My child," he said with feeling in his voice, "come and read, I beg you, what I've just written. I don't really know if it's worth anything!"

I collect my tools: sight, sound, taste, smell, touch, mind. The evening has fallen; the day's work is done. I am returning home like the mole in the earth. Not that I am weary of working. I am not weary, but the sun is setting. . . .

This time it was my own eyes that dimmed. My voice choked. As I tried to finish reading it, I kept thinking: Whatever has gotten hold of him to make him think about death today? Why today, for the first time, does he accept death?

I pretended to be annoyed and scolded. He remained calm, resting his hand on my shoulder, as always. "Be calm, Comrade. I'll live another ten years. We've said so! People don't die when they have a purpose to accomplish!"

But that same evening he wrote the following to his friend, Pandelis Prevelakis:

---

* G. Nazos, journalist, who died very young.
† Pandelis Prevelakis, very young at the time, a poet and student. He became an esteemed writer, and professor of the history of art at the Fine Arts School in Athens.

Today I'm sending you the prologue of Report to Greco. *Eleni could not read it all the way through; she burst into sobs. But it is good that she becomes accustomed to it, and that I too become accustomed to it.*

But let us pick up the thread where we broke it off—in the year 1906.

Athens, 1906

Dear Mother,

You'll forgive me for not having written you till now, but you can't imagine how much I've been studying and working, and I don't even have time to eat. I don't go out of my house at all. A boy brings me food at noon and in the evening, and I eat at home, holding the book open in front of me and reading. I go to sleep early, but wake up in the middle of the night, at two or three. Fortunately this won't last long. In about two weeks I have my examinations and can rest easy.

I'm really very happy that I'm going to be with you for Christmas this year. I'll go to church in the evening, make the sign of the cross, light a candle—"Kyrie Eleison! Kyrie Eleison!" And I'll come back home, and the table will be set and the stuffed pork will be steaming. Then we can drink a glass of wine, Anestasia? "Welcome! Welcome!"

Now as I'm writing you, it's noontime, and I'm terribly hungry waiting to see what fare the shoeshine boy will bring me.

I leave him to his own discretion. One day it was raining and he didn't come, and that noontime I gulped down five cups of tea, three cups of hot chocolate, and five hard biscuits.

Here he is now, bringing the food: bean soup—oh no, now I've fathomed it with my spoon, it's pea soup. He brought some fried codfish too. You see, it's Friday today, and as you very well know, I have no intention of breaking the fast. Ah, that's all we need!

Let me eat now. I'll write you later.

I can hear you far, far off, calling to me: "A good appetite to you!" Thank you; thank you.

1906.   Family spleen, books, the coat of tar his mother glazed his linen with to guard against sickness, the "grand project"*—these were

---

* She wanted him to marry a Heraklion girl.

the themes of this correspondence. About the Turks who refused to relinquish their hold, or Greece's fear of being drawn into an unequal war he had very little to say.

A fertile year, an "egg with two yolks." Kazantzakis received his diploma from the University of Athens. It bore the signature of a great poet, Kostis Palamas, who was a mature man at the time. The family was elated. The father, like all Greek peasants, dreamed of making a lawyer, or perhaps a politician, of his only son. The mother was weaving the web of the "grand project," which would keep him a prisoner at her side. The sisters ordered little gifts—powders, fashionable laces. They stayed up late around the oil lamp, drinking tea and chattering about the approach of Christmas, when the prodigal son would be coming home. What must they set about doing to give him pleasure? White-wash the house from top to bottom? Groom the little dog, Karmen? Set out some new fragrant plants in the courtyard? That's what he asked them to do in his letters. About his other concerns, his writings, his insatiable thirst to learn and understand, to see as much as he could, to fill that head of his if it could ever get its fill, they guessed next to nothing. The only son came and went again, the affection remaining as solid as ever. But the bitterness of parting increased, and as life flowed on, a chasm opened between him and his native city, bridged only by his death.

In the year 1907, Nikos Kazantzakis became the hero of a curious adventure: The University of Athens presented an award to his play *Daybreak*, while at the same time attacking its advanced ideas. "Though we crown the poet, we expel from this abstemious temple the young man who dared to write such things!" Such was more or less the pronouncement made by the venerable university professor, Spyridon Lambros, who was presiding over this strange coronation ceremony. And what did our laureate do? With perfect dignity, he walked out of the "abstemious" hall, neglecting to bang its doors, carrying his wreath of laurel leaves. At a later point he used to enjoy telling how he took the award and used it to season a *"stifado"* (a kind of stew made with onions, herbs and tomato sauce).*

---

* In Switzerland, with his friend Iannis Stavridakis, a young Cretan aristocrat of vast culture, in whom N.K. had vested great hopes. Greek Consul General in Zurich, he died in Tiflis of pneumonia in 1919 while N.K., who was on a special mission at the time, was trying to repatriate Greek refugees from the Caucasus. See *Zorba the Greek* and *Report to Greco*.

When he learned the results of the university competition, Vlassos Gavriilidis, an epoch-making journalist, raised a hue and cry:

> The young playwright, Mr. Nikos Kazantzakis [he wrote in his newspaper, *Akropolis*], received the award in an essential rather than an official sense for his genuinely beautiful and symbolic work, *Daybreak*. He is a Cretan, therefore a revolutionary. His play is a literary Therisso,* as was also true of his last year's work entitled *The Serpent and the Lily*, painted all in red, with a scattering of pages full of force and the south wind, and dizzying, penetrating aromas, Arabian aromas in fact, just as the writer's pen surges forth like an Arabian horse. . . . This work contains an unsubduable rebellious spirit. It is a kind of battle against nature, woman, love, and his own self. . . .
>
> What is most important for us is that in the person of the author of *Daybreak* and *The Serpent and the Lily*, our poverty-stricken modern Greek literature acquires a new writer, who will most probably go far and take his place in the front rank, or perhaps indeed go beyond it. Anyone who peruses these two works of his attentively must perceive in them a literary fountainhead. He enters our literary world bearing new demons: intellectual, aesthetic and linguistic. . . . He is the new writer, the writer of fire and the writer of life. . . .

Gavriilidis summoned the young Cretan and entrusted him with editing his newspaper. Kazantzakis accepted, but resumed his liberty a few months later in order to go to Paris and finish his studies. From Paris he sent several rather indifferent articles to an Athenian daily. A month later, he published the third act of a new play, *Fasga*, in the periodical *Pinakothiki*. He immediately submitted it to a competition at the University of Athens, in hopes of winning the first prize.

In a letter dated October 1, 1907, we find his first impressions from Paris. To his father, the young Kazantzakis spoke of the trouble he had when he found himself alone, lost in the hubbub of a great city—"Carriages, cries, crowds, very high houses, thousands of things oppressing you . . ."—and on the reverse side, as usual, to his mother and sisters:

---

* At Therisso, Venizelos proclaimed the union of Crete with Greece on May 10, 1905.

Dearest Mother and Anestasia and Eleni,

I still haven't recovered from Paris. I come and go all day long without stopping, seeing new things all the time. Above all, it's a fine thing to see how the women work here. In all the sweetshops, grocery stores, in all the shops, you see women managing and serving. Others draw carts and sell newspapers. They all work day and night to earn their bread. It's not like home, where you sit and embroider and, when you hear a carriage, rush to the door to receive your visitor.

I kiss you sweetly, sweetly, my dearest Mother and Anestasia and Eleni. You can't imagine how much I love you.

On January 25, 1908, in answer to a question from his sister, Kazantzakis said in a bantering tone that he was taking some philosophy courses in both universities*—"I'm happy," he wrote. "I'm learning the ABC's."

On February 23 of this same year, he wrote his father:

I want to ask you a strange favor. Recently I've read several books about bees . . . and I had thought of asking you to set up five or six beehives in the middle of our vineyard, underneath the fig trees. Here, "the people who study" by and large have beehives with the one side in glass and they observe myriads of things. . . .

Paris [no date]

Darling Mother, Anestasia and Eleni,

The French women aren't ugly, like the ones you have at Kastro. They are very, very beautiful. They all have wonderful ways of wearing their hair . . . And they have very white, delicate skin. When I remember our own women . . . I burst out laughing . . .

Paris, June 1908

Darling Mother, Anestasia and Eleni,

I'm sorry that they didn't accept the Fasga, and so I didn't get the prize, but I'm happy too, because in a few days I'll be seeing you. Because I hope Father will agree to let me come back . . . (Expenses, expenses, Marigo!)† But what's to be done? You can't imagine my joy

---

* The Collège de France and the Sorbonne.
† N.K.'s mother.

when I feel that in a few days I'll be coming. To see Karmen again, the banana tree, the neighbor women, the watering trough, the mulberry tree, the portraits of the warriors,* everything, everything. . . . To get up early, early in the morning with Eleni or Anestasia (if she condescends, now that she's got a wrist watch), and we'll go to Knossos or the vineyard. . . . Then I'll go up and write. And then I'll come down again. Well, what were we saying? . . . And we'll tell jokes and eat grapes . . . You'll hear my laughter from far away, and Karmen will wag her tail and bark, and Father will be happy.

And then one day, Mother will come up to my den and sit on the chest and the front part of her stocking will be new, darker than the rest of the stocking, and she'll rest her cheek on her hand and say to me: "Well, child, what do you think of our plan?" And then—very seriously, as befits my age (Marigo, whatever you do, I am 26 years old!)—I'll say this and that to her. . . . And then some afternoon, I'll take Father to the vineyard and talk to him for two and a half hours. And we'll start action. . . .

And another day, I'll call Eleni to talk over another plan we know about. And to keep Anestasia from grumbling, we'll call her in too . . . Ha-ha-ha! What a joke!

And so, at the end of June, I'll be leaving Paris . . . So paint the walls pale blue below and rose above. A good dark tablecloth on the table. Take care of the banana tree. Give Karmen a bath. . . .

How strange this world is! This very moment the street is roaring away beneath my window, carriages, railway train, the river, high-high churches, ladies in décolleté, voices, houses six or seven stories up, theaters, music—a hubbub of life—and in a few days, peace, the banana tree, Three Kamares,† and the portraits of the warriors! That's how I like life to be. From one extreme to the other. No monotony. I am happy.

Paris [no date]

In my room (Anestasia, thank you for not frowning), there's a fire burning all day long. And it's very fine to sit in the warmth, drink your tea and read while it snows outside, and from time to time you open the curtains of the windows and see the world all white. The only bad thing is that my friends like my room too, and there they are often coming up

---

* The portraits of the Heroes of the Wars of Independence.
† The principal square in Heraklion.

43

the stairs and ringing the bell . . . for me to open up. I pretend I can't hear, and hold my breath so they'll think I'm out. But they understand and call out to me, "We won't budge from here unless you open up. . . ."

What can I do? I get up and open for them, scolding them as I let them in. They sit on the couch or in the easy chairs, set about lighting the stove by themselves, find the sugar, tea, biscuits, and make tea . . . "Do you want any?" they call to me. Do I want any! And in the big cup, to boot!

And so we drink our tea. Sometimes they have some cognac or champagne outside and we sip away . . . and in this way we waste quite a few evenings! And it pleases my landlady, because, she says, they make me let off a bit of steam after my studying. If you saw her, Mother, you'd kiss her, and make her put some tar in her clothes to keep her strong.

Paris, spring, 1908

Darling Mother, Anestasia and Eleni,

. . . Last night I went to bed late. . . . We'd gone to the café, shouting away, and the French people staring at us. I was one of the first to shout and laugh. A student friend of mine came to Paris the other day, and he didn't know I was here. Suddenly I saw him running like mad through the crowd, shouting "Niko!" I stood still. "Moré,* you here!" he said. "I heard you laughing from the other end of the street, and I said, No one else can laugh like that. And here you are!" . . .

Paris, 1909

Darling Mother, Anestasia and Eleni,

How beautiful the whole world out there must be now! The gorse must be as big as the sea, and the poppies and sun and flowering trees and crickets. And above all, the fruit. Some days ago I saw some red cherries here, wrapped in cellophane, in boxes, as though they were pills. And I remember our big platefuls, and my delight when my lips would get red from the blood of the cherries, and when I used to count the pits at the end and there were 150 of them. . . .

To tell the truth, what else shall I write you about? Ah, Mother's worried about the twopence for the postcard. . . . You see, I wrote

---

* "Dear fellow"—an exclamation uttered in an affectionate, familiar tone in Greek conversations.

Father again day before yesterday to send me five 20-franc pieces. You get my meaning? Napoleons! And you give a thought to the penny? Ah, if only I were rich, I'd show you how scornful one can be of Mammon and how far above money a human being can be. Since we must all die anyway, what does it matter whether you have a thousand francs more or a thousand francs less. . . . Ah, Marigo, Marigo! As a fine, here's how I'll punish you. I have great need of a book called Cretan Civilization, by Xanthoudidis. It costs one franc (horrors, O Lord, ten whole pennies!) . . . I need it very much. I'm going to give a lecture here on the antiquities at Knossos. . . .

Paris [no date]

. . . I have no greater joy than to get a letter from you. Really, many times I say to myself that no one in the world loves his mother and his sisters as much as I do. The other day, after getting your letter, I went to the University. A friend of mine said to me the moment he saw me: "What's wrong with you? What's come over you?" "I got a letter from home!" I shouted to him. "From my mother and my sisters. That's what's come over me!" . . .

1909.   Along with his philosophical studies and extraordinarily varied reading, Kazantzakis had prepared two new novels, Imperial Life and The Theanthropists, which, along with Broken Souls, were supposed to form a trilogy. But spring was there; the brain desired one thing, the heart and body another. The demon of travel won the match.

Paris, 1909

Darling Mother, Anestasia and Eleni,

. . . Yesterday and today we've had sun, and I'm all upset, nervous, restless. You know, when I set my mind on something, I don't rest until I do it. I thought that instead of spending two more months in Paris, I might spend them in Rome. That way I'll benefit much more and see things I've longed to see ever since I was a child. . . . Ah, if only I had money, now, this very minute, I'd stuff my books and linen in the suitcases. I'd call the coachman, climb aboard the train, and next morning I'd wake up in Italy. That's how I like life . . . to make my decision manfully like that . . . Not to go over to the Kastrinaki mill, and dress myself in spats and a wide-brimmed hat and a brow-band and

45

a gourd of water and make the sign of the cross before setting out. . . .

If I stay here two or three more days, I'll die of suffocation. The black sky, heavy air. Mathilda* hasn't seen the sea yet . . . and she doesn't believe it's as blue as indigo. . . .

Letters full of imagery, addressed unfailingly to Kapetan Mihalis, who in actual fact must not have been so hard to deal with, inasmuch as he merited all his only son's teasing and whimsical sallies. Merely to keep up appearances was enough. As always, a first page carefully penned:

Paris, January 25, 1909

My dear Father,
 I am well and hope that you and the whole family are likewise. . . . My only joy is to learn that you are well. I often reflect on what would have become of me if you had not been there. Whatever good I have learned, I owe to you.

With respect and affection,
Your son, NIKOS

And on the back of this same page, the dialogue in fragmentary phrases with his mother and sisters:

Paris, 1909

Beloved Mother, Anestasia, and Eleni,
 . . . Sometimes at night, when I'm reading under my lamp with the green shade, and it's snowing outside and the fire is lit, Mathilda comes in or her sister, Susan, holding their embroidery, and they ask me, "Will you let me keep you company a bit? I'd embroider this band a bit more, but I'm sleepy. Here I don't feel sleepy. So will you let me?" And I raise my head and say to her, "With pleasure. But if you want to oblige me, light the stove and make some tea because I'm not in the mood to . . ." "Ah, avec plaisir."
 And all the time the water's boiling and Mathilda or Susan is bending over her embroidery, I keep saying to myself, I'd give half my

---

* The young manageress of the *pension* where N.K. stayed in Paris.

life to have Anestasia and Eleni sitting here and Mother sitting on the couch facing me, crocheting the tips of her stockings. . . .

I'm terribly upset because it's taken so long to get the money and I have to borrow every day. And worst of all, I have my books in the suitcases, and my room's like a boat ready to sail, just like at home, every time you do the laundry. . . .

And from Florence, two weeks before Rome, without date:

Beloved Mother, Anestasia and Eleni,

. . . And so the tale begins: "Good evening!" The first day I wandered up and down, trying to find a place to stay. I was tired out, didn't know anybody, and you can imagine the howde-do! Just then a signor approaches me: "Signor," he asks me, "Cercate una casa?" (As much as to say, "Are you looking for a house, sir?") "Si, signor," I say to him. "Sapete una?" (As much as to say, "Do you know of one?") And he says to me, "Yes." And he takes me to a house. Three sisters make their appearance, one uglier than the other. The youngest is forty-five and the oldest sixty. . . . I remembered the Focadopoules.* They showed me the room. Small, with long lace curtains, three big mirrors and full of ikons, fragrance of incense, branches and sprigs, a real chapel. And now I'm enthralled. . . . In the evening I eat macaroni by the meter and make conversation in Italian. At 22 o'clock (here they count to 24) . . . we go to sleep. "Buona sera! Buona sera, signorino!" This is my life inside the house.

Here the people don't talk. They sing. Their language is musical. Everyone polite, happy, lazy. . . . Every day I go to three or four churches, regularly. I go to admire the superb paintings of the saints made by the great painters. . . . Next door to my house is San Marco, further down San Lorenzo, and then Santa Maria Novella . . . You see how beautiful their language is? You take delight in just pronouncing it. . . . I'll be here Holy Week, and I can imagine what all-night vigils I'll be keeping. . . .

Florence, 1909

. . . I'm very happy . . . I often say to myself, Ah, if it weren't for the tar, I would be nothing! What does it matter that my linen's all

---

* Heroines of the novel *Freedom or Death*.

black, and that I smell like a harbor pier full of barrels and tar and ships' cables. In the course of my walk today I saw flowering almond trees. You can't imagine how I felt. I'm wearing a green hat, a green suit and a green necktie. I'm like a grassy meadow. I don't know anyone, no one knows me, and I do as I like. I eat oranges on the street, and stand for half an hour staring at a painting. . . .*

Kapetan Mihalis must have been troubled by his son's peregrinations, and for the first time his son wrote him a long letter in a direct style, without having recourse to the purist language.

Rome, March 24, 1909

. . . I assure you, dearest Father, that I'm not roving about the foreign cities, and suffering so many, many things, just for my own caprice, like a tourist. . . . While all the young people—all my friends —enjoy life, I've been staying alone with my books in my room or at the universities, trying to earn back whatever you have spent on me. . . .

I was not happy to leave Florence, but I had to see and study Rome. . . . I'm being sparing of money, even for my food. . . . You know that I'm not one of those young people who fail to think of their obligations.

Dearest Father, forgive me for this long letter I am sending you. But I don't know how to tell you that I am extremely well aware of all that you have done for me, and no other father has done so much. And here abroad, I am suffering very much and studying very much and not at all roaming about to pass my time—because one day I want to make our name illustrious. Nikos.

When he returned to Greece several weeks later, in his luggage he brought back his completed thesis, *Nietzsche in the Philosophy of Law*; a one-act tragedy, *The Overseer*; and another one-act play entitled *Comedy*. Had not this last play been published in 1909, Kazantzakis might have been accused of plagiarism, so closely does it resemble

---

* Letter to his parents.

Sartre's *Huis Clos*.* But with Kazantzakis, the eleven dead men shut up in a room that has no exit only hope for the arrival of the Saviour, who, needless to say, does not come.

A philosophical essay entitled "Science Has Gone Bankrupt" was also published by Kazantzakis in the periodical *Panathenea*.

1910–1913.   What would be the good of advanced ideas unless one put them into practice? Nikos loved Galatea; Galatea loved, or thought she loved, Nikos. How to prove to oneself and to other people that one is what one is—that one soars above the stagnant pools of one's own small town?

In 1910, they decided to live as man and wife against the will of their parents and without the blessings of the Church. Kapetan Mihalis gritted his teeth and tightened his purse. The taciturn man must have allowed some imprudent word to slip. The son with the delicate ears and the touch-me-not skin shrank into himself. Though he continued to revere his father as the magnificent man he was, he never again gave him the opportunity to come to his help.

"ἔρως ἀνίκατε μάχαν . . . [Love unconquered in battle . . .]" All sails to the wind, the young lover went on ahead to search for the ideal place to live in. In this respect he was strangely like the water sorcerers. Throughout all his long wanderings, always without any money, he managed to find vast, sunlit houses surrounded with gardens and in pleasant neighborhoods.

To earn their living, he buckled down to hard labor. He was simultaneously stubborn and patient, full of trepidation and possessed of a legendary capacity for work. Now he glued himself to his chair for four years, rushing to translate the maximum number of those works he considered worthy of himself and of the reading public of Greece. Among the titles:

Friedrich Nietzsche: *The Birth of Tragedy*
Friedrich Nietzsche: *Thus Spake Zarathustra*
Johann Peter Eckermann: *Conversations with Goethe*
Charles A. Laisant: *Education Founded on Science*
Maurice Maeterlinck: *The Treasure of the Humble*
Charles Darwin: *The Origin of Species*

---

* *No Exit* was the title of the American translation of Sartre's play.

Ludwig Büchner: *Force and Matter*
Henri Bergson: *Laughter*
William James: *The Theory of Emotion*
Plato: Alcibiades I, on human nature
Plato: Alcibiades II, on prayer
Plato: Ion, Minos, Demodokos, Sisyphos, Cleitophon

One year of hurling defiance at society was enough for the young woman. In 1911 she demanded and obtained a marriage that was celebrated in the chapel of the cemetery in Heraklion, with a schoolmate acting as witness. They slipped onto their fingers weddings rings improvised out of a bit of rusted iron picked up from a grave.

Through oral and written accounts by the people around them, we know that the young couple's life was not always serene. Though they did pass difficult moments, they also knew repose and exhilarating vacations in Crete, where laughter intermingled from all sides—that laughter which Kazantzakis used as a shield against all the evil impinging on him. Everything might have been saved except that their natures were so divergent. Except that—but it is too hard to vivisect the human soul. Having despaired of creating harmony in their own household, from that point on, Kazantzakis seized every opportunity to go away, so that he might, if possible, preserve intact the deep affection he bore his wife.

Before long, Greece—and the entire world as well—was to encounter difficult days: war against the Turks in 1912 and 1913; then against the Bulgars, who coveted Thessaloniki; and immediately after this, the world-wide conflagration and the fratricidal hatred splitting Greece into two hostile camps—that of the Venizelists and that of the royalists, a curse which still weighs heavy upon this country torn between the one and the other.

Kazantzakis volunteered his services. He was assigned to the prime minister's cabinet, and accompanied the future King George II on a tour of Epirus.

"You should have seen how those Greeks welcomed us," he told me at a later point. "They were delirious. They rushed upon the heir apparent, kissing his hands; and not content with unrolling their finest carpets in the mud, they threw themselves down on the ground and offered their own bodies to be trodden on by the foot of the liberating prince."

"And how did the future King of Greece act?"

" 'How much is this carpet worth?' he kept droning in his monotonous voice. 'How much is this carpet worth?' Like a broken gramophone record. 'How much . . . How much . . . How . . .' "

From this period, I have nothing but a postcard dated October 1, 1912, and bearing the stamp of the Athens post office. It is addressed to Harilaos Stephanidis, the old school fellow and most warmhearted friend of Nikos, who used to tease him about his hypersensitivity.

My dearest Friend,

Apparently war is inevitable. If we get there before England, Crete will be occupied by Greece—perhaps on Wednesday. Here, desolation, calm, dust. We will do all we can to get as far as the borders. . . .

Nineteen fourteen arrived with its joys and its sorrows: The long-sought victory—at long last Greece was to have land for fields, no longer left to wither on her ancient rocks. Prosperity. And, above all, a gift of the gods, a kindred spirit, Angelos Sikelianos.

In 1914, the Minister of National Education had opened a competition for textbooks. Any book accepted for teaching purposes was retained in use during four consecutive years in all Greek schools throughout Greece, as well as abroad. To the authors chosen, this meant reputation and considerable income.

Kazantzakis participated in this competition, and all five books of his were accepted. Perhaps his wife did help him to a certain extent. But as though he mistrusted the jealousies which even then his name aroused, he begged her to sign these books in her own name alone. Later on, she sold them without his knowledge.

To this very day, all Greeks honestly believe that Galatea wrote those textbooks. Several recently found letters from Nikos Kazantzakis to his friend, Stephanidis, reveal the truth:*

---

* Two Cretans, Mr. Tzordzaki and Mr. Papadaki, saved these letters of N.K.'s at the time of the auctioning of the house of Harilaos Stephanidis in Crete.

Dearest Harilaos,

. . . I'm taking the baths* because I'm a bit tired, or rather because I can afford 200 drachmas. I can imagine your deadly boredom in Heraklion. Only one cure I know: for you to write educational books. . . . I told you so years ago, but my idea will seem less chimerical to you now that 60,000 drachmas have filtered their way into my pocket. . . .

And what's more, just imagine this: In Constantinople last year, a competition was announced by the Patriarchates for the four grades of the public school. Ah well, I submitted two and . . . both were awarded prizes. . . . Well, the other day, I got a telegram from the Patriarchate asking me to write two more books (on commission!), because none of the others submitted was worth anything. Within ten days, I hope to have finished them here and sent them off. . . . There you have my affairs and my fanfaronade. . . .

Here . . . I'm alone. All day long I play with the sea, stark naked . . . and this fills my entire existence. It seems to me I desire nothing else. It fills my heart like love. If you can create such joy for yourself down there in Heraklion, you'll be able to grow enthusiastic again about life. You lack intensity, love for something, whatever it is—the sea, a woman, your pharmacy,† your own self, etc., etc. . . . I always adore something. I'm full of gratitude and affection for existence. Since this conception of mine is useful for me, I nurture it carefully and persistently. Now that I'm alone . . . I just barely avoided boredom and weariness. But I threw myself into the sea. Gradually I managed to persuade myself that the sea has everything and can give me everything. I found myriad beauties in it. I adorned it with symbols and ideas, and dressed it with all the passion of my own imagination. And now suddenly, after sage preparation, it appears to me in the guise of a flamboyant, omniscient mistress, moistening my body and my soul, and inundating even the loftiest roots of my mind.

Things have the value that we ourselves have the capacity to give them. Everything is blank paper, and we write a foolish or an enthusiastic phrase. . . . I try to observe the following motto: "The more value I find in life, the more value I myself have." And I always try to use my enthusiasm as a tool for my own perfection. . . .

---

* Sulphur springs at Methana, a well-known spa.
† H. Stephanidis dreamed of a pharmacy, which he was to obtain a bit later on.

My very dear Friend,

    . . . You, Manolis,* Androklis,† and I must definitely undertake some joint enterprise. Without you, pleasure rolls off my back like water. But don't worry: I'll find something. It suffices that you help me. . . ."‡

It would be criminal and idiotic to attempt to confine certain human beings within the prevailing molds. When they believe themselves to be God the Father, they do not make themselves ridiculous. When they believe themselves to be the hub of the world, they do not expose themselves to jeers. They are entitled to be visionaries.

Angelos Sikelianos was of their kind. Nikos Kazantzakis described their meeting in 1914 as a "lightning bolt." "First impression," he jotted down: "a spritelike body, a marvel of beauty and freshness. Eagle-eyed, not handsome; laughter, nobility."

To vibrate in unison with the cosmic forces, to master one's mother tongue and ply it in new forms, to keep one's thought and imagination fertile, to aspire only to the heights—both of them possessed these gifts, each manifesting them in a different way: the one as a prince to whom everything was due; the other as a soldier of some future army.

Immediately following their first meeting, Sikelianos and Kazantzakis set out for Mt. Athos. For forty days the two poets roamed through the Sacred Mountain in a state of exaltation, anguished and blissfully happy. That God existed in each form—in Dionysos, in Christ, in Herakles—they hardly doubted. Their great terror, the only doubt they allowed, was whether they would be able to find adequate words for grasping Him and for erecting a cathedral to His glory worthy of Him and their own impulse.

In opposition to Goethe's verdict that life has no purpose and that we ought not even to ask any questions, Kazantzakis believed that human impulse was by no means individual. He saw it as the will of the Cosmos manifesting itself for the first time in man. Whence responsibility, heroism, struggle. Later on, he added: "No hope, absolute freedom, therefore joy!"

---

* Manolis Georgiadis.
† Androklis Xenakis, another schoolmate, who later assumed responsibility for the business at N.K.'s mines.
‡ Letter to H. Stephanidis.

Nikos Kazantzakis kept the record of his pilgrimage to Mt. Athos. A few extracts follow:

Mount Athos

November–December 1914

November 14: 7:30 A.M., we left Athens.

November 19: A superb, early morning view of Athos. Our ascent to Karyes genuinely celestial. . . . Three temptations of the monks: beardless boys, love of money and love of power. Remember how secretively the concierge of Athinaidos betrayed the perverse doings of Mt. Athos to us. . . .

We reached the Iviron Monastery. Magnificent. What a godlike moment on the balcony there when we watched the echoing sea and the moon. Now the moon is in truth fulfilling its predestination—illuminating things eternal. . . .

November 20 (Iviron Monastery): Yesterday evening, we found a most cultivated bishop from Leondoupolis. But he is also writing a novel. Civilization ruins everything. Pictures of kings, foreign landscapes, electric lights, etc., etc.

"Ogni mattina io rinasco. [Each morn I am born anew.]" Life a metaphysical endeavor.

Monastic life, even the way it is now, uncultivated and immoral, is more elevated than secular life. Tradition, even when it is limited to external gestures, is capable of helping the artist create a great work whose social influence may be infinite.

When we have a grand idea, we advance constantly toward a higher form of youth.

Night of November 20, 1914: In the moonlight we came down the stairs, our beads in our hands, to attend the all-night vigil. An eternal moment—as though we were borne aloft on the wings of angels.

November 21: Matins. We read the litanies to the Virgin:

> Heaven and earth cannot contain Thee
> and yet a woman contained Thee.

Often we humanize God instead of deifying man.

The monks' cells: three- to four-room apartments. Electricity, a bell under the lamp, curtains, tea sets, stoves, silent domestics. . . .

November 22: Conversations with the monks on the balcony overlooking the sea. . . . Lack of faith. Fear of poverty. Love of the world. Pseudo-scientific spirit. Ah, simplicity! . . .

An idea: to reorganize Hellenic asceticism. How to make Mt. Athos a hearthplace for the life of the spirit.

November 23: . . . At night in bed, we talked about creation. In the briefest moment, a second of time, as soon as we reach the high point of emotion, there comes an anguish that is full of joy and mystery and curiosity. In what direction will the free creative force independent of us turn? When we reach the high point of an emotion stemming from some specific theme ("Dionysos"), suddenly another cycle on another theme springs up, with great clarity and transparency, ready to become a work of art. And we take this one, abandoning the original theme.

Down with philology, the narrow molds of genres. One salvation only: a religion. This alone is capable of containing all my soul; only in this way is it worthy of revealing itself. . . .

November 24 (Stavronikita Monastery): . . . To create a perfect work, like the bee fertilizing the queen bee, then dying. And this is how I must fertilize the empress—life.

Not scattered and rambling. All my power concentrated on Dionysos-Christ-Tha . . . [?]*

November 26: Bread is not as indispensable as the Idea. . . .

We are more rested than when we started out.

A breath fecundating the ages and giving a certain direction to all spirits—Christ still reanimates the believers.

November 28 (Panagouda Monastery): . . . Make a program of how you ought to be at the end of ten years.

November 29 (Karakallou Monastery): In the evening in bed we talked again about the essence of our supreme desire—to create a religion. Everything is ripened. Ah, how can we externalize whatever is most sacred and profound in us?

November 30: Ah, if I could live always at the peaks! Ah, the humble humdrum of habit! How can I liberate my spirit, how can I break the arrows in my flesh? . . .

Here the people are writhing from the fear of hell. Thus religion is no consolation. To one person I mentioned that Christ had laughed, and that person got angry. . . .

---

* Probably the first letters of the title of some prospective work. N.K.'s biographer P. Prevelakis thinks that they signify "Theophano," and that this was the early title of the verse tragedy which eventually was published as Nicephoros Phocas.

Friday, December 5: *We must add to the essence of life, express the summit of our desire. In the grip of a superhuman will, we must surge forward. There is no moral problem binding us. This has been solved for us, whereas for Nietzsche it was insoluble and extremely painful. . . .*

December 6 (*Iossaphaion Monastery*): *I must concentrate; render in images and religion my heart stirring like the sea. A work with an original form and spirit that will embrace all the love and warmth of my breathing. Something that will open the secret of life, as the sun opens the lily. . . .*

December 7 (*St. Paul's Monastery*): *Eros: the only way to creation. Not with spasms and outcries, but deep, serene, balanced (Plato, Dante, Beethoven, Rodin).*

December 8: *. . . Tonight Tolstoy affected me deeply. His tragic escape: a confession of defeat. He wanted to create religion, and all he could create was novels and art. His finest essence—he knew this well— failed to be expressed.*

Sunday, December 14 (*Dochiariou Monastery*): *. . . One monk, an ex-policeman, told us how he became a monk. He was reading the life of a saint in a village where he'd gone to arrest someone, and the words seemed to him sweeter than honey.*

(Chiliandariou Monastery): Panaretos said to us, "I became a monk not out of piety, but out of poverty. . . ." "And are you happy?" "Thank God! And if sometimes you see me sighing, I'm not sighing for the things of this world—them I execrate, and every day I execrate them—but I sigh for the things of heaven."

December 14: *There are some people who kill their souls and die altogether.*

Saturday, December 20: *This morning we read the third canto of Dante. I shall never forget the impression it made.*

And the conclusion:

Mount Athos. To make a book like the Cathedrals of Rodin. Our spiritual pilgrimage to Mt. Athos. How we lived our race and the faith of our fathers; how we everywhere elevated the soul, how we hailed life rising like an arrow of divine grace toward things heavenly.

The art and faith guiding the vitals of the painter, the architect, the musician, the stone-carver. Religion elevating all things. How we read

Dante, Buddha, the New Testament. How we talked about Greece and life. The Virgin, Christ, the Angels, Nature, the air uncontaminated by woman. . . .*

1915.   The year began well. In a mood of self-confidence, Nikos Kazantzakis jotted down the following comment:

I have entered the cycle of creation. Everything is going well. My body is healthy. The almond trees have blossomed in my garden and my brain is full of light and sureness.

I must conquer two enemies:

1. The flashy, spasmodically lyrical: i.e. the temporary and non essential.

2. The abstract. Each conception must become a plastic image.

I shall conquer everything through asceticism. To summarize a throng of thoughts in a vigorous, striking image. To give the creatures of the imagination the same relief possessed by living reality, like Dante.

January 20, 1915: A profound emotion in the Acropolis Museum.

February 2, 1915: For each subject I must not content myself with my own slipshod, or even studied, thought. I must tense myself and say, "What is higher, always higher?"—until my power reaches a peak of sharpest penetration.

February–March 12: I am studying Dante. His ambitions overwhelm me and spur me on.

After the trip to Mount Athos in 1914, Angelos Sikelianos and Nikos Kazantzakis undertook a historical pilgrimage—"to discover the consciousness of their history," as Kazantzakis recorded in his notebook. They visited Mistra, Sparta, Taygetus, Mycenae, Delphi, Thebes, Mega Spilaion, the Acropolis.

Frequent separations followed by reunions, soaring discussions, a burning desire to work out the synthesis between Byzantium and the civilization of ancient Greece. Sikelianos lived in comfort on the edge of a forest near the sea, worshiped like a god by his wife, the magnificent Eva. Kazantzakis lived with Galatea in a bourgeois apartment in Athens, happy to be at her side again, still vainly hoping for harmony, though

---

* Notebook, 1914.

57

anticipating the catastrophe. Occasionally Galatea accompanied Nikos to Sikelianos' home, where Eva, dressed in the ancient style, her long red tresses grazing the floor, used to welcome her friends in the manner of a great lady—and taught them to weave and braid sandals.

On March 19, 1915, Nikos Kazantzakis commented in his notebooks:

A young man, Merkati, told me tonight that my face is like Tolstoy's. This moved me, because the essence of Tolstoy's endeavor is my own work.

All this new evolution of mine I owe (a) to my expeditions to Mt. Athos, Mistra, Delphi; (b) to my recent reading (Dante, Rodin . . . Bergson, Claudel . . .); and (c) to the company of Angelos Sikelianos.

That same night of March 19, after hearing the twelve Gospels of Holy Thursday, Kazantzakis noted:

Great feeling in the church. The crucified Christ seemed to belong to me more, to be more my own self. I was profoundly aware of the "suffering God" inside me, and I said, "With perseverance, love, and endeavor may the Resurrection come." Joy, conquest of passion, transubstantiation, freedom. Simplicity and serenity, composed of the essenza of all the passions subjected to the Eye of God. Spirit like light and like the clear water of the fountain.

A "Christian" fervor, the like of which we shall not find again in Nikos Kazantzakis, except in his book on Saint Francis. But the soul "like light and like the clear water of the fountain" he knew how to forge for himself and to preserve intact until the end.

March 20: I thank You, my God, because You have freed me from Science, Truth, Art, Duty; from all words and all ideals. I thank You because You have saved me from the death which I could not endure because it was against my higher nature. Only You, eternal and serene One, can give rest to the exalted turmoil of my heart. . . .

But the storm was there, lying in wait:

June 8: *Ah, if I could only go away—go away and be delivered from the society of men; escape to my house by the seaside,* and be "μόνος πρòς μόνον [alone with myself]." This evening once again my spirit broke from incessant coarse contacts: vile, mean things; ugly things; petty passions . . .*

My God, how can I save myself, how deliver myself? I am stifled with disgust, disgust because I am degrading myself. Because if I do not go away, I shall not be saved! I feel like crying, like bellowing, "Ah, would I had never been born!" Lord, I have cried unto Thee. Hearken unto me, Lord!

And he did go away—to a small island, Siphnos, and the Monastery of the Virgin of the Mountain, where he isolated himself from the ninth to the nineteenth of July.

I'm writing, I'm writing . . . The knot has loosened and the sob has burst. I feel happy, as though I'd never known people. . . .
July 18, noontime: *I've finished the whole work. It's the skeleton, but it has relieved me because it was written with absolute sincerity. I fell ill immediately—vomitings and fever—but it's nothing. The flesh gets a little angry, ma soeur la chair [my sister, the flesh], but its anger will be spent.*
July 24: *I'm leaving the Monastery. Tomorrow Athens, where I'm eager to see Galatea again.*
July 25: *The joy of return. I always return better. With more tenderness, more calm, more goodness. . . . Until people and base habit revive my bitterness, and I go away again in order to heal again.*
August 10–25: *In Sykia, where the joy of living is balanced in a godlike way, I lack nothing. "Laudato si, mi Signore, per il fratello Angelo che è bello e robustoso e casto e forte. [Be praised, my lord, for Brother Angelo who is beautiful and robust and chaste and strong.]"*
August 25: *I'm leaving for Athens. In the evening when she saw me all of a sudden sitting at the iron-grill gate, how wonderful it was, the furtive kisses. But the 30th of August a ghastly day. Terrible scene . . . We're both leaving for Sykia.*
September 3, 4, 5: *Horrible days. A guilty letter . . . And I felt that only one thing exists: the light. . . .*

---

* N.K. was planning to have a house in Sykia, next to Sikelianos.

The moral problem has been most clearly laid before me, and I have accepted it with a severe kindness after a tremendous struggle, wherein the lower elements revolted against the summit. I won out, and grew thin as Herakles after he'd seen Hades and come up to the light again, in a reflective state of mind.

Still in the groove of Olympian Herakles, Kazantzakis noted:

How people misconstrue the sacred figure of Herakles, who is altogether a mystical hero: holy, all spirit, asceticism, struggle, profound grief, and ultimate inner purification.

September 7: A marvelous walk on a hill from which we could see outlets of the Alpheus River. Along the river bank on the way back, we saw scattered red fires like flowers. It was the people at the festival who were caught out in the dark. Tonight I was filled with love and the simple things of life.

May I escape from the webs of society to find deep joy in silence and grace, like God before the Creation. . . .

September 8: There's nothing left for me any more except my work. Woman has behaved unworthily; man has fallen in my presence. All forms of ugliness have been cast upon me. There is only one salvation: my work (art and religion, the essence of my will). Flight. Facing myself alone. Escaping from details, pettinesses. "Omnivergente, rinnegator di tutto, da me maestro. [One who turns toward all things and disowns all things, my own teacher.]" Not forgetting the highest models of virtue: Christ, Buddha, Michelangelo, Beethoven.

September 11 and 12: Sykia. One of the worst days of my life. This kind of life is unbearable, and life together utterly lethal for us both.* Nos sublimes ne s'amalgament plus. [We have ceased to merge on our highest levels.] The end is coming—horrible, calm, inevitable. . . . She will be relieved, and I shall become once more master of myself, free.

All my work will have as its motto and aim "Come l'uom s'eterna [How man makes himself eternal]."† This is where I've wound up.

---

* That is, for him and his wife.

† Four of the works planned at this period were published as verse tragedies: Christ, Nicephoros Phocas, Ulysses, and Herakles. The last of these, Herakles, appeared only in a periodical in Alexandria, Egypt, and cannot be found.

To found a religion, to found a religion at all costs, this was the obsession haunting Kazantzakis over a long span of years, driving to the furthest extreme his innate tendencies toward asceticism and renunciation sanctified by laughter. After harsh struggles, he came to realize and know that the "new myth" had escaped him. At that point it was poetry that acted as his spinal cord.

Not to scribble verses, but to confine his spirit in the from-time-immemorial "Ah!"—the beginning and end of all human life:

My God, heaven and earth cannot contain Thee.
Only an "Ah!" can do so.

In the *Symposium* (written probably between 1918 and 1920), Kazantzakis evoked in an extremely Biblical style and in the form of a confession an ascetic exercise to which he would have liked to have devoted two years of his life in the silence of Mt. Athos. He was able to accomplish this only in a fragmentary way and over the course of several sojourns in various retreats.

What was he seeking in this imaginary hermitage in the depths of a gorge as deep and narrow as a well?

. . . To obey a strict rhythm, to enlist in an army animated for the purpose of attaining the maddest hope. . . . Like the ascetics, I too wanted to conquer pettiness, fear and death, through faith.

To begin with, he had divided his ego into two enemy camps: the higher and the lower, the clear and the obscure, the soul and the body, and he had declared war between them—

. . . I said to myself: I shall humiliate and insofar as I am able confine the desires of the flesh. Does the flesh want to sleep? I shall remain awake. Does it want to eat? I shall fast. Does it want to sit down? I shall arise and climb the mountain. Is it cold? I shall make myself naked and walk upon the cobblestones. . . . When I have conquered the flesh, I shall turn to the soul, and I shall distribute it too into two camps, lower and higher, human and divine. I shall fight the petty pleasures of the

spirit: reading and recollection, pleasure in victory, justice, friendship, tenderness, joy and grief. Then, once again, when I have won for the second time I shall proclaim a new division within myself: Down with hope, the ultimate enemy, and up, high up, with God's flame, for it shall consume me, without smoke or movement, in deep darkness and silence. . . .

No! No! I shall never express the martyrdom and pleasure in this deep pit of the hermitage; not because I do not want to or dare not do so, but because the martyrdom is inexpressible, and there are no human words to grasp its voluptuousness.

The inexpressible martyrdom described by Kazantzakis is by no means an imaginary one. Though he never spent two consecutive years of asceticism on Mt. Athos, he did ply himself with various forms and intervals of asceticism whenever he succeeded in isolating himself on some mountain. There he could exercise his body, teaching it to obey the exigencies of his soul.

The *Symposium* has a surprise ending, to put it mildly. At the very moment when the ascetic believed himself prepared, when the time had come

for the tumultuous festival to break up and the scourge to swish through the air, and for my soul, that vast spark, to burst upon your ramparts, Babylon, and soar through the streets, burning the wooden gods, melting the golden calves, and enveloping your vitals, and you roaring out for mercy—at that very moment, a dream came to light up the darkened mind of the anchorite.

I went into my paternal home and saw my father sitting, as was his custom, cross-legged, in the corner of the divan. When he caught sight of me, he leaped up fiercely, calling out:

"You've come to me in a cassock? You're weary of the world? And where have you learned to know the world? Have you been married? Have you lost a child? Have you had a high old time? Have you worked? Get out of my sight."

Ever so slowly he turned around, staring at me, and he remained silent a long while. A wave of sweet and tender feeling overcame him, and he began speaking plaintively:

"How have you come to me like this, without blood or strength?

Your hair's already begun to fall out, my child; your eyes have gotten dim; you've gotten hunchbacked; you've wrapped yourself in a cassock; you knock on doors like a beggar. Has my race gone barren? What have you done with the blood I gave you?"

Then it all dissolved in mid-air, as quietly as dew. The vision faded and the voice vanished. . . .

Ah, how suddenly this loomed in my solitude as the greatest temptation of all, greater than woman, the voice of my father:

"Rise up. You seek God? There He is: Action, replete with mistakes, fumblings, persistence, agony. God is not the power that has found eternal equilibrium, but the power that is forever breaking every equilibrium, forever searching for a higher one. Whosoever struggles and makes progress by the same method in his own narrow sphere finds God and works with Him. Rise up and go out among human beings. Learn to love them and to kill them—love is respect, affection, loathing. Do not expect to give birth to anything by yourself alone. You will rise only by struggling along with human beings, by pitying and hating our unhappy heart. Come with all your weaknesses and your pusillanimities, all your chimeras in their entirety. In the course of your struggles you will become pure. Descend and choose your own panoply and strike. The enemy is the God dressed in cassock, fingering the rosary, unwashed, unmarried, indolent. . . ."

The days passed, and the months. Illnesses came, delirium . . . And spring came. . . .

On that day I'd taken a long walk, I was reveling in the heat of the sun as the worm on the ground; I was reviving. It's spring, I thought to myself, the great Temptation; the monks cannot keep it from treading upon their solitary places.

I grew dizzy and leaned back upon a tree. I saw the birds gathering earth, hairs, twigs, building with haste; all the earth was stirring, abounding with myriads of live things, working away. I felt the tree I was leaning against pumping the sap up to its tip, struggling to transubstantiate the mud, stone, water, air and sun and make them into flowers. I saw substance, that great whore with her wide thighs, fall like Mary Magdalene at the feet of Christ, and, in tears, she too became transubstantiated.

Deep compassion overcame me for Earth, who sustains us all upon herself and gives us nourishment. Inexpressible sadness weighed upon my heart, because I had spoken ill of you, O Mother Earth, I who prance amid your vitals, full of earth and dew.

O Lady Amazon, when his horse charges through the obstacle course, the good equestrian holds his cup of water full to overflowing, but does not let a single drop spill. And in the same way, in your own impulsive ascent, you must hold the human heart level, solid, full. . . .

A song from the earthen heart of life outweighs the most deadly sin. Lord, Lord, hearken unto the song warbled by the earth caught in the snares of death. At that instant, weakened as I was by illness, enchanted by the spring, I was aware of the song of the earth arising from thousands of mouths, from insects and wild beasts, from water, grasses, human beings, bounding upward, loud, swift, distant, and within me like a summons, a command, a complaint.

Ah, the sweetness of life. With what nonchalance it sings—like the red-throated goldfinch, sitting and warbling, carried away by the fragrance of the wild pear tree in springtime and by the hot nest stirring overhead with two shiny eggs in the middle. . . . And it lifts its red throat and cries: "Let me sing and then warm them. Let me sing first!"— unaware that it is sitting upon the snares of the bird hunter. . . .

In all the houses we ever lived in, he always had his own retreat on the upper floor. There, from dawn on—or sometimes from three o'clock in the morning on—he used to wage his battles. But how he loved to come down with the last rays of the sun and bite into the other half of the fruit he had turned his back on all day long.

Conversations, walks, frugal meals, laughter, nights of love and tenderness. It was not an exhausted man who came back to me, or a sullen, morbid man, but the lovable mischief-maker, the patient schoolmaster, the torrential inventor of new tales to lighten my solitude. And then the color came back to my own cheeks, and I in turn picked up my pen to sing my happiness:

> *I have chosen my beloved,*
> *A high citadel of granite . . .*

About the year 1916 we do not have much information. We know only that Manolis Kalomoiris' opera *The Overseer*, from Kazantzakis' tragedy by the same name, had its world premiere in the middle of March. We also know that on the twentieth of August of the same year, Kazantzakis became a member of the Society of Social and Political Sciences.

In 1917, there was Zorba—Zorba and the famous lignite mine, whose actual location was not in Crete at all but in the southern part of the Peloponnesus, at Prastova, in Mani, near a stunning bay with fine sand and fresh-water springs spurting in the sea and along the beach. Nikos often told me how the goats would come and strike the sand with their hooves to make the fresh water spurt out. The old people of Mani, who still remember Kazantzakis, Zorba, and their cabin, proudly point out the grotto where Nikos used to take refuge to do his reading and writing. They also remember Sikelianos and how his voice reverberated as he recited his poetry and how he slept on a kind of platform that had been constructed for him over the waves.

I found this little bay of Prastova just as Nikos had described it to me. But (and I am annoyed at having to record this) the tiny hamlet of Stoupa did not have a single slice of bread to offer us. Nothing but olives and tomatoes and a few figs. Abandoned by the government in Athens, the inhabitants of Mani may well say that they live "behind the sun."

When the mine collapsed, Zorba and Kazantzakis abandoned it, the one setting off for the mines in the Chalcidice peninsula, then to Serbia, and the other for Switzerland. From this period, we would know hardly anything, except for the letters preserved by Kazantzakis' friend, Iannis Angelakis:*

Vienna, May 25, 1917

[post card]
My dear Angelakis,
   . . . I am surheureux [hyperhappy], i.e., a kind of unhappiness and agony. I'm alone and can't laugh, i.e., rest. Enormous musical activity. This week, Beethoven's Ninth, Brahms, Strauss, Max Reger. And dances.

Always, N.

Grindelwald, October 5, 1917

Dearest Angelakis,
   "Οὐρεάτε σκιόεντα, Θάλασσα τε ἠχήεσσα [The shadowy mountains and echoing sea]" are between us, and our voices can't be heard. I cry out

* A lawyer and native of Asia Minor, intimate friend of N.K., who unhesitatingly gave up his career and followed N.K. on his special mission to the Caucasus.

every day. I write, sometimes to Galatea, sometimes to you, sometimes to Pharantatos.*

Please write me regularly two letters each month . . . one friendly one, wherein the spirit can talk of the eternal things that used to agitate us both in our evenings together, and one purely business. . . .

My spirit has not yet found serenity. Like the cat who wants to give birth and rushes to all the corners of the house, into the drawers, the cupboards, underneath the beds, and nowhere can feel happy because inside her there is a heavy agony, an ineffable awe, so I rush from mountain to mountain looking for a place where I can give birth. But no, I think Switzerland is not for my particular disposition. If, at least, Sphakianakis† were only here . . .

Zurich, Freigutsstrasse 14
October 27, 1917

. . . Here I get along as follows: 1) materially—food-rations with cards, very expensive; 2) spiritually—only the music is great. There are libraries, but as you know, from books we no longer expect much. There are a few very good paintings in the Museum. This spring, God willing, I'll go to Paris. Only there will my brain feel at ease. . . .‡

Zurich, November 15, 1917

My dear Angelakis,

. . . I'm staying in Zurich here at the Consulate General, because the consul§ is a very good friend of mine. . . .

An intellectual movement worthy of us doesn't exist either here or anywhere outside Paris. What I need is a circle of vibrating human beings, a soaring impulse, a flaming atmosphere of belief, joy, discipline. I work alone, wandering through the mountains, and sometimes Nietzsche's face appears before me, troublante comme un pressentiment douloureux [disturbing as a painful premonition]. That's why I want to become good and strong and go up to a very high mountain, so that I'll be able to carry the weight of my anxiety and desire without bending. I

---

* Iannis Pharantatos, Athenian lawyer, friend of N.K., and partner in the mine at Prastova.
† Kosta Sphakianakis, a composer and professor of music, descendant of a great Cretan family and intimate friend of N.K. They spent a summer together in Kifisia.
‡ Letter to Iannis Angelakis.
§ Iannis Stavridakis, the Cretan friend we met earlier.

think of you always with profound feeling, because we are united, I believe, by a very mystical thing, in which we are alike, the same raging passion for our alma mater, the Orient. Here I'm fully conscious of the superiority of my race. And when all this Frankish civilization vanishes from the brilliant face of the earth, we will come back—we Orientals— to renew the seed of life. I sit here, I the Oriental, and, like the spider, eat my heart out in order to weave the strong fabric, the new warp of hope.

. . . What's become of the Prastova mine? What profits will we have from the textbooks, and when? What's become of the lumber; what's happening with the Chalcidice mines? . . . Here I'm living my own intense, inner, retirée [withdrawn], self-sufficient life, . . . but I'm consumed by worry over what's to become of our affairs back there, and this robs me of my serenity. These past days I've finished some work, and now I'll begin something new, and I have all the nausées [feelings of nausea] and nervousness of a pregnant woman. And I'm leaving for Arosa tomorrow. . . . God willing, there I'll find out whatever I'm looking for, and so once again begin rolling my Sisyphean rock, in the compulsory labors of my own exquisite punishment.

Like the praying Moslem, my whole spirit makes its namaz* facing the Orient. Ah, in the midst of this heavy fog and damp and snow, how the blue mountain wells up, the sea, a red rag on a date tree, the hot sand, the Moorish arch, the fellah girl with the jug on her head, bare- foot, dark, her breasts taut! All my spirit burns like Damascus at noon, and an Arab dance on my ten fingers carries me away, while I quietly sit in their theater observing their anemic little ideas and their fat pale women and their gold teeth. Ah, the smell of the Oriental port with its rotting oranges and watermelons, its caïques rocking to right and left, and the bare, mud-spattered legs! This is what living abroad has given me—disgust for everything which is not the Orient and my own race. I have found myself again, the descendant of the Arabs on the African island of Crete. Please God, our journey to the Orient may take place now while our blood "is still alive and reigning."

Kazantzakis was to believe more and more in the omnipotence of the spirit: If one knows how to desire a thing, one obtains it. One even creates it out of the void—an idea frequently expressed in his work. For instance, in his tragedy *Christopher Columbus*, or *The Golden Apple*:

---

* Moslem prayer.

COLUMBUS [who is trying to persuade the Prior of the Monastery of the Madonna of the Atlantic, Captain Alonso and Captain Juan]:

> Faithless generation, defiled, ungrateful, doomed
> to death.
> This generation mentions the earthly Paradise
> And bursts out laughing!
> Never, Captain Alonso, never Captain Juan,
> You will never find the new land—know this from me—
> Because you do not have it within your own vitals.
> The new land is born first inside our own heart
> And only then emerges out of the sea . . .

And to Isabella, who is skeptical, and refuses to believe Columbus' promises:

> "Nonexistent" we call whatever we have not yet desired. . . .
> If the islands do not exist, then why was I born? They
> exist because I exist.
> Let him exist, my Queen, who preserves the dreams of
> the night by day, and struggles to put them into
> action!
> This is what youth means, this is the meaning of faith.
> Only in this way can the world grow!

1918.   On this first of January, Iannis Stavridakis, Mihalis Gunalakis, a young woman and Nikos Kazantzakis set off on a long peregrination through the Swiss mountains: Chur, Maran, Peter Molinis, Davos, Pontresina, Silvaplana—high peaks, high aspiration and discussions; occasionally a disagreement or a poignant regret, never a platitude or a vile thought.

Kazantzakis commented on the color of the mountain tops, the form of the crystal-covered trees, the icy torrents, the moon, the dawn, a lonely bird flying over the immense, snow-blanketed expanse, a little girl offering him a bouquet of flowers. . . . On the evening of January 9, in a deserted hotel at Pontresina, conversation was lagging. At that point, Nikos suggested they talk about love. They drew lots, and he had to open the debate:

"I identify love with élan vital," I said. "1) Plants, 2) animals, 3) human beings, 4) the uniting of male and female spirits, and 5) the founders of religions. . . . The relationships of our Order must not be physical intercourse, but rather an intercourse of the spirit comprising all the pleasures of a higher intercourse." A rousing debate blazed up. They all shouted that this was contrary to nature, a horrible sacrifice, and that I was giving a religious tendency to our Order. *I answered that we must sacrifice individual happiness, transmute lust, and have inferior contacts only outside our own Order. We must redouble our powers in order to preserve the virtue of our aspiration. . . .*

January 10: We have reached Silvaplana. I have an intense recollection of Nietzsche and Lou Salome. Gunalakis is leaving us. Sadness at his departure.

The days went by—St. Moritz, Bevers, Tiefencastel. Enchanting landscapes; half-serious, half-erotic conversations with the young woman. Return to Zurich, concerts, banquets, fits of unhappiness.

On February 13, we meet her at Bellevue:

It was raining. We went to Hall-Stube. She was wearing a simple black velvet dress, an ambre [amber] necklace, white lace showing. Beautiful eyes, large and intelligent. We drank two bottles of Dezaley and ate fondue. High spirits, laughter; I bought her a big red rose: the Annunciation.

Four months of love were to follow, with high points and low points; moments when it seemed they had been grasping happiness, and other moments when there was a desperate feeling of aloneness. On the fourteenth of June, at daybreak, the young woman went away. The notebooks resume their thread of excursions through mountains and valleys. Not another word is ever mentioned about this scholarly young woman who for four months had accepted the gift or—according to the Chinese—the "curse" of "living near an interesting man" . . . To convey the state of her companion's spirit at this precise period, I quote at random a few phrases scattered through the six pages torn from a school notebook, which I have before me as the only testimony of this brief interlude:

February 15 and 16: An impulsive communion with her. I pour my spirit feverishly into her.

February 17: When we sat down in the restaurant in the village of Uster, the sun shone on her through the window, lighting her with shadows. She was red, her neck white against the black velvet: very beautiful, and I told her so.

February 18: Around the dining-room table at the Consulate . . . I motionless, pale, at the threshold of death. I was suffocating. I said: "Would that I might quietly open the door and depart from this world. I want to hide myself!"

February 20: This afternoon I walked with her. I told her that what attracts me is the supreme incandescent circle of the divinity; art is too limited for me. I renounce the certainty of profit, because I accept as my supreme commandment "Better two in the bush than one in the hand." I told her that Eros, as I imagine him, treads this sacred earth with muddy feet, a sunburned body, and two enormous wings of many colors, predominantly green. I told her about my ancestors, the Arabs, and that like them my own supreme command is to burn the ships of my hopes, and to conquer my new Crete by compelling my spirit to lunge toward new heights.

March 11: A superb day. Our hearts leaped at Gandria. We said, "Here we shall be happy." We came back happy. . . .

March 13: We talked about love. I read Plato's Symposium: "Better to make love openly than in secret." . . . I tease her about her learning, and I say to her: "I'd love to be on the boat the Queen of Sheba used to send the wise Solomon every three years, full of monkeys and peacocks."

March 17: Sunday. A very beautiful day, walking, convalescence. I'm consumed by worry that I must find a new justification for my existence. I told her that now I understand God much better, because I'm working as He works each and every moment, with innumerable faces (plants, animals, human beings), and that we are taking together the same path of love. I am no longer capable of doing anything ephemeral or disjointed. At each point, I give myself all the way. . . .

March 19: Great intellectual exaltation. My body melts, wax in the flame. I feel God like a woman mincing and gliding about me, and I want to grab hold of Him, all flesh and blood. At the fireplace in Seehof, I was trembling all over.

March 20: Today I told her, "Ah, if only I had four men at my table, so we could talk together and create God." She shuddered, seeing how far I am away from her; farther away; terribly separated. . . .

Nine years later, the young woman was to return, married and the mother of a child, hoping for the impossible. But Kazantzakis, having cut his moorings, was sailing all alone, on the ocean of his *Odyssey*, which she detested so much that she refused even to hear him read it. Kazantzakis suffered very much because of this, and he complained of it in his letters. It is interesting to note that all the women he had consorted with till that time had been a driving force in his active life. All except one—Elsa. And Elsa was far away . . . inaccessible. Each in her own way had loved him and hoped to see him change his nature. "As though one could expect a banana tree to produce oranges!" Yes, he had suffered a great deal at that time and in various ways. But not a drop of bitterness remained in him. No creature once loved by him could ever complain of any lack of regard or affection. And more than that, he taught me to feel affection for all these women who had enriched and polished him, each in her own way, as the wave polishes the pebble and knowing fingers the amber bead. . . .

Four months of joys and griefs shared, and then once again, at the end of this year, 1918, Kazantzakis tried to solve the problem of his finances:

Athens, November 28, 1918

My dear Angelakis,

I came to Athens to see the Foreign Minister. Unfortunately I did not reach him in time, and so once again I am left hanging in the air, supremely disgusted by the changes I see in Athens, the nouveaux riches and the hungry. I've brought permits with me from the Swiss government for 500 tons of carob-tree fruit. . . . I'm a member of a society composed of Swiss and Greeks for exporting carob fruit, oil, and tobacco, and importing into Greece iron, machines, fabrics, pharmaceutical drugs, lumber, etc., etc.

If you think you can, take your holiday and come to Athens for a few days . . . so we can reach an understanding once and for all. . . . For we're about to undertake great enterprises. . . .

Great "enterprises" or little "enterprises," commerce or literature, it must have been written in the Great Book that you would never profit from it, Nikos. Do you remember the "cemetery of our hopes"? The famous five-year-plan you pinned up over our bed at Gottesgab "at the

71

pinnacle of happiness and of Czechoslovakia"? It contained the list of the things we were supposed to accomplish and the aims we must pursue for a better future.

How I used to wait for the postman in those days! He came from a great distance, in sunshine or snowstorm, and when his steps creaked on the narrow wooden staircase, I would rush out to meet him. But from all directions the letters were negative. There were no checks; the editor wasn't paying. And yet your ideas for films, scenarios, books, for the establishment of university chairs and for an International of the Spirit to safeguard peace have all been carried out by others. Sometimes even in accordance with your own plans, your own adaptations, but always without any mention of your name. This we did not surmise at the time. All I remember is how you would get up, a bit more stiffly than usual, and put a big red cross over the disappointed hope. Before the first year had slipped by, we had a perfect cemetery confronting us, very droll-looking with its scarlet crosses.

Though tangible riches forever eluded you, the miracle came many times, kneeling before your door like a camel waiting for your to mount. From Zurich you had cried aloud for help from the Orient. And it came "in a different form," as it should have done; without folklore or faded dreams; but with problems that were burning ones, the only kind worthy of virile thought. . . .

Having been appointed Director of the Ministry of Public Welfare by Venizelos, Kazantzakis prepared feverishly a vast plan for rescuing the Greek refugees from the Caucasus:

Athens, June 10, 1919

My dear Angelakis,

I am enthusiastic because I have much work and I do good without finding many obstacles. Today I got a telegram from Aidepsos from the Minister. He says he approves of the note I submitted to him about organizing a department for reinstating the refugees.*

The struggle and contact with people do me a great deal of good, and just as you strengthen yourself by swimming in the sea, so I do by struggling with the human element.

---

* Greece had sent military troops against the U.S.S.R., and the Bolsheviks had begun harassing the Greeks in the Caucasus.

. . . I'm working very hard at the Ministry, even at night. And within me the whole face of God shines.

[no date]

. . . The journey to the Orient is going well. I study every question for five or six days, and then I submit a statement to the Minister, wherein I mention all the possible or proposed solutions and formulate which is the correct one according to my opinion. In this way I give him an opinion, and he is very pleased. He sends my notes on to Venizelos regularly with great pleasure. That is why he has accepted all my organization for the Mission and now he's awaiting telegraphic approval from Paris* so that it can be submitted to the other Ministers. . . .

Don't tell me not to get tired. My joy and liberation is to work over and above my duty. When working hours are over and all the "subaltern" employees have left with relief, I remain free and work away beneath the wing of the great God. I think of you at regular intervals, and pray for the great trip—the sky of the Orient at night, the new moon, the squalid villages, the colorful calico draperies and the shadowy fountains at noon. . . .†

[no date]

My dear Friend,

Your letters I welcome in the same way that I do your words, all pluck, power, passion. Your letter strides into my office just the way that you yourself come in, dusty from some great march, with your thick walking stick and your forehead burning.

And I sit in front of my desk, and the whole Orient dances over these documents and payment orders and booklets of the refugees. I'm working divinely. I'm exhausted, and when I go to the office, I prance like a deer as I say to myself, When will I begin to work, to govern human beings, to see my will become tangible in daily action, and consequently to observe the value of my own spirit? . . .

I eat dinner at Sfikaki,‡ and return immediately to the Ministry till midnight. I have the voluptuous giddiness of overexhaustion. I've gotten very thin—this too is a method of giving one's blood for the Fatherland. . . .§

---

* Venizelos was in Paris for the Peace Conference.
† Letter to Iannis Angelakis.
‡ A restaurant near the Ministry.
§ Letter to Iannis Angelakis.

In great haste, June 25, 1919

My dear Angelakis,

  Most probably we'll be leaving in ten or fifteen days' time. I'll set you up in Constantinople as chief of our department there. I'll go on to Russia, the Caucasus, the Black Sea, where I'll set up other departments.

  You must be our administrator . . . You'll be assigned the post as head of Section A. When I leave, I want you to replace me as Director, because I regret leaving half finished the activities I've been involved with here. . . .

  "I sow to all the winds" might have served as Nikos Kazantzakis' motto. The man of the iron will, this inexhaustible man, was never capable of remaining at his post once his task had been successfully accomplished. Body and spirit revolted; fever shattered him. It was by no means the fanatical work that exhausted him. On the contrary, routine and the easy chair were repugnant to him. Like the pilgrim who comes across a quagmire and flees it for fear of seeing his own face debased by the stagnant water. And if one wanted to see him flourish again? A cell by the sea or on some mountaintop, pen and paper, plenty of fruit, a loving human being at his side, and he would become fresh and fit again, mocking time and himself, hoping for nothing, demanding nothing, indomitable—days, months, years if necessary in pursuit of perfection.

  With the 1917 Revolution, the Greeks of the Transcaucasus—Armenia, Georgia, Azerbaidzhan, as well as those of Ekaterinoslav and Novosibirsk—were persecuted by the Bolsheviks and the Kurds* and had asked the Greek government to repatriate them. For the most part they were peasants accustomed to rich lands, and to make it possible for them to live on the meager soil of Greece became a challenge. Nikos Kazantzakis understood at once the scope of the problem. Venizelos also understood and approved the decisions taken by his new Director of the Ministry of Public Welfare.

  Kazantzakis did not like to speak about himself. When the conversation would turn to those years of public activity, the main recollection he mentioned used to be the touching reception that the Greek committee in charge of the repatriation of the refugees had been given at Baku, at Tiflis, at Sohum, at Yerevan, Constantinople—yes, in

---

* N.K. saw Greeks who had been saddled like beasts of burden by the Kurds.

74

Constantinople too. For Greece was still nurturing her great dream, which she almost saw become a reality in the time of Venizelos—that is, the foundation of an autonomous state in the Black Sea region, where the Greeks of the Caucasus, those marvelous "sentinels of the frontiers," might become established.

Three of his great friends who helped him carry out his task successfully are already gone: Herakles Polemarchakis, a colossal Cretan lieutenant colonel; Iannis Stavridakis; and Giorghos Zorba. Still alive are Iannis Angelakis, who will soon be ninety years old, and Iannis Konstantarakis, another of Nikos' schoolfellows. Both their accounts agree that everything had gone well, according to the plans drawn up by Kazantzakis; that their mission had lasted approximately one and a half years; that they had brought assistance to hundreds of thousands of Greeks; that they had organized hospitals; and that the transporting of the people desirous of leaving Russia was carried out with the greatest efficiency—human beings, domestic animals and implements all transported on Greek boats.

But Venizelos was forced to resign, and the refugees settled in western Thessaly and Macedonia suffered a great deal. Might this be the reason why Kazantzakis avoided the subject?

And once again he withdrew into his solitude. Some people might think him insensitive, because he kept his distance. But the man who, "in order not to forget," mentioned in his notebooks the kindness of Sikelianos in getting up at dawn one day to wake him up, and a tear at a moment of farewell, and the timid gesture of a child offering him a bouquet of field flowers—this man who regarded forgetfulness as a deadly sin and a coward's way out registered the whole world's suffering. Injustice upon injustice, crime upon crime, catastrophe upon catastrophe, the sparse victories, his own defeats, were all recorded in his brain, nothing obliterated.

Stavridakis reaped by death in the flower of his age; Varvara Nikolayevna from Tiflis, with the enormous boat-shaped eyes—the only woman, as Nikos noted, "who ever asked me to give up everything for her" and who filled his cabin with red roses on the day of his departure—I gladly imagine him carrying off with him in the way depicted in a canvas of Moreau that he had so loved in his youth. Far away, yet exceedingly close, stretching their hands toward him, one of them with a face as brown as the bread of their childhood, the other pearly and mysterious and ethereal, her long hair a black veil in the wind, forever lost and forever his own.

Absorbing every emotion, he was often on the point of breaking from the wealth of memories. Yet this man of letters who scorned literature kept the floodgates closed until his visions had become clarified and freed, without any loss of richness, from whatever suspended material might make them opaque. Clarity was necessary to him. He has sometimes been compared to Victor Hugo. He is closer to Homer. When he was composing his frescoes with big brush strokes, he was the Picasso of *Guernica*, or even a cave man.

Elaborate scaffoldings of words he came to love less and less, even when they resembled cathedrals. He had confidence only in the "verb" duly labored over and ripened in the depths of his being and passed through the alembic of his own vitals.

"Why have you torn it all up again?" I often used to ask, saddened at the sight of so much hard work thrown into the wastebasket.

"It's dictated too much by the brain, Lenotschka. It hasn't come from the vitals yet."

Twenty years had to go by before *The Greek Passion* came out. Priest Grigoris-Who-Eats-Alone, the crucified refugees, Priest Photis-the-Just, Manolios the visionary rebel and his fellow apostles, there was nothing there, and yet everything converged in it. The foreign press at once recognized this novel as a masterpiece. Albert Schweitzer declared that he had never read anything more moving. Roman Catholics and Protestants acclaimed it, even promoted it; but the Greek Orthodox Church cried "Blasphemy!"—except for the Patriarch of Constantinople, who went so far as to recommend to the Church of Crete that Kazantzakis be buried with the rites of the Orthodox Church.

1920. After a short stay in Athens, Kazantzakis took refuge in a monastery at Delphi on Mt. Parnassus, and then in another monastery in Crete. There he resumed his tragedy *Herakles*, finished it, and sent it for publication to a periodical in Alexandria.

In his notebook, he made the following entries:

August 21, 1920: I often used to go to our house in the country to see my parents. Mother sunburned, radiant, determined, holy. Father pitch-black, "bilious," fussy, heavy, overseeing the workers as they gathered the grapes. I watched him lean over, absorbed in the work, and I said: "How like me he is in his forehead, his determination, his attentiveness.

And how far away! The grapes will become a dance of women in Vienna or an ascetic hut where, at peace, I shall devote myself to my work." . . . August 29, 1920 (Vrondissi Monastery): Through the open window a breeze came into the church and turned the pages of the psalmbook on the pulpit. That evening, by the fireplace, the Hegoumenos [head of the monastery] held the oil lamp to give me light while I took notes for the Herakles."

1921.   Kazantzakis returned to Athens only to resign together with the Venizelos government on February 6, 1921. And then he was off again to Paris, Germany, Venice. Having returned once more to his own roost, where he found the fire quenched, he left with Kosta Sphakianakis for Kifisia in the plain of Attica and the clear shade of the pine trees. Work, fruitful conversations with his musicologist friend, visits, long walks fragrant with the perfume of the masticha trees, wild thyme and sage. This light earth, stirred by the wind into a fragrant, transparent cloud, is propitious for meditation. Here in Attica, Christ might have been born just as well. In any case, during the summer of 1921 in Kifisia, in the verse tragedy of The Christ, He did return to the world, crucified and resurrected in Nikos Kazantzakis' thought.

In the course of that faraway year, at the age of thirty-seven, Kazantzakis already divined his own limitations. He recorded a conversation he had in Crete with Manolis Georgiadis on August 18, 1921:

My aim is not Art for Art's sake, but to find and express a new sense of life (remember Nietzsche and Tolstoy). In order for me to attain this aim, there are three paths: 1) the path of Christ—inaccessible; 2) the path of St. Paul—the combination of Art [the Epistles) and Action, but a Christ is needed; 3) the path of Art or Philosophy (Tolstoy or Nietzsche).

I am following the third, and that is why whatever I write will never be perfect from the point of view of Art. Because my intention transcends the limits of Art.

In the process of writing I feel increasingly relieved. And yet I know that this is by no means enough. To attain my aim, I must make a leap. As soon as this leap is accomplished (which can only be an example of life and not one of Art and writing), I shall find the expression of my soul . . . which will probably be an action and a form of preaching rather than writing.

*Will I ever be capable of making this leap? Almost impossible.
And therein lies the tragic sense of my life.*

He described his unexpected arrival at his parents' house:

*Mother was getting ready to go to Vespers. When Father came
back, and caught sight of me suddenly, he had to prop himself against
the door. He was so moved he couldn't speak.*

In company with Lefteris, Kazantzakis began his long excursions
once again. "I often used to visit my parents on their land," he records.

*August 22: A sad separation from my parents. For the first time, Father
kissed me on the forehead. Mother wept and followed me as far as the
dirt road. Unbearable bitterness. Better not to have been born.*

Inasmuch as Kazantzakis' letters to Sikelianos have been lost,* I am
inserting at this point two letters from Sikelianos to Nikos corroborating
the deep friendship binding them as well as the divergence between
their natures and the methods they adopted to reach the same result.
What result? That of attaining their own fullest development.

April 4, 1921

My beloved Friend!
    Last night—I didn't know this when I boarded the boat—I set
foot in Heraklion, more poised and ardent than the *Kybisteres*
[acrobats] of the Minoan bullfights. In what a godlike way I felt
warmed upon your soil, and to the very marrow of my bones I
breathed in the perfumed scent of Leukas,† as I had prophesied.
My first step upon the Cretan sward was a dance linking heaven
and earth, and my mind was like unto that big double-edged ax
familiar to you.

---

* There are only about fifteen of those letters remaining from the years
1940–1950.
† The birthplace of Angelos Sikelianos.

I went to Knossos with Lefteris, spent the evening in the Turkish coffee shop—amid the camomile plants—and talked about you and me—oh, how much! Now that I'm sailing once again, your mind keeps me company like a brother—like the dolphin springing from the depths alongside my ship. Love me infinitely and write to me. . . .

Angelos

Sykia, evening, October 11, 1921

When I came back alone (you had seemed to me like the bird winging off in search of food), like a father or a mother I held the whole responsibility in my arms. The sun of energy radiated deep within me with such brilliance as it had never manifested while you were near me. And yet I felt that you were living the same experience and that the whole universe was ablaze with the sacred fire of our souls. No doubt, no doubt at all can be allowed. The slightest misstep on our part, I believe, will hurl us into the antipodes. Remember me, just as I, remembering you, meditate upon "all things and all people." . . .

I await your letter with what godlike longing!

Angelos

1922–1923. Of all the letters Kazantzakis wrote his first wife, she saved only eighty, covering a period of a few months during the years 1922 and 1923. What we had already surmised comes clearly to light in this correspondence: that Kazantzakis still preserved a great affection for his first wife, and admired her for her leftist ideas; that life in common was becoming impossible; and that she used any pretext to avoid coming to a husband who was ill in Vienna and insistently appealing to her.

Before leaving Greece once again, Kazantzakis wished to set his finances in order. Seeing the tremendous success of the five textbooks, he arranged with a publisher to produce a series of history books for the primary-school level. His correspondence shows that he wrote them and that he also posted them by registered mail. His wife never received them. Once again, long and painful labor had been cast to the four winds by blind fate.

Between May 19 and August 19, 1922, Nikos Kazantzakis found himself in Vienna, where, among other things, he wrote a novel, *A Year of Solitude,* which he later destroyed, and the first version of a tragedy,

Buddha, which he was to mold and remold over a long period of years and bring to its final form only in the last years of his life.

Vienna, Saturday

I was overjoyed to see Egyptian Art again and the Museum of Natural History, the evolution of animals as well as another miracle: a great amethyst. But I'm alone and feel stifled from not being able to speak about my emotion.

At present, according to our new conception, you don't know how deeply I'm affected when I see the hunger and despair that the people here are suffering. My God, what misery! And how long will it last? Today, for example, I went to buy a newspaper. A young girl about fourteen years old came in and heaved a sack full of packages onto her shoulder . . . I went over to help her arrange it, and I couldn't lift the burden. The girl smiled, but her body was already deformed, her shoulders stooped, and her legs like reeds.

Yesterday there was a woman sitting on the pavement with one leg raised up over the other, and her whole body was showing, stark naked, up to her navel. She looked sad and cynical and terribly pale from hunger.

"Modesty" is a luxury for the wealthy. Ah! How well I've come to understand this "sister" of our new religion! Better that the earth should be destroyed, that the firmament be purified of the shame of modern life.

I gaze at the paintings, at the trinkets in the shopwindows. At other times, even last year, they gave me joy. Now I feel they are contrary to nature, superficial masks to hide the truth. Charming shams for cowards. My God, I cry out inside myself as I walk along the great streets, when will you descend like a violent wind, like the Megas* descending from the peaks of Parnassus, and clear the earth!†

Sunday, May 21, 1922

. . . The horror of Vienna in a state of collapse is indescribable. A special police force has been organized to keep people from jumping into the Danube at night. But many escape the observation of the police and do jump, especially mothers with their children. At night, thousands of women roam the streets, begging for something to eat. Starving Eros. (There is no more horrendous anguish!) The other day a rally was held

---

* Megas: the great wind sweeping down from the peaks of Parnassus.
† Letter to Galatea, Vienna, 1922.

attended by 800,000 of the common people. There will soon be a revolution here. . . .*

Wednesday, May 25, 1922

. . . My God, how I think of you and how tragic my life seems to me. I am, as Buddha says, il sempre alzato [the one who is always up]. Always on my feet, always setting forth.†

The women were very beautiful in Vienna, and while Buddha was spurring him on to absolute renunciation of the flesh on the one hand, on the other, in the concert halls, in the streets and restaurants, in the libraries and museums, various caressing, oblique glances were summoning him to enjoy himself. Whether it was by coincidence or, as Dr. Wilhelm Stekel, a disciple of Freud, had told him, by the force of his own spirit, a hideous eczema suddenly broke out over his whole face, prohibiting all contact. Loving beauty as he did and loathing sickness, there he was, imprisoned in a repulsive mask. When he was alone, he was very clumsy—as I have verified a thousand times—incapable of taking his own temperature or making a cup of camomile tea or putting a bandage on himself. When he wrote his wife as follows, he spoke nothing but the naked truth:

Vienna, June 1922

Chérie,

If you were suddenly to open the door of my room and set eyes on me, you'd sympathize with me very much. I'm lying in bed, my face wrapped in compresses, which I change every half hour. . . . You don't know what I'm suffering. . . . Alone here in my hotel . . . I fix bandages, antiseptics, etc. ineptly, and you'd look at it all with great tenderness. I can't eat or go out. But I endure it all with calm and patience. I don't get upset, even though I despise illness.

This letter I'll send you only when I am absolutely cured, so that you won't worry. My only regret is that I've lost a chance to have you see me ill and to divine in your concerned glance that you love me a little. Une larme bête [a foolish tear] has just come into my eyes, perhaps because I'm sick, perhaps because I love you very much. . . .

---

* Letter to Galatea, Vienna, 1922.
† Letter to Galatea, Vienna, 1922.

Chérie,

Today, thank God, I'll be going outside. How joyously I'll breathe!
What happiness to be strong, not to hate anyone, and to have a great
aim before you, and to be striving toward it! My God, how much I have
suffered—but with calm, because I have felt that what I am suffering is
nothing, a caress in the face of the infinite unhappiness of the world.
The vision of the great Unhappiness must not be inundated by our own
small, insignificant miseries. This idea has given me patience and calm.
No more to be said. I think I'll accept death with the same serenity.

. . . By all means, send me newspapers. I don't want to cut myself
off from the Greek agony. . . .*

June 18, 1922

. . . Come! You can't imagine what joys await you. But have your
lady friends with you, because otherwise you'll feel bored with me.†

Clairvoyant and self-critical, he himself analyzed their state of
mind:

Vienna, July 3, 1922

. . . Then again, I say: "How boring my company must be. And
how can Galatea breathe near me? She will always be looking in the
direction of Athens, of her own familiar habits. She'll get nervous. Our
life will become unbearable and finally she'll go away, and love and interest from a distance will begin all over again." This is our martyrdom,
and I feel it every day.

What shall I do? Tell you that I'm ill? What's the use from my
point of view? You'll come, you'll suffer with me, you'll take care of me;
and when I'm cured, history will repeat itself. Do as you like. "They're
throwing us out in the streets"; you "despise people"; you "don't have
any joy."‡ And yet you stay there, out of cowardice.

There's nothing festive about my life here. I have sorrows I don't
tell you about—to what avail? . . . The great cure, the total change of
front, cannot be made. And so, no salvation. Will we get at least a
chance to be killed in some kind of heroic fashion? Once and for all to
expend this tedious residue of our life? I doubt it very much. But let us
wait. You won't believe it, but were it not for this hope, I should have

---

* Letter to Galatea.
† Letter to Galatea.
‡ Quotations from his wife's letters.

killed myself recently. I work from four o'clock in the morning on, because I can't sleep. And I have such lucidity that I'm not led astray by vain illusions. My thought and my heart have long since gone beyond all the permitted bounds. I say this with all simplicity because I know it's true.*

Was it another coincidence? Dr. Stekel's prediction came to pass: The horrible sexual "mask" (the psychoanalytical term he had used to describe Kazantzakis' illness) vanished as soon as Nikos left Vienna.

One knows the condition he was in when he arrived in Berlin in the autumn of 1922—Vienna, Buddha, the overexciting women, the sexual mask. His Arab blood (by dint of telling himself this over and over again, he had ended by believing it) did not always adapt itself to the twin rigors of Byzantine asceticism and Hellenic rationality.

At a later point, he would talk about his "Jewesses," and he succeeded in making me love them all: Rahel, Elsa, Leah, Itka, Dina. However, it was mainly with the first two—one the daughter of a rabbi from Warsaw and the other a pure Aryan from Jena—that he played. Mischievous yet disciplined, ardent yet circumspect, he was a young dolphin gamboling on the waves and at the same time an old fisherman with his mind set on how to catch them. But what of them? Did they also spread their nets to catch him? I see no sign thereof. Setting his happiness above their own, they let him act in his own fashion—or, rather, in the manner of the tiger riding him,† that same beast that had befriended me, heaven knows why, allowing me to follow him.

Rahel, Elsa, Leah, Itka . . . Once upon a time . . . A new tale is beginning.

NOTEBOOKS, 1922–1923

October 1, 1922: *Congress of Radical School Reformers. I went with Daniilidis.‡ A throng of young people, teachers, dressed like proletarians.*

---

* Letter to Galatea.
† An allusion to the Hindu proverb about "the man who rides a tiger." It refers to the obsession driving a human being. N.K. used this image often, and made it still more terrifying in the reversed image of "the man who *is* ridden by the tiger."
‡ Demosthenes Daniilidis, a sociologist who returned to Greece about the same time as N.K. and wrote a book entitled *Preconditions of Modern Greek Sociology and Economics.*

A blond giant about twenty years old ate heartily before speaking. A lame woman, pale, with a splendid head like Galatea's. Another spoke sweetly, crystal-clearly, sensibly, with balance, heftig [forcefully]. An ugly blond woman poured out intense passion and grief, and the moment she got back to her seat, began eating Wurst greedily.

October 2, 1922: I went to the Congress . . . and when I turned around, I saw a girl wearing an orange-yellow silk blouse, and without seeing her face, bezaubert [enchanted] by the color, I went over to her . . .

"Sind Sie eine Jüdin? [You're Jewish?]"

"Jawohl [Yes, indeed]." Wunderbare orientalische Augen [wonderful Oriental eyes].

We talked.

"Und Sie? [And you?]"

"Ich bin ein Araber [I'm an Arab]."

"Und dieser Ring? [And this ring?]"

"Ein Zauberring! [A magic ring!]"

We laughed. Finally I said to her: "I want to give you a book. I'm curious to see what book you'll choose."

"So you want to make a gift, not as a favor to me, but as a favor to yourself?"

"Of course, out of selfishness."

She chose several children's books and said to me: "I'm a poet. I'll give you a book of mine too."

On the street we talked heartily. Today was a great Jewish holiday, Versöhnungstag [Yom Kippur, or Day of Atonement], and all day long she hadn't eaten anything. I said to her:

"Bitte, tun Sie meinetwegen eine Sünde, die letzte, oder, lieber, die erste: Kommen Sie mit mir zu essen. [Please commit a sin for my sake— the last one, or, preferably, the first: Come and eat with me.]"

She refused, but finally accepted. We ate in a restaurant—thick warm soup.

As we walked, I talked to her about God. The God outside is a heavy, imbecilic, lazy one. But we (i.e., the most advanced and liberated God) keep vigil and do not let him fall. We talk to him as soldiers talk to their general. We say: "You ought to do such and such. When the sea recedes, the seagulls, fish, crabs have no water. You ought to bring the sea back. I pray; you ought to listen. And if you haven't any ears, you should create some to the right and left of your head. . . ."

She recited some marvelous songs of hers: Psalms, dictates to God.

She recited The Song of Songs to me in Hebrew. What a dulcet rhythm, like a mixture of Spanish and Arabic.

Exultation. She was leaping up and down in the street, embracing me, and crying out. Her hair is blue-black, her nose slightly aquiline, her skin touched with red.

She said to me: "Jede meine Nacht ist wie ein offenes Fenster aus dem immer ein andrer Mann auf meine Träume blickt. [My every night is like an open window through which another man is always looking at my dreams.]"

How sad! I could have sat next to any other girl in the same way. The crust of the body would have been rent, and the recognition as brothers would have occurred. For a few moments indeed (Sexualität . . . is not the end, but the means) the fetters do burst. The souls are liberated. We feel that not only, as Plato says, were man and woman at some point one, but all souls—men, women, and even all the animals, plants, matter—were at some point one, and are struggling to become reunited. Love (that is, the bondsman of the flesh) makes the beings one. What joy and exhilaration at the first moment! Bodies find release, flesh becomes light, the spirit leaps along the pavement among all the sullen, foolish people in their prison-houses, sunk in the Hell of non-recognition.

If only human beings could maintain this intoxication! Yet not with screeches and Dionysiac capers, but with serenity, discipline, and immobility. Such were the great magnetic personalities. Why did Christ attract people? Because his body had opened up, and his soul inclined toward all human bodies, like the key-bearer, and he tried to open them with persistence, violence, and the ultimate in sweetness.

The soul is capable of taming even the beasts. Who knows what is hidden in love?

October 3, 1922: The next day I went to the Congress two hours late. I didn't see the orange color. Sorrow. Suddenly, in front of me to my right, I felt two eyes watching me. I turned and saw her smiling, and her face sparkled like marble in the sun. She was wearing a shabby, charcoal-colored shawl. Her collar was raised, because it was cold.

Suddenly I felt remorse for my Dionysiac outburst the day before. I no longer felt any warmth toward this creature, who was radiant with feeling. I didn't turn around to look at her. On our way out, she gave me the little book of her poems, laughing and sustaining our union of the day before. But I was in a hurry to get away. She was utterly meaningless and foreign to me. For a moment as I bent down, I saw her eyes scanning me—uncertainly, with a slight terror . . . Her body had contracted . . . And at that point, a great wave of pity swept me away.

"What is your Weltanschauung?" I asked her, taking her as usual by the shoulder blades, kneading her slender shoulders.

"Bruder, zerstören die Welt! Bruder, der Hass! [Brother, destroy the world! Hatred, brother!]"

"O Mitkämpferin [fellow combatant], Sister," I answered her, "hatred is but the cruel progenitor of love. Hatred is the ugly, laughterless forerunner going ahead to prepare the paths for love. . . ."

"You raise up my mind and cleanse my heart, O Unknown One. How have you come like this from the Orient, how have you found me? Ah, you open horizons for me. My mind broadens! The other day, before you came (ah, that is how my life is divided now—before you came and after) I was reading Plato's Symposium. I imagined I was walking early in the morning beneath the olive trees I've never seen, in the sun, and all the world was awaking. Eros was leading the way, with a smile. But somehow it was all romantic images, aping old statues I had seen; an opium I was inhaling to become intoxicated and forget reality.

"But now in your words I feel that reality is far deeper and more beautiful than anything I have ever imagined. Eros leads the way, but no longer as a young child, with wings and a quiver. Now he's a tall, black man who has no wings or quiver—and is dressed like a man of the present day, wearing a big ring on his hand."

"I'm thinking of writing a Symposium," I told her, "to which only we two will be invited. We two; i.e., the whole world. Ah, man and woman, God's couple. We'll talk about hate and love, about God and war—calmly drinking the sacred wine that fills the clay urns of our bodies."

"We two are capable of destroying and creating the world!"

She laughed and grabbed me by the arm. Then she began softly reciting The Song of Songs in Hebrew. Through the hubbub of the streets and the ugliness of the tall houses, at the moment we were going down to take the subway, I listened to this Hebrew chant. And it was the Church, the Bride of God, talking to her Lord.

October 6, 1922: . . . In the evening we sat in a Russian pastry shop. She spoke to me about the Talmud traditions and about her distant fatherland. . . .

And I told her that I am entering her life and her soul, as I would *enter a forest. Slightly terrified. The merest sound becomes gigantic. Words with us are like bombshells, a hidden and frightening power, and we liberate it. The words "bread," "God," "fish," "stone," "sea" explode in our hearts. My head feels like the Ark. When it rains and snows and I walk bareheaded, alone on a mountain or by the edge of the sea, I feel that the whole world is drowned and that the curse of God, like a cataclysm, has risen up to my neck. But on the surface of the water, my head floats, containing all the seeds of good and evil. . . .*

Her eyes had filled with tears. She wrung my hand and kissed it.

"How I was waiting for you!" she said.

One time she had said that she would come, Nikos recorded in his notebook, but at the last minute sent him a note to tell him about some aggravating obstacle. For a second, in his vexation, the man had thought of never seeing her again. "Good riddance to future bitterness and shame," he commented. "But a voice, perhaps that of God, was guiding me!"

And he wrote her, still in the flowery Biblical style:

O God, look upon this charming maiden, Rahel. Her forehead shines like a bright thought, her eyes are sweet and wild as those of the sacred lioness who watches at the anchorite's feet. Her heart is of flesh and tears and pride. And her delicate hands, O God, keep your great Universe up over the Abyss. . . .

October 16, 17, 18, 1922: *I told her about my Buddha. We ate chocolate, then talked about our relationship. I said to her: "You are Jewish, a predatory spirit, Spinoza and Shylock. You want to benefit as much as possible from knowing me. When I have nothing left to give you, you'll abandon me."*

We spoke of the influence of fleshly lust upon the spirit. I told her: "There are only two ways for brave spirits—either to separate at this very instant, or else never in this life to separate. Whatever you decide, I will make it bear fruit. At present, I'm writing the Buddha. If we do unite physically, I shall feel all the bitterness of bodies which long to become one in a complete sense, and are not able to. I shall perceive the limits of voluptuousness, and my work will be bitter because of the vanity of all effort. If we remain only friends, at every moment I shall be conquering desire inside myself and I shall be aware of the frontiers of every happiness, and my work will be as deep as a dream. If we separate, this entire life will become unbearably bitter, and Buddha will gaze on the mean spectacle of life with a shudder. Like the bee, I shall turn everything into honey. You are perfectly free. You must choose the way you prefer to take. I shall always bear fruit."

I shall never forget how delighted she was with this liberty I gave her.

October 27, 1922: I went to her home. How moved she was when she told me that it was only the evening before that she had freed herself from the dreadful apprehensiveness she used to feel when she came to my home. . . . And now she regards my home as her urvaterliches Haus [ancestral home]. . . ."

November 15: Despairingly she told me: "I shall never leave you, for I shall never be able to plunder all of you."

November 19: If her mother were to learn that she was living with me, she would die of it.

And so by this most delicious ruse, disguising Himself as a slender young girl, exquisite, vibrant, a visionary poet as well, Jehovah had taken the Cretan in hand, allowing him to apprehend certain mysteries of the Bible—of the Bible in which he was already thoroughly versed, this man enamored of Judaism. "The Jews are the salt of the earth," he proclaimed as a mature man; and as a child, he had gotten his father to let him penetrate the ghetto, so that a rabbi could give him Hebrew lessons.

While the young Jewish girl was initiating the Cretan into the rich traditions of her race, the Cretan for his part was gradually revealing to her his conception of the world. He talked to her of Homer, Dante, Buddha, and "his" Crete. He took her to the Völkerkunde Museum (Ethnological Museum) and, after imbuing her with African legends, they spent hours staring at the grimacing masks.* There was nothing missing. States of spiritual exaltation, visions in the middle of the

---

* Notebooks for 1922–1923.

street,* pleasant chatter in pastry shops, amorous interludes punctuated with remorse and conflicts between Jehovah and Christ,† the flowery Biblical style, a touch of grandiloquence (isn't that the sign of youth anyway?), all in the blazing fire of the great injustice, where all the apostles of violence and all the apostles of nonviolence are forged. . . .

The years passed. The young girl returned home and was imprisoned. Our efforts to have her come to Greece were unsuccessful. She married and had a son. When the war broke out, she was in Paris. She stayed there to help in the work of rescuing the children of her race. She had given up Communism and the gospel of hatred. But the poet wanted to immortalize her in her original flamelike guise. And so, both in *The Odyssey* and in *Toda Raba*, we encounter Rala in her orange blouse, sacrificing herself to her revolutionary ideal and choosing to die rather than compromise with Socialism, whose weakness had allowed the present state of things to come about.

The wheel of Destiny turns fast. At the same time as a new world was being born in Soviet Russia in the midst of blood and privations, in Asia Minor a world three thousand years old—once flourishing Ionia, the first Christian Church—was vanishing in flames and carnage. The First World War had come to an end for the whole world, except for the Greeks, who had been fighting ever since 1912. Letting themselves be carried away by the immoderate optimism of a Lloyd George and the vague promises of the French government, the Greeks, instead of halting at "Smyrna-the-Greek" and Constantinople, had begun advancing on Sangarios and Ankara. And the inevitable happened. A total reversal of our allies' political and economic views occurred before King Constantine and his generals even realized it. And precisely at this point, Kemal Ataturk, armed and aided this time by the very same people who had been impelling us to change our war of liberation into a war of conquest, swept the Greek army into the sea—and along with it, a million and a half Greek settlers, who cursed us with perfect justification. A million and a half haggard refugees, repatriated at a whirlwind pace in Greece, were forced to share the stale bread of six million undernourished, tubercular Greeks, who themselves had just emerged from four centuries of slavery. The Greek refugees and remnants of Wrangel's army were joined by some 200,000 Armenians, who had escaped the sword of the Young Turks.

---

* *Ibid.*
† *Ibid.*

Mme. Hryssoula Poirier, an eyewitness, often used to speak to us about the tragedy of 1922. The fire consummating the end of Ionia became rekindled in her great black eyes:

"I had married a Frenchman, as you know. I did not want to leave Brussa. But the French forced me to board a warship and gave me a pistol. 'Do you know how to use it?' they asked. 'I do!' 'Then fire on them!' 'You dogs, I am Greek and a Christian. Do you want me to kill my own brethren? Pity on them, have pity!' I cried, throwing myself at their feet. But they would not listen to me. They fired on them. . . . And I saw some of them being scalded. The Gulf of Smyrna was full of corpses. Then I blasphemed and prayed God to do the same to them. . . ."

The tragedy in Asia Minor and the peculiarly inflammable atmosphere in Vienna and Berlin had a profound influence on Nikos Kazantzakis' spirit and work.

Radical educational reformers, grand figures like Kaverau, Oesterreicher, Hilker, were preaching school reform at their Congress, hoping to achieve the renovation of society as a whole by changing this matrix of the new generation. But Nikos Kazantzakis, disdaining halfway measures, demanded an attack on the root of the evil:

"We should not begin with the school system," he proposed to this Congress, "but rather with the foundations of society itself—of which the school is an emanation. If we are going to help society to advance, we must one day make up our minds to sever its rotten roots and free men from their shells, which prevent them from growing. . . ."

And so, the *Spiritual Exercises*—the credo that Kazantzakis had begun in Vienna—was put into final form in Berlin; except for one chapter, the last chapter, entitled "Silence," which was added a few years later during a trip through Siberia.

He was no longer satisfied with the *Buddha*, and he destroyed three thousand lines of verse and began the whole thing over again in rhythmic prose. He wanted it more sober, more "African."

His spirit was changing too. He no longer had any great hope of finding the God whom he was seeking. So much the worse. He still went ahead, as though hoping to find Him. And he was to feel himself more and more solitary.

At the same moment as Angelos Sikelianos had launched his appeal from Delphi—in hopes that Apollo the Hellenophile would achieve the miracle—Nikos Kazantzakis recognized the future savior of the world beneath the proletarian mask of Lenin. Delphi would never be the navel of the world. For him the new Pythia held sway in the north, in a red capital, with crenelated battlements alongside a mad cathedral full of many-colored turbans.

Nikos Kazantzakis loved Sikelianos deeply. All the more reason for speaking to him with an open heart. He copied the following letter, which he had sent his friend, into his notebooks:

December 4, 1922

I too am thinking of you. I too live in fervent expectation, awaiting the fruits of your victory.

However, our paths have diverged. Not because at a difficult moment, you distrusted the purity of my judgment; nor because you have forgotten all our resolutions and resumed the old path.

These pusillanimities belong to the human part of our existence and are insignificant, ephemeral, without any weight for anyone who sees beyond detail and temporality. . . . But because I sense that God is sinking more and more into the desert and wants to transcend the last form of combat, Hope.

During these years, 1922–23, he approached the native Germans only as one human being sharing in the suffering of other human beings. Through Daniilidis, he met some young Greeks, and for a certain period he had hopes of a modern Greek Renaissance. Painting, literature, theater, music, Chagall, Franz Mar, Schönberg, Piscator, Klabund, Barlach—what an artistic effervescence! And through Rahel, he laid his finger on the Jewish passion. In unison with the rebels, he swore to work for a better future.

Hasidism and in particular the great lesson of Rabbi Nachmann; Frobenius and the African *Decameron*; Rahel, who as a little girl had painted her knee and played with it as though it were a doll; Itka, who had gone to the hairdresser and sold her long tresses when she did not have money enough to treat herself to a concert; Leah, Rosa, Dina. And the "silent little woman" from Jena, who arrived with the golden keys. How could he part from this world to go and find Zorba, who was trying to get him to come to Serbia?

The letters of Kazantzakis to Zorba no longer exist. But we do have the ones Zorba wrote to Kazantzakis, and it is a great joy to be able to reread them. Here are several excerpts selected at random:

. . . I have received your letter yet again and seen that you praise me most awfully. You think it funny that we have some other value and are seeking something beautiful, Greater than all the others. All the people I have ever knowed, I knew them to stop short at money; once they manage to get money, they stop straightway. They avoid their friends, demand a dowry, go get married, begin the usual things of householdish life, are managed by a woman (Good or Bad) and nothing else.—In this department, please note, I don't mix you, only me myself—

Because as for me, I got married all for a joke.—My lady wife she died, and that was one good thing she did—I'm still laughing, when I think of my friends of them sending me their condolensaries—And now, I have got children, only you know what Idea I have concerning my children, I amn't moved by them one little bit. I don't feel sad or glad as the rest of the world sets its Hope in its children. I love them same as what I love my friends and if I give ten drachmas to one child of mine, I feel as glad as when I give it to somebody else, the same signification of joy I get.

I have no hope in any child of mine, I don't want to have and that's why. I reckon it a grave thing indeed for any old man to be depending on some young person, which is to say, I consider every old fellow miserabilious when he's got to be living with his daughter-in-law or son-in-law, however good she is or he is, they will be strangers, because it's not the old fellow which has loved them. Now on the one hand, it was the son who loved the daughter-in-law and on the other, the daughter who loved the son-in-law, and the above-mentioned love originated from Lust and from the physical impulsation,* it was not the love of a Friend, because Friendly love, I do believe, is depending on the Spirit.

So be it; all this you know far, far better than me . . .

Now me, I'm not afraid of God one bit, for as much as I believe I do practice His Commandments. I'm not afraid of death neither, because it's not a bad thing, it's not anything at all, just as me too, I'm nothing neither. I amn't afraid of the greatest Elements of Nature which or whatsoever they may do, even were the tail of some thingum-mybob comet to come colliding with the Earth and make too-may-toe salad of us all, I Laugh. I know o so, so well—even should the Earth be all beat up, anyways the Devil's going to get me some day. I will die, I'll

---

* The underlining follows the actual marks made by Zorba himself.

Turn into a stinking corpse, an Unconscious Rag I'll be—I'll be smelling up the whole wide World and that World'll be compellerized to bury me to keep from being discombobulated . . . I am very well awares likewise, that all this too you know far more seriouswise than me. . . .

And now, I have to ask you one thing what I am afraid of and I feel it very hard—Old Age frightens me tremendrously, I can find no invention to chase away this Fear—I consider it terrible bad to say I am an Old Man, then I shall be subjectated to everything I Hate, I'll lose my freedom. My daughter-in-law or my daughter will be giving me orders, bidding me take care of some Monster—her child—to keep it from burning itself, stumbling itself, letting the devil get into itself.

I find this same narrow, very narrow—I who can go through Fire and Brimstone, I who roam roundabout and everywhere without a shudder, I whom you write me and you laudify me like unto the forests of Mt. Athos, like unto all Russia, etc., etc.—I to end up a Watchdog over some few monsters—my wee grandchildren—and they peeing on my smock and I not having the Right to have my say and say I feel disgustated, poor miserable wretch I am—

Concerning all these imbecilities I am writing you, I am taking care to liberate my Self, wherefore and why, I am rushing up into the Mountains to earn a Great Lot and so my folks at home will be fearing me and thinking of me even when I shall have died.

Otherwise, I shall prefer whatever death so ever, at the hands of wolves or Bears, whatsoever beast is there in front of me—bravo for it!—If we succeed not in obtaining our afore-planned Cell, to boil Soups, potatoes, green vegetables, whatsoever's to our taste, woe betide us!

Always with Love, I greet you and
always the Same,

G. Zorba.

About the Work, I shall be writing you in an Other letter.

Mine, Village of Gribevsta
November 13, 1922

Dear Mr. N. Kazantzaki,

I received your letter of 20 October, '22 and I am answering.

I am in helth and creeating things. I have an Aim of quite some interest even for you. (Namely, you have only to follow my own Life to become persuaded that any Person who has a Will (and with the help of God reinforcing him) can achieve all things!)

For some time previous, I've been being aware as I was not entered into this world a <u>Horse</u> or an <u>Ox</u> (by way of example). Only the Animals live for the purpose to eat. In order to Avoid the above category, I am creeating Works night and day, and with this I am most felicitous as well as with my own tremendrous Struggle-for-Life. . . . But hence and whence, I manage to get into some Serious Confusations. . . .

Look here—From the trading in Horses and Cattle, I lost and went to Debt—From the oil and Coal, I had no success to find a Capitalist to carry off that bit of Work. And it's me myself as am still paying off all these expenses. I have Hopes to manage things little by little and succeed my Aim, namely, to form a Company. . . .

Last August, Another Serb embraced me . . . More or less an Adventurer like myself . . . whom I straightway followed up into the mountains and in said manner, God helped me to uncover a most splendiferous bed of calamine, very adaptible for my economizing some Capital and amalgamatating with a certain Z . . . merchant-in-bronze of London and America. . . .

Now, as to about the question of our Native Land Greece: We have one sole Aim. Greece is always Greece. . . . You know very, very Great things (far more than all the World, I do believe) and it is shameful for me to be telling you about Hellenism. So then, I shall only be writing you what I took cognizance whereof a few days since . . . in the case of my own Relatives. . . .

Well, just imagine that: My own brother—a Greek Doctor— worshipping a Beast—holding an ikon of a . . . Good-For-Nothing- Human-Being!* How much more should not I, the Illiteratored, be idolaterous? But the World would be Happy if it were like me—For example, when I see a Big Big tree, a beech-tree or a chestnut-tree, I marvel at it and likewise, when I am seeing the Calamine now belower the earth—deep-deep green, the color of oxyde, ever so brilliantish—I Worship it or rather, I Marvel in the Creation of God and Nature.

It were not possible for me to be admiring or Worshiping a mortal being lower to myself, for as much as I believe as any Human Being as does not have his mind on doing Something Good—or discovering

---

* Zorba refers to the King of Greece.

Something, without taking away the labors of the other Human Being—such a one is not a Human Being at all.

The Party in Greece is Interest and the King is the instrument of Interest and every evil instrument must be destroyed—weapons, Cannons, pointed knives, etc., etc., etc. Imagine that, Mr. Kazantzaki: A Doctor of Macedonia not understanding the Game of Europe; not realizating that this same Europe has found a Persecuted People and has gone and formed two Un-Paid Police Forces inside Greece—on the one side, the Royalists to kill the Venizelists and on the other side, the other party to kill the Other Royalists—and the People itself to be proclaiming that Venizelos is a Friend-of-the-Entente and Gounaris a Friend-of-the-Germans!

And the People has not understood . . . or taken care to find a Phil-Hellene Minister to attend to what is the Interest of Greece! Namely, that the People become reconciliated and deliverated from their Slaughterings. . . .

We shall meet and confabulate all this. . . . At the present now, I am fighting so as maybe to be able to guarantee a Livelihood and shake a bit of the mud off me and write you to come here, you'll see how fine and beneficialary it will be that we be Together. For on the surface of this Earth there is Life and it has its Flowers and its Abundantated Good Things and Beautiful Things. Howevertheless, they cannot make me Happy, for as much as everywheresoever, I find intermingling all the Bad Things habitating the Surface of this earth. Whereas the Pickaxe digging brings up wealth—regardless if it's gold or silver; if it's Iron, it may be still more useful: It will Become a tool for you to Sow, to reap, it will bring forth Coal for you to warm your House, etc., etc.

So be it. When you write me, I shall see what Sort of letter you shall be asking for. I Laughed at your letter:—You tell me to write you a Big Letter, namely as though I have all kinds and sorts of Letters, Size 1 and Size 2. . . . It's Droll; happily we're not in Greece for the postman to be Laughing when he sees my Big-Size Letters.

No more.

I greet you with love,
Giorghos Zorba.

Nish, Serbia, December 30, 1922

Dear Mr. Nikóla Kazantzaki,

I received your letter three days ago. I am happy for it, and when we'll be traveling together, I shall be happy too.

95

We shall have a very Good trip, we will go together to the Azof Sea. My first Wife was from that city in Russia and we shall go and find her Relatives, we'll find my Father-in-Law, my mother-in-law and all the Family. And even if she do be married again, my Wife will welcome us, because as her First Husband that I was, I have the Right—I'll say lies, that we've come for her sake.

And then, we'll go all round "Bela Russia"*—we'll find my second Wife, the beautiful one, and we shall Enjoy all her relatives and friends, they'll all kiss us . . . because they loved me, I was a Good Person, that's what they used to say then.

So be it. I have a deal of Work, I won't write you a Big Letter. . . . I've come to Nish to buy some Sacks and I am starting in to send Stuff to England and as soonest the Stuff reaches the factory, I know the miracle will Happen, it will not be at all strange if very soon there'll be some Grand success and then, the aforementioned will all be Verificated. . . .

1923.   If Rahel had blown on the flame, hoping to see it take the form of some new prophet, Elsa, nourished on Hölderlin, Novalis, and Rilke, knew how to catalyze in Kazantzakis τό ἤπιον δάκρυ—"the gentle tear."

Elsa's first meeting with Nikos took place in June of this year in Dornburg. A "decisive" day, Nikos commented in his journals, underlining it in his own hand. For he was far from expecting such happiness, especially during this period of revolutionary exaltation. And as he wrote his beloved, he kept hiding himself from the gods, who might be jealous of so much happiness:

Your hands in my hand, I walk upon this earth, at every moment taking leave of the sun, the air, thoughts, butterflies, and I sing very softly so that God will not hear me, a joyous song of love. . . .†

In company with Elsa, they visited most of the medieval cities of Germany. And then Kazantzakis took his beloved to Ravenna and Assisi, to be near his favorite saint. And there, their erotic liaison was to end, to be transformed into a lifelong friendship.

---

* White Russia.
† Letter written in German, copied by N.K. into his 1923 notebook.

Dornburg, Goetheschloss, Pension Fischer. June, 1923. Decisif my stay at Dornburg. The first evening: garden, light rain. I found a green scarab and a sea shell. In the salon, two lady pensionnaires. One a thickset, blond, masculine woman . . . And the other, calm, dark, silent, Elsa. . . .

On June 2, Elsa and I went to Naumburg. . . . We had an impassioned talk in a sweetshop. "Don't get lost," I told her. "Link yourself with some courageous movement; never allow your soul to become extinguished." She listened with agitation and amazement. Suddenly we noticed that the time had been passing, and we wouldn't be able to catch the train. We ran. Too late. It had gone. We stayed over in a hotel.

In the morning, tired and happy, we went back to Dornburg. Slowly we climbed the slope, lay down in the grass and talked. Several days later, we made another expedition, this time to Weimar. . . . Again we missed the train on the way back. We spent the night in Kösen. . . .

We read Homer, Buddha, the Hasidim. Phrases we were always using: "Unrewarding!" "Das Winken des Schicksals vollenden: unsere Pflicht. [To answer the wink of Fate, that is our duty.]" The last words: There is no response yet. Let the response ripen like a fruit."

Rahel came. Stormy meeting. I was with Elsa in the salon, and we were talking about my childhood. Suddenly the door opened, and Rahel came in with L. How I received her! Cruelly. (She was returning from Poland.) "What did you see?" I said. "What progress have you made? What do you have to add to what we had already said?" (Like a general receiving an officer on his return from a mission.)

On July 2, 1923, Nikos Kazantzakis copied in his own hand a letter he had just sent to Elsa:

Thank God for the marvelous full moments, our moments in Dornburg; our strolls in the magnificent garden, our talks and laughter, the silence, the rain, and above all, embracing all, the great rainbow with its many bands of color. Everything inside my dark head was transformed into light and sun and love. Today, as I was writing my Buddha, the words came like those little horses of Franz Mar, clear and simple, with big Oriental eyes and burning throats like a young girl's. The human heart is marvelous, that muscle full of secrets, devouring everything insatiably; that extraordinary smithy heating and hammering the common metal of life and transforming it into a brilliant saber or a golden goblet.

This morning Buddha danced in my arms like a woman.

A few pages farther on, addressed to the same person:

My life has once again assumed its ascetic aspect. All day long I wrestle with words; I compel infinite thoughts to become confined in these poor, incomplete, cramped bodies. I give the shadows my own blood, and I suffer profoundly, ceaselessly, because often I achieve only a caricature of my most cherished, grandest conceptions.

. . . For me, Art is a sort of cowardice; a great, great sin. It bewitches my powers. To it I give my brain and blood. I revel in its beauty, because I do not have the strength—not yet—to transcend beauty and ugliness. Ah, to see you again, to laugh and talk and walk and be silent! What is this earth? Where? Whence? Why? Thank God, there is no answer. We create this answer each day, with our laughter and our tears and our blood. Thank God. We are free, without hope, without a master!

From Putschow, a humble fishing village on the Baltic Sea, where Kazantzakis stayed from July 13 to 21, in the company of Rahel and her friends, Dina and Eugenia Kulbis, he wrote again to his beloved:

The limitless sea roars on before me, gray, devoured by the sun, restless, strong, like a great heart. I'm neither sad nor joyous nor impervious. For all these days when the sea has once again invaded my eyes, petty human reason has become silent and tremulous, and the great breath of the Cosmos has penetrated my sturdy brown body.

Dear universe in my caressing hands! It feels warm, vain, and mysterious to me, like a human body. There are moments when I cannot restrain my tears. No, the deeper I delve into my own heart, here on this desolate seashore, the more I feel a boundless sadness passing into my blood and perturbing it.

Blessed be the sea which kills the weak and gives austere thoughts to the strong. Blessed be the heart of man, the great struggler who struggles with death and wrenches speech from it. Thrice blessed be the awesome moment when two bodies—a man and a woman—meet and play at the brink of the abyss, like two children at the edge of the sea.

At the end of November, Galatea arrived in Berlin; at the beginning of December she went away. "Was it worthwhile setting off on such a long trip, just to see things I already knew from the cinema?" she grumbled.

Kazantzakis stayed on in Berlin until December 31, except for a few days when he went to Leipzig to help Karl Dietrich, Professor of Hellenism, translate the *Spiritual Exercises*. His friend Daniilidis accompanied him.

PART TWO

THE ODYSSEY

1924–1938

1924.   On the first of January of this year, Kazantzakis started out on what seemed to be a sort of pilgrimage to the places where he had been happy with Elsa.

It was snowing at Dornburg. The previous year at Goetheschloss, the lady who ran the *pension* had offered him Goethe's bed.

She'd been told I was a writer, and she thought I'd be overjoyed to sleep in the bed of my fellow artist.* But I'm neither a Romantic nor a woman, and I refused to occupy the Titan's bed.

I slept in my own bed, the same one as last year, and in a dream I had the following vision: There was a war going on, and the General looked at me and said: "Don't go away! Come and fight too!" A sort of terror passed over me. (In dreams, when I'm going to war or into danger, I'm always seized with fear and trembling, whereas in my waking life, on all the occasions when I've been put to the test, I've always shown myself to be brave. But since I'm not at all brave in my dreams, I believe that deep down I must be a coward. Only because I'm ashamed of myself, out of pride I succeed in controlling my fear and am therefore brave. I stood there, quaking, determined to fight. And my dream proceeded.) The General thought a bit and resumed: "But you can't fight on the right, because you look to the left. Nor can you fight on the left, because you also look to the right! And so you will have to carry ammunition to both right and left, to both camps." . . .

---

* This passage is an excerpt from the Notebooks for 1924, as are the following quotations on pages 104–5, 106, 108–9, 110, 111, 112.

On January 2, Kazantzakis took a walk through the snow. He rested in front of a stove, smoking and looking at a statuette of Nefertiti, which was intended for his dear friend.

I set Nefertiti in front of me . . . gazing at her with such joy that I became aware of Time as something indeed profound . . . beyond the rich, colorful, sacred, flowing eternal realm of touch and hearing with all its surprises—like music, like water . . .

In the afternoon a woman [Elsa] . . . threw a snowball at my window. . . . How had she found out that I'd come? All the dark voices of the earth speak and command in woman's hot body. In man the spirit seeks an exodus, to get out of this beleaguered world, to be saved. And woman, divinely incarnating all the adverse powers, comes and stops him with her embrace.

. . . She [Elsa] was born in a little snow-blanketed town of Germany, and yet inside her burns a longing for the Orient. When she is overcome by love . . . a longing for tropical countries possesses her, as also happens in her dreams. As though sleep and erotic love were of the same substance, as though both were a kind of reminiscence, a sudden discovery and liberation of the memory. There is a race of sheep which, the moment they feel the pangs of birth, rush and jump over the wall, and race madly toward the place where they were born—often days away. In the same way love awakens extremely ancient memories in this small, silent, Northern woman, and after thousands of years she charges southward, where our human parents were born. . . .

That evening, when I went back to the pension, I found a new guest at the table. An old Prussian, dry, square-set, looking as though he'd been carved from a piece of solid wood, worn out by toil. When he stirred, he creaked like the ruins of a wooden house. He did not speak. He ate, stooped and joyless, without chewing—like a person throwing logs into the stove. Once again I was watching a human being regress to an animal state, and still further back, to matter. The spirit had returned to matter, motionless in the burnt-out bit of flesh, devoid of sap, bereft of memory, bereft of imagination. . . .

Ah, if only I could revive this old man! Suddenly I felt a terrible surge of anguish inside me. I seemed to be making an effort whose aim was not this old man . . . but to save all the matter within this small area and to transform it back into spirit. . . .

When we'd finished eating, the old man dragged himself over to the stove and leaned his back against it. His eyes grew heavy. I controlled my terror, and approached him and began talking. He was bored, didn't want to listen. I tried to awaken in him the image of the village where he was born, I tried to evoke for him his wife, his children and grandchildren. But everything had faded from his mind. His wife had died. He hardly remembered her. "Was she a brunette? A blonde?" "Her hair was white." He remembered her only with white hair. His children had behaved ungratefully, parceling his fields before he died. His grandchildren bothered him and got him dirty. "Have you traveled?" "I have traveled." "Where?" "Here and there—how should I remember?" "Do you remember where you drank the best wine, where you saw the most beautiful woman?" "Hi-hi-hi-hi!" He laughed softly; his eyes played—so he did remember. Little by little, he was coming to life. All this array of people he had known—friends, relatives, women, enemies—he suddenly realized were now down beneath the sod. . . . Unconsciously the bitter futility began softening his voice, warming his knees, lighting up his eyes. A kindness that was not his own began illuminating him.

He was looking behind him; now he could see everything dispassionately, disinterestedly, like a superior mind. For a moment. And then he relapsed once more. He was tired. He wanted to lean against the stove, to go to sleep. But I didn't let him. I drew him away from the heat, took hold of his knees, questioned him, tormented him, gripped him with anguish. . . .

At midnight I let him go. I too was tired and I lay down to sleep. I always make an effort to remember my dreams because they have always been a great help in my waking life:

Before me a dark ocean was foaming; the sky was low and pitch-black, and from the shore I was gazing far off into the distance. A boat was bobbing up and down, with its triangular sail puffed out in the head wind, shining as though self-illuminated. And when I saw it, I cried out inside myself in awe: "My own heart!"

From the fourth to the tenth of January, "die kleine Frau"* reappears:

I still haven't gotten used to this miracle—that two people who were strangers yesterday, from different races, different climates, different

* "The little lady"—this is how Elsa was called at the Goetheschloss.

kinds of life, suddenly meet and merge and become one and get to know each other better and more deeply than mother and daughter, than brother and brother. "I have only you in the world!" she told me. And this simple sentence made me shudder at the mystery enveloping us. . . .

On January 18, 1924, Kazantzakis left Germany. Italy still attracted him, and he had decided to wander again through the cities he had come to know in the course of his student years.

January 21, 1924: I wander through Naples and still cannot believe my eyes. Yelling in the streets, hurdy-gurdies, orange peels, colored rags on all the balconies—a life full of smells and filth and cries and curses. People spit, stick their fingers in their noses for hours on end, gesticulating and talking to themselves. They're all like prestidigitators and old-style theatrical players, wearing feathers, capes, Napoleonic hats—serious and ridiculous at the same time. Beggars in the churches, as well as others, sketching the Madonna in chalk on the pavement, collecting pennies. At noontime I saw a woman sitting in a chair with her head thrown back, while another woman hovering over her was kneading her. I rushed in terror to see. It was her hairdresser!

Later on, when I saw the first donkey in the street, I almost ran to embrace it, as though I had seen a Greek. . . .

Sadness. How brightly the big eyes shine, all fire in the midst of the rags and laziness. This spirit is all wasted. For lack of being used, it evaporates in flamboyant improvisation, jovial ballads, futile exhilaration. . . . "Why should we think?" one pale, magnificent youth said to me. "All's in vain in the presence of so much beauty. Here thinking would break the harmony. The people of the North think in order to protect themselves—for their own self-preservation, in order to replace the ugly world around them with the world their own brains invent. Thought is superfluous here."

This city, this sea, is indeed a Siren. And I too am carried away calmly, surely, by a sweet sensation. I wander about blissfully happy and idle. I must leave quickly.

On June 10 of this same year, Angelos Sikelianos, on a pilgrimage to Jerusalem, thought of his friend and sent him a long letter overflowing with poetic images and mystic impulse. He attached a photograph as well, "to remind you of my face," as he said. A few extracts follow:*

Beloved friend,

. . . At the time we parted, I should have let my head become the crossroads stone and the tempest that the wheels of the age might create around me a maze of roads dense enough to render in a form of mystic completeness the problem of my own freedom—I had ascertained that a certain force, however slight its spiritual endurance, was capable of absorbing the world-wide passion and transforming it by its own means and displaying it one dawn over all the horizontal waves of time, like the body of God crowned with lilies and flooded with a new, invincible rhythm. Throughout all this period, as I have written somewhere, my tribulation was like that of the steed the ancient Scandinavians used to dedicate to their Goddess of War and it was confined in a distant temple and it never stopped sweating and foaming so long as any battle was under way at any point on the earth; but for this very reason, it was also like the incarnation of some boundless mystical serenity. After this tribulation, my spiritual body, no longer erected like an inimical God . . . but perfectly emancipated on the pure level where the Great Action is alone possible (the only thing deserving to be called Action)—this Action which will transcend all the present layers of substance and restore unto each thing its own most splendid honor— if this spiritual body denies all manner of "mixed life" (nowadays, invariably the life of all "thinking" people)—then you will not only perceive that I am not in any wise exaggerating, but I am convinced you will accept it at once in the very depths of your own respiration, just as you would accept the wind of some immaculate dawn. . . .

I might address myself to people who could have sacrificed the decorative surface of their own ostensible gnostic kingdom and who, being animated by a movement to intensify all their vital and intellectual essence, could strive to augment the vigor of their own higher being. . . . But such people—the people absolutely elevated to a full and conscious spontaneity—do not exist, as you know. Or, if they do exist, are there more than three of them? I don't think so. As for the others, I am convinced that the roots of their thinking being are diffused so superficially through the contemporary pulp of history, they

---

* The translator has intentionally followed the labyrinthine style of the original.

are so foreign to the concentrated center of struggle that the stones and the trees would be more profoundly shaken by the Word of higher life, assuming that [such people] could ever manage to achieve within themselves the identity of thought and action demanded on this level. . . .

If the arena wherein I could now struggle and act were not simultaneously the whole world's and my own, and if it were not destined that all its profound problems would ascend with me in the end, I would tell you unhesitatingly that I am weighed down by the monolithic activities with their myriad sad conventionalities whose sole trophy is the preservation of some idol—call it Thought, call it Art (its name has always been foreign to my own full breath)—If the Action allotted me with unimaginable palpitation by my own heart were not capable of pumping its own pure vibration from my mind out toward the masses—of dragging the "Many along with the One" into the arena where I do anticipate that some day they will breathe as a single body— the respect for life I have acquired even in its slightest prerogative would prevent me from wresting my soul out of its own "God-nourished" silence. But the arena I have in mind does exist intact, and at the same time, in all its being, is demanding to be illumined.

Whenever I tried to elevate the tiniest pebble in this [arena] in order that all the space around me might sparkle like an emerald, I always had you in my mind, precisely as my grand desire first grasped you and holds you always. If it would not tire you, indeed, I would like to know your own deepest desire, in the face of your own problem, just as You would have formulated it to me. You know that I have never asked this of you, that I have always remained silent in the presence of your own silence; but now it is time and I do ask it. You will not hesitate to force your Self to a full confession, which my perfect—my superhuman—devotion to you is entitled to demand, for the first—and if needs be—the last time.

Yours always,
Angelos
Answer me at Sykia.

The following letter, copied by Nikos Kazantzakis into his notebook, seems to be the answer to Sikelianos:

. . . I understand your struggle. I know that it takes great courage in Greece to remain standing up in the same place, inasmuch as collapse is the natural, recognized, prudent, and fruitful development of man there.

When I was in Greece, I used to say: "Let us unite, the three or five of us who want not to yield. Let us strive to resist the steady current. Let us not only resist, let us also work actively by transforming as much substance as possible, and whatever belongs to the opposite current, into spirit."

I felt this to be premature in Greece. We are still at the preliminary stage, and whether we like it or not, we will struggle and work and die in isolation—isolated no longer by the plebs, but by our own defenders. I too, like you, am isolated, struggling alone. And if I have chosen life abroad as my own position in the battle, I do so not out of cowardice, but as a result of deep, laborious study of my own powers. God has given me a spool of instincts, impulses, light and dark, matter and spirit, and I choose the terms most expedient for me to transform as many of the dark ingredients inside myself into spirit as I can. Only in this way can my life and personality become worthwhile—insignificant, but all that I was capable of—for the totality. The vital precondition of a fecund harmony is that we recognize the era it is our lot to be born in and work in, and that we regulate our own views and acts according to the nature of this era. . . .

I live ascetically, serenely, on very little. I work by day and sleep at night. I have no ambition. I hate no one. I would like to do good to whosoever it might be. I'm like a silkworm that has eaten all the leaves of the mulberry tree allotted to it, transforming them into silk, and now it nods its head to right and left as it unwinds the precious essence from its own vitals and solidifies it in mid-air.

My best friends have left me. No one in the world is interested in me any longer. That is why I am interested in everyone. I feel I am free and can dispose of my life as I want, without causing anyone sorrow. This is the supreme independence, a fortifying solitude, a godlike silence for him who works. God willing, this solitude and silence may last throughout my whole life. . . .

Let us seize everything we can from each place. Let us exploit to our utmost the crust of this beloved, embittered, eternal Earth.

On February 7 of the same year, 1924, Kazantzakis recorded in his notebook a meeting with Marinetti at the Hotel London in Naples:

"What is Futurism?" I asked him. "To find the beauty and grandeur of motors, railways, airplanes, modern life in general," he answered. "An ancient Greek saw the human face and wanted to crystallize its beauty. I do the same when I see the motor."

"To crystallize the human face," I answered, "or the motor, or phenomena in general, is the means employed by art. But its essence has always been what the craftsman divines behind these phenomena and endeavors to crystallize through these phenomena. According to Futurism, what is the essence of all these phenomena? How does it envisage the eternal, mysterious force acting behind man and the motor?"

"'Futurism hasn't found this yet. It is still struggling. Through looking at the motors, railways, etc., it does its best, gradually and methodically, to arrive."

"This is the method of science," I told him, "not of art. Art, on the contrary, has its first source in an intuition, establishing a contact with the great reality. A vision. And then quite simply and effortlessly all the details fall into place and find expression."

Marinetti was pensive. His is an explosive nature, militant, simple, brave. And then all of us—a whole phalanx of his disciples—went off to the theater. A lecture by Marinetti, an exposition of painting (interesting). Expressionist dances and a play: "Two steam-engines inamorate del capostazione [in love with the stationmaster]." A little play by Marinetti: a Madonna on the wall, a table, and a garbage pail.

All the efforts ridiculous. Only the painting was worth anything. The music was banal, not even absurd. But Marinetti's courage in bearing ridicule is admirable. Shrieks, whistles, interruptions, guffaws—and he went on answering. The entire hall was the stage and the play was this man trying to introduce something new and the people opposing and cursing him. One old man kept shouting furiously: "No vogliamo capire! [We don't want to understand!]"

One also finds in Nikos' notebook a letter transcribed in his own hand and addressed to Rahel after he visited Pompeii on February 18, 1924:

The cellars of Pompeii were full to bursting. The women were beautiful, carefully bathed in the Roman baths, sterile; the men exuberant, sensual, spiritual, ironical, weary. All the gods—Greek and

110

Asiatic—had convened there in democratic misery, laughing, devoid of faith, in a cowardly fashion distributing among themselves the offerings and the souls. The whole city, stretched out along the seashore, was there, stinking like carrion. . . .

And the grand and magnificent vultures smelled it in the air. The heavenly spirits seethed, and God's mouth spoke like a volcano.

Rahel, never have my nostrils known such delight as in recent years, ever since I've been able to perceive the stench of the world. I feel some godlike vulture dwelling inside my own skull, its great wings open; it is hungry and has no love for human beings and thinks of Rahel, Dina, Itka as Mitgeierinnen [fellow vultures].

And to Leah, on his return to Naples:

Naples, February 12, 1924

Leah, my fish-sister, my fig-comrade! There is no Time and Space. The heart is all! I feel you near me, near this fish-filled sea. I hear your extraordinary voice and gaze at your round, brown eyes. At the end of February, I'm leaving for Assisi. I'll live in the house of an old countess near the monastery. Write me, Leah. Don't leave me alone in this sanctity. . . . Are you still with the same troupe?* When will you be going to Russia? Perhaps I'll go with you. Rahel? She's written me only a postcard. Ah, Rahel, Leah, Dina, Rosa, Itka, Eddy!

And he signed himself "Nikos Salomon."

. . . The bells [of Assisi] have a profound harmony. The heavy bell of San Rufino begins and after a bit, the robust, masculine limbs of this sound become intermingled with the supple, delicate, silvery bell of Santa Clara. They are perfectly easy to distinguish in their union, like a dark-skinned man with a white woman. And soon they pause and then —"Ding!"—Santa Clara rings one bell, as though with a provocative intent. Then, a bit afterward, another ding! And at that point the heavy voice of San Rufino comes down, and from the distance the voice of St. Francis joins in. And then it begins all over again—a delight, a game through the air, a dance.

---

* Leah was an actress.

Elsa came to meet Kazantzakis in Assisi, but there is no mention of this meeting in the notebooks, though they are rich in such reflections as the following about the Poverello and his native city:

I'd been reading the Fioretti, or legends of St. Francis; his scorn for this life; his love of ugliness, modesty, poverty; his fervent desire to return to heaven and leave the world's misery. And suddenly I opened my Anthology at random and began reading our own popular ballads:

> And bring me my lute that I may softly sing:
> "O my sable mustache and my fine-arched eyebrows,
> And you, my strand of hair, proud down my back,
> Ah, the black earth, the desolate soil, will devour you!"

If the fundamental ideas of St. Francis—poverty and chastity—had been disseminated throughout the world; if everyone had become a Franciscan, the world would have been ruined. If Francis had preached more accessible ideas, his teaching would have had no influence. The ideal must be preached in absolute terms, higher than human powers can reach. In this lies its mystical power, the painful, fecund straining of spirits to attain it, the impossibility of attaining it and consequently the concern, contrition, weeping, the eternal dissatisfaction. This is the only way that the momentum can become as strong as possible: by refusing to yield, or to make any compromis after [first] defining the goal.

And once again to Leah:

. . . I'm wandering amidst all these terrestrial beauties—spring, the air, the flowering branches—and I miss the untidy little room of L. in Berlin. A herring on the table, and mismatched, chipped cups of tea to be drunk by Jews and Russians who smoke and talk about God and the Revolution. Tranquillity, idylls, terrestrial springtimes are not for us today. The spirit is suffering, demanding to burst into bloom. . . .

On the 13th of April, I'm leaving Assisi. The Countess* is weeping.

---

* See Report to Greco. The Countess Erichetta Pucci, aged but still beautiful, coquettish, witty. N.K. used to stay with her when he went to Assisi.

The farewells to Italy lingered on in Padua and in Venice, whence another brief letter to Leah:

Here in Venice, I'm happy, tired and insatiable. . . . I know that you are strong and determined—you know what you want and you are a Jewess! May God, the Master-of-Armies, be with you! . . . I am always with you, in your somber little room. Au revoir.   N.

And finally from Brindisi (where he stayed from April 29 to May 3), a letter to Elsa, from whom he had separated in Ravenna:

I love seaports, the salty air, the dirty old women on their doorsteps in the evening, the girls of the port strolling back and forth in their short dresses, with their painted eyes and raucous voices. I'm not impatient. I sit by the edge of the sea and savor our days slowly, deeply, sweetly. I see everything, sort everything out and arrange it. I feel God leaping and growing inside me—like those cucumbers in the Cretan gardens. Everything is burning. Tar, onions, and the fat people are already decomposing. The sea is indigo blue, the sailors drunken; the little houses open onto the street with their gigantic bed right in the middle—the only battlefield for the indigent proletarians. In just such an Oriental port, Aphrodite was born one evening, ungirdled, ample-breasted, with painted eyes and nails and lips. This was a revelation from the sailors.
I'm leaving Brindisi on May 3, 1924.

Like a pillager fleeing the enemy for fear he may be the next to be plundered, Nikos Kazantzakis hastened to entrust the new seed to his own ancestral soil. An Annunciation in the futuristic style, the Angel having assumed the features of Lenin, and the lily having been reduced to a stem of fire in his hands. The Madonna: Crete in a widow's veil, hands folded over her belly teeming with the corpses of her own sons.

A brief interlude in Athens. Our first meeting, recognition of each other, the seeking one another, the first chaste kiss, a brother's kiss.

And then Leda; alone with the sea. Constraint and delight intermingled; amazement at discovering, beneath a mask hacked out of the wood of a twisted olive tree, an authentic Prince of Knossos. Constraint at his refusing any wisp of clothing that might come between our bodies and the sea. And yet he was of an extremely modest nature, and I had to wait, live by his side on an island, to understand the motives of his behavior at Leda and his veneration for the regenerating element.

"Furchtbare Qual [terrible martyrdom]," you had commented in your notebook. You had suffered then in order to give me time to unfold. And I can still see my face in your own hazel pupils, magical mirrors reflecting an idealized portrait that gave you strength and confidence.

Heraklion, [1924]

Liebe, liebe Genossin!

I've been in the sea since this morning, waiting. Today Elsa will be coming to Heraklion. She'll stay a few hours and leave at once. The weather is cloudy; it is sprinkling. And I'm ashamed to have Crete appear in this murky light to the eyes of this remarkable woman. Sometimes I regard Crete as my own body and believe that I am personally responsible for whether it looks sparkling, bathed in sunlight, smiling or not. But perhaps we shan't see each other at all, because in her last letter from Italy, she told me she hadn't yet decided whether she ought to see me or not. So I'll wait at the port . . . and I will write you. For you have come to love this woman from two or three phrases of hers, this ganz geschlossene, heftig, und still [utterly closed, intense, and quiet] woman. She is pleasing, dark-haired and not at all beautiful, silent and stubborn.

Genossin, Odysseus keeps growing, devouring my vitals. By working, I am struggling to drown out the terrifying little voice that cries incessantly inside me, telling me that life is something different, more profound, more brilliant, more ensanguined than these exercises in ink.

How should I, the person of touch, I who believe that only those things I can touch really exist, I who have concentrated all the value of my life in my hands and not in the babbling, hashish-drinking imagination—how should I end up a pedant, writing books, transferring the aim of my tremendous struggle from the hot and sacred body of man and animal onto inanimate, anemic paper? . . .

I remember when the evening would fall and we lay on the hot sand—you sitting and I lying on my back on the ground—how I trembled, struggling to balance into an outward stillness the frightening conflicting forces of the universe, which for a moment had taken refuge

114

and acquired consciousness inside my own hard skull. What was it? A man and a woman, the evening, stretched out by the sea. And yet, is there anything more sublime in all the universe? We were the two primeval armies, full of love, hate, curiosity, anticipation. I knew this, and with meaningless, futile human words, I was striving to initiate you into the mystery, taking you by the hand through this dark catacomb of God.

There were moments when you hated me, when you loved me, when you wanted to leave; others when you wanted to stay with me eternally, and alternating thus, you experienced all the contradictory, sacred essence of God's agony. And later, when the stars came out, the strain was eased. Your heart was soothed because involuntarily you had adopted the same rhythm as the calm, sacred movement of the sky—of the sky, i.e., of the earth.

I talk and I am still in the grip of the idea that we are together by the sea in solitude. It's evening now, raining monotonously, despairingly, and I'm letting the letter grow so as to be with you a bit longer. . . .

The boat stayed in Heraklion two days, and there was such a storm that none of the passengers could land. And today the boat left for Alexandria. So I didn't see Elsa. I'm definitely sure that it was better this way. . . .*

Heraklion [September, 1924]

Liebe, liebe Genossin,

I'm staying all alone in Georgiadis' house by the sea. At times in this absolute loneliness, watching the waves, the rocks, the crows passing by overhead, I have a sudden feeling of happiness. I write all day long. Sometimes I'm full of joy because what I write seems to me full of warmth, pain, love; so true a cry that whether He likes it or not, God will hear it.

Ah, if only I might have a little calm and enough time to get there. I find myself at the height of my powers. I don't want to lose a single hour. From daybreak on, I'm bent over the paper, battling away to save my soul. As long as I am able to. Not in order to let people know that inside this black head there is a warm and palpitating vision, but genuinely, in order to save my soul after the transient body has disappeared. Genossin, every day I feel my mind is progressing, my heart is growing crystal-clear. And if it should happen that we could live

---

* Letter to E. Samios.

together again, I would be better with you, more peaceful and warm. If I chanced to die suddenly now, the sea at Leda would come before my eyes, our rock, the hot pebbles, the burnt lemon trees, your slender, supple body, your tight-pressed, silent lips. Ah, this earth is full of miracles. My heart is an insatiable, terrifying mystery metamorphosing all the inferno of life into a sacred intoxication. You remember our anxiety to transform Leda into Paradise?

I'm writing The Odyssey; my heart is melting. Odysseus, Eleni, Nefertiti—my God, what anguish it is to save them by finding refuge in a perfect line of verse! This is the book that I'll carry with me in the grave—as the ancient Egyptians used to hold a small wooden boat to pass through Hades. Ah, if only we were together in the same boat in those dark subterranean waters! Genossin, all these days and nights I have you so strongly in my mind that if you are not aware of it, human feelings must be most imperfect. I tell myself that it is the sea that is thundering incessantly before me, and that is why all my dreams these nights are full of your presence, d'une façon inavouée et inavouable [in a manner not admitted and inadmissible].

So in my heart you are fused with an eternal element, the sea. Blessed be the Libyan Sea, Genossin, Genossin!*

. . . Several days in bed—fever, difficult breathing. I know it is a psychological reverberation. I am freeing myself of certain people, especially of Lefteris, whom I loved, and this never happens without bodily exhaustion. I suffered the same thing when I freed myself of Sikelianos and of Sphakianakis later on. The body follows the spirit faithfully and attentively; understanding slightly later and striving to follow the footsteps of the spirit.

Today I'm a little better. Tomorrow I hope to go as far as the sea. The sky is autumnal, sparse clouds; in the evening mute flashes of lightning. I have the Odysseus notebook in bed with me, and take notes all the time. Several dreams these nights have helped me. This is a good sign; it shows how the inconscient [unconscious] is working for Odysseus, and in this I have absolute confidence—not in the miserable, narrow, deceitful human logic. . . .

These days and nights, the vault of my head sparkles with the vision of Cretan and Egyptian civilization—for these are the first two stages of Odysseus' second trip—I'm happy in a very cruel, inhuman way. In my fever I closed my eyes and I saw and I took my leave of all

* Letter to E. Samios.

116

the figures I have loved. They were all women. If I should die, only women would come to bid me farewell and weep. I know that. Not a single man. Not even my father—because he would see so many women around me.

Liebe Genossin, write me many things. Your letters are dry, disciplinées, like compte-rendus. As though you were afraid someone else might read them. Ah, lassen Sie das Herz bellen! [Let your heart roar!]*

Heraklion, Autumn, 1924

Liebe, liebe Genossin!

Once again, I am dominated by the bloodthirsty, rapacious bird— the Spirit. All day long I'm bent over the paper, writing, suffering more than I shall ever be able to tell you. "Like a skull rattling and crackling on the funeral pyre, I hear in the quiet of my own steady mind the whole earth being rent." These words, which I wrote at one point for Buddha, are imbued for me with deep and painful feeling. I am the earth and the funeral pyre and the quiet mind. I have no hope, no joy, no chimera.

I know that all this marvelous play of light and shadows upon the earth, all these warm apparitions—flowers, women, sea, insects, ideas— are transitory vapors rising out of the crossroads of our five senses.

And yet I rejoice. I have an irrational love for all these shadows. I give my blood to bring them to life, to have them live inside me eternally, in a moment, to save them from wretchedness, degradation, death. Even though this hard, intoxicated skull of mine will, I know, be shattered and the seven waves of worms pass over it and empty it.

I'm striving to experience the vanity of all endeavor and simultaneously the eternity of every moment. Ah, Genossin, how few were those hours at Leda! Ah, when will I be able to live with you again—so that you will no longer ever be worried about my silence or my words; so you will live my agonies and my joys and hold my mind in your hands calmly, luminously—like a bronze sphere, like a bronze mirror?

Now I'm writing The Odyssey. My heart is a ship with a yellow sail, from prow to stern filled with Odysseus. He has set off on his second and last journey—passing through Crete, Africa, the Mediterranean. He encounters the ideas and women and labors he has longed for. He transcends human limits and goes on—creating God with the prow of his ship.

---

* Letter to E. Samios.

You think, Genossin, that in this awesome last journey of mine, I am forgetting you. And you cannot see that you are sitting inside the ship, calm, silent, disciplinée, mistress of your own heart, with your lips sealed tight, insatiable and proud. Where are we going? We've set the rudder toward the abyss, but unwearyingly our eyes revel in this world. I look at you with a trembling heart, but my hands are steady as they hold onto the rudder, and I smile at you to give you courage. . . .

Last night I was with you the whole night through in my dreams. I woke up with the taste of your all-night presence on my lips and my eyelids. Is this the reason I'm writing you today? I don't know. It's evening. I've been working all day long. I'm full of despair and calm; the whole day's frightful struggle is concentrated into this warm, insistent greeting to you. This is the reward for my day's work: these are my day's wages.

Genossin, I thank God that you exist. I thank the 18th of May when I saw you for the first time, and our sacred days and nights in Leda.*

The past rolls and unrolls like an endless belt, drawing me back into the land of memory. I am no longer a tree whose sap is protected by long years' growth of bark. I am a bee tangled in the web of some monstrous spider and at its mercy, a mummy with a heart still beating.

Was I at my post on the "ship" carrying you off to the other shore? Instead of our sinking together into the black sands, why have I become a new Dybbuk?† What diabolical trap was this name you dubbed me in the land of Israel? Another of those plunges into the future that you were so good at! And so, here I am, prisoner of a charioteer shadow holding me by the reins.

How often I've forgotten that you are absent, and hurried home to bring you the latest news. To tell you that the flag was at half-mast on the Castle at Antibes because you had just passed away at Freiburg . . . to bring you a letter from Albert Schweitzer calling you his brother, or a brave word from Alvarez del Vayo at the time when Cyprus was taking the same sanguinary way as Crete.

But can you see the quintessence of things through my eyes, which are still engrossed in insignificant details? Do I have, could I ever have,

---

* Letter to E. Samios.
† A legendary figure in Hebrew literature of a young girl in whom the dead fiancé went on living.

those magical eyes that guided you throughout your long solitary wanderings?

January 27, 1925

Liebe, liebe Genossin!

I think of you all the time, every moment, divining all your sorrows, weaknesses, vacillations, violent desire—your whole individual adventure is growing inside me into a universal horror and futility. And at the same time, all the rhythm of the world is becoming incorporated, assuming a countenance, voice and sweetness in your own pale, determined, beautiful face. How shall I write you? How shall I make you eternally aware that I forget nothing? That our three stars shine forever inside my dark skull and that I am with you—whether you want it or not, whether I want it or not?

Usually, in order to be aware of a feeling and to see distinctly that they have it, people need to find a name for it. I'm not seeking a name. But what I feel is a mystical, dark union, replete with all kinds of tenderness and cruelty, without beginning or end, a recognition of two tremendous impersonal forces whirling and battling to become liberated within our own ephemeral bodies.

We are not pursued by some destiny. Rather, all of us—strong and weak, worthy and unworthy—depend upon countless coincidences, on chance meetings, on a word, on a breath of air, on a dream. And whosoever has a more delicate nervous appareil [mechanism] is all the more dependent upon them, because he is aware of all the mystical messages. Indeed, the idea of the savages and of the ancient Persians is absolutely true: The air is full of demons, good ones and evil ones. In the process of walking, we traverse a sea of spirits.

Genossin, lieber Kopf [Comrade, beloved head], I too wish I were with you. I have suffered so much, I have inside me so many bitter and joyful things eternally renewed, that I think I understand well all the joys and bitternesses of my brothers and sisters. We would talk. I would strive again to break the ice of your individuality, and you would feel how good it is to be alive, to look, to listen, to walk in the rain or sun, to tremble from despair or pleasure, and to feel a human being beside you springing along in the same sacred, quivering rhythm.

Liebe Genossin, shall I ever see you outside Greece? Shall we ever walk together again the way we did on that horrifying shore of Leda? And by our patience, persistence, love shall we succeed, the way we did there, in transforming hell into paradise? . . .

I am afraid of nothing, because I hope for nothing. I have located my joy beyond all joys, and my serenity is composed of all the agonies in the world. I do not seek "happiness"; on the contrary, I consider sorrow and unhappiness indispensable elements for exercising my determination and my love. . . .

Sometimes as I walk, I feel the wind and the rain beating on my hard Arabian head, and I shudder voluptuously. Ah, my God, I'm alive, I can hear the wind and the rain. I'm suffering, I feel pain. The whole vision of the earth and sky is ripening like a flaming fruit in the dark leaves of my existence! . . .*

And to Leah:

Candia, March 10, 1925

Leah, Leah, dear herring-comrade; beautiful, marvelous Jewess. . . . How often and how deeply I think of you. I hope to see you this year. I'm going to Palestine this summer—I've become a Zionist. Ah, why am I not a Jew? I feel no affinity at all with my own people. I find myself at home, in my own climate, when I talk with Jews, when I laugh and am silent with them. . . .

Heraklion, May 2, 1925

Liebe Genossin,

. . . In the evening up until midnight, I read whatever I come across—philosophy, Communist material, poetry. I have ceased to attach any importance to the selection. Odysseus is still growing, still consuming my heart. Nefertiti† sent me a beautiful German edition of R. Rolland's Gandhi, and she writes: "This is a human being—not you, who still love words and write!" This little Jewish girl is right. But she doesn't know—she's Jewish and very young—that it's a mistake to hasten the unfolding of the spirit. I've always developed with great difficulty, very slowly. The spirale [spiral curve] of my soul is very tightly wound up and unwinds at an inexorably slow pace.

Recently I've reached some unexpected conclusions about the Communist ideology, leaving my old theories behind. Always the same thing. In the same way at an earlier time I escaped from science, by

---

* Letter to E. Samios.
† Rahel.

which I'd been possessed, and later on from philosophy. And so now I'm going to emancipate myself from art too—only by working for it passionately, dedicated to it in my entirety will I succeed in liberating myself from it. This, I think, is the method of God. This is the way He too liberated Himself from the plants and animals. And it's the way He is struggling today to liberate Himself from man. I've always tried to unite the two great enemies which are each other's complement: Raserei und Klarheit. Violent passion (mania) and, at the same time, crystal clarity. Let not the mind chill the scorching heat of the heart, nor the heart dim the clarity of the mind. . . .*

[Heraklion] May 21, 1925

Liebe Genossin!

Today is your name day and I wouldn't like this day to pass without talking to you. I too bless the day—that evening in the station—when I first saw you. Please God, till the end of this transient, most bitter life may we always be companions, liebe Genossin—with many griefs and many joys, as is fitting for a vital human heart. . . .†

[Heraklion, spring, 1925]

Liebe Genossin,

I'm so submerged in the work I've begun that for the first time in my life I feel a power and maîtrise like this. I write all day long, sleep all night long, live all alone, look out on the sea, the mountains of Crete, the earth that has molded my body, the air that has created my soul— and I am profoundly united with all this island, as is the flower with its roots. . . .

These days as I write, I'm striving to resurrect the primeval souls of our ancestors at Knossos. I live the entire vision, gaze at the faces, weep, laugh, die and love along with all these painted women showing their bare breasts—and all these slender-waisted, proud men. Odysseus passes by and devastates their decadent civilization.

Two or three times in my life I've had this overwhelming creative intoxication: once, very violently, on Siphnos; another time on Mt. Athos; and then in a village in Switzerland near Lugano; and then in Germany, near Jena. So, not two or three times, thank God; several times—and I feel as though I've just been born. I'm liberated and

---

* Letter to E. Samios.
† Letter to E. Samios.

*henceforth, I shall try to keep this intoxication at an everyday, extremely simple level.**

Breaking his creative surge of his own accord, Nikos Kazantzakis would at intervals go for brief jaunts in Greece itself or, better still, to some faraway, inaccessible land. This time, after a month in Athens and a brief visit to Aegina, he was able to realize his dream of making a trip around the Cyclades. His letters of that period exude all the flavor which he had the capacity to preserve intact for some twenty years, so as to convey it to us in his Zorba:

The sea, autumn mildness, islands bathed in light, fine rain spreading a diaphanous veil over the immortal nakedness of Greece. Happy is the man, I thought, who, before dying, has the good fortune to sail the Aegean Sea.

Many are the joys of this world—women, fruit, ideas. But to cleave that sea in the gentle autumnal season, murmuring the name of each islet, is to my mind the joy most apt to transport the heart of man into paradise. Nowhere else can one pass so easily and serenely from reality to dream. The frontiers dwindle, and from the masts of the most ancient ships spring branches and fruits. It is as if here in Greece necessity is the mother of miracles.

Toward noon the rain stopped. The sun parted the clouds and appeared gentle, tender, washed and fresh, and it caressed with its rays the beloved waters and lands. I stood at the prow and let myself be intoxicated with the miracle which was revealed as far as eye could see.†

Tinos, August 9, 1925

Liebe, liebe Genossin,

"Glory be to God for all things!" The sea was good at daybreak at Syra. *Clean and whitewashed, the houses were shining like a pile of skulls, with black holes formed by their open windows.* At eight o'clock in the morning, Tinos. A dry, typically Greek island, without any trees or water, full of clean houses, whitewashed or else colored with indigo or yellow ocher. We sat down in the café; Athenian types, *en villégiature*

---

* Letter to E. Samios.
† Zorba the Greek (New York: Simon and Schuster, 1952), p. 16.

[on holiday in the country], trousers pressed, hats, foolish ladies who are supposed to be having a good time, but are bored without admitting it.

We didn't find any lodgings. The hotels are full. We found a stretch of sand where we shall sleep tonight. The moon will be late in rising and we shall have stars. Heavenly white figs. It makes me happy to hold these sweetest of earth's gifts. Tomorrow we're leaving for Mykonos by caïque. So we shall go au petit bonheur [to the little happiness]. . . .

The mountains here are as I love them: naked, sun-baked, thrusting into the deep-blue sky. But the people are disagreeable. Except that on the sandbank I found two young fishermen, and we talked about octopuses, mermaids and witches.

I'm sitting in the café at high noon as I write you, watching the ladies strolling along the fire-hot quay with their little sunshades, serious, all painted up, unbearable. My heart is torn with pitié. No salvation. If only I could blow one violent gust of wind into the Greek fenlands before I die!*

Mykonos, August 11, 1925

Miraculous Mykonos, Genossin. Rarely have I felt so profoundly happy as the moment when I confronted this little snow-white city, with its flat, whitewashed roofs, sparkling like a city on the moon, over a dark-blue-and-green sea. And when I entered the narrow lanes, around each corner inexpressibly delightful discoveries: white, white staircases, columns, arcades, wells in little squares, fig trees, plane trees, and all around windmills slowly, idly, peacefully stirring their wings. The whole city a miracle—the air, the color, the arid mountain, the simple people, their speech, the figs, the grapes, the thyme, the mint. . . .

[continued] August 12

. . . I slept superbly. The sky was revolving once again around my head; the caïque was dancing lightly in the harbor; and a dog was barking alongside the prow of a ship. Nazos couldn't sleep. He was cold. . . . He's not very sturdy. Today he can't walk and I had to climb the mountain alone to get to the Panomeria Monastery. Inside the church, I found five village girls adorning the ikon of the Virgin (barely recognizable on a piece of charred wood). They were dressing her in wax flowers, gauze veils, flowers and ribbons. And they were laughing

---

* Letter to E. Samios.

and singing softly, as though decking out a bride. I am always thinking of you. I am striving to have you get well and come with me. Then the days and nights will be beautiful. We will talk quietly and walk. The whole island will take on meaning and sweetness. O God, may you get well and may we have time to live a few days together again.*

Naxos, August 15, 1925

My heart trembles when I gaze at the medieval castle at Naxos. I wander through the familiar old streets, remembering everything—making out familiar countenances. Some houses have collapsed. Some fountains have run dry. Some fig trees I used to know have been uprooted. The city is dying. Lots of old men and old women; very few young ones, the lazy ones. At night very few lights are burning. All the houses are bolted very early, and the people crawl like spiders behind their own thresholds. I saw the house where we stayed, the school, the windows of a few girls—Augustina, Kleo, Iakova—with their shutters broken and dangling. Some have died, some have emigrated abroad. At night, two lanterns like funeral torches are lighted at the entrance to the port.

My heart is heavy and exultant, like Odysseus' heart when he returned to Ithaca. Several traits [characteristic touches] will go into The Odyssey. I wander through the streets seizing whatever I can from the well-loved corpse.†

Like the sun identical in its course each day, yet never twice the same, our actions and our innermost desires created circles in infinity, crystal balls, iron rings, a magic eye mirroring universes in the process of becoming. . . . How many births can man experience in this way, even the most poorly endowed man on earth?

Master and disciple, elder brother and younger sister, man and woman in love, we shed these cocoons at the world's crossroads and took our time as we slowly passed through the prison-houses of our own shells, separated and united anew with each new birth. Chrysalises painfully unfolding our wings in idyllic Amorgos, butterflies with scorched wings in incandescent Palestine.

I arrived at Amorgos on the ninth of September, more dead than alive. According to our secret pact, we were to "snatch" ten days a year

---

* Letter to E. Samios.
† Letter to E. Samios.

from our God to live "alone confronting one another in solitude." I had boarded the ship lightheartedly in spite of the fury of the *meltemia*,* that scourge of the Aegean Sea. Later on, Nikos confessed to me that when he caught sight of me all pale on the deck, he had been seized by a wild impulse to throw me overboard.

Amorgos, for other people an island of the Cyclades, typical in its milk-white nakedness. For me a lean man with a swarthy complexion and a small, round head. But look at the warrior in Uccello's *Battle Scene* in the Louvre. No one but Uccello could paint this man's portrait. Amidst the tumult of knights and armored horses, he alone has his face exposed, he alone remains impassive, his feet fixed firmly in the battle, his eyes gazing beyond mundane things: it is the very face of this faceless crowd which is still unaware of its own destiny.

A man who had a teasing, caressing way of looking you over, a distant air, as though he were lost in the contemplation of the heavens under the starry sky, and then lapsed into voluble talk or taciturnity for the rest of the day. Drawing you into the heart of his silences, as succulent as some ripe fruit, letting you follow him with no caviling up his precipitous path.

When he was not working on his *Odyssey*—from dawn on I could hear him scanning the lines, counting the syllables on the tips of his fingers—he was translating Tagore. And while I was resting, he would be writing letters, those confessional letters he wrote to his dearest friends. The following one to Elsa was composed in German:

I've already completed the whole cycle of the Aegean islands. This trip has been splendid, full of light, color, harmony. The real Greece shines in these islands between Europe and Asia. For the first time, I think, I've come to understand these two things: what the Greek spirit is, and how this spirit became a luxury, too remote from our spirits of today. This divine beauty acts like opium on our bodies and our enkindled, hungry souls. I hope I have liberated myself from it at last. These months I've been culling the most sublime flower of Greece. I've understood everything. I am free.

For me, freedom has always been the fruit of the highest use of the human understanding. The ultimate act of love. My method, as I explain it in Spiritual Exercises, *does not involve a denial of spirit and*

---

* A north wind blowing in the summertime.

body, but rather aims at the conquest of them through the prowess of spirit and body.

This method is very difficult and very dangerous, because this earth is marvelous, and the fear in our hearts is deep.

Every evening on the threshold of her little house by the sea, how this old Calypso* listens to the tales of the many-souled Odysseus! I talk to her about the stars, insects, love, God, butterflies, bees. I'm a "Diali," an [African] rhapsodist; and I love and understand profoundly, like a blind man, all that is visible on this earth.

Sometimes I feel disturbed because I realize how dangerous I may become to a spirit. I love and understand too well . . . I am too vehement for the practical rhythm; but I also know that I am a precious seed of God, an eternal element, a red flame, beyond logic in the geometry of the universe. Without these red flames, God would have remained forever among the plants. Siva, the Hindu god of love and destruction, is the true countenance of my heart. . . .†

On September 4, Kazantzakis mentioned a dream in his notebooks. A dialogue with his friend, the Cretan professor and poet, Mihali Anastassiou:

Anastassiou: What we feel for you is hatred and love. We say bad things about you. We consider you a monster. We don't want to talk with you. All your actions seem somber to us, full of egoism and cruelty. But the moment you appear, the whole rhythm changes: You seem to us full of love. We see sacrifices in all your acts; an exemplary struggle in your whole life. When you leave, we see the same darkness again.

I: Your belief in what you say is so unshakable; all your words seem to me such expérience vécue [experience actually lived] that I am forced to make the following confession:

When I see a worthwhile spirit, I am seized by a weird passion. I feel upset, exultant, hungry and full of love. Some carnivorous bird inside me launches out toward this spirit, refusing to let go of it. Every human soul, regardless of the person's sex, appears to me feminine. A fierce Annunciation, a tempestuous erotic love. I make haste. The spark

---

* Marioritsa, the proprietress of the hotel on Amorgos.
† N.K. copied this letter into his notebooks.

I have found in the other body I strive to kindle so that it will burn as much substance as possible around it—bodies, ideas, habits, established laws—so that it will rise into a flame thrusting upward and merge with the gigantic conflagration I call God.

This need of mine for kindling the spark is by no means based on calculation; it's a carnivorous instinct consuming both myself and the others, and it's higher than myself. I am not concerned for riches or for a goal or for salvation. This is a dark power, inconsciente qui se déclenche [unconsciously unleashed].

Can I leave Amorgos without a word about the majestic Marioritsa —"another catafalque," as Nikos used to exclaim at the sight of her many voluminous veils—and Antonaki, her epileptic son, sometime chef of the Grande Bretagne Hotel in Athens?

It was Antonaki who gave Nikos swimming lessons. And rigged out in the paraphernalia of his art, with hieratic gestures, he used to serve us baked sea bream, small fry, and *poulet à la milanaise*. And their tiny "Grand Hotel," with its two spic-and-span rooms, frequented by mosquitoes and other undesirable intruders. And the brief September twilights, fragrant with the odor of white figs, the long starry evenings when our hostess used to come and sink down exhausted beside "my Kyrios Nikos," cooing as she plied him with her eternal questions:

"Do the angels live in the stars, my Kyrie Nikos? Doesn't Santorini have more scholars than Athens, my Kyrie Nikos?"

Milk and honey for her Kyrios Nikos; and a dose of poison for the young stranger who was expected at any moment.

"Couldn't you write her there's nothing to eat, my Kyrie Nikos? No milk, for instance, no fish, not a single egg, nothing at all? Aren't we happy without her?"

But the moment she saw my bedraggled state, her mood changed.

"Ah, my poor little lady!" she cried. "What a trollop that sea is! Antona-a-a-aki! Pay attention! Nothing fried today. Something good, something tender; get a move on. A diet for our angel!"

A few months before Amorgos, while in Crete, Nikos Kazantzakis had made the acquaintance of three very interesting people: a young Italian archaeologist, now well known; his Greek fiancée, Anna, and his sister Edvige. Majestic and beautiful, Anna was very impressive. Edvige had jet-black hair, rose-petal skin, and a slender figure, one more jewel in the renowned collection of *extraordinary* Jewish girls.

We shall come upon the lovely Athenian in several letters Nikos wrote between 1925 and 1927. During his brief sojourns in Athens, he used to look her up, liking to have a solitary chat with her. As was his habit, he introduced us to one another, and I had a chance to admire her elegance and ease in conversation. Edvige, who was settled in Trieste, I did not meet until several years later. A spontaneous friendship developed, which has lasted to the present day.

I haven't yet spoken of Nikos' mania for playing the role of matchmaker.* The moment he met any good, eligible person, his one thought was to find some sisterly soul, if possible a partner in marriage. This was his secret hope, I think, when he gave the young girl a message to be delivered to his friend, M. G. Three days before his first trip to the U.S.S.R., Nikos wrote Edvige:

[Athens] October 16, 1925

. . . A great piece of news! In three days, I'm leaving for Moscow!

Everything was ready for my trip to Africa, but at the last moment, they gave me the chance to start off for Moscow, and I seized it with delight. . . .

There is some one governing our destiny, my friend, and this some one is ourselves. Everything I've desired in this bitter, ferocious life I've attained because I've desired it bitterly and ferociously. Reality—I experience this every day—is an extremely fluid thing, without a face, without a will; a blind, stupid, supplicating fluid, begging our will to give it a face and character. . . .

Arrivederla! [Au revoir!] May my God, that barbarous, sanguinary Warrior, guide your steps and mine. N.

And from the boat carrying him off to the U.S.S.R.:

October 25, 1925

Liebe, liebe Genossin!

I left on Tuesday. I didn't want to—and I couldn't—say goodbye to you. I shall never forget that Sunday twilight we spent together, so

---

* He was even planning to write a comedy, to be entitled "The Matrimonial Bureau."

128

calm and intimes, quite, as we said, like two almonds in the same shell. I didn't want to change that last moment. . . .

In the Black Sea a huge storm has broken out. The captain doesn't dare to brave it. Perhaps we'll stay in the harbor at Constantinople a long time. . . .

It's night now and raining. The city is all sparkling with lights on both the right side and the left, in Europe and in Asia. It doesn't make my heart beat faster at all to look upon this city embodying "the aspirations of the Greeks." I realize how far I've gotten away from the nationalistic ideal. Underneath the shelter of these houses shining in the rain, I sense the whole of the human struggle, independently of national labels. I suffer, love, rejoice with them, feeling the cares of the men and the sweetness and bitterness of the women and the yearnings and drives of the Young Turks. And I am with them, a human being like them, full of anguish, love, hopes. I relish the bitterness of this rainy evening. Around me in the little salon I hear the two young Russian women talking, and the Russian men are drinking their tea. And I am bent over a piece of paper, trying to bring you close to me, to conquer distance, to grab you this very moment, wherever you are, and take you with me, Lenotschka.*

Moscow, November 10, 1925

How many, many years is it, liebe, liebe Genossin, since I have seen you! The end of the world, the end of time, that's the way this feverish city I'm wandering and living in looks to me. I still haven't been able to catch its countenance. The golden domes of the churches and the red flags with the sickles and the extremely ugly women, abîmées by work and freedom, and the men possédés by the idea—all these things are chaos and I who love chaos (but on condition that I find the rhythm that will produce order)—I am happy; I'm struggling and I've gotten thin.

All day long in the museums, the ministries, at workers' meetings, Marxist universities, I'm observing the attempts to create a new art. Here I'm experiencing the new world's effort to create and annihilate, to find a rhythm, and to set a rhythm for the whole of life. And life, that carefree trotteuse [sidewalk whore], laughs and weeps and plays, going her own way, and mocking whoever wants to save her. I remember my poor, beloved Jean Jacques Rousseau. He'd found a trotteuse on the

---

* Letter to E. Samios.

street in Venice—Giulietta was her name—and that night he took her up to his room. And when they lay down in bed and Giulietta got undressed, poor Jean Jacques began catechizing her, begging her to take the straight and narrow path. This is the way I see the Communists who preach morality and strain to build an honorable, just and good world. . . .

I'm staying in a house called "The House of the Sages," because only scholars are accepted! There are some twenty men and women. The house is splendid, overlooking the river, very clean, comfortable, peaceful. But I still haven't met any "sages." I'm working alone in the little blue salon with a potted palm in front of me. The other "sages" work in the big green salon, each at his own little table. I never talk to them, and it's wrong of me not to, because perhaps one of them is worth something.

The women here in Moscow, I repeat, are all extremely ugly. From time to time, I meet a woman who reminds me of Rahel, but the illusion quickly vanishes. I've met several girls who are clever, but since they are physically unattractive to me, I don't feel like talking to them.

The other day I went to a dancing school . . . I was the only spectator, and for three hours thirty almost naked girls danced in front of me. The air got saturated with the smell of sweat and powder. I watched "mes chers frères, les corps des femmes [my dear brothers, the bodies of women]" with anxiety and despair. I'll not touch any of these bodies, I said to myself, as though they were ghosts, as though they didn't exist. The dancing was in the familiar style of the Russian ballet; nothing new or unexpected. I remarked on this in a quiet tone to the directress on the way out. "Well, what do you want then?" she replied. I told her what I want, what I demand, from dancing; and she got afraid. And then I laughed and told her I'd just said that to tease her. I was nervous and upset. The dance, woman, death bear for me the same immediate, bitter-sweet sensation of life. . . .*

Moscow, November 20, 1925

Liebe, liebe Genossin,

I've just gotten your letter and our whole life springs up amid the snows, in grief and joy, in very brilliant color and mystery. Underneath my window, the river "passes by," frozen. At this twilight hour, thousands of crows sit over it and caw. On the other bank a church dome, all

---

* Letter to E. Samios.

of gold, glitters among the naked poplars. My life immediately re-assumed its rhythm here, as though I'd been born in the midst of this snow, among the crows and the golden domes. I'm working very hard, studying the organization of each Ministry . . . as though there were a possibility of its all being useful to me some day in tiny, miserable, godlike Greece. This trip has come at the right time—at the very moment when I was struggling to free myself from the enchantment of Art. . . .

When will we in Greece be capable of making an organized attempt to achieve the unachievable? What moves me in Russia is not the reality that they have achieved, but the reality which they long for, and do not know that they cannot achieve. All human value roosts in this chimera; for this intoxication, it is worthwhile to act and die. For the human masses—workers, peasants, women—to enjoy themselves, to eat better, to become enlightened is certainly a goal worthy of man. But I regard all these things as petty, practical illusions, crumbs for my heart, which when it has eaten is hungrier than before.

Liebe, liebe Genossin, will we ever be able to celebrate Christmas together? I seem to find myself on the edge of the world, and there is no bridge. I'll spend Christmas alone, in a warm little church I know, with little green domes, among good old women with blue eyes. I'm courage-ously breathing the air of solitude, and all the while it seems to me I'm about to sink into incurable isolation. . . .

My God, what solitude! What a harsh, heroic intoxication over-whelms my heart! I have a perfect memory of you. In my left hand, I can feel your whole face, nose, mouth, chin, neck—how can they ever be lost? Even if you should go away and forget me, I shall clasp your memory to me like a body.

Sacred, holy, mysterious this city, and here your whole face takes on a new brilliance, as though the phosphorescent snows were lighting it, and the golden domes across the way. . . .*

November 27, 1925

They've just this moment telephoned me from the Embassy that they're sending my mail over to me. I'm standing at the window, waiting, hoping to have a letter from you. A terrible snowstorm, every-thing drowned in fog and deep snow. The river is invisible. Like shadows, a few loaded carts pass heavily and slowly by. The crows are

---

* Letter to E. Samios.

131

cawing, and all the sad, deep Russian soul is crying out. A strange uneasiness is catching at my heart. My whole life seems like an aimless, painful, tumultuous fever, and the only natural condition of man, beast, or god seems to be death. What's the point of all this struggle? What's the point of all the warmth and mystery of man and woman? Why should our hearts and hands get so agitated? . . .

And when your letter came and I read it, all this sorrow grew and found an echo, as I thought of you bedridden once again, struggling with the invisible enemy. Ah, if only I could be sick as well, so as to have the right to talk. Once when I was ill in Vienna, as I have told you, how proud and elated I felt that in that critical moment my soul proved it was not easily overcome by panic, and if it were to die, it would face death, without anger or supplication—the way we get up from some gathering, open the door, and cease to exist.

If I were near you, I would tell you the kind of stories that you like, and so the unhappy moments would pass happily. Do you remember how we won at Leda? . . .*

Moscow, December 20, 1925

. . . Here in Moscow I've been talking with various "leaders." Their worthiness consists in their action and in their holy impulse with all its flame and smoke; their thinking seems to me too simple-minded. I never weary of looking at the snow, the crows, the Oriental churches, the heavy peasants, the painted women—my heart writhes at leaving Moscow.

Rahel wrote me that she is coming. I wrote to her. A month has passed. They won't let her cross the border. I can hear the beating of her heart outside Russia. This girl really lacerates my heart. If only I could do her some good! If I could make her happy, make her laugh, for a single moment! . . . . I'd like her to come to Athens and for you to meet her. But will she ever see our sun? Will we ever find ourselves, all three of us, on a Greek island? Difficult, dark, full of uncertainty this life of ours. How to rise up and utter a cry? . . .

Today at the house of an old man, who is a very fine human being, I saw something beautiful. This rare person lives all alone, an old aristocrat, and he has the most beautiful collection of ikons in the world. His Madonnas, angels, saints are inexpressibly beautiful. He has discovered a process of his own, and now, as Director of the museum that has the

---

* Letter to E. Samios.

132

ikon collection in Moscow, he has put it into practice. He performs miracles, removing from the old ikons the various layers which subsequent ikon painters painted over the divine originals. The original ikon he finds under perhaps eight layers, and often ten. He showed me one large Madonna of the nineteenth century. By removing eleven layers of color, he discovered the original ikon—from the eleventh century! How can I describe to you its beauty? An angel on the right side is the loveliest I have ever seen in my life. I roamed for hours through the scholar's chambers, listening to him talk, his voice quavering with love for the ikons. He never shows his collection to anyone. But he had seen me at the museum. We had talked a bit, and he invited me. Ah! An erotic love, a passion for something other than yourself—I believe, Genossin, there is no other salvation. This is the only way that destiny can be conquered; the only way we can forget, and conquer death. This old man promised me he would come to Greece in the spring. He wants us to go to Mistra together and to Mt. Athos. You will meet him. My God, how many marvelous spirits there are in the world! What power this earth has to engender and nurture so many beautiful women, so many splendid men!*

Moscow, December 24, 1925

I went back to the home of my elderly friend. Tonight he showed me a marvelous ikon which he had hidden the first evening. In the fifteenth century, according to a Russian tradition, a young peasant boy went for a walk through the countryside one spring day, and was struck by lightning and killed. And he became a saint. The sixteenth-century ikon is as follows: Green, green grass. In the very center, wearing a violet-pink chiton, light and graceful, stands a young boy with bare legs touching the grass, as though he is dancing. Behind him shadowy darkness full of delicate gold flowers—like stars. And overhead, the sky is all fragmented clouds, of a menacing aspect, charged with electricity. This is the human soul dancing as it treads the sacred sward of the earth, while the sky above dangles its death-bearing thunderbolt. . . .

Genossin, liebe, liebe Genossin, how I wish we could be together tonight! All these very bitter and divine images are filling my heart, and manifold riches well up inside my hard skull. At least, keep well. Be happy—and may the New Year come, good, abundant and discret, with its ten days!†

---

* Letter to E. Samios.
† Letter to E. Samios.

1926.   Faithful to his "herring comrades" as well, he sent them ardent dispatches:

Moscow, January 20, 1926

Dear marvelous Jewess!

. . . How close I feel to you and how I should like to hear your extraordinary voice again! Surely, this year we shall realize your plans: Egypt, Syria, everything!

I attend the marvelous Jewish theater assiduously. How happy I am among these unknown women who look like you and Rahel and Itka and Rosa. . . . I relive our herring evenings and our talks about God, Tchaikovsky, and the Revolution. . . .

How beautiful, profound, frightening this world is, Leah. I have a purpose that I pursue relentlessly. Everything, both joy and pain, I subordinate to this one flaming point; there is no longer any pain or joy; there is only a step in the direction of this purpose. Otherwise life would have no meaning, and my heart would be empty and tranquil, therefore dead.

Leah, I do not forget anything. Everything burns, living and present, inside this black head of mine. . . .*

Invisible fingers are telling the beads for me on the rosary of time—1924, 1925, 1926, drops of honey on my outstretched palm. The ten days of our secret pact have become a thousand, ten thousand, innumerable.

From January 27 until April 25, 1926, Nikos Kazantzakis lived in Athens in the center of the business district. Having become officially divorced, he had taken refuge with his younger sister, Eleni. There in a kind of monk's cell, the walls lined with books and ikons, the death mask of Nietzsche above the door, he began clarifying his impressions of the U.S.S.R. Not mincing words, perceiving the pros and cons and expressing them without the slightest equivocation, for he was not of flatterers' stock, he outraged both the left and the right wings. The center merely praised the beauty and force of his style. Nevertheless, his fame was growing. Nikos Kazantzakis was coming to be recognized as a master in the field of "travel journals."

---

* Letter to Leah Levin Dunkelblum, in German in the original.

The articles appearing in the Athens daily *Elephtheros Logos* were subsequently published in two volumes entitled *What I Saw in Russia*. A bit later, after Kazantzakis' third trip to the U.S.S.R., he deleted all the statistical material and published them in a single volume, which was included in the *Travel* series.

As we already know, Kazantzakis detested Athens. Even while he was writing down his impressions of the U.S.S.R., he was getting ready to escape again. This time *Elephtheros Logos* offered him Easter in the Holy Land.

"If you like, you can come with me!" he proposed to me one day, watching me out of the corner of his eye.

"Go off to Palestine alone with a man! Even if you were God the Father Himself, my guardians would shriek 'Scandal!' "

"Try to get a journalist's identity card. Your guardians would be flattered and give you their blessing," advised Nikos, his affectionate side occasionally displaying an ingenious streak.

"I'll mention it to our good Aunt Chariclea."

"No. Better go see Vlachos."

Giorghos Vlachos, proprietor of the newspaper *Kathimerini*, agreed: "All right! If I like your articles, we'll publish them! Come around tomorrow to get your journalist's card."

My two closest friends, Ketty and Marika, were overjoyed. "We'll come with you," they said. "Mama has already consented, on condition that we bring her a splinter from the true cross."

"And your father?"

"He's sulking. Aemilia will lend us the money we need."

"Don't worry," Nikos put in. "You'll give concerts, taking turns or playing duets. I'll write Elsa at once to ask for her help in Jerusalem."

I was the only one of our little group who had never set foot outside Greece. Should I admit it? I used to suffer from it as though it were some infirmity. At school I used to invent surrealistic capitals. "In Paris, I'd get lost, carried off by a moving sidewalk. . . . When you get to the top of the Eiffel Tower, you slide out onto an ebony parapet. . . . The men sit astride it, their straw hats on strings like paper kites. . . . The women wearing riding habits and some of them carrying open parasols in their hands. *Parisian* parasols with platforms one on top of the other: one for the sun and one for the moon. . . ."

On April 25, with an absolutely calm sea, we boarded the ship *Naxos* and set off for Jaffa.

Palestine. The Book, with its message of love and murder perpetuated for all time, once again became flesh of our flesh. Naked Golgotha, a lunar landscape. Not a bird in the sky, or a tree on the earth. The wind had no shepherd's pipes to make a song, and the sun was ripening three corpses hanging from the leafless trees.

On the broad pages of ivory-colored parchment, the imprint of Christ still fresh on them, four tiny midges appeared, barely visible for the space of an instant—three girls and a man. What part of our experiences should I draw from oblivion?

We followed His shadow through the souks sweet with the scent of cinnamon, as mysterious as the veiled countenances, as fresh as the desert wells. We saw Him crouching by the fire, on the edges of the Sea of Galilee, sharing the meal of the fishermen. We scrutinized His multiple metamorphoses. At times we felt as if we were being sucked up by the cyclone of His gentle blue-green eyes, as blue-green as the eye of the Dead Sea. We murmured funeral laments over His tombstone, and summoned Him triumphantly with the muezzin, our necks bent back and our palms over our ears.

We forgot God and His prophets in order to become better acquainted with our traveling companion. We reveled in his enthusiasms and endured his heavy silences. And last of all, we had a chance to touch two of his "Jewesses" in the flesh: Elsa, the reticent, impassioned woman from Jena in her scholarly circle in Jerusalem; and Leah, the superb Pole settled on the seashore in nascent Tel Aviv.

The concerts of Ketty and Marika having been proclaimed a success, we added Cyprus to our tour, though we came within a hairbreadth of missing it on account of our traveling companion, who was prostrated by parting from Elsa.

Cyprus is indeed the native land of Aphrodite [Kazantzakis wrote at that time]. I've never looked upon a more feminine island, or breathed an air so saturated with voluptuous and dangerous suggestions. I feel enervated. In the evening when the sun goes down and the sea breeze rocks the little boats and the women stroll along the seashore, my soul capsizes and gives up, like Aphrodite, the holy prostitute. You become deeply permeated here by a sweetness like the scent of jasmine. A voice caresses your ear, and you listen to it enthralled. "Thought is an impulse that runs counter to the will to live." Tension of the soul, exaltation of the spirit, are great primordial sins. Eat, sleep, walk by the seaside. . . .*

Ah, life has changed very much since then in Cyprus. Only the words of hate spoken by the old Sultan of Hejaz in exile there are still, alas, up to date:

"From the Judaic sea to the Atlantic, from the Judaic sea to the Pacific, all the Moslems will rise up to cast the Jews into the ocean. If not this year, then it will be next year. If it is not next year, then it will be in a century. . . ."†

When we had come back from Jerusalem and Cyprus, we fled Athens and its scorching heat to take refuge with my sister on Mt. Pelion. Nikos stayed on in the capital, working uninterruptedly. Kavafakis, proprietor of the newspaper *Elephtheros Logos*, would have liked to turn over some big reporting job to him, but he didn't have a penny. Nevertheless, he did propose Rumania and the Balkans. Kazantzakis preferred Spain and Egypt. Taki Kalmouko, a painter and our friend and neighbor on Aegina, wanted to accompany Nikos and was urging him in the direction of India. To keep from losing Nikos again, we invited him to come and rest in Tsangarada, the village at which we were staying. If he brought a typewriter, we would teach him to use it.

[Athens, June 1926]

Liebe, liebe *Lenotschka!*

May "God" be with you in this loneliness of yours; our God. I've been at home all day long. I can hardly hold my pencil—my hand is so tired from writing. I don't see anyone. . . .

Find me a little house. I will come as soon as I can. Learn Russian. Supplement me. Above all, keep well. Die Hauptsache [The main thing] . . .

I haven't written to anyone yet—neither Elsa, nor Leah, nor Rahel. You write them. . . .‡

---

* From an unedited text by N.K., translated into French by himself.
† *Ibid.*
‡ Letter to E. Samios.

[Athens, end of June-early July 1926]

   . . . Bakasha* has just left my cell. She stayed a long time. We had a good talk and made plans for them to come to Tsangarada too in July. . . .

   By now my desk has gotten cleared of Hebrew and Russian books and has filled up with Spanish ones: Don Quixote, Calderón, Lope de Vega, Saint Teresa, the Spanish Baedeker, El Greco, Kultur der Araber, etc. I hope I'll be able to phone you that I'll be coming this Sunday (July 4). . . .

   Curious characters, people I don't know, come or write me that they like my articles. If I published anything really good, they'd all be silent or abuse me. "Leur verre est petit. [Their glass is a little one]."

   At night, I go out alone under the bright moon and roam about. All is well on this earth. I feel elated because I can fervently merge myself with the earth and sky, and make the brief moment of my own life eternal. Thus liberated of hope and fear, free of all ambition, serene and feeling very profound emotion, I wander around greeting the world and taking leave of it. In these solitary moments of mine, I always think of you; and sometimes my body casts two shadows on the moon. Ah, may you too see this same moon in the same way—with fire and serenity —all these nights in your own solitude! . . .†

[Athens, end of June 1926]

Liebe Lenotschka,

   A heap of plans are passing through my mind, and I haven't yet made any decision. Kavafakis is offering to let me go anywhere I want—I told him Spain, Egypt, India, and he had no objections. He suggested that I might want to go to Rumania and Serbia first. I refrained from answering. . . .

   Now this July I'm thinking of coming to Tsangarada. If I can buy one, I'll bring a small typewriter, so you can teach me. Before I leave, I'd like to have my book on Russia typed so it can be published. If I have time, The Odyssey too—because I have only one copy. . . .

   I've collected all the books I have on Spain, El Greco, etc., and

---

* Ketty Papaioannou. In Palestine we had given ourselves Hebrew nicknames: Toda Raba, Bakasha, Shalom, Dybbuk.
† Letter to E. Samios.

*now my head is full of Spain. I want to free myself of these countries so that I can work calmly, without tentations. . . .**

So here at last we were under our own roof. Finding joy in everything, so shy, so discreet, he was like a child who has just been offered a red balloon.

His first typewriting lesson. But how much easier it was to do the work in his stead, leaving him to plunge, as he used to say, "into the sea of horizontal verses," interrupting him only for the little cup of coffee and the stewed fruit—green walnuts were the specialty of Diamantoula, our landlady's daughter. Waiting till he came down to go walking with us under the beech trees and the chestnut trees. Resting in the roughly plastered little courtyards of the chapels; quenching our thirst in the numberless springs, keeping silence in order to hear their dialogue with the insects and the breeze in the branches. All the while smelling the humus of the woods and the salt air of the sea. Glimpsing in the distance the blurred outlines of Skyros and, when the wind blew a certain way (so we fancied), the peaks of Mt. Athos.

In the evening chatting away with Diamantoula and Fanny and their mother, lean and slender as mountain goats, sober as only southern races know how to be. Discovering that the apparent wealth concealed a poverty here on this magic mountain all the more tragic because it was ashamed to show itself. In wintertime, they often had nothing to eat except a kind of chestnut paste. Three of them had to share one egg on meat days. They longed for a taste of rancid bread again! "On Christmas Eve," Diamantoula confessed with a sigh, "I stand in front of our door, waiting. Fanny and Mama get annoyed. I know very well that we aren't expecting anything from anybody, because we haven't anyone who could think of us. But it's stronger than I am. Like everybody else, I wait for the postman. . . ."

Kazantzakis' articles on Cyprus and Palestine enjoyed great success. Kavafakis decided in favor of Spain. Not being able to take me there, Nikos worked out a plan for us to meet each other later on.

Giorghos Vlachos liked your work [he told me] and would like to appoint you Paris correspondent for Kathimerini. What joys you're

---

* Letter to E. Samios.

going to find there! What riches for your spirit! Only don't go by way of Marseilles. Go by way of Rome. I'll wait for you there on my way back from Spain. And we'll walk hand in hand through the streets of Rome.*

And suddenly, just at this point, Galatea came looking for Nikos, asking him to help her get away to Paris.

Athens, August 14, 1926

. . . I don't know exactly when I'll be leaving. Galatea wants to leave and at the same time she's panic-stricken at the thought of staying abroad all alone. I feel sorry for her and I understand her, but I have no right to insist. . . .†

[Athens] August 17, 1926

. . . I remember you and want you every moment, Lenotschka. "Ah," I say to myself, "if the door of the cell were to open and she were to enter!" But let's face necessity heroically, calmly. All will go fine—only get well. . . .‡

[Athens, August 20–24, 1926]

Beloved—

Athens is quiet today. The unfortunate people are happy because Pangalos has fallen and Kondylis has taken his place.§ The same soldiers who guarded the old regime are guarding the new one, with the same savagery and lack of understanding. Es ekelt mich. [It disgusts me.] These people, and all peoples, are ignorant of the root of the evil and rejoice in the change of master, without understanding or dignity.

This change will probably postpone my trip. . . . I'm ready for both good and evil, looking on with a steady and independent gaze. External events impinge upon me now without upsetting the difficult, tragic balance of my own soul. The thing I care about is keeping my soul upright, intransigeante. Of all the definitions of God, the one I like

---

best is this one: Dieu est un coeur debout à son heure! [God is a heart that is upright at the given hour!]

Beloved Lenotschka, I remember you and abide with you so intensely that if you do not feel it, it must be because the human soul is too powerless, too miserable. I'm striving to consolidate my life—first within myself and then in my external life. To leave Greece, to work very hard, to finish The Odyssey, to plunge into some seminal international movement. And you must be with me as much of the time as possible, more and more my collaborator. Life is very short; it's very precious, and it's a shame to waste it in petty squabbles and petty pleasures. . . .*

[Athens, probably August 19, 1926]

Beloved Lenotschka!

Everything was ready for me to leave day after tomorrow, Saturday—when Galatea came to see me, to beg me to stay and wait for her so we can leave on Thursday, August 26. Her papers aren't ready yet. I agreed, because of my conviction that if Galatea leaves Athens, she will be saved. I'm doing all I can. I go to her house every day and iron out all the difficulties so that she can make the decision to leave. She is so worthwhile that I can't bear for her to be lost and die every day. . . .

When the trip to Spain is over, if Kavafakis can't send me to Egypt and India, I think I might get a post as correspondent and stay in Paris. Instead of going to Spetsai, etc., to work, there are peaceful, heavenly suburbs in Paris where one can live for 2,000 drachmas per month, so they write me. And then recently . . . Paris is becoming a great center of intellectual and spiritual life—Russians visit it; the famous Hebrew theater of Moscow was there this year, etc., etc. . . .

Our "God" be with you, Lenotschka. Get well. Have faith in the strange power that struggles inside us and that we give light and heart to.†

August 24, 1926

. . . Galatea has disappeared. . . . We took the passport photos together, got the official stamps etc., but she never came back. Beyond a doubt she will not go. I did everything I could—with such warmth and affection on my part—in vain. Substance conquered the spirit. . . .

It has begun sprinkling. Once again I'm flooded by the profound,

---

* Letter to E. Samios.
† Letter to E. Samios.

dark, bitter tingling sensation the first [autumn] rains always give me. I wish we could be together at this critical moment I'm passing through. I'm all alone in my cell and all the earth smells like a newly dug grave.

This morning I went down to Piraeus and got my ticket for Marseilles. . . .*

S.S. Attiki, August 29, 1926

Beloved Lenotschka—

This trip is marvelous, like the ones when we were together: the sea, the cool weather, the joy of leaving Greece. The passengers insignificant human beings, the women the same. Only one blond, élégante Jewish woman, with very beautiful hands. People's conversations miserable. I'm reading about El Greco, and I think of you so much, so intensely, with such love! . . .

I'm sitting in the salon. They're playing wretched music, and a lady in green is dancing. In Piraeus, I saw her saying goodbye to one man in a heart-rending way, and my heart broke. As soon as we had left, she was surrounded by a number of men. She laughed and that evening went up to the bridge with a man—lithe and gay—and once again my heart broke, remembering Leda.†

This life is awesome, mysterious, above our own power, and in order to preserve the unity and elevation of our spirit, we have to make an incessant, laborious effort. There is an inhuman law, superhuman, governing the world. And if we want to embrace it within ourselves and endure it, our heart must break. How I have suffered in my own life, in the effort to adapt this horrifying law to my own ephemeral body, I shall never be able to tell you, Lenotschka. If we could live together, you would see what an enormous effort I make to preserve this balance in my life. I feel great relief because you exist; because I shall see you again; because we shall remain together again, talking and keeping silent. For how long will this joy last? I ask and a frisson of voluptuous pleasure and death overwhelms me. May God be with us. May God keep our soul ever awake, pure, and free of unworthy compromis.

How brief this life is, and how we squander it in wretched petty squabbles! Let us conquer pettiness; there could be no greater blessing. I looked at Venus as it set, and afterward at Jupiter rising in the sky; and

---

* Letter to E. Samios.
† The Leda of mythology.

now, a short while later, Mars has risen out of the sea, all purple. All these stars belong to us now, marking the heavenly moments we have spent together. When will that night come when I shall look at these eternal specks of light without a trembling in my soul?*

Madrid, September 4, 1926

Beloved Lenotschka!

I am waiting for my impressions to crystallize a bit, so that I can write you with calm. Crossing the Pyrenees at daybreak on September 1, I ran into danger. A terrible downpour. Many trains in Spain were derailed; many people killed. Our train escaped. An Armenian woman on the boat . . . had foretold this danger to me. And also, that the goal of my life will be attained, but late.

Madrid is a big European city . . . The museum is a great miracle. How shall I describe for you my feelings as I entered the big hall that has some thirty El Grecos? I'm impatient to set off for Toledo. My God, what joy to be alive and to see!

But what a joy if you were with me. On the night of the first to the second of September, in Barcelona, I had a frightful dream about you. You were trembling in a horrible way, a delirium tremens, horrible— and I came and at once you laughed, got up, and we went out for a walk, laughing and talking as though nothing had happened. Did anything occur that night? . . .

The men here are very ugly; the women—so far—are too. The old women monstrous; the young ones warm, fuzzy, garbed in mantillas, all painted, and full of vehemence. But so far none of them has stirred me. Perhaps because I'm absorbed in El Greco and the first violent contacts with this new land.

All the men I've met so far are insignificant. I feel here an inferior cultural niveau [level]. Aged, superficial, sex-obsessed bellâtres [dandies]. But the countryside teems with austere, ascetic character—you feel that all the Knights of the Woeful Countenance have been born here and have died for the disembodied, abstract Idea. A violent hallucination is begotten by the Castilian plateaus, like the exaltation we felt in the mountains of Jericho. The Spanish villages are very similar to the Arabian—without water, without a single tree, out of the same stone as the surrounding mountains. There are very few people here, and they are fashioned out of the same rock, bony, sunken eyes, shaven heads. I

---

* Letter to E. Samios.

never anticipated this resemblance, and I'm glad that now I can better understand the ascetic, tragic history of this glorious, fallen land.

I wander through the streets alone, speechless, with burning eyes, taking in this African vision. . . .*

Madrid, September 6, 1926

. . . I'm overjoyed to come home and sit down to write to you. Today I had a deeply moving experience. I made the acquaintance of the founder of the El Greco Museum, the Marquis de la Vega Inclan. He invited me to dine at his home. We talked about El Greco, as though he were a very dear and intimate friend of ours—about his wife and child, about his work, anecdotes about him, about his character. I was the first Cretan to come to visit El Greco, three centuries after [his time]. And suddenly at the moment we were eating the fruit and drinking the heavenly Malaga wine, the Marquis made a sign to his servant, and shortly, the servant came in bearing a large covered picture. As he swept the velvet cover back, my heart leaped. Before me stood what is surely El Greco's masterpiece: Saint Louis in Jerusalem, with Toledo in the background. Several months ago the Marquis discovered and bought this painting from a Spanish monastery. I've never seen a more spectral face, flesh more ivory-colored, eyes more caverneux. The sky was gray and green, like a stormy sea.

The old Marquis was emitting gentle roars, like an animal, he was so ecstatic. He has donated some twenty of El Greco's works to the state, but this one he won't part with until he dies. When he goes away on a trip, he sends it to the treasure-vaults of the Bank of Spain, to keep it from being stolen from him. . . .†

September 7, 1926

. . . I've just seen Primo de Rivera . . . a mediocre person, who is nevertheless inspired by an impulse higher than himself—the impulse that is stirring men of today to organize themselves fanatically either on the extreme right or the extreme left. . . .

I'm doing an astounding amount of work here. All day long I rove through the Ministries, study legislative acts, examine what has happened in Spain since the war in the fields of economics, politics, commerce, industry, agriculture, science, art, etc.

I'm studying a pile of books, hardly sleeping at all, once again in

---

* Letter to E. Samios.
† Letter to E. Samios.

the grip of the mania to exhaust the subject I've undertaken. Blessings on my father, who gave me the health of a wild beast! . . .*

[Madrid] September 10, 1926

. . . The days are full—and at night I do not sleep. I have a nervous excitement. There is no one with me any more to hold me in check, and I don't let my mind rest day or night.

The other day I went to a bullfight. The shock I experienced is indescribable. And I don't even want to write you anything about it, because I'll remember it all again and I'll relive all the horror. . . .

Now I've just come back from the Escorial. . . . I went mainly to see the five paintings of El Greco which are there. Ah, my God, you must see and touch the work of El Greco. Touch and sight—you remember how I love the human senses? The sacred human body? And so I touched this Cretan today in the Escorial and every day in Madrid and day after tomorrow in Toledo. I'm exhausted and happy. El Greco is becoming a great lesson for me, a model, a direction that I must follow. After three centuries, I'm the first Cretan to come to hail this stupendous fellow countryman of mine. May God grant that our encounter bear fruit! . . .

I've met Spain's greatest poet here: Don Juan Ramon Jiménez. We talked for hours today by way of farewell. I'll tell you about it when we meet.

My separation from El Greco at the Madrid museum was painful. I was battling to hold in my mind all the forms, the wings, the angels, the people, the colors . . . I shall never see them again. . . .†

Toledo, Monday, September 13, 1926

I've reached the towering, ascetic stronghold of El Greco. My heart was pounding violently all the way from Madrid—this visit to the awesome Genosse [Comrade], how I had longed for it ever since I was a small child! "At a mature age to make a reality of whatever you have desired as a child, that is the destiny of a real human being." A great many things—almost everything—that I've desired I've turned into reality by wrestling with difficulties, by the sheer impetus of my own soul. And when I came face to face with Toledo and entered it and began slowly and with exhausting intensity wandering through the

---

* Letter to E. Samios.
† Letter to E. Samios.

streets, bringing to life the old buildings; and when I crossed the threshold and made my way into El Greco's garden and went up to his house in the ghetto—El Greco loved the Jews so much that all his life he lived in the Jewish quarter—when all these things had gotten inside my hard skull, once again (my God, how many times before!) I blessed the moment I was born.

And yet my judgment was not dimmed: Toledo is not what I had expected it to be—where, oh where, are Jerusalem, Mykonos, Moscow! Those are the three cities that have amazed me. Toledo does not present as tragic a landscape as I should like (remember the mountains of Jericho!). It's very reminiscent of Crete—near Knossos. Olive trees, red earth. The little city is situated on a slight elevation and down below flows the River Tagus. There—there only, on the rocky cliffs of the Tagus, did I have a profound sense of El Greco's spirit. The rocks are gray, élancés [high and narrow], utterly dry, rising out of the green water, desolate—like El Greco's figures. This is the most moving experience I've retained from Toledo today. And at twilight another joy: I went into the superb Gothic cathedral, and all the light of the day had gathered in the splendid medieval vitraux [stained-glass windows]. The whole church was shining, and the saints in the vitraux were floating in the midst of purple, green and blue light. This was the second moving experience. And the third: when I went to the post office and got the letters, I had one from you, one from Elsa, one from Leah, and three from Rahel. . . .

Today I only roamed through the city, went into a few churches, laid siege to El Greco. Tomorrow I shall see him. I'm todmüde [dead tired]. I feel as though the excessive tension will cause my body suddenly to vanish. The following message is sent to me by Elsa: "Ihren Körper sorgen und ihn nicht ganz vergessen, damit noch etwas bleibt zum Fassen! [Take care of your body and don't forget it entirely, so that something will remain to cling to!]" And I do love the human body and feel compassion for it. But I always consider it as a means, and that is why I allow it to dissolve. One thing only I do want: for it to endure and bear the spirit without giving way. . . .*

Toledo, September 14, 1926

One of the most glorious days of my life. The moment I entered the El Greco Museum and with one violent glance grasped the images,

---

* Letter to E. Samios.

colors, splendor, godlike hands—my heart began pounding so hard that I turned to talk and joke with the old caretaker. And laughing and talking like that, my heart had a chance to grow calm. And then I gave myself up in entirety to each work. No photograph, nothing, can convey any idea of what El Greco is. The colors—blue, green, lie-de-vin [wine-colored]—gleam like metal, the whole body is athletic, solid, all panoply; and then suddenly the emaciated face, rising, vibrating like a flame. Today as never before I was aware of my own soul. This meeting of the two Cretans was so violent, Lenotschka.*

Pisa, September 28, 1926

All day long I wandered through this marvelous little city—the river, the superb cathédrale, distinguished for its Gozzoli frescoes and the Orcagna cemetery. All these beauties are so contrary to the harsh Spanish flame! Everything here is harmonized, discipliné in the spirit of Art. I recollect El Greco. How can I ever love all these beautiful things now, after the Cretan's terrifying and holy intoxication? My spirit well understands the harmony in these Italian Renaissance works that I am viewing. But I raise a cry along with the cruel Spanish priest, who said to Philip: "Fagamos un templo tal que nos tengan por locos! [Let us create such a temple that they will take us for madmen!]" Insanity, i.e., the breaking up of the old harmony, the passionate urge to foresee and establish the supreme balance of the future—here is the flame licking at my brains and searing them.

I go around Pisa, and tomorrow I shall roam around Florence. My heart leaps, longing to escape these tentations of beauty which do not belong to our age, but are so enchanting they can paralyze even the bravest spirit. The method used by Odysseus, of binding himself to the mast, annihilating his own freedom in order not to be led astray—this is contrary to my own nature. I want to hear all the song, feel the whole dizzying sensation—and for this reason I have to be free. I want the frisson, the awareness that at each and every moment I am in danger. And as you know, I've been following this way in my life up to now; and that is why my development has been so painful, slow-moving, insatiable—but at the same time, also so unyieldingly upward.

Now as I return to Italy, I realize how far I've come these past two years. All this Italy is behind me now, far from the sharp summit of my own will! I hear the Siren's song sometimes (like this evening at twi-

---

* Letter to E. Samios.

light, when I was gazing at the river, whose deep waters were all on fire, and the light was damp and blafard [wan], and my heart most bitter)—and I shudder, because I feel that I am in danger. Do you remember once in Tiflis, Varvara Nikolayevna saying to me in a garden full of big pebbles from the sea and yellow-flowered rock cress: "What do duty, fatherland, and art matter? Come, let's go away!"

If I were hardheaded, dry, prudent, unfeeling, I would not be in any danger. But I do feel the danger every moment. And now throughout this journey another Siren—the sweetest and most faithful of them all, la Mort [Death]—has often overwhelmed me. If I could only die! If I could only die! There could be no greater happiness for me, I think. Because I love this earth too much, the air, woman, thought, the sea— and I cannot get my fill of them.

Lenotschka my love, it's better that I shouldn't say anything more to you tonight. I cannot restrain my heart. If you were with me, perhaps I shouldn't have said anything, but you would have seen the tears suddenly brimming in my eyes. And then I would have laughed and shaken my head. . . .*

Florence, September 30, 1926

I arrived this morning. Pension Savonarola.

Surprise and delight on Anna's part; she hadn't expected me so soon. Edvige was already there.

We roamed around the pleasant old city. I'm looking at Giotto again, at Masaccio, and at Michelangelo. . . . All this is beautiful, but far, far, far away! I'm in a hurry to get away from Italy. On the twentieth of October, I'm leaving for Assisi. . . .†

Taking leave of his charming friends, Anna and Edvige, Nikos Kazantzakis left for Rome, where he was to meet me. . . . From his letters he might seem like a tormented man, forever torn between two desires. Actually he was a man who conveyed the feeling of marvelous stability. "For and against," "right and left," incessantly battled each other in his mind. But his instinct or his reflective reason made a quick choice of the road to follow and rejected all vain regrets. The inner struggle was revealed in the letters alone. They constitute a kind of

---

* Letter to E. Samios.
† Letter to E. Samios.

autobiography, a technique of liberation engendering that harmonious and radiant poise which impressed people who came near him.

From Rome, on October 10, 1926, he wrote Edvige:

> . . . Mussolini has given me an appointment for the day after tomorrow, and I'm leaving immediately afterward. . . . I've too much to do in Athens. . . . I'm ashamed that I haven't done anything so far. A few sentences, a few grand ideas, and great personal sorrows. But life is a more vast, a more profound duty. I must begin the last assault to do my duty before I vanish underground.
>
> Must I bid farewell to all the people I love? This is the great agony that's been strangling me these past weeks? . . .
>
> Is this the path I must follow? Renunciation of all personal joy? Is that the way to force my soul forward? Or better, to force the world's soul a bit further forward? . . .

I was about to embark for the first time on the great adventure. Marika accompanied me to Piraeus. "There's no use being on time" was the advice given us by a friend who knew all about traveling. "Greek ships say 'noon,' but they raise anchor at nightfall."

Nevertheless my ship did raise anchor on schedule. The gangplank was quite up and away. A few latecomers were still waving their handkerchiefs on the docks. Frozen with despair, I watched my one chance slipping away into the distance.

But one must believe in miracles.

Suddenly this extraordinary ship began trembling, slowed down its engines, spat out some black smoke, and stood there, imperceptibly swaying. A big mustachioed fellow, cursing father and mother alike, thrust us into his boat as though we were sacks. A few strokes of the oar and there we were, hurtled against the tar-stained sides of the ship.

What delight each time we met again! Nikos was as overjoyed as if he had been afraid of never seeing me again. He caught hold of my shoulders and squeezed them until I cried from the pain. Adjusting his steps to mine, he dragged me out at the crack of dawn to the museums, the deserted streets and lanes, the churches and pagan temples.

Kazantzakis had refined tastes and when he could afford it, he used to choose *pensions* in the private-hotel class—that is, with personnel well-trained and reserved in manner; with separate tables, soft carpets, and lighting that was ample but not garish. Such a *pension* existed at that time in the Piazza Barberini. We were overwhelmed with attentions there. Rome was showing herself at her best. We looked at Titians, Tintorettos, Michelangelos. Nikos went into ecstasies before Moses and his little horns. "Just think! It was a five-year-old child who made me understand the mystery of these horns!" exclaimed Nikos, referring to something said by our niece. "One day we were standing in front of a shopwindow displaying Easter eggs, and our little niece Alka said to me: 'Hold me tight, Uncle. Get some glue and stick it on me here. I'm happy, so happy I feel I'm growing horns.'" Alka sprouted horns of joy before the Easter eggs; Moses before God, or else before his own power.

Anchored to his idea that good and evil collaborate and in the end join forces to help overthrow this unjust world, Nikos Kazantzakis had not yet guessed the hidden, megalomaniac, weak aspect of Mussolini, with whom he had just had a brief interview.

"What strikes you most about Fascism?" I asked him one evening as we were resting from a visit to the Rome museums.

"That it has several points in common with Communism."

"How so?"

"The same suppression of individual liberty, the same faith in a better future. Only . . ."

"Only?"

"Fascism zigzags between past and future, uses means that are often out-of-date and ineffectual, seeks to have its cake and eat it too. This does not prevent Mussolini from being one of the tragic figures of our history, a man who believes in his historical mission and is ready at every moment to die for it."

Nikos Kazantzakis was mistaken in his judgment of the Italian dictator, and perhaps also in his prediction of Italy's future.

"What will happen when Mussolini is gone from the scene?" I asked.

"Considering the chaos that will follow the collapse of Fascism and an unhappy war, considering how the hopes of the Italian people have been inordinately inflated and then deflated in a minimum of time, and bearing in mind also all the people who have been oppressed during the Fascist era, and the hatred that will erupt between the previous masters and those who will try to take their places, perhaps we may predict that Mussolini will have been merely the best collaborator of a future Meta-Communism."

The promise he made me at the moment of farewell in Rome, Nikos kept to the letter. I was not at all dismayed by the dismal, rainy weather in Paris, or by being without a coat (in the confusion of my embarkation at Piraeus, my coat had been left behind) and without friends. For there he was, through his increasingly fervent letters building the bridge that enabled us to see one another every evening.

S.S. Mykali, Brindisi, October 25, 1926

My love,

. . . The sea is sparkling; I've been given a cabin all to myself and I'm stretched out to read—but my mind is with you, my love. Be brave and confident, in the conviction that love and heroism have the same source. If will power, determination, faith in the omnipotence of the human soul are capable of crossing seas and mountains, then you will feel at every moment that I am leaning over you, infusing my soul into you. Everything will turn out as we want; it suffices that you do not lose your courage. I have so much determination myself, and I consider external life so far subjected to the inner life that I have no doubt you will get well; you will get organized; I'll come to Paris; I'll work all day; I'll see you, and in the evening we'll eat together and enjoy ourselves. And afterward we'll set a new goal—and we shall achieve it and again we'll pass it—so long as our soul remains alive and we have love.

I'm elated that yours is a heroic nature, sobre and reticent, full of understanding and energy, and I feel you walking along with me ever more harmoniously and lithely. Nothing else is required for all this ephemeral life to become transubstantiated into a miracle. Let us believe, love, and each one feel the other's breathing, narine contre narine [nostril against nostril]—this is how "God" is created and saved.

Lenotschka, at this moment you are on the train,* and I send you this warm voice, as solid as that of the flesh. I remember you as though I were touching you—and I love you.†

Corfu, Thursday morning, October 21, 1926

Greece hasn't given me any joy. The people seem to me stunted, ugly, submerged in petty politics. On the streets they talk eternally about Venizelos; on the walls, election posters and the wretched faces of the candidates. Corfu marvelous—but only for a short time. The

---

* The train taking me to Paris.
† Letter to E. Samios.

mountains, the sea, the colors all exquisite, but pathetic, amolissants [devitalizing], soporific, fatal to any fighting soul. It reminds me of Naples and Andalusia; and as you know, Saint Teresa herself, the great guerrière [warrior], when she went to Andalusia, felt her soul was being diminished and appeased in that exceedingly sweet, damp, warm landscape. And she left it.

I bought some grapes, red ones and white ones, and some marvelous apples. Then I sat on top of an iron post near the seaside and ate them in peace and quiet, like some ascetic eating and all the while blessing God for sending the grapes and the apples—and hunger. I was thinking of Odysseus; a mass of images rose in my mind. The triangular sail of his black ship was hoisted once again inside my breast. I heard the seamen around me blaspheming. The painted whores ambled around the newly arrived vessel on the quay. I smelled the rotten fruit decomposing in the briny harbor, and out in the open sea I could divine the gleam of the heavenly blue waters. All this is holy, it has an immortal soul, and I must save it. A good line of verse, a brave deed, a sudden élan—if only I could produce them amidst all this futile, squalid stream of everyday necessity! And my mind perched like an Oriental seagull atop Notre Dame, like some new gargoyle, watching the approach of springtime with you, Lenotschka, and all the delights of unremittent toil and the night's love.*

Cell, Friday evening

I felt deeply affected when I entered the cell. Everything in its place—the Madonnas, the books, the couch, the Cyprus Aphrodite. . . .

I got here at noon, and at once began the awful, aggravating labor. I arranged the notes, wrote down the plan of the articles, and now it's evening and I'm tired and I'm writing to you to give myself a little joy. . . .

It will be days now before I go out—because I have a great deal of work and because I don't have any urge to see anyone. I should only like to find out when I shall be leaving and where to.

This cell is very dear to me and that's beginning to worry me. I shouldn't like to be tied to any point on the earth. But perhaps in Paris in the spring you will find me what I want—another cell. I'm impatient to end the cycle of travels and to begin the work. . . .†

---

* Letter to E. Samios.
† Letter to E. Samios.

By the time evening begins to fall and the outlines of the Madonnas in the cell grow dim, all the twilight air fills with your presence, Lenotschka. I'm always tired in the evening, and I find relief in writing to you. Have you gotten comfortably settled? Have you found new joys and sorrows in Paris? . . .

Sometimes I go out at noon and walk in the Zappeion* awhile—marvelous sun, Hymettos naked like a god, the sea shining—and I'm glad that I've found a way to live in Athens without having to say "Hello" to anyone. And so I live in a deserted, godlike city. . . .†

November 8, 1926

. . . Nothing yet about the trip. They still don't know the results of the elections, and the newspapers are all crazy. . . .

The articles‡ will be published in a few days, once the Greek souls have calmed down a bit. I write you with difficulty, because my fingers hurt from copying. . . .§

Athens, November 15, 1926

. . . Please write me long letters. . . . There's no joy in my life here. I write a great deal, and sleep hardly at all; I'm in a state of intellectual turmoil.

In a new periodical which has just appeared, I've written two chapters on Russia. They've stirred up quite a revolution here among the intellectuals. A philosophical battle is beginning: The Communists call me a heretic and a mystique. A few young people come to my cell and avow that for the first time they feel a new expansiveness in their hearts.

Various matérialistes are going to answer me in the periodical, and I'm pleased, because I have a sense of great strength and clarity of mind. An incredible intellectual and psychological confidence.

I still don't know whether I'll be going for a trip. I haven't seen Kavafakis yet. He wrote me a very polite letter and says that he'll notify me as to when we'll see each other. I've written 40 articles and haven't turned them in, because at the present time all Greece is a

---

* The main public garden in Athens.
† Letter to E. Samios.
‡ The articles N.K. had written on Spain and Italy.
§ Letter to E. Samios.

stagnant marsh. People's minds are on nothing but the elections and the government.

If I don't travel, I'll try to come to Paris earlier. A number of things have to happen. In Paris I must find Communists, in the broad psychological sense that I attach to the word Communism. And a new formulation of the Idea must begin.

In three years' time I'm thinking of going down to Crete and presenting myself as Communist candidate for deputy in parliament. This will give me an opportunity to talk to the poor people and the hungry, in simple words. That's the modern way to proclaim our religion. . . .*

Athens, November 22, 1926

. . . Night had fallen, and I was in the cell, stretched out on the couch, thinking of you in the dark. And the maid came in with your letter. I ask one favor of you: Don't work too hard. . . .

I feel a profound affinity with Africa. I've often talked to you about the masks. Rahel felt her brain being lambasted by them for many months—so intense was the impression left in us by the African masks which we had seen together, and then by Sent M'ahessa. . . .†

Nothing new about my trip. . . . Logos doesn't have any money. Vima refuses, because they consider me a Communist.

I'm impatient, Lenotschka, to finish my trips and to rest myself in Paris. Nevertheless I must stop by to see Rahel, from whom I receive disturbing letters. I must see her. How? By coming to Paris? And Elsa is happy because she expects me to be in a kibbutz this spring. The Israelis are writing me officially and inviting me to come. . . .‡

November 27, 1926

My love,

. . . All these days, I've been going through an extraordinary crisis in my inner life. I'm undergoing some difficult psychological phase, and I've grown very thin and can't sleep. A doctor friend of mine who came the other day was alarmed and wants me to take some X rays, etc. He's made me take cod-liver oil, eat a great deal, etc.

---

* Letter to E. Samios.
† A famous African dancer who performed African religious dances.
‡ Letter to E. Samios.

But I'm tranquil because I know the why of all this exhaustion and when it will pass. . . .*

November 29, 1926

. . . When I come, I'll tell you about the uproar I've caused. These articles† *have been regarded as dangerous by the orthodox Marxists here—as mystiques. They're going to answer, they hold meetings, although certain ones are on my side. In Heraklion, Lefteris continues writing against me. . . . My God, what provincialism, what narrowness of spirit! What a lack of the divine breath!* . . .

An interesting article of mine is about to be published on the theme of the "modern Greek crise," and I shall send it to you. You see, involuntarily I have found myself in the center of a movement. I have hopes that in two or three years Greece will be ripe for some great movement. Get well, for we are going to have a great deal of work. . . . Debout! [Stand up!] This word at the end of your letter pleased me and fortified my heart. There used to be a Buddhist sect which called itself "Those-who-are-always-standing." Let's be like them!‡

December 13, 1926

. . . Elsa doesn't write. I'm worried.

I've finished the essay on Metakommunismus that I wrote you about. That's the name I give it. It will be published later on—because it's a décisif step in my life, and I have to weigh it well. It's a big rupture with Communism—not in a backward direction, of course, but terrifyingly forward. All my Communist friends will be furious. Those who are in agreement will misinterpret once more. . . .

B.§ described to me the life of his friends in Paris. . . . I was horrified by the young people who are satisfied to live in such a sterile way. . . . Like the debris of some fallen race. They read, get drunk, gossip, try to shine—wasting their time in mean and fruitless concerns. Spengler is right when he calls us Fellaheenvolk.‖

---

* Letter to E. Samios.
† The articles on Spain.
‡ Letter to E. Samios.
§ The elder brother of the Papaioannou sisters.
‖ "*Fellaheen* people," the term used by Oswald Spengler to describe a society after its culture has collapsed. *Fellaheen* means, literally, Egyptian peasants. "That which follows a culture," he says, "we may call—from its best-known example, the Egyptians of post-Roman times—*Fellaheenvolk*."

Thank God, we Cretans are not Greeks. I'm glad for the African blood in my veins. I work with conviction, determination, and at the same time, as I like, without hope of reward. . . . Lenotschka, there are days when I cannot bear people at all. Only a few women whom I feel near me and on the same level with me, and they too, like me, do not feel comfortably established.

Well, the other day I walked from Alyssida to Tatoi, and then back to Kifisia, so as to get my body a little tired out—and to calm myself. The sun was heavenly. The fields were green. The mountains sparkled blue and transparent. I quieted down and went to sleep at last, having felt some joy. . . .*

December 20, 1926

. . . I'm writing now—that is, correcting—my autobiography, a few pages of which I read you at St. Stefano's in Tsangarada. . . .†

January 2, 1927

My love,

Yesterday, the first day of the year, the old dream was reborn in me with intensity: to make St. John the Hunter a workshop of the spirit. . . . I'm once more gripped by the idea of the monastery. . . .‡

January 7, 1927

My love, a good, unexpected New Year's message: I'm coming to Paris very soon, perhaps at the end of January!

Many cares, Lenotschka, many worries. I must get myself settled at last near some trees, with a lot of sun, on a straight and level road, and begin working. And see you in the evening to talk and dine together and go for a walk.

I have an absolute need of concentration and work.

Today as I write you, I'm terribly sad—when I come, I'll tell you about it. I'm struggling to overcome a crise. . . .§

January 18, 1927

. . . I'll have to delay the trip a bit, Lenotschka. . . . First I shall go to Egypt, as far as the Sudan. I'm leaving day after tomorrow with Kalmouko.

---

* Letter to E. Samios.
† Letter to E. Samios.
‡ Letter to E. Samios.
§ Letter to E. Samios.

Elephtheros Logos suddenly decided to have me go first to Africa. It's good because (a) it's indispensable to me for The Odyssey, and (b) it cures me of my worry about going to Egypt. So I'll get rid of that country and will be able to stay peacefully in Paris for a longer time.

. . . Russia and three of my tragedies have been given to the publisher and they'll be published in the spring. . . .*

January 20, 1927

However much I yearn for a harsh, ascetic life, the human heart in me is insatiable.

And the thought that you are in Paris makes my heart jump and beat fast. In three days I'm off for Egypt, the Sudan, as far as Khartoum. I'll take one swift, rapacious glance at that world and come back immediately, so that by the middle of March I'll be leaving for Paris. I tremble when I think that I'll be a few steps from Jerusalem, and that I cannot—I must not—go back there. Elsa will be frightened if she sees me, and I will do her harm if I leave again immediately—perhaps forever.

Lenotschka, my heart is breaking. Life is very burdensome, very deep; it's almost too much for my body. When I come, I'll tell you why I've been so sad all these months. You mustn't worry. That's the way I am. I've suffered a great deal, thank God, in my life. But I discipline and restrain my heart as much as I can in order to keep it from bellowing. Only sometimes I don't succeed and my agony becomes apparent.†

January 22, 1927

. . . I'm leaving tomorrow. Egypt and the Sudan with Kalmouko. I hope to heaven that our being acquainted will do him good. I give him as much power as he can take, God be with him! If he does make something of himself, most probably he'll disavow me—like Lefteris and Sphakianakis. If he ruins himself, they'll all jump on me on the grounds that I've destroyed him. Either way I accept as the reward that genuinely suits me. Ohne Belohnung! Ohne Belohnung! [No compensation! No compensation!] That's the cry of my heart.

Lenotschka, I'm also leaving for Egypt—though I have so longed for it—with a heavy heart. I cannot articulate clearly all my sadness. Part of it is fassbar [tangible], the rest of it is not conscious. When I come in March, we'll talk about it. . . .

---

* Letter to E. Samios.
† Letter to E. Samios.

I'll take a violent look at Africa and lay hold of whatever I can for The Odyssey.* And so, heavily laden with booty from Russia, Palestine, Cyprus, Spain, Italy, Egypt and the Sudan, I'll come to Paris to work. Ah! If only your presence could soothe a little this wild, insatiable heart!†

The Palace Hotel, Cairo, February 1, 1927

Once again my head is full of the Orient. How I miss you! I'm wandering through the mosques and bazaars. A marvel, this city; it still hasn't crystallized inside me—but everywhere, with an indestructible intensity, I've been longing for your presence. . . .

Now I'm going to the Museum for the first time, and I'm tremendously impatient. Ah, this heart, greedy, insatiable, all warmth, turmoil, bitterness—how long will it go on trembling? God willing, till I die! For this earth is inexhaustible; a flower, a scent, a woman, an idea will always—please God—stir my mind. . . .‡

Cairo, February 2, 1927

The treasures in the museum are indescribable. Tutankhamen's tomb all gold, all his royal ornaments, vessels, guards, all in gold; a mysterious, troublante splendor; a feeling of horror because all human endeavor is in vain and the earth swallows it up, just as it will also swallow our own hearts which love one another and our own insatiable eyes.

You know how much I love Egyptian art. I wandered for hours en frissonant [quivering]. What joy, what pain; what effort my heart makes to preserve all this terrifying life! I roved about like Odysseus, trying to plunder all this wealth and carry it off in my sailboat.

Lenotschka, always you were with me, and I held your hand so that I could endure it all. This whole life seemed to me a vain tale, a mirage of the desert, and I needed to feel your warm body so as to find a grip-hold—just the way some one falling into the abyss might clutch at a bush. About the Sphinx I'll tell you when I see you. The pyramids are ridiculous, but the Sphinx is an awesome eye looking out on the desert

---

* In this same letter N.K. remarks that the pedants in Athens have been troubled by the 17-syllable meter of The Odyssey. They demand 15 syllables. But N.K. says that he himself feels at home in the unconventional 17-syllable line.
† Letter to E. Samios.
‡ Letter to E. Samios.

in wide-open terror. I've never seen a more profound image of the brave, lost human soul. . . .*

Lenotschka, the moment I opened the hotel window, I saw in the garden across the way an exquisite bougainvillea covering the whole wall. My heart leaped because in my mind now bougainvillea qui enguirlandait votre enfance [which garlanded your childhood] symbolizes you, Lenotschka. And it seemed to me that you had come to Luxor before me and were waiting for me. Oh, God, when shall we be able to do this whole marvelous swing around Egypt together? This is the Orient as we love it, teeming with light, color, scents, and the ashes of innumerable generations that have passed, suffered, loved and vanished.

The Nile flows quietly on, watering and fructifying whatever soil it touches. This is the way the Mind flows, watering and fructifying the Abyss. Lenotschka, here I've loved you very much—in this warm, most ancient land steeped in effort and futility. Were we together, we should have lived this moment when we love each other—before we die—with intensity. Here the contact with death—a violent, voluptuous contact— is apparent at every moment and makes you shudder. What are we then, and why do we get lost in trifles and petty passions? Miraculous this graveyard of the great Pharaohs. Miraculous this horrible, hot, barren sand beyond the waters of the Nile; and miraculous this Nile with its verdure, its animals and its fellahs. I who love so violently both the "yes" and the "no" revel in both of Egypt's faces—the greenery and the gray of the sand.

The supreme sight I have seen is the Sphinx and far off, behind the trees, the desert lying in ambush. . . . I gaze at the wide, slow, kind Nile; in its waters float the sharks with their abominable open maws and above it fly blue birds with red bellies or yellow-yellow birds like canaries. Seeing these many-colored birds set the air aflame, I tremble in exultation. What a miracle this world is, all things arranged to make our eyes and minds rejoice! Lenotschka, the bitterness of your being so far away is transubstantiated into a profound frisson as I look at all this world alone. God be with you . . . and may He let us wander once again together over the earth! How much life is left for us? Instead of burning it stingily and miserably, let's burn it at both ends.

---

* Letter to E. Samios.

The ancient Egyptians were in the habit of setting a coffin on their banquet-tables so that they could look on death and abandon themselves to their delights. Like just such an immense coffin, all this Egypt lies before me and I shudder in agitation and impatience. . . .*

Arabia, camp in the desert, February 13, 1927

Beloved Lenotschka, I'm writing you at night, under a tent in the desert. For three days now we've been traveling by camel, and tomorrow, God willing, we'll be at the Monastery of Sinai. Outside the tent, our three Bedouin guides, along with seven other Bedouins we met along the road, have lit a fire, arranged their baggage in a circle, tied the camels up all around it, and begun cooking. . . . Our Arab servant-boy is making some pilaf and I'm lying on the camp bed the monks from Raïtho gave us, writing you and longing for you very much.

Dreadfully cold; huge drops of rain are falling. Today we've entered the fierce and desolate mountains, all granite. Sometimes a half-dried-out palm tree, sometimes a gray bird. We're traveling on high, high camels. I stare at everything greedily. Kalmouko is slightly sleepy. We don't talk at all. In the evening we sit by the fire with the Bedouins, and I use the few Arab words I know and we laugh. All of a sudden last night I uttered the famous sentence from the Koran: "There is one God and Mohammed is His prophet." At once their eyes sparkled with happiness and they lifted their arms on high.

For three days now I've been thinking to the slow, monotonous rhythm of the camel, attuning my mind and memory to it. My whole life is passing by—what I've done, what is still left for me to do. Bitterness because I haven't done anything valiant; and abruptly I decide that I will change and not die like this, without having done my duty. I think of the people I've loved, the joys and pangs I've brought them. Very bitter and very pale, Elsa emerges within me, as usual shedding big hot tears on my hands. Ah! I shall never see her again. I had the premonition in Jerusalem, and my heart is torn. Always when I think of her, I am overcome by a violent, irrepressible desire to die.

Lenotschka, here again I'm overwhelmed by terribly bitter thoughts —here in this desert, in this Oriental tent where I've stopped to rest. I'm thinking of you so intensely and I so long for you to be here that tonight I absolutely must force you to remember me. . . .†

---

* Letter to E. Samios.
† Letter to E. Samios.

I'm writing you from the "Holy Summit," 2,500 meters altitude, where God gave Moses the Ten Commandments. I can see the whole Arabian Peninsula—on one side the Red Sea, on the other the Persian Gulf. In between, the fierce, gigantic mountains, and beyond, fuming and white, the desert. Today, on my birthday, I'm happy, and my eyes are taking delight in what I've longed to see for so many years—Arabia. . . .*

Red Sea, March 6, 1927

The glorious dream—roaming the coasts of Arabia; dipping into the sea; rolling in the desert sands; seeing the palm trees and the camels far, far away; gathering the wonderful mammoth shells from the Red Sea—is over. . . . The other day in the desert, when evening came on, Taema the Bedouin and I pitched our tent near a little spring under the palm trees. We lit a fire, made tea, and ate together. Then I lay down, gazing up at the starry desert sky. Great dangling stars. Profound tranquillity. Taema was saying his prayer, kneeling at my side, his countenance turned toward Mecca—and I was thinking of you with intensity and eagerness and I desired you. I remembered our nights at Leda and I still recalled the evening when we were lying on the grass at Tsangarada, and you wept because you couldn't make out the stars clearly. For hours I couldn't—didn't want to—close my eyes, lest I should lose you from my thoughts. I listened to all the tiny, mysterious voices of the desert; I heard the camel near me munching a bit of dry grass he'd found in the shade of the date tree. I saw the stars revolving, and inside me, I reconstructed my whole life, all my determination and intensity, all the wildness and voluptuous desire of my soul furrowing the earth. Ah, how should the dust ever succeed in smothering my eyes?

And so tonight in fury I felt the humble fate of man, and I do not want to accept it, Lenotschka. I do not want you ever to be extinguished; I do not want this flame that burns us ever to cease. Irrational decisions spring up inside me, and, under the sway as I am of this wild desert, I would like to change my life.

The next evening we entered a horrible rose mist—the simoom had risen. The camel stumbled this way and that; the sand beat on my face

---

* Letter to E. Samios.

and hands, and wounded them. And I loved it, because Odysseus should experience this sensation. It was a great torture—and an enormous joy when we reached a Greek monastery at the edge of the sea—the joy of a fire, stewed fruit and coffee, laughter, food, clean sheets, and a big sleep. Five divine days I spent at this monastery of Arabia Petraea, waiting for the boat. A balcony over the sea, purple and yellow caïques, swarthy women with silver rings on their ankles, unending sand in back of us, and in front of us a boundless blue-green sea. . . .*

Alexandria, March 9, 1927

. . . I'm leaving Egypt on March 12, and I'll do everything in my power to start for Paris as quickly as possible. Here many warm friends, a literary movement, etc. I like them very much, but I would like to be alone. The sensation of Egypt is very acute inside me and I don't want to talk with people.

I'll write you again from Athens. . . . Don't get worried if I'm once more overcome by sadness in Athens. You see, I escaped it a bit, by traveling. And now it's lying in ambush for me in Athens. But I'll get away again. I'll tell you about it when I come. God be with you, Lenotschka. May God keep us ever alert, good, and on fire. . . .†

In Athens, sadness was indeed lying in wait for Nikos Kazantzakis. Not wanting to make anyone else suffer, he himself suffered very much. Fortunately, at this precise moment, Pandelis Prevelakis, a young Cretan, eighteen years old and a talented writer, entered the scene. From this point on, Kazantzakis would have a younger brother, who was to remain faithful to him through death. Several months later, referring to the significance of their meeting, Kazantzakis wrote to Prevelakis:

That you should appear on my horizon, to stand by my side and help me at this critical moment of my life—I do not consider a coincidence. For both of us, this event must acquire great value. . . .‡

---

* Letter to E. Samios.
† Letter to E. Samios.
‡ Letter to Prevelakis, August 1, 1927.

Beloved Lenotschka,

God willing, this will be the last letter I send you from Athens. I've been here several days. The dream of Arabia is over—as though I'd now awakened—and once again I'm oppressed by the stifling air of Athens.

I'm writing the articles on Egypt and Arabia now, and I'll leave immediately afterward. . . . I'm overjoyed because I'll be seeing you, my love. I want to get settled and work. This way my life is being wasted here, and I must hurry. The Odyssey must be finished in Paris. . . .*

[Athens] May 16, 1927

Beloved, beloved Lenotschka,

I am desperate. Here it's two months now that I've been rushing around and struggling. They make promises to me, then take their promises back. I've gotten ill from it. I can't sleep any more. The day before yesterday everything was ready and I was waiting to sign the contract, and suddenly the whole thing fell through. I don't see any salvation for this summer. . . .

Right now God is against my getting to Paris. Never have I encountered so many difficulties. I've never struggled so hard to arrange a trip. I've found thousands of ways and they've all failed. Isn't this a sign that it shouldn't take place? I'm tired out, half the size I was. I'll go to an island and stay alone. Perhaps the bad fate will be exorcized. . . .†

Aegina, May 25, 1927

I got your three letters and my heart broke. Oh God, be as patient as you can. It isn't possible, I'll come unfailingly. I want to leave Greece forever. Perhaps I'll find some other way. . . .

Let's wait a little longer. I'm living all alone, I'm working, I'm hurrying to finish The Odyssey, to get rid of it. . . . I get tired and that lulls my grief a bit. . . .‡

Aegina, June 4, 1927

. . . I'm still living all alone. I'm still working terribly hard in order to be delivered and to be free. I never go out, and no one comes to

---

* Letter to E. Samios.
† Letter to E. Samios.
‡ Letter to E. Samios.

see me. I don't write to anyone, and I feel very badly that I haven't written to Rahel or Elsa for so many months.

Just these days the printers are finishing Nicephoros Phocas, and I'll send it to you. . . .

Lenotschka, if I could be with you for one moment now! Write me a lot; that's the only consolation there is now. . . .*

Aegina, June 14, 1927

. . . I'm sending you the articles on Africa to ease your monotony a little. Also two pages of a review in which I published a few lines of poetry. I'm working so hard I'm afraid I won't be able to hold out much longer. Many, many hours a day, with great feverishness, as though there were some question of my dying tomorrow. In a few months (not in two years as I had calculated), the 24 books of The Odyssey will be finished. And then I'll be a free human being. Here in Greece, they're sure I won't carry it through. The other day one periodical wrote: "Goethe could not finish a similar epic. So will Kazantzakis have the stamina to?"

Kazantzakis will have the stamina to; if only I have a little peace. Sometimes on Sunday some friend or other comes to see me here and leaves the same evening. I don't know if what I'm writing has any value. I write it because otherwise I'd be suffocated by it. An organic need.

Aegina is rather like Amorgos. But I never go out for a walk. The sea is ten minutes away and I don't go, because I don't have time. I write from five in the morning on, and when I stop at eight in the evening, I'm very tired and I go out on my terrace and look at the mountain across the way, at the garden around me and the first stars, and I think of Tsangarada, where we stretched out on the grass and played a game to find out who would see more stars first. . . .†

Aegina, July 30, 1927

. . . I have your little photograph in front of me, and I'm glad to see you with your slightly bitter, slightly ironical smile that I like so much. . . . If the turmoil I feel when I think of you is the essence of this little earthly life of ours, then blessings on it. This morning, as I wrote the beginning of Book XIX [of The Odyssey], I marked the following two lines:

---

* Letter to E. Samios.
† Letter to E. Samios.

>   Ephemeral warm games of the brain; puffs of blue smoke
>   from the head, phosphorescences on the damp plain—human beings

and I felt so bitter that my eyes got misty. What are we, tottering a few hours over the earth, our body remaining warm for a time—and we cry out, feel pain, and love, and then in a flash it all disappears?

In this mortal disaster, I think of you with so much sadness and happiness and warmth that all of life and death become concentrated into the brief moment when I shall see you at the station in the dim light and squeeze your hand. . . .*

September 9, 1927

Dorogaya moïa:†

. . . The Odyssey is finished. I'm relieved. . . .

I hope you've received the Spiritual Exercises. Here it's doubtful whether three souls can be found in agreement with it. Mme. Lambridi has translated it into English and sent it to the publisher. I wish it could be translated into French, so that it might be published in some periodical. When I come, we'll make an effort.

. . . These days I'll be writing articles for the Elephtheroudakis encyclopedia‡ on Buddha, Lenin, Gandhi, Dostoyevsky, El Greco, etc. So once again endless work ahead of me. When I come, you must be well so that you can help me. Don't forget, you'll be my Secrétaire. . . .

Aegina, September 30, 1927

My beloved Lenotschka,

I'll be coming to Paris in December. . . .

Yesterday again something unexpected happened. . . . For the tenth anniversary [of the Russian Revolution], some extraordinary festivities are going to take place in Moscow, and the Russian government has invited one or two people from each country. Only one person was invited from Greece and it happened to be me. I'll go to Moscow at the expense of the Soviet government. I'll stay 20 days. They'll take us everywhere in Russia and I'll come back to Greece! Perhaps I'll publish a series of articles. . . . I feel deeply moved about seeing Russia again, and very sad because I wish we could be together. . . .

---

* Letter to E. Samios.
† Russian term of affection.
‡ The publisher K. Elephtheroudakis was preparing an encyclopedia, and P. Prevelakis had procured for N.K. a large share of the work on it.

I'll take some English copies [of the Spiritual Exercises] to give to people I find in Moscow. It's a bit dangerous to make propaganda for Meta-Communism, which the Communists hate so much. But it's necessary.

. . . I'm drowned in manuscripts, very tired and énervé. My God, when will I ever rest? . . . I'm very uneasy, I don't know why. . . . Write me; don't forget me till December. . . .*

Aegina, October 5, 1927

Dorogaya moïa,

. . . I'll write a book, Meta-Communism, in Paris with you. All things are developing calmly and painfully, and I feel that I'll see you in December beyond a doubt. I've worked hard and suffered a great deal this year, and I'd like to get settled in Paris in such a way that I won't have to set foot in Greece again for years. All these months I've been aware of my soul's acquiring a definite countenance and of my life's acquiring a unity. The whole past seems like a zigzag, and the gropings along different paths are finally beginning to get harmonized and to converge in a single, incandescent, motionless point. May it please God that I shall go on developing and enriching myself in this way until I die, and that, without anything being rejected, my whole life may become what the Byzantine mystics call "a rich unity." No illusions, no cowardice, staring chaos straight in the eyes without a tremor. I desire nothing more.†

October 8, 1927

It's pouring rain. From my window I'm watching the plain fading into dimness, the soil exudes vapors, and the little courtyards are gleaming with the water. I'm content and slightly cold. My senses are saturated in the scent of the earth. . . . I'm thinking of you quietly and passively as I think of the sea, the earth, death, eternity. My head feels as if it were shining and pitch-black, like a big rock that has been inundated and is reveling in the rain and the sun.

. . . I'm sending you three acacia blossoms my sister sent me from our father's house. . . .‡

---

* Letter to E. Samios.
† Letter to E. Samios.
‡ Letter to E. Samios.

166

Beloved Lenotschka, this afternoon I'm leaving for Odessa. The weather is calm. I'll have a splendid trip. You're with me every moment. . . .

I sent you several copies of the Spiritual Exercises. Here this "Cry" is beginning to arouse a commotion. Politis is writing a pile of eulogistic articles. Glynos' Renaissance is beginning a series of articles, some expressing a favorable response, others a critical one. The modern Greek waters have gotten ruffled a little, but I'm leaving. I don't answer, I'll not hinder them. . . .

No newspaper has agreed to take articles of mine about Russia. A violent anti-Communist wind. I finally managed to persuade Proïa to take ten articles, and I'll submit them when I get back from Moscow. . . .*

October 22

We've entered the Hellespont. . . . For two days now, on the boat I've been reading ancient Japanese and Chinese literature, and my heart swells with storms of emotion, hearing these ancient cries of love and pain. My God, if I could only crystallize perfectly all the emotion my heart feels and so preserve it in The Odyssey.

I know Moissi† and like him exceedingly. I used to see him often in Vienna. How did I fail to tell you about him? He's especially marvelous in Oedipus. This slender, sickly man with the whining, delicate voice plays the role of the awesome king of Thebes in hair-raising fashion. . . .‡

Sunday, October 23, 1927

Dawn found us in the harbor at Constantinople. The minarets, St. Sophia, the gardens, Europe and Asia at their juncture, the morning mist—all that stirred and gently enchanted my heart. On my way through Constantinople in 1919, I had declaimed: "After ages and in time, once again she shall be ours!"§ Now I've gotten far away from this patriotic tirade. I enjoy Constantinople for herself without ephemeral patriotic regrets. Like an animal basking in the sun, I enjoy her and I

---

* Letter to E. Samios.
† Alexander Moissi, a German-language actor who came originally from Albania.
‡ Letter to E. Samios.
§ A popular Greek proverb about the return of Constantinople to Greek hands.

don't care to whom she belongs. Some day we must see this miracle together too, as we saw Jerusalem. How many things are "musts"! Life, health, simplicity, love—and all the rest will come! Sometimes I feel myself a center of forces, a whirlpool, a tourbillon [whirlwind] of invisible elements, and they are all whirling around my own immovable will. And so I hope that whatever we desire will happen.*

Odessa, Tuesday, October 25, 1927

A few hours only in Odessa, but I've had time to see my beloved Jewish features—black eyes, hooked noses, thick lips—and now I'm writing you from the compartment of the train taking me to Moscow. . . .

Kiev: We got here early this morning. I met a Jewish woman in the train—not young, but very interesting—and we went out together in the city and laughed and talked. And now I'm back and continuing the trip. Ah, if we were only together; that's what I keep saying every minute. To be happy we would have to take a big trip together. Only in this way, by combining companionship with movement, can I feel all the facets of joy. I'm deeply affected by setting foot on the Russian earth, the black, fertile soil; by breathing the cold, still air; by gazing at the mute, enduring masses. The soul dilates; the mind longs to transcend its own limits, to fuse with all these herdlike souls and blow upon this fertile human clay. Whatever I've written seems to me unworthy and provincial. My cry has been heard by only a very few people in one meager little corner of the world—and most of them faithless and malicious. And I look at these women and muzhiks, and I know that my voice will never reach them, because the means I use are weak.

What do art and a beautiful phrase and a good simile and a brilliant line of verse matter? All these things are little; and they don't touch the great waves of humanity. Only religion and action—only a Christ or a Lenin—deserve to live today. The others exist in order to wait for him, or at most to prepare the way for him with their inarticulate, provincial cries. . . .

Ah, if only I could burst the bonds not only of Greece but of art; emancipate myself from beauty; channelize all my warm love for woman; dedicate myself to some fierce and mortal action. Will I ever be able to do it? Will I have time? I don't know. I am serving beauty as much as I can, and I shall make The Odyssey as beautiful as I can—there's no

---

* Letter to E. Samios.

other way to emancipate myself from beauty. Lenotschka, I'll see you again tomorrow, in Moscow. . . .*

Moscow, October 27, 1927

My love, I've reached Moscow. . . . It's raining, faces shining in the dark air. I've seen what I love, hastily, avidly. I've been wandering all day, and now I'm writing you from the warm room where the Soviet government is lodging me. Tomorrow I'll go to Kameneva to see if I have a letter from you. I'll see Istrati and Barbusse. I've much to do these twenty days, and I want to bid farewell to this land which perhaps I shall never see again. . . .†

Moscow, October 28, 1927

Horrible rain and fog. Evening falls at 2:00 P.M. I wander through the museums and the churches, gazing hungrily. . . . Tonight I'm going to the theater, and I've left them a message to reserve me theater tickets every evening. I'm all alone, and that gives me a sensation austère de volupté [severe feeling of sensuous pleasure]. It's only you whom I desire to have near me.‡

Moscow, October 29, 1927

I was just coming back to the hotel when Kameneva's secretary pulled up in a car, bringing me your letter. She gave it to me with a smile. "This morning," she said, "I saw that you changed color when they told you you didn't have a letter, and I thought I'd make you happy by hurrying over with it. Perhaps this is what you're waiting for." I looked at the envelope and answered joyously, "This is it." . . .§

November 1, 1927

Once again I've begun working with frightful intensity. I'm seeing people, discussing, trying to sort them out. I'm meeting different foreign writers. Just now I've been with an excellent Japanese man; in the evening I go to the theater. And then I've met an Italian, an extraordinary person and writer, who suffers from insomnia, and we sit and talk and drink tea. Heavenly women on the streets, dangerous ones, and

---

* Letter to E. Samios.
† Letter to E. Samios.
‡ Letter to E. Samios.
§ Letter to E. Samios.

I'm making an effort to keep my head. Or else, should I decide to renounce the world?*

November 3, 1927

The days and nights go by, and I hardly eat or sleep. I'm in the grip of a violent impulse to stop looking at things and institutions and to see people. Chinese, Japanese, Swedes, Americans—innumerable souls. And with an eagerness at once indiscrète and barbarous, I go out of myself to see what they are bringing. So far . . . I haven't found anyone with so high a tension of the spirit as my own or so lofty a form of psychic torment. But all these people have completed a work and have an influence that I lack. . . .†

November 4, 1927

The tempo of life in Russia has changed. It's different from 1925 now. The official rhythm is calmer. There is a certain embourgeoisement. The arrivistes are arrivés, and they no longer even budge. The women have begun relapsing to their lower natures. The men are tired. Fortunately, the great internal struggle between Trotsky and Stalin gives new life and fire to the Russian spirit. Russia finds herself at a critical moment. They're all expecting Europe to make war against them, and every day throngs of men and women stand in queues in front of the shops to get supplies of flour.‡

November 5, 1927

I've just had a terrible piece of news. A very beautiful poetess I'd known here, Lilian Georgievna Harassova, died two weeks ago. I had a little gift for her, and I'd written her to ask when I might see her. And her aunt came and told me that she had died. . . .

I'm sitting in my room, and from my window I can see the snow-covered roofs and the people's breaths in the cold. Moscow is decked out all in red. The great pilgrimage is approaching. I'm glad that I've been able to be in Moscow right now. What force is it that is bringing reality to me according to the boldest desires of my own soul? I shudder, knowing that this force will suddenly hurl me to earth and fill these insatiable, incandescent eyes of mine with dust. At times these days my

---

* Letter to E. Samios.
† Letter to E. Samios.
‡ Letter to E. Samios.

heart feels like breaking, and I cannot hold back the tears. Slowly the death of Lilian Harassova is working upon me inside. There's a shadow falling across me, and my light is dimmed. Of course, I did not love this woman; but I saw her vibrancy when she recited her poems to me. I saw how she longed to come to Greece, to see the sun and the light, not to die! Ah, Lenotschka, how can the human heart keep from being crushed? How can it endure? A pall has been cast over this whole Soviet celebration by the shadow of a woman who died young. . . .

Everything I see, hear and touch in this land—the snow, the steppes, people, ideas—must be converted both into lines of The Odyssey and material for my work on Meta-Communism. I must seize, plunder, get there in time before I die!

The Spiritual Exercises is a terrifying, blood-steeped cry that will be heard after my death. At present people understand only its poetic form. But within these similes and lyrical phrases, there is projected in luminous tones and in full panoply, beyond despair and hope, the future visage of God . . .*

On the tenth of November in Moscow, Kazantzakis was to have a marvelous surprise. As he was leaving the Congress in the company of the Austrian writer Arthur Holitscher, he became aware of a woman's voice calling him: "Nikos!" It was Itka.

"Great joy, emotion, agitation," he commented in his notebook. "We went back to the hotel, drank tea, and talked. The *intuition* and judgment and *sensualité* of this woman are miraculous. She has all the powers inside her."

Between bear hugs, Itka told Nikos about her life, her past sufferings, her divorce, her little daughter. And Nikos remarked in his notebook: "How she works in the Party! She's learned children's medicine. She's a fanatical Marxist."

On November 12, we find just three words: "Congrès. I spoke." Nothing else. Only through his letters and later conversations do we learn that he had used strong language and that he was afraid that his passport would be taken away from him and that he would not be able to return to Greece.

He did, however, have more to say about Itka in his notebooks:

---

* Letter to E. Samios.

171

I went to Itka's home. She was playing with her child, Yvonne—a deep maternal joy—and I felt moved as I watched this marvelous woman who has roots in the earth. Ah, would that I could be so primitif and simple! This evening there was an enthusiastic session at the Congrès. They awarded medals to Clara Zetkin, Bela Kun, Marty, Sadoul, a German, a Chinese. Emotion, war cries. The night at Itka's. At daybreak, she talked to me once again about her life, how she loved, how she wants to write. . . .

On November 13 Kazantzakis met Panaït Istrati, in the latter's room at the Hotel Passage. Istrati received him by shouting: "Moré, welcome! How goes it?" Nikos Kazantzakis described his new friend as "full of life, high spirits, strength." And he added: "We're both thinking of staying in the U.S.S.R."

But already on the fifteenth, we find a strange note revealing his perplexity: "Very sad because I find myself with two or three possibilities of staying in Russia." Are we to explain this remark by the feeling he had already expressed that he was not yet mature enough to settle in the U.S.S.R.—or by his fear of no longer being able to return to Greece?

The notebook abounds with the names of people of all nationalities with whom Kazantzakis spent time in the U.S.S.R. and with conversations whose quintessence he has given us in part in his books and travel journals. But always he returns to Itka, "to the Marxist department of his soul," as he calls it in his notebook.

I should not like to close these notebooks without quoting a conversation Nikos had with one adamant Communist:

He went to the Caucasus last summer and for the first time enjoyed the sun, the Oriental sweetness of the air and the sea. And he'd come back a changed man. "The North is barbarous," he said to me. "All this Russian Communist fever bothers me now. Communism needs to be adjusted in terms of the geographical latitude of each country and of each soul. Life is not everywhere so fierce and dark as we imagine it here. I lived, stretched out in the sun, ate some fruit . . . played with the sea and became reconciled with nature. A new Weltanschauung has begun flowering inside me."

The same thing was told me by Olga Markova B. She too had spent the summer in the Crimea and had come back transformed. . . .

[Moscow] November 16, 1927

Steps are being taken for me to stay on in Russia for a long time. . . . I'm making thousands of plans: about staying here, about your coming to Moscow, about giving a new direction to my life. But I still don't feel quite ready for Moscow. In any case this week I shall decide. . . .

In the meantime I'm leading an intense life: theaters, music, people. The most sublime theater I've seen is the Jewish one. Stanislavsky is a great personality, but his theater—where they play superbly—is now a "former beauty." People who live in Russia feel that Stanislavsky, by insisting on his own marvelous acting method and on the kind of plays he offers, is behind the times. . . . I regard it as very difficult to perceive what is best in our own time; because this "best" still has deficiencies of technique which the older conception has overcome. . . .*

Kharkov, November 17, 1927

. . . A few of us guest-delegates set off suddenly, and now we're on our way toward the Caucasus. Istrati and I have a compartment to ourselves, and we stretch out and chat all day long, or read or write, looking through the window at boundless, snow-covered Russia. Day after tomorrow we'll be in Baku . . . after that, Tiflis, where the grave of my beloved friend awaits me, the one who died there.† The whole journey will last sixteen days and I'll go back to Moscow again. . . .

I feel very deep emotion at the thought of being able to bring you to Moscow. Istrati doesn't want to let go of me. He's making plans for us to live together in Russia, and I feel that my whole life will change and will be renewed if I find a way to live in Moscow. I can't say anything yet, and I don't yet dare to hope that we will walk together on Russian soil. . . .‡

Caucasus, November 20, 1927

We're crossing the Caucasus. These mountains which are the first that ever saw Man are looming all covered with snow. In primitive times these gorges were traversed by the races migrating from Asia to Europe. . . .§

---

* Letter to E. Samios.
† Iannis Stavridakis, the Greek consul at Zurich, who died in 1919, at the age of twenty-two, while N.K. was in charge of repatriating the refugees from the Caucasus.
‡ Letter to E. Samios.
§ Letter to E. Samios.

It's raining. The Caspian Sea is gray and sad. My heart is full of Sehnsucht nach Ihnen [longing for you]. My only joy is Panaït Istrati, who is with me and who will be, I have a premonition, a faithful, warm, and stimulating companion throughout the rest of my life. We'll go down to Greece together. I'll give lectures, then Istrati will be off to Egypt for two weeks; from there he'll return to Moscow. . . . We're considering buying a little four-room house in Moscow, hoping for it to be ready in February. He'll keep two rooms and I the other two, and I think we're going to have myriad delights. Because then you'll come to rest with me, and you'll help me a great deal in the work. You'll have your own room, and all the rest will go well. . . . As soon as the réalité becomes substantial—it's still so fluid around me at present—I'll write you. Lenotschka, I cannot tell you how much I miss you. . . .*

Moscow, December 6, 1927

Dorogaya moïa!

I think of you every moment, with grief. I don't know what's going to happen. A thousand plans are passing through my mind. . . . Tomorrow I'm leaving for Kiev, where I have to stay with Istrati until December 20, and then we're both leaving for Greece. Istrati will go on to Egypt. I'll stay in Athens-Aegina until he gets back, and then we have in mind to come back to Moscow together. . . . From Athens I'm thinking of sending you the traveling expenses to Moscow, where you will come in the spring. . . . The climate here is splendid, life broad and deep. . . .†

Kiev, December 10, 1927

My beloved Lenotschka,

The days here are passing calmly. Istrati is a bit sick, and I stay with him most of the day. I see a lot of people, and everyone has dreadful, tragic stories to tell. These Russian eyes have seen great and frightening things. Every soul here has lived, rejoiced, and suffered as has no other soul in Europe. That's why even the most insignificant person here is full of interest, shining from the reflection of a great blazing fire. . . .

On Sunday we're leaving for Odessa. I'm afraid I'll experience difficulties in Greece because I took an active part in the Congress in

---

* Letter to E. Samios.
† Letter to E. Samios.

Moscow and spoke in strong language. If they don't give me a visa to leave Greece, it will be a great misfortune for me. . . .

Istrati loves a brilliant woman who lives in Paris. She is supposed to come to live with him in Russia. It would be a good thing for you to see her. Istrati is writing her at this moment to tell her to write to you. You should write to her too and arrange a meeting. She's an extraordinary woman, he tells me. It would be marvelous if you became friends. . . .*

Kiev, December 15, 1927

Dorogaya moïa!

I'm still writing you from Kiev. The sun is brilliant; dry cold weather; the rivers frozen; steam coming from the nostrils of people and horses. My heart is full of sadness and passion. My desires are boundless and I feel unsatisfied. It seems to me the time is drawing near when I shall die and I am in a hurry. Lenotschka, I'd like you to be with me because you have a brave soul and a pleasing body. . . . I'm glad we're going to meet on Russian soil. Only keep well. . . . Life here consumes people; it's too headlong and harsh—but we'll bear everything together. My head swims when I reflect that time is passing and I still haven't done anything at all.

Istrati's companion will talk to you. . . . Well then, do you want to come to Russia? Can you come in March to Odessa, where I'll wait for you?

I'll be expecting your crucial letter in Athens. . . . Our life will not be easy. You already know how boring the life of a mondain person can be with me. I'll be working all day long. I'll see you only in the evening—sometimes sad and taciturn, sometimes expansif and joyful. I'll have contacts and a regular correspondence with people I love, which will be disagreeable for you. Material life will be simple and poor—as it has always been since I left my father's home. But you are not mondaine; you are simple and heroic. Life in Russia will strengthen these virtues of yours and our daily collaboration will perhaps do you good.

Lenotschka, I'm impatiently awaiting your letter in Athens. My life has become irrefragably linked—I believe forever—with Istrati. We'll live and work together in Russia. . . .†

---

* Letter to E. Samios.
† Letter to E. Samios.

Constantinople, December 24th, 1927

We crossed the Black Sea comfortably and have arrived in Constantinople. A cloudy sky, fine rain, St. Sophia, the Byzantine ramparts, the mosques, the cypresses—all this old enchantment is no longer capable of winning my heart. I'm glad that seven years ago I had time to enjoy it with all the warm, romantic force of my soul. Now I evade it. All these bewitching Sirens seem very far behind me now, not because I've liberated myself from all the Sirens, but because I've found the modern Sirens, and perhaps even the future ones, and I am listening feverishly to the most modern of songs, that of the Abyss. The grand Siren is now seated in the north, amid the snows, with green eyes, a heavy Slavic voice, a blood-stained breast. I'm returning to Greece to take my leave of it. . . .

Nevertheless . . . there are still a few people on Greek soil whom I love—my sisters, my mother, one or two women. I think of Anna K. and feel torn at having to leave her. We've never uttered a single word of love, nor will we ever—and yet I feel that her whole being frissonne [quivers] and rejoices when I go to see her after each of my peregrinations. We lock ourselves in. No one comes. We drink tea. We talk for hours, and after much time has passed, we part with difficulty, I to continue my rambles in the light and she to sink back again into silence and darkness. And now, never more. Another woman who will be hurt—you know. She wrote me in Russia how she's waiting for us to collaborate in some great active work together, telling me to return quickly because she has great plans in her mind and can no longer live far away from the "monster," as she calls me. And now I shall tell her goodbye forever. . . . One or two souls will be sad—perhaps even Galatea; everybody else will be glad to be rid of me.

A grand, difficult life is opening up before me with Istrati. We have very many hard things to do, traveling around Russia. Articles, books, organizing, propaganda for abroad. I consider you my collaborator, at my side throughout all this exacting life. You must get entirely cured. You must learn many things in order to help me. You must work with me and share as much of the toil as you can. Will your body be equal to it? Write me in Athens all your thoughts, unreservedly. . . .*

---

* Letter to E. Samios.

We're still in the harbor at Constantinople. . . . I've written the newspaper articles here, and now Istrati and I are writing the lecture that is to be given in Athens. I've sent you a telegram from the boat. . . . I pray God to lead us along the best path. I'd like to change my life. I'm not at all happy about the way I live. It seems to me too easy, too comfortable—I'd like to be able to suffer, to go hungry, to love, without hope. . . . Everything comes to me conveniently, and I'm ashamed. Perhaps life in Russia will give me some very agonizing experiences. Perhaps some great misfortune will visit me, and it's high time now.*

1928.   Events unfolded as anticipated.

Panaït Istrati was being awaited in Athens with impatience and curiosity. For the benefit of the people who didn't know him yet, Nikos Kazantzakis had sketched a hasty portrait of him, which appeared on the last day of the year. And so, 1928 was laid open for the action the two comrades in arms were hoping to bring to a happy conclusion.

The lecture they had planned took place in the Alhambra Theater, with throngs of people flocking to it. The theme was captivating: To find a spokesman who could at long last describe precisely and boldly the hidden miseries endured by the greater part of the Greek people—a spokesman to denounce the injustice rampant in the land.

The two friends seized the bull by the horns, and the enthusiasm of the audience approached delirium. The people who claimed to be the guardians of God, the Family, and Freedom on this earth also reacted as anticipated. Dimitri Glynos, who according to them had committed two serious errors—that of sponsoring this lecture and that of publishing the Spiritual Exercises in his periodical Renaissance—was summoned to appear in court. So was Kazantzakis, charged with having committed an offense against the state and religion. As for Panaït Istrati, he was asked to leave the country at the earliest possible date, at the same moment when the members of the upper bourgeoisie were dispatching their emissaries to bring this "savage" to them, urgently insisting that he come just the way he was, dressed in his high spats and lime-green hunting-breeches.

---

* Letter to E. Samios.

Meanwhile a great joy was in store for me at Meudon: Bilili. What kind of person would she be, this woman chosen as a companion by our bewildering vagabond? I could readily imagine her as a fiery, flamboyant Bohemian. Instead, I found myself face to face with a medieval cathedral Madonna—the same wise smile; the same persistent, piercing gaze; the same voice emerging out of some *Stabat Mater*, even and velvety and deep and at the same time crystal-clear.

"Would you like to take advantage of our bathroom?" she suggested to me a few moments after our first meeting. I looked myself over anxiously. Did I really look so unkempt? Bilili scoffed. "I offer all our friends this little luxury," she said. "In Paris, one gets weaned away from it, doesn't one? Here there's hot water in profusion. . . ."

After the bath and some tea and descriptions of Panaït as a man and Panaït as a writer, and his plans and hopes for the future, I was no longer surprised by anything. "When shall we leave to join them?" I asked. "As soon as possible." "Agreed, Bilili. I promise you, you will find me more than just a traveling companion—a sister."

Arriving in the harbor at Piraeus, we found Panaït standing erect in a frail craft. He began gesticulating and yelling when he saw us—"On for the U.S.S.R.! Quickly! On for the U.S.S.R.!"—all the while prancing about like a man possessed. Nikos was trying to keep the boat balanced; the boatman looked on in amusement, cursing away; and the passengers began to eye us with distrust written on their faces.

A third cure at Plombières,* considered indispensable by my doctors, as well as my hopes of keeping the *Kathimerini* job, made it necessary for me to return to France. I lost *Kathimerini*. On the other hand, several French newspapers and periodicals did accept the articles I was to send from the U.S.S.R.

How were we going to live in Russia? This problem troubled me very much. Would I become a burden to Kazantzakis? Would we be under "obligation" to the Soviet government?

Athens, January 3, 1928
. . . *How are we going to live in Russia? Absolutely no dependence on the Russians. The economic situation is as follows: Through his*

---

* The illness involved was a variety of intestinal infection, which necessitated systematic cures throughout my later life as well.

books and his articles Istrati will have all he needs and more. I too will have money from:

(a) writing the articles I've accepted for the Elephtheroudakis encyclopedia;

(b) writing articles for Russian periodicals (they are asking me and they pay very well);

(c) I'm being asked to let my books be translated into Russian;

(d) I've agreed to produce scenarios in collaboration with Istrati for the famous Russian cinema.

Thus we, like Istrati, will have all the money we need and at the same time be free.

My ideas on Communism you know, and I've formulated them in a difficult but clear way in the Spiritual Exercises. I'm neither superficial nor narrow-minded nor a Marxist. When you come to Russia, you cannot fail to agree with me. . . . Our work in Russia does not impose any slavery on us, nor are we the tools of anyone. We may perhaps encounter difficulties on account of not being orthodox. But these philosophical reservations are secondary. Our first duty is a different one—and this we are doing. . . .

Istrati, as a writer, is very interesting—read in particular Oncle Anghel (and in that, above all, "Cosma") and Codine. That's what I like. Your judgment is severe and just. But he's a marvelous human being. All simplicity, vivacity, high spirits, good, pur. He has many qualities that I love. . . .*

Athens, March 8, 1928

Beloved Lenotschka,

The trial has been set for April 3. There are two tendances [trends]: the judges, for the sake of publicity, want to make a big sensation out of it, and to condemn us, while the politicians want to end quickly and noiselessly a case that is not to their advantage. Which of the two tendances will win out? We shall see. We're ready in either eventuality. We shall do nothing at all to give provocation, but if we are provoked, we shall speak our conviction with firmness.

Marika is leaving on the 27th of March, desolate because she can't be here for the trial†. . . .‡

---

* Letter to E. Samios.
† The trial dragged on for some time, then ceased being an issue.
‡ Letter to E. Samios.

Beloved Lenotschka,

Overjoyed when I get a letter from you. How long will this joy last? I'll do everything in my power to make it last forever. I know the limits of human beings and how narrow they are. I know the law of germination, flowering, fructification, and decay. But I also know the power of the soul which has but one goal, the loftiest one: to conquer Nature instead of continuing it.

My Lenotschka, we must both make this effort to preserve the intoxication on the highest level in our soul, our heart, our body!

I remain here like a prisoner of war. The trial is going to take place, and it will be a fierce one, because the judges want to strike Glynos and me mercilessly in order to put fear into the others. I hope that the trial will take place before the end of March. We're preparing clear and energetic pleas for our defense, without cringing or bravura. This medieval trial is apparently going to be interesting. They can put us in jail for six months at most. If it's only three, then I'll be able to leave at once, obtaining a stay of judgment. . . .

The second volume of the Russia will be in print in ten days. In twenty days the Christ will be finished. And thereafter I'll begin your Odysseus.* Ah, when will our service in Russia be over, and when can we take refuge in some calm hermitage full of tall trees, with straight streets, near some vast city? How ready I feel now to write the second version of The Odyssey! . . .

The prosecuting attorney has bought everything I've published, in order to prove that I want to destroy religion, morality, fatherland, etc. It's a disgrace to live under the same sky with such creatures. . . .†

[Athens, no date]

. . . Yesterday I got a letter from Barbusse, asking me with great insistence to send him a piece of work for Le Monde. If he sends me any remuneration, keep half and give the other half to the translator. . . .

What men call "glory" is beginning to surround me in Greece. I receive letters. Critiques are being written about me. Young people come to see me. My God, how far removed my soul is from all this

---

* This refers to two tragedies in verse, the Christ and the one N.K. called my Odysseus because he dedicated it to me.
† Letter to E. Samios.

wretchedness! Solitude, violent labor, several brave souls in a female body—I don't need anything else. . . .*

Aegina, April 14, 1928

. . . I'm writing you from my little house in Aegina. The windows are open. A light breeze is blowing, very fragrant because the fields roundabout are full of flowers—enormous yellow daisies, camomile plants, sage, thyme. . . . Prevelakis is sitting opposite me, reading the Christ. Tomorrow at daybreak we're going off to the Temple of Aphaia. Kera Zoe lit up when she saw me and asked for news about Kyria Eleni. The children are fine. I had some Easter eggs for them, some chocolates, and some yellow Japanese birds, and we all played and laughed together. Monday morning we're going back to Athens—nous déménageons [we're moving] from Aegina now for good. May it shine in my memory forever, in spite of the inhospitable welcome it extended at the time of your visit. I've lived here with unique intensity; I've written good verse; I've had the inconsolable, inhuman happiness of the human being who creates utterly alone. . . .†

Easter Day, April 15, 1928

. . . Prevelakis and I have just come back from the Temple of Aphaia. We started the trip at daybreak. The whole island was filled with the perfume of camomile and flowering broom. I lay down half naked on the burning marbles of the temple and dozed off for a few moments. I was delighted to see you in a dream. I dreamed that you had written a very beautiful poem entitled "How I Slept with Him." I still recall all the details and I'll tell them to you when we meet. I saw you with such marvelous vividness that I felt upset when I woke up, as though I'd had an apparition. . . .‡

I had forgotten this letter and this dream when, several years later, ill and far away from him, I sang my love in verses that were perhaps awkward:

> When you go far from me, my love,
>> our house is haunted, and I cannot touch anything,
>> cannot touch anything without touching your hand . . .

---

* Letter to E. Samios.
† Letter to E. Samios.
‡ Letter to E. Samios.

April 17, 1928

So here is my last letter from Athens. The cell is full of suitcases. I feel no joy in my heart. What I'd like now above all else would be to remain quietly in one spot and work. And later on, to travel. . . .*

S.S. Lenin, April 19, 1928

Lenotschka,

I'm now on my beloved sea, passing by the temple at Sounion. The sea is heavenly, calm, my brow is cool, my heart tight as though divining some evil. But my mind propels me far away from Greece, and I would to God that years may pass before I see it again. . . . I'm the only passenger on this fine boat. I've got a pile of books. Tomorrow we'll be in Smyrna, day after tomorrow in Constantinople. . . . Istrati sent me a telegram yesterday, saying that he has heard nothing from me and that he's leaving for Kiev. In the meantime, he's in Yalta, the superb Crimean Kurort [spa], waiting for Gorki. . . .

It's absolutely essential for me to finish the scenario in May, and I foresee that Istrati is going to want me to go to Yalta. I simply cannot live at the beck and call of a person who changes his mind every minute, and who, on every occasion, lets everything depend on the way the wind happens to be blowing. Anyhow, I have to complete a number of things this year: scenarios; a trip on the Volga; a book [about Russia] in French; and then, next spring, the journey to Siberia and perhaps to Japan; and finally in Germany, the writing of the Buddha scenario, which I'm counting on to provide us with material security and peace of mind. Near Vienna, for The Odyssey. These are my plans, en route to Russia. What will actually be achieved? We shall see. . . .†

Smyrna, April 20, 1928

A marvelous voyage. In front of me now are the coasts of Ionia, Smyrna, a dulcet sun, harmonious mountains, all the trucs [tricks] to cast a magic spell on the simple human heart. For a moment my heart does pound—but at once it becomes aware of the artificiality of it, and soars upward again, insatiably, like a flèche de cathédrale [cathedral spire].‡

---

* Letter to E. Samios.
† Letter to E. Samios.
‡ Letter to E. Samios.

April 22, 1928

We've entered the Black Sea. Calm but dull and dreadfully cold; a light sleet; the sun has vanished. . . . All day in my cabin reading and writing. An enormous amount of work can be done in such godlike solitude. . . . The parting with Ketty was moving. Prevelakis I didn't see—better that way. We'd arranged a meeting for the afternoon, and I left at noon. I felt very sorry for my sister. I've left no one else behind me. . . .*

Kiev, April 24, 1928

. . . I'm with Istrati and Bilili, a thousand plans boiling. In three days they leave for Moscow, in fourteen days for Paris. . . . Istrati promises to return in three weeks. A wonderful chance for you to come back with them, if you want. . . .†

April 27, 1928

. . . I shouldn't write to you at all, or I should write to you not every day, but every hour, every instant. Our plans change from one second to the next. All this comes from Istrati's character and the situation here. This afternoon, new decision: Panaït isn't going to Paris; perhaps we'll all go in ten days' time, perhaps I'll stay in Kiev, or return to Odessa to finish the screenplay, perhaps I'll go to Moscow, finally perhaps we'll all go to Germany! My God, when will this whirlwind settle? . . .

How quickly life goes by here. The tempo is so swift that you don't even have time to feel it before it's changed! And so it's a most logical consequence that every human being decays very rapidly, like things burning in a great deal of oxygen. Living here, the only kind of acts that can be performed are dynamiques. The atmosphere audessus de l'éphémère [above the ephemeral] needed for The Odyssey does not exist here.‡

April 28, 1928

. . . Today there's some tentative stabilization. We're staying in Kiev four more days, in order to participate in the May Day festivities and the pilgrimage which is made from all over the Ukraine to its

<hr />

* Letter to E. Samios.
† Letter to E. Samios.
‡ Letter to E. Samios.

greatest poet, Shevchenko. On the third of May, we'll leave for Moscow. . . .

The plan as of now is to make a trip to Siberia that will last three to four months. Instead of writing a book about Russia (and by now innumerable ones have been written), we'll write about Siberia. . . .

At the moment I'm writing you, I'm in my hotel room; it's 7 P.M. and very light. A table, in the center of which is the samovar, very high, like an altar, and steaming. On my left, Bilili is turning the robinet [faucet] on to prepare tea for us; she's calm and radiant. . . . On my right, Istrati is smoking and drinking coffee and tea, and opposite me is our beloved Chekist, who is telling us stories. At 8:30 we'll go to a splendid cinema, and tomorrow for an outing in the country. The trees haven't come out yet, but in a few days the chestnut trees will be all in bloom.

Midnight: We've just come back from the cinema. I'm extraordinarily interested in this art now, and I realize how difficult it is to write a scenario. When it becomes necessary, I'll collaborate with a Russian friend of mine who is a film-régisseur [film director].

In Russia, you will feel powerful sensations, because life here flows on a lofty level, it's harsh and heroic. Possibly your body will also grow strong, and obey the soul. . . .*

By the Dnieper River, afternoon, May 2, 1928

Stretched out on the grass around Shevchenko's statue . . . we're watching the crowd, the brilliant Ukrainian costumes, and we're reveling in the sun. . . . We're talking about our life, how much time we waste, and how our life slips by as if it had no purpose.

Evening: The celebration is over. There were speeches, Ukrainian songs, and joy for me because I saw many Jewish women. I'm impatient to get off by myself and work. All these days, life in Russia has been very external, and my soul has not become full. . . .†

May 3, 1928

We have traveled all night on the river to get back to Kiev . . . Istrati half dead from fatigue. It is raining today, the river is full of mud and waves. It is cold. This kind of life will devour Istrati, for he is sick

---

* Letter to E. Samios.
† Letter to E. Samios.

and won't rest. He must be quiet, work, return to the land, take up a peasant's life and renew himself. . . .*

May 4, 1928

Today Istrati and Bilili left for Moscow. How long will they stay? We settled together on ten days, but I don't believe it. . . .†

Kiev, May 5, 1928

. . . I am terribly tired. The day Istrati left, our program was . . . What will come of all this, I don't know. Istrati has no will power and his desires are constantly changing. . . . Life is impossible because of Istrati's wastefulness. This has to be set right, or we are lost. Bilili sees this, but she is pathologically powerless to do anything about it; she simply follows him, like someone who has been hypnotized.‡

[Kiev] May 6, 1928

I'm working quietly in my room, not talking, not seeing anyone. At last, I've found my own rhythm. The scenario is coming along, developing every moment. It's much more difficult than one thinks; it requires a terrible intensité visuelle [visual intensity], as well as logic, to make the action evolve. But I hope it will turn out well, and then I'll begin the new scenario on which I'm basing all my hopes—the Buddha.§

[Kiev] May 8, 1928

. . . My life here has acquired a great serenity. Ever since Istrati left, it seems as though I've escaped from some extraordinary hubbub. My room had turned into a public thoroughfare; people were incessantly coming in and out, eating, shouting, bothering me. Now all day long I'm silent. I work, I don't see anyone. I'm not happy, but this cadre [framework] to some extent takes the place of happiness. The scenario is not at all historical, as you fear. It is assuming a human and dramatic character. The elements composing it are the man who struggles, the woman who loves, the sea, the sun. . . .

Russia is no longer giving me any joy. My only hope is for us to travel in Siberia or Turkestan, or to live in Moscow. That's the only

---

* Letter to E. Samios.
† Letter to E. Samios.
‡ Letter to E. Samios.
§ Letter to E. Samios.

place where life has the color and fever that I like. Here it's provincial, and only my great love for everything Russian makes me able to stand it.*

May 9, 1928

God is not a song that flies through the air and fades away
but a rough, hot gullet full of nerves and blood!†

Those two lines have been obsessing me all day today. They express my warm contact with the earth and my emancipation from the anemic abstract ideologies.

Ah, if I could only find peace somewhere and scud along in The Odyssey!

Today a warm south wind is blowing from Turkestan. I've not gone out all day. I lean out the window and feel the whole Orient upon me. I don't see anyone, I don't talk to anyone. With awe I am feeling what people call "solitude" and what I have always called "beatitude." At such moments I feel profoundly that I am free. I admit that I would like to see just you; two or three others, but them for only a brief time. My love for you makes me a "human being"; that is, an organism capable of distinguishing and saying: "This person I want, this one I don't want." When I cease to love, I shall acquire an inhuman autonomy. God willing, I shall respond to you until my death as I do now, and you will bind me to human warmth—so that I may not be lost. I love you and I marvel at this, and I experience tenderness for my own self and pitié and unbearable grief and joy. I am living my human nature, which I have fought so hard to conquer; and I hold your face in my palms as something warm and fleeting, precious and dearly loved, and I shudder when I think of my own death, because my fingers will no longer be able to feel your mouth, your nose, the fluttering of your eyelids and your marvelous high breast . . .‡

[Kiev] May 15, 1928

My love, I wish I could send you the scenario, so that you could see it. This exercise will do us much good. I believe that the new modern style is going to be profoundly influenced by the Kino [cinema]. . . .

A great visionary power is required, logic and, at the same time, madness. Logic alone would produce films of an extremely humdrum

---

* Letter to E. Samios.
† Lines composed for The Odyssey.
‡ Letter to E. Samios.

186

kind; madness would produce chaotic ones. It seems to me that, if I were well versed in the technique, I could do some interesting things, because I have both the requisite elements. But I content myself with sharpening my visual power, and so I shall use it with a more incisive effectiveness in The Odyssey. . . .

By myself, I can live very well on 100 rubles. For the two of us, 200. We shall find them. Our permanent residence must be either Moscow or Petersburg—everywhere else is provincial. In Moscow there's the difficulty of the house. But we'll find one in the suburbs. It suffices that you accept this life and can live with a human being like me. You already know me well, and you can decide in full consciousness. Work, quiet, laughter, kindness, trips when we are able, simplicity of life, frequent solitude—life héroïque et simple. . . .*

Kiev, May 18, 1928

. . . I feel very sad today and am talking to you to find a bit of relief. It's twilight. I haven't gone out all day. I've been reading a brilliant book on the cinema by Moussinac. Certain sections open up great perspectives, and as long as I am in Russia, I tell myself, I must dig deeper into this most modern expression of the spirit. This power man has to create people, ideas and passions out of light and shadow, and to annihilate them, is beginning to affect me. I've been gripped by the thought of Buddha, who, in the cool domes of his own brain, similarly created the world out of light and shadow. . . . To succeed in transforming the abstract conceptions into simple, clear images is my great aspiration. The Odyssey is to be full of images. Odysseus' eye is an appareil [apparatus] for creating the universe in the dark room. . . .†

Panaït Istrati's way of envisaging life in the U.S.S.R. upset Nikos. Wishing to avoid any ambiguity, he wrote Panaït the following letter on May 17, 1928:

Dear Panaït!

On a little card you wrote me, you repeat the word "réussir" [succeed] three times, and you have conveyed to me the impression that you are exposed to great danger. For me, "to succeed" means "to

---

* Letter to E. Samios.
† Letter to E. Samios.

produce a great work." For you too. But you squander yourself too much in ephemeral, harmful things. Neither you nor I have time any more to waste our powers on purposes inferior to our own spirits. We're both at the decisive turning point in our evolution—we're capable of creating this great work and we're also capable of ruining ourselves. Seeing personalities, learning Russian, talking, waiting, listening, gradually and unconsciously yielding to the methods that are imposed on this outlook and way of life—this is what your card suggests to me.

Panaït, I love you too much not to do my utmost to lead you back to the "forest," that is, to your own soul. So far, we've done nothing— barely a few exercises for learning this magic; for learning to express in words the terrible, obscure, marvelous power that consumes us. Now we're mature; we've loved, suffered, felt joy. We're at the peak of the life cycle—let's escape the decline!

The endeavor to escape it is the sole object of our friendship. I personally am determined to concentrate all my powers in order to transform the curve into an arrow. If you leave me to myself alone, I shall try to "succeed" alone; if we try it together, the task would not be easier, but it would be deeper and richer.

With an inhuman clarity, I see both paths which, at this precise point in our life and friendship, diverge in front of us. And now, as I write you, taking you by the arm and pushing you, I feel moved in all my being.   N.*

Your Name Day, May 21, 1928

Spring has made its entrance today in Kiev—sun and a warm wind. The women have donned their white embroidered blouses; in a few days, the trees will be full of blossoms.

At this moment a hard rain, warm and heavily scented, has just broken loose. . . . Summer rain arouses in me the tenderest of feelings. The sense of death gently inundates my soul. . . . Love, death, the great futility, the terrifying sweetness of the passing moment. Ah, my whole heart is throbbing. I remember, once at Mani and another time at Assisi, two summer rains falling on flowering trees. Ah, if I could only have died at that moment! Never did my bond, my identity with the earth seem to me so simple and so desirable. The return: rising out of the earth for a second, casting a glance at the light, the sea, woman, man, and once again sinking into the earth! Tonight when I'm all alone

_____
* Letter in French to Panaït Istrati.

188

and it is raining and there's a tree across the way from me prematurely in bloom, death beckons to me, gently bewitching me, and I don't know why I don't rise to follow her. My mother, you, Lenotschka, and two or three other people are all that hold me back.*

Kiev, May 26, 1928

. . . I don't know Istrati's plans, but more and more, I think, he is inclined to join the Party and become an homme d'action [man of action]. If his writer's vein has run dry, that would be the best solution. Anyhow, if he does devote himself entirely to action, this means that the vein has already run dry. As for me, I've firmly decided to remain aloof from any ephemeral action, however valuable it might be, and not to betray my supreme guide, "Odysseus-Buddha."

It is natural that Russia should have ceased to awaken the same raptures in me that I felt at the time of the virginal encounter, (a) because it has passed beyond the heroic phase itself and moves more and more in the direction of a normal equilibrium—an overwhelmingly significant one certainly, but one which cannot produce any violent excitement in my soul; and (b) because I am not an homme d'action and cannot be unremittingly interested in the amelioration of a social order. I love the first descent of the Spirit, the violent event that brings the fire. The rest of it, the way that the dread moment gets channeled into prudent, everyday necessity, does not interest me very much. My deepest joy is to see how the mysterious force seizes hold of man and shakes him like a lover, an epileptic, or a creator. Because, as you know, what interests me is not a man himself, but the being that I so imperfectly designate as "God." . . .

About the cinema I've done a great deal of thinking, and I'm glad I'm having a chance to make this expérience too. As I wrote you, it helps me with The Odyssey, which is the goal of my existence until 1933, because (1) it compels me to transform every abstract idea into an image; (2) only the cinema can grasp the inconscient [unconscious mind], the dreams and the visions; and (3) I feel a very wry, Buddha-like pleasure in creating passions, loves, and collisions among shadows, and then in a flash, while they remain as mute as phantoms, annihilating them. Isn't that like the vast écran [screen] of the universe?

Now I'm beginning work on a new scenario: Lenin. . . . It's a vision lasting but a single second. . . . Ah, if you only knew the delight

---

* Letter to E. Samios.

I feel when I think of being able to express this flash of lightning in images, so that millions of eyes will see it. But I must find a great film director. In Moscow perhaps. I know perfectly well what the film must be, but I lack the technique. Only with a specialist can I write the scenario. The flash of lightning I have. . . .*

June 1, 1928

My love, where are you? Have you left Paris? Are you at Plombières? How I long for you here! It's spring, and every day for half an hour it pours rain on the flowering chestnut trees, and the earth is tapestried with white flowers. Fortunately, time passes quickly, and here we are already in June. There's only a little time still separating us. Every day I go through an intense reliving of our days and nights in Palestine and Cyprus. The godlike night in Jerusalem with the white rose and the red rose. All my life, I think, even at the moment of my death, this night will shine in my mature thought—and I hope to God that you will be near me at that instant so that I can tell you so! What a terrifying mystery this life is—when I recall the vertiginous experience of that night, I shudder, thinking of the irresistible filters used by the dark force in order to subjugate man.

To annihilate these filters would be horrible; to let oneself be overcome by them, degrading. We must taste them, en les dosant [measuring them out] in a noble way. . . .†

And Nikos set off for Bekovo, the large suburb of Moscow, to resume life with Panaït and Bilili, in a chalet Itka had just found for them. In November, 1927, he complained in a letter to Leah of the implacable law of maternity, which in his opinion had made a slave of the marvelous Jewess. A year later, Itka, who also lived in Bekovo, saw Nikos often. She translated Russian newspapers and books for him, discussing with him the burning problems of the contemporary revolutionary reality. At that period, Nikos wrote the following to P. Prevelakis:

. . . Here I've rediscovered one of my Jewish girls from the fiery circle of Berlin. . . . Full of drive, strength, and faith, and a fanatical

---

* Letter to E. Samios.
† Letter to E. Samios.

member of the Party. This encounter has been useful for me and has refreshed my heart. . . .

Panaït, however, took umbrage at Itka's frequent visits. He was uneasy about my future and he wrote to me. Panaït did not know about our pact for "ten days a year." And Nikos and I did not yet know our own hearts.

Upon my arrival in the U.S.S.R., Nikos was to say to me: "If you agree to become my companion, I promise you to break with my past. There will no longer be any other woman." And indeed there was no other woman. But by common consent, we were able to link past, present, and future by hyphens, preserving always a warm contact with friends of times past.

[Bekovo] *June 14, 1928*

My Love,

Right now we have to make a boring trip to Yalta, near the Rumanian border, where Istrati has to be. We'll be back in ten days. So stay a few days at Elsa's and rest. . . . If I weren't afraid of having our trains cross, I would come to Minsk to fetch you. . . . Beloved Lenotschka, in these final moments before our meeting, I feel a slight frisson. May "our God" guide us at this difficult moment. . . .*

Bekovo, June 15, 1928

. . . I'm now in Bekovo, one hour outside Moscow, in a boundless forest of fir trees. This place has two faults: innumerable mosquitoes and dampness. Istrati is a bit sick from the daily changes in the weather, and now he's obsessed with the idea of setting off for the Crimea. . . . Yesterday I got a letter about the scenario I had submitted, saying that the committee approved it and considered it the best scenario that has ever been submitted to it. Heaps of praise and they're going to film it immediately. Today we're going in to Moscow to give another company the idea for three other scenarios. Two of them mine and the third one taken from Oncle Anghel. . . .

I've written several articles for Pravda about labor problems in Greece, and I can send you 1,000 francs, but with great difficulty. . . .

---

* Letter to E. Samios.

Leningrad, June 26, 1928

. . . Our stay here has been extremely interesting. First, the White Nights; then several paintings I love in the Hermitage—Rembrandt, El Greco, ikons; and two or three people I've met, especially one great poet mystique, a Christian.* He gave me a beautiful ikon, and we talked for a long time about the human agony.

I had a long talk with Istrati the other day, in a forest, about your coming. I presented the case to him very simply and very ferme [firmly]. He's afraid we may have money problems. But I explained to him that we can both live on a modest scale and work. With the train [pace] of life he leads, he's constantly getting stranded. He has no rhythm. If needs be, we'll separate from him. . . .†

June 30, 1928

. . . The trip is almost certain to take place now: Volga–Japan. We'll send articles to the N.R.F. [Nouvelle Revue française] as well as to German and Russian newspapers. We'll have a lot of work, a terrible amount of it, but I've purposely assumed full responsibility for it, in order to contribute as much as I can to the economic side of our life with Istrati. When this trip is over . . . we'll go back to somewhere near Paris . . . where we'll write three or four volumes about the trip and where I'll isolate myself in an inexorable way to rework The Odyssey. If at that point, you still want to live with me, Lenotschka, we'll share the work. You will begin writing with me, and you will help me, and when we want and are able to, we'll make excursions to Spain or elsewhere. If you no longer want to breathe the same air, then—free and unperturbed—you may leave me, and I shall sink into perfect solitude. I'm very strong. I can stand anything; whatever happens, I'm entirely ready for it. So no one is ever obliged me ménager [to take care of me]. . . . Before you leave Paris, Bilili will write you to bring her revolvers[!!!] and some other things. . . .

Life here with Istrati is going well. Only Bilili—who is a perfect companion for Istrati—gets into humeurs [moods] sometimes, and as she told me, she has a mortal hatred for me sometimes. I understand and explain to her the reason why. I hope that my influence will do Istrati good—and that consoles me.

---

* Nikolai Kliouev. N.K. translated certain of his poems. For the poem "Joy is a caravan of silk . . . ," see Toda Raba.
† Letter to E. Samios.

Heraklion, 1899. NK (left) in his gym class

1902. NK (center, hands clasped) as Creon in a school production of
Oedipus

2 _ Οἰδίπους Τύραννος ἐr Ἡρακλείῳ ὑπό Μαθητῶν τοῦ Γυμναδίου (1902)

Heraklion 1905(?). NK with his mother and sisters

As a student. NK second from right

Right: 1902

Below left: 1912. NK and Galatea

Below right: 1919. NK in Constantinople, during the repatriation of the
Greeks from the Caucasus

Zorba. A photograph taken in 1920

Left: Rahel, Berlin, 1923

Opposite: Elsa and NK, 1923

Below: 1926, Tel Aviv. NK talking to Leah (far right) in her garden

With Panaït Istrati in the Soviet Union, 1928-1929

On the Dnieper River with Bilili (far right) and Panaït Istrati (center)

Eleni Samios, 1928

Athens, 1928

NK and Pandelis Prevelakis, Gottesgab, Christmas, 1931

NK in the Aegina, 1931, working on his translation of the Franco-Greek dictionary

With Eleni Samios at the Colonial Exposition, Paris, June 1931

Aegina, 1933. Prevelakis, NK and Renaud de Jouvenel

K. KOUTOULAKI

1946. NK returns to Crete to see the devastation of the war

Antibes, 1953, Villa Manolita. NK with Eleni Kazantzakis and Mme. Y. Renoux (right), his secretary at UNESCO

1955. With Albert Schweitzer at Gunsbach

1956. NK on his balcony at Antibes

Right: 1956

NK with Eleni Kazantzakis, just before his last voyage to China

CHAILLET, ANTIBES

Beloved Lenotschka, our fate is amazing. If our dream about the trip really comes true, this life gives more than we ask of it. Never did I expect, when we met, the fulfillment we have today. We've given life a big chiquenaude [fillip], and it has acquired a superhuman impetus. God grant that you will experience great joys and great griefs with me, and never mediocrity or boredom. . . .*

Toward the end of the month of July, in hopes of contemplating the aurora borealis, Istrati, Bilili, and Kazantzakis set off for the land of silence in the Great North.

At Murmansk, at that time of year, the sun never sets. But our tourists were besieged by battalions of mosquitoes in such dense array that, deeply impressed as they were by the midnight sun, they had to give up walking beneath it. As for sleep, it was out of the question. Myriads of bedbugs infested the little polar inn. And Panaït requested permission to spend the night in the Murmansk hospital.

About all this, we find not one word either in Nikos' letters or in his notebooks. Only the terror and awe inspired in him once again by the human struggle, the unequal struggle against the elements of stubborn, death-dealing Nature.

"God, do not kill me!" he jotted down in his notebook. "This is the only prayer the Eskimos say to their God." And further along: "In the museum we saw the rags of this God thickly soaked in blood. . . ."

If I were asked to describe Elsa, I should repeat what other people called her, "the silent little woman," such was her way of creating silence around her—dreamy, ocean-deep, rich, hypnotic silence. Yet Elsa did talk too; she talked copiously, in fact, in a muffled, or, I might say, mysteriously smiling, voice. Her eyes and the curl of her lips from time to time stressed such or such a significant word. Her head thrown slightly to one side, she sought above all else to express your own inmost thought—or, rather, to complete it. So that one had the impression of carrying on a monologue with one's own soul.

The few days I spent under her roof on my way from Paris to Moscow were tremendously important to me. Happy to find an attentive ear, Elsa gave free rein to her most cherished memories. She had

---

* Letter to E. Samios.

not loved for a spring or a day; she loved for always, in the only way that one does love—without asking for her due.

With a sure hand, she stroked in the finishing touches on the portrait I had come to submit to her. "Yes, you can have confidence in him, Eleni. In spite of the flame consuming him, he remains balanced and perfectly normal. Go. And whatever happens, never regret that you have gone. I'll be following close behind you, and I'll always be with you when difficult moments come. He is naked, without armor. He reminds me of Saint Sebastian just as the arrows are about to fall on him. Shield him; protect him from these arrows."

She enfolded still closer this "rich unity," this thought which resented flesh: ". . . There are also some ambivalences, of course. But he's the first to admit them and struggle against them. He might have been selfish. But he is so only for the sake of his work. He might have been hard. But he isn't hard toward anyone except himself."

"He is rushing toward self-destruction," I cried in agitation. "The way I've seen him, he will destroy himself by the very act of trying to sublimate his soul. And yet the strange part is that I feel rested when I am with him, as if I were beside a fountain."

"Eleni, do you remember the old Cretan who left such a deep impression on him? The odds are a thousand to one that he's spoken about him to you many times. As he bent over a stream, this man a hundred years old saw his life flowing by. This was his answer when Nikos questioned him:

" 'Life, my son, is like a glass of fresh water. . . .' "

" 'Do you feel your thirst has been quenched, grandfather?' I carried on, laughing."

" 'Curses on anyone whose thirst is ever quenched!' " Elsa quoted, her eyes on fire. "Eleni, my friend, you are going to hold this cup of fresh water between the palms of your two hands. Curses on you if you let a single drop escape. . . ."

After a week in Düsseldorf at Elsa's home, I took the train for Moscow, armed with Bilili's two revolvers, as though I were on my way to the U.S.S.R. for some anarchist exploit. A balalaika welcomed us as soon as we had passed the station at Minsk. A jubilant, winging song, scented with the fat smell of the Russian earth.

Man's effort to surpass himself, to scratch the thick crust of egoism from his own carapace, to open his ears to the plaint of the hungry, to fortify his heart against his own unhappiness—this I would soon touch at close quarters, with all its high points and its low points, its undreamed-of successes and its inevitable reversals.

"If you have two shirts, give one away and buy yourself a rose!" say the Chinese.

"What are you carrying there, madame, in that big case?" we asked our traveling companion, a woman still beautiful, who had gotten on the train at Batum on her way to Leningrad (seven days by train). "Why do you seem so worried?"

"It's a gift for an old friend of mine," she answered. "She used to be rich; now she's poor—very, very poor. . . ."

"Oranges and tangerines, of course!"

"Not exactly . . . Two hundred white roses—she loves them so much, and how could she ever get them for herself now?"

"To Bekovo? You can't go there alone. If they don't come here to fetch you this evening, I'll get someone to go with you."

The stationmaster smiled at my embarrassed explanations. "Nichevo! [No matter!] Drink some tea, eat some blini, and wait here nicely. I won't forget you!"

I sat there perched on my suitcase as though on a rock inundated by dense waves of comrades in sheepskin boots, red shawls and white jackets. I was just calculating my chances, when a slender, swarthy man appeared, gesticulating, bursting into noisy laughter and squeezing the ample shoulders of a dumbfounded matron as he spun God-knows-what tale in God-knows-what dialect of his own invention. It was indeed Nikos, who had come to the station to pick up some information about the train schedules. After catching sight of me, he was trying to gain time before rushing toward what must have seemed to him an apparition.

Bekovo fitted his descriptions: a dacha (a Russian chalet) set in a dark forest of fir trees; dark ponds, in which Panaït and Bilili hoped to swim one day; clouds of mosquitoes; frequent rain; Itka;* and an unanticipated enemy—lice—of which I was the only victim.

I liked everything about Nikos Kazantzakis and was not frightened by the warnings in his letters about "correspondence and visits I might find disagreeable." I was afraid of only one thing: not measuring up to my task. But the joy we felt at being together again and the desire, each

---

* At a slightly later point, she vanished to Siberia.

time we separated, to be united anew—a desire overpowering everything else—seemed to me a very good omen.

Bilili I loved already, and Panaït's charm worked away. There was no one to equal him when he began telling us his stories from Braila and Ploesti. But it would be sheer fantasy to pretend I didn't suffer from his unpredictable moods, at times even to the point of losing my head.

Gathered around the samovar every evening, we used to draw up minutely detailed plans. As soon as we had gone to bed, Panaït would begin gleefully knocking them all down again. At daybreak he would summon us to his room in our nightclothes to work out the same puzzle all over again. New detailed plans, new "final" decisions, which he respected only for an instant. Bilili alone preserved her medieval Madonna smile. I could see the serpent of anger crawling along Nikos' spinal cord, though he preserved his equanimity and didn't show anything.

I still remember one day in Tiflis when I fled from the hotel in exhaustion, expecting never to return. But when I reached the top of the bridge and wanted to carry out my intentions, I lacked the strength. On another occasion—and this amused Nikos until the end of his life—I got so provoked myself that I drove Panaït to exasperation by stubbornly insisting that "back home" our potatoes emit water in the course of cooking. Not daring to raise his hand against me, Panaït almost choked with rage.

Nikos had done something imprudent. Having no confidence in his own practical sense (he had hardly any at all), he had promoted Panaït to the post of treasurer. But Panaït was incapable of keeping a cent in his pocket. He used to offer some form of financial aid to every person who happened to come along. One person received a certain sum to have a denture made for himself; another to buy a pair of spectacles; a third, at the far end of the U.S.S.R., to come and live near us. I saw one poor wretch arrive like this one day from Odessa.

"Here I am, *Tovarishch* Panaït! You are my savior! I shall never leave you!" he cried, kissing Panaït on both cheeks. And Panaït, that *enfant terrible*, just opened a book and thrust it under the nose of his guest, who was a worker as he himself had been and, like him, had tuberculosis.

"*Tovarishch* Nikolai Vasilievitch, when we spoke in Odessa, we were at this page here. Now take a good look. The pages turn fast. Today we're at that page there!"

To describe our peregrinations in the U.S.S.R., our trip down the Volga, our excursions to Georgia, Azerbaidzhan, Armenia and the peaks of the Caucasus, our sunlit stay on the enchanting shores of the Black Sea, I would need a whole volume. The happiness and the troubles involved in becoming a woman. The joy and the weariness in traversing one sixth of the world's surface, with its mountains, its rivers and lakes, its steppes, its deserts, its mammoth black fir-tree forests, its light-colored woodlands of birches, its vast tea plantations and citrus groves, its silent snows and torrid heat, its factories, its ancient cities with their Byzantine frescoes, its mosques decked out in turquoise, its theaters and films, its ballets, its opera—the whole sweep of art from the modern to the most ancient, the vitality and diversity of the Russian people. And finally our traveling companions, the impetuous Panaït Istrati and the imperturbable Bilili.

Once the money Nikos had set aside with such difficulty had been squandered, our pilgrimage in the U.S.S.R. met a pitiful end. And it was in Tiflis, in a state of perfect euphoria, in the midst of Gargantuan meals, with the *tchemadan** and *shashlik*, and *Napareuli*† and *Tjinandali*† flowing in torrents, and with an elite of ardent young poets around us, that Panaït dealt us the final blow, laughing a yellow laugh.

"My friends, *finita la musica!* Ha-ha-ha! We haven't got another cent! Unless we want to go back to Moscow tonight, we'll have to ration ourselves. Ha-ha-ha! Just one dish at noon, preferably a soup, and a good thick one, a cup of cocoa in the evening. *Bolshe ugoshchat' nichem* [I can't offer you anything else]."

How did Nikos keep from smashing his head, since, according to Panaït, this was the only honest way for friends to act with each other? And how did we forget our righteous indignation and go on loving him to the end?

Farewell, beautiful dreams! How many tears I shed in secret at parting with our tiny coupons, granted by the Soviet government, allowing us free use of all the Russian *poyezdi* and all the *parokhudni*.‡

Only Nikos succeeded in completing the pilgrimage we had begun under such good omens. Panaït, Bilili and I were forced to leave the

---

* According to an old Georgian custom, someone is always designated chief of the banquet.
† Georgian wines.
‡ Russian railroads and steamships.

U.S.S.R. early in the month of January 1929. Panaït certainly did not suspect that he would never return.

Before resuming Nikos' letters, I should say a bit more about Panaït Istrati.

In the last stages of tuberculosis, though refusing to admit it, he deceived us all by his extraordinary endurance. He reminds me of another writer, famous and fanciful like himself. I'm thinking of the Englishman who disappeared at about the same time, D. H. Lawrence —great traveler, impenitent preacher, hoping to persuade the world to sacrifice its petty personal interests to the Great Cause; indulging himself in outbursts of anger against his friends, his Frieda, and his enemies; getting along with everybody in just the same shattering, generous, noble way, without hypocrisy and with enormous verve; unbearable and at the same time utterly lovable.

Panaït, shod in high leather leggings, wearing riding trousers and an ill-fitting semimilitary jacket full of pockets, roamed about bent beneath the burden of his old itinerant photographer's gear. His pockets were stuffed with the oddest conglomeration of objects: fountain pens, penknives, scissors, pliers, files (he was very fastidious and loved to care for his delicate hands), cigarettes, lemons, half-consumed red pimentos, a flask of olive oil, the famous box of lozenges which had been sucked on and spat out—and no trace of a revolver, after all their insistence that I bring those revolvers. (I had set eyes on them only once, the day I unpacked them on their table.)

Woe to us if the lemon happened to be missing. While the tea turned cold in the *chainaya*, we had to scour the village in all directions, looking for that cursed citrus fruit.

"*Yest' limon* [Do you have a lemon there], *Tovarishch?*"

"*Niet!*"

"What do you mean, *niet?* Isn't there a lemon in the whole U.S.S.R.?"

How many times did we cross the wooden bridge at Nizhni Novgorod in the pelting rain? How many times did we tramp from one end of town to the other in Kazan, Astrakhan, Baku or Batum? Five? Six? Ten? Always hunting for lemon, while our teeth chattered with the cold or our brows dripped with sweat and Panaït howled like a Cephalonian boatman, suddenly recalling all his father's oaths: "Let me —— your mother and your father!" . . . "Let me —— your great uncle's mustaches!" . . . "Let me —— your Soviet Russia!" Then, collecting himself, he would rummage through his pockets and offer us one of his lozenges, which he'd already spat out several times, trying to pacify our righteous wrath.

Like a toy loaded with lead to keep it from toppling over, Panaït never allowed himself to be toppled over by anything or anyone. He obliged us to follow him, often anxious and sometimes exhausted as we were, astonishing us each time with his new resurrections. After one long excursion on horseback to the Turkish frontier, when we had left him at death's door and when we ourselves could neither get up nor sit down except in slow motion, he suddenly turned up triumphantly, waving his tenth tube of aspirin. "A whole tube in one night!" he cried out at the top of his lungs. "There's nothing like it for bronchitis. Take my word for it!"

Aspirin after aspirin, coffee after coffee, scene after scene, each one more violent than the previous one, he recouped his strength just at the moment when the rest of us had reached exhaustion and were ready to scream for mercy. And what an orchestration of journalists, photographers, and politico-philosophico-socialists. And what a rumpus!

After returning from Leningrad, overwhelmed by having seen an insignificant, malicious *Komsomol* destroy the family of a distinguished old Bolshevik, Panaït, in a paroxysm of rage, picked up the telephone and cursed a blue streak at anyone who cared to listen—up to the Secretary of the Party himself. Then at once he collapsed on the bed, prostrated, waiting for the thunderbolts of the ignominious bigwigs to strike. The game, dangerous as it was, was cut short by a nice journalist, who in a bantering tone put the following question to our traveling companion:

"Dear *Tovarishch* Panaït, have you heard about those poor Western journalists who took the boat the other day to go home? What an atrocious drama! It tears my heart to think of it! . . . Oh, how sorry we all are! A storm, an accursed storm, and it was impossible to save anyone . . . anyone. All vanished without leaving a trace."

Once we had returned to Moscow—after the Volga, Azerbaidzhan, Georgia, the Caucasus, Armenia, and the blissful shores of the Black Sea, Leningrad and a brief meeting alone with Nikos in the old city of Novgorod—I took leave of him, going on to Berlin. There, in a place near my friend Marika,* I stayed to wait for him. Panaït and Bilili

---

* In the home of Fania Lippmann and little Johnny, who were later burned at Dachau.

stayed in Berlin briefly, then went on to Vienna, where they separated for good.

Several years later, Panaït, penitent about his attitude toward the U.S.S.R. and toward his companion, wanted Nikos to forgive him, longing to see him again. In one long letter, he described to Nikos the separation from Bilili. According to his account, he had gone off his head because of it, and had been picked up in a provincial railway station, carrying a sack on his back crammed with an unusual quantity of sticks of sealing wax. He wrote a book following this, in which the mood of spite hid the finer aspects of his soul.

The winter of 1929, when Kazantzakis went off to Siberia alone, was one of the most severe on record. In Moscow, the thermometer often sank to 45 degrees below zero. The milk dangling from a piece of twine like a block of ice or the stalactites hanging from the horses' nostrils and the coachmen's beards had made no impression on us. Only one young eccentric wandering through these frigid scenes in his shirt sleeves attracted our attention.

I cannot remember Panaït with any other protection than his flimsy, soiled, gray-green coat. Nikos wore a heavy, fur-lined coat, the *mamochka*, which he had kept from his previous travels in the U.S.S.R. It was too heavy for a woman's shoulders. More sensitive to the cold than to ridicule, I decked myself bizarrely in a coat tailored for a former Tsarist officer, whose "trimmings" and stars we stripped off. Unable to treat ourselves to boots, we wore our wretched galoshes, which skidded on the snow. And I didn't have Marika at my side to warm my shoes for me, exchanging them with her own every five minutes, as we did a little later, in the ice-glazed streets of Berlin.

In fact, this voyage across the white immensity of Siberia acted on the poet as a convalescence. It was as if a soft and refreshing sponge had removed the dusty imprint of the past few months.

Instead of meeting the Russian people, Nikos once more communed with his own heart. And it was probably here, in the dazzling whiteness of the Russian steppes, that he conceived the end of his Odysseus, and his disappearance among the icebergs of the South Pole.

> O mind, since all your wiles and tricks won't work here now,
> turn dread Necessity to pride here, if you can,
> and with no swoons or false bravuras bravely mount
> that pure-white elephant that passed, and let it take

me where it will without vain protest or surprise
*as though I had myself selected the same road.**

Perm, February 4, 1929

Beloved Lenotschka,

I'm at the gateway to the Urals, about to enter Siberia. I'm all alone in a compartment. . . . The celestial silence which does so much to purify and nourish man's soul is flooding me, as the Nile floods Egypt, bringing calm and fertility. Of all the coaches for Siberia, only one is very badly heated: the one I happened to get. They suggested that I change . . . I preferred to suffer rather than to be with people. It's beastly cold at night, in spite of the protection I get from the mamochka. But that doesn't matter. It's the price I pay for my solitude.

I read, write verses and meditate. Ah, how good this silence cure is! The landscape is all the same: snow, fir trees, hamlets, sleighs, valenki [felt boots], shubas [sheepskin coats]. This monotony is a kind of silence, très discret [a very subtle form of silence], and it rests me. Tomorrow we're entering Siberia, and then I'll continue this letter; it consoles me, because it gives me the illusion that you are with me, Lenotschka, and your pale, proud, beloved face is shining in the corner.†

Krasnoyarsk, February 7 (I think)

Since Krasnoyarsk the terrain has been accidenté [varied] and very beautiful. A great delight is the vast Yenisei River. Other beauties: sunset and sunrise in Siberia, soft, tender, virginales. . . . Today I talked for the first time. I sat down in the dining car with a French missionaire who has lived in Manchuria for fifteen years. He talked to me about the way that people live there, about their souls and their sufferings, and it made my heart pound. I don't know why people who are far away seem closer to me and more like brothers. . . .‡

Irkutsk, nighttime, 8 P.M.

Nighttime, izvozchiki [coachmen], I crossed the frozen Angara River; desperate cold; a tiny, very warm hotel, tea. I took a walk. It was

---

* Nikos Kazantzakis, The Odyssey—A Modern Sequel, translated by Kimon Friar (New York: Simon and Schuster, 1958), Book 23, Verses 684–689.
† Letter to E. Samios.
‡ Letter to E. Samios.

dark. Low houses; sturdy, rosy-red women; cinémas. I lost my way in the very bitter cold, finally found it again, and now I'm stretched out on a velvet sofa (most probably full of fleas). As I write you, I am remembering you with love. I long for day to break so that I can pick up your telegram. . . .

I went to the post office. Not a word. I'll go back. . . . The cold here is frightful. They cut the milk with a knife here when they sell it. It's solid, like cheese. It's a life of torment. The river is superb, the way its waves have frozen. The museum is mediocre; the city dull. . . .*

February 10, 1929

. . . They suddenly informed me that the train was about to leave, and I rushed and just caught it in time. And now I'm writing you from the train. I thought it might be wise, if not necessary, to write Panaït to send a letter to Berlin, saying that the articles belong to me and that I can take care of them. . . . Do everything you can so that we can stay in Germany. . . . I have an Angst [anxiety] about Paris† to the point where I have nightmares about it. . . . Something else: I'll do my utmost to be with you by early April. We must see a great miracle together: the flowering cherry trees at Werder, near Berlin. The day I saw them is one of the loveliest treasures of my life: April 13, 1923. I'm happy that we shall see them together.

See Nefertiti in the Museum and Rembrandt's Krieger [Warrior]. Also the superb Egyptian and Arabic wings in the big museum. As well as the Ethnological Museum, unique of its kind in the world. Read Frobenius. When I come, I'll buy a lot of books. . . .‡

Chita, Manchuria, February 11, 1929

My Lenotschka, a word from this little city in the middle of China. Baikal is beautiful, but Lake Sevan is more so. Beyond Baikal there begin some very beautiful mountains. . . . It's almost spring. The snow has almost entirely melted; the flocks are beginning to pasture. Chita is very pleasant, Chinese. My hotel owner is Greek. Tomorrow morning I'm leaving for Khabarovsk. . . .§

---

* Letter to E. Samios.
† The expensiveness of Paris.
‡ Letter to E. Samios.
§ Letter to E. Samios.

Waiting at the railway station for Khabarovsk
Daybreak, February 12, 1929

. . . Last night I had an unexpected joy. Here at Chita there are one hundred and fifty Greeks. When they found out that I had come, they congregated in a house and took me to it, and for long hours I had a most interesting and warmly affectionate discussion with them. Simple people, bakers, cobblers, bootblacks. They put endless questions to me in that lonely place, and as they told me, they got together every evening but never succeeded in finding any answer. "What is Communism?" . . . "Why has Greece been conquered?" . . . "Why was man born?" . . . "What does honor mean?" . . . "Will there be war?" . . . "Where are we going?"

If I were Christ, surely my apostles would be people like these. Love, warmth, trust. The intellectuels are barren, dishonest, doomed. I had felt tired and sad. And with these simple people I regained my confidence in man. Chita! A little city in Manchuria. A thing that until yesterday did not even exist. Ah, "Reisen! Reisen! Reisen! [Travel! Travel! Travel!]"* as Rilke says.†

Manchuria, February 20, 1929

We're crossing the Manchurian border, following the course of the Amur River. Monotonous landscapes, desolate plains with little bouleaux [birch trees], and now and then a village. Everybody gets off and runs to the kipitok [hot water], fills his teapot and goes back to the train on the run. Yesterday the temperature was 36 degrees below zero, but the coaches are well heated, and a different kind of martyrdom is commencing: we suffocate. The windows are weather-stripped and frozen fast. . . . Yesterday I worked well on the book, or rather on the two books, about Russia, with the title you know, En suivant l'étoile rouge [Following the Red Star]. Volume I will be Homo Bolshevicus and Volume II Homo Meta-Bolshevicus. I now have the complete outline, with a mass of details. . . .‡

Khabarovsk, February 15, 1929

I arrived very early this morning, a beautiful city. Frightfully cold again, and not a single room in the hotels. I shall sleep in the corridor.

---

* An intentional paraphrase of Rilke, who says, "Reiten, reiten, reiten! [Ride, ride, ride!]"
† Letter to E. Samios.
‡ Letter to E. Samios.

. . . I'm roaming about the city, which is full of Chinese people and snow. It's dreadfully hard on the face. A moment ago someone stopped me and informed me that my nose had turned white. I got some snow and rubbed it a long time. So far Siberia hasn't given me any intense sensation, and you mustn't have too many regrets about not having seen it. . . .*

February 16, 1929

. . . The train was twenty-four hours late, so I'm staying here another day, a byezprizornyi.† Last night I went to the cinéma to see Genghis Khan. I saw parts we hadn't seen in Moscow and liked it better. . . . The twilight was marvelous: the snow very blue, the Amur River azure-blue and very wide, and over it all a green star was shining. I'm trying not to feel sad, and I go looking for everything that has beauty and cling to it in order to keep from falling. . . . I slept very badly in the corridor. Thank heavens, I'm familiar with greater misfortunes. . . .‡

Vladivostok, February 18, 1929

. . . Last night I arrived in Vladivostok. Together with a Russian I'd been traveling with, I looked for a room till midnight: everything zaneta [filled up]. I slept in a corridor again in a miserable Chinese hotel. But today I've got a very fine room.

Wind, snow, cold. The Pacific Ocean frozen, plunged in frosty mist. The city teeming with Chinese people and Chinese shops. "Commissions,"§ but I've found nothing, nothing at all. . . . But I assure you,‖ there is a great abundance of butter, tea, of anything you want, and above all of bread! I assure you, moreover, that if I could, I would stay here forever. . . . What worries me is that I don't have a single book and can't find any. I'd hoped I might here in Vladivostok, but there isn't a single foreign book. I asked if I could at least buy a Chinese grammar, to look at the structure of the language, but not even that. . . .

It's the first time I've seen so many Chinese people. . . . They stare with their small, sly, querying, mocking eyes, ready to grab, shriek,

---

* Letter to E. Samios.
† This was the name given to the little street urchins, victims of the war.
‡ Letter to E. Samios.
§ Big Russian shops.
‖ We had agreed that any sentence beginning with the words *But I assure you* would have the opposite meaning of what it expressed.

leap—like monkeys. You feel they are cruel, inhuman, thieving, clever, without any impulse of the spirit. . . . And yet the other day in Khabarovsk, while I was watching the sunset over the ice of the vast Amur River, I heard an old Chinese man softly singing, as he sat all curled up gazing at the river. A monotonous, plaintive song, like a lullaby, full of passion. Suddenly I realized that he too was my distant and alienated brother, and my heart bounded. I looked at him—he looked exactly like a consumptive ape—and when he turned around and caught sight of me he fell silent and curled up still more.*

Siberia, February 20, 1929

I'm on my way back, crossing Siberia in the opposite direction. In just a few days the snow has already diminished. Once again I've arranged my things for a week in the compartment—as far as Krasnoyarsk. Alone, mute, sometimes staring out at the unending steppes, sometimes correcting The Odyssey, sometimes meditating and smoking. . . . In Vladivostok I didn't find a single book to read and so I'm left alone to my own resources. I mustn't let boredom and sadness get the better of me. The days and the nights must pass without the brain's growing dim and sleepy. I'm thinking of many things, ripening decisions, outlining inside myself paths of work and of conduite de vie [conduct of life]. I feel that this heavy isolation and silence will do me a lot of good. . . .†

February 21, 1929

. . . I'm well, my spirit calm. Whatever happens, the solitude has done me good; my vitals have been refreshed by the silence.‡

February 22, 1929

. . . I've not uttered a word all day long, and my mouth feels pure and sanctified, as though I'd taken Communion. I believe that there's nothing more sublime than silence.§

Evening, February 23, 1929

This day is over too. All alone in the compartment, I've been working on The Odyssey. Ah, if I were free to begin all 24 books at

---

* Letter to E. Samios.
† Letter to E. Samios.
‡ Letter to E. Samios.
§ Letter to E. Samios.

once! I feel so elated that the days go by like lightning. Do you remember how our own days used to fly like lightning? Do you remember how our hours would fly in Moscow when, before we went to sleep in the evening, we would correct a line of verse? When will I see you? When will we correct together again, and the hours pass for the two of us like lightning? Everything will come true; all will go well. I am very hopeful. . . .

I forgot to tell you, this morning I got off the train and bought a roast goose. The weather was 42 degrees below zero. I touched the iron knob of the train to climb up and the frozen iron burned my hand. The coach is well heated. Every night I get undressed between the pink sheets* and have a good rest. These sheets and the teapot† are precious. But not the nose-protector, because the moment I put it on, my breath forms a crust of ice on my eyeglasses, and I can't see. My body and legs are very warm at all times. And my hands and ears. Only the face suffers now and then.‡

Krasnoyarsk, February 28, 1929

A pleasant, insignificant city. Everywhere, Soviet uniformity. Whatever is local, picturesque, primeval has been abolished. . . . Everything is a bad provincial copy of Moscow. In Vladivostok, there used to be a brilliant old Chinese theater. I wanted to go. "Remont!"— They've "restored" it; i.e., made it Soviet, à la Moscow. I'm afraid I'll find the same thing in Turkestan. We're seeing Russia too late. . . .§

On the way to Novosibirsk

. . . I'm in a hurry to get inside Old Russia and stop in a small town, perhaps Rostov, to rest and see everything we saw together in Novgorod. All the cities of Siberia are new, copies of the imperial style. . . .‖

March 4, 1929

. . . We're just approaching Omsk. . . . It's 3 p.m. and perhaps, if I don't like Omsk very much, I'll leave tonight for Sverdlovsk. What is

---

* Bilili and I had devised some pink sleeping bags.
† A miniature Sterno-fueled teapot, a gift from the Greek writer and friend of N.K., Theotokas.
‡ Letter to E. Samios.
§ Letter to E. Samios.
‖ Letter to E. Samios.

most tiring is having to wait for the train at every station three, four, five hours, because they never know exactly how much delay there's going to be. Yesterday I waited for the train from 8 p.m. until 1 a.m. I smoke my pipe, of course, and drink tea, eat, write—but the atmosphere is so polluted that I have to look out to avoid getting a headache and to keep my stomach in a state to resist. I'm glad you aren't here to suffer like this, without any worthwhile recompense. . . .

Another bad thing about Siberia: everywhere, strong wind! How the légende of windlessness was born I don't know. Today it's 15 degrees below zero and the wind is so violent that it's torture to stand outside. And when we were in Irkutsk, it was 45 degrees below, and windy. . . .

P.S. Besides the book of Berdyaef, Un Nouveau Moyen-Age,* which I already wrote you to order, please order also La Trahison des Clercs by Benda. I'll need them very much for the works on Russia.†

Vologda, March 6, 1929

I've entered the ancient Holy Russia. A Jewish woman from Poland grabbed me at the station and took me by force to her home, where she has a bed for foreigners. So I spent the night in a Jewish family, spoke German, rested. The city is marvelous, full of churches with fig-shaped domes, all green and indigo and gold. Along the right and left banks of a little river running through the city, the monasteries—très élégants, très élancés [very elegant, very delicate]—are reminiscent of Novgorod. But rassurez-vous, Novgorod is more beautiful. . . .‡

Jaroslaw

A pleasant city, nothing extraordinary. Lots of churches and, above all, a monastery in the middle of the city, like the Kremlin. Its churches are now warehouses, the columns collapsed, the doors dangling. Beautiful discrètes frescoes, buried in snow, half effaced. The view of the frozen Volga is superb; a small, small bell tower with a saxon-blue dome is a miracle. In the museum I saw our ideal samovar, in red. . . . I keep always on the lookout for beautiful kustari,§ a samovar, etc.—but

---

* Literally, A New Medieval Period.
† Letter to E. Samios.
‡ Letter to E. Samios.
§ The famous wooden objects—bowls, spoons, boxes—painted by the ikon painters when they no longer had a clientele for ikons.

nothing. Only in houses in the villages can you find them, they tell me. . . .*

March 9, 1929

Today I have you very much on my mind. I saw two marvelous things: two churches painted from top to bottom with frescoes that are inexpressibly sweet and refreshing. Identical with the ones on the boxes† we saw in Nizhni Novgorod, only the colors were unusual. Remind me to tell you about these churches in Jaroslaw, because they're one of the most beautiful things in Russia. . . .‡

Rostov, March 10, 1929

A pleasant old town—but not so prenante et intime [engaging and intimate] as Novgorod. All day long I wandered through the churches— a uniquely Russian type, beautiful ikons, a wonderful angel's head. But nothing overwhelmed me. Tonight I'm leaving for Moscow. The weather is horrid, wind, snow, frost. . . .§

Moscow, March 11, 1929

The moment I reached Moscow, I went to Itka's, where I found your two letters. . . . I was glad to read them and to see that you are well and are not forgetting me. I roamed all over Moscow to find a hotel. . . . Itka told me, bursting with anger, that Istrati gave a dreadful interview to the Nouvelles Littéraires. She says that everyone here is against him and says that one had best keep an eye on friends like him. . . .||

From March 13 to March 20, Kazantzakis waited in vain for the permit he needed to go on to Turkestan. He finally decided to dispense with it.

Moscow, March 21, 1929

My love, tomorrow I'm leaving for Turkestan, and I'll just let them send me back. I hope everything will go all right. . . .

---

* Letter to E. Samios.
† Again the painted koustari.
‡ Letter to E. Samios.
§ Letter to E. Samios.
|| Letter to E. Samios.

[Stefan] Zweig is a splendid critic. I don't like so much any of his novellas that I've read. Try to read J. Roth's Die Flucht ohne Ende.* One more book I want you to order for me is Guehenno's Caliban Parle. . . .†

I'm thinking of The Odyssey day and night. My God, what imperfections! What dreadful lines! How shameful! A terrifying, cruel, épuisant [exhausting] reworking. You witnessed the history of the first line: saw what I went through till I reached the final form. And you have seen how rich it is now, how mature, immediately conveying a breath of fresh air. . . . That's the way I must suffer for all the 33,333 lines that are to make up The Odyssey. And that's why I need a high mountain and tranquillity—in order to come out alive.

My Lenotschka, I am always hoping that you will help me and that we shall suffer together many times for these verses. . . .‡

Orenburg, March 24, 1929

. . . Snow everywhere, occasionally landscapes of a very soft blue; the Volga frozen, and Samara, which we went through yesterday, looked different. It's hard to believe that this desolate, snowbound wasteland could ever give birth to the watermelons, apples and pomegranates we saw last year. . . .

We've come into Kazakhstan. There's snow—but I saw a black horse and a rider racing as though it were a sandy desert; and suddenly in a village to my right I spied the green cupola of a mosque. My heart leaped—we've entered a Moslem land.

A marvelous camel on the endless, snow-covered plain, drawing a wagon. The isbas are starting to be whitewashed, and the sight of the white houses on the snow is wonderful. The Orient is commencing. In one station a woman with yellow pantaloons. An old man has come into the compartment, and now I can hear him singing Oriental songs in a melodious, rhythmical voice. I absolutely must go to Bukhara.§

March 25, 1929

Daybreak found us on a desolate stretch of yellow sand, with sparse patches of snow. Small, undulating hillocks, rows of stumpy reeds struggling to restrain the rippling of the desert—like on the desert of

---

* Literally, Flight without End.
† Literally, Caliban Speaks.
‡ Letter to E. Samios.
§ Letter to E. Samios.

Astrakhan, you remember? A tepid wind, springtime, houses with low terraces, camels, people wearing colorful Tartar caps—we're shifting terrain; at last we're plunging deep into Asia.*

March 26, 1929

We've reached a little city at the border of Turkestan. When I got off at the station, there were people with odd wigs, wrapped in green and red quilts, and an efendi† with his legs crossed, reciting the Koran and begging, his lap full of potatoes, onions, apples and pennies.

By evening we'll be in Tashkent. There the fate of my trip will be decided. I've made up my mind to succeed at all costs.‡

Evening, March 26, 1929

. . . We've reached Tashkent. Now we're going on toward Samarkand. No one has asked me for my permit. I hope there's no danger now. Tomorrow around noon I'll set foot in the celebrated city of Alexander the Great and Tamerlane. I feel strongly moved, and at the same time sad that you aren't with me. . . .

I got off for a minute at the first station after Tashkent, famous for its apples. It was night. I caught sight of some marvelous apples and ran. Just as I got my hands full, the train began pulling out. I clung to it and caught it. I was just in time. Marvelous huge apples and once again I feel that when I die—you will be at my bedside—you mustn't forget that one of the greatest delights of my life has been fruit. And bring heaps of them, for me to bid them farewell. . . .§

Samarkand! March 27, 1929

My love,

I'm in a fairy-tale city, out of the Thousand and One Nights. At daybreak I opened the curtain of the compartment onto a meadow of flowering almond trees. Sun, heat, trees budding, gardens and water, Moslems with multicolored jelab cloaks, colored blankets, good-natured donkeys, camels. It's noon now, and I'm wandering around—the bazaar is superb, Moslem, a flamboyant throng, Mongol faces, women wearing thick feridgi veils, and all around, heavenly ruins all of Saxon blue and

---

* Letter to E. Samios.
† A Moslem.
‡ Letter to E. Samios.
§ Letter to E. Samios.

green majolica, like those at Yerevan, the tomb of Tamerlane and the Bibi Khan in the middle of the city, around the bazaar. . . . From time to time, a splendid minaret, a turquoise cupola. Everywhere people in bright-colored rags, hubbub, mud, an exquisite fragrance from the flowering almond and at the same time a vile stench of stagnant water and urine. It's very hot. I'm walking about without a jacket. Hodja Mouratof has found me and taken me to his home—a cool house made of mud, very beautiful carpets on the floor, and on each side four little lace-covered cages of canaries. Old coffers, Arab ewers, the women out of sight in the female quarters. He opened one coffer and showed me coins from the time of Alexander the Great, etc. . . . I bought a large embroidered tablecloth from him—an old Indian one—and a beautiful piece of majolica that came from the grave of the Bibi Khan. I also bought some skullcaps. . . .*

Samarkand, March 28, 1929

. . . All day long today I've been wandering around—mosques, "tsarsia,"† streets—eating melons and grapes, wearing an embroidered skullcap, reveling in the indescribable exotic spectacle. As for mosques, the one in Omar is superior because it is intact. Here there are several huge ones, but they are in ruins—half a cupola, heavenly green in color, broken columns, minarets that are already leaning at a slant in the Yerevan style. . . .

But as a city, as couleur asiatique, it is infinitely superior to Jerusalem. This is the heart of the Orient. An exotic vision, these colorful quilts and capes, these green and white and yellow turbans, and these red slippers turned up like gondolas. As in the Persian miniatures. . . . How I longed for you to be with me! . . .‡

From Samarkand to Bukhara

Noon, Friday; I'm leaving. A very sweet plain, a summer's day, bedeckt [cloudy]. Flowering almond trees; clay villages; people garbed in festive red; light, hot clouds. My heart is pounding because in five hours I'll be in Bukhara. . . .§

---

* Letter to E. Samios.
† Shop districts.
‡ Letter to E. Samios.
§ Letter to E. Samios.

When I arrived (the station, you know, is 13 kilometers from the city, to keep the women of Bukhara from being seduced), it was already nighttime. The burning heat had waned and a very sweet, cool breeze was blowing. Suddenly I found myself in the heart of Bukhara, swarming with Moslems taking their evening stroll. Imagine them all dressed as bishops and archbishops, wearing high miters. Zurna pipes;* the shouts of café waiters; chick-pea vendors; beggars; a santuri;† the cafés strewn with carpets, and thousands of people sitting on them, legs crossed; the singers in the middle—a beautiful young boy and three old men with very shrill voices; intermingled scents (as you know them)— spices, jasmine, urine. The whole old city covered with a wooden ceiling, as though you were walking in a house. Only one hotel and that a horrible one. . . . I strolled around until midnight, discovering in the faint light the mammoth, shiny, desolate mosques. I slept very badly.

At dawn I was roaming around. And now, here are my conclusions: Bukhara is more Oriental, more of a desert [city] than Samarkand. The houses all lower and all of mud, the walls with only one tiny window, high up like a loophole. When the wind blows as it did today (already hot and horrible), the houses peel and the dust is unbearable. The people here do not wear such a mixture of colors as in Samarkand. Everything is gray, like the dust, like the sand; the houses are low and terraced. And suddenly, out of this gray, muddy surface, there dart the turquoise miracles: the round cupolas with a discrète pointed peak (like beautiful female breasts), the exquisite mosques. Here one realizes to what extent the great moments of civilization sacrifice all individuals in order to glorify an idea. All these people's houses, built of mud and straw, have been sacrificed in order to erect the house of their God in their midst. What élégance in the mosques of Bukhara! While those of Yerevan [and even the one in Omar] are slightly trapus [squat], here they are slender. Their cupola rests on a delicate belt, which gives it airiness and lightness.

The bazaar not worth mentioning, Soviétisé [Sovietized]. I searched for your ring all day long, in vain. The jewelers now are Russians and Caucasians, and you can imagine the miserable pacotille [junk] . . . Conclusion: Samarkand was a revelation of the warmth and color of the Orient. Bukhara has something of the classical

---

* Russian bagpipes, called zurna pipes in the Caucasus region.
† A stringed instrument of the Orient with a melancholy sound.

Oriental: line, color, it is discrète [restrained]. It is thrice-enchanting to a soul in love with the desert. Only both are now coming to their end; they are beginning to become civilized, that is, they're losing their soul and have begun aping Moscow, which apes Europe, which apes America.

I'm leaving for Merv [Mary], the great city swallowed up by the desert a century ago, the Pompeii of the desert. I don't want to stay in Bukhara any longer, because I know I shall lose the feeling it has given me. . . .*

March 31, 1929

I passed through Merv; I stayed there only one hour, needed no more. When an Oriental city is destroyed, the ruins don't amount to much. Walls of mud stretched out over the desert, barely distinguishable from the earth. Only the mosque (if it exists) preserves traces of beauty. In Merv, there is no mosque. . . . I'm traveling in the direction of Ahmedabad, to catch the train for Tashkent. . . . A horrid desert, Kara Kum, unbearable heat. I'm suffocating in my compartment, the dust penetrates into it, and I keep breathing the earth. I can imagine what it must be like in summer. The temperature goes up to 80 degrees [176 Fahrenheit]! And all the natives here are like savages—dressed in heavy clothes, thick pink stockings, and huge sheepskin caps, three times the size that the Caucasians wear. To my left now, a very short distance away, gleam the mountains of Persia. A few hours on foot and I could reach them. If I could only climb the mountain and look at the plain below! Clouds, muggy heat, a few trees in bloom at the stations. . . .†

Tashkent, April 2, 1929

A dull city after Samarkand and Bukhara. . . . I've done with Turkestan. What remains? The colorful human flood of Samarkand; the compact, exquisite vision of Bukhara; and the terrible desert of Kara Kum. With these three treasures, I'm returning to Moscow, to get ready for Berlin. Perhaps I'll be in time for us to go together and see the cherry trees in bloom in Werder. . . .‡

---

* Letter to E. Samios.
† Letter to E. Samios.
‡ Letter to E. Samios.

. . . All these long hours in the coach, I've been reflecting how my life is going to waste. I've done nothing of the things I might have done. If I were to die tomorrow, the world would be none the poorer. I've scattered my power over a multitude of roads, instead of concentrating it on one single point with all the determination and passion I'm capable of. It's high time for me to concentrate. My great thirst for travel has been appeased by my overdose of it for the whole past year. I must now take advantage of my glutted state to concentrate. At all costs I must be able to keep a long way away from Greece. I must write the two books, and they must be published, and then The Odyssey. But even this no longer gives me enough room. I feel an inexpressible bitterness. What I want is something else. What I want I can attain if I impel all my powers in that direction. I would have to presuppose that all these years have been merely preparation, and that the preparation must now end. I still have forty years left to live. They're enough, provided that I cease to dissipate anything on ephemeral matters outside my own purpose. "It is not human beings that interest me, but the flame that consumes human beings." This brief sentence which I have come upon in recent months sheds light upon my spirit in a perfect way and helps me a great deal in the decision and the scope of the decision. All that is monstrous and inhuman about me, as well as all the super-human impulse sweeping through me—all the Dämonisches [demonic] —is explained perfectly by this sentence. My contact with people and ideas, and my distance from them, become comprehensible in these terms. And through all the thronging details of my own individual life and of the totality, I can in this way distinguish the "Red Line" which I am following and which is following me.*

April 5, 1929

Last night at midnight our train was slightly derailed. The coach I was in was hurtled off the tracks and got disconnected from the others. Women's shrieks, etc., but no one suffered any harm. And so I narrowly escaped having my sadness end for good.

The return trip goes on with some difficulty. . . . I can stand everything except the stench. . . . Ever since I clarified my idiosyncrasy in that brief sentence I quoted to you yesterday, I understand why I cannot have any external contact with what we call the "people,"

---

* Letter to E. Samios.

popular feeling, equality. And so I'm not making any effort today to accommodate myself for Communist reasons. If I do accommodate myself, it is because I can do with my body as I like and not because I enjoy being with the people. Thus, sometimes a dream (this was often the case in my development as a young man) or a sentence (as now) clarifies my soul once and for all, carving a line that is at long last straight, free of zigzags and rationalized sophistries. And along this line we walk—my thought, my action and myself.

This feeling is not to be identified with what we call "aristocraticism," etc. I feel an extremely deep contact, as well as cohesion and continuity with the masses. But this union is so internal that it bears no relation to external contacts at all. Indeed it is contrary to them. Just as the diamond is the primeval crystallization, the essence, of coal, and yet has no external relation with coal, and indeed is the opposite of it in appearance. And all the same, the diamond is the essence—the sweat or the tear—of all the coals.

My Lenotschka, this letter is coming to sound like a confession and a monologue, precisely because I'm writing you at a moment of crisis. I hardly even noticed that since Orenburg there's once more unending snow, the rivers are all frozen, it's cold and horridly muddy in the stations. The streets of Moscow will be impassable. . . .

I'm eager to see you and touch you. . . .*

1929.   Once in Berlin, forgetting the cherry trees in bloom at Werder, Nikos had but one concern: to acquit himself of his debt to "crucified Russia" and with all possible speed to pick up again his Sisyphean rock.

He gave just one lecture before a select audience. As his custom was, he spoke unequivocally. But whereas in a small group he could hold his listeners under his spell, from the platform he had no gift at all. His throat got tight, his voice faint, and, worse still, he lost his ability to talk extemporaneously. Conscious of his own limitations, he refused to make a second attempt. Friends like Helene Stoecker, Arthur Holitscher, Egon Kisch tried in vain to keep him in the German capital. The hubbub of big cities exhausted him. He found nourishment for his creative energies only in contact with the primeval elements—earth, water, fire, sea.

---

* Letter to E. Samios.

And so, one evening we took the train for "somewhere" in Czecho-slovakia. Could anyone believe me if I insist that we had no idea where we would be getting off?

Huddled in a corner, Kazantzakis was smoking his pipe, indifferent to the smells of garlic and badly digested beer. Suddenly casting aside his usual reserve, he leaned over toward his neighbor, extended his tobacco pouch to him, and picked up a conversation. Fate, in the shape of a Czech miner, was serving as our guide.

"Don't go to Prague! Get off with me at Joachimsthal. And don't be frightened when you see our enormous cemetery. Radium is no joke . . . But three hours' walk farther on, 1,200 meters up, there's Gottesgab. Even if you wanted to, you wouldn't be able to die there."

"Gottesgab . . . Gottesgab . . . Gift of God . . . ," murmured Nikos, nudging me with his elbow. "Lenotschka, my love, do you still believe in miracles?"

We meditated a long time before the impressive cemetery of Joachimsthal. The path was steep, and it was nightfall by the time we reached the outskirts of the village. Dead tired, we slept at the first inn we came to. Next morning, without even investigating what possibilities Gottesgab might offer us, Nikos led me onto a long, straight road.

"I've got a hunch, Lenotschka," he said, "that the miracle is waiting for us, curled up like a little animal. It's up to us not to come back empty-handed."

I've always trusted my companion when it was a question of finding us new lodgings. This time, once more, he had taken the shortest path to discover what was to become for us synonymous with happiness. A vast sunlit clearing, rimmed by fir trees and larches; here and there, sprouting like daisies, the substantial rough-plastered, whitewashed homes of the foresters.* Tiny Mr. Kraus and his wife A-n-n-n-n-a listened deferentially:

"Jawohl, Herr Direktor! Come this way, Frau Direktor! Be so kind as to look at our house. You won't lack anything. . . . We'll tend to that."

"Director" and "Directress" of the wind, we took possession of our new quarters. And thus began life with the solar rhythm.

Two spacious, many-windowed rooms on the second floor; plump

---

* This little agglomeration of foresters' houses was indeed called Förster-häuser.

eiderdown quilts we used to struggle with every night to make them cover both our feet and our shoulders at the same time; meticulously clean and everything, including the service, at the most modest price. On the ground floor stood the cattle shed—washed twice a day with great sprays of hot water—a gurgling spring, and the kitchen with the fire that never went out. No disagreeable farm odors, but an animal warmth in the air, the house breathing in unison with the distended breathing of the cows. There was also a rooster like all the roosters in the world, a few white hens, a tawny goat. Some deer strolled beneath our windows, and trout leaped in the stream flowing across our meadow. The foresters did very little coming and going among themselves. The farms became linked to each other only when the postman made his morning rounds, invisibly interlacing them.

In this profound peace, Nikos wrote his book on Soviet Russia. On the trans-Siberian train taking him to Vladivostok, he had been planning to write a two-volume work of 800 to 1,000 pages, with the forbidding title *Homo Bolshevicus, Homo Meta-Bolshevicus.* But all that emerged from his pen at that point was one tiny volume, "stirring and apocalyptic," according to Grasset, midway between a novel and a book of confessions, with a title that still amazes people—*Toda Raba.* Why *Toda Raba,* which means "Thank you" in Hebrew? Quite simply because it sounded well to the ear.

This confession in the form of a novel [Kazantzakis wrote on the first page of his manuscript] *has but one hero. Azad, Geranos, Sou-ki, Rahel, Amita, Ananda, and the Big-Jawed Man are merely different facets of a single consciousness that experienced and mirrored the complex, fluid, many-sided reality of the Soviet Union. . . .*
Only the Negro is outside—and above—the hero.

The Negro in question is Toda Raba; his creator Nikos Kazantzakis, the man who in 1929 foresaw the awakening of Africa at Lenin's call. Just as in 1927, he had foreseen the role that Egypt would play in the Islamic world, the decline of the British Empire and the ideological war destined to break out between the old Communists who had "arrived" and the young Communists who were still struggling and felt betrayed by their own precursors.

The state of his own soul and his conclusions on what he was able to see and understand in the U.S.S.R. Kazantzakis described to Mihali

217

Anastassiou,* to whom he was in the habit of writing long letters for Anastassiou to read to their mutual friends. Several excerpts follow:

After my big trip to Russia, where I saw and studied a multitude of people, events and landscapes, after my solitude here in the tranquillity of a lone mountain, and on the eve of a great moment for me, when I am about to begin The Odyssey again—I feel genuinely compelled to speak to you.

The Russian reality I am just beginning to feel—I'm just getting a sense of all its complexity, lack of clarity, contradictions, and above all the necessity it undoubtedly serves. That's why it is now extremely difficult for me to speak about Russia. Before, when I was only imperfectly acquainted with it, I could talk for hours on end and with assurance, supplementing whatever I did not know with my own desires or my own ideas. . . .

I shall merely make a very inadequate attempt to give you an inkling of the general outline my mind is following in its desire to contemplate this great problem. Many things in this outline supplement or make explicit certain of the directions I have previously followed in my own intellectual development. And for this very reason you must scrutinize my conclusions with skepticism. For am I perhaps forcing all the events and ideas I have been experiencing during these years into [the framework of] my own intellectual and psychic necessities? But perhaps this is the human being's inevitable plight. Only some one who has no violent motion inside himself—i.e., the person without soul—can confront ideas and the world with impeccable impartiality. But in that case, the person's opinion is worthless.

Therefore I'm appealing not primarily to your logic, but to the movement existing in your own vitals, longing to stir the world in harmony with its own rhythm. . . . Look at the words I use as "substance"—a very hard, dry kernel, but containing explosive force. In order to find out what I want to say, you must make each word explode inside you and thus free the soul imprisoned in it. Maybe you know the marvelous anecdote about the great Rabbi Nachmann. When he used

---

* This old friend of N.K. (whom we met in the 1925 notebooks from Amorgos), himself a fine poet, used to read these "Reports" to their "circle" in Heraklion. Unfortunately the entire Anastassiou–Kazantzakis file has been lost. Only this particular document remains, owing to the fact that copies of it had been circulated.

to go to the synagogue to pray, he would make his last will and testament and bid a tearful farewell to his wife and children, because he didn't know whether he would come out of the prayer alive. Because, as he used to explain, "When I utter a word—for instance, 'Lord'—I'm overcome with terror. I melt. I don't know if I'll ever be able to leap on to the following words, 'Have mercy.' " Ah, if one could only read a lyric in that way, or talk to one's wife, or scan the letter of a friend.

. . . Experiencing Russia face to face—that is, turning a dream into reality—I reached the following conclusion: Attainment is inferior to the assault. A dangerous, painful conclusion, which can never be useful as a practical basis for human action. The exalted moment of intoxication cannot last long. Inspiration necessarily becomes constricted and humiliated when it has to be solidified in a word—all this we know. However, it is most painful when you observe this terrible law of human incapacity in the present-day Russian consolidation of the tremendous inspiration. The realization of the ideal has weakened the spirit of the person struggling. And these souls, having reached a balance that appears convenient to them, no longer want to advance. The revolutionaries have become comfortably established; the comfortably established soon wind up as conservatives and little by little the conservatives become reactionaries.

I don't want to rail against this curve, which is necessary and sometimes useful to the evolution of man. It's natural that the human soul cannot long endure a constant tension, and that it wants to rest, to live at last without anxiety, like a plant, and forget. . . .

But here in Russia in particular, we have the following twofold evil: . . . (a) this natural evolution of the spirit toward matter is working itself out too quickly; and (b) since the Russian proletariat is profoundly united with the world proletariat, a premature collapse such as this involves great danger for the comrades who find themselves still at the stage of upsurge preceding the assault. . . .

In order for the masses to be swept away . . . (not only the masses—even the most chosen people) . . . into an assault teeming with so many hazards, it is necessary to find the appropriate slogan. . . . Every era that has created a civilization has had such a slogan, which has often taken the form of a religion. For our own era, the slogan is, beyond dispute, the Communist one. This embraces all the elements of contemporary reality, corresponds to it and magnifies it, as it must do—otherwise it would not be a slogan. The classes of proletariat and bourgeoisie do not exist in such a sharply defined way. There are not two camps with such distinct boundary lines and such a deep chasm between them. But by suddenly defining the two classes with such crystal-clear logic, Marx helped them to achieve an abrupt separation and to acquire the class consciousness they had previously lacked. And in the course of acquiring this class consciousness, they began to range themselves in camps which Marx had assigned to them a priori, by means of his own logic. . . .

It might be useful to recapitulate certain key passages from Nikos Kazantzakis' notebooks and letters of the period 1922–1929 for the purpose of appreciating more clearly how much he suffered to create order out of his aspirations and to leash his heart in a state of permanent ebullience.

The old world was collapsing. In the U.S.S.R. a new world was being born. Man's duty, according to Kazantzakis, was to help this new world grow strong and flourishing.

Under the influence of Galatea and, later on, of his Berlin "Jewesses," he struggled to atrophy the contemplative man and the poet in him—that is, half of his own being—and to hypertrophy the other half, the man of action he was hoping to become one day. Clairvoyant to excess, ever since his first trip to the U.S.S.R. in 1925, he had foreseen what would be the great obstacle for him:

For the human masses—workers, peasants, women—to enjoy themselves, to eat better, to become enlightened is certainly a goal worthy of man. But I regard all these things as petty, practical illusions, crumbs for my heart, which when it has eaten is hungrier than before.*

He was equally clairvoyant in regard to himself:

Whatever I've written seems to me unworthy and provincial. My cry has been heard by only a very few people in one meager little corner of the world—and most of them faithless and malicious. And I look at these women and muzhiks, and I know that my voice will never reach them, because the means I use are weak. . . .†

---

* Letter of November 20, 1925, supra, p. 130.
† Letter of October 25, 1927, supra, p. 168.

The exclusively materialistic content of Communism did not satisfy him. He was vainly seeking for something else among the innumerable delegates who had come to Moscow for the tenth anniversary of the October Revolution:

I'm in the grip of a violent impulse to stop looking at things and institutions and to see people. Chinese, Japanese, Swedes, Americans— innumerable souls. And with an eagerness at once indiscrète and barbarous, I go out of myself to see what they are bringing. So far . . . I haven't found anyone with so high a tension of the spirit as my own or so lofty a form of psychic torment. But all these people have completed a work and have an influence that I lack. . . .*

And he foresaw the curve that was still invisible but, alas, inevitable:

The tempo of life in Russia has changed. It's different from 1925 now. The official rhythm is calmer. There is a certain embourgeoisement. The arrivistes are arrivés, and they no longer even budge. The women have begun relapsing to their lower natures. The men are tired. Fortunately, the great internal struggle between Trotsky and Stalin gives new life and fire to the Russian spirit. . . .†

At the same time that the revolutionary half of him was clamoring for a militant life, the other half—the poet—was suffering from having to languish in inactivity:

I feel no joy in my heart. What I'd like now above all else would be to remain quietly in one spot and work. . . .‡

And again:

Ah, if I could only find peace somewhere and scud along in The Odyssey!§

---

* Letter of November 3, 1927, supra, p. 170.
† Letter of November 4, 1927, supra, p. 170.
‡ Letter of April 17, 1928, supra, p. 182.
§ Letter of May 9, 1928, supra, p. 186.

Kazantzakis' wish for peace was at last to be granted. And in the silence and seclusion of Gottesgab, he would be able to complete his "mission" toward the U.S.S.R. No sooner had *Toda Raba* been tied up and sent off to Rieder's than he plunged into another novel, which he also wrote in French, *Kapetan Elias*, whose hero was his own father. And he began preparing himself, over a long period of time, wisely though not without impatience, to immerse himself in *The Odyssey*, the great adventure.

I had to leave Gottesgab for the cure at Plombières. Left alone, Nikos passed through brief fits of anguish. And yet Gottesgab remained for him a sparkling memory, so unbelievably beautiful and beneficent that he came to wonder later on if it had ever existed except in a dream.

Nikos Kazantzakis was not indifferent to Istrati's revolt against Russian Communism in general or to the important role played by Victor Serge in that development. If Istrati had a brain "no bigger than a linnet's," Victor Serge on the contrary was a tried and tested revolutionary. We had stayed in his home in Leningrad, just before his exile to Siberia. He had translated Trotsky. He had known Lenin intimately from the early days, and all of Lenin's comrades. You could have confidence in him. But, undoubtedly under the influence of Istrati, he became wary of the Cretan poet who used to lose himself in long "mystical" discussions with the poet Nikolai Kliouev. . . . Now that Panaït Istrati's writings had stirred up resentment against the U.S.S.R., Kazantzakis felt even more regretful that he had not tried to break the ice between himself and Victor Serge. Which explains the querulous tone in the following letter, something that we rarely find in his correspondence.

Gottesgab, August 10, 1929

Dear Serge,

You have given me up on the grounds that I always bring something very poignant and painful back to your mind. We hardly listened to one another at all. There are a lot of reasons for it; about some of them "il tacere e bello [silence is golden]." One admissible reason is the following: I am not a Marxist, and consequently in your eyes I lack the capacity to grasp the contemporary reality. I am not a Marxist, first of all because the metaphysical sense is not sufficiently to the fore in me; I cannot content myself with hypersimplified affirmations and negations. Next, because I am not a man of action. If I were a man of action, Marxism would be very suitable for me and for our own time, a most rigorous and seminal rule of action. The only one.

You have seen nothing in me but a mystic! Or, rather, a Bücherwurm [bookworm]! I've just written a confession in the form of a novel about the U.S.S.R. There's a character in it, a Negro, Toda Raba. I hope that you will read this book, and in this Negro you will then see my own real countenance, profound and alexandrinophagos. . . .*

All the other masks—the seven that act in this book—are but convenient masks I wear in order to be able to circulate in society and to be able to converse with my own kind with a certain rational, calm civility.

In me you have discerned only the most superficial masks, and that is why, when I think of you, dear Serge, I feel this bitterness. It is because you are not a matter of indifference to me, and I wish I could love you as a brother in arms. And now this is not possible.   N.†

Gottesgab, Thursday, August 1929

I read Panaït's article immediately. Horrible! The article is very well written and vivid, impressionnant, reportage sensationnel [stirring, sensationalistic journalism]. But everything he says about Russia and the unfair, superficial way he has of generalizing from a single cas [case] make this article revoltant and macabre. Beyond doubt what Panaït says is true. But it's one side—out of many—of the truth. Anyone who generalizes the evil or the good in this way is either superficial or dishonorable. Panaït is merely superficial, passionnant [arousing passion] and [himself] passionné [responding with passion]. This article will do harm in Russia. In general il me révolte [I'm disgusted with it], because by getting bogged down in a single cas Panaït has forgotten whatever good he saw and touched in Russia. This is ingratitude, triviality, a pose. . . .

Whitman is a great joy. This is a great work‡ and we shall read it together regularly. It's all wind, sea, light, joy. . . .§

---

* That is to say, anti-scholarly.
† This letter to Victor Serge was in French in the original and was copied in N.K.'s hand into his notebook.
‡ Leaves of Grass.
§ Postcard to E. Samios.

223

I'm working well; in a few days Kapetan Elias will be finished, and then I'll begin it again for the final version. But if we don't manage a contrat, I shan't be in the mood to finish it. The agony with the publisher all over again will exhaust me. . . . Whatever happens, I beg you not to worry. All this is dans l'ordre des choses [in the order of things]. . . .

*Look for good books on Africa, the Pole, wild beasts. . . . Yesterday I corrected a few lines of The Odyssey. Ah, what a difference! Involuntarily I've adopted the rhythm of the popular song. And this has always been my ideal: sublime content and simple form. . . .**

Friday

. . . It's raining today and it's morning and I'm waiting for the postman. This agony is unbearable, and if we don't have a contract for Kapetan Elias, I won't send it. The torment of waiting will ruin all the quality of the year, and I won't be able to devote myself single-mindedly to The Odyssey. . . .†

Calling me sometimes his "Feminine St. George," and sometimes "little fish," Nikos exaggerated the effectiveness of the steps I was taking. Helene Stoecker had had little or no success in Berlin. Grehtlein and Drei Masken Verlag had loved *Toda Raba,* but did not dare to publish it. A very small number of articles about the U.S.S.R. were published in the German newspapers. Fortunately, they paid well, which allowed us to prolong our stay in the mountains. But in France our great hope—Robertfrance—was procrastinating. Did he want to gain time so that the volumes of Panaït Istrati could be read before the disturbance that would eventually be provoked by a testimonial such as *Toda Raba?*

While he felt gratitude for any pertinent criticism, Nikos had little taste for French irony. Obliged to keep him informed, I could hardly spare him the bitterness of some of my encounters. The reception reserved for me, for example, by the director of Editions Montaigne, Mr. Aubier, who received me without ceremony—"Come back in a week for my answer."

I had made the mistake of handing him along with the manuscript a laudatory letter from a German publisher, in which "genius" was

---

* Postcard to E. Samios.
† Postcard to E. Samios.

mentioned. After a week that seemed to me longer than a year, I knocked on the door at the appointed hour, and heard his "answer":

"Ha-ha-ha! A genius! Allow me to laugh! Who is this gentleman who speaks in the first person? Whom does he take himself for? Oh well, tell him from me that he will never be read in France!"

As I write this, a far more sinister adventure comes back to my mind. The year 1940—Hitler at our heels—Paris in chaos. The ministries were burning their archives. Radiodiffusion française had crumpled, and the broadcasts devoted to Greece hit bottom—a knife they twisted in our wounds. With the intention of being useful, I presented myself at the Hotel Continental. After a lot of interminable corridors, I found myself face to face with the director general. A general of the familiar type: stuffed and glib. "You're Greek, you say? Hmm . . . Greece and the Greeks! At the first cannon blast you'll all fill your breeches!" Fortunately history proved the contrary!

[Gottesgab, August 25, 1929]
Sunday

Beloved,

   . . . I've just read the biography of Cromwell. Run-of-the-mill. . . . Rimbaud, Stevenson, Molière very good. Jeremiah* criard [shrill], garrulous, mediocre. Several good scenes, but no condensation, no dash, no bold originality. Zweig is a superb critique. We must get his Dostoyevsky at Rieder's. . . .†

On September 1, 1929, from Gottesgab, he wrote his friend Edvige:

Ah, how good it feels to be talking a bit with you! For a whole month I've been absolutely alone and virtually not a single word has left my mouth. I feel elated and sad and free, like a rabbit dancing away under the full moon. I feel that life is terrifying and simple, and only human beings are petty and complicated. I could live here, on this abandoned mountain, for years and generations on end. There is everything I need: air and wind and forests and a few cows; and my head is

---

* A tragedy by Stefan Zweig.
† Postcard to E. Samios.

teeming with landscapes, dreams, flowers and monsters, and with nuova ed antica pazzia [new and ancient folly].

From time to time a slight shudder passes across my contented back; this frenzied love of solitude fills me with a sacred terror. I remember another time, when I was on the peak of Mt. Taygetus. I had a little house. I was alone with a few tall pines in the courtyard. Every evening when I drew the great iron bolt and locked the door and heard the grating of the bolt, I shuddered with happiness; and I promised myself that when I die I would take this bolt and try to find a way to smuggle it into Paradise along with me. . . .

"Frenzied" love of "inexorable," "implacable," "sacred" solitude— these cries return again and again in your correspondence. And yet there are also such admissions as these: "I'm not sleeping well." . . . "I have nightmares." . . . "I don't know why, there's a horrible anguish gripping me." . . .

You thought you didn't know why you couldn't sleep well, you who always slept like a child. You thought you didn't know why you were gripped by the horrible anguish. But your own subconscious knew: the demons laid siege to you as soon as you remained alone, and you could find your equilibrium again only near some friend or, still better, some loving woman, provided that the "mating" was consummated. For with the descent of the spirit—recall the spark of fire implanted by the angel in the Apostle's skull—each time the work acquired its original form, spread out on the virgin paper, there followed fever, nausea, exhaustion. . . . Then only the solitude of "two almonds in the same shell," the miracle sung by the awe-struck Cretan rhapsodist:

> What then this miracle?
> A man and a woman—strangers
> Become one another's own
> And trusty friends as well.

Only this miracle could come to your help.

Gottesgab, September 28, 1929

My beloved:

. . . I avoid writing you letters, because, I don't know why, but the moment I start to write, a bitterness insurmontable m'envahit [an

226

insurmountable (bitterness) invades me], something inexplicable and so deep that I cannot control it. And so I would upset you to no avail. Whereas you must have all the insouciance [freedom from care] to look after your own body and get cured. . . .

My life goes by calmly here, without any change. I wake up early, lie in your bed, correct The Odyssey. The milk comes. I eat. The weather—curses on it—is marvelous, forcing me to go outside. I rove far away, beyond the forest, four or five hours. Then I come back and eat. They don't even ask me what they should cook any more: Erbsen [peas], Bohnen [beans], potatoes. The biscuits you made are still here. I don't drink tea at five o'clock, because I don't like it. Tea, as you know, is just an excuse for me to join a person I love, and no more than that. I go to Wiesenthal* often, to get tired and perhaps be able to sleep in the evening. . . . I come back and sleep badly, even though all the windows are wide open and a heavenly breeze is blowing. I have nightmares, I long for day to break, and yet tremble at its coming; and the same life begins all over again. . . .†

Gottesgab, Monday morning
[September 1929]

My love,

I got the books this morning. . . . Since very early I'd been copying and correcting Kapetan Elias. And suddenly, here before me, the pile of books! I abandoned the manuscripts, and didn't know where to begin. You know about l'âne de Buridan [Buridan's ass]. That's what happened to me. I leafed nervously through all of them, and finally selected Les Bêtes qu'on dit sauvages. . . .‡

I want the vision of Crete to emerge perfect, and that's why I need to leave Kapetan Elias a few more months; I mustn't be in a hurry. I wrote Robertfrance to thank him, and told him how vital it is that Toda Raba be well launched, to keep it from getting submerged in the mass of books being published about Russia. . . .§

Monday evening

Is Mary going to the Congo? How could we get to go there too and spend a month? That's enough for me to acquire the vision I require for

---

* Oberwiesenthal; a five-hour trek to go there and back.
† Letter to E. Samios.
‡ Literally, The Beasts We Call Wild.
§ Letter to E. Samios.

The Odyssey. And will she leave the little house in Paris? What a pity that we can't be sure we'll be able to live in Paris, so that we could take it. A thousand things now on our minds: your books, my books, publishers, plans, Papandreou, the Congo, India, Kalmouko's arrival, a little trip to Italy for you, The Odyssey, Kapetan Elias, Fieramosca.* . . . Life begins to be something to relish, and I rejoice at feeling you near me. . . .†

1930.   The second version of The Odyssey, begun on October 1, 1929, was nearing the end. And so was our nest egg. This led to new measures, without much hope of success. At regular intervals, P. Prevelakis was sending newspapers, periodicals and books to Nikos, who used to read them and answer, sometimes in a bantering tone, sometimes in the guise of a confession.

He knew that both his young friend and he had all the advantages needed for representing Greece in Paris, at the Institute for Intellectual Collaboration. But he also knew that his friend Papandreou was not omnipotent and could not sway the Minister of Finance‡ to intervene on his behalf. He was also aware that Venizelos did not like him. So how could he find work that would enable him to be useful to his country and also carry on his own creative labor?

At the beginning of this year, Prevelakis was getting ready to write a book about El Greco. His elder, living on a high, snow-enveloped mountain, where a "supraterrestrial tranquillity" reigned, took him under his wing, lavishing advice and encouraging words on him. Kazantzakis had not abandoned his own old plan of writing a book on the great ancestor. He thought so much about it that he even saw a dream about it, and at a later period this dream was to serve him as the starting point for his own book.

Gottesgab, March 15, 1930

. . . Yesterday evening, I had a magnificent dream about El Greco. All night long we were together in his home. We ate, spoke Cretan, laughed. Afterward, I woke up, then fell asleep again and continued the dream. Naturally, I cannot talk about it in words. But I

---

* A novel I was working on at the time.
† Letter to E. Samios.
‡ Maris, a fellow Cretan and supposed friend of N.K.

remember well a throng of details and I've found a plan for later on—to write conversations with El Greco. I felt great joy. . . .*

Sitting at his worktable in summer; in bed with mittens on his hands and 20 degrees below zero in the wintertime, this devil's organist played his organ stops—epics, novels, humoresque comedies—with a fierce air and a steady temper, never ruffled when I used to come in to interrupt him for some trifle or other.

His forearm suspended in mid-air, holding his pencil aloft, he would raise his head with a smile. "We-e-e-elcome," he used to hum in amusement. "Till when?"

Then I would set the cup of coffee, the fruit, or the page for correction on his worktable, happy at his own happiness.

When he abandoned *The Odyssey* to "let it cool," he attacked eternal problems, themes recurring again and again under his pen, like fugues of Bach, never quite the same, always renewed.

He loved to laugh and make others laugh. He loved to stretch out in the sun. He loved to look at the stars, being first to discover them. This used to amuse him, because I would get annoyed.

Long walks along straight paths set the rhythm of his thoughts. He needed words to develop his themes: "English people smoke their pipes. 'Yes,' they say, pensively. 'Yes.' They take their time. The solution matures in silence. We Mediterraneans begin with the word. Our 'yes' or our 'no' is the click setting our thought in motion. Step by step as we invent the word, our thought takes shape."

Toda Raba, Kapetan Elias, the second version of *The Odyssey* (containing no less than 42,000 verses), the *History of Russian Literature,* ten other projects all hurtling against one another to see which would come first. Not a moment to lose.

But even the most robust body, even the best balanced spirit needs a change of climate. After the mountain, we long for the sea—our sea, the Mediterranean, limpid, scented with watermelons, familiar.

The hour for farewells came. Once again, Nikos Kazantzakis' subconscious took a plunge into the future. Just as he was crossing the doorstep, he changed his mind. He opened his suitcase, searched for the one and only copy of *The Odyssey* and laid it in the arms of Philip Kraus.

---

* Letter to P. Prevelakis.

"My friend, I entrust my work to you. Keep it, please, till our return."

"Hadn't we decided to say goodbye for good?"

". . . God took us by the hand and led us here. Let's let him take the initiative again. His paths are unpredictable. . . ."

We had been thinking of staying in Paris awhile, so that Nikos could write the new series of articles for the Elephtheroudakis encyclopedia. On these articles our main hopes were based. To keep our expenses at a minimum, I stayed with my cousin Mary. Our friends Luc and Mily Castanakis found Nikos a pleasantly luxurious room in the Fifteenth Arrondisement.

Unfortunately, Paris proved very inconvenient. To his friends Nikos never complained about the tortures inflicted on him by the demolition of the next-door house or by his landlady's vocal exercises. But he did complain, and rightly so, of not being able to obtain the books he needed for his work. No library—not even the National Library—had any large foreign encyclopedias. Equipped with a letter of recommendation from our embassy, he presented himself at Larousse's. "On principle," the door was shut in his face. And so he was obliged to hand the work back to Elephtheroudakis and for the tenth time we lost a chance to settle in Paris.

On April 19, 1930, Nikos wrote to Edvige from Paris:

Amica cara!

. . . I find myself in this hell of Paris and I'm trying to get out of it as soon as possible. I turn my gaze upon all points of the horizon and know not where to pinpoint it. Ah, "l'isola nostra! [our island!]"— Crete. How like a ship she is, beaten by all the winds. 1930 is here, and we are so far away, so inaccessible. At times, I am seized by a longing to return to Crete and stretch out along her coast and listen to the bitter waves. Or else, to go very far away, in the direction of the islands—the Marquesas, Tahiti, Samoa . . . There is a maritime demon in me, rending me, devouring me, high tide and low tide. I do not want to hear it and I do hear it and I do not know its name and I tremble and smile. Might it be Death, Our-Lady-in-a-Dress-from-beyond-the-Seas? . . .

After three years of freedom, I must work [to earn my living]. . . . Paris oppresses me and depresses me. I feel my spirit dwindling here, like a wild beast being tracked. . . .

And so it was impossible to work in Paris. Kazantzakis did not fold his arms, however. An assiduous correspondence resumed between Paris and Athens. Kazantzakis made suggestions, while Prevelakis examined each possibility at close range and gave advice about which path to take.

The Greek government had just enacted a law which authorized monetary grants as a means of encouraging and regulating the translation of our great classics. Kazantzakis, optimistic as always, exclaimed: "Let's ask to be given the translation of Plato. And why limit ourselves to translation? Let's also make a French-Greek dictionary. Let's translate it into both languages, demotiki and katharevousa.* There is no dictionary of this kind in existence. And it will facilitate the efforts of foreign translators." And as though this were not enough, he went on: "Let's also make a 'Blue Series' of high-quality books destined for the public at large. And what's more, a series of children's books—the best ones, including that grand old devil, Jules Verne."

Kazantzakis wrote to the editors. His young friend tried to persuade them by word of mouth. Two contracts followed. One was from Elephtheroudakis for a series of children's books, leaving Kazantzakis free to choose the books, the language and the kind of adaptation he intended to make. The other contract was from Dimitrakos senior and involved compiling the famous French-Greek dictionary. Each of the two men was to translate approximately 40,000 words. And then each would check the other's work. These two contracts brought back the sunlight. Nikos bristled with impatience.

"I'm going off to look for a beach. It's out of the question not to find the counterpart of Gottesgab near the sea. . . ."

"Let me come with you. You've suffered so much recently."

"Me? . . . Suffered? . . . Where do you get that? You remember only the unpleasant things, Lenotschka, whereas I think only of the joys I've had."

And he laughed, squeezing my shoulders till they ached and embroidering upon Plelo Street and the singing prowesses of his landlady:

"She was a 'singing teacher,' so she told me, and had 'flocks of pupils.' I never saw a single one. Only her toy poodle Hector, who kept the basso continuo while Madame settled herself at the piano. In order to be polite, the first day I tried to pet Hector. . . . 'No, no! Don't do

---

* The spoken tongue and the purist tongue, as we have already seen.

231

that! And what's more, don't come too close to me. He's jealous, my little Hector, a real Othello. . . . By jingo, he's even jealous of my deceased husband! Every time I decorate his photograph with flowers, Hector begins weeping. . . . And d'you know what my name is? I'll give you ten guesses . . . Madame Rossignol [Nightingale], the finest little songbird in the Fifteenth Arrondisement.' "

Sanary, June 11, 1930
noontime, on a little bench

Beloved Lenotschka,

I've just arrived, left my things in the checkroom and rushed over to the agence. The agent was eating . . . I made him come down from the first floor and said this and that to him. "À Sanary, cher Monsieur, tout est pris. Addressez-vous ailleurs! [In Sanary, sir, everything's taken. Look somewhere else!]"

He showed me the road for Le Brusq, an hour away on foot. But there's a trolley halfway there. I made the rounds of the port and found the trolley stop—a little bench—and now I'm waiting. The port is pleasant; the heat awful, but there's a sea breeze blowing. . . .

Provence is very beautiful, absolutely Greece—cypress trees, pine trees, vineyards, anemones. But without the sea, the heat would be unbearable. Here, Sanary reminds me of Aegina; pleasant, boats and kaikis and fish frying. The right trolley's just arriving. A fisherman yelled over to tell me so. God be with me, I'm off!

2 P.M.

Not a thing; everything's rented. I got there too late . . . And the village is charming, peaceful, right in the sea. How sad. I'm going back and then I'll go right over to La Seyne and from there to Les Sablettes and Fabregas. This way, I'll do the whole peninsula this evening. Heat, the earth fragrant, the gorse in bloom as well as the osier plants and the thyme. Masses of fig trees. Exactly like Crete.

Sanary, 7 P.M.

I'm just back from making the rounds of the entire peninsula. I'm very tired, sunburned, hungry, thirsty. Not a thing. . . .

It's a blessing we didn't come together, because you would have gotten very tired. I can stand it. I often think how much we might have gained if we were rich, and at the same time, how much we would have lost. I feel elated at suffering like this to find a meter of sand for us to lie on and be near each other on.

8 P.M.

I've come to a good hotel, because I was tired and unwashed. There's hot and cold water; I washed myself thoroughly and rested. The femme de chambre is Italian, and we began talking Italian. She was touched by this and told me that she would give me her house. . . . But Sanary is not the solitude and simplicity we want. . . .*

June 12, 1930; Saturday noon
Côte des Corailleurs

. . . I've been walking for 5 hours now, looking. I went along the entire coast as far as Agay; magnificent villas, where the rich people stay. . . . Everything rented. . . .

Saturday evening; Cannes (alas!)

. . . Thousands of thoughts passing through my mind. Here, the coast that we are searching for—a seaside Gottesgab—does not exist. Of course, somewhere in France it must exist . . . but where? Everything here is civilisé and inaccessible. . . . I'm exhausted. You can't imagine how I've been rushing about. . . . I keep pondering on what we can do, and the notion that I cannot communicate with you increases my agony. If we were together, we could make a decision. After Nice, it strikes me that I might set off for Bordeaux and start investigating there. Meanwhile, time is being wasted. I'm not working. I'm spending money and fretting. But always the idea that I can find a stretch of sand for you to sun yourself and grow strong on gives me courage. . . .†

Sunday morning, Juan-les-Pins

I slept on the famous plage [beach] here, because the cheapest hotels in Cannes cost 40 francs per night! An abominable night. The plage was full of mosquitoes, horrible heat. When I asked the girl from the hotel why this constricted, mosquito-ridden coastline is so famous, she answered me (almost everybody here speaks Italian): "È la reclama, signore! [It's the publicity, sir!]"‡

---

* Letter to E. Samios.
† Letter to E. Samios.
‡ Letter to E. Samios.

Sunday afternoon, Villefranche, beyond Nice

In despair after Cannes and Juan-les-Pins, I've come here. A small, agreeable, absolutely Italian city. Very few French people. By the edge of the sea, few people, palmiers, flowers, laurel, etc. . . . I've found an excellent hotel, and I'm sitting in the garden here, writing to you. Tomorrow, I'll ransack in all directions. I'm wearing the yellow shirt (it was dirty and I washed it) . . . and now I'm wearing the other yellow one (the beautiful one) you sewed for me and white shoes and my forehead's pitch-black. I wander around all day in search of our retreat. . . .*

June 16, 1930

. . . I've just found a superb villa, garden, peace, all to ourselves! To be sure, it's not ideal, i.e., au bord de la mer [right next to the sea]. There's nothing like that left. . . . I'm impatient to see you and touch you. Our God willing—the Great Oriental God—we shall spend these four summer months as we deserve, remaining by ourselves, working again and talking and being silent together. Life is good, because we are "good people," and we love one another. . . .

Come as quickly as you can. Our villa is splendid, peaceful, full of roses, two peach trees all laden, lemon trees, orange trees, all ours. . . .†

Things always came "in another way." In the snows of Gottesgab, we had been dreaming of the day when we would burn the soles of our feet in the incandescent sand, then rush to cool them in the new wave. Fate decided differently. Neither beach nor incandescent sand to revel in the sun. Instead, a Mediterranean garden painstakingly cloistered, where only the cats could see us. It was full of the favorite fruits of our youth—tomatoes, eggplant, peppers, white grapes, pink peaches. And also rhododendrons and mounds of periwinkles.

And in Paris a piece of very good news. Jean Cassou had liked *Toda Raba.* He was not only a good writer; he was a good person as well. He wanted to help his unknown fellow writer and proposed to have the book published at Fourcade's.

Exultant, I rushed to the Gare de Lyon, sending Nikos a triumphant telegram in advance. But my telegram never reached its destina-

---

* Letter to E. Samios.
† Letter to E. Samios.

tion. "A bad omen!" I murmured, disappointed. "A good omen!" answered Nikos, happy to hug me in his arms. "God willing, I shall always learn good news from your own lips!"

Settled alongside "his" tomatoes, his torso bare in the sun, Nikos had already plunged into the children's books. Tanned, rejuvenated, resplendent-looking. And our life of work, strolls, fragmentary talks and long silences resumed on Montboron, in Periwinkle Villa.

But the great temptation of Nice was its market. Nikos, who didn't like interrupting his work in the morning, was now just looking for excuses to get out and wander among the fruit and vegetable stalls. If we had been rich, we would have been buried beneath mountains of fruits. Not being rich, he used to come back to me laden with the "most fragrant cantaloupe in his whole life," the "crunchiest watermelon," figs "tasting like a drop of honey." Hand in hand, we used to market for fish. We went through the "fresh-herring phase," and enjoyed marinating them in white wine. Yes, there were all the luxuries—for we also had a wine-cellar, discovered by the gardener one day after he had condemned us to drinking dirty water on a long excursion to Eze.

During these four summer months of 1930, Nikos translated or adapted some twenty books for children, lovingly selected from world literature: Alphonse Daudet's Le Petit Chose; Harriet Beecher Stowe's Uncle Tom's Cabin; Kari the Elephant, by Dhan Gopal Mukerji; Waldemar Bonsels' The Bee; Charles Dickens' Oliver Twist; Gulliver's Travels, by Jonathan Swift; et cetera. He also drew up a detailed plan for his new novel, A Day of Rain. The vision of an entire life concentrated into a single day, situated between two dreams (ones that he had actually had): the visit to El Greco and the apparition of Buddha—the inevitable gulf.

Toward the end of September, Prevelakis announced his imminent arrival in Paris, where he wanted to complete his studies. Would it now be possible for us to settle somewhere in the Paris suburbs, so that the two men could work together on the dictionary? In hopes thereof, I began arranging our things, before setting off to scout around Paris.

Confronted with the Tartar slippers that had come from Kazan and once upon a time had been resplendent with all the colors of the Russian earth, I stopped, pensive for a moment.

"They're very tired, the poor girls!" murmured Nikos, as he glanced at the pile ready to be thrown into the trash bin. "Lenotschka, you're not going to—"

"Let's bury them in the garden," I suggested, just to say something.

"Like a cat? If you really decide not to take them with you, let's give them a more fitting burial."

And so it happened. Nikos rummaged through the drawers till he found the richest embroidered cloth his sister Eleni had sent us and some tissue paper, which he smoothed with his palm.

"Tonight, we shall cast them into the sea," he said, when the package was all tied.

"We mustn't forget a stone. Otherwise, the undercurrent will bring them back to shore."

"Oh, I almost forgot!"

He went back to pick the last pomegranate in the garden, opened the package and laid the fruit in the little old ladies' lap.

"As an offering to Charon," he murmured again, with a sad air. "Unless he has a gift, he won't ferry them over to the other bank. . . ."

In my ears, I can still hear the muffled *plop* in the waves. I can still see sketched against the backdrop of the night the slender silhouette of this man who knew how to add relish to all things. Only the indifferent stars and a quadruped friend were there to attend our biped folly.

Nice, September 1930
Sunday afternoon

My St. George!

. . . I'm eager to hear your account of the interview with the Comtesse de Noailles. . . .

All this must end, Lenotschka. My life is becoming meaningless like this, like other people's lives. As soon as the work with Prevelakis is done, we'll take our leave of all these petty miseries. Mountain, peace, very little correspondence, pas d'affaires [no business]. Neither I nor you nor The Odyssey can follow such a train [pace of life] any longer.

In the meantime, let us . . . accept Necessity temporarily, and let's force it to give us the best it is capable of giving. And then, we will be able to liberate ourselves from it. . . .

*Votre absence est douloureuse [Your absence is painful]. I kiss your toes which grow so tired. . . .**

---

* Letter to E. Samios.

Nice, September 1930
Tuesday evening

My St. George,

. . . In Le Temps yesterday, I read an article on the Institut. Valéry has gone to Geneva et présente un rapport sur la Coopération intellectuelle [*and is making a report on intellectual collaboration*]. Well, is it possible for us to have this rapport? Please, my St. George, work on it. . . .

I wish you could find a good price for the ivoire.* Let it turn into one room of our house! And let's make another room with Elephtheroudakis, and another one with the dictionary. And in this way, we too shall have a home! By now it's a necessity for us to be somewhere chez nous. . . .

And as we used to dream about having a house—now in Salzburg, now in Nikolassee near Berlin, and now again in Meudon or Fontenay-aux-Roses—Nikos continued:

For the present, our "flying" house is made of mist and will power und Schwert [*and sword*]. But it shall become a solid one, because you are with me and I fear nothing. . . .†

Obliged to leave for Greece, Nikos wrote to me before his departure:

Nice, September 1930
Wednesday evening

May, May Gwan,‡

My last evening in Nice, Periwinkle Villa. I don't want to take leave of it without writing a word to you; how you are with me at this

---

* A Byzantine miniature carved in ivory, that we were hoping to sell.
† Letter to E. Samios.
‡ Heroine of a novel by White, which Nikos was in the process of translating.

moment and how hearty, profound, happy our whole life here was. Without you, all this beauty, sun, sea, solitude would have been extremely cruel for me and my life would have been genuinely inhuman. You are the cause of sweetness entering my life.

Within myself, I feel terrifying, dark, misanthropic forces. With difficulty I keep them in balance, because I believe there are few people in the world capable of feeling so deeply the horror of life and death. No illusion deceives me. No naïveté makes me forget. I have no hope. And even when I create a good verse, there is someone inside me whistling and jeering and reminding me where I come from, where I am going and that there is no salvation. And only when I raise my eyes— how often this happened here at Periwinkle Villa—and see you writing at the machine or doing the simple, human, household chores (washing a dish or serving tea), only then am I consoled. The ephemeral moment suddenly assumes scope and the intensity of eternity. And I say to myself, For this moment which is so simple and human, perhaps it is worth being born and does not matter that one will die.*

Marseilles, October 17, 1930

Beloved Lenotschka,

Since yesterday evening, I've been in Marseilles. A most interesting city around the old port, dangerous at night. . . .

Yesterday I went to the Agency. . . . They've got me a cheap berth, but I can't even afford that. I've barely enough to manage a thrifty second-class [ticket].

I got your letter and thank you for all the good things you tell me. I wish I could work only on The Odyssey. Let's hope so. Since you are with me, I can hope. . . .

The poems of Noailles are very fine, but how can they be translated? I shall try.

Superb, exactly like Sicily the old harbor of Marseilles. Abundant fish, fruits, clams, etc. Painted wanton women, narrow streets, beams holding up the houses to keep them from collapsing. Colors, cries in Italian and Spanish, crafty modern-Greek eyes. I'm eating grapes, a piece of bread, black olives. . . .†

---

* Letter to E. Samios.
† Letter to E. Samios.

238

When he returned to Greece, Kazantzakis took refuge near his mother. A month of vegetative life with faintly perceptible caresses and words barely articulated, scented in clove and honey and cinnamon.

Then, once again, back to work. Before Prevelakis set off for Paris, the two friends signed the definitive contract with Dimitrakos. And we went on to Aegina, with 40,000 index cards in our luggage. Each of these had to be filled in by Nikos with a French word and its equivalent, both in *demotiki* and in *katharevousa*.

We were invited by Angelakis to stay in his old country house set among olive trees and pistachio trees, fig trees and vineyards. Beneath the balcony, there was also an old *masticha* tree, whose anise flavored our pastry; a palm tree and a magnificent umbrella pine tree.

The sea sparkled through the luminous foliage of the olive trees. With the first stars rose the cry of the prison sentinels—reminding us that human beings shut other human beings into cages.

From the wooden balcony where Nikos worked on the dictionary, we could take part in the sunset inundating the world with cataracts of gold and vermilion. As soon as this imperial procession disappeared, Venus appeared, pale as mother-of-pearl.

For the first time and surely for the last time, I saw my companion suffer and complain—not a complaint about the thankless task, but a muffled anxiety whose causes we couldn't yet guess. Later on, we came to understand. This new labor was going to be sacrificed to the greed of a publisher and his advisers. To this day, the huge work is unpublished —an unforgivable shame.

1931. From dawn till night, immersed in the dictionary index cards, Kazantzakis was working away without even raising his head. During our evening strolls along the seaside or inland regions of the island, he often used to sigh. "What makes me saddest of all is to be wasting these best years of my life . . . not being able to lose myself in the inner richness."

Nikos tried to transmit a part of his own personal experiences to Prevelakis, who was at that point in Paris at the mercy of his own anxieties. "The vulture that has gripped our skull," he wrote, "is drinking our blood to keep from bursting. And we must leave it free, for if it should ever fly away from this earth, we too shall be lost. . . ."*

---

* See letters to Prevelakis from 1931.

Rumors about the Colonial Exposition in Paris had reached as far as Aegina. In one direction, Paris; in the Bois de Vincennes, an agglomeration of all the splendors born beneath the black or yellow sun, in the sand, the forest, the monsoon or the tropical rains—all of non-Europe. In the other direction, a high mountain, Turraherhöhe, whose marvels Bilili had lauded on her way through Athens. Nikos needed nothing else to raise anchor.

"I'm a migratory bird, Lenotschka. I'm neither laborer nor fisherman. I wait for an auspicious wind." As he said this, his nostrils distended.

But there was still the trial over the *Spiritual Exercises*—a trial destined never to take place, though every so often the threat was brandished over our heads. And now Glynos was asking Kazantzakis to prepare his defense.

Nikos disinterred from among his papers a text written in 1925 in Crete,* where everything is stated. This time, he added a few words to it and shoved it back into a drawer again. And to divert the course of his bad mood, as always, he looked for the comic side of the matter:

"My God, how funny people are! It's so hot . . . and the judges, magistrates and lawyers are all going to bury themselves in a narrow hall. They'll get all flustered and perspiry, everyone shouting at the same time. . . . And then they'll feel so proud, because they will have served . . . Justice!"

And then he laughed his great liberating laugh.

When we arrived in Paris, Prevelakis accompanied us as much as he was able around the Bois de Vincennes. From morning to night, the rest of us preyed on the honey. It was hot, very hot indeed. The various exotic woods—bamboos, papyrus—water lilies in the ponds and the human bodies in unison exhaling the aroma of the South. Night and day, the drums reverberated—the tam-tam drums and the acrid flutes. At every turn, a mask, a lion or some other wild beast—half-man, half-beast—a red or black column, a hut or a temple . . . Several years afterward and alone, I was to touch the actual Angkor Wat, not a flower picked in a vase. Nevertheless, at this Colonial Exposition, France offered us the vision of a dream.

Once again Nikos wanted to spare me useless fatigue, and he set off alone to look for a place for us.

---

* See the *Appendix*.

My St. George,

. . . I am writing to you and if it weren't for you, I would have wept with exhaustion. . . . I got off at Turrah too. Nothing. One or two horrid houses, which accept you after hesitating a long time and looking you over from head to toe. . . .

What can I do? The only salvation is once again Gottesgab. . . .

Tomorrow, I'll take the bus as far as Prelitz, St. Michael, and, last of all, Linz. A dreadful detour, expenses, exhaustion. I'll go close to Czechoslovakia. And if I don't find anything, I'll go back to Gottesgab. . . . My only consolation is that you didn't come and have to pass these hardships too.

With relief, I recall the good Kraus household, where they know us and are so serviables [helpful] and discrets [circumspect]. I'll get them to put in a stove* . . . and joyfully we shall resume our happy life in these same rooms. . . .

My love, I'm tired; I'm tired. My feet are swollen from climbing up and down the mountains, going from hotel to hotel in the rain. And so I look to Gottesgab as an oasis. . . .

I'm writing you as I wait for the bus to leave, and it's raining monotonously, despairingly. I think of you with warmest love and tenderness. And, may God be my witness, only when I think of you do I feel assuaged. Our sacred life will begin again. Work, the sweetness of evening after toil, in these same beloved rooms. So was it fated. Impecunious people like us, when they do find something extraordinary —like this house we have at the high peak of Czechoslovakia—must realize it is a gift of Destiny and cannot happen again.

Meanwhile, I shall look toward Aegina, to our own home over the sea and the cliff.

I rejoice that you exist. May "God" grant I die before this joy dies. . . .†

Gottesgab, June 1931
Sunday evening, "at home"

. . . The closer I got to the house, the harder my heart pounded. The landscape sparkled in the sun. The peasants were threshing. A very

---

* The first time, there hadn't been any stove in Nikos' room.
† Letter to E. Samios.

sweet scent, the "je sème à tout vent" [dandelions] all white like grandfathers; the chardons [thistles] still open with a dark-blue bud.

I traversed the same paths and with deep, deep desire felt you by my side. As I crossed the bridge, a fish leaped high out of the water. A good sign; just the way my own heart was leaping.

Hilda was the first to recognize me from the high turret window up on the roof, where she was stacking the Heu [hay]. She lit up like a red flag and shouted: "Ojè! Ojè! Ojè!"

Kraus was threshing with the great sickle of Charon.

"Herr Direktor!"

The old lady rushed over. Delight, tears.

"Und Frau Direktor?"

"Im Juli! [In July!]"

I went up to my room. They brought me a liter of milk. For the evening I've ordered milk, butter, potatoes. Now I'm sitting on the couch in my room; and I feel a calm, gentle, happy feeling. The birds are warbling. The house smells of Heu, fir trees, meadows, the setting sun. . . .

Wednesday, Thursday, Friday, Saturday, Sunday—I didn't stop, day or night. I slept only one night. . . . Yesterday in Linz, I lay down for a moment on a . . . little bench on the banks of the Danube and fell asleep! As soon as I closed my eyes—even in the middle of the street—I felt as though I were falling asleep. . . .

Now today, it's the first day I have a pleasant sense and feel relaxed in spirit and body. All the landscapes I have seen are no better than here. . . .

I also saw two things which delighted me: a rabbit springing straight up among the crops, perking up its ears; and an Admiral in Turrah, an old retired army man, friend of King George—half-mad, garrulous, interesting. I'll tell you about him. . . .

I have good premonitions . . . feeling sure of good work, sweet calm, and happiness, when every evening we'll talk again like two privileged, good, unspoiled spirits and like two bodies which love one another and want one another. . . .*

And to P. Prevelakis:

---

* Letter to E. Samios.

242

July 17, 1931 (I think)
Gottesgab, Erzegebirg, Czechoslovakia

My dear brother,

I shall never forget our evenings in Paris. They have left an ineffably pleasant sense in my vitals. . . .

Write me often, please, and forgive me if I am reserved in my words and my letters. I want to, but cannot, overcome the hard shell enveloping the nut of my heart. . . . In this way, I've acquired a mask that has deceived almost all the people who have "known" me. And I shall leave behind me a legend extraordinarily different from my own real countenance—which is severe and tender and implacable and despairing. . . .

It was agreed that, after I took a cure at Plombières, I would go on to meet Nikos on the mountain. But Salzburg was exactly on my way, and the temptation was too great. Thanks to my journalist's card, in the twinkling of an eye I could obtain all the invitations for a musical fortnight. More than thirty years have gone by since then, and I still cannot forget my elation and the ensuing disappointment. For, in spite of all my supplications, Nikos did not want to come and share my delight. Neither Stefan Zweig (who wanted to meet him) nor Bruno Walter and Mozart nor Max Reinhardt and Alexander Moissi could tempt him.

Gottesgab, July 1931

Saint George of the Mandolin!

Unfortunately, I am out of spirits; no joy, no desire to meet anyone. I am very tired and slightly ill. My soul is not at all in the mood to talk. I'm sorry to cause you this bitterness. I'm sorry not to see Ketty.* From daybreak till 3 in the afternoon, I work on The Odyssey. Then I drink a little cold milk and begin translating Jules Verne. This life does not leave me in a state of spiritual exaltation to endure even the supreme good I have always longed for—music. Next year. . . .†

"Patience." . . . "Grit your teeth." . . . "Next year." . . . A sad

---

* By coincidence, the first person I had met at Salzburg was Ketty Papaioannou.

† Letter to E. Samios.

leitmotif even when uttered playfully. When we could not afford something—an excursion, music, clothes, a visit to some friend—we would do so unfailingly "next year." When Nikos was submerged in his *Odyssey*, only a trip to some distant, virtually inaccessible country could bring him back to earth.

For the first time, Nikos' resonant laugh did not boom out when we met again. He had come down to fetch me at Joachimsthal with a morose air. His soul was really "not at all in the mood to talk." But he loathed sadness, and so he soon found his good humor again and Gottesgab appeared to me paradise regained.

We were still in August and Nikos was alarmed. "What will I do when I've finished the third version of *The Odyssey?*"

On our way down the steep slope to Joachimsthal and on our way back up, laden with pears and apples and smoked herring, he spoke little and disconnectedly. But up along the straight paths on the high plateau, his chest thrust out and his head thrown back, he gave his thought free rein. And we had a hard time following, amused and perplexed by all its prowesses.

To resume *Kapetan Elias;* to write a new tragedy on several levels; to rework the *Buddha;* from A *Day of Rain* to make a novel that would take place within a few minutes,*While Smoking:* "A lonely man lights his pipe after the day's work. His eyes half closed, he watches the spirals of smoke. At first barely discernible, then more and more tangible, through the penumbra of his dreams, his failures and his successes loom up, his most hidden and his most spectacular acts, his renunciations and his deepest aspirations, the delights he has tasted, the bitter cups he has drunk, the prowesses of his childhood, the sinking in the quicksands of old age. . . ."

Also, to write a theatrical piece where time and space and causality would be vanquished as though men were marionettes; having madness as the essence. . . . And so much more. In a little notebook entitled "Seeds," there are many projects which never saw the light of day.

"Ah," Nikos used to say with a sigh, "if only I had ten arms. Or, still better, a dozen disciples. So many ideas, so many ideas which might have assumed flesh and bones. . . ."

On December 4, 1931, the third version of *The Odyssey* was already completed. Cut off from the whole world by a violent snowstorm, two days later, we celebrated St. Nicholas' name day. Snows and fog enveloped us; and on the inside, human warmth—a "supraterrestrial peace."

If we had been able to, we would have embarked for distant lands. Not being able to, Nikos invited his young "brother" for Christmas. Meanwhile, he was wondering what new beast he should turn loose to feed upon his spirit. He did not like to scatter himself in minor works. Even his novels, twenty years later, would have the dimensions of epic murals.

They say that in order to relax, Lenin used to translate dictionaries or learn some new language. Nikos let himself slip into the bottomless pit, the unfathomable gulf of the human soul.

"Choose some great spirit," he used to counsel me, "and dedicate yourself wholly to it. See how elated you are when you write your book on Gandhi. When you finish it, I'll help you find another great spirit. . . ."

"And you?"

"I don't know yet. Buddha keeps me from sleeping. I'm seized by the impulse to write a tragedy in seven parts. The first six parts will be six different exercises; then the vision of Buddha will come. I'm not in a hurry. I'm letting the subject ripen inside my vitals. What is important is to let oneself be grazed on by some great beast. Only in this way can one escape the petty vermin. . . ."

The year was drawing to a close. Once the hay, peat, potatoes, onions were stored away, the Kraus family set about making lace. Gathered around an oil lamp magnified by glasses of water, four pairs of hands skillfully manipulated the crochet needles. Parsimonious in all other respects, they generously fed the greedy stoves with the thick clods of peat they themselves had extracted from the ungrateful soil that had seen their birth and all of whose secrets they had pried into.

Strangers to winter, we let ourselves go, reveling in the sport of it. The first snows enchanted us; the sudden disappearance of the somber forest mass amazed us. In a single night, enclosures and barriers fell. Henceforth, we were floating in a boundless foamy white ocean.

Deafened by the great stillness, we lowered our voices for fear that the slightest cry might shatter us like glass. Taste, smell, sight, touch, everything changed, even our pulse.

The Kraus family lent us skis. Hopelessly pedestrian, we never learned to fly easily on these great gliding wings.

Passengers aboard an icebreaker that cracked away beneath the storm and spat out thick black smoke, with our noses stuck to the windowpane, we kept a lookout for the mailman. He alone was entitled to split our day into two equal parts like a frozen fruit and lay the pit in our hands—a fistful of burning coals.

"Lenotschka, Pandelis is coming!"

Exultation; consultations.

Drawn by our handsomest cow and accompanied by Philip Kraus, Nikos went down to Joachimsthal to meet his friend at the appointed hour. While I attended to the ovens, Kraus junior prepared the surprise. And once again it was Hilda who shouted her triumphant "Ojè! Ojè!" and then rushed to light the sturdy Christmas tree.

Kliouev was right: "Joy is a caravan of silk and embroideries that comes unto us from the Orient." Our first Christmas tree was indeed redolent of the three wise men. The friend, his gift of rum we sipped as we rambled on and on, the stalactites garlanding our windows—so many unforgettable delights.

Talks, strolls, photographs, Cretan laughs, lion-cub hugs, Greek meals with garlic—plans, replans, unplans—two Cretan flint stones casting sparks.

1932.   Was it destined that all these unpublished, bold, humoristic or tragic ideas, that all this range of the human temperament, would be butted against the lack of understanding, the mistrust, slackness, bad faith of the people aware of it? Or was God-the-Great making sport by poking his little finger in our wheels and keeping them from turning?

An unprecedented series of calamities beat down upon ourselves and the rare friends who were hoping to help us.

And so the publisher Fourcade went handsomely bankrupt. And, after him, Haumont. Renaud de Jouvenel (a young friend we still hadn't met) proposed to publish *Toda Raba*, barely escaped a hideous death and was laid up for several months thereafter. Fire broke out in the studio of the "most highly qualified film maker in France," whom Mady Humbert-Sauvageot* had succeeded in interesting in Nikos' scenarios. Last of all, Robertfrance, who was still hopeful of having *Toda Raba* published at Rieder's, was struck down in the bloom of youth. Not to mention the death of people very close to us, occurring at a more and more rapid rate.

---

* Mady Humbert-Sauvageot, N.K.'s agent, who later became a very close friend.

Meanwhile, the two Cretans harnessed themselves to their *Piatiletka*, or Five-Year Plan.

To begin with, Nikos went back to his scenarios. Within several weeks, *Don Quixote* and *Buddha* were ready. A third followed—*An Eclipse of the Sun*—showing the absurdity of contemporary life, the horror of war and the need for brotherhood among peoples.

I no longer know which of the two men first got the idea of taking the Persian and Hindu miniatures as a source of inspiration for films. "On with it! We'll study these too!" exclaimed Nikos. "But when I come to Paris. The mysteries from the Middle Ages too? Why not? Agreed, right down the line! First, though, let's try to make arrangements for *Don Quixote*, *Buddha* or the *Eclipse*. . . ."

At the same time, according to habit, Kazantzakis resumed work on his *Buddha* in the form of a tragedy.

"I would love to give him wings, Lenotschka," he used to tell me in the evening, as he stuffed his pipe with some coarse tobacco. "Superangelical wings, like the ones El Greco puts on his angels. But to do this, I must imagine it will never be read. I will feel freer."

This time, the news of a fresh disaster reached us from Greece: Dimitrakos had reneged. He no longer wanted the dictionary. He no longer wanted the children's books that he had commissioned. Nikos was sad. He suspected who was at the bottom of this new injustice but didn't let this new disaster even touch him. The first three scenarios completed, he now thought of *Madame Bovary* and Boccaccio's *Decameron*. The latter seemed to him a find "that will undoubtedly take us out of our straits."

On March 15, 1932, in this unhappy atmosphere (Fourcade had already gone bankrupt), Lefteris announced his arrival. The winter was still dragging on and we went to the German border to meet him in the same cart harnessed to our handsomest cow. And once again, along with the other little people at the station, tiny Mr. Kraus gawked at the spectacle of Cretan effusiveness, shoulder pounding, embraces, noisy guffaws and the rest of it.

"There's Crete for you! There's Crete!" I thought in amusement. "There's the Cretan measure!"

Lefteris was happy. Three years of Germany had worn him out a bit. He was glad to come and rest at his elder's side, glad to hear his elder's opinion on what he had written. For Nikos loved him and he himself adored Nikos, whenever the venomous influences of Dexameni were far removed.

Nikos listened, enchanted. The novel was good, and so were the two plays. The translation of the *Aeneid* (if I remember correctly) honest. Nikos, who was not blind, always tried to encourage his fellow writers. When I showed my amazement at his leniency, he used to say to me: "When I was young, I too didn't know how to write. I developed very slowly. I think all we Greeks need a great deal of time to develop. And so we must not cut the wings of anyone who is struggling."

The barometer registered dead calm.

Convinced that tiny Mr. Kraus would derive pleasure from hearing the trios and quartets of Beethoven he had brought along in his luggage, Lefteris invited our host to attend a musical evening. Philip Kraus listened, his eyes agog, sunk in profound meditation. Lefteris was jubilant.

"Yes, yes, Herr Direktor," our guest murmured. "But all the while that was playing, I kept thinking to myself, Where are you going to throw all those needles? And what if my cows should happen to swallow a few of them?"

Perfect harmony reigned throughout the household—until the day Lefteris suddenly burst out in a rage and tore up his manuscripts, in the water closet overhanging the snows. It was dawn. We were waiting for him over the steaming coffee. He came in with a depleted air, his eyes red. How could his work be salvaged, now that it had been siphoned down the big hole and scattered by the winter wind? After a few seconds, some strange little things began whirling around the house. In consternation, Nikos bit his lip. I burst into tears, knowing that Lefteris had just torn out his own heart.

Minor adversities slipped over Nikos, barely grazing his skin. The disappearance of Marigo—the mother he adored, who was not prematurely aged or suffering from any long illness—touched him to the quick.

"These days, I am incurably sad. One of the greatest unhappinesses that could rend my heart has happened to me. I keep strong hold of myself in order not to cry aloud. Though I know that only the cry of a wild beast could ease me," he wrote to Prevelakis.

Nikos was suffering, but he did not dare to admit the cause of it. To utter or write it would be in some way to admit it. Death, death, death—how often had he talked to us about it in his letters. Alas, one admits death only for oneself, never for the people one loves.

As I peeked at him out of the corner of my eye, I kept asking myself thousands of questions. What can the squirrel or the ivy do in the presence of an oak tree struck by lightning?

From Paris, increasingly insistent letters were arriving. Prevelakis was preparing for his examinations. Our friend Mady, whom we still hadn't met, could no longer handle our affairs alone. Moreover, as the Greek proverb asserts, "The [actual] face is trenchant as a sword."* Kazantzakis' presence in Paris was becoming indispensable.

But, more than ever, Nikos longed for solitude. And so we decided that I would go on to Paris alone by a roundabout route, to see Romain Rolland and to offer him my manuscript on Gandhi, since it was thanks to him that I had come to love the Mahatma. We naïvely trusted that with a letter from Stefan Zweig in my pocket everything would go splendidly. Unfortunately, Romain Rolland refused to receive me. He also made it clear that he never read manuscripts. Nikos reared up:

> Gottesgab, May 6, 1932
> Friday morning

> My beloved, wounded St. George,
> I just got your letter and am furious. You must not write to Romain Rolland supplicatingly, as though you were to blame. Write the two phrases I herewith enclose, so that the Grande Conscience may realize that he has wounded a living organism and behaved unworthily. . . . This will be the first time he has received such a noble, proud letter, and he will not forget it easily. . . . I am angry and disgusted with great men who do not have the flair even of a dog to realize who is knocking on their door. . . .†

With the enormous manuscript of The Odyssey under his arm (1,984 pages, 42,000 verses, written in his own hand) to offer Prevelakis, Kazantzakis arrived in turn in Paris on June 1, 1932. Cousin Mary, in her high-perched quarters, invited us to stay in Boulogne-sur-Seine this time. Prevelakis came to settle nearby. He suggested making a screen adaptation of Cardinal Bibbiena's La Calandria and Machiavelli's Mandragora. No sooner said than done . . .

Our finances were tottering. I pawned whatever little gold objects we had. While I attended to our home life, Nikos walked about in

---

* Perhaps the closest English equivalent is: "Out of sight, out of mind!"
† Letter to E. Samios.

Boulogne, carrying with him his miniature Dante. He invariably "erred," straying into the cemetery. After getting lost, he would come back dead tired. Was he really "erring," or was it a tomb freshly opened in Crete that was unconsciously drawing him there?

When he wasn't working, he read Valéry, Mallarmé, his own little personal anthology. From this period dates an unpublished translation into demotic Greek of the short poem of Moréas:

> I who can lift Apollo on my ten fingertips have faced the scorn
>   of the plebs.
> Justly I pay this tribute now and forever, as in the past, so that
>   order may reign on earth.

In a Greek periodical, he stumbled across a bad translation of Rainer Maria Rilke's narrative poem *Die Weise von Liebe und Tod des Cornets Christoph Rilke.**

"Demotic Greek is still incapable of rendering texts such as these," he murmured thoughtfully. "Do you remember the 'sea, the sea, always begun again'?† I've tried on many occasions. There's nothing to be done with it."

"And 'reiten, reiten, reiten?' "

"To translate it literally would mean nothing in Greek. 'Trot-trot, trot-trot, trot-trot,' perhaps? That remains to be seen."

Leaping from theme to theme, we mentioned the name of the great Florentine. Electrified, Kazantzakis seized his pencil, the first scrap of paper in reach and began scribbling urgently.

"Do you want to listen, Lenotschka?" And he recited to me the opening verses of Dante's *Divine Comedy*:

> Stò messostráti apáno tís zoís más
> sé skotinó planéthika roumáni. . . .

This was a gala day for Greece. Nikos Kazantzakis was to offer her a matchless translation of the *Divine Comedy* in demotic verse, without a single omission or enjambment. He polished it over the course of many long years. But the first spurt took him only forty-five days.

---

* Translated later into English as *The Tale of the Life and Death of Cornet Christopher Rilke*.
† Paul Valéry, *Le Cimetière Marin*.

With the patience of Job in the presence of his manuscripts, Kazantzakis felt anguished in the big cities. Four months of Paris had exhausted him, in spite of the efforts of his young "brother," of the exquisite Mady and her mother, of some other friends of Prevelakis, and of my own efforts. Moreover, all the doors our friends battered against remained hermetically sealed; hermetically sealed all the ears. Gongora, Cervantes and El Greco—that ancestor who had also become a grandson, flesh of his flesh—stirred the solitary man to break his moorings. In late September, taking leave of his friend with heavy heart, he set off alone for Spain.

Madrid, October 1932, Wednesday
Calle San Bernardo, Pension Abella

My beloved Lenotschka,

. . . I took the trip at one go: two nights and a day. At Bayonne, it was raining so hard that I lost all desire to stop there. . . . I saw the Atlantic for the first time. Cold, muddy-yellow, antipathetic. I didn't like Biarritz at all. From Irun, I traveled with a Frenchman who has some land in Morocco. Very young, clever, cold, interesting, enthusiastic about Morocco. Voices, women, children, foods, songs. At midnight, someone woke us up, playing on a flute and picking up pennies. At 7:30 this morning, we arrived in Madrid. At once, I began doing chores. I rushed around for five hours, looking at fifty boardinghouses. The very cheap ones aren't for us; the very expensive ones are inaccessible and disagreeable. At last, I found a superb boardinghouse, exactly like the one in Rome—perhaps a bit more aristocratic. . . . I may be slightly tired, but I don't feel it. . . . I remember you every moment. . . .

The first thing I did in Madrid was to buy a kilo of magnificent black figs . . . and I ate them on the street. Cold and sweet, they went right down to my vitals, and in this way I felt rested from the whole trip. The grapes are also superb, 80 Spanish centimes. Melons and bananas in abundance. . . .*

Madrid, October 8/9, 1932

. . . My life has found a rhythm again, as though I've been living here for years. But so far I haven't been able to begin writing. All day long I rush to the museums. We have abundant sun (only today for the first time it's begun sprinkling). The pension is superb. . . . I haven't

---

* Letter to E. Samios.

made friends with anyone. I don't say a word. I wrote to Rubio* . . .
but so far I haven't gotten any answer. I haven't seen Jiménez† yet. I
want to feast my eyes on Madrid—her streets, museums, people—and
then. The other day, I was at a bullfight. The spectacle magnificent and
terrifying. Impossible for you to see a bullfight, Lenotschka. I'll go again
day after tomorrow. For many reasons, I have need of this spectacle.

Spain's greatest playwright, Benavente, has written a play, Russia,
Holy Russia, and yesterday it was performed for the first time. Before
the curtain was raised, the author (who's about 70 years old) recited a
Prayer to Russia, a miracle of warmth, love, compréhension and véhé-
mence. Fortunately, it's in print. I bought it and I'll translate it for
kyklos,‡ so you can read it. And then I'll send the text to Prevelakis.
He's said exactly what I say, and he too has called it "Crucified Russia."§

Madrid, October 9, 1932

. . . Yesterday evening, I went to the theater where Benavente was
supposed to recite his Prayer to Russia. I waited for him a long time at
the exit. It was sprinkling; the wind was blowing. At last, he arrived, got
out of his car and I recognized him from the caricatures of him published in the newspapers. An old man, slender, sturdily built, élégant,
with a little beard, short and refined. I sent my card and a letter. And
after a short while, his secretary came and gave me an appointment at
his house tomorrow (Monday), between 2 and 4 o'clock. . . .‖

And so Benavente was reading Toda Raba. Another Spaniard,
Lopez, was supposedly in the process of translating La Calandria. And
Boris Bureba, who was apparently very dynamic, had promised to read
the scenarios. Everything seemed to be going well.

But now, Odysseus—who kept returning more and more intract-
ably—was joined by another great shadow: Dante.

And Kazantzakis, after each visit to Goya, El Greco or Velázquez,
began mentally scribbling terza rima verses that would one day con-

---

* Timoteo Perez Rubio, painter, Director of the Museum of Modern Art in
Madrid, and husband of the Spanish poet Rosa Chacel Rubio.
† Don Juan Ramón Jiménez, the great Spanish lyric poet.
‡ A literary review, published in Athens.
§ Letter to E. Samios.
‖ Letter to E. Samios.

stitute a canto to Dante. He also investigated all the pleasantly isolated sites where he might take refuge and resume his work.

At this period Kazantzakis, for the third time, narrowly escaped death. The danger over, the recollection remained engraved upon his memory:

Could this be a warning, Lenotschka? Must I make haste? I shudder at the idea that I might leave The Odyssey unfinished. . . . If I had died in frjnt of the Atocha station, my soul would have been lost too. . . .

Madrid, October 14, 1932

My beloved Lenotschka,

. . . I'm hoping to begin soon on Nicephoros Phocas.* *. . . If I do succeed in fixing something up and no longer need to stay here, I'll move southward, to a more peaceful little town. Perhaps I'll be able to work there. Madrid is beautiful and has museums, but you can't find any peace here. In the evening (7 to 9), I go to the cinema. I saw a marvelous film, Congorilla: life in the forests of Africa, the splendid expédition of Johnson. Tonight, I'll go to see [René] Clair's À Nous la liberté.*

I spend as little money as possible. I go wild when I see fruit. Just imagine, a cantaloupe (and there are mounds of them on the sidewalks), a superb 2-kilo melon, can be bought for 30 centimos! The same for watermelons. The bananas heavenly, for a penny. Apples, figs, pears; my room is filled with them and I can't get at them quickly enough. . . . If we only had money! But let's hope Gandhi will save us! . . .

The main streets are full of people as at a demonstration—fiery, big black eyes; men and women. Cries, laughter, like a bazaar. The people are kind, warm, eager. . . . This year, Goya has made a great impression on me. El Greco has remained at the same height, no further progress. But some of Goya—his last ones—have risen very high inside me. . . .

---

* *Nicephoros Phocas*, a verse tragedy by N.K., which he was in the process of translating into French, at the same time reworking it to make it more "dramatic."

One more favor: Before you give Valéry back to Prevelakis, make me two copies of the Palme and the Cimetière Marin. We'll put them in the Anthology. . . .*

. . . The news you write me isn't pleasant. But we'll hold out a bit longer, and perhaps the wheel of Fate will turn. Here, I economize as much as possible. For everyday expenses, I don't spend more than 2 pesetas. . . . At this rate, I'll last till December, and perhaps then we'll have something pleasant. Jiménez came home yesterday. . . . Always the same: grand seigneur possédé [a great lord possessed] by his work, profound, serious, sweet, distant and cordial. He promised me to speak to his friend at once. . . . He'll certainly do his utmost, and perhaps we shall succeed. . . .

I saw Benavente in his home. Taciturn, old, élégant but cold. I don't know how he managed to write such a beautiful Prayer. His play Rusia, Santa Rusia [Russia, Holy Russia] I saw; mediocre, tirades, old-fashioned trucs, but warm and correct. As literature, it is of small value. Ortega [y Gasset], the greatest penseur [thinker] here, I shall be seeing one of these days at Jiménez' home. . . .

I am constantly reading useful Spanish books. But this isn't enough. When I go back to Paris, I must have the manuscript of Nicephoros Phocas. Perhaps something might be done with Pitoyev. The death of Robertfrance nonplussed me. Is Toda Raba perhaps to blame? I'm beginning to be anxious about the destiny of this Negro. I hope he won't strike us as well.

I don't know what we can do about D.† . . . But what can be done with a scoundrel who wants to drag the case to the law courts? There are certainly not many ways for an honest man to defend his own rights. We must be patient and hold out as long as possible. . . . I am sorry you aren't near me, so that I could relieve you of everyday worries now. Patience, patience, patience sur la terre.‡§ . . .

---

* Letter to E. Samios.
† The Greek publisher who had commissioned the French-Greek dictionary and a series of children's books. It is interesting to observe that several Greeks were found—men of letters—to testify in the courts that N.K. did not know French well!
‡ Paraphrase of the famous verse of Valéry.
§ Letter to E. Samios.

Madrid, October 26, 1932

We talked at length with Rubio; warm, sentimental, I like him. . . . Now that Herriot's coming, do you think I should send you an article to offer Le Monde or the Nouvelles Littéraires? What can we do about money? Do you think I should write Renaud about payment for the article? When you're left without anything (and I suppose this will be very soon), I'll set aside my shyness and write him. . . .

My God, how I try to hide my anxiety over the misfortune in our external life. . . . I pluck up my courage, grit my teeth, and don't say a word. But the idea that we're separated like this . . . exhausts me. . . .*

Madrid, October 31, 1932

. . . Thank you very much for your two letters. They gave me great joy, even though their contents were not pleasant. The main thing exists, l'essentiel: notre existence si unie [the essential thing: our existence is united]. All the rest is a shadow passing by without casting any black mark upon us . . .

I read Grasset's letter calmly. He is very right: grouillant et apocalyptique [agitating and apocalyptic] and without adultères [adulteries].† I'll write to Rieder. . . .

Here, Jiménez hasn't written me yet about whether he's given Toda Raba. A month has gone by since I've been here and not a thing! I'll approach other editors as well. I think the genre I write is more suited to the Spaniards than the rationalistic French. We shall see. . . .

Yesterday, I had a terrible piece of news from Alexandria. One of my best friends—a strong, powerful, marvelous man, G. Petridis—is dead. . . . This life is terrifying, meaningless, full of horror. All day yesterday, I was trembling with rage. And now I cannot talk about it. . . .

I haven't moved over to Rubio's yet, because he wants me to go without paying. He's poor and this can't be done. Where can we find money till I have to come back to Paris? How can I be calm with this miserable necessity? . . .‡

Having learned that in Athens witnesses had been found to testify that he didn't know French and didn't make good translations, Nikos wrote to Prevelakis:

---

* Letter to E. Samios.
† This is how Grasset had described Toda Raba, which he refused to publish.
‡ Letter to E. Samios.

Madrid, November 1, 1932

. . . All our practical endeavors lost. The whole world has joined together to consume us. At times, I am impelled persistently by the idea to climb a mountain and never come down again. We have nothing in common with human beings. We do not need them. They cannot reach us. They besiege us in myriads of ways, even the finest of them, in order to make us capitulate. It's as though we are the first specimens of some future race, and the physical and psychological conditions around us are still hostile. Neither the air nor the aspirations nor "human beings'" thought are our "climate." This is not "romanticism" or "révolte" or weakness or merely strength. I feel that it is something deeper, more mystical, more organic. We shall see!

And to his young French friend, Renaud de Jouvenel:

Madrid, November 1932

The two extreme poles of the Spanish spirit—Nada [Nothingness] and Passion—offer me the austere climate that suits me. Here, I breathe with ease. If I could, I would settle down in this old Castile, as my compatriot El Greco did. I love and admire the clarity and unbefogged rationality of the French race. But I feel rather stifled within their precise horizon. To stare straight into the Nada and to have a burning love of life (of the path leading to the Nada), this is what I love and find here in the earth, the air, the windmills of our Lord, Don Quixote.

Madrid [no date]

Beloved Lenotschka,

. . . Here, negotiations are taking their own course with Spanish fervor and nonchalance. Today for the first time, the sky is clouded and it's sprinkling. But it's pleasantly warm. . . . If our affairs could only take a good turn and if you could only come! But let's not talk of dreams any more. It becomes shameful. . . .

I too am thinking of Prevelakis all the time. Will we always be moored to the profession of Ananghe [Necessity]? We've done every-thing in our power. What more does Luck demand in order to come? What's to be done? . . . I cannot sleep any more; I'm beginning to get thin again. Unconsciously, secretly, care is devouring me. What are we to do to avoid having to go back [to Greece]? I so long to give some

256

good news from here! . . . My answer to Grasset was that he should excuse me if I remain faithful to the countenance of my own race. . . .*

From Trieste, Edvige had told him that she was invalided with a fractured arm. He wrote to her:

Madrid, November 6, 1932

Amica cara,

You speak to me of Chance and individual virtue and their multiple combinations . . . mysterious things which I haven't been able to answer in any precise way. From my own personal life, I know this well: There is something awesome in the human soul, a spear of fire and light, piercing the enormous weight of substance and shadows. . . . There is a sarcastic, provocative little laugh emerging victorious from every tribulation. I have never met "happiness" except at the peak of the greatest despair.

And why? Because I have persisted (my lips pressed, scorning death in my heart) in climbing till the very end. All around me, everything was always organized against me. And at the sight of so many enemies, I felt myself ready, gay, scornful, silent—and ultimately victorious. My friends believe me happy, because they do not know the struggles preliminary to every victory; because they do not know that my happiness is the supreme flowering of my own despair and my scorn for all things "terrestrial." I am not a Romantic in revolt, nor a mystic scorning life, nor an insolent belligerent against Substance. I love life, the earth, man, animal, ephemeral things. I know their value very well, and yet their limits too. I do not feel possessed by any illusion. I have not fallen into any trap; and at the same time, I enter into all traps—like some extremely elastic rat, which enters the trap, eats the mixture set in the background to catch it, and then goes on to other traps, well aware that the last trap—the trap of Death—is there waiting for it and it will enter and never come out again.

Dear friend, . . . words are traitors and simplify all things excessively. That is why I always loathe speaking. But you are refined and will understand all the inexpressible aura vibrating around the words. This is why (and not only because your arm is broken) I am talking with you, unveiling a little of my "secret" to you. . . .

---

* Letter to E. Samios.

He also wrote to Leah during this same month, also from Madrid:

Dear, dear Leah,

At last, I got your good letter. How often I have turned in all directions of the earth to find you; like a blind man, seeking you beyond the mountains and the seas. Ah, you're in the Holy Land again, which I am unable or unwilling to forget. When shall I see your marvelous face again? At times, the earth seems too large to me, too broad, and my various souls forever scathed. But some time surely, our laughter and our voices will resound together again, happy in spite of everything.

I am almost happy; which means I don't need happiness at all. I see, hear, think, make good verses, remember, avidly devouring, as always, this magnificent deep life. . . . Everything is sacred and good, and I am never sated. I am not playing, as Rahel insists. But I advance as far as the frontiers and there, in front of the abyss, I feel that everything is a fairy tale, aimless, marvelous—beyond all aim. For Odysseus, Ithaca is not the little island, but the voyage toward the little island—which does not actually exist at all. . . .

I know nothing about your life. Please believe me—I love you very much and am a good friend. Panaït Istrati says that I am strong. I don't know. I know only that I am capable of being happy and suffering with all the people whom I love. I forget nothing. I feel myself solidly bound to a few spirits I love. The terrible life of our present day cannot touch me at all. I do not let it. . . .

Now that Robertfrance was no longer there, Rieder came back with a new proposition—alas, untenable—that we buy in advance 500 copies of *Toda Raba* (which he intended to publish at 15 francs per copy). So we would have needed 7,500 francs, a sum which, needless to say, we did not have at our disposal. Fortunately, the financial debacle did not drain Nikos' creative verve. In his letter of November 15, 1932, he wrote:

Today, I finished the canto to Dante. It's 166 verses (a bit longer than I wanted). I'll send it on to you in a few days so that you can make 5 copies of it. And give Prevelakis a good copy for his trip. Unfortunately, at present, I can't make him any other going-away gift. . . .

I'm on my way now to the Ateneo [The Athenaeum], where I'll meet a few friends and see Unamuno. . . . At the last minute [Bureba] arrived. We came to an agreement. . . . He's optimistic; the cinema director was enthusiastic about Don Quixote and made an appointment for us to talk in . . . 15 days! This is how time passes and I don't know whether I'll be able to hold out. . . .*

Madrid, November 18, 1932

. . . A woman here (once again a woman!) is taking steps to find a way for us to stay in Madrid. . . . I have little hope, but I'm doing my utmost. . . .

Yesterday evening, I saw Mädchen in Uniform [Young Girls in Uniform], the most beautiful film I've ever seen in my life. Perfect both as performance and as scenario. Simple, profound, bitter, human, sobre, vibrant. . . . I've stopped eating fruit now, buying books, everything. And now at Rubio's, I'll stop eating food as well. I realize that to succeed in something here, one must have patience and endurance. . . . I gave an option for the scenarios and Lidio to Bureba until December 31. . . .†

Madrid, November 1932
Midnight, Sunday

Mary's just gone out of my room. . . . Relaxed, fresh, in a good mood. . . . She gave me your letter, and I was delighted about Gandhi's letter.‡ May dawn break! I was also glad that Prevelakis passed his exams. I'd been very worried about it. . . .

Madrid, November 1932
Plaza del Progreso 5

P.S. I've settled myself in the new room. It's large and full of sun. . . . I've just this moment gotten the enclosed letter from Angelakis. He says the book trial is over and we've won it. Only the letters [in the words] have to be recounted. . . . I'm thankful for this, though for now it won't help us financially. . . . By the time we touch the money, the drachmas will be worth nothing. The gain is mainly a moral one. . . .§

---

* Letter to E. Samios.
† Letter to E. Samios.
‡ Gandhi had written me a letter about my book on him.
§ Letter to E. Samios.

Madrid, November 30, 1932

. . . I'm sleeping badly—a restless sleep which doesn't relax me at all. My only joy is to get letters from you and from Prevelakis. In the meantime, I'm collecting as much material as I can for the fourth version [of The Odyssey]. And I'm impatient to see when we'll be able (perhaps here in Spain?) to go to the sea to some peaceful place where I can begin the fourth labor [of Herakles]. . . .*

Madrid, December 3, 1932
Evening

. . . A folk song I heard the other day has made me feel that my life's been wasted all in vain. If I were to return to the earth, I would surely take another path. But I would not want to come back to the earth. When I feel the damp earth like this, my heart contracts and I am filled with bitterest elation at returning into the earth. I remember as I was going around the corner of the road on my way down to the harbor, I turned back and saw—for the last time—my mother standing in the doorway, weeping. Now she's on the other shore, drawing me that way. The earth is no longer loathsome to me. Not a single day passes without my sinking into this vision. Not a night goes by without my seeing my mother in my dreams. . . . Hades has taken on an unexpected splendor, and I believe that only you still hold me to the surface of this earth. . . .

But let me not talk of this. . . . The Odyssey? I need it now more than ever to keep my heart from crumbling. It's like wine, to make one forget. But I've never been able to get drunk and lose my memory. . . .†

Madrid, December 8, 1932

. . . Yesterday evening in my dream, I saw that I was talking about you to someone. When I woke up, I remembered only this phrase: "When Eleni is near me, she sheds light on me, whereas the other one (I don't know which other one) casts a shadow on me." . . . I felt happy, because this is true. . . .

On this scrap of paper, I'm making the corrections you have very rightly suggested to me.‡ Some parts I like very much, as well as the calm, hushed ending. Go on correcting it, and later on we shall see. . . .

---

* Letter to E. Samios.
† Letter to E. Samios.
‡ This is in reference to several comments on the Dante canto.

The NEP [New Economic Policy] *is going very well! The day before yesterday, on my name day, I decided to go out to dinner. Impossible to describe the impression made on me by cooked food now! Precious, delicious, rare. Usually I eat twice a week in a restaurant and the rest of the time at home: tea, cocoa, butter, superb olives, salted sardines, and fruits. . . . So I've put on weight. My body's no longer worn out, the way it was at the boardinghouse. . . . So don't worry at all. In this way, I spend half as much and am better nourished. . . .*

Bureba read Lidio *to a theater manager, but they find it obscure. . . . For* Don Quixote, *he has hopes. . . .* Lidio *will certainly be a success if it is accepted. But recall* Topaze.*†

Madrid [no date]

. . . The other day I went to Toledo. . . . Here the days are exquisite, all sun, like summer in Aegina. I hope the weather will turn bad so that I can work. . . . And now, how can I mention the following to you? I'm ashamed to. . . . Do you perhaps have the time and inclination to copy the Spiritual Exercises in English? . . . I feel ashamed to be giving you so much new trouble. . . . But you're a good companion and you will help me once again. . . .‡

Calandria, Don Quixote, Boccaccio's Decameron, the Mandragora of Machiavelli, *An Eclipse of the Sun,* the Chair of Modern Greek at the University of Madrid, a literary prize I had been hoping for for *Gandhi,* the new Rieder proposition for publishing *Toda Raba,* and *Nicephoros Phocas,* which Jouvenel was supposed to submit to Pitoyev —everything slipped through our fingers like sand.

With any other traveling companion, I would have cursed the day I was born. But Nikos—even if he did not dance like Zorba at the most critical moment—retorted so unexpectedly, grimaced so disarmingly, became so "alchemistical," transforming the basest metal into gold, that you joyfully accepted continuing the steep ascent.

"Blessed be the obstacle!" he cried out at that point, exasperated by all these venomous turns in succession. "Blessed be adversity, for it allows us to judge our own souls and find them worthy!"

---

* Letter to E. Samios.
† *Topaze,* one of the first theatrical pieces by Marcel Pagnol; no one accepted it in France.
‡ Letter to E. Samios.

But he too had moments of profound sadness. "Death encircles me on all sides," he wrote me after Erichetta Pucci passed away. "Not a day or a night goes by without riveting my spirit, mute, to the first death—the one that struck me in March, shattering my heart. . . ."*

Left to himself alone, Kapetan Mihalis spent his time feeding the birds and drinking. Seated in his favorite place in front of the window, he cut the bread in crumbs and spread them out in his handkerchief on his knees. Anestasia was worried. Her father was eating next to nothing. Slowly, with monotonous gestures, the old man sipped his raki. No one could guess what thoughts were crossing his solitary mind.

Counting on the affection he bore his grandchildren, Anestasia persuaded him to come and live with her. Klio, his granddaughter, was his favorite, the only person who could still make him come out of his mute state.

"He was very solicitous as far as I was concerned," she told me in a moved tone. "Whenever I went to Grandfather's I always found the warm frantzola† and the fruits I loved and above the safe-chest a bar of perfumed soap for my hands."

"And afterward?"

"Afterward, he didn't want to stay with us. He preferred his solitude, his birds and his raki."

The last days of Kapetan Mihalis were not at all like the last days of the hero in Freedom or Death. The actual Kapetan Mihalis died in his own bed, in a state of euphoria familiar to doctors. Throughout his final days, he imagined he could see his other son, the one who had died as a tiny baby one night when they had been fleeing from the Turks. In her frenzy, Marigo must have given it a bit too much of that "sleeping herb" they used to give babies to keep their cries from attracting the Turkish guns.

And now Charon was coming to look for him in his turn, with velvety soft tread. Kapetan Mihalis called to his daughter: "Anestasia, bring some chairs—more chairs! Can't you see them? All the relatives and friends are coming to greet our Yorgaki now he's back." And he addressed "Yorgaki," thinking he could see him: "Welcome! Welcome!" he whispered, inexpressibly blissful.

---

* This refers to the death of N.K.'s mother.
† A kind of white bread.

In Madrid, the news struck Nikos like a thunderbolt. To keep from sinking into the void himself, he took to flight. The first days he couldn't write to me. I was anxious. He knew this and asked forgiveness.

Valladolid, December 27, 1932

My beloved Lenotschka,

I'm writing you a word from Valladolid. I'm wandering through northern Spain, trying to exhaust my body. Day before yesterday, I was in Salamanca. Tomorrow, I'm off for Burgos; day after tomorrow for Saragossa and after that, I don't know. I am seeing new throngs, cathédrales, museums, Christs, paintings. I am sleeping little and eating almost nothing at all. In a few days, I hope to get as worn out as I need to, and this will do me good. At every single moment, I am thinking of you. There's no one else left in the world except you. When will we see each other? When I go back to Madrid, I'll have a letter from you, and that gives me joy. Perhaps everything I'm seeing now is beautiful, but my soul is opaque. I can't discern clearly and my mouth is full of ashes. . . .*

Miranda (near the Pyrenees)
December 29, 1932

. . . At 4:30 A.M. I left Burgos, and I've been waiting here three hours . . . for the train to Saragossa. The cathédrale of Burgos is a genuine fortress, all upward thrust and warlike breath. It lacks the grace and nobility of Notre Dame, but it is masculine, fierce, aggressive—and I liked it. An old fifteenth-century palace where the King and Queen welcomed Columbus back from America, exquisite. An old manor house, very simple and precious; I liked it very much. . . . I'm wearing the cache-col [scarf] you gave me (gray-red-blue) and the thick undershirt and I'm not at all cold. Perhaps from Saragossa, I'll go down to Alicante. . . . My body is still not as tired as I would like and as it should be. At every moment you are with me. I have never thought of you with so much love and longing. I no longer have any other joy except to see you.†

---

* Letter to E. Samios.
† Letter to E. Samios.

Saragossa, December 30, 1932

Fearful cold. I come and go in the streets, aimlessly. The city is pleasant up over the river, but it doesn't interest me at all. Its famous cathédrale immense, incohérente, foolish. The miraculous idol of the Madonna dressed in gold, encircled by a heap of tapers, candles, priests, women. Her footprint in the marble is worshiped by the weeping women, and alongside it there's an empty tray. Out of all this throng I saw going in and out, praying away (many of them stretch out their arms like crucified figures for hours on end), I saw only one who seemed to me to have genuine faith—a peasant who put his hand in his pocket, took out a penny and set it on the tray.

Narrow little streets like Naples; wash hanging on the balconies, ugly girls wearing ribbons in their hair, a crowd of priests and beggars, sidewalk bazaars. All these things I've seen over and over again. My heart remains unmoved. . . .

Saragossa, Night of December 30, 1932

. . . I've just this moment received quite a pleasant piece of news from Madrid: The Foreign Ministry of Spain is giving me 400 pesetas per month on condition that I write some articles on the intellectual activity in modern Spain. . . . To be sure, 400 pesetas are not much, but it's enough for us to live on in Madrid and, in the springtime, to make our pélérinage of Spain. I was glad, because in this way you'll see El Greco, Toledo, Madrid, the Escorial. And I was glad, because in this way I shall see you and in Spain at that!

May light dawn! May this horrid 1932 never return! May we live together and far away from Greece! . . .†

At the very moment Nikos received this "quite pleasant" proposition from Madrid, I had been offered in Paris the chance of going to England to study English, with the promise of a certain position after several preliminary months. Our letters crossed. We would both have loved to be able to live in Spain. But both Nikos and I believed we should best choose the offer that promised most for the future. Often one asks one's God for a single thing and He gives us several, amused—I imagine—at our inability to make the right choice.

---

* Letter to E. Samios.
† Letter to E. Samios.

At the same time, Iannis Angelakis, who was acting as our lawyer, demanded my presence in Greece—to testify to the precise number of letters contained in each manuscript of Kazantzakis'! As though they couldn't be counted by someone else. I wrote to Nikos, begging him to decide himself. I had more confidence in his subconscious than in my own. He replied:

Madrid, January 1933
Midnight, Wednesday

My love,

I just this instant got back from the trip and I found your three letters and the telegram.

You certainly must not lose the chance of going to England and learning English. I tell you this with much calm and conviction. . . .

I won't go back to Crete; it's superfluous now. . . . Now what's done is done. The property remains, but it's of very little value at present. The cash they've either taken already or else, as I told you, everything may be hidden in the ground.

Tomorrow, I'll see what I have to do about the work I've undertaken here. I'm sorry now. But I did it in order to avoid Greece. Perhaps in this way, some path will open. But what path? For myself, my own work is not to see anyone at all; not to live with human beings. Every contact is painful for me and—what is worse—superfluous. "O mon coeur, suis ton chemin comme le rhinocéros! [Follow thine own path alone, O my heart, O old rhinoceros!]" . . .

Forgive me for having taken so long to write you. The pain was unendurable . . . as though half my body had collapsed, as though half of me had sunk into the ground before my time. That's why I hurled myself into flight. I traversed 2,000 kilometers almost without stopping, eating rarely, sleeping very little and with horrible cauchemars [nightmares]. I was struggling to occupy my spirit to keep it from crying out, to tire my body and so tame it. Yesterday by the sea in Alicante, in the sunlight, I felt relief for the first time. And now I have come back calm. Only, I wish it were possible for me not to see a single human being, not to have to speak for years; to sit upon the ground—if possible, before the sea—staring at the desolation. But where? And how? How can I escape human beings? How can I disappear? The moment is crucial, and I no longer have many years to play. The roots, you see, have begun dragging me into the earth.

When I got back, I found a card from Panaït here. I copy it out for you:

> Neamtz Monastery, Carpathes, Moldaves; December 5, 1932.
> What's become of you, my dear Nikos? I miss you. I'm seriously ill
> and still cannot forget your great unique face. If you're still angry,
> forgive me. And give me a sign of life. Your Panaït.

I'll write to him one of these days. . . .

Tomorrow morning, I'll mail this letter. . . . I haven't hurt myself
in any way. This body does not crack. What more must it suffer if it is
to collapse? I am well, neither thin nor tired from all the bad conditions
under which I've been living voluntarily. It is certain that some day my
body shall crack all of a sudden. We shall see. I'm beginning to wait for
it with a certain impatience. . . . I believe that you are the only root
that keeps me still standing. . . .*

Madrid, January 5, 1933

. . . Lenotschka my love, I am aware of what you're telling me,
but I cannot—cannot. A harsh voice inside me will not let me go back
to Crete to see what inheritance my father's left me. How can I explain
what is beyond all logic? I feel ashamed inside myself to do so. I feel
ashamed and do not want to. . . .

Perhaps in the meantime you may find something for me too in
England—ancient or modern Greek in some college, etc. . . . Perhaps
we shall both find something stable here. . . . But for the moment we
cannot live in Paris. Who knows? Later on. For in any case we must
wind up in Paris.†

Madrid, Evening of January 5, 1933

. . . The sensation given me by this death is indescribable. I've
said nothing to a single person, not even to Rubio. And I've been forced
to preserve a calm countenance. And this has exhausted me. Only by
being silent, only by going away, only by racing as I raced through
Spain, only by fasting as I fasted could I keep my faculties sound and
prevent them from cracking. I tell you once again: It was not love that
united me with Father, but a thick deep root, which has been cut now.

---

* Letter to E. Samios.
† Letter to E. Samios

The whole tree has tottered. This event will have profound effects upon my life. And now that I am beginning to calm down, I feel them emerging one by one. First and foremost, the unholy, horrifying feeling that I have been liberated. A bugbear has been oppressing me my whole life long. Now I shall begin to breathe. Many of my works, many of my vacillations will be swept away. I shall become brave and proclaim my independence and my autonomy. I shall be able to do whatever I want, without having to account for myself inside myself to anyone. I feel as though I'm now a vulture whose moorings have been cut. The shadow over me has dispersed, gone down, sunk into the earth. . . . And now that he who engendered me has vanished, I am being born.

These words are terrible and I say them only to you, because you have sensed them all these many years we've been living together. And I beg of you, burn this letter so that no evidence shall remain.* Because no one will be able to judge this complexus as I really feel it. I am eased. I am liberated. My soul shall wax strong. I no longer fear anything or anyone. And this liberation has shaken me and torn me. The loss of my mother was an utterly emotional embitterment: the complaint of a child left alone in the dark when the well-loved hand's gone out of reach. The loss of Father was a relief that rent me. Freedom, breathing eased, as with a little child being born and its lungs must be ripped in order for it to breathe and it hurts. . . .

Impossible to talk. I could only cry out. But I didn't want to. Forgive me for having worried you. But I shall never again experience such an earthquake [that will] close my mouth. I write all this to you, and it is nothing—says nothing. But you shall give it whatever contents are missing and cannot be uttered.

. . . As I've told you, I don't see any reason for my going to Crete. . . . I should have been there before the fatal end. But even then, I'm sure it would have been superfluous. If nothing is found, it's certain to be hidden somewhere in the ground. Will they find it? Once when Father was very ill, he did this and then afterward dug it up again. And now he must have done the same. A heavy, somber, cave man's instinct. And then there was his obsession: That his children should not rejoice after his death and because of his death. The ancient fierce feelings of the ogre. . . .†

---

* But he himself made this same confession in Report to Greco, just before he died.
† Letter to E. Samios.

This letter was so moving that I endlessly put off the moment to destroy it. Twenty years later, when I reread it, I felt myself freed from the demand by Nikos' own confession in *Report to Greco*—a confession which is illuminated and amplified by this letter written under the burden of overwhelming pain.

He also wrote to Prevelakis on January 5, 1933:

. . . Were it not for Eleni, this would be the moment for me to make my decision: I have no need of cities and conversations and endeavors with men over men. Soledad, soledad, pureza! [Solitude, solitude, purity!] . . .

Yesterday evening, I found your two letters. I shuddered for Athens as I read them—with disgust and at the same time elation—at our finding ourselves absolutely alone like this, unknown. . . . What we want—because it is eternal—seems to everyone unreasonable and anachronistic. . . .

Forgive me for not being able to follow your advice. What you tell me is correct, reasonable, indispensable. Nevertheless, there is a voice inside me bellowing to prevent me. I know that it is absolutely unreasonable, demanding things that are perhaps beyond my powers. It wants to make my life unbearable, full of anguish, uncertainty, martyrdom—and at the same time more heroic. I say "heroic" for lack of a better word. Perhaps "pride" would suit it better. Perhaps "pureza." And in this particular case, the bellowing roar is amplified by the scorn I would have felt for myself had I rushed in such haste to my father's grave—not to grasp a handful of earth and rub it on my head, but to open his safebox and see what it contains. I am familiar with all the arguments—absolutely all of them—that impel me not to act in this manner. But the invisible grandeur of man rises up above these arguments and bids me "No." . . .

Madrid, January 10, 1933

My love,

I like your novella* very much, with all its sobriété and bitterness. This novella is more than littéraire. It is rather a document humain [human document] and that is why I like it. . . .

As I wrote you yesterday, I insist and believe it is right and

---

* This novella was entitled *The Orphans*.

necessary for you to go to England. What Angelakis says is stupid. To what do you have to testify? How many letters there are? But the manuscripts are there. Let someone count them. . . .

Our separation embitters and exhausts me, but let this be the last time. If you don't feel at ease in England, then you can come here. I hope I'll have gotten settled. Everything depends on whether I find a newspaper in Athens to publish my articles on Spain. I've already written to Elephtheron Vima and Kyklos.*

The day of your departure is drawing close, and I'm writing you at regular intervals like this to help you leave unhesitatingly. I am terribly sad at the long delay in seeing you, but I feel it is right for you to learn English and to see something beautiful (London, the British Museum, etc.) that will rest you from the martyrdom of life in Paris. I was glad at what you tell me about Prevelakis. God willing, he shall surpass me. That is the only way for us both to be saved. . . .

My love, take a sponge and erase all our past worries. Nineteen thirty-three will be better. . . . Courage, calm, faith, joy that we both still exist, united like this. "God" is blowing furiously all around us. But he will only crack his teeth. . . .†

Madrid, January 27, 1933

St. George of England!

At long last, I got your first letter and my heart leaped. For a long while, I just stared at the English stamp, thinking to myself that we are utterly mad, penniless like this, leading a tourist's life, exploring foreign worlds with incredible bravura. And everyone will say that somewhere we must be finding unlimited funds for traveling. . . . They'll all be topsy-turvy. And only we ourselves know, for years now, that all this is soul. Time is soul, nothing more. I have never wanted a more daring companion than you. One word perfectly conveys our rhythm: Ortsa [Onward]! We are not afraid of anything, not only because we are united in this way; even before we merged, our nature was like this. Especially ever since the day my father died, I feel a freedom and unexpected intrepidity. When I get a letter, knowing it is almost certain to announce bad news again, I just smile scornfully at dark, hostile Destiny and say: "You shall not touch me!"

---

* Kyklos, the literary review edited by Melachrinos, a symbolist poet. In actual fact, seven Greek newspapers wanted these articles.
† Letter to E. Samios.

I think of you like this so far away. England, because I'm not familiar with it, seems to me at the very edge of the world. And I only wish my spirit could make its presence felt, transcending distance. Then you could see me near you, by the English fireplace, calm, stretching my palms out to the fire and smiling at you. My well-loved comrade, may our God be with you in these difficult months of separation!

Here, it's very cold and snowing. The other day, all Madrid was utterly white. I sit in my heated room taking notes for the articles I have to write on Spain, reading and translating the modern Spanish poets. I have already sent the Jiménez to Kyklos and they've accepted enthusiastically that I write as many pages as I want each month. And so part of my obligations here are being fulfilled. . . .

Kyklos is publishing the three cantos of Dante. I'll also send them my own [canto on Dante]. . . . Prevelakis' criticism of it is ecstatic, but I don't know whether he's right; I've got another one in mind that will come at the end of the Dante translation and will be the Resurrection of Dante. . . . When it's ripe, I'll write it too in a few days. Time, Time! Ah, if only all Time were my own—9 months alone with you and 3 months for a quick trip with you! . . .

How I live here, not even I know. A real miracle: the multiplying of Christ's five loaves of bread. . . .

Panaït writes me enormous letters. He's laid up sick in a monastery and can no longer speak or walk. His wife, who's very beautiful, 22 years old (a chemistry student), is with him. He talks to me about Bilili's behavior most vehemently, with passion and hatred. . . . But what am I to believe? We know Panaït. And last of all, he suggested that we write a book together and that he give it to Grasset and we'll get 10,000 francs straightway and meet and set about making a new trip together! . . . Utterly madcap, but as always, with his "seven lives," warm and full of vitality. . . .*

Madrid, February 1, 1933

My beloved Lenotschka, my St. George!

. . . I got an enthusiastic letter from Kathimerini telling me to send them as many articles as I like. . . .

Today, I saw the Minister of Education here; he was cordial. These days, I shall be seeing a throng of personnalités. I'm gradually turning into a Hispanologist, I'm working so hard. I see only Rubio. There's no

---

* Letter to E. Samios.

fear of my meeting any "sourloulou" [flibbertigibbet] here. Don't worry. You are my last joy in life. Schluss [Finish]; then death. . . .*

Madrid, February 7, 1933

My love,

. . . Prevelakis writes to me in despair. He feels confined in Greece. He wants to get away. But how? He's writing Greco and this relieves him a bit. . . .

Still nothing from Crete. Only some newspapers telling anecdotes about my father's gallantry, stories I didn't know. Someone is going to make a book about him, about his brave deeds. I know little, because he never spoke. But a few old men in Heraklion still remember and tell about him. . . .

Panaït hasn't written me for several days. I wrote him a warm letter, telling him that it's impossible for us to write a book together on Russia, but perhaps some other [book]—our conversations. . . . As soon as I get a letter from him, I'll write to you. I too feel compassion for him and would like to see him again. . . .†

Fearing the worst, Nikos wrote frequently to Panaït, hiding his anxiety beneath a bantering tone.

Madrid, February 8, 1933
Plaza del Progreso 5

My dear Panaïtaki,‡

At the moment Abdul Hassan, the great Moslem ascetic, was on his knees, praying to God, he heard a voice—"Abdul Hassan, Abdul Hassan, if I reveal unto men everything I know about you, they will stone you to death!" And then Abdul Hassan answered: "Eh, God, You too beware! If I reveal unto men everything I know about You, woe betide You!" And then the voice of the Lord made itself heard: "Sh-sh-sh! My dear Abdul Hassan, keep your secret well, and I'll keep mine too, O brother mine!"

When I think of our own life, our words, our acts, our meeting and

---

* Letter to E. Samios.
† Letter to E. Samios.
‡ The suffix -aki (meaning "little") added to a name constitutes an affectionate form of address.

the hallucination in Russia, this dialogue often occurs to me and I laugh happily, my eyes flashing kindly and roguishly, as your giant Cosmas* (whom I love) would laugh. I am sure that in thirty (I had written "twenty," but, seeing that was too little, quickly corrected it to "thirty") years when we do finally decide to vacate our lodgings on this earth, we shall find ourselves seated in some Oriental café—very thin, very cunning, very garrulous, with long white beards—you smoking your narghilé, and me my pipe, and we shall talk with God, that Oriental mirage of ourselves, in the words of Abdul Hassan and the laugh of Cosmas. Oh, how beautiful and brief and impious and sweet and worthy of us both is life, O Abdul-Hassan-Panaïtaki!

No, you will not go before me. We shall go backstage together— like that memorable evening in Baku when we both jumped up on the stage, arm in arm, and bucked our way backstage to see at close quarters and to touch with expert fingers that unimaginable, simplest of miracles —the young dancing girl dressed in gold like a bishop, that "petroleum flower." We'll do the same then: We'll buck our way like this on earth and finger the other mysterious dancer, who's so seduced us on stage— the little wench Life.

Do you still remember my Ben Jehuda? The doctor told him: "You'll live only two more months!" And Ben Jehuda said: "Me? But I cannot die. I have a great idea!"

You, Panaïtaki, have still more: You are a great idea. In a natural, happy way without your knowing it, O Great Ignorant One! I'm sure of you; I'm not afraid. I shall die at the age of 83, in the month of March. And if you want to, come along with me. The black Volga's waiting for us.

How delighted I would be to see you suddenly in Madrid. I won't show you the museums—don't get in a huff! Just some little corners of the city, half-African, and some little Spanish girls with spit curls at their temples, wiggling their hips fit to kill. And I have a heap of devilish things you love to tell yourself about. My black head is full of beautiful things, and I'll give them all to you. But Rumania is too far away, your monastery impregnable, your companion watching over you. And if you should wake up at midnight and take the key to the open fields, she'll catch you by your shirt—O my Don Quixote—this all too real Dulcinea, and bring you back to the straight and narrow path—to bed.

I'm counting on spending the summer on some deserted coast of

---

* Cosmas was the hero of a book by Istrati.

the Atlantic. I'm going to write the fourth version of my Odyssey. Oh, why don't you know Greek! You could have read all my soul in this epic. In Greece, who could understand it? Only Prevelakis! To cry, to cry in the desert gives me a most acrid joy, very pure, very bitter—the only joy I love—inhuman, monstrous, solitary—everything I need. You know (or, rather, you don't know at all) the saying of Buddha: "Follow thine own path alone, O my heart, O old rhinoceros!"

Till we meet again, my brother! Take care of your body; our soul has no other donkey on this earth. Take care of it. Don't tire it too much. Feed it well. Don't give it wine (or cognac or raki, of course). Don't give it too much to smoke. (Since when have donkeys smoked!) Don't think. Open your eyes. Look on everything benevolently. Breathe calmly. Say: "I am a plant! I am a plant!" At a later point, you'll evolve. You'll climb another stage; you'll say: "I'm an animal! I'm an animal!" Then later on, another stage; and in this way you shall be cured. You'll become a thinking man again, drinking, smoking, traveling—and we shall find one another again.

Dear brother, once more, until we meet again!

N.

Madrid, February 20, 1933

My beloved Lenotschka,

I'm glad you're seeing so many beautiful things. But why are you forgetting the Persian and Buddhist masterpieces in the British Museum? They are superb. Also, our beloved Leda is there. Go and see her. See the horse again and the Parthenon friezes. See them well and with my eyes. Because I'm afraid there's no hope of my seeing London soon. . . .

I'm sending you Panaït's book tomorrow. . . . Very good, clean, true. His prologue all fire, genuine Panaït; only he shouldn't talk so cruelly about Bilili, a woman who gave him so many delights and made so many sacrifices for him. But Panaït is immune . . . and, as with a madman, one forgives everything he does. His is human substance seething without control or form.

I've received several letters: From Harilaos [Stephanidis], moving, embittered, full of nostalgia. He's offered us his house in Messara* (huge aristocratic gardens, cellars, doves, etc.). Also [a letter] from a

_____
* Messara, a place in Crete, where N.K.'s childhood friend had a large house.

friend of mine, the publisher from Alexandria. This letter too is full of bitterness and asks me for moral support. . . . Also a very noble, warm letter from Patra. . . . I'm thinking of sending you the canto on Dante. . . . And keep it in your purse to read. . . .*

Madrid, February 1933
Monday

. . . Here it's Carnival; drums, masquerades, confetti. How insipid all this seems to me! Surely because it lacks any genuine, animalistic exaltation. For all these rites have lost their content. They're worse than the religious processions, because here in the churches you suddenly witness spectacles of bigotry that make you shudder. The Church derives its life and prestige from these backward, dark spirits. But the carnivals nowadays have become melon rinds without any melon! . . .†

Madrid, February 28, 1933
Tuesday

. . . I tell you this: Never worry about the future; it's useless from a practical point of view. We only lose the present. The future may not exist; or something may happen that will suddenly change everything. The right thing is to exploit the present moment to its very marrow. Now that you're in England, how can you profit from it? . . . Let your mind think of nothing else. The best way for the future to turn out well is for us to work the present moment well.

If I were to think about what's to become of me tomorrow and the day after tomorrow, I would be nothing at all today. And being—à force de forger [by the very act of forging]—what I am today makes me unafraid of the future. A simple philosophy, and yet it's no mere sentiment. It is also a system that can be taught. If you reflect a great deal on all this, you will make it your own blood and action.

Panaït still hasn't written. I'm alarmed. How I wish I could see him again, because I'm afraid he may be leaving [us]. And I don't dare write him again, for fear he may sense my alarm. . . .‡

---

* Letter to E. Samios.
† Letter to E. Samios.
‡ Letter to E. Samios.

. . . Here, the political news is alarming. A new war is brewing and it may break out suddenly. . . .*

. . . I like Prevelakis' poem very much. But I have a few comments. I'll tell them to you in person. . . .

In the course of waiting these days, I'm thinking about the canto I am going to write about El Greco: The moment at the Palace when they tell him the King has not accepted his St. Maurice. Noontime. He is holding a little clot of scented resin between his fingers . . . Thronging details . . . Till the Angel comes, the one he painted during the last years of his life in Toledo, to lift him upward—"and his wings smelled of balsamed resin"—and carry him off to Toledo.

If I have peace of soul, the [canto] will turn out well; on two levels, like the Burial of Orgaz.

I don't know whether you're reading the newspapers. The war is approaching. The danger was never greater. We must bear this in mind too, for we must choose where to let the storm hit us. . . .

· Solitude, solitude! The whole fourth version [of The Odyssey] has grown too large and is piercing my temples. . . . Do me a favor: Write me how to make marmalade. The other day, I tried to make some orange marmalade, and it turned out just plain boiled oranges. I put in a lot of sugar—no result. What's wrong? . . .†

Parallel with the modern poets, while he was still in Madrid, Nikos Kazantzakis also began delving into the old philosophers, poets, novelists, and mystics: Garcilaso, Fray Luis de Leon, Gongora, Ruiz, San Juan de la Cruz, Quevedo. And he was also watching, listening, inhaling the ferment of the Civil War. He wrote:

Everywhere the smell of gunpowder; even in the tiniest villages, ammunition factories are being discovered. Bombs are exploding and wounding people, especially in Andalusia. . . . But the University City

---

* Letter to E. Samios.
† Letter to E. Samios.

is splendid, the students full of life and enthusiasm. A new Spain is struggling to extricate itself, monarchists and anarchists alike. . . .

The cantos thunder with rebellion and gunpowder. All Nikos demanded of the gods was a healthy body, stubborn determination and physical verve. But he suffered as he saw time slipping through his fingers. To give himself courage, he summoned to his mind his beloved kindred spirits. For the important thing was to bring to a good end the great adventure haunting him, his *Odyssey*.

"Life is brief," he wrote to Prevelakis on February 6, 1933. "We must not dissipate it. We must have one perfect thing to leave behind us, when they come to lower us into the ground at long last and the 'huge butterfly' of Jiménez begins to unfurl itself."

And he quotes Gongora's marvelous verses so well suited to his mood of a "free-besieged."

> Ven muerte, quando quieras; no me espanta
> la tronadora voz de tu eloquencia,
> porque frente a su fallo, se levanta
> el sereno latir de mi conciencia.

Were it not for Nikos' strong desire to let me see Spain, he would have long since set off for the sea or a mountain. And when he thought of Gottesgab, he sighed:

"Was this Gottesgab a dream? Calm, sweet air, fir trees, snow, incessant work, companionship and solitude—Paradise!"

On March 14, 1933, he wrote to Prevelakis again:

. . . Your fervent letter full of indignation and pride found me immersed in the construction work of the new canto on El Greco. The other day, I went to Toledo to see a new friend. . . . And as I was walking through the little streets, a crowd of voices, words, verses swooped down upon me. Ever since then, I've been able to think of nothing else. . . .

And to his dear Panaït, who lay dying inexorably:

Madrid, March 15, 1933
Plaza del Progreso 5

Dear Panaïtaki!

At last, I got your letter and find you in Bucharest. How I'd love to appear there suddenly before you to drink the fragrant black coffee of life together again for a few days. Give God and the Devil two or three of your seven souls and keep the rest for yourself and your old brother who loves you and for the great pathways of the vagabond. Just now, our real life's about to begin.

"We have become genuine hearthplaces of wisdom, for we understand absolutely nothing!" says another Oriental poet I love, Mirza Abdul Bider. It is only now we shall begin kneading all the mud we've gathered and playing on the seashore of this world. I think of you with such voracity that you shall never be able to go away alone. Perhaps there is some other, subterranean Volga; we shall explore this together, as we wait (let's hope in vain!) for Eleni and Bilili.

I read your book in one fell swoop; I love it very much—alive, profound, human. But what I love best is the introduction—pure Panaït —vehement, insolent, prophetic, thirsty for justice and—injustice. It's unfair to Bilili; you've been too harsh. Or, if you prefer, too just—which in the case of women is supreme injustice. Women (you know this well) have another universe—material, moral, intellectual. Their spirit is laden, all rippling with flesh. They are innocent, even in their greatest infidelities (especially then), for they obey a subterranean drive, prehuman and extraordinarily profound. They are always faithful to this drive and, to be sure, therein lies their grand, sad virtue. Man can sometimes be free, in a moment of heroism and intoxication; woman— never. Freedom such as this (which in a man is honor) would be for her insubordination to her destiny—a vice. That is why I find your anger against Bilili unjust. And also: Mustn't we pardon everything in a woman who has given us a single moment of happiness? . . .

At Easter, as we had agreed, Nikos came to Paris for a brief encounter. Cousin Mary lodged him again, on Erlanger Street, up on the seventh floor. Two little rooms, a sunny balcony. Mary was away, and Nikos shut himself up alone, waiting for my arrival from London. He bought himself tomatoes, fruits and bread, and to keep from feeling idle, he began the canto on El Greco.

A brief, all too brief encounter—ten days: and yet they were to glow in our hearts till the end of our lives. And Nikos never wearied of talking about them:

Ah, Lenotschka, Lenotschka, as soon as you go away I shrink back into a corner, into a tree hollow, and, like a bee, set about making honey. But when you are there, I feel all of me full of honey, and I bless the day I was born. . . .

Where could the two Cretans find the solitude they longed for? As though by chance, Cousin Mary had just acquired a charming country house by the sea in Aegina. Prevelakis and Nikos Kazantzakis settled there and resumed work enthusiastically.

Aegina, April 23, 1933

My beloved Lenotschka,

. . . Our life here is very simple, as you might guess: The house is comfortable, new, very clean. We've been to some expense to make it habitable. I've brought my desk and a few books, stools, etc. Facing me so that I can see you, a big photograph of you. Over my bed, a nude by Kalmouko. To my left, Elsa. The 4 plates on the walls and some ikons. I wake up at 5:00 (A.M.) and work on The Odyssey. I still haven't gotten into the rhythm, but I shall. . . .*

Aegina, May 7, 1933

. . . I had reached Book 7 of The Odyssey and now for two days I've had to leave it, to write the articles they've asked me for. I'm writing from morning till night. My hand is worn out, because I have to make a copy of them and send the same articles to other newspapers in Egypt and Kavalla, etc. . . .†

Aegina, May 30, 1933

. . . The other day I went to Athens. . . . To avoid people, I rushed to the museums . . . but by chance, I did run into several acquaintances . . . all enthusiastic about the Spain articles. They say they're magnificent, masterpieces, etc., etc. All this saddens me, because

---

* Letter to E. Samios.
† Letter to E. Samios.

it proves that anything good you write is beyond them and only when you write bagatelles do they understand and the enthusiasm begins. If I had a bit less will power, or a weakness for success, I would have slipped into these easy laurels. . . .

Here, life in Aegina's the same: sea, winds, work, talks about El Greco. And I feel a deep nostalgia for you. I couldn't stay in Athens, because they don't leave me in peace to think about you. I'm very glad my heart pounds like this when I think of you. All things assume meaning and a halo [aura] of desire.

When will we see each other again? And where? The ten days [in Paris] "qui ébranlèrent la terre [that shook the world]"* remain immutable, eternal in my blood. When will they glow again? . . .†

Aegina, June 8, 1933

My beloved Lenotschka,

. . . Prevelakis came back from Athens this morning in despair. Only enemies . . . all Dexameni pounced on him. "Why should he be staying with me?" "Why should he be in isolation?" . . . All of them organized against us. Terrible slander against Marika (they learned that she had spent a night with us). The fire had been kindled by N. It was a lamentable sight. Prevelakis disgusted, never wants to go back! . . .

I'm working hard on The Odyssey. . . . Yesterday, I interrupted it for a moment and read the newspaper avidly. You surely must know that the Royalists tried to kill Venizelos. . . . For five kilometers, two cars full of assassins pursued his car and shot at him with revolvers, pistols and machine guns! Venizelos wasn't hurt at all. Four bullets struck his wife, but she's out of danger. A Cretan bodyguard of his was killed and his car riddled. Everyone is topsy-turvy. Crete is seething. I (who have no great love for Venizelos) feel disgusted and abashed at their tracking down like a wild beast this old man who doubled the territory of Greece. . . . The Greeks are brutes!‡

Aegina, June 13, 1933

. . . Here in Greece, the situation is abominable. The country's on the brink of the abyss. I feel disgust and anger. Beyond a doubt, there are two Greeces and the soudage [soldering] hasn't occurred yet.

---

* Paraphrase of the title of the well-known book on the Russian Revolution, John Reed's Ten Days That Shook the World.
† Letter to E. Samios.
‡ Letter to E. Samios.

Perhaps it will soon. There are two spirits which are very different; it's not that the one is good and the other bad. The one is bad and the other worse! And it is very sad to watch the imbecility and passion and malice with which the one Greece pounces on the other Greece. . . .*

Aegina, July 4, 1933

. . . I still haven't gotten any letter from you. They must be holding it up in Thessaloniki, where two days ago fierce senatorial elections were held. All Greece was in an uproar; violent hatred between the followers of Venizelos and the Royalists. But finally Venizelos won out. Better this way, because the others intended to bring the kings back. . . . I am deadly disgusted at the sight of all this. And it's only because I am enclosed in this solitude, possessed by a work, that I can escape and all these things just graze my skin. . . .†

Aegina, July 12, 1933

. . . Intense heat. I plunge into the sea around 3 in the afternoon, bake myself, work a great deal. . . . These few verses I'm sending you describe my peaceful state. If I only had financial peace too, my God, how I could work!

I'm impatient to write the 24 bodyguards of The Odyssey. (Dante and El Greco are finished.) And I shall try to write a canto for you too, Lady-Generalissimo-of-All-the-Bodyguards—to tell you all my rich, multifarious, imperishable love. Will I ever be able to? It's difficult, because I am living all this emotion. If I were not living it, it would be possible. But, then, it's better for me to live it than for it ever to become a reminiscence. . . .‡

Aegina, August 7, 1933

. . . I've delayed a bit [in writing you], because all these days we've been having visits. . . . All this hurly-burly is contrary to my own soul. What's the need of talk and cries? And to what avail, all this peacock parading? I long for only two things in this world and they fill my heart: Creation of the Obra§ and you. All the rest seems to me futile, a tiresome hubbub. I listened to them talking away; and I talked too.

---

* Letter to E. Samios.
† Letter to E. Samios.
‡ Letter to E. Samios.
§ The Odyssey.

But I kept thinking of only one thing: to get back home and write you a long, warm letter; to open all the water taps so that love might flow unhindered. The more I love you, the more useless the world is to me . . . because I can replace it with another, better, warmer, more simple world, as I would have created my entire life if I had been the Creator.

Now I've launched into Dante again. I'm correcting it verse by verse, and it's becoming much better and more faithful. I wish I could print it. But where can I find the 30,000 drachmas needed? In two months, it will be entirely ready. . . .

Here, the cantaloupes have begun, and the watermelons and the figs and grapes. Yesterday, we cut the first two figs and the first grapes on "Mary" Estate. Simple delights which, as you know, for me are very great.

Lefteris sent me the first canto of his Dante: dismal. And he insists that it's incomparably superior to mine. This will be another new source of grief and hatred, when he becomes aware of the truth—as though I were to blame, as though I had challenged him to the battle. The fact of my existence will always be a cause for his enslavement, hence devotion, and at the same time hatred. But I'm not to blame. I try my utmost to help him liberate himself. But he cannot. . . .*

Aegina, August 15, 1933

. . . In ten days, I did 33 cantos [of the Inferno] and tomorrow I'm entering Purgatorio. [The translation] is improving a great deal. I want this translation to be at the same level as Pallis' Iliad. And I shall surely succeed in this, if I live. If I have some free time to myself and a few years longer, I feel I am now ripe to leave a work solidly founded in the Greek—i.e., the Cretan—earth. And all this confidence, high spirits, elation—secretly and without your knowing it—I owe to you, my love. . . .

Having once again tried to play the matchmaker and not having succeeded in bringing two of our dearest friends together, he added:

Life with a human being is collaboration, adventure, an excursion into an unknown land, intoxication and, at the same time, an incredible

---

* Letter to E. Samios.

dream, bringing you tears of gratitude and emotion. You remember how often we used to say in amazement: "What then this miracle/ A man and a woman—strangers/ Become one another's own/ And trusty friends as well."

Grapes are growing in the vineyard. Every morning before dawn, when I wake up, I go down and cut a big, big bunch and eat away, like Odysseus, blessing the earth and the vines and the sun and the rain. All the powers have collaborated to give birth to this superb miracle of the plump grapes. . . .

Around 8:30 [A.M.], Pagona comes up (she's our young merry-widow servant) and brings the milk. I'm sunk in my papers and don't even lift my head. I say "Good morning" to her with an absent-minded glance and she goes off. God knows what she must think of me, since she's never seen me except when I'm writing, absorbé [absorbed], unsmiling, untalking. And then all of a sudden, when anyone comes on Sunday, the whole seashore reverberates with my laugh. . . .

At night, I lie on the terrace and look up at the stars a long time. I can't tell you how I wish you were by my side at this hour. "Il tacer è bello," says Dante. "Silence is beautiful." But the night will come when I will stretch out my hand and—O miracle!—touch your body. And then I will say nothing, but my heart will be pounding fit to burst. Because I am well aware that this is the great happiness. . . .*

Aegina, August 20, 1933

. . . Today, Harilaos [Stephanidis] came unexpectedly and you can imagine my delight. We cut figs and grapes and laughed. I tried to animate him a bit. But he's aged. He is all worries. Now the Royalists have dismissed him and he doesn't know what will become of him. I felt heartily sorry for him and did my best. He's thawed out a bit, but when he leaves he'll fall back into the void. . . .

Here in Greece the atmosphere is abysmal; impossible to describe the misery, vulgarity, dishonesty of the people who are governing. Nowhere a single light. If I didn't have the Odyssey, Dante and you, I would be suffocated with disgust and rage. But now nothing can touch me: Mon pain est cuit! [My bread is baked!] The "bread of angels," not the other bread.

---

* Letter to E. Samios.

Day after tomorrow, I'm expecting Skouriótis* to spend three days here. The Royalists have dismissed him too, and he's out on the street. The best and most honest person in the employment of Greece. . . .

On Sunday, Haritákis† the doctor is coming. . . . And now he too is poor. In a little house he's built among the pine trees near Daphni, he's struggling to nourish his two "creatures."‡ He's impatient, he says, to see me and let off some steam. I wish I could be useful to my friends in a more positive way. . . .§

Aegina, August 22, 1933

. . . If the letters of these past months do survive, one day when they've turned all yellow and someone is leafing through them to supplement my biography it will be said that surely I never loved any human being as I loved this girl with the initials E.S.—who must, of course, be Eleni Samios—and your name will be uttered. And, of course, they'll go on to add: the author of the celebrated Gandhi, and the first woman to introduce stenotypy into Greece!‖ As far as her character is concerned, we have no clear evidence. But the fact that she was capable of living to the end of her life with a person like the poet of the Odyssey proves she had great virtues—and her greatest virtues of all: patience, endurance and courage. For, needless to say, life was not easy with this person so harshly judged by his contemporaries—Lefteris and the great authoress Madame Galatea!

And no one will ever know (unless these letters are preserved) what you are for me, "7 women in one, 17 women in one," last joy of my life. . . .¶

Aegina, August 28, 1933

O coz, coz, coz, my pretty little coz!
. . . This whole year—except for the ten stars in March**—has been

---

* Panayís Skouriótis, General Director of Jurisprudence in the Ministry of Justice. Active in the democratic cause and prison reform in Greece.
† A Cretan doctor, and childhood friend of N.K.
‡ This was how he referred to his wife and daughter.
§ Letter to E. Samios.
‖ N.K. was teasing me in this reference to stenotypy. I had actually studied the Granjean method in London and had been planning to bring it to Greece, but never managed to do so.
¶ Letter to E. Samios.
** The ten days in Paris, once again referred to.

all dark and bitter, and may it never come back again! My ideal you know: 8 months' isolation and work, 4 months' traveling. Perhaps we will manage this when the inheritance is settled.* Meanwhile, I am passing difficult months, because I have no money. . . .

Today, Skouriótis came to see me. He gave me great pleasure, telling me, on behalf of Papandreou, that if I want to accept a position (the post of Library Director will soon be vacated), it will be easy, so long as the present government falls. . . .

Abundant grapes in our vineyard. Every morning at daybreak, I cut a huge [bunch] and refresh myself. Yesterday, it sprinkled. The first [autumn] rains have begun. . . .

A great joy that you're now reading English books. . . . This language has a troublante harmony like flowing water. Read the superb verses of Keats, Browning and Tennyson; they're a great delight.

I love you very much, ineffably much. . . . "O coz, coz, coz, my pretty little coz, that thou didst know how many fathom deep I am in love."† What a godlike language, what harmony! How well this phrase suits the feeling of my heart! . . .‡

Athens, September 2, 1933

My beloved Lenotschka,

Renaud sent me a telegram to say he had arrived by airplane and he says he has come to see me. All day yesterday, I was with him and his wife. . . . Today, we'll go to the museum and the Acropolis, and tomorrow we're leaving for Delphi; day after tomorrow for Mycenae, and last of all Olympia. They'll stay here 8 days, and I'm obliged to be with them. I'm worried both because I can't do my work and also because I don't have any money to show them a bit of hospitality. I borrowed a thousand drachmas and I'm spending them savagely. I don't let them pay for anything, and I'm désolé [dismayed] at not being able to pay for their hotel too. (The rascals are staying at the Grande Bretagne, 600 drs. per day!) . . .

In addition to Toda Raba, Renaud wants me to promise him three other books! . . . In spite of this, all my mind is turned toward

---

* A hope never realized.
† This line is from Shakespeare's As You Like It and was quoted by N.K. in English.
‡ Letter to E. Samios.

London, toward the woman who's the only one who interests me in the world. . . .*

Aegina, September 8, 1933
. . . After a week of touring, fatigue, receptions, I came back to Aegina yesterday. Two hours later, by another boat, the Jouvenels arrived. We ate lunch, talked, bought some figs, grapes, honey, sweets, cheese, olives, stuffed vine leaves, etc., and they were enthusiastic. In the evening a stroll in Aegina and at 11 P.M. we separated. . . . Jouvenel is thinking of setting up a Greek publishing house in Athens. . . . Maybe this will become a reality next year. But I wouldn't like to get involved, because I don't want to confuse friendship with business. I gave Mme. de Jouvenel a pretty copper object, as well as the "Virgin of the Roses."†
. . . She's a very vigorous, clever Jewess. . . . If we stayed in Paris, we would go to their home occasionally. . . .

Two nights ago, I saw Papandreou and he told me that as soon as he assumes office in the government, he'll recommend a chair of modern literature at the University and I'll be appointed. . . .‡

Aegina, September 10, 1933
Here it's autumn. The evening cool, the nights cold. The sea foamy, no more swimming. The earth is turning bare. The clouds are gradually emerging up over the mountains. We need a stove in the study and some new repairs on the windows and the doors to keep the waters and winds from coming in. All this will be done when you get here. Because otherwise I'll stay like this; I'm not in the mood to attend to my own confort. . . .§

Aegina, September 18, 1933
. . . "When man and woman unite, the heavens rejoice." Perhaps this is the greatest human joy on earth, the only happiness, which so long as it lasts is not a chimera. All the rest riffraff or air, profoundly loathsome to me. So may the best befall us! At times, I enjoy leaving myself in the hands of the awesome powers we call Chance, Coin-

* Letter to E. Samios.
† Our most beautiful ikon.
‡ Letter to E. Samios.
§ Letter to E. Samios.

cidence, Destiny. And I have confidence in them. May they smile upon us now.

Now that Prevelakis is gone, I'm all alone. The clouds pass by very white and autumnal. Occasionally a drop of rain falls. I go up to the terrace, stretch out my hands like Buddha and receive my day's wages in my palms, thinking of you.

The neighbors . . . have gone, and so there's no voice contaminating the air. A way farther on, two or three little houses, dogs barking, a peacock shrieking.

Tomorrow, I'll be finishing the second draft of Dante and I'll begin the commentary. Apparently, it's going to be printed before Christmas. Melachrinos* has bought the paper for me (very fine paper) and we hope to find the money soon.

If I am in Greece and so desire, something is sure to turn up. Most likely, professor of foreign literature at the University. . . . If this does happen, at last we shall have a home and one sure trip per year. Meanwhile, I am hoping to arrange the inheritance matters, etc. . . . Not to mention the fact that I'm working splendidly here. . . .

All the German-Jewish intellectuels are in Paris: Holitscher, Kisch, [Thomas] Mann. Erich Baron (do you remember him in Berlin?), the Director of Russland,† committed suicide in prison. I read about it in the Nouvelles Littéraires. . . .‡

Aegina, September 27, 1933

. . . Here the internal situation is becoming increasingly anomalous. But this doesn't bother me at all. I've found my own rhythm now. I'm living in Greece as though I were on some little island in Japan. Whoever comes here does not disturb me. Whoever used to disturb me has stopped coming. They cannot touch me and they've left me absolutely in peace. . . . The Jouvenels wrote me that they're "follement heureux [madly happy]" with their trip. . . .§

Aegina, October 4, 1933

. . . I got all the Nouvelles Littéraires and the two letters inside, niché [ensconced] like the sweet fruit of the almond inside the shell.

---

* The symbolist poet and director of Kyklos, already met earlier on.
† Russia, a literary periodical.
‡ Letter to E. Samios.
§ Letter to E. Samios.

I was overjoyed with everything and went down to the sea at once—heavenly, transparent, all sandy in the depths and hot—and I lay on a rock and dried off. A light, pleasant weariness and all this afternoon I won't work; I shall be tasting the future joy of your coming here and beholding this sea and the celestial panorama of the Saronic. Sublime solitude and sweet air here, as though you're at the edge of the world and there's no one to bother you. Athens is at the other end of the world and, as I wrote you, when her inhabitants have come once or twice and seen no crack in the fortress, they go away again and settle down placidly to their own little affairs. Never has Greece been so good to me, so expedient and so hospitable. My way of life and ability to live happily and without any rancune [animosity], remote from human beings, disarms them and they leave me alone. When you come, the fortress will be even more solid and the diamond wall all the more impregnable. From time to time, we'll allow some loved person to enter. And then he'll go away again, peacefully, preserving only the vision of an incredible existence, because it is so simple and good in the midst of all the complexity and malice of the world. . . .

Besides our own individual reasons, there are also general reasons that impel you here. . . . With Hitler, the world is once again in a state of upheaval, and I fear that some great harm may break loose and you may be far away in the very center of the fire. . . .

Please don't forget the schoolbooks. . . . It's vital that you write some too. I feel you'll manage it better, because you have a simpler, more patient style. I'll tell you some ideas and you'll make them into a book. If one of them is approved, it's very important. . . .

If Renaud's revue [periodical] paid, it would be splendid. . . . But will it pay? He writes me over and over again, asking me to send him some manuscrits. . . .

I don't want anything from Paris. Here, we have all the bounties of God: olives, honey, cheese, sun, sea. . . .*

Aegina, October 15, 1933
. . . Here, preparations are under way for your welcome. With Kalmouko the other day, we repaired the path down to the sea to keep your feet from being hurt. We've bought some fishing poles and lines, and you can relax that way, doing nothing. I set some workmen to plastering the outside walls where they'd gotten a bit banged. . . . I've

---

* Letter to E. Samios.

ordered food so the cupboard will be full. I'm doing my best and there's still a bunch of grapes hidden away somewhere, waiting for you. . . .

How I've longed for you to be here with all this sun and beauty of the Saronic. Fishing boats with red-and-white sails pass by, the fish leaping and sparkling. The mountains like paintings on glass. What a pity for me to be reveling in all this without you. But you will come and the sun will come and all the good things of earthly life. . . .

I feel tremendously stirred as the day draws near when we shall see each other. My ten fingers frissonnent. I kiss you, my love, on your shoulders and the palms of your hands.*

Aegina, October 31, 1933

. . . Waiting for you like this, I have no appetite to work, because the joy of soon seeing you robs me of all power to concentrate. And just as I diverted myself while waiting for you in Paris in March, so the other day I also wrote a canto, like the one to El Greco, on Genghis Khan. I don't know whether it turned out well. It's very harsh, sonore [resonant], forceful. How I'd like to know whether it's good! You'll tell me when you come. . . .

Heavy the solitude, now that I'm expecting you. Indescribable how sweet these autumn days have been—tender, gris argent [silvery gray], the sea calm, with showers of rain now and then. Abundant quince, and my desk is full of them. . . . Greece has never appeared so sweet and good to me. The reason is surely that I'm on an island, in a beautiful site, far removed from all contact, as though I found myself on the Pacific islands—Hawaii or Tahiti. . . .†

If I had been a Japanese calligraphist, after bathing and fasting to purify my body and my soul I would have donned my finest kimono, taken hold of my paint brush in the traditional style and depicted our failures and our triumphs in two kakemonos.‡

Multifarious, variegated, floating in the autumn mist, as they have become traced upon our memory, demolishing the prison of walls, inviting the visible and invisible world to penetrate my room. : . . Clusters of wisteria, undulating serpents, perpendicular waterfalls,

---

* Letter to E. Samios.
† Letter to E. Samios.
‡ Japanese paintings that unroll vertically.

moving images swelling with sap; ethereal, barely perceptible states of soul and body, expanded and compressed by our own writing.

The El Greco discovered by Prevelakis, though authentic, found no buyer. Stenotypy was not introduced to Greece by me. Papandreou did not assume power and, therefore, could not offer Kazantzakis any post. The subscriptions for the edition of the *Divine Comedy* translation did not bring in the money needed to publish it. The National Theater did not perform the translations of the plays they had commissioned. In France, two editors had already gone bankrupt, a third had died, and a fourth came within an inch of losing his life. In Greece, there were certain individuals who behaved indelicately. Nikos finally yielded up his part of the paternal legacy to his younger sister. And to complete this black sequence: in Paris, I was the victim of a theft, robbed of my last thousand-franc note, which I had intended to use for my return ticket to Greece.

So many, many misadventures counterbalanced by so few successes. . . .

In the other *kakemono*: As though traced on water, a face simultaneously stern and smiling, with the enormous, receding brow and the incandescent, amused eyes; and as a backdrop, changing in successive waves, the countries we visited together: Palestine, the U.S.S.R., Czechoslovakia, France and England, Italy and Spain, China and Japan—and our Aegina, transparent as an aquamarine—and also, the sea and the mountains and the clouds and the sky with its constellations; the coming and going of our friends of always, the ones we've already met in this book as well as several others I shall not even be able to enumerate—and all the foreign friends, such as Jean Herbert, Mady and Pierre Sauvageot, Yvonne and J. Pierre Métral, Sir Sidney Waterlow, Josephine MacLeod and Marie Bonaparte. The last-named, as we shall see, befriended us at the most crucial moment of our life. . . .

A life full of savor, serene in spite of its perturbations—in the rhythm of the great wave leading toward the abyss. . . .

Left penniless in Paris, after much hesitation, I ventured to admit the new disaster to Nikos. He replied:

Aegina, November 8, 1933

My beloved Lenotschka,

I just got back from Athens yesterday evening and received your letter about the theft. . . . Don't worry, my love; all this is nothing. It will all be set right and we shall pay our debts. These are trifles that vanish and leave no sting or poison, in the presence of the unshakable fact that we both exist. A single moment of our being together is worth more than all the base, inimical acts of dishonorable, stone-blind Chance.

I think that when you come here and stretch out on the chaise longue (Kalmouko's going to give us one) and listen to the peaceful soughing of the sea and close your eyes and I'll be talking to you by your side, all these things tormenting you now will fade away like mist when the sun falls on it. All this time, I am not afraid of anyone or anything— on one sole condition: that I feel you near me.

In Athens, I saw no one except my sister, a marvelous person, a real miracle of kindness and love. She bought me various things for you to find in the cupboard when you arrive: honey, Quaker Oats, olives and a kerosene stove. All this is in place, waiting for you. . . .*

Aegina, November 8, 1933
Afternoon

Kalmouko came home and I interrupted this letter. We took the hoes and dug the little path to the sea so you can walk evenly. We worked a lot and got all perspiry. Then we came back and I lit the kerosene stove and fried some fish. We made a tomato salad with garlic and I drank to your health. And now Kalmouko has taken the pole and gone off fishing. A peaceful, gentle day—the sea calm. I'm happy that the day will soon be here when you will walk here and see the exquisite vision of the Saronic, without being tortured by any cares. And all the bad things will become distant memories and we shall never again be separated for so many desperate months. . . . Don't think about anything; don't worry about anything. We have what millions of human beings do not have. Whatever may befall us, no one can touch our happiness.

My love, I kiss your hands, your feet that have walked so much, your large eyes that have wept so much, your knees that I love so much, your slender shoulders that have borne such a burden, your lips that I long for. I kiss all your beloved body.†

---

* Letter to E. Samios.
† Continuation of preceding letter to E. Samios.

290

Elena Konstantinovna!

All day long today I've been arranging your room and I've been very happy. *Everything here is waiting impatiently for you. . . . My heart is trembling, and I won't be able to utter a sound when I see you land. . . . This life is a great, unanticipated miracle. We need no future life, no other Paradise. This is enough for us, more than enough.*

I'm sleeping downstairs now, in your room, to have a foretaste of all the delight of your presence. I look at the space that is empty now and I conjure you here to walk back and forth, making all the well-loved, familiar motions in the evening. And I know the joy I am feeling now will be a thousand times more intense when the reality is actually here. I've put a Madonna on the wall, two Spanish plates and strung some pomegranates up. On your big table I laid a few books, some postcards, the Nouvelles Littéraires, and a few quince. These are sacred, tender moments as I prepare your room, alone like this. My beloved Lenotschka, at times I shudder; this joy is greater than any human being is entitled to. But then again, perhaps—I say to myself—we are such "good people" that we have the right and power to transform this fallen earth and make it into Paradise. We have been well tried in sorrows and in joys and have emerged victorious from the trial. May God keep our hearts thus, always upright, pure, invincible. . . .*

1934.   Aegina was sought after by the ancient Greeks for her dry climate. Aristophanes supposedly was born there, and Plato used to go there to rest. Our contemporaries relish Aegina for her porous pitchers, her pistachios, her unique fish† and her sponges. Her Doric temple of Aphaia was pillaged by learned archaeologists practicing a "civilized" brand of brigandry—following Elgin's example. Its metopes severed from the brushing strokes of the pine trees and the sea breeze are desiccating in Munich. In their fragmented dance, the austere columns facing Sounion bear witness to the raping ravage.

Earth of Attica's earth, Aegina awoke one day, her cables cut, a cloud fallen from the sky, laden with promises, floating unanchored.

---

* Letter to E. Samios.
† A goldish flat fish delicate in taste, called by the Aeginetans katsóula.

Small, though not too small; remote, though not too remote;* popular, though not populous, spared tourism "made in Europe." Her port is aristocratic, her capital a "poor relation." Her hills are strewn with almond trees and ruined chapels. Her mountain is bare and her vineyards chalky. Her populace smiling, loving jokes and laughter. Arid on the side facing Athens, full of olive trees on the side facing Epidaurus, African further southward. . . .

In antiquity, she knew the glory of victories as well as the devastation of armed warfare. Only 140 years ago, the Greeks—Eaters-of Garlic—having driven out the Turk with cutlass and slingshot, chose her as their capital. No sooner done than Athens was preferred and her first school was converted into a Common Law prison.

And so passengers for Aegina had one chance in two of traveling in company with policemen and some "bandit"—often young, wearing handcuffs, smoking and chatting with his jailers, or taciturnly twisting his mustache. . . .

Who would ever have told me that after all these years, as I evoke these brief crossings, my pulse would beat in the rhythm of the *santuri?* Who remembers? His head tossed back, his eyes fixed, the stout man singing the sorrows of our islands; the hail-like notes of the *santuri*, like fine rain, soaking the deck. At that period, even the very music was redolent of the Terror. Nowadays, the knob is turned and fake sighs reeking of plastic and prefabricated ads flood the air. . . .

It would have been natural for Kazantzakis, who was Cretan to the very tip of his fingernails, to have chosen Crete. But he was only a human being after all, a human being afraid of succumbing to the temptations of the family embrace. And so he chose Aegina, an island whose bridges were cut for the rest of the day once the boat had passed. Solitude, within close range of the capital city.

I would have preferred Attica. Our floating rock terrified me at first. Slowly, I learned that if two beings so desire—if they take the trouble—they can be happy even on top of a pole.

I am neither idealizing my companion nor disparaging him. It was not always easy to breathe his fiery air. But if he preferred the bare branch for himself, he never imposed it on others. Between convenient compromise and his own dignity, he never hesitated. He proudly refused the easy chair.

---

* Aegina is 18 miles from Piraeus.

I loved this charming and wise man. And I believe that under his discipline I blossomed as much as my nature was capable of.

"You've lived thirty years by my side and haven't learned a thing!" he said plaintively one of the last days at Freiburg, as I lamented on our catastrophic rashness: "What had we been doing in China? Why had we allowed that cursed vaccination?"

His hands transparent, resting on the arms of the easy chair, he raised astonished eyes, as usual. "Why look backward, Lenotschka?" he asked.

"Because . . . because you've suffered the martyrdom. . . ."

"How funny you are, you other people!" he murmured then, shaking his head. "I think only of the joys I've had; the rest is of little importance!"

I loved this man because he never asserted his superiority, never insisted on transforming me into a "lady philosopher." I was a simple person. He left me as I was, respecting my nature. He did, however, liberate me from the complexes created by inept guardians. He taught me to be ashamed only of my own shortcomings. He didn't offer me the possibility of the university diplomas I had aspired to. But he offered me love, confidence, affection, the fields and the forests, the mountain and the sea, undreamed-of travels, Cretan and African tales, his own example of perfect nudity before God. Only with Gandhi could he have lived and governed, with the great doors open: "The man who governs owes the whole truth to his people. The people have the right to read his thought and his life as they read a book."

Our "silence" by the sea was but a euphemism. In summer, myriads of invisible flutes played. In winter, the nights were sometimes anguished, the north wind roaring like mad over the rocks and the waves splattering our house. Since it was itself a rock extracted from the sea, it could resist them. The window blinds cracked as though a whole caravan of old wagons was passing by beneath our windows.

If I had been alone, I would have been panic-struck. But he was there, serene, near the fluttering wick of the oil lamp, caressing and holding my hand, reading out loud to me to keep me from tiring my eyes.

"Today, I'm going to initiate you to philosophy."

"If you'd only tell me a Cretan tale!"

"Philosophy" I had there in front of me in the flesh and bones: to be good, not to envy anyone; to possess only what was strictly necessary (*hm-hm*—well, there were a few ikons, some ivory or some little trinket brought back from the far corner of the earth); to make an idealized image of yourself, to nail it on the wall in front of you and to try to be like it; to forgive those who do you wrong (it is thanks to them that you mobilize your own forces); to revel in the earth, the sky, the sea, the rams and the cows, the bread and the olives ("*Cuando perdices, perdices; cuando oraciones, oraciones!*"*); never to let comfort dull you; and if a child at the far limits of the earth is hungry, to feel responsible for it; to keep one's soul always ready; to remain upright when the time comes; to have an Occidental brain and an African heart.

Yes, "philosophy" did have an African heart. It knew how to laugh, caress, tuck the covers under you. It smoked a pipe, treated itself to fish soups, went for a bathe and dried itself in the sun, strolled down to the town to make its purchases and returned, its sack full of anecdotes:

"Good day, Stratis! When's the marriage set for?"

"What's that you're saying, Kyr Nikos? Don't you know my wife's demanding shoes?"

Stratis, the village idiot, had strung the shoes around his neck like a collar. He sighed with contentment at having had typhus as a young boy thereby escaping school.

No person could ever claim to have knocked on our door in vain. More than the sanctity of his own work, Nikos honored hospitality and friendship. But a serious friendship, remote from coffee shops and public meeting places, free of raucous scenes.

He was also a father-confessor and people who had been humiliated and offended used to come to ask his advice:

"Kyr Nikos, my husband caught me in the act . . . He would get rid of me if . . ."

Kyria Maria was already old and toothless, wasted away by her multiple births. Her husband had accused her of being the mistress of their daughter's lover!

"If what, Kyria Maria?"

"It's like this: He wants me . . . to the . . . by boat. . . ."

"By boat?"

"By boat, but on one condition . . ." And in Nikos' palm she laid

---

* Saint Teresa of Ávila's famous dictum: "When partridges, partridges; when prayers, prayers."

a little package of dynamite* wrapped up in newspaper. "To do it or not to do it? What do you think, Kyr Nikos?"

1933–1937. Once again Cousin Mary gave us shelter, this time on a tiny spit of land on the north side of the island facing Salamis and Megara. To the west, a bit south of Aegina, lay the crenelated mountains of the Peloponnesus over Epidaurus and Methana. To the east, like some good-natured, round-backed, domesticated animal, our Mt. Hymettos. We also had a vineyard, our own private terrace up over the waves, a fig tree and a belvedere designed as an ivory tower.

Intense work by day, tea about five o'clock, walks at nightfall. Rose-tinted awakenings, amber noons, vermilion sunsets, nights of golden constellations, sleep cradled by the salt waves. North winds in winter, *meltemia* winds in summer and the mad west wind to remind us of the absolute felicity of the calm.

More than a few visitors of all sorts and varieties—painters, sculptors, poets, young and old, novelists, long-term friends and newly made friends, Greeks and foreigners alike. And we usually invited them to stay and share our frugal meal.

Within a single year—1934—Nikos wrote two schoolbooks, in collaboration with Professor Panetsos; a third schoolbook on which I collaborated to a large extent; a reader; and a new version of his *Odyssey,* nine cantos in *terza rima,* dedicated to the "bodyguards" of his *Odyssey:* "Lenin," "Don Quixote," "To Himself," "Mahomet," "Nietzsche," "Buddha," "Moses," "To Rhyme" and "To Eleni." He also was commissioned by the National Theater to translate Cocteau's *Infernal Machine.*

In January 1934 Nikos put down in his notebook, in a telegraphic style, a dream which deeply impressed him. Twenty-three years later, he recalled it in *Report To Greco:*

Two stony lips, woman's lips, suspended themselves in the air without a face. They moved, and I heard a voice: "Who is your God?"

---

* At that period, they used to use dynamite for fishing, and several accidents had been recorded.

"Buddha," I unhesitatingly replied. But the lips moved again: "No, no. Epaphus!"*

. . . Epaphus, the god of touch, who prefers flesh to shadow and like the wolf in the proverb does not wait upon the promises of others when it is a question of filling his belly. He trusts neither eye nor ear; he wants to touch, to grasp man and soil, to feel their warmth mix with his own, feel them become one with him. He even wants to turn the soul into body so that he can touch it. The most reliable and industrious of all the gods, who walks on earth, loves the earth, wishes to remake it "in his own image and after his likeness"—that was my god.†

The fig trees were sprouting their first leaves like tiny hands stretched up to the sun. The meadow was strewn with poppies, big yellow daisies, blue and white irises. . . . The wild violets were clinging to the rocks, sweetly scenting the coast.

The lawsuits with the publisher were still not at an end. And Angelakis was begging Nikos to come to Athens and see the publisher. "Out of sight, out of mind," he had written, quoting the popular adage. But Nikos loathed having to speak with anyone he did not respect. And I had to go to Athens in his place:

Aegina, spring 1934, Wednesday

My beloved Lenotschka,

As you must know, the latest Nouvelles Littéraires dedicates a big notice by Finberg on your Gandhi.‡ It is most laudatory; one phrase: "For her book is written with a gentle passion in a surge of love." . . . I was very happy. This will do the book a lot of good. . . .

I'm also writing to Angelakis. . . . We need money, and God knows when we'll be free of the law courts. . . .

Having unwillingly accepted a small loan from Kalmouko, Nikos was regretting it.

---

* Epaphus was the god of touch. N.K. often used to say that he was a man of touch.
† Report to Greco, translated by P. A. Bien (New York: Simon and Schuster, 1965), p. 418.
‡ The book had just been published by Delachaux and Nestlé Editions, Neuchâtel and Paris.

I was moved by Kalmouko, but I wouldn't have accepted it, because I know he doesn't have it. Let's hope we'll be able to give it back quickly. . . .

Come now and begin the new book* and everything will come about. . . .†

Aegina, summer 1934, Wednesday

. . . You've got a letter from the publishers et je me suis permis [I took the liberty] to open it, because I was impatient. . . . Very pleasant: Gandhi will be translated into German too! Bravo for L., à la langue si pure, l'émule de Tagore [of the utterly pure language, emulating Tagore]!‡ . . . I am overjoyed, because in this way you are opening a path for . . . our travels. Come quickly and plunge into Schliemann. It will grow still better. . . .

> Onward, Lenio! And so long as the air stirs my hair,
> I shall never leave you masterless; I shall hold your hand,
> And we shall roam the whole wide world; do not complain!

I wrote these verses in the Odyssey today and I was thinking very much of you. . . .§

At the end of July, I felt sharp pains while swimming in the sea. . . . At first, I dragged back and forth between Aegina and Athens. In the end, I had to remain bedridden once and for all in Athens.

Aegina, August 8, 1934

My beloved, ailing St. George!

Early, early this morning, a little donkey stopped outside our door. A lady dismounted, followed by a servant carrying blankets. I jumped up and opened the door.

"Miss Mazur!‖ Ach, Eleni ist nicht da [Ah, Eleni isn't here]."

---

* I was planning to write the life of Schliemann, excavator of Troy and Mycenae.
† Letter to E. Samios.
‡ One of the phrases from the French reviews of the Gandhi book.
§ Letter to E. Samios.
‖ Miss Mazur was a young lady archaeologist living on Aegina.

She had come to fetch us both and had gotten two rooms ready at Dr. Welter's,* and we might have stayed there till you got well. . . . I was very moved by her kindness; she's a rare person. . . .

Don Juan† took the third pill and tonight I tried to give him the castor oil through the dropper. Impossible. So I got a kataïfi,‡ poured all the castor oil into it and he gobbled it right up, licking his whiskers. . . .

I've been working on the canto and decided that it will be the Prologue to the [other] 12. . . .§

Aegina, August 11, 1934

. . . I read your letter several times and my bitterness grew and grew. . . . I think of you every moment, and my love and grief are inexpressible. . . . I'm ashamed to be repeating défendus [forbidden] words. . . . Writing is a necessity that gives me no joy, because I am no dry intellectuel type, nor am I fatuous enough to believe that whatever I write is worthwhile. And so, writing is no consolation for me. You alone in the world can make me rejoice in being alive; you alone justify my existence. And once again I am unbearably sad at still not having been able to tell you what you are for me. On the contrary, often, precisely at the most intense point of my tenderness, I have behaved brusquely to you in order to hide my feeling and I haven't wanted or haven't been able to explain the cause. Ah, get well and come quickly to Aegina and I shall never do so again. . . .

It's windy and cool, and I go swimming. I've finished the canto. I'm reading Point Counter Point [by Aldous Huxley]—it's very good, very rich, very fine; but trop intellectuel [too intellectual]. . . .

Marika's wanting to come and take care of you touches me. . . . The days she spent here remain very dear in my memory. . . .||

Aegina, August 15, 1934

. . . Miss Mazur wrote me today saying that she had seen you and that you are still in pain. I pace up and down at home in despair. I can't think or work. The canto to you¶ that I'm writing in order to find relief comes out drop by drop, like blood. . . .

---

* Dr. Welter, a German archaeologist settled on Aegina.
† Don Juan was our cat.
‡ Kataïfi is an almond cake full of syrup.
§ Letter to E. Samios.
|| Letter to E. Samios.
¶ The "Canto to Eleni."

One of our schoolbooks has met with success and perhaps this will help us take care of things for some time to come. When you're up and around, go to the special shops and ask about a radio with batteries. I'm hoping that in this way we'll be able to have music in our solitude this winter. . . .

Here, nothing new. You've received only the French periodical from Egypt publishing an excerpt from Gandhi. About Toda Raba not a word. So it won't have the good luck of your book, about which quite a great deal has been written. In this way, I'm liberated from the temptation to write in French again. . . .*

Aegina, August 18, 1934

My love,

I'm writing you again today . . . to keep you company before coming in person a few days from now. . . .

I'm sending you the last part of your canto. I don't know whether you'll like it, but how can the word ever equal the human heart! "God," as a Byzantine mystic said, "is a sigh and a sweet tear." The same is true of love; only in a tear and a sigh can it be contained—and in action. . . .

The other day, an emissary from Madame Ralli† came to Aegina for the express purpose of bringing us some gifts: capstan tobacco for me, and for you a big jar of peach jam; and a fiery letter. . . .

Katina comes just for a moment and rushes off again. I do the washing and sweeping and watering. . . . I am with you always and love you. Para siempre, siempre, siempre! [For ever and ever and ever!]‡

Fortunately, his sister Eleni came to Aegina to take my place. But, still, Nikos couldn't overcome his bitterness.

Aegina, September 1, 1934

. . . I've read the Vie intime [Intimate Life] which Ts. sent to me. . . . It's interesting. . . . If he has the other book by Keyserling, Meditations sud-Américaines [South American Meditations], please ask him to lend it to me for a few days. This would interest me extraordinarily. . . .

---

* Letter to E. Samios.
† Maritsa Ralli, a talented writer, whom we had just recently met.
‡ Letter to E. Samios.

There's a competition for children's poems. I wish we could take part. . . .*

Aegina, September 13, 1934
Thursday

. . . I am not reading your new poem just now, because I feel upset. I'll read it tomorrow. I will surely like it. . . .†

Aegina, September 1934
Friday

. . . All goes well. Our guests‡ enthusiastic. . . . They stay up on the terrace for hours, writing and reading. We went down to the town today, and I bought some fish and an abundance of fruits. The table is full of simple, good food. . . .§

Aegina, September 1934
Sunday

. . . We read all your poems again—superb. "Music" is miraculous, one of your best poems. A different note, profound, exquisite. You are one of the most profound and best poets in Greece. In a single stride, you have reached the very top, without any missteps or groping. . . .

Mady sang a bit today. Her voice is still voilée [veiled] but superb. . . .‖

Aegina, September 1934
Thursday

I received your poems. . . . They are all excellent. I've translated some of them and given them to Pierre [Sauvageot]. . . . And today I'll translate some more. . . .

It seems to me that Pierre and I have become friends. I've gotten over my antipathy to his theosophies and futile, syrupy-sweet hopes of

---

* Letter to E. Samios.
† Letter to E. Samios.
‡ Mady Humbert-Sauvageot, a fine singer of folk songs, and Pierre Sauvageot. They had just been married and were spending part of September 1934 in our Aegina home.
§ Letter to E. Samios.
‖ Letter to E. Samios.

300

metempsychosis; and I take the splendid, clever, warm, pure human being existing behind the crust of Buddhist sugar. . . .*

To spend seven months bedridden, between life and death, is not easy. To conjure away the evil spirits, I had set about composing some short poems. In each of my letters, I used to send Nikos one of them, to lessen the pain of being apart. And he was overjoyed with them and, of course, exaggerated their value. Luckily, it was also he who one sleepless night had told me the adorable story of Ali-bey:

Sitting in front of his miniature shop, Ali-bey, the old Turkish spice merchant, was fanning himself in the shade, waiting for his rare clients (mainly children, who used to come and buy a few pennies' worth of pepper and cinnamon). He was finding life just beautiful. And just then a friend stopped in front of him and the sweet prattle began:
"Where've you come from, friend?"
"From Istanbul, Ali-bey."
"And what were you up to in Istanbul?"
"I went to visit the Sultan."
"To the Patishah?"
"May God take our days and add them unto his days; to the Patishah, Ali-bey! And the Patishah (so great is his mercy) wanted to hear news of you: 'Tell Ali-bey I love him well and am sending him along with my salutations a cargo of cloves and cinnamon—100 okas of cinnamon, 200 okas of pepper, 300 okas . . .'"
Ali-bey swooned, forgetting to fan himself. The visitor talked and talked; the okas kept piling up and up. Megalo-Kastro was smothered in cinnamon and cloves.
"Go on talking, go on talking, friend," murmured Ali-bey at long last, licking his chops like an old tomcat. "Talk, talk forever. I know it's all lies but I li-i-i-ike them!"

Talk, talk, Nikosmou; I know that you're exaggerating. But I li-i-i-ike it!

---

* Letter to E. Samios.

. . . My term as an enlisted man is over now. . . . Our guests are going and I'm glad that everything went well—even if I haven't been able to work at all these days. . . .

Yesterday, when I came back home around midnight, there was a delight in store for me: The Sauvageots had bought the Gorgon* and carried her up to the entrance of our house! The figurehead we often used to see (painted all green) down near the port, where they repair the boats. Now she's standing upright in our entranceway, facing the sea. She'll stay here now as Notre Dame of our house and we shall never part with her. Ah, if only it were possible for everything we long for to come about: you to get well quickly and Pierre to help us go to Paris, and then to build our little house in Aegina!

We have indeed made friends with Pierre. . . . I got a telegram from Minotis,† but no money. It's a good thing you sent me the 1,000 drachmas, because Vekios [the grocer] took more than 500 this month. But I'm very happy, because the hospitality came off incredibly well. . . .‡

Before he too left Aegina, Nikos received a letter from Roger Martin du Gard. He was one of the rare men of letters in France who, along with Jean Cassou, Jean Herbert and Renaud de Jouvenel, had appreciated *Toda Raba*:

"My sincere thanks to you for sending me your book. I read it in one go, with the greatest concentration and sustained interest. It can be read in a single surge just as it was written. A troubling and violent book, vibrating with accumulated strength and belief; a human, moving book, making one love its author. . . ."

1935.   We had often commented on the "miracles" that came from time to time to take us out of trouble. Nailed to my bed, I had begun to

---

* Throughout Aegina, our new house was known as "The Gorgon's House." This Gorgon is now in the Museum of Historical Studies, Heraklion.
† Alexis Minotis, a Cretan actor, at present Director of the National Theater of Greece. He had taken steps to have translations commissioned from N.K. and performed at the National Theater. Not one was ever played.
‡ Letter to E. Samios.

lose confidence both in my own organism and in our tutelary deities. Just then, the director of the Athens daily newspaper *Akropolis* commissioned Nikos to do some articles on Japan and China—this very Orient he used to dream of with almost painful intensity.

Before he embarked for the Orient, Kazantzakis thought of his most Oriental friend, Panaït, whose recent messages had been exuberantly optimistic.

Athens, February 6, 1935

Moré Panaïtaki, dear *Lazarus-who-hast-no-need-even-of-Christ, O Super-Lazarus, All Hail!*

What a joy to be alive upon this clot of earth and to love. To love this sacred haidouk* with the leaden pelvis, who after each somersault still remains standing. Hail, O brother, O companion-in-tricks, O eternal Odysseus!

In three days, I'll be leaving for China and Japan. I'm happy I shall see the yellow face of God, those monkey eyes, dissimulating smiles, mysterious masks of our future masters. I'll be back in five months. But in the meantime, I want to offer you my little house (three or four rooms, kitchen, veranda, terrace, vineyard, well and a fig tree) in Aegina, by the edge of the sea, a splendid coast! Come, dear Panaïtaki; you'll be happy there, with this dazzlingly beautiful young woman of the dangerous smile and teeth. We're happy, both of us, the only happy people in this world, because we're playing with fire and we need only our own magnificent, avid and ensanguined heart. We devour it every day, and every night it is reborn. We are Prometheus and, at the same time, Prometheus' wings; we are whole beings.

Seven months ago, I sent you Toda Raba with a very tender dedication. (When I think of you, my throat catches with tenderness.) And now you can dispose of it in your own way. And if there's anything left for the author, then drink a toast to my health, your own health, the health of your wife and of Bilili and Eleni! . . .

S.S. Cyprus, February 18, 1935

My beloved Lenotschka! My St. George!

The coasts of Egypt have come into sight; far off beyond my cabin

---

* *Haidouk*, a Rumanian word, probably meaning "gallant lad," is the title of one of Panaït Istrati's books.

porthole, I can just make out a very faint, dark line. . . . I'm the only passenger on the whole boat . . . my own yacht!

I'm lying in my cabin today—my birthday—thinking of you and recapitulating my own life; once again, taking new decisions, struggling to purify myself still more, expel my weaknesses, strengthen whatever good there is in me, so that I may be lighter and cleaner for the climb toward my peak, which keeps shifting place.

And you are with me, great Love, and I shudder with a sensuous proud exultation.*

Port Said, February 20, 1935

. . . By chance, I met a Cretan, the customs director here, who knew of me through Galatea! "You're the husband of Madame Galatea?" "Yes." What ensued is indescribable: An easy chair, coffee, shrieks of delight, and this noon he's taking me home by force for lunch. . . . I'm afraid Madame Galatea may be known even in Tokyo. Páli kalà!†‡

Port Said, evening of February 20, 1935

. . . Well, I did go to the Greek's house, and we ate pheasant! How can I describe the parlor for you? I was in a fright and lost all my appetite: As a girl, Madame had dabbled in painting. Well, she had made huge copies of criardes [gaudy] postcards and plastered the walls with them. Revolting dolls on blue pillows. Celluloid Negroes in the corners. Frightful Chinese vases. And after a while, Madame herself appeared—cold, collet monté [collar raised], not knowing what to make of me: a tramp, a savage, or a superior creature? A radio was blaring away somewhere, droning amanédes.§ At a later point, Madame told me that she was mad about good music! . . . And so we sat down to table: Barboúni fish and the famous pheasant. . . . The servant girl, Katina, is Cretan. And then a live partridge began cooing in the next room and the master rushed over and brought it in. It's Cretan too; he had brought it from Crete to remind him of the Cretan mountains. He set it on the table and just as we began admiring it, it soiled the tablecloth.

---

* Letter to E. Samios.
† "Páli kalà" is an untranslatable Greek idiom, roughly equivalent to "Well, it might have been worse."
‡ Letter to E. Samios.
§ Amanédes are droning chants, typical monotonous airs of Moslem countries.

Madame jumped up and put it back in the cage. The meal resumed: Cretan wine, Cretan cheese. Gradually the ice broke. I asked the lady what her aim in life was, and she asked me whether God exists. I told her "pas encore, Madame [not yet, Madame]" and she told me to give her a good recipe for life, how to find happiness. I told her: a) a clean conscience; b) to love some one thing in life with a passion, whatsoever thing that be; and c) never to wound a human heart. She was very pleased and promised me that when I come back in 4 months' time she will be happy. At that point we turned off the radio, and I felt ineffably relieved. We went out on the balcony. The sea in front of us was stormy; there was a cool breeze. I breathed deeply. At four o'clock I left and have been wandering through the streets till now, seven o'clock. I filled my pockets with sweet, sweet tangerines and ate them on the streets. A little Arab approached me around evening and spoke to me in Italian. He took out of his pocket some very obscene photographs to sell me! And then he proposed taking me home where he has a very pretty sister. I told him I didn't want any women, and then he proposed his brother to me—at his home again. I told him I didn't want any men either, and then he just looked at me in horror and left. . . .*

[At sea] February 21, 1935, noon

. . . The Japanese [ship] Koshima Maru has arrived. . . . Short and silent Japanese, a big ship, mysterious Japanese characters for every sign. The Captain has assigned me a superb cabin all to myself, 2nd class. I've arranged my books and things, and settled down for a month here. . . . We're in the Canal; full of ships; date trees along the boulevard in front of us. Fellahs with their boats loaded with tangerines, flat unleavened breads, olives, cigars and hashish pipes. My fellow travelers are Japanese, some dreadfully ugly Japanese women, consumptive Indians, and a disagreeable Frenchwoman. Apparently she'll be getting off at Suez, because I heard her say, "Ah! Je tiens à ne pas perdre mon petit déjeuner demain matin! [Ah! I insist on not missing my breakfast tomorrow morning!]"

A naked fellah has been diving again and again from the bridge to the sea. Everyone was laughing, and afterward the poor man dragged about, begging for a pourboire. I averted my eyes, because I am disgusted by everything that humiliates another human being. They all stare at him and laugh, and I'm in a corner, smoking my pipe and

---

* Letter to E. Samios.

thinking about the trip that's about to begin. Yellow men beget a slight terror in me. Will I be capable of loving them? How will my heart be when I get back?*

Night of February 21, 1935

We're still passing through the famous Suez Canal. To our left, the Arabian desert, monotonous, treeless, houseless. To our right, the plainland of Egypt with its date trees and its little villages. And so here we are, between Asia and Africa, on our way down toward the Red Sea. . . . I've met a Japanese Christian! We talked at length (in English!) about religions and his brain has been stimulated and he's begun writing a book, Kokoroman (kokoro in Japanese means "heart"). This is how I called Christ for him, and he liked it, and he's going to write a book now, The Way the Japanese Feel Christianity. . . . Everywhere, people are thirsty for a good word, and often the good word fecundates. . . .

At the dinner table, the Frenchwoman's sitting next to me, but I haven't said a word to her, nor am I going to. . . . We're eating half-European, half-Japanese foods. The Frenchwoman sniffs at them, fait la moue [grimaces]; she doesn't like them. I eat them with relish and have already adapted myself. . . .†

Red Sea, February 22, 1935, evening

Atzuma ha ya!

We're still crossing the Red Sea. We've passed Mecca on the left and Abyssinia on the right. Splendid mountains, deserted, rose-colored, inaccessible, the way I love them. I feel that here is where my ancestors were born, men of the desert. And when I look upon the unending sand, my ancient heart pounds hard as though seeing its ancient fatherland. My God, how different I am from the other Greeks, whose ancestors were born amid greeneries and waters.

I'm learning a bit of Japanese. "Atzuma ha ya!" is the famous, mythical phrase of Japan and means "My wife!" When I come back . . . I'll tell you the légende.‡ But this is how I'll address you from now on. . . . I cannot tell you how much I'm thinking of you, my love.

---

* Letter to E. Samios.
† Letter to E. Samios.
‡ According to this legend, the young woman cast herself into the sea in order to save her husband.

On all these rose-colored mountains, I saw our two shadows passing by like clouds in mid-air, hip to hip, eternally—eternally, i.e., until we die. . . .

I've written two or three articles. . . . I'm thinking about the canto I will write on the Yellow Man. . . . I have four eyes and four ears and two hearts—and we are traveling together, my love!*

February 24

I read, I write. I spoke to the Frenchwoman. I saw her boredom . . . and asked if she would like me to give her a beautiful book about China. Annoyed, she replied, "But since I am going to China, why should I read a book about it?"†

At sea, February 25, 1935

. . . Now and then a dolphin bounds. Seagulls engulf us, and early, early today a red bird from Abyssinia came, chirped two or three times and went back. This evening . . . we'll be coming into the Indian Ocean. The passengers are bored. Nobody reads. They sprawl about on the deck chairs, play deck golf and at night put on the phonograph and dance. The first days, everyone lived separately and didn't talk to anyone else. But now they're uneasy, looking for conversation, and wherever you're standing one of them is sure to come up on the pretext of wanting to know what time it is. . . . In this way, I met a vigorous Englishwoman, heavy-jawed and wealthy, who's going to China with her husband. . . . From time to time, I play deck golf. . . . But almost all day long I read. . . . In eight days we'll reach Colombo, and we need 15 more days to Shanghai. A long, boring journey, especially now that we no longer see any land, only sea, unending and uninteresting. . . .‡

At sea, February 27, 1935

The trip is becoming decidedly monotonous. One gets the sense that the passengers are beginning to go crazy. . . . And what is worst of all, the passengers don't read. They continuously play the same games, make the same jokes; only, each day they laugh less.

Every day, I read two or three books from the miserable ship library

---

* Letter to E. Samios.
† Letter to E. Samios.
‡ Letter to E. Samios.

and I keep rereading your poems, correcting them slightly, but usefully.

I would like to begin some canto, but the atmosphere isn't congenial. Heat. Every day now, we set the clocks half an hour ahead. My love, only you exist. And this journey over the Indian Ocean, this too has been a myth. . . .*

At sea, March 1, 1935

Atzuma ha ya!

. . . Henceforth, all our hopes are hung on Colombo. The Chinese opposite me at the dining table has turned pale; he doesn't talk and he can't stand it any more. The Englishmen and the Englishwomen are fed up and lie sprawled out on their chaises-longues all day long, staring at the sea, which has grown choppy. Whenever a ship passes, everyone feels relieved, grabs his binoculars and gazes avidly. The French lady picks up conversations; she's unbearable. The Viennese lady flirts with a Japanese man who's fat, like a chimpanzee. The Hungarian violinist plays the violin and cards, and walks back and forth half naked, and the German keeps waiting in vain for a glimpse of a shark. . . .

The Japanese Christian wrote my name in Chinese, and it means "Soft and merciful light" (Nikos) and "Flowermountain cape" (Kazantzakis). And now he's working on yours too. If I can, I'll make a joint seal in ivoire.

This afternoon, a great storm. For hours, I stood watching the sea. Sprays of foam kept dashing up, turning to rainbows; flocks of flying fish were leaping playfully. I felt elated.†

At sea, March 3, 1935

Yesterday evening, the famous constellation of the Southern Hemisphere appeared in the sky: la Croix du Sud [the Southern Cross]. Large, very clear; its shape is

*

*   * . I felt great joy.

*

The Japanese man wrote your name in Chinese characters. It means "Pretty little night, thou only choiced" (sic). . . .

Yesterday, I got the idea of writing the French book, the pendant

---

* Letter to E. Samios.
† Letter to E. Samios.

[companion piece] of Toda Raba. Let's hope it will be good. It unfolds very quickly, within five minutes. . . .*

At sea, March 5, 5:00 in the morning

Daybreak. We've arrived in Colombo. In a little while, I'll go out and mail this letter to you. Overwhelming heat; the sky dense, mauve. Chocolate-colored, slender Indians, full of vitality. . . . Always with you, Pretty-little-night-thou-only-choiced!†

At sea, March 6, 1935

Atzuma ha ya!

All day yesterday in Colombo. A magnificent spectacle the Indians; godlike, lithe bodies; dark-chocolate-colored; multicolored pagnes [loincloths]; fiery, large, sweet eyes. Very early in the morning they arrived in high boats with big oars. They rowed, standing upright, half naked. . . . On the quay, repulsive buildings, hotels, banks, customs, warehouses, toute la vermine [all the vermin]. But I got away quickly and climbed into a rickshaw. . . . Swiftly, noiselessly through wide streets, I found myself in the old city—little shops, full of fruits (bananas, pineapples, mangoes and masses of grapes). I bought a mound of them.

The greatest delight is to see bodies and colors. Everything we've seen so often in paintings is coming to life now in front of me. But it is terribly hot; I'm melting. A smell of rotting, of sweat and of musk. Flowers everywhere, red, mauve, snow-white. A Buddhist altar in the middle of the street and a woman offering red flowers, intertwining her hands, gazing at the statue of Buddha.

At this very instant, a cable from Athens has just been posted on the bulletin board, saying that revolution has broken out in Greece.‡ I'm fearfully upset. . . .

Some hundred Indians have come and settled themselves on the deck: silent, chocolate-colored, very beautiful women with violet and orange veils, gold trinkets in their nose and hair, indolentes and very clean. The men are handsome. They cook, play cards, smoke, talk cross-legged, calmly, with the sweetest flame through their entire body. . . .§

---

* Letter to E. Samios.
† Letter to E. Samios.
‡ An attempted coup by followers of Venizelos, very quickly suppressed.
§ Letter to E. Samios.

We're passing Sumatra, a huge island, all trees. The sky is strewn with clouds, and a violent tropical rain has begun. The sea has a weird, metallic color, like melted iron. The clouds are dense, heavy, tasseled. . . .

My love, I am in anguish. The ship cables are most alarming about Greece. . . . And I'm so far away, and I can't find a single detail. . . . I dreamed of you tonight; you were wearing a kimono and we were together, joyful. . . .*

Gulf of Siam, March 12, 1935

Atzuma ha ya!

Singapore is almost at the equator. We arrived at four in the afternoon and right away I went out on land. . . .

Marvelous scene: First of all, the streets are teeming with Chinese people and Chinese signs. Huge white letters against a black background, or gold letters on green, or black letters on dark cherry-red. The Chinese wearing their familiar, cone-shaped, broad-brimmed hats; the Chinese women wearing pantaloons and long jackets made of calico or alpaca or silk. Everywhere, open-air eating places and barbershops; vile stench from the shops and sewers (you can't make out which stench comes from the people and which from the sewers); exotic fruits (and when you eat them, they're all sticky and excessively sweet); heaps and heaps of children wallowing in the filth; and everywhere heavenly, deep-green trees with clusters of red flowers like wisteria. I smoke my pipe, moving slowly, slowly forward, reveling in this unprecedented yellow vision.

I am most impressed by the unexpected élégance of the Chinese woman: simple, well-tailored pajamas, without any trinkets; hair sometimes in long braids and sometimes in tight buns (the married ones). Their faces are as though they've just been licked, carved on shiny, unblemished wood; and they walk lightly, resolutely, like ephebi. . . .

We were hungry and sat down at an open-air restaurant. . . . A crowd at the tables, everyone holding a bowl and eating, using their chopsticks, like magicians, in complete silence and a sickening stench. . . . The eggs were rotten, and in the center of the yolk one could see the outlines of the embryo chick. The soup was thick, halfway between hot chocolate and tea, and horribly sweet. . . . We left in despair and

---

* Letter to E. Samios.

luckily, all of a sudden, came across a bakery full of bread. Each of us got a loaf, and we bought some bananas and began dinner as we walked along.

And so we reached the big entertainment center, the famous Amusement Park, where the radios were blaring away. Some Chinese bagpipes set the whole air howling like a cat making love. What was to be done? We went in. . . . But what was ineffably enchanting was the throng seated there or walking back and forth inside the park—mysterious figures, eyes all fire, harsh, extremely clever; a scent like cheap soap; a peaceful, incessant humming sound like silkworms feeding.

By ten o'clock at night, the new moon was shining, deep-green in the tropical sky. We were sitting facing the door of the cabaret, watching the Chinese prostitutes enter. This was the most troublant spectacle, the most intense vision given me by this trip so far. Imagine slender, tall Chinese women like snakes erected upright, dressed in very simple, unornamented silks . . . green, orange, sky-blue, black silk sheaths. Never did the human body look so like a sword. And through the dresses slit open at the sides, at each step, the yellow blade of the leg glistens—slender, strong, irresistible—right up to the pelvis. And to top this snakelike, slowly swaying body, imagine an extraordinary mask: pie-shaped, heavily powdered, with dagger-sharp, very fine eyebrows, an immobile orange mouth, the eyes slanted: they too are motionless, staring at you indifferently, coldly, mercilessly, as the snake looks at you. I watched them gliding by, one by one, and disappearing under the arched doorway of the cabaret, snakes slithering into a cave. And from inside, actual hisses could be heard: woman with woman, woman with man, dancing on a shiny, polished floor, an invisible flute leading their dance in low, sibilant tones. An exotic, hair-raising spectacle; lust arrived at the lethal point of hallucination; exhausting identification of opium and woman.

The time passed like lightning. The moon had already set when we got up and left. I felt tired and elated and revolted—a dim, dense sensation as though I'd been smoking hashish and had just awakened, heavily, longingly, in horror, remembering the lost paradises. Like their streets, all stench of sewers and scent of jasmine; like their fruits, repulsive and fragrant; like their women, full of charm and syphilis— this is the way their paradises attracted and repelled my spirit. This is the way I also imagine the Sirens, in any brave and honorable spirit that is unwilling to lose the temptations of this earth and yet, at the same time, is unwilling to slip downhill. Of the methods discovered by man—to give all of yourself and to rot, not to give any of yourself and to become holy—once again, the method of Odysseus is the best. . . .*

At sea, March 19, 1935

My beloved, far-off Lenotschka!

. . . I'm eager to set foot on Japanese soil. At once, I'll start looking for a fine pearl to give you a bit of joy. If I could only lift up all Japan and bring it to you and wrap it around your beloved shoulders like a kimono! . . .

Life here aboard ship, identically the same, like a clock. No joy! No land again. Boundless sea, and now there's fog and the boat keeps tooting its horn to prevent our crashing. Today I wrote an article describing the boredom that has weighed down upon our ship, suffocating us. By now everyone's out of sorts, and my sole joy is that today, at long last, the Frenchwoman's getting off. . . . So, I'll be slightly relieved. She was sitting next to me at table.

What can I say about my anguish when I look toward Greece? There's a telegram here informing us that the revolutionaries have been defeated and will be sent into exile.† . . .

For ten hours now, we've been stuck in the middle of the sea, unable to move. Thick fog; we can't see anything more than a few feet away and the Captain doesn't dare move ahead. . . .

My beloved Lenotschka, I dreamed of you yesterday. We were going to Nazos' house in Kifisia. And along the way a girl met us and gave us an exquisite, transparent alabaster bowl, and in the bottom of the bowl was a very light, très discret carved relief of Buddha. . . .‡

Waters off Japan, March 24, 1935

. . . We had a big storm after Shanghai, but the sea didn't bother me. . . . Tonight we'll be entering the inner Sea of Japan, which is like a lake full of islands.

I'm feeling terribly queasy. Tomorrow I shall be plunging into the unknown. Without the language (very few Japanese people know English), without very much money, how shall I manage things? The worry of finding a good and cheap hotel, finding a restaurant, getting settled is troubling me a lot again. . . . But let us hope that I shall

---

* Letter to E. Samios.
† Venizelos went into exile in Corsica.
‡ Letter to E. Samios.

see extraordinary things that will make me forget the queasiness. Already the vision I've taken with me from China has been a great compensation. . . . What a different world, what another sort of earth has molded these people; and there is no communication. To be sure, song, erotic love, pain—and, above all, death—unite us with them. But from how far away must we come in order to meet at these eternal points?* . . .†

March 25, 1935, Kobe

. . . It's raining softly, despairingly. Terrible cold and mud. I went outside and came back after three hours. . . . I went into a bar; the famous geishas, three of them sitting around a little table, waiting for clientele; insignificant, tiny, ugly. . . . All the women here seem to me ugly and good-natured, contrary to the Chinese women, many of whom have lethal charme, but you sense they're sinister. . . .‡

Nara, March 26, 1935

The tour has begun. Very difficult, because I don't know the language. I left Osaka in the morning. In a miserable little village . . . all of a sudden a cherry tree sprang up, all in bloom. . . .

We've reached Nara . . . I'd thought of going to a Japanese hotel, to see if I could manage things. Impossible! I went in. Two or three women in kimonos were warming themselves around a deep bronze brazier. They took a long time to understand what I wanted. When they did understand, I took off my shoes and put on some sandals before going up the staircase. The room like a cage of fragrant wood, sparkling clean. They set out a pillow for me and I knelt down and they knelt down around me and began talking with me. I opened my notebook, where I'd written a few phrases. And I said, "I'm hungry." They brought me some rice and some other suspicious-looking things, smelling medicinal and all yellow with saffron. Impossible to eat. . . . I packed my suitcases and went over to . . . the only European hotel in Nara. . . . There are more than a thousand deer in the park. I've gone to all the temples, lit candles, hit the gong, lit a large, scented bâton [taper] to your name—whispering a particular prayer for you. May Buddha hear me. . . .

---

* N.K. later came back to this first opinion—as shown in his articles in Akropolis, June 9 and October 19, 1935, and in his Japan, China (New York: Simon and Schuster, 1963).
† Letter to E. Samios.
‡ Letter to E. Samios.

I'm very tired. All day long, I've eaten two apples, because I didn't dare go into the local restaurant. . . . I don't know why; so far, this journey hasn't been very exhilarating for me. Perhaps because I've been so long without any letter from you. I'm upset; I can't concentrate. We're too far apart; how can I be happy? . . .

Nara, March 27, 1935

I went from Nara to the renowned Monastery of Horyuji. Exquisite. Peaceful, pagodas, springtime-sweet air, Buddhas smiling in the half-light, paintings on silk, dancing girls and, above all, the goddess Kwannon, the goddess of mercy. This is the most beautiful statue I've ever seen. . . . I came back to Nara and wandered through the superb gazelle park. Splendid avenues lined with stone lanterns. What a spectacle it must be when they are all lit up for the great rituals. . . .

I got tired and came back to the hotel with my pockets full of apples. Tomorrow morning, I'm leaving for Kyoto. . . . The weather is bedeckt [cloudy], but tender, like springtime. . . .†

Kyoto, March 31, 1935

. . . Yesterday evening I arrived in this old, extremely beautiful city. I was with a Japanese friend of mine, and so I managed to find a handsome Japanese hotel. I communicate in gestures and one little word, and I'll be staying for 3 days! . . . I eat in the local restaurants and am beginning to get used to it. . . .

At night, the city is absolutely irréelle. All multicolored lanterns as at some ritual and you hear only the clog-slippers hurriedly clacking by . . . (I've bought you a pair of very beautiful cherry-red ones.) I've also gotten you a waterproof paper umbrella and a kimono, also one for Anna. . . . The pearl I'll get in Tokyo.

In Osaka, I went to the main newspapers and saw the huge machines. The Japanese newspapers announced my arrival and my comments on Japan without asking me.

So far, the Japanese people are agreeable and most polite. Their life has a gentle Oriental charme. The women all seem ugly to me, but they do have a charme. They're constantly smiling, bowing and they walk as though dancing. . . .‡

---

* Letter to E. Samios.
† Letter to E. Samios.
‡ Letter to E. Samios.

All day long today, I wandered through Buddhist temples and museums, seeing superb paintings, superior ones. Above all, on a sixteenth-century paravent [folding screen], a series of bambous in water. All the color gris argent [silvery gray], both background and painting alike, a difference only in tone. Very simple, but I believe I've never seen a more beautiful painting.

I came back to the hotel, worn out. The girl brought me some tea at once and prepared my bath for me. I ordered some food (all with gestures), rested, lit my pipe, and all my soul and all my life are turned toward Lenotschka. Higher than everything, better loved even than the bambous, sweeter even than traveling, a grand delight, all the delight of my life, all my hope. I am afraid of nothing because she is with me. And I want nothing except for her to be with me. Delight, sweetness, eternity—when I think of you, my heart trembles and all my mind flowers with a great joy.*

Along with Nikos Kazantzakis, another correspondent from a Greek newspaper had also set off for Japan. For fear of being eclipsed by his illustrious colleague, he had denounced Kazantzakis to the Nipponese authorities as a dangerous terrorist on his way to Japan to make an attempt on the life of the Mikado!

And so the "Japanese friend" mentioned in these letters was none other than a secret agent assigned to spy on the poet and, better still, with instructions to bar him access to any hotel along the itinerary planned for the grandson of Amaterasu during those particular days! Through this intermediary—this "guardian angel" with the bridled eyes—destiny once again took Nikos Kazantzakis in hand—we recall his anguish in Kobe as he confronted the unknown country—acquainting him with whatever was essential, helping him avoid all fatigue and useless expenses, initiating him into the heart of the Chrysanthemum.

"At first," Nikos recounted, "it had been very painful. I'd no sooner fallen asleep than they would come and wake me up, jabbering at me in Russian, asking me thousands of hocus-pocus questions, wanting at all costs to make me contradict myself. Gradually, they calmed down. I

---

* Letter to E. Samios.

could sleep in peace and my police guardian was transformed into a guardian angel. A perfect traveling companion, enamored of his own country, capable of making me see what the ordinary tourist almost never sees. . . ."

Tokyo, April 8, 1935

. . . I'm seeing a great deal of Kabuki theater; seeing many dances, hearing much music, seeing godlike paintings. And I've bought a splendid old book of Japanese engravings. . . .*

Tokyo, April 9, 1935

. . . I went to Kamakura today. A delicate, clear rain; all the cherry trees in bloom, huge allées all in flower, and underneath the trees the women with their multicolored, rainproof paper umbrellas unfurled, circumambulating silently. Sweetness, silence, inexpressible tenderness. With difficulty I refrained from weeping, because at that moment I was longing so for you to be with me. I moved slowly-slowly as though wanting to regulate my own step with yours. Unendurably sad to be seeing superb spectacles and not to have the person you love near you. . . .†

Tokyo, April 10, 1935
Evening

Japan is giving me many delights, but quelque chose y manque [something's missing]. I haven't yet been able to allocate the new treasures inside me. At the present moment, I am looking, listening, walking, exhausting myself. The springtime exhilarates me, the life of the street, the painting, a few temples, the paper lanterns. Another world, more silent, more stylisé than our own. The theater, the singing, the dances, the women are as though you're seeing them from afar, from very far away, on some other planet. Charme and indifference, a strange sadness, a monotony that is très intéressante. Love of the bibelot [little trinket], which is so alien to me, choque [shocks] me here. When I see the dwarf trees, my heart contracts. Oaks in flowerpots, flowering cherry trees as small as basil plants, fir trees ten centimeters high. . . .‡

---

* Letter to E. Samios.
† Letter to E. Samios.
‡ Letter to E. Samios.

Atzuma ha ya!

. . . I got the newspapers and, inside the envelope, the horrible news of Panaït's death. I'm waiting impatiently for your new letter to learn details. Life is hideous and we are not aware of it, and we waste it in petty, wretched acts, and only when a person we love dies do we realize that we are walking along the brink of the abyss. I'm in haste to come back near you and we shall walk hand in hand. This is the only consolation. . . . In China, there are new wars on again, but I'm hoping to be in time to see Peking and to leave Shanghai on May 6. . . .*

Tokyo, April 17, 1935

It's raining, raining, cold. All day yesterday, I was in Nikko. . . . Magnificent mountains, huge cryptomeria trees (a kind of cypress-pine tree) splendid old temples, statues, paintings, allées of stone lanterns. . . . And now, I'm in my own long, narrow room in front of a beautiful, bronze brazier and on the wall the . . . kakemono of Buddha I bought. . . .

The other night, a friend of mine and I went to the house of some geishas. Indescribable the purity and exhilaration of the atmosphere. A wooden house like all the houses. In the entranceway, two huge paper lanterns. As soon as we rang, the door opened and a bevy of girls sprang up to welcome us, as though we were some old, well-loved acquaintances. They bowed to us, touching their foreheads to the ground, took off our shoes and led us into the parlor. Straw mats, the wood burning, not a single piece of furniture except a low little table, two bronze braziers, and some pillows. On the wall a religious kakemono: Buddha meeting a woman and their colloquy in the midst of flowers. We sat cross-legged, the geishas surrounding us. I spoke my bit of Japanese and they all laughed. They brought us pistachios and sweets and hot sake. . . . And we drank. One of them took the samisen and, seating herself cross-legged, began playing. A little one got up and danced. Grace, serenity, modesty, dressed in brilliantly colored kimonos, their eyes gay and innocent as I have never seen in any European family. My friend spoke excellent Japanese and joked with them, and they all laughed like seven-year-olds. I have never, never sensed to such an extent the

---

* Letter to E. Samios.

innocent sweetness of women. . . . I sat calmly watching them, my arms folded like Buddha. I didn't stretch out my hand to touch them, I was so afraid the enchanting vision might vanish.

It was late when we left. They bent down to the ground and, doing homage to us, helped us put on our shoes. Then once again they did homage, warbling gaily like birds, "Arigato kozaimas! Arigato kozaimas! [Thank you very much! Thank you very much!]"*

Tokyo, April 20, 1935

I haven't had a letter from you again in many days and again the world's all dark. . . . Yesterday I had dinner with a former Japanese ambassador to Athens, in a Japanese restaurant. When we entered, once again the girl came to the threshold, bowed down, resting her forehead on the flagstones. Then we climbed the sparkling clean steps and sat down cross-legged on pillows. Each guest has the right to a private room, because very few people come here. The room is absolutely bare. On the floor, straw mats, three pillows and three bronze braziers full of lighted coals. On the wall a kakemono of painted reeds and a vase with three flowers. Nothing else. The serving girl came in, wearing a mauve kimono and her hair in a strange sort of architecture. She prostrated herself: the rite of the meal had begun. . . .

The charme of these dinners is beyond description. There is something religious about the mute rituel. The girl who does the serving—a grande dame—retreats into a corner, attentively surmising our every gesture and gliding noiselessly back and forth, bringing us sake or tea or a napkin, whatever we had just been turning over in our minds. . . .†

Tokyo, April 21, 1935

I've got the pearl for you! A superb one . . . I was overjoyed. . . . Tomorrow morning, I'm leaving Tokyo. . . . "Never more!" Little by little, I'm bidding farewell to Japanese soil too. . . .

I'm not sleeping well, and two days ago I woke up in terror. It was as though I'd heard a voice telling me, "You are sitting on granite, yet you do not realize that everything is air!"

Almost every day here, we have a small earthquake. A short way outside Tokyo, the mountains are full of hot, smoking springs. We are

---

* Letter to E. Samios.
† Letter to E. Samios.

surely sitting on top of a volcano that is still active. But the voice I heard in the night had a metaphysical meaning, of course, in harmony with my whole vision of life. . . .*

The Yellow Sea, April 26, 1935

. . . I feel a little tired as I turn my gaze backward to survey what I have seen and felt during the month I spent in Japan—and I can't yet form any harmonious conclusions. Multitudes of joys and bitternesses, weariness, exaltation, nostalgia, freedom, godlike colors, paintings, statues, theater, women, forests, temples, seas—all this is still seething in my chest and I cannot express it. But of necessity I will have to be able to, because I must write the articles. And all the essence will crystallize and go into The Odyssey. For its sake, I have suffered this difficult— extremely difficult—trip; and I hope to be able to preserve whatever magnificence I have seen in a few verses. . . .

On the ship I've come into contact with the Chinese. Exceptionally repugnant. Of course, there are some splendid types—raffinés, grands seigneurs—but where can you find them on the ship or on the streets? I'm eager to see Peking, the mysterious city. . . .†

Bay of Peking, April 27, 1935

. . . The journey goes on, monotonous. We've entered the big bay of Peking now, and tomorrow we'll be arriving in its harbor, Tientsin. Fog, cold. I lie down all day, reading. Ah, if only I could write some verses, I'd be assuaged. But I'm not comfortably settled; voices all around me, radio, stupid noise offensive to my spirit and it has no will to work. Moreover, the Japanese cooking here m'écoeure [takes the heart out of me]. . . . In Japan, I found only some fine apples and delicious bananas. I've brought a basket of them with me, and aboard ship I'm living on them. . . .‡

Tientsin, April 28, 1935

At this very moment, daybreak, we're arriving in Tientsin. We're waiting just outside till the water rises and we can enter. . . . The weather is cloudy but pleasant. . . . I can dimly make out the coast of China. Little boats gliding back and forth with strange sails like straw

---

* Letter to E. Samios.
† Letter to E. Samios.
‡ Letter to E. Samios.

mats. I'm preparing my things, my books and my eyes to set foot on this new land. . . .*

Peking, April 29, 1935

My love, at long last—today—I believe that I am happy! Peking is an inexpressible city, the pendant of Moscow. All morning, I wandered around the "Forbidden City." . . . The richness, the colors, the raffinement, the treasures, beyond description . . . and the grass growing on the rooftops, and the paintings on the walls all peeling away, and the yellow porcelain bricks breaking and falling. I'd never hoped to see such a miracle. I've just come back and my eyes are éblouis [dazzled]. And it's a marvelous day, whereas yesterday, they tell me, there was an ouragan [hurricane] that uprooted many trees. . . .

I've seen some exquisite works—inconceivably simple painting, without any colors, unsurpassably perfect. . . . Kalmouko must come here. Also, godlike vases, pottery. I have never seen more beautiful or finer forms; never such volupté in touching substance. Frosso† too must come here. And, above all else, we must come here together, my love, the both of us, for I am ashamed and cannot contain this vision by myself alone. And, along with all this, acacias, unending avenues of trees in bloom, and wisteria too. . . .‡

Evening of April 29, 1935

I went with the secretary from the Belgian Embassy (a friend of Herbert)§ to a Chinese nobleman's house. The grandmother, 80 years old, was celebrating her birthday. A vast house, the courtyard decked out with red silk banners full of good wishes from the relatives and friends, wishing her to "live a hundred years." The tables were laid; there was a throng of people, and they'd also brought the Chinese theater, and it gave a performance in the main courtyard. . . . Some children acted plays, comedies. Caterwauling voices, rich costumes, primitive themes. Chinese music, fascinating and monotonous. We made our salutations to the old lady—a charming, pourri [spoiled] creature—we ate sweets made of criardes colors. And I smoked and

---

* Letter to E. Samios.
† Frosso was a sculptress friend of ours, now well known in various countries.
‡ Letter to E. Samios.
§ Jean Herbert had given N.K. several letters of recommendation for both China and Japan.

watched and listened, wondering when these holes in my face [that is, eyes] will at long last be sated. . . .*

Peking, April 30, 1935

. . . I've just come back from various superb temples and my eyes are flooded with blue colors—because the tiles in these temples are made of dark-blue porcelain. But I've come back happy, because when I went by the post office, I had three letters from you!

"Tom,"† I shouted, "quickly, let me home!"‡

Evening of April 30, 1935

I've just come back from Herbert's Princess [the "General"]. A magnificent aristocratic Chinese house, closed garden, Oriental chambers in inégal [uneven] taste: Alongside an exquisite Chinese kakemono, a piece of French junk. The Princess enters—about 50 years old, très svelte, mince, élégante [very lithe, slender, elegant]. A coquette, dressed in a handsome, gold-embroidered, tight robe. Long jade earrings and perles. Fânée [withered] but very soignée. She's a dancer and mad about music. She wants to write a series of books, and as her model and ideal she has Alexander Dumas's The Three Musketeers!

But she's clever and pleasant. She's seen and lived a great deal, and we spoke like old friends. I'll see her again the day after tomorrow, and we'll go together to a closed palace, where entrance is no longer allowed. Tea with rose leaves, Manchurian sweets, etc. . . .§

When Nikos returned to Athens, it was a shock for him not to find me waiting on our threshold. But on my doctor's express orders, I had had to leave for a cure in France. And Nikos had had enough of this lingering illness.

Athens, June 5, 1935

Beloved Lenotschka,
. . . The atmosphere here is irrespirable [suffocating]. Unutterable horror, misery, barbarism. I'm impatient to take refuge in Aegina,

---

* Letter to E. Samios.
† Tom was the coolie who drew N.K.'s rickshaw.
‡ Letter to E. Samios.
§ Letter to E. Samios.

till we see what is to become of us. . . . The Prevelakis affair is progressing splendidly. . . . Extraordinary zeal of Mme. Ralli and Paxinou, and their omnipotence is also extraordinary. This noon, I'll take them a Chinese bowl as a gift and some estampes [engravings].

One of the German publishing houses that read Toda Raba is reminding me of my promise to send them a new manuscript. . . .*

Athens, June 8, 1935

. . . Tonight, I'll be dining with Papandreou, and I'll give him an estampe too. And so I'm giving away whatever I have with me and I'll wait for you to give you the rest. . . . I admit that if you delay long in coming, I shall be extremely upset. . . .

Tomorrow elections. Misères. All my friends have been dismissed. I don't read the newspapers, I'm not interested, and yet I am breathing in all this decomposition and am upset by it. . . .†

Athens, June 12, 1935

. . . I am very uneasy. Athens upsets me very much. And this is why the letters I am writing you are so embittered and depressed. . . .

I'm dragged from dinner table to dinner table, and I have no appetite; and with difficulty I preserve my mask. . . .

How I wish I could write you a warm letter, Lenotschka, full of joy, so you could read it abroad and feel a little joy. But I cannot. I am very bitter and cannot overcome my bitterness. Many things are to blame, and one thing is this air of Athens, déprimant, dégradant [depressing and degrading]. And I would prefer not to write you at all and just wait mutely for your arrival. . . .‡

Athens, June 13, 1935

. . . Try to work on the 4th-grade reader, because I won't be writing it. I must concentrate all my attention on the 3 readers. . . .

The articles on Japan are also impressing people. I must write on China too, as soon as I get to Aegina. A great deal of work, but I shall

---

* Letter to E. Samios.
† Letter to E. Samios.
‡ Letter to E. Samios.

be in time. I only need calm and a happy heart. These do not exist at present, but you will come and they will come with you. . . .*

With an able-bodied companion, Nikos Kazantzakis would never have guessed the range of tenderness, patience, magic he was capable of. With a cozy-soft companion, I would undoubtedly have taken better care of my own body and might even have cured it once and for all. "It's a lucky thing you're ailing," he would say, teasing me. "If you were in good health, you'd have turned the world topsy-turvy!" I did not turn the world topsy-turvy. But with a guru like him, my spirit fortified itself and I was able to taste unstintingly the joys and sufferings of this earth.

Aegina, June 22, 1935

. . . From the moment I set foot on Aegina . . . I've become another man. Exhilaration, almost happiness, sea, solitude, there is no more perfect climat for my spirit. I go to and fro in the house, thinking constantly of your splendid poem, changing only the [gender] of the adjectives—"When you go far from me, my love, our little house is haunted. . . . The whole house is hanté [haunted] by your beloved shade. I dare not touch anything, because it seems to me I touch your hand and I shudder at the invisible presence." . . .†

I'm deeply moved by your things, the way you left them here. . . . I'm cooking for myself again. I've filled the big table with books. I'm reading about China, thinking about The Odyssey, planning the a-b-c-readers and from tomorrow on (Monday), I'll begin writing the articles. . . .

The day is endless. I sleep on the terrace and all the stars hang over me. The Scorpion superb whirls over my head, and at daybreak I wake up elated, and the sacred labor of the day begins. . . .

The "garden" at home is miserable. Everything's all dried up, and only the thick-leaved plants are still growing. Babbit [our new cat] came back at once, and he keeps me company. In the evening we walk up and down together on the terrace. . . .

---

* Letter to E. Samios.
† He was quoting my poem.

Heavenly days. I've grown bright red in the sun. I swim, dry myself off on the rock, watch the boats passing by, smoke Japanese tobacco, remembering all the things I've seen. I'm waiting for you to come, so that sacred conversation and sublime caresses may intertwine again. . . .*

Aegina, July 5, 1935

. . . Please save me all the speeches delivered at the Anti-Fascist Congress. I received an invitation to go, but it's impossible.

Splendid, full of vitality your 2nd article too. I've just read it. . . .†

Aegina, July 15, 1935

. . . I'm immersed in the reader and am just about out of my mind. I keep writing and rewriting. Kalmouko comes over. We work together here and then I rewrite. And I have to make one or two more readers, for the second grade. . . .

I like your new poems as essence, but their form is not at ease and simple. They need reworking, because the style you follow is so concentrated that unless it attains absolute simplicity (Nachmann), it is incomprehensible. You want the simplicity that is found after complexity; not the other sort of simplicity that has not yet been contaminated by complexity. An extremely difficult feat, the supreme ambition and you must suffer very much. It is a steep ascent. . . .

Today I had a well opened on our "estate," and 30 centimeters down we struck a rock. . . .‡

Aegina, July 20, 1935

. . . In Athens, once again political upheaval and miseries. I'm not at all upset by it. I only feel disgust at the collapse of the race. . . . Lefteris is in Athens . . . and he wants to come to Aegina. So be it! But nothing can be done with a person who is inégal [unstable]. . . .§

All the pains of parting were well worth the joys of return. Inexhaustible, sparkling with mischief and innocence, Nikos used to evoke for me, down to the tiniest detail, his life as a hermit, empha-

---

* Letter to E. Samios.
† Letter to E. Samios.
‡ Letter to E. Samios.
§ Letter to E. Samios.

sizing the comic side, sidestepping the anomalous or morose part. On such and such a day the color of the sea had never been more revitalized; on such and such another day the cactus had flowered like fireworks. A friend had promised something extraordinary; the cat had battled with a big snake; new topics jostling one another, demanding priority in his "vitals." And he was the first to laugh as he told me his own misadventures or some involuntary blunder.

The winter was coming on. Chills like lizards rippled up and down our backs. The first chilblains appeared.

And I went to Athens to attend to everything—to see publisher friends; editors in chief who promised work; actor friends from the National Theater; Duras, the architect who was drawing up the plan of our future house. For, more than ever, we were longing to have a house and, if possible, a radio. And a stove . . .

Aegina, November 5, 1935
Tuesday

. . . This winter, we must have music. I go to bed at 6 o'clock now and sleep little and badly. I have insomnia and have no urge to get up at midnight and work. If we have a radio, we'll be happy. . . .

I'm working on The Odyssey. I'll write Mon Père whenever the need drives me to it. But I'll be sure to write it, for your sake. . . .

And so I sleep at 6 o'clock and Babbit comes and sleeps at my feet. In the morning, I find him curled up on my chest. About 5 in the afternoon, he comes up to my desk, meows for me to open up and looks at me as much as to say, "Well, on with it, breadwinner! Come on down! I'm hungry!" And so I go down and he gobbles up the dry bread with ineffable pleasure, drinks plenty of water and rushes over to my bed. After a little while, we meet. And in this way life goes by, waiting for the Mistress. . . .

May the God-Devil (this is the new synthèse) be with us! . . .*

Aegina, December 6, 1935

My beloved L!

Today, I realized it was my name day from the following event: Early this morning, Mr. Katsimingos† came to wish me many happy

---

* Letter to E. Samios.
† The spice and coffee merchant of Aegina, who had a plaque over his cash register written in ancient Greek, "Fear those who are indebted to you!"

returns, dressed in his ceremonious black suit and a clean blue scarf around his neck.

And so I decided to celebrate too, and I've made an exception by putting a few grains of coffee in the coffee grinder! And so I drank . . . my coffee and wished myself a better year next year!

It was a marvelous day, but I didn't feel at all elated. I set off on an excursion and passed through Aegina, where a gift was waiting for me at the post office: a beautiful edition of Hamlet in French and English, sent me by Prevelakis. I was delighted with it and went on toward Messagro. There I found a splendid beginning for my book Mon Père. I noted it down and . . . came back. On my way through Prokopi, I bought three cakes—a gift from the three people who love me most: you, my sister Eleni, and the unknown X! At home, I ate yesterday evening's greens and half a herring. At first, I said to myself I wouldn't heat the greens and I'd eat them cold (and you know how revolting they are cold). But after that I remembered it was my name day, and so I said I might as well celebrate and I heated them.

And then you can just imagine how the Copenhagen pastry tasted. And I drank a sip of Anna's liqueur, to her health. And in this way, December 6 came to an end. . . .

The whole outline of En Fumant [While Smoking] is ready, down to the tiniest details. What does it need in order to catch fire? The spark. I'm waiting for it, but my heart is still closed and refuses to surrender. Every day, I beg it in vain. . . .*

Aegina, December 1935
Saturday

. . . I've made my outline for En Fumant, but I don't know when I'll begin it. All these months my heart has been heavy. I don't know why, and I cannot get into the incandescent atmosphere needed for creation. I've outlined perfectly how the book will be. . . . It will take place in Japan, where a geisha lights my pipe, casting into it un tout petit grain noir (a very small black seed), a tiny bit of hashish. And all at once, the idea that travaillait [had been bothering] me secretly all the while leaps up and within a few minutes I live all my father, Crete, my childhood . . . until the pipe goes out and we hear the laugh of the geisha, who'd been looking at me, absent-mindedly, as though for a moment I'd forgotten where I was.

---

* Letter to E. Samios.

The hashish justifies my évasion perfectly, as well as the saccadé [brusque], violent and jerky style the book will have and the mass of hallucinantes images: extrême Orient [Far East] and Crete inextricably interwoven, paysages, slanting eyes and Cretan head-bands, a difficult and fascinant enchêvetrement [fascinating intertwining].

I have it all, all in my mind. I lack only the God-given moment of carefree intoxication. But that will come too, this winter, in our solitude. I have been worn out by the visits and talks and cares of life. . . .*

Aegina, December 24, 1935

. . . The days are extremely sweet, tendres, embués [tender and misty]. I am calm. The nervous crisis is over. Perhaps the agony inside me to begin En Fumant was to blame. Everything irritated me; the slightest contact hurt me. And now, I am calm. Childbirth has begun.

I shall begin on Mon Père immediately afterward. As I've written you, I've found a superb beginning, serene and original. . . .

I've written to a specialist to make me a relief map of Crete, if it doesn't cost too much. I'll have it mounted on the wall behind my desk. . . .

Our house m'obsède [obsesses me]. Day and night, I'm thinking about it and correcting the Duras plans. When you come I'll submit my corrections to you, and if you approve we'll send them on to Duras and he'll make us the definitive plan. . . .†

After the rising staged by Venizelos' followers in March 1935 and Venizelos' subsequent exile in Corsica, Greece fell into the hands of the rightists. It can be said, without exaggeration, that since General Kondylis' coup d'état in 1935 the Greek people has not known a single day of liberty.

Kondylis' first act was to abolish the republic and to stage a crooked plebiscite, in which there were more votes for the return of the monarch than there were citizens entitled to vote! King George was invited back to reign. The rest—Metaxas' fascist dictatorship, the war, the two civil wars, the fact that Nazi collaborators were retained in key posts after 1944, the attack against every vestige of democratic thought—all this was too bitter to be described in a few words, yet it must be noted here.

---

* Letter to E. Samios.
† Letter to E. Samios.

1936–1937.   The two ensuing years were to be difficult years. What-ever adversity had not been capable of destroying was almost under-mined by the crystallization of a dream: The Nest, the haven every man longs for. The popular proverb goes: "Whosoever never had a daughter to see married or never built a house knows not the afflictions of this world!" We knew the proverb but were far from suspecting the afflictions.

From the very start we encountered difficulties. We wanted—so we claimed—a little peasant house, in harmony with the style of our islands. No roof, nothing but broad terraces—so deliciously simple when the sun bakes them white or the rains inundate them and they begin leaking over your beds; so adorably in harmony with the sea and the broad back of Mt. Hymettos.

We also wanted a cistern under the house, since we were building on rock. And an outdoor stone staircase, the steps carved out of a single block, needless to say, for greater simplicity. A living room on the ground floor, rigged out to give the impression of being on a boat; our bedroom, supplementary rooms; and up above, a belvedere encircled with terraces—the eagle's roost.

I had proposed a ⊓ shape, which would give us the prospect of a patio sheltered from the winds. The architect found this disastrous and amputated one of its legs. Nikos crowed with delight: "My word, aren't we the canny ones! The new form is perfect and we're still strictly in the style of the surrounding houses. And what's more, it's a Gamma, ⌐, the third letter of our alphabet. Three, thirty-three, three thousand thirty-three—the number I love more than all others."

We wanted "Nature to come into our home." Yet at the same time, Nikos also had the vision of a fortress out of carved, unplastered stone that would become one with—be the flesh of—the cliff on which it stood. The architect had provided for four doors "communicating with Nature." Nikos demanded that three of them be done away with. We split the difference; our veranda was "cut off" from the rest of the house. As far as the kitchen was concerned, I had my way.

No sooner had the storm over the doors subsided than another storm blew up: the indoor staircase. Nikos was obstinate. "One staircase is enough! I loathe opening holes in houses. We'll move about by way of the outdoor staircase." He was answering our imprecations with a plan for a *trap!*

The problem of the windows was the last straw!

On paper, we were enchanted with the large bay windows, supposed to be 4 to 7 yards long. But when I had to go off to Athens and our two masons (I'll say more of them in a moment) came face to face with these gaping apertures, they were panic-stricken. "Kyr Nikos!" they cried. "Your architect's crazy! With openings like these, we'll never be able to cast a single block of cement. It'll collapse."

They managed things so well that by the time I got back I found myself confronted by tiny square windows, all lamentably higgledy-piggledy.

To build, tear down, rebuild, tear down again. This martyrdom lasted many long months. For two whole years, we kept cutting the Hydra's heads, but they kept growing back, each time more vigorous. Through Nikos' letters, our troubles can be observed at closer range. No one will ever know our anguish when those damnable Saturday paydays used to arrive and the workmen would stare us in the eye, their stomachs empty and their backs broken.

Our masons, Theodoros and Ignazios, were two colossi from Asia Minor. With an infallible instinct, Theodoros (the elder one) sized up his "boss's" wallet as being no larger than his own—whence his firm resolution to economize on everything. "We've settled our price, Kyr Nikos; we won't go beyond it!" he announced, as he clinked glasses with the boss. "And when shall we start?" "Well, right this very minute!"

No sooner said than done. He rose and went over to a corner of our field. There, Theodoros and Ignazios had laid two long iron bars. What was our astonishment when we saw them go off, fetch the bars, and head down the path to the sea. Were they about to perform some sort of ablutions?

Unaware that they were being spied on, Theodoros and Ignazios stripped up to the navel and went into the sea. They shoved their long bars under the cliff and, heaving gigantic grunts, began hacking away at it. After a little while, they started back up the path, each one laden with a thick block. This time, they stripped in the opposite direction (covering their navels, uncovering their torsos) and set about carving the salty boulders. Some beautiful, good-sized stones bounced out, ivory-colored and slightly rose-tinted. A few days later, our walls went up, as appetizing as a candy house.

In his own way, Theodoros had also just solved the problem of the sand: "Why buy sand, Kyr Nikos? Here it is at our feet. We'll wash it in fresh water and it'll be fine!" At a later point, this overoptimism turned to vituperations; a glittery, snow-white powder had devoured our poor books.

329

To reach our promontory, our two artisans had to pass through the little town of Aegina. Like true Orientals, they never forgot to bring some meager gift—fish, fruits, some fresh almonds from their almond trees.

When the time came for laying the flagstones, Theodoros sent me off to Piraeus with solemn admonitions: "Above all, don't let them cheat you, Kyra Elenitsa! We'll need dry flagstones of the highest quality!"

I came back with a *kaiki* full of materials, among them the famous flagstones. Theodoros, who was always skeptical, frowned. He leaned over, took one, put it in his mouth and bit it hard with his teeth. It was the flagstone that snapped in two! In *Freedom or Death*, we find the eater-of-plaster. He is still alive and his real name is Koukis. Theodoros and Ignazios too might well appear among the Cretans of "Kapetan Mihalis."

As he had done with *Toda Raba* and the U.S.S.R., so in the *Rock Garden* Kazantzakis wanted to give the quintessence of his experiences in Japan and China—two countries that were so foreign and yet so close to him. The travel books, appearing regularly after each of his major trips, contained the essential part of what he had written for the newspapers that had sent him. The *Rock Garden*, as his biographer Aziz Izzet* so appropriately calls it, "is a sort of laboratory where all the author's experiences are put harshly to the test. It is not without reason that certain extremely important passages from the *Spiritual Exercises* are incorporated into the web of the narrative. Beyond a doubt, Kazantzakis had in mind to bring his *Spiritual Exercises* within reach of his reader. But he was equally interested in ascertaining just how solid the results of his own ascetic exercise were. Out of this intermingling of dreams, observations, action and passive receptivity—all in a realm of total alienation—results a book of capital importance for grasping the thought and profound, sensual vitality of Kazantzakis."

Along with the *Rock Garden*, Kazantzakis was also writing a reader for the Greek schools in Egypt, to satisfy the insistent demands of his friend Marselos, who ran a bookstore in Alexandria. Nikos called it "The Grand Project" and insisted on my signing it with my own name alone, though I hadn't worked on it at all.

---

* Aziz Izzet, *Nikos Kazantzakis* (Paris: Plon, 1965).

... I've received the manuscript from Marselos for the Egypt book. Enormous, all rewritten in pencil, chaos. And I have to correct it and recopy all of it.

All day long, I've been writing the Felsengarten [Rock Garden], and I'm eager for you to come and tell me whether it's good or whether I have to begin it over again. . . . I've been seeing some strange dreams. I'm impatient for you to come. Only one thing pleasant: The King of England's dead! . . .*

Nikos had just finished the *Rock Garden* (written directly in French) when the state of my health deteriorated. And then for the first time the man at my side—to whom the gods should have given a companion as strong as a rock—abandoned himself to despair. Throughout our long correspondence, there are only two letters that evince such a state of abandon. Thank God, neither in speech nor in writing did he ever let me guess that I made him suffer.

Aegina, May 1936
Friday evening

My beloved Lenotschka!

I still can't recover; as though I've fainted and my nerves are still quivering with fatigue and overexcitement. . . . The idea of your still being sick, after the operation and after the Plombières cure, is unbearable for me. . . . My only relief would be if I got sick too and had to stay a while in bed, forced to look after my own ailments. That would rest me and perhaps might do you good. . . .

When I got back home, I was hoping at least for une crise de larmes [a fit of tears]. A very simple thing, so many human beings have. But not a thing. The eyes dry and the heart taut, like a clod of lead weighing on me. . . .

I'm waiting impatiently to hear what the doctors will tell you. . . . I pace up and down on the terrace, unable to do anything. Rarely in my life have I found myself in such détresse. . . .

I went to the masons, in hopes of being able to shout or scold, but I didn't even have the strength for that. I came home, sent Katina away

---

* Letter to E. Samios.

for the day, drank some tea and sat down in the sun. A bit of ricqlès*
did me good. . . .†

Aegina, May 7, 1936
Thursday

. . . And don't forget to tell him [Duras] at all costs not to make
a kitchen door. We don't have to have absolute confort. Remember
Carel: "Syphilis, alcoholism, and confort will be the death of our
civilization. . . ."

The day you left, I got a letter from Chile. The editor [Ercilla]
tells me he's enthusiastic over Toda Raba and he proposes translating
and publishing it, and offers 10 per cent of the price per copy. He also
asks me to send him the Rock Garden.

Please send me 50 grams of ordinary tea, because it's a pity for me
to use up the good tea by myself. . . .

I'm getting along well, peacefully, working a great deal. By the time
you get here, the 1st version of Mon Père will be finished. . . .‡

Aegina, May 10, 1936
Sunday

. . . In three days, I'll have finished Mon Père. And after that, I
don't know what I shall do. A new book has gotten into my brain, but
I'd rather be able to make a trip—within Greece, of course. For without
my realizing it, the body may get worn out, the way I keep writing one
book after the other like this. . . .§ .

Aegina, May 1936
Thursday

. . . Mon Père finished since the day before yesterday! It happened
more quickly than I'd calculated. Now I'll put it aside in a drawer and
forget it for a little while. I'm not in a hurry at all, though I ought to go
to Crete too for a few days. . . .

Now I'm uneasy, idle. I'm thinking of the next book: Felsenkloster
[The Rock Cloister]. This must be good. But it should take place in
India (as the Felsengarten took place in China). . . .

---

* Ricqlès, a brand of mint alcohol used for medicinal purposes.
† Letter to E. Samios.
‡ Letter to E. Samios.
§ Letter to E. Samios.

Tomorrow, I shall begin a canto on the Japanese person I love—Hideyoshi.*

Nothing new here. Only the big cactus is about to bloom. I'd water it with raki, if I had any, to make it delay.

Nothing else, my love. God be with us! But whatever happens, our motto is always: "High thinking—hard work—adventurous excitement!"†

Aegina, May 20, 1936

My beloved Lenotschka!

God be with you and with me tomorrow, on your name day. I was extremely moved by the blossoming of the cactus flower two nights ago, on our 12-year anniversary. A good sign, mystique and real and utterly simple. May this present year be perfect—health, home, readers, Hasidism‡ and French novels and French children's books, etc., etc. . . .§

Aegina, May 1936
Thursday

. . . Renaud writes to tell me he's read only the first pages of the Rock Garden, but he was upset because I'm in favor of Japan, i.e., in favor of fascism! Whereas he . . . etc., etc. I answered him that it is superficial juger une oeuvre d'art en homme d'action [to judge a work of art in terms of a man of action]. They are on two different levels. In any case, he does promise to attend to it. . . .

I don't have any money for the house. . . . I don't know how we'll manage to put at least a roof over the ground-floor area. . . .||

Aegina, May 1936
Wednesday evening

. . . I get worn out; all day long I'm at the construction works. I neither eat nor sleep any more. Most of the walls have gone up. This is no house: it is a fortress and it shall become a superb Schloss [castle]. I feel certain and happy that you'll be delighted by it too. Only Duras must give in about the apertures. . . .

---

* Kazantzakis did in fact write this canto on the great Japanese hero.
† Letter to E. Samios.
‡ Hasidism and the French books for children I had begun working on.
§ Letter to E. Samios.
|| Letter to E. Samios.

*I tire you with the house, but Buddha is right: "He who builds a house becomes a door and a window." . . .**

Aegina, June 2, 1936
Tuesday evening
. . . Because of the house, I can't work. . . . I've written only a few cantos: Shakespeare, Leonardo, Hideyoshi. . . . Let's hope the [school] books will be approved. Only in this way will the house be finished. In Crete, there's such poverty that it's impossible to sell any land. . . .†

If the house-in-the-process-of-construction caused us a thousand worries, friends—old and new ones alike—gave us delights never to be forgotten.

Around this time, we met Helmut von den Steinen and Conrad Westpfahl, both German Jews—a good omen for Nikos. One a writer, disciple of Stefan George, and a Homeric scholar. The other a painter, with a magnificent gift for poetry, married to a German poet.

It was a joy to hear them discussing the eternal themes with Nikos and, as a refrain, always returning to their favorite poets—from Shakespeare to Hölderlin, from Valéry to Rilke, moving through the Chinese, Japanese and Arabic poets, and never forgetting the mystics of all countries and all ages.

Through Westpfahl, we also met a Dutch couple—the Blijstras; he a writer (at a later point, he translated the *Rock Garden* into Dutch), she a teacher, both of them young and full of fantasy, both of them adoring Greece. To help them stay as long as possible in Greece, we offered them our place for several months and we took refuge in Angelakis' house. A stray mongrel acted as our postman at the time:

"Come and taste our new fig jam!" Attached to the neck of our four-footed postman, the message reached its destination.

"Expect us Thursday at four o'clock!" The good dog started back over the same path, traversing the island from one end to the other. Exactly on time, the tea would be waiting on the table.

Jean Herbert, soaring a full head over everyone else, always smiling, his hair blowing in the wind, also came to visit us on Aegina. In

---
* Letter to E. Samios.
† Letter to E. Samios.

company with Nikos, Marika and Kalmouko, we reveled incomparably with him.

Solitary to the very depths of his soul, Kazantzakis honored his visitors and usually asked them to share our meal. He had a weakness for the young people, in whom he had set all his hopes for the rebirth of Greece. And there were not only friends from Aegina—the young pharmacist Mitsakis, the Justice of the Peace Kindzios, Madame Persakis (she was a writer too)—but also the friends who came from Athens or still farther away.

"I'd so love to come and live awhile with you," Tellos Agras confided in me one day. He was an excellent lyric poet who worked at the National Library in Athens and who died during the great famine. "They tell me Kazantzakis knows how to live on nothing. I'd like to learn to do that too!"

And then there were the young poets and novelists from Thessaloniki, who arrived in a group. While Nikos was shaving (to give them a proper welcome), one of them—the elder of the band—offered me his book with a dedication:

"Would you be so kind as to give this to Mr. Kazantzakis?" he asked me, but corrected himself at once: "Please give it back to me, madame. I've made a mistake. I wrote the dedication in the present tense, whereas I am dead. . . ."

And V., grandson of our national poet of the last century, young, robust, handsome, who, without blinking an eyelash, informed me he was "thanatophilophilos. . . ."

In spite of these foibles of youth, they were genuine talents. How can one mention them all—all the ones ignored by foreign literary critics and various anthology compilers? There were so many, many of them who came to visit their elder. And there were so many, many of them whom Kazantzakis loved from the start and whom he would have liked to see going far beyond the frontiers of Greece. . . .

At that time, there were no transistors and automobiles on Aegina. We had horse and carriage, mules and donkeys—and our feet.

When there was company for us aboard the boat, Kapetan Stamatis used to sound three blasts on his foghorn and sail so close to our cliff that we could see our friends with the naked eye. Otherwise, Nikos' binoculars came in handy.

"Look! There's Mihali and Eleni Anastassiou! Minas Dimakis; Manolis, Frosso, Giorghos Loulakakis!"

Just enough time to rush down to the port and welcome them.

During this summer of 1936, with the help of Helmut von den Steinen, Nikos revised, polished, and repolished his verse translation of Goethe's *Faust*. He was still hoping (most naïvely) that the gentlemen of the National Theater would accept it for their repertory.

Aegina, June 1936
Saturday

My beloved Lenotschka,

. . . I can't understand very well what you told me about the Academy. They're going to give me an award? What for? If it's for the Dante, of course I'll accept. In any case, last year I submitted it for the very purpose of winning this prize. If they give it to me for my other work, I'll reflect on it. In that case, it would be better for me not to accept. . . .

Here I'm working constantly on the cantos now. A huge struggle, terribly difficult. Tomorrow, I shall finish Alexander the Great. . . .

I'm impatient for the Faust to be printed in Kathimerini. It will be extremely useful . . . (a) everyone will be able to see how much better this translation is than Hatzopoulos'; (b) the National Theater will be intimidated and will find it more difficult to act unjustly. . . . *

The National Theater, however, did act unjustly. And Kazantzakis wrote a protest destined for *Kathimerini*.†

. . . I have learned as much as possible from the efforts of the translator preceding me. As for myself, I have done my utmost to keep my own endeavor close to the immortal prototype, in a more rhythmic verse form, a purer resuscitation, a language that is richer and more

---

* Letter to E. Samios.
† I do not know whether he actually sent this text or whether it was ever printed.

universally Greek. May some eventual successor of mine profit likewise from my own efforts and so progress still further!

Starting from today, the work . . . will be published every Monday in the newspaper Kathimerini. The readers will be able to judge whether I have succeeded. I would be very glad and grateful to them if they can point out any errors to me, offering proof to support them. In so doing, they will help me in this vital but discomfiting task. . . .

And so I dedicate this translation to the Areopagos of Time and from it await justice. Any honest man, in this miserable Sodom, where the intellect grovels nowadays, can set his hope nowhere else. . . .

Immersed in the past, as I relive these happy years, I can hardly believe they were so cruel. My God, the struggle of them and the S.O.S. to friends, in order that Nikos Kazantzakis should be able to live by his own pen.

Aegina, July 1, 1936

. . . Life here goes by peacefully. . . . I've already finished the second act of the Matrimonial Agency and I think it's good. . . .*

The director of this agency was none other than Jupiter Kazantzakis, who had taken pity on all the lonely women. . . . Unfortunately, this comedy has been lost.

At the same time as the Matrimonial Agency, Kazantzakis had begun a new tragedy, Mother Mary, based on the life of Mary Baker Eddy. But it didn't come from the "vitals," as he used to say, and he never finished it.

While Nikos Kazantzakis was tenaciously constructing a work in Aegina that would resist the winds and tides, Metaxas,† with the aid of certain forces too well known to mention, was subjecting the rest of Greece to demolition. Everyone who was progressive became suspect. The humble people—the "faceless" ones—experienced the quaint pleasures of police interrogation. The young University professors, the

---

* Letter to E. Samios.
† Metaxas was dictator from August 4, 1936, until his death on January 2, 1941.

337

ones who had the largest audience, were shipped off to the islands. The "anhydras," the islands where the only water was mud, were reserved for the hardened men. After several years of internal quagmire, one came back home to die.

The army was "purged." Every Venizelist (hence liberal) officer, every officer believing in the Allied victory, was dismissed. When the Italians invaded Epirus in 1940, these officers demanded to be allowed to serve the nation. Instead, they were told to go and offer their services to Haile Selassie! Germanophiles alone were left in the echelons of the army.

With horror, we were also observing the tragedy of Spain: the Germans and Italians testing their new weapons; France, under Blum, wanting to come to her rescue, and England preventing this.

But we ourselves were living between sea and land, in a purity that in the long run was more unhealthy than life in one of those city-infernos of Europe or America.

Autumn was already there. The sponge fishermen would soon be returning. And with each return there were dead men to be mourned— or, even worse, "touched ones," paralyzed ones, who henceforth would move about on donkey-back, their limbs dangling, useless puppets on this earth.

At that period, the most joyful moment for the sponge fishermen was the eve of departure. Taking leave of the "kaïméne kósme [poor dear world]," they would squander nearly all of their wages in a single night, leaving wives and children utterly destitute. In the Dodecanese, Manglis told us, the divers used to play the game of which could look the richest. They went so far as to stick gold pounds on their heels. . . . In Aegina, which was closer to Spartan sobriety, they contented themselves with violins and sandoúris, mezés and retsína in strong doses. And the day of departure arrived in a state of bliss. At the time of return, joy could be read only in the eyes of a few wives or mothers, "melted away," like a leftover bit of soap, from their long wait.

Yannoúla, the elder daughter of our housekeeper, had just married a splendid specimen of a diver, for whom everyone predicted a brilliant future.

"Are you happy, Yannoúla? Did you celebrate your husband's return well?" I asked her one day as she was sorting out the salad greens, a white scarf covering three quarters of her face.

"What a question, Kyra Lenitsa! Of course I'm happy." Some-

338

thing in her voice, however, suggested a hidden thought she hadn't expressed. This intrigued me.

"Well then," I said, staring straight at the young woman with the noble bearing and patrician gestures, "well then, Yannoúla, do you like married life?"

"I like it," the young woman answered. "I like it. But . . . there's something I miss."

"What's that?"

"The distance, Kyra Lenitsa. We've lost our sense of distance—if you know what I mean."

October on a Greek island is ineffably sylphlike. After August, burgeoning with cantaloupes and watermelons, grapes and figs; after September, sunk up to its knees in wine vats, enamored of laughter and salty jokes, October comes, elflike, with a light shadow, lulling the winds to sleep, setting the sun like a night lamp, transforming the sea into an iridescent cloth of mother-of-pearl.

A single cloudburst completed the miracle. In the silence of the night, the tender crocus petals, stronger than our steel pickaxes, pierced the hard, sun-baked biscuit we euphemistically called "our field." After the crocuses came the violets gripping the cliff and the dandelion greens among the blackberry bushes.

Quiet calm, light air, light shadows, everything clamoring for happiness. And yet, there was Spain and the impossibility of helping her. And the oil in our lamp was about to run out. No prospective hope, the horizon of our "affairs" blocked, and before us the walls of a house that was still being built and was in danger of being knocked down by the December rains.

We were sitting in front of the somber sea, with the flotillas of *grigris** winding their way with their powerful lamps lit. There, Nikos and I let ourselves go in our favorite after-dinner game:

"If we had, if we had . . ."

". . . an omelette with forty eggs . . ."

"And a *tschiek*, of course." *Tschiek* was how Nikos used to pronounce *check*.

"And a trip with it. And a tiny steak to go along with that . . ."

---

* The *gri-gri* was a chain of seven or more little *kaïkis*, each with its bright *pyrophári* light to enable the men aboard to fish through the night.

But that evening, Nikos didn't even have time to get up and dance the beefsteak dance. A young man on donkey-back arrived in the night.

"Eh, Kyr Nikos! Come and see! I've got a telegram for you!"

The telegram, bearing the signature of Vlachos,* was urgently summoning Nikos to go and report on wartime Spain.

Vlachos, extremely cynical and intelligent, had a weak spot for Kazantzakis. He welcomed him with a mischievous smile.

"I know you'd prefer to go among the Reds, but I want to send you to the 'Blacks,' as you call them."

"And just why do you want me?"

"Because you'll tell the truth. Your friends and enemies will avoid you like the plague. I'll be delighted. Will you leave now at once, yes or no?"

Marseilles, October 9, 1936

My beloved Lenotschka,

. . . I'm sitting in a café now . . . waiting for the rain to slacken a bit so I can dash over to the hotel, get my suitcase and go down to the boat. I'm not at all in good spirits. I'm longing for Aegina, and only necessity has made me leave her—and the desire to see this new wound in the world, Spain. I'm paying for it heavily, but I keep thinking to myself, it's only for a month and it will pass and turn into recollections with the sweet patina of Time. . . .†

Marseilles, Evening of October 9, 1936

. . . The ironical, refined, insufferable, feelingless, penny-worshiping Frenchies are not my psychological climat. At every single step, they make me furious. You can't say a thing without having them stare at you with a scharfe [sharp], scornful glance. Just now, I got out of the boat and went over to a baraque [little shack] near here to buy some tobacco. The patron just looked at me and scoffed. "A trois kilomètres, monsieur! [Three kilometers from here, mister!]" he blared at me. And all the Frenchmen who were there drinking their colored liqueurs were ridiculing me. And why? Because I'd asked for some tobacco, and they didn't have any. . . .

Spain never leaves my mind. I feel grief and pain for her as though

---

* Vlachos was still the director of the newspaper *Kathimerini*.
† Letter to E. Samios.

340

she were a concret [specific] person. I'm impatient to see what she has suffered, what has happened to her, whether something irréparable has been lost. And I shall be inhumanly impartial in everything I write. Both sides will be displeased, but I cannot do otherwise. By now, I am beginning—and this is my absolutely final évolution—not to be preoccupied with left or right ideas. One thing alone interests me and gives me joy and pain: man, that human, exquisite worm that creeps along, struggling to create wings—"la farfalla angelica,"* as Dante says. . . .†

Lisbon, October 16, 1936

. . . All day yesterday I rushed around and finally got the permit. I met quite a few people, got some letters, and hope to manage. The difficulties are in the means of transportation; automobiles and railways don't exist everywhere; not even hotels, etc. But I'll manage. . . .‡

Segovia, October 22, 1936

My love, we've just come back from the front. Many long hours on the front lines with the soldiers. . . . Along with several officers, I'd gone up to an elevation, from which we could see Madrid and, a short way off, the enemy lines. . . . "It's dangerous for us to be standing here," one of the officers said. "They'll shoot their cannons at us." He had hardly finished speaking when a shell whistled over our heads. They all fell flat. I remained standing a moment to see the shell—it had fallen close by, stirring up a terrible smoke and dust and breaking some trees too. And then soon after that, a second and a third cannon blast, but, luckily, without hurting anyone. . . .

We want to go to Toledo, but there are difficulties. . . . Here, the great events (barbarous acts, etc.) are over. The other great event, the capture of Madrid, has not yet come. Crowds of reporters (mainly Germans) are sitting in Salamanca, waiting. . . .§

Burgos, October 26, 1936

. . . There's a strict censorship . . . that's why I'm sending you cards in French. . . . Here my life is full of spectacles that are most oppressive for us, as you can well understand. In one week, I traversed

---

* Farfalla angelica means "angelic butterfly."
† Letter to E. Samios.
‡ Letter to E. Samios.
§ Letter to E. Samios.

the entire northern front by car. I went to the front line in the midst of cannon shots and bullets. Maybe I was slightly in danger, because several bombs did fall alongside me. At first, I remained standing. But afterward I got used to it and as soon as the whizzing was heard I fell flat too, along with the rest of them. . . . I went into the trenches and could see the Reds across the way from me, and I lived a week of the war. Villages in ruins, mothers weeping, people in black, dogs still faithful to their own thresholds, their eyes all red.

Tonight, I'm going back to Salamanca, where my quartier [head-quarters] is. I'll stay there a little while and then I'll make another tour by car again—of the southern front—Toledo, etc. . . .*

1937.   The Spanish "gifts" never left us: the tiny red flag dipped in the blood of a young man killed because he believed in the possibility of Freedom; a letter and photograph of Francisco Lopez' wife and their daughter Carmencita, calling her father to come and see how the cat had given birth to four kittens; and a thick key from some violated church.

Too much has been said about the horrors of the Civil War in Spain. Too little has been done to remedy them. The "little sardine," which had reared its head in Nikos' dream to beg God, "If you are good, O Lord, do not give power to the big people; give it to the just ones!"—that little sardine has never been heard.

Aegina, a fortified island, was under military censorship. But this did not prevent some turbulent meetings as soon as Nikos returned.

"Do you agree with what Unamuno told you? Must we hide the truth from the people? Is Unamuno right to invoke the words of the Old Testament—'He who looks God in the face will die'?"

"The ancient myths are dead. Our duty is to create new myths."

"And in the meantime?"

"Unamuno's words have a practical side. How can one unveil the truth to these thousands of young or old women whom the priests and the various governments have kept in a state of total ignorance? For these women, a Communist or anarchist son, father or brother is the devil."

---

* Letter to E. Samios.

"Why did they have to go and burn the churches?"

"Don't forget that if the Reds did burn the churches, the Spanish Catholic priests burned the Church. . . . In Christ's name they have sanctioned and desired a thousand crimes. They have sided unhesitatingly with the devil."

"Is there any hope that Spain will be able to pull herself out of trouble?"

"I don't think so. All the forces of evil have aligned themselves against her."

"And yet, one day our turn will come!"

"It will come, I'm sure of that!" said Nikos, with that little spark in his eyes we knew so well. "I repeat over and over again the following: We are passing through a new Middle Ages. And it will last a very long time."

"Ten years? Twenty years? We'll hold out well."

"Two hundred years, perhaps—I'm very pessimistic for the near future."

"But the people will rouse themselves. Were those Spanish mothers you mentioned a while back happy to see the Moroccans pillaging their houses, killing their sons, carving crosses with a knife blade on their husbands' noses?"

"The Spanish officer acting as my guide bowed down in admiration of them. 'They can hear sounds we barely catch,' he told us. 'Even in the blackest night, they can see things we can barely glimpse. They're more agile than we are. They fear nothing and fight better than anyone else.'"

"Isn't it dangerous to teach them to kill Europeans?" I asked him, nonplussed by his unconcerned air.

The officer shrugged his shoulders. But I could already see an historic law in the process of evolving and I knew that the descent of the barbarians had begun by way of Spain.*

Summer was approaching with great strides, as it always does in Greece. There were still neither doors nor windows on our house; and we were going to have to settle down in it, in view of our Dutch friends' declining to leave the little house we had lent them. To speed up

---

* N.K.'s report on wartime Spain appears in the "Viva la Muerte" section of *Spain* (New York: Simon and Schuster, 1963).

delivery of the frames, etc., etc., I went off to Athens again. A little later I left for the Pyrenees.

Aegina, July 1937
Tuesday

Lenotschka my love,

N. [Papaioannou] arrived just a few moments ago, and he had your letter for me, but not Europe. He was afraid, he says, of being searched. . . . I wish they'd give me the prize for Dante so that I could accept. . . . I doubt it.

Early, early yesterday morning, Blijstra came. We took a little walk and talked about plays. I told him an idea for a play and he was enthusiastic, and he'll write it. And I began organizing my own play today—Othello Returns. I've found the plot and it seems to me it will be extraordinarily passionant [thrilling].

I've finished the Alexander the Great canto and I like it. . . .

Today, Kyria Photini* made bold to suggest that I buy some . . . butter! I said to her in an amazed tone "Butter!" and the poor thing was mum. A bit later, and there she was back again. "Well, at least, can I bring you some spinach and rice this noon, Mr. Niko?" I accepted cheerfully, and her heart went back to its right place.†

Aegina, Summer 1937
Monday

. . . This morning, the sea was flooded with cantaloupes! A kaïki loaded with them had broken down and cast them about outside our house. A crowd of women and children ran down and began collecting them. Boats were scurrying about, and some people dove after them. Sophia carted up two sacks stuffed full and she brought me a huge melon too. . . . Great glee and piratical shrieks—I can just imagine what would happen if they were to sack a rich city.

I finished the canto, and now I'm studying the tragedy Mother Mary. . . .‡

---

* Kyria Photini was the housekeeper and the mother of Yannoúla, previously mentioned.
† Letter to E. Samios.
‡ Letter to E. Samios.

Aegina, August 1, 1937

. . . Yesterday, I came to an agreement to send Kathimerini a piece of work every day, and I'm buried in work.* I'll get 3,000 drachmas per month. However, I'm still hoping the Theater is going to be reorganized and I will get the post I have wanted. If this does come off, our everyday life will be secure. . . .†

Aegina, August 2, 1937
Evening

. . . I have in front of me 7 new books by Communists who've come back from Russia déçus [disillusioned], like Panaït. And that's why I say your book will‡ find a publisher. Il est à la page [It's up to date]. The same for J. des Roches [Rock Garden], with China and Japan, at the present time. . . .§

Athens, August 17, 1937

My beloved St. George,

Today, I came into Athens to negotiate with Kathimerini about a tour of the Peloponnesus in September with 20 French people from the Budé Society. For Kathimerini, I'm not writing my own articles, but an anonymous column and a series of articles is already under way: Gide, Céline, Russia, etc., etc. . . .‖

Aegina, August 23, 1937

. . . Prevelakis has been sworn in, and he has assumed office and is in full glory.¶ And I get reverberations from the glory! Everyone keeps writing to ask me to intervene on their behalf, etc. . . .**

Aegina, August 24, 1937

. . . I'd been working away all day long, and in the evening an extraordinary thing happened: I was just drinking my evening milk and

---

* N.K. wrote unsigned fictionalized biographies for *Kathimerini*.
† Letter to E. Samios.
‡ I was writing a book about Panaït Istrati—*La Verdadera Tragedia de Panaït Istrati* (Santiago, Chile: Ercilla Editions, 1938).
§ Letter to E. Samios.
‖ Letter to E. Samios.
¶ Prevelakis had just been appointed director of the Fine Arts School, a branch of the Ministry of National Education.
** Letter to E. Samios.

getting ready to go to bed when a carriage appeared. A lady wearing a broad-brimmed straw hat alighted. . . . "I've come to seek your hospitality!" she announced, laughing. "Who are you?" "Don't you remember me?" . . . Aliki! It was Kyveli's daughter!*

She sat down on the couch in my study, said various things, and finally: "But aren't you going to ask me why I've come?"

"The ancient Greeks asked their guests only after three days. I'm an ancient Greek!"

"But I'm in a hurry. I've come because my theater's going to the dogs. We don't have enough to pay anyone; we owe money. Tonight I was supposed to perform, and I just threw everything overboard, without anyone's knowing where I was going, not even my husband. I wanted to commit suicide, but then I thought of you and came running at once. Let me live here near you several days. I'll take courage and start on a new road."

"Let's go and eat at Marini's," I said. "I don't have anything here."

We went to Marini's and ate some tomatoes and cheese. He didn't have anything else. . . . I fixed her bed on the studio couch, and now it's 9:00 A.M. and she's still asleep. I'll go down now and prepare her milk for her. (She doesn't even know how to boil an egg, she informed me.)

I got her milk ready, laid the table, and we ate. She couldn't sleep, she says. She didn't bring a comb with her, or soap or a towel or nightgown. Nothing. . . . I gave her some books, and now she's sitting in the studio reading. She doesn't say a word or even budge. She doesn't know how many days she'll stay, she says. . . . She seems desperate. I feel sorry for her. A strong, autumn wind blowing. . . .†

Aegina, August 26, 1937

The guest is still in our home. Luckily, she doesn't bother me at all. She sits calmly in the studio (where she's also sleeping), reading, not making a sound. Every day I leave an order at Marini's and he brings us some food (tomatoes, eggplant, green beans, etc.). We eat at noon. I go upstairs. At 5 o'clock, tea. I go back to work and in the evening we talk about theater, her life, etc. She's a calm, good person. She didn't have a

---

* Kyveli, along with Kotopouli, was one of the great dramatic actresses of Greece.
† Letter to E. Samios.

nightgown, and I gave her one of yours. She came with only her straw hat. Today, the newspapers published in big capital letters: ALIKI DISAPPEARS! HER FATE UNKNOWN! POLICE SEARCH FOR TRACES OF HER, IN VAIN! etc., etc. I told her to send a telegram, but she doesn't want to. . . . However, I'm getting ready to leave on September 1, and of necessity she'll have to leave too. She's a pleasant person and extremely discrète [circumspect].

The Dutch people left yesterday, promising to do their utmost for our manuscripts. . . . I haven't finished Mother Mary yet, because —what with Kathimerini and preparations for the Peloponnesus trip— I've lost the atmosphere. But it will turn out well. It's better for me not to be in a hurry.*

Aegina, August 28, 1937

The Aliki adventure horrid! What happened with the newspapers is beyond description. The police topsy-turvy . . . fears that she may have committed suicide, articles, etc. . . . Now that's all over. . . . Since yesterday evening the house has been full of reporters and photographers. . . . Today her husband came at last—tears, etc.—and they've just left. Her stay here was very pleasant. Last night we had dinner with Kalmouko. We laughed. I'm sure I did well—very humanly —to take pity on her and give her a good welcome. . . .†

Aegina, August 29, 1937

Today's newspapers are all full of descriptions: "This is the 'villa' that was Aliki's hideaway!" . . . "This is the window of the room where she slept. This is where she drank her milk. This is the figurehead flanking the chaise longue where she lay and looked at the sea," etc. . . .‡

Aegina, August 30, 1937

Yesterday, Mrs. Angelakis brought a pretty little green tablecloth, embroidered discret in white. . . . You can imagine her excitement when she asked about Aliki. Lots of people believe she was my mistress! What a hubbub enveloping my name again, and all for nothing! Kathimerini telephoned me to say I should have phoned them immediately to

---

* Letter to E. Samios.
† Letter to E. Samios.
‡ Letter to E. Samios.

inform them she was at my home—and they'd have had a first-class scoop! I answered that I'm a bad reporter and an honest man.

In any case, Kathimerini is enthusiastic. . . . No masterpiece I could ever write, they say, could have made me so well known, etc., etc. . . .

When will you come back? Our "villa" is superb, and the winter will be happy when we are both here. I have throngs of themes to write, but how can I find time?

Christ, the canto, made a great impression. . . .*

Patras, September 6, 1937

. . . You know Patras. Provincial. I wander around the little streets all day long, like "the Pope's dog," drinking coffee, eating loukoumi, watching a garish dancing girl on the platform of the main café. The men ugly, their manner of talking abysmal. Alongside me today . . . an old lady with her two plump old-maid daughters, chattering away: "Potatoes . . . our aunty's mystery . . . the pots and pans . . ." The young people are even worse. I haven't heard a single word that comes from the spirit. Food, flirting, money. . . .

Everyone knows my name now. Every time they hear it, they jump up: "Kazantzakis?" "Yes!" "Aliki's?" "Yes, indeed!" I might be a great writer; my name would never be so well known. And now, with the . . . abduction of the actress, I've become renowned! . . .†

Kavassila, afternoon of September 6, 1937

I set off by myself; I couldn't stand Patras any more. . . . And so, I'm moving on toward Olympia. At present I'm in a station in a miserable little village, where I'm waiting . . . for the train to Kyllene. There I'll climb up to the Hlemoutsi Castle . . . Today, wretched villages . . . and in the Middle Ages they were most splendid, full of knights, tournois [tournaments], luxury, colors. . . .

Swamps, eucalyptus trees, cypresses, vineyards, fertile black earth, dense air, heat, mosquitoes. Talk without any élan, without any humor, without any stamp of the spirit or the soul. Women with low rumps, short legs, waddling around like geese. And all the faces surly, heavy,

---

* Letter to E. Samios.
† Letter to E. Samios.

servile. . . . My only consolation now is my pipe. A vital, warm, silent companion.*

Kyllene, September 7, 1937

. . . Last night I arrived on a beach with two or three shacks. "Is there any hotel?" "Let's go to Nikoletta's," suggested the railway man; he's very helpful and garrulous. "Are there any bedbugs?" "Our only products here are grapes and bedbugs." "Are there any mosquitoes?" "There are." "From the swamps?" "It's full of swamps." "Let's go," I said, sealing my lips.

We reached a seaside inn. Nikoletta fat, squalid, cheerful. She brought us some boiled fish and garlic sauce as strong as gunpowder and some rosé wine. Five or six tramps, peddlers, policemen. One of them picked up a conversation and, lowering his voice, told me: "Hide your ring. They're all convicts and thieves here. I want to ask you a piece of advice." And he began telling me an amazing story about his wife who hates him and doesn't want to have intercourse with him. She keeps remembering her uncle, with whom she'd had sexual relations . . . An incredible story, with very weird details. I felt drowsy and the garlic sauce had made me dizzy. I gave him the advice and went off to bed. "Do you want to be by yourself or with other people?" Nikoletta asked me. "By myself!" "Then you'll sleep in my bed. . . . But I won't turn the light on, because of the mosquitoes. . . ."

Next morning I found the bed very clean. The parlor's full of pictures and photographs, towel racks, plaster statuettes of King Constantine, paper flowers, green vases and handicrafts stuck with sea shells. . . .

I went up to the celebrated fortress of Hlemoutsi . . . and now it's afternoon and I'm sitting by the sea. A cool breeze blowing and I could see before me the ruins of Glarentza, where in the Middle Ages the Frankish ships bearing knights used to cast anchor. Delicate sand, bulrushes, reeds, mountain laurel, masticha trees, myrtle. . . .†

Olympia, September 9, 1937

I'm just arriving in Olympia. A big fair: thousands of people, selling mainly horses. . . . At the hotel, they tell me they're expecting 12

---

* Letter to E. Samios.
† Letter to E. Samios.

French people tomorrow. Will they be mine? We shall see. I went to the museum again and reveled in the grand bas-reliefs. . . .

A heavenly day. I'm wandering about with my pipe, feasting my eyes slowly, lingeringly on the plain. I don't yet know what I'm going to write, but inside myself I'm agitated and various motifs are seething. . . .*

Athens, September 20, 1937

. . . I've just this moment come back from the expedition; it lasted 17 days. I saw exquisite landscapes and was delighted by several fortresses, above all, Monemvasia. The French people didn't come. . . . Along the way, I came across two French sisters: splendid (one the Itka type, the other Elsa).† We stayed together for a week, and then I left them at Mistra. . . .

And now, I don't know what to write. Greece is a difficult theme. And I cannot write whatever I want. It's too cruel, too humiliating for the modern Greeks. . . .‡

See Victor [Serge]. I wish our government would permit him to come to Aegina and do whatever he wants. . . . Give him my warmest greetings and tell him again how much we love him. . . .

I think we must never again travel separately. . . . I've been collecting images, sensations, bitternesses and I've come back full. This is how you'll come back too, and you'll have much to tell me. We shall exchange merchandise. . . .§

Aegina, September 25, 1937

My beloved Lenotschka!

I've just this instant received your letter telling me to come to Paris. I don't know whether Kathimerini will accept. . . . But even if they do accept, I don't consider it right, because . . . I've come to an agreement that as soon as I get the telegram I'll take a flying trip up to Athens to be sworn in as Director of Repertory in the National Theater. . . .

---

* Letter to E. Samios.
† The two sisters were Yvonne Métral and Lucienne Fleury; they became faithful friends of ours.
‡ N.K. wrote some extraordinary pages on the Peloponnesus. See *Report to Greco* and *Journey to the Morea* (New York: Simon and Schuster, 1965).
§ Letter to E. Samios.

Your manuscript was printed front page in *Kathimerini*, and Hourmouzios asks me why you haven't sent any others. . . .*

Aegina, October 5, 1937

. . . Your letters calling me to Paris have upset me in various ways and I've decided to send someone to *Kathimerini* to ask if they do accept—personally, I don't want to come to Paris, although I do realize there'll be many joys there for me and that it is necessary for the books. . . .

About the Theater position: After your letter, I decided to find a way not to accept it. I had accepted only for your sake, so that you might have a little bit of comfort. Personally, for myself, it was very irksome. But since you don't care . . . I'll find a way to get out of it. . . . I'll try to lay my hands on some pretext for refusing, without throwing cold water on Prevelakis. . . .

I'm writing the articles on the Peloponnesus now.† There'll be 20 of them. They're overwhelmingly difficult, whereas they might be overwhelmingly easy. But I don't want to slip into platitudes and I'm being very careful. Impossible to write more than one a day. . . .‡

Guernica refused to let me sleep. Everything I loved in Nikos' work I saw there, concentrated onto a few meters of canvas. How could I enable the solitary man of Aegina to see it too? When I got back to Athens, I left no stone unturned. And for once my efforts were crowned with success. In his own turn, Nikos could now set off for Paris.

Waiting for the ship that would take him away in the simultaneously satin and translucent night fringed with the light of day, we were taking our leave—lingeringly, gently, sharing in silence the fruit of coming joys. Suddenly, three little knocks rapped on the glass-paned door of the studio.

"Hola, Westpfahl!" called Nikos, who could see in the night like a lynx.

"Hear the great news! Nikos is on his way to see *Guernica!*"

"*Guernica*," sighed the painter . . . "*Guernica*—I would so have loved to see some Picasso again. Especially now that I've reached a turning-point."

---

* Letter to E. Samios.
† See *Report to Greco* and *Journey to the Morea*.
‡ Letter to E. Samios.

"Sell some canvas and hep-hep-and-away!" I rejoined, overflowing with optimism.

We had reached the point of discussing the possibilities of a sale when Nikos interrupted.

"Do you know Picasso personally?"

"Almost. I know his work perfectly. What a stimulus for me . . ."

"Do you really want to see *Guernica?*" asked Nikos, already a little stirred by what was about to ensue.

"And how!" replied Westpfahl.

"Ah, well then, there's nothing easier. You shall go to Paris!" And he took out of his pocket the ticket so arduously won and the few foreign-exchange bills needed for the trip.

1938.   The year came in like a fairy tale. "Once upon a time, there was . . . there was not . . . and yet there was . . .

"Tantine,"* a very, very rich American lady, extremely intelligent, extremely eccentric, a devotee of Vivekananda. With her, Jean Herbert had begun publishing works of Swami in Europe and I was to translate two little tomes into Greek. Our friend had spoken to Tantine at great length about Nikos Kazantzakis.

"Stones don't interest me one bit!" she announced to me the very first moment we met in Athens. "Neither the Acropolis nor any of your old treasure troves. I like to meet human beings. Who's this Nikos Kazantzakis you're living with?"

Lithe and erect in spite of her advanced age, the lady from America sprang out of her armchair.

"Let's go on to Aegina at once! I'm burning to meet him."

"I'll sleep in a different room every day," Tantine announced to us once she reached Aegina. "And please leave all the doors open. I love to know what's going on around me!"

She did not change beds, but she did inspect the house from each and every angle. Clinging to the narrow staircase, she climbed up to the highest terrace, reveling in the Saronic, stubbornly refusing all assistance.

"You've known me only since yesterday," she said, "and you suppose

---

* The name by which her friends addressed her.

you can help me? I've known myself for eighty years; I can do it better than anyone."

At table, Tantine ate only the white of the egg.

"Eleni, that yolk is clean. You mustn't throw it away!"

"Of course, Tantine," I answered, without budging.

"Eleni, that yolk is clean! Are you going to throw it away?" she repeated with a severe air. In a single gulp, I swallowed the little amber ball. Tantine had given me my first lesson in economy.

"When I was a little girl," she said, "I used to hide my pennies over my door whenever house-cleaning day came. I don't like waste. Even today, if I see a match drop, I still pick it up! Make economies, Eleni. Don't allow any waste. But learn to give for the great causes. And then give with both hands! And God bless you! I see you need it."

"And what's that 'huge' manuscript on your table, Nikolo?" queried Tantine, as she suddenly came face to face with the "Monster." "Could it possibly be *The Odyssey* Jean's been telling me about?"

"Yes, it's our child, Tantine."

"Tell me what you say in it. Why don't you publish it if it's ready? What are you waiting for?"

And Nikos began unraveling the extraordinary story of his corsair. The trips, the devastations, the burnings of the palaces, the flights of exodus, the building of the Utopian city, the destruction, etc., etc. Tantine listened in stupefaction. Night fell and they were still sitting face to face like conspirators, *The Odyssey* spread out on their knees like some ill-gotten plunder, all the more cherished for that reason.

I came to interrupt their tête-à-tête.

"Come and take some sustenance. The table's set."

"You there," Tantine, almost angry, ordered, "go and get my purse. It's on my bed. And come back quickly!"

"How much do you need to print *The Odyssey*, Nikolo?"

"Hm-m . . . approximately 1,500 dollars."

And Miss Josephine MacLeod signed a check for 1,500 dollars! And we were able to produce 300 in-folio copies, the first edition of *The Odyssey* in Greek! The second edition, more modest in its format, I laid on Nikos' bier on the day of the great departure. He was not in time to caress it, according to his habit.

Once the check had been entrusted to the printer, Nikos asked me to be in charge of correcting the proofs. I accepted and called on another Eleni, the young wife of Mihali Anastassiou, to help me. We were allowed a total of only two corrections, and they had to be made at

353

once! They brought us the pages. We corrected them; they were printed; and we had to check them the very same day, on the spot, working more than eight hours a day. For, they warned, unless we kept up this pace, the book would wind up much more expensive.

Occasionally, we became aware that two syllables were missing from a verse—the 15-syllable verse was very much like the 17-syllable verse. Or we had doubts about a word. How to solve such problems? To telephone to Aegina took longer than to go there. The slightest delay discombobulated the typographers. And, what was still more comical, Nikos himself was astonished:

"Is it so difficult," he wrote me, "to correct a verse by yourself? Add or take away several syllables? Change one word for another?"

At about this time he began to suffer recurrent attacks of an allergic facial ailment which was to plague him again in the last years of his life.

Aegina, Winter 1938
Friday
. . . Just yesterday, the fluid stopped (in any case, it was very slight) and there's nothing else wrong with me. . . . I'm sorry to have caused you so much worry. And I promise you, if the fluid does reappear, I'll come at once. If I don't come, it means that all is well. . . .*

Aegina, Winter 1938
Wednesday
. . . Your letter a great delight. How I wish they'd accept Melissa. This would give me courage and I should write other theatrical works. Otherwise, . . .

The biscuits are still untouched, not so much for you to find them [when you come back] as to test my own will power. I'm looking at Mother Mary again, agonizedly, but I haven't yet begun on it again. I'm waiting to see what's to become of Melissa. A theatrical work is something utterly different from a poem. Poems I can write even if they are never published and even if no one ever reads them. But a dramatic work is like that incarnation of thought occurring in Tibet: It is an autonomous organism that becomes detached from yourself and

---

* Letter to E. Samios.

*hankers to climb up on the stage. If it does not get there, your power to make another birth cracks. . . .**

In spite of the new troubles caused by the excessive thriftiness of our mason Theodoros, Nikos was working well as always and on several fronts at once.

> *Aegina, Winter 1938*
> *Wednesday*
> *. . . All these days, I've been writing the Second-Grade Reader. By the time you come, it will be ready. Bring me everything the censorship† has returned to you: Books XX, XXI, XXII, XXIII, XXIV, . . . Here, calm. Heavenly weather. . . .‡*

And from this same period, he wrote to Leah, who, with her little daughter Ruth, had recently visited Aegina for a few days.

> *Aegina, November 17, 1938*
> *. . . The times are fearfully heavy. For several years now, we have entered a total Middle Ages. Wars, shadows, hatred, pogroms, they're all there. There are still a few magnificent, fiery hearts left, but without any tangible results. What is our duty? To remain faithful to the Flame. At present, it remains hidden, infirm, diffident. But the time will come when it shall rule again upon this awesome, marvelous earth. We must remain strong, Leah, and faithful; this is the only salvation. Our cry in the desert today will later on once again change stones to men. There is something in the human heart that can never be extinguished, and this something is our only hope. . . .*

> *Aegina, Winter 1938*
> *Monday*
>
> *My beloved L!*
> *All day today, I've been carrying water from the well, pumping water [in the cistern] and helping to fill in the chinks. A strong wind, very cold. Luckily, it's not raining, and so we'll finish quickly. . . .*

---

* Letter to E. Samios.
† The censorship of the Metaxas dictatorship.
‡ Letter to E. Samios.

I read your Spanish book on Panaït* twice. Fascinant, written with vitality and great artistry. It was very difficult for a book to emerge out of so many events and be so clear, alive, passionant. . . . Not only have you done a good deed in memory of Panaït, but you've also written a fine book. And now, let's see your third book. . . .

One disagreeable fact: Peter Gray† has had to leave Aegina, i.e., the police told him that foreigners aren't allowed, etc. So the poor boy has had to take refuge in Poros again. When he left, he gave me five or six very handsome books: Keats, Shelley, Lafcadio Hearn (etc.). He was dismayed at having to leave. Barbarities! . . .

You've seen what's happening in Germany? I am right: we have entered a Middle Ages. We are in a Middle Ages. All the symptoms. And what are we to do? Daydream, plan, work for the coming civilization. We are holding a "tiny lighted candle," and we must not let it go out. . . .‡

It is human—all too human—for an artist undergoing a nervous breakdown to avoid his neighbor like the plague when the latter goes on with his own work imperturbably.

One day, our dear Kalmouko warned us, "If you see a pot of basil on my doorstep, you may pay a visit. If not, stay away; for I'm in a state of absolute creative euphoria." In actual fact, Kalmouko was spending his nights drinking, coming back at dawn when Nikos was already settled at his worktable. All day long he spent sleeping, his shutters closed. We were sad that we couldn't do anything to help him out of this crisis, especially because we liked his painting immensely.

"Kalmouko has built high walls [screens] all around his entrance patio," Nikos wrote me, "to avoid seeing us. . . ."

Once again, Minotis reassured me that *Melissa* would be performed, and I wrote to Nikos, who celebrated the good news with the poor-man's champagne.

---

* La Verdadera Tragedia de Panaït Istrati.
† We had given him the use of Cousin Mary's house.
‡ Letter to E. Samios.

Aegina, Winter 1938
Monday

. . . The moment I read your letter, I rushed to the cupboard and ate a good big spoonful of cherry preserves. . . .*

Aegina, Winter 1938
Wednesday

. . . I received the four miraculous edibles, all delicious! . . . With this new method of yours, I eat better when you're away! . . .

Madame Lambridi sent me the article she had presented on the radio. She lauds me to the heavens, declaring that Sikelianos and I are the two great realities in Greece today! My God, if only I believed all that, how eased my heart would be! But I believe nothing, nothing, nothing of any of the good things people tell me. Other things I longed for; other things I should have done; other things I could perhaps have done—and my life has been wasted. Everything I write—and I repeat this—is Ersatz. . . . †

The task of correcting the proofs continued. The wife of Timoteo Rubio, the Spanish poet Rosa Chacel Rubio, a woman who radiated goodness, arrived in Athens. Together with Nikos, she began a verse translation of The Odyssey.

I'm glad Rosa has come. She is most certainly a rare woman. What she writes—and, above all, the rhythm in which she writes—is rare. She might have done great things. . . .‡

Aegina, December 5, 1938

My love, Qué tal?§

A superb day. Young St. arrived . . . bearing three "fire flowers," plants full of orange drops. . . . We planted them; if they take root, they'll be marvelous.

---

* Letter to E. Samios.
† Letter to E. Samios.
‡ Part of letter immediately preceding.
§ Spanish for "How are you?"

Your translation of Peter Gray excellent; it was published and given the best space. I sent it on to him at once. He'll be delighted with it, of course. Your language perfect. . . .

Tomorrow's my name day and I'll wake up at midnight to begin work. I'm working tremendously hard to have the manuscripts ready in time. . . .*

Aegina, December 1938
Friday

. . . I'm eager to come and see you. You've finished the entire Odyssey without my having to step in. Perhaps I'll be in time for Omega. . . .†‡

Aegina, December 8, 1938

. . . From night to night, I'm writing the Hapsburgs. I want to finish most of it, so as to feel easy about time during the holidays. That's why I shall come to Athens only when the moment has come . . . for me to write the signatures. . . .

Today for the first time, I lit your stove. It got very hot and I put some beans on to boil. This roucoulement [glug-glug sound] makes me feel strangely peaceful. . . .

I'm waiting to translate the theatrical piece; it too was a windfall. . . .§

Aegina, December 9, 1938

. . . The ailing cactus that I took to Sakiotis' is recovering, growing new shoots. It had suffered a sunstroke! If we leave it in the sun, we must put an umbrella over it!

I forgot to tell you that on St. Nicholas' Day I wore the jacket you made me from your coat, and je me pavanais [I paraded about] like a child. . . .||

1939.   Hereafter, it was a festive occasion to set off for the printer's at dawn—in the midst of the vegetable gardens in southwest Athens.

---

* Letter to E. Samios.
† That is, Book **XXIV**.
‡ Letter to E. Samios.
§ Letter to E. Samios.
|| Letter to E. Samios.

Was it the sight of the first flowering almond tree or the raw smell of the bitter dandelion greens mingled with the invisible, violent violet? Or the joy of having completed our task in record time?

Bursting with pride, like benevolent godmothers, we two Elenis held the plump newborn baby* on our knees, eager to present it for public adulation. And just then we caught sight of the first boners! Blushing to the roots of our hair, we called Nikos to our rescue.

"Printing errors? Serious ones, you say? . . . Don't panic! . . . Yes, of course, I'll come. Meantime, please consult Kalmouko!"

"Only one possible remedy" was the latter's verdict. "Scratch out the letters you don't want, and in your own handwriting put the correct ones in their place."

Fortunately, there were only three hundred copies in all and, in more than thirty thousand verses, fewer than thirty mistakes! But there was one good-sized one! In the Greek alphabet, the letter o lacks a single stroke to become an a. Distorted in this way, the adjective assumed so unexpected a meaning that even the rest of us could hardly keep from laughing. O Nikos, Nikos—ideal boss! Instead of swearing, he just clucked away in amusement: "Well, well, well! Just imagine, I'd never even thought of that one!"

This reminds me, by the by, of our young niece Alka's mad urge to play on the typewriter every time she came to visit us. Nikos was upstairs correcting the pages that had been clearly typed from the fourth version of The Odyssey. Alka was carrying them up to him bit by bit. One can well imagine the writer's relief in seeing his text freed of all the layers of crossed-out mistakes and erasures. Alka and I used to amuse ourselves by suddenly adding to the original verses other hocus-pocus verses—hocus-pocus, but perfect in form. Holding our breath, we would await the "Master's" reaction.

The first minutes would go by in impressive silence. And then the cackle of laughter would explode. Hurtling down the narrow steps four at a time (Nikos hadn't gotten the "trap" he had wanted, but the most inconvenient staircase in existence), brandishing the telltale pages in his hand, he would begin pounding and pommeling our shoulders, lifting Alka in his arms and twirling about with her.

"It's pure surrealism! It's a masterpiece!" And he would offer us a little glass of homemade kirsch to toast the health of the burgeoning poetess.

---

* This first edition of The Odyssey actually weighed about fifteen pounds!

The grand day arrived, at last. On the eve, a centrally located display window was painstakingly arrayed by two friends who ran bookstores.* And the "Monster" was enthroned—a monster from all points of view, Moby Dick gone astray in the buoyant waters of the Mediterranean.

"Give me 100 grams, please!" demanded M.A. at the head of the line, the most bilious of the detractors, with the most deceptively amiable smile.

"Me too; 350 grams, please!"

"And me, one pound!"

The game was long and drawn-out. The persons vomiting abuse against the man "who would not follow his own times" were precisely the ones who never read him. But even the most refractory cities cannot escape poetry. Of the three hundred copies, Nikos gave approximately half of them away. Hyperpessimistic, I was counting on five buyers. There were a hundred. And the young people managed to find a way to read the river epic, passing it on from hand to hand, while clamoring for an edition on their own financial level.

Our friends exerted themselves. One of our finest painters, Nikos Hadjikyriakos-Ghika, for example, without uttering a word, began translating into French certain passages of the poem he wanted to illustrate. Upon these first drafts of the translation, Robert Levesque wrought his own translation, published later in *Permanence of Greece*.

"I had invited Levesque and Kimon Friar to Hydra," Hadjikyriakos confided jovially one day at a vernissage. "And I 'belabored' them till they realized what work they were confronting. With all the rumors spread by anti-Kazantzakis circles in Athens, believe me, this was no easy task."

Hourmouzios, editor-in-chief of *Kathimerini*, used his prestige to promote *The Odyssey*. A long series of articles bearing his signature appeared in his newspaper. Among the most alarming dispatches from that year, one found impassioned diatribes for or against *The Odyssey*. Once the initial excitement had died down, Nikos' only thought was to get away. But before going away, he conceived an astonishing idea.

"I'd like to buy a baked earthen jar, my love—a big one!"

"To do what with?"

"To put oil in—let's say about 90 pounds of olive oil!"

My shriek of horror did not keep him from carrying out his idea.

---

* Stamos Diamantaras, who became a close friend, and Ganiaris.

He looked far and wide and found his jar. And, what's more, he filled it himself with excellent olive oil!

"This oil will go rancid," I protested.

"Please, Lenotschka, don't get upset. At home, we always used to have a large quantity of oil."

I knew that in his father's household bread was never allowed to run short. The father used to buy so much of it to hand out to members of his family that he was nicknamed "Kapetan Bread." Nikos, I thought to myself, was about to become my "Kapetan Olive Oil."

It was a lucky thing that Nikos paid no attention to my grumbling. For, thanks to this oil, we escaped the festering sores left by the famine. And we were also able to save a few children in our neighborhood.

PART THREE

THE WAR

1939–1945

During these troubled times, there was an English diplomat in Athens, a genuine country gentleman, Sir Sidney Waterlow. Nikos had made his acquaintance through a mutual friend. Sir Sidney was impressive of stature, vastly cultivated, interested in metaphysics, and he loved Greece—the Greece of today as well as that of bygone days, something we weren't at all accustomed to.

The two men took pleasure in each other's company now, their minds alert, discussing politics, art, religion. The sharp-sighted Englishman understood the dangers incurred by the Greek poet in his "paradise" and promised him a trip to England. Sir Sidney was also interested in his friend's ideas and began translating the *Spiritual Exercises*.

The National Theater, the schoolbooks, the translations promised —nothing came of all that. Only the Englishman kept his word.

Nikos was not indifferent to the fact that, in spite of everything, *The Odyssey* was enjoying a certain success. And from Aegina he wrote to his new friend Stamos Diamantaras on January 6, 1939:

. . . *I rejoice that there have been a few spirits who have felt a little joy in reading what I've tried to save of my own soul—by dint of great effort, by giving flesh to it in words. I desire no other reward. There can be no greater reward for a hermit.*

Far more people have bought The Odyssey than I'd anticipated, and so Pyrsos* should facilitate things for anyone who wants to pay for it in installments. . . . The aim of The Odyssey is to be read by the

* Pyrsos, the publisher of *The Odyssey*.

young people at all costs. *This work was not written for old men. It was written for the young people and those who have not yet been born.* . . .

While waiting to set off for London, Kazantzakis went back to Aegina to work.

Aegina, February 17, 1939

My beloved L.,

. . . *The gillyflowers are all in bloom, purple and yellow. I found some fifteen olive trees planted.* . . . *A splendid sun today; peace and calm. I am happy. The day is full of hours. I work and I work, and the sun does not set. Here, time is profoundly meaningful. It doesn't drift by distractedly and emptily, as it does in Athens. I'm stretched out on the couch in the atelier, gazing at the beauty of our house—good, simple, full of light. The sea glassy; the mountains serene and good-hearted; the earth covered with greenery. I owe everything to solitude. I would have done nothing, I would be nothing, were it not for solitude. "Soledad, soledad, soledad!" as Jiménez says.* . . .

I've been reading English all day. I'm making thousands of "escape" plans. Would that we could cast anchor on the English cliffs for several years. . . .

Tomorrow—Saturday—it's my birthday. I'll go down to get the cutlets you'll be sending me. God be with you. Don't forget me. . . .*

Aegina, February 20, 1939

. . . *Here, everything is calm and peaceful. I'm working on* . . . *Nicephoros Phocas for the theater and studying English.†* Waterlow sent me a letter for my birthday and wrote at the end, "Il faut absolument nous revoir bientôt [We simply must see each other again soon]."

I wish you could see him too and I wish the day would come soon when we can leave for London. This is the gate to salvation. . . .

Some Carnival masqueraders came around again, but I chased them away, saying I was in mourning. "Mourning for what?" they asked me anxiously. But I didn't tell them it was for Spain.

---

* Letter to E. Samios.
† N.K. knew English well, but spoke it poorly.

*God be with you, my beloved, precious Comrade! Without you, I
would be lost.**

Nikos set off alone for London. He stopped in Paris to see his dear
friend Segredakis and our Spanish friends, who were already in exile
there, among them the two children of Valle Inclán. Nikos was
entranced with Mariquina, who was very slender, very beautiful and
particularly endearing. In her company, he felt as though he were back
in his beloved Spain.

In due course, I too arrived in Paris, with the prospect of a new
piece of surgery in the offing. We found ourselves on the eve of the
Second World War.

One of our great delights in Paris was to revisit Manolis Segredakis,
a Cretan antique dealer, robust and very much of a peasant in the good
sense of the word, an optimist, who thirty years before had arrived in
France barefoot. And now he had just opened one of the finest art
galleries in the capital.

In Nikos' correspondence, we do not often come across the name
of Segredakis, unless to announce some new batch of exquisite postcards. But whenever we were in Paris, what delicious prattle!

Segredakis was extremely generous. When he came to the station to
see you off, a huge box of fruits was a must, enough to quench the thirst
of the entire compartment. And after the Liberation, if you asked him
for a comb or some paper or a pen, he sent you enough to open a
whole shop.

We thought he was rich. When the war was over, he sent clothing
from New York, enough to dress his entire village in Crete. But at about
the same time he jotted down in his notebook the five, or even two,
dollars he had had to borrow to pay for a coffee or a sandwich for
himself. Alas, he died suddenly, while visiting his birthplace, and we
wept bitterly.

How often in the past Nikos Kazantzakis had described to us his
amazement at suddenly penetrating from the dream to reality, at

---

* Letter to E. Samios.

"holding" like a pomegranate opened in his palm, as he used to say, Palestine, Egypt, Sinai, Jerusalem, Yerevan, Bukhara, Moscow.

And this time it was London, the England he was to meet under the best possible conditions—in its full grandeur, at the most critical moment of its existence: the moment when Hitler's hordes were hoping to invade it.

Kazantzakis smelled the sulphur of Inferno burning his nostrils. Yet at the same time he reveled in the English grass lawns—the most pleasant sensation left in him by the land of Britain. His gaze caressed lingeringly and forever such and such a painting he had loved and was now encountering for the first time at close range. Then he matured and lost himself in Asia, among the Arabic and Hindu and Persian miniatures at the British Museum.

He also visited several country gentlemen on their estates, wistfully reflecting what a tonic this space and isolation might be for spirits such as his.

To his friend Prevelakis he wrote:

Bedford Place, Russell Square, London W.C. 1
July 23, 1939
. . . Every day, I bring you to mind, telling myself that we should have been born here—rich, silent, isolated squires like the lords I've met, living in distant English country districts, inside comfortable old castles, with the portraits of their ancestors—austere, white-wigged, red-cheeked—hanging on the walls. When I die, some biographer of mine will write (the idiot!) that I was of an ascetic nature, having few desires, a human being who thrived on living in an abandoned, impoverished state. And no one will realize that if I wound up an "ascetic," it is only because I preferred nakedness to the cheap, humiliating livery of the bourgeoisie.

"Be strong and play the man!" These words pronounced by the Archbishop as he crowns the King of England here encircle my forehead like a crown. I knew them, but I was delighted to find them here, consecrated in a rite that is so solemn. . . .

Hitchingbrooke, Huntingdon
August 1, 1939
My beloved Lenotschka,
I'm writing you from the famous Sandwich castle, and when you come, I'll tell you all the details. Incredible wealth, libraries full of

Cézanne, Van Gogh, Derain, Corot, Modigliani, Picasso, etc. Gothic statues, Buddhas; in the gardens, stone lanterns brought back from Japan; and, best of all, hothouses with splendid vines laden with huge black and white grapes, peach trees and pear trees on trellises against the walls, fig trees, etc. . . . .

When I arrived, the Countess was at table—fat, about 60 years old, sweet, yellowish (she has heart trouble), kind and clever and very simple. He's slender, about 60 too, with one eye poché [puffed up]. He is refined, esthète and understands a great deal about painting. The two daughters charming. . . .

The house is full of servants in livery and tail coats, the walls laden with tableaux of the ancestors. The countryside serene and good. Sometimes it rains, sometimes the sun shines. Tomorrow, I'll be going back to London with the old Countess, in her car.

The room they've given me is huge, full of precious furniture. . . . The bed is 16th century, with an old bordure [ornamental border] embroidered with medieval musicians playing all sorts of instruments. The washbasin and ewer are antique faïences [enamelware] of the kind one sees in museums.

The park enormous. A forest surrounding it and a river with various canots [canoes]. Unlimited library . . .*

London, August 2, 1939

I'm back in London. This is the only place one should stay if one has to be away from Aegina. Peace, calm, green grass—nature—one can have in Greece too.

I read books incessantly, taking notes, preparing my own book on England. It might be translated into English and it must be good, and it's very difficult. What can one write that's new on such an usé [worn-out] theme?

Here, it rains every single day; monotonous, sad, gray weather. I'm impatient for the great fogs to come, so I can at least see something new. . . .†

Birmingham, August 14, 1939

My love, this is one of the ugliest of cities: smoke, provincial, laughterless people, poverty and vast wealth. Oxford yesterday—beauti-

---

* Letter to E. Samios.
† Letter to E. Samios.

ful, medieval, province. The weather marvelous, sun, heat. I'm worn out because I rush about all day long, to see and sate myself and leave. . . . Tomorrow morning on to Chester; day after tomorrow Liverpool, where I'm hoping to rest for two days at Vlastos' home. . . . I am not much benefited by all this; my heart has not even once felt resilient. But I had to see it all. In Scotland, I hope we'll find some joy. . . .*

> Chester, August 15, 1939

. . . Exquisite this small medieval town: a beautiful cathédrale, old houses, arcades and promenades along the ramparts. I arrived this morning and now before the sun sets I'm writing you a word. After abysmal Birmingham, I've felt happy here. The women are very ugly, prematurely aged by poverty. Laughter nowhere. The faces are tormented. . . . The trip will soon be over, sooner than I'd reckoned on. . . . I rush all day long, and the cities are being exhausted. . . .†

> Liverpool, August 16, 1939

. . . I'm at Vlastos' home, in a large park; and tomorrow I'll be leaving "as though someone were chasing me," as Vlastos puts it. A manor house; a clever, pleasant wife; two very pretty daughters. Liverpool is a big, antipathetic city; all coal and only in the Art Gallery one or two paintings—Cranach and the old German and Italian [painters]. I'm off for Manchester, then Sheffield, Petersborough, and by the 19th or 20th I'll be back in London. . . . I'm well, though terribly tired. . . .‡

> Sheffield, August 18, 1939

. . . I went to Manchester, wandered around all day long. At dusk, I left and came here—to Sheffield. Horrid cities, all smoke and coal and surly faces and uniform barracks. I move to and fro in this Inferno, unwilling to let anything escape me. I want to revel in all the ugliness— so that I can come to know it. Each city has its own Art Gallery and in it there are two or three beautiful creations of Man, and they make all the deeper impression on one, nichés [ensconced] as they are in the lap of ugliness. . . . Tomorrow, I'm leaving for Petersborough, where there's a beautiful cathédrale, and by then I'll be near London. . . .§

---

* Letter to E. Samios.
† Letter to E. Samios.
‡ Letter to E. Samios.
§ Letter to E. Samios.

London, August 23, 1939
. . . Come as quickly as you can, because I'm afraid we're about to have war. The sudden Russo-German pact increases the likelihood. Here, they consider it certain. And it's better that we be together at this terrifying moment, to see what decision we must make. . . .

*Be as thrifty as possible, for I foresee difficult hours ahead. . . .**

Birmingham, Manchester, Liverpool, Sheffield—Kazantzakis was discovering these grime-stained entrails of proud Albion. He watched them consuming and digesting mountains of coal gas. He scrutinized the faces—eyes, nostrils, coal-smudged mouths, lips no longer knowing how to smile. The quicker the machines pounded, the grittier the human watchworks grew—that marvel of delicacy and precision. Tense, as one feels several seconds before an earthquake, Kazantzakis swept his brush over England's circle of Inferno in broad strokes, like a painter in haste to pinpoint his vision on his canvas. In the wake of the Second World War, in Cambridge, he wanted to write a book on the intellectuals in postwar England. He tried but did not succeed—not because the men of letters he had met in this country were unworthy, but because he could no longer understand them—he, the great dissenter. The questionnaire he submitted to them rubbed them the wrong way. Very few of them went so far as to answer it. Most of them, one could sense, were annoyed or indifferent. And at that point in Cambridge, Kazantzakis brought to mind the nightmare of the industrial wheel, whose headway he had observed before the war. He recalled his uneasiness and depicts it this time, in the form of a letter to an imaginary mistress, in a book that by his own wish shall remain unpublished.†

My beloved, distant joy and companion,
I shall not tell you all that I have seen and felt as I wandered through the black cities of England. I was blind and I saw. I escaped things fleshless; I saw the flesh working and, tightly attached to the flesh, spirits which feel pain and hold in their hands the fate of the world

---

* Letter to E. Samios.
† Most of the passages of this letter can be found almost verbatim in N.K.'s travel book *England* (New York: Simon and Schuster, 1965), pp. 86–95, 108–14.

today. When I see these real human beings laboring in the factories and at the machines, working on ships and underneath the earth, and when I recall those intellectuals gathered at Lewis' home and my naïveté in speaking to them of my dismay, the blood rises to my head in shame.

I kept thinking about the forlorn scribe who, thousands of years ago, sat cross-legged and motionless where the roads met before Memphis, his wide-open eyes filled with angry, hopeless amazement as he stared at the massive, evil city. Wretched human beings would come along, aged fathers and mothers without enough to eat, women abandoned by their husbands; and he would go on writing the letters they wanted, from morning until evening, every day, telling about their miseries. The mighty would also pass in front of him, reclining in the arms of their slaves, weighted down with their own flesh, their expressions dim from drowsiness and too much food and kissing. The scribe rolled his eyes and saw and saw, from morning until evening. And he did not forget and his outcry is still preserved, carved upon the rocks: "I have seen! I have seen! I have seen!"

Would that our own Industrial Age could engender such a scribe, before we sink into the abyss! For there are voices surrounding us, lamenting, and they must not be lost.

We arrived in Birmingham on a Sunday. Everything closed tight—the faces laughterless, having the toil of the past week imprinted on them, as well as the horror of the week that would begin next day. The wheel, the torture wheel, the eternally rotating wheel.

Today the sun was shining and the glare made the streets two or three times as ugly as before. I walked hastily through them, then climbed up to the large Aston Park to get a breath of air. Marigolds, violets, flowers in every hue. I caught a smell of Greece. Of all the circular forms, the rose that blossoms in the heart of hell may well be the most pitiless and inhuman. Because it reminds the damned of how life might be and isn't.

Early the next morning, Monday, I took to the streets again.

Fortunately, that day the sun had vanished. A dense fog had descended, smearing the walls and concealing the ugliness. Once again the city had become transformed into an array of mythical symbols, a hyperborean scene. For a person born in the lands of the wanton sun, which lays all things bare without mercy, this veil-draped day exuded a discreet nobility and mystery.

Throngs of working men and women scurried along, each holding a little package in his hands—his lunch—and disappeared behind the soaring pitch-black doors. A bitter Frankish song of the twelfth century seemed to arise from inside the factories—a dirge that constricted the human heart.

> We will always be weaving silk cloth
> And we'll always be dressed in rags.
> We'll always be rotting in black poverty
> And we'll always be dying of hunger!

As I roamed from factory to factory, the feeling of cramp in my heart grew sharper and sharper. "Merrie England" has ceased to be merry; the wheel has gathered momentum and no one can stop it. The machines have triumphed. In his enthusiasm over his possession of his new iron slaves, modern man, kindled by irrational hopes and naïve optimism, has rushed headlong to conquer matter. In this way, he believes he will attain happiness and liberate the spirit. The eternal battle to replace the inhuman laws of the physical world by the laws of the heart is the emblem of man's nobility. Man has fashioned ideals that are entirely human, for they were created in man's own image and likeness: justice, equality, happiness for all men. These do not exist anywhere except in man's desire. The jungle that has become man's heaven and earth is ruled by different laws diametrically opposed to these: injustice, inequality, happiness for the few—and even this happiness flits away and vanishes like a flash of lightning.

And still man battles against the laws of the physical world, refusing to accept them. He regards the world as inferior to his own heart, and he longs to make his own better world. The prudent and the prosperous resist. "We're well fixed," they shout. "The world is fine. Don't destroy it." But when did the flame that burns in the vitals of man ever become degraded to the point of heeding such people as these? This flame has never consorted with the well-off. A wayfarer traveling among human beings and in a hurry. Hungry, thirsty, he has seen mirages of cool oases in the desert—justice, equality, happiness— and he has hurried on. He was impatient to arrive. The horses pulling him in the past had seemed to him to be dragging along at an intolerably slow rate; and he was in a hurry. So he made new steel horses that crossed the continent, the sea, the air, swiftly. And the spirit mounted so that it might pursue its chimera. But as sometimes happens in our nightmares, the horses suddenly mounted the riders and took a diametrically opposite path and they are rushing and we are rushing with them.

I walked through Birmingham and the next day through Liverpool, looking at machines and factories, at the thin, atrophied shinbones on the children, at their sad smiles, at the rags hanging from the dark, dank windows of the working class. I was struggling to give nobility and meaning to the ugliness, to find hope for the hopeless, to locate the present horror—so far as I could—within the complete circle, and in that way to transmute it into joy. Since we can't change the world, let's change the eye that sees the world!

"A dangerous marsh inhabited only by wild pigs, bulls and wolves" —this is the way an old chronicler describes the stretch of land where the enormous, monstrous city of Manchester sprawls. So it was then, and so it is today. Here we see the face of our industrial civilization: fierce, bereft of human sweetness and tenderness, merciless and bitter. As I gazed upon the anthills of human beings hurrying up and down the unsmiling streets, I felt overcome with anguish. Could I, I asked myself, be having some hideous dream? Or could it be that humanity was being destroyed in some collective nightmare? Where were they going? Why were they rushing? Why had people's lives ended in this dehumanization?

This tragic moment of destruction or salvation resounds with nerve-racking noise and outcries and conveys secret hopes as well as nameless terror. You feel an overwhelming intoxication of a weird kind. The most insignificant event, the most fleeting human form produces in you a disproportionately intense excitement and emotion, as though in reality we were all one and our end had arrived and we were rushing pell-mell with a great sob in our throats and with shouts of "Farewell! Farewell!" Nowhere is this atmosphere so heavily charged with messages as in the great industrial cities. Whatever happens, however trivial it might seem to be, has an appreciable weight and takes its place with a thud, for all time, on the scale of destiny.

On thousands of occasions, in a multitude of cities, I had seen the faces of young girls glued to the shopwindows, their eyes yearning. But that day in Sheffield the same event made me feel indescribably bitter and certain that we have reached the end. One poverty-stricken young girl, wasted away from hunger, had pressed her little face against the well-stocked window of a butcher shop. Desire shone in her eyes as she stared greedily at the meat. Through some mystic transubstantiation, all this horrid meat might become yellow hair, fluffy curls on the nape of the neck, red lips. But where could this half-starved little girl find the money to undertake the divine transubstantiation? And so the little girl withered and the meat rotted, and the union never took place.

Only one unexpected delight lay in store for me the other day in Manchester. I had gone into the museum. . . . I stopped suddenly. Something you would never have expected to find in the steel heart of Manchester: a superb old Chinese statue made of wood, the Chinese goddess of mercy, Kuan Yin. She was sitting, a charming figure with folded legs, on a lion whose reins were being drawn by a slave. She smiled calmly, all sweetness and compassion. Serene and graceful, she was hiding in the smoky entrails of Manchester, waiting astride her tame lion for her turn to come. . . .

And all at once all the agony I had experienced in Manchester found relief, as though this little goddess were our own soul and it was now riding her tame lion.

One day Giorghos Zorba—the actual Zorba, not the one in the novel—told his "boss" his version of how the First World War broke out:

"A few giddy young gadabouts had read a few patriotic books and turned patriots. Then they read socialist books and turned socialist. Then they read anarchist books and became anarchists and decided to kill. But whom? This they didn't know yet.

"One of these underage boys (Princip was his name) went to Sarajevo. . . . Well, he went to Sarajevo and sat down in a café. The waiter rushed up. 'What do you want, sir?'

" 'I'd like to ask your advice. Whom do you think I should kill? I say the Governor—or the Bishop—I don't know. Tell me.'

" 'Well, my boy, wouldn't you do better to kill the Crown Prince? He'll be coming this morning.'

" 'All right then, the Crown Prince!'

"He took up his post. The carriage passed. Princip threw a bomb at it. The bomb went off all right, but it killed two other people. Princip asked a professor nearby: 'Was that the Crown Prince?'

" 'No,' a deacon answered. 'It was somebody else!'

"Then the Crown Prince went to the Cathedral to make a doxology

375

for having been saved. He made the doxology, came out of the church, said he was going home because he was hungry—it was noontime, you see. There were two roads.

"'Right or left?' the chauffeur asked.

"'Right,' the Crown Prince answered.

"The chauffeur failed to hear him. 'To the right?' he asked again, stopping the car. He stopped and some demon brought him face to face with Princip. So Princip brought out his revolver. Bang-bang! Down went the Crown Princess Sophia. 'Sophia,' cried the Crown Prince, 'you must live for our children's sake!' Bang-bang! Off went another bullet, and the Crown Prince fell. They were picked up and carted off to the cemetery. The father of the Crown Prince heard of it—his father or his uncle, I can't remember which—and got angry and drew his sword. Then another relative of the deceased drew his sword too. Everyone began drawing swords. And that's how the European War, as you call it, came about, damn it all!'"*

Damnation indeed! For the second time now, war was assaulting us, just at the moment Nikos was walking on the lawns or through the industrial infernos of England—but alone, without Zorba to spice the sauce.

As a guest of the British Council, he was offered the opportunity of approaching a few rare specimens of the British aristocracy, as well as many personalities in the field of literature and in the arts and sciences. It was a most propitious moment for this man who hated stagnation, for he could watch Robin Hood (long dulled by too much comfort) rouse himself and set off now, to defend his own liberty this time (rather than other people's liberty)!

The English no longer have any appetite to make any offensive or attack [wrote Nikos Kazantzakis in his England]. For what purpose? What do they lack? . . . The English have arrived. Their old offensive slogan—"Action over all!"—has now become the slogan of indigent nations ready for the offensive. . . .

Now the danger has emerged. The English people have seen it. They are biting their lips, clenching their fists. They sense that the

_____
* From N.K.'s *England*, pp. 200–1.

376

moment has come for them to play their fate all the way, heads or tails. "Wake up, John Bull!". . .

They are slightly behind time, but this is their rhythm. . . . I learned one of their extraordinarily characteristic proverbs: "Don't cross the bridge before you get there!"*

"What will England do?" [Nikos Kazantzakis asked this question of a professor sitting next to him at a party given by a Lord on the terraces of Parliament in London.]

"She'll follow her own interests."

"And at the present moment, what are her interests?"

"War!" he whispered with a solemn air.

We both fell silent. This terrifying, bloodstained word seemed to have fallen between us like a corpse.

"Are you afraid?" my friend asked me, watching my eyes darken.

"The human mind is not easily frightened," I rejoined. "It knows and looks Necessity straight in the eye and is not afraid of it. But my heart felt afraid."

"I was afraid too," my friend admitted, "because I know what war means. . . . But it is necessary." . . .

"Surely, it must sometimes happen that the individual morality of the English does not coincide with the official morality of England" [comments Nikos Kazantzakis slightly further on]. "What happens then?"

"At that point, the Englishman plays a slightly woebegone role," the professor rejoined. "Or else he is inconceivably unhappy, trying desperately to persuade the others (and, above all, himself) that his nation's policy is moral; that it is dictated by the loftier interests of humanity; and that it is in harmony with the Ten Commandments. . . . Many Englishmen, the most sensitive or the most violent of them, are aroused and raise a hue and cry, denouncing the immorality. . . . Our government suffers too, and it too is composed of Englishmen— namely, Puritans. It too is afraid of the voice inside it. It too is afraid of public opinion. And so, in all sincerity it calls upon morality. And that is why we are called hypocrites. But even if we were still more immoral, we still would not be hypocrites! Do you get my meaning?"

"I understand very well" [answered Kazantzakis], "and I like this psychoanalysis. But in this present war, now—if the war does happen?"

"Now, if I may say so, the English will be happy. Not happy—

---

* Passage quoted from pages 205–6 of same 1965 edition of England.

*because they don't want war at all. They will just feel deeply calm. Calm because in this present struggle they feel that they are in the right; that they are defending England's interests and, at the same time, the interests of the whole world."** *

In his *England*, Nikos Kazantzakis does not conceal his respect for the civic character of the English people. He was impressed by the spectacle of the rich people graciously offering their own homes to shelter bevies of evacuated working-class children and their readiness to take care of the children.

As soon as I reached London, Nikos wanted to introduce "Akritas" to me along with his companions in arms, the wise men and musicians goodheartedly accompanying him on his legendary exploits.

Sitting alongside one of those "penny-hungry" English stoves, Nikos spread out on my knees several dozen Persian and Arabic and Hindu miniatures. And he pointed out the ones he had chosen to give flesh to the heroes still crystallizing inside his mind.

Akritas, Akritas, Akritas—is it not abominable that people like Nikos Kazantzakis use themselves up and die, so full of seeds still ungerminated. If Nikos had only had a few more years to live, we would have seen *Akritas* growing too, forging a fine place for itself in our lives, nourishing itself drop by drop on its creator's blood. We would have watched at close range Nikos' dream of "changing"—of giving his creatures wings like El Greco, of disburdening his words, of liberating himself even from the weight of reason—and of becoming a "dance without a dancer"—we would have seen how all this became crystallized. But Akritas remained a dream, and Nikos is now no more than the shadow of a dream upon this earth.

Long after this introduction to Akritas' companions and Akritas himself, Nikos mentioned to me the sirens that had alerted London just the evening before, telling me of his apprehension for the future of the white race. Early the next morning, hand in hand, we found ourselves already confronting the heavy doors of the British Museum:

"You see?" he said to me. "This whole immense wing of the 'British' belongs to Tantine. Her niece, Lady Sandwich, has invited us for several weeks to Halls Croft in Stratford. That's the house of Susan, Shake-

---

* See pages 215–18 of same edition of *England*.

speare's daughter; it belongs to Tantine too. She asked me how many valets we would need!"

I too knew the British Museum well and wanted to show Nikos the famous Etruscan couple, comfortably seated on their tomb, staring out at the world. "When we get rich, we'll have a copy made!" exclaimed Nikos ecstatically. "I love seeing us seated like this by each other's side, Hymettos facing us, the Saronic Gulf at our feet, wandering for ever and ever."

Hitler did not leave us time to visit Scotland, where we had been invited to stay by a Scotch scholar. The implacable London blackout complicated our lives to the utmost. In Russell Square, there was no external mark to differentiate our own house from all the other houses. And Nikos had the experience of going into the neighbor's house, climbing the staircases, arriving in front of "his" door, before realizing that he'd set foot on forbidden territory. To move about in this tar-thick darkness became a challenge.

"Let's take the bus," suggested Nikos one night. "It passes right in front of our door."

"Are you sure it's the right one?"

"Absolutely sure. I take it every day." And to the conductor: "Toutanghamon Court, please!"

"Sorry, sir! Never 'eard of it!"

Only after the third mishap, Nikos burst out laughing. The passersby stopped short; and others who were in more of a hurry turned around to see what insolent person dared laugh on a night like this.

"It's Tottenham Court, my love, where we have to go! Forgive me. That reminds me—" And new roars of laughter rebounded, intermingled with reminiscences from Madrid:

You remember the howdy-do I had in Madrid to meet that person who was supposed to introduce me to the cinema people? Well . . . I'd set off in the night, found the house without any trouble and rung on the right door. An old lady, half-deaf, opened up: "Mister Goudonov, please." "Ousted's mistaken. There's no Mister Goudonov here!" "Ousted, I assure you I'm not mistaken. Mr. Goudonov's expecting me." "I repeat, ousted, there's no Mr. Goudonov here at all!" And she slammed the door in my face. Furious, I rushed down the stairs to look for the night watchman. The serano listened to my story. "No gentleman by that name in this district. You must be mistaken, ousted!"

The blood had risen to my head. I'd spent a month trying to find him; and now I was about to lose him, and so imbecilically! "If you don't believe me," I said to the serano, "just read this letter then!" And I thrust the envelope with my friend's address right under his nose. "Well, is there or is there not a Boris Goudonov in your district?" "Boris B-u-r-e-b-a!" The night watchman spelled the name slowly: "Boris B-u-r-e-b-a. . . ."

I had often dreamed of living a few days out of a fairy tale. But I had never thought Tantine would offer them to us against the current of the times, in the very days when the last myths were being killed.

Halls Croft was more than an old Shakespearean home—an entire museum lay at our disposal; we could roam freely and eat our meals in front of fireplaces where trunks of trees hundreds of years old burned slowly, over a period of several days.

Nikos went without lunch, so as to be able to write one more tragedy, *Julian the Apostate.* But he loved to walk along the banks of the Avon with its white swans and its rose arbors and through the medieval lanes, where quaint characters chattered on their doorsteps. The English countryside with its beautiful black-and-white Holstein cows enchanted him. We also wended our way into the vast domains of those country gentlemen who do not barricade themselves behind high walls. One of these strolls gave us occasion to admire the civic spirit of the English—as long as they're in England.

For the evacuated children, the landowners used to set boxes of apples on their doorsteps. Some had even thought of leaving baskets there to help the children carry the fruits more easily. A sign was left on top of the pile of apples: "These fruits are intended for the evacuated children!" In front of us, two little boys aged five and seven had stuffed their pockets with red apples and were just about to set off. Then with a very serious air, the elder began spelling out the words: 'T-h-e-s-e a-p-p-l-e-s a-r-e i-n-t-e-n-d-e-d—"

"We don't have a right to these apples then," he told the younger boy. "Come on then, John; let's empty out our pockets."

Stratford-on-Avon, September 1939
. . . More fortunate and more penniless hordes than ourselves do not exist. At just such a critical moment as this, we've found ourselves

again in the center of the whirlwind and in the midst of a marvelous, self-possessed, sure people. . . .

Eleni must have written you about the house we're living in, full of precious things, statues, paintings, faïences, historic beds and the most important thing of all: fireplaces. At this particular moment, Eleni (wearing some marvelous slippers and a ribbon in her freshly washed hair) is sitting in an armchair-of-foreign-forefathers, knitting a new sweater with thick English wool (mulberry-colored). The huge fireplace is lit; a tree trunk is burning and the flames are dancing on the walls, over the precious tables and on my pitch-black (not from the smoke, but from the sun of Aegina) brow. And I am writing—what else could I write here, beneath the shadow of my fellow writer, Shakespeare?—a tragedy. And so I'm writing a tragedy in verse even if the whole world is on fire. I watch myself bent over the paper, far off on some other star, arranging words rhythmically, struggling to invest them with my breath before it is extinguished.

From time to time as she reads The Times (her great love!), Eleni raises her head and says to me, "Hitler . . . Stalin . . . Halifax . . ." "Who? . . . Who?" I exclaim in amazement. And then she realizes I'm "inhuman," and she doesn't answer. Or else she says with tight-sealed lips "Nothing! Nothing!" and plunges back into The Times.

Such is our life—a strange, incredible miracle. Aegina, of course, remains sparkling in the middle of the sea. She is the immovable focal point of the universe. When will I see her again? Open the windows, feel the sea turning my thoughts blue? God knows—sooner or later; all is well. I no longer know what to wish for. Everything in this world seems to me marvelous. "But isn't there anything ugly?" I say to myself, nonplussed. "Nothing? Nothing? Thank you, my God, for having made my heart so inhuman."

One of the best "things" in this world, beyond a doubt, are you and Ketty. Often as we walk along the banks of the Avon, with its white-white swans, we say to ourselves, "If only Marika and Ketty were here!" And we both sigh. . . .*

The green-velvet countryside, the scarlet apples, the white or black swans, the delicate scent of the roses, Shakespeare and the treasures accumulated in the home of his daughter Susan—all these many

---

* Letter to Marika Papaioannou, now Madame Hourmouzios.

beauties were pierced by the corroding acid of war. We too had been mobilized; only we were more helpless than ever, without any resources, strangers among strangers. How could we take our share in the responsibilities? How could we enlist in some useful task?

With Nikos' permission, I wrote to Tantine in New York. If we could manage to support ourselves in London for two or three months, we could find the solution to the problem.

Tantine did not answer. Halls Croft was requisitioned by the army. We packed our bags.

Nikos refused to dally in Paris. Once again he teetered between action—descending into the brawl, as his brain longed to do—and plunging into the future of his verses. And once again I saw the Beast of the Apocalypse appear. We had hardly finished *The Odyssey*—for fourteen years, the best years of our youth, it had devoured us—when Nikos conjured up another, *Akritas*, vowing to devote the rest of his existence to it.

Already, long before war was declared, Nikos had written to his young friend at the bookshop, Stamos Diamantaras:

Bedford Place, Russell Square, London
June 1939

. . . Once again the heart is beginning to overflow; the chest is swelling; and like an awesome embryo, Akritas is knitting itself in my vitals. I must go away. I no longer have time to lose. It's questionable whether I shall be in time. My aim is neither glory and recognition, nor confort, nor pleasant chitchat—but to transform as much earth as I am able into a cry. . . .

July 17, 1939

Over a month ago I began this letter. I am continuing it now, elated at talking with you. Travel is good; but it should pass like a vision, like love pressed for time, like a great gulp of wine. I'm in haste to sink back into solitude, the sober source of work. I have seen superb things, met human beings, seen new stones, collected new plunder—a travel book will emerge—and then several verses in the Akritas. Nothing else. I am not made for Europe; it's too poor and the plunder too meager. It's the Orient I long for, a stroll along the Tigris and the Euphrates, an ascent into Tibet, an expedition to Central Africa. There lie the great riches; there are the thousands of verses waiting, clustered like bunches of bananas. I must—I must go. . . .

Once again, I resume this letter, but this time I shall finish it! I'm ashamed of not having written to you and Mr. Ganiaris for so long, my two great friends and allies. But I'm submerged in excursions, books, museums, people, and I don't have time. Several friends are trying to find a way for me to stay. But deep down, I feel I must not; it's not to my soul's advantage. I would stay if it weren't for Aegina, namely, my fortressed, sea-girt Solitude. . . .

On reaching Paris, I knelt down to kiss the ground.

God created London, old maid of Britain, I thought, just to make us better appreciate this adorable coquette, who smiles even in the deluge.

Here, too, the curfew law was in effect, but on a human scale. The police didn't rush on top of you to snuff out your lighter before you had time to light a Gauloise. The Parisians, in spite of the incredible lies blared at them by the newspapers and the radio, were aware of the danger. And yet their capital still preserved the graces of a stylish salon.

How often in the course of what followed we set ourselves the dilemma: Should Paris be declared an open city? Or should it be sacrificed along with Rome and Athens—ten, twenty, a thousand Stalingrads—in order to achieve victory one day?

The heart refuses the demands of a "just" mind. A Europe in ashes, and in the smoking ruins everything that is most beautiful in man's creation—in a gray plain, bereft of birds, bereft of grass, bereft of sky or clouds, human wrecks hideous in their downfall.

Infuriated anew, I decided to cast anchor in Paris. The only effect was to have the proposition thrown at me of going to Germany—to spy on the Nazis!

It would take too long to enumerate my maneuvers and failures. And I have often wondered: If God, the "nonexistent," had granted my prayer to him, would I still be alive? And Nikos—would he have been able to survive the famine? In Aegina itself, out of 10,000 inhabitants, 2,500 died of malnutrition! What would have become of this man if he had been left absolutely alone—this man who forgot all about his body or shunned taking care of it?

1940.   Nikos Kazantzakis was now fifty-seven years old, though no one would have thought him more than forty. Straight as the lighthouse on his Aegina promontory, his eyes full of light, his hair increasingly fine and silky, his body and mind agile, ready for all feats of daring.

By virtue of his intelligence a pessimist ("We come from a black abyss; we end in a black abyss"), disgusted by the politics of the great powers ("We have entered a Middle Ages that will last two hundred years"), a tragic optimist and hence no pessimist ("We know the future does not depend on us, and yet let's act as though it did"), and, last of all, promoter of "man, the creator of God."

> *Hail Man, small biped cock!*
> *Unless you crow, the day shan't rise!*

he cried, certain that the day exists because the human consciousness exists.

Ever since 1938, the *Obra* had been finished. Having reduced it from 42,000 verses to 33,333, Nikos Kazantzakis relished it, pleased by the almost miraculous elasticity of this millipede army: 33,333.

If he had allotted fourteen years to model his Odysseus, the "future man," Odysseus in his turn had allotted fourteen years to model the future Kazantzakis. And when the umbilical cord was snapped, there were two men—mature, serene, walking hand in hand along the rim of the abyss. The osmosis of life and death took place gently, "admirably," open-eyed.

His worktable was laquered in black with strips of carmine and looked like a bookseller's stall. Among the books, notebooks, postcards, envelopes already addressed to friends who were expecting their letters; among the Baedekers and countless schoolboy's notebooks (he had a craving for them) and the finished or unfinished manuscripts, there was a chiseled platter from Skyros and a handsome red-and-gold wooden bowl from Nizhni Novgorod, the former filled with pencils of all colors and all sizes, the latter filled with raisins, walnuts and almonds. Nikos, who disliked meat, had enjoyed nibbling on fruits ever since his childhood. In one of the hiding places of his desk one could sometimes find oil and cinnamon biscuits or figs pressed between laurel leaves.

There were also tin boxes containing treasures such as a ball of labdanum, which he used to knead with his fingers, making the whole room fragrant with it; a clod of Cretan earth; a miniature flea market in several square centimeters: scissors, pincers, razor blades, innumerable tiny bottles empty or filled with exotic essences, erasers, buttons, old eyeglasses . . . One of these boxes (filled with cinnamon bark, cloves and nutmeg) still scents my cupboard.

In a niche facing him and to his right, a *kakemono* six hundred years old, a Japanese Buddha and a fine seventeenth-century print of a fierce rider in the moonlight. To his left, encircling the Byzantine crucifix, ikons of less value—since Nikos used to offer our best ones to the visitors whom, for one reason or another, he had come to like.

Behind him, tacked to his bookshelf, two reproductions: one a Saint Francis by Giotto and the other a representation of Dante. Above them, two Madonnas—one from Mt. Sinai, the other from Mt. Athos—the one copied by Kalmouko and the other by Kondoglou.* And Elsa of the full lips and the prominent brow, over the little staircase that led to this ivory tower. . . .

Akritas, My Father, fictionalized lives to appear in serialized form, new cantos, two books for young people—all this could not appease the devouring energy of this woodcutter from the Bronze Age. Ever since Stratford, Shakespeare had become the "tiger riding him."

"I would love to translate a tragedy of Shakespeare's into demotic Greek. But which one? Before deciding, we must read everything that has already become translated. Our library is poor. Let's enlist our friends to make contributions! . . ."

And Nikos wrote to Stamos Diamantaras, "You would do me a great favor by sending me Rotas' *Hamlet* and *Lear* and Karthaios' *Romeo and Juliet*." And a bit further on he wrote: "I am well, working hard, casting my glance over the map of the world, looking to see in what direction I should embark. India attracts me very much, but will I ever be able to get there? *Hazain pirouit!*"

Hazain pirouit! Stamos Diamantaras, born in Russia, had told Nikos about the baker from his childhood days—who used to work for long months on end, without ever raising his head. Then, suddenly, the demon would grab him by the neck and he would hurl off his white blouse and long-handled shovel, let his fire go out and set off to celebrate, hanging a sign on his door: HAZAIN PIROUIT! (The master's out on a fling!)

I forget the bakery I've opened and the breads I knead and I write in

---

* Fotis Kondoglou, an excellent hagiographer and writer on Byzantine art.

big red letters on my door, *HAZAIN PIROUIT*, and I do as my mood bids me. I laugh, utter coarse words, spin truths with lies, resurrect the beloved dead, men and women both. I set the violins and fifes to playing away inside me. And so I too can burst out a little; so my lips too will be in time to laugh; so my mind too can turn its back a moment on the abyss and gaze upon the green world overhead, with its fine embroideries—its people and its trees and insects and its empires—and for an instant roll about like a tiny donkey in the springtime in the green grass. And then, all eased, I'll open up the bakery again; I'll light the great fires and once again turn my face toward the abyss.

Nikos Kazantzakis was not afraid of repeating himself. The old man a hundred years old, bent over the stream, thinking he sees his own life flowing there "fresh as a glass of water," and cursing any man who thinks he's quenched his thirst; the shepherd from Crete who ran down the mountain to learn "how Norway's faring," and who goes his way elated because Norway had said "No" (a "masculine word")—"*Hazain Pirouit*." The baker from the Caucasus became identified with his own father and recurred in his conversations and his writings. Eight years later, Kazantzakis had the idea of using him as the Preface for his series of great future novels.

To have a fling—why not? Between two labors—the one completed, the other in the process of construction—why not take a holiday?

And he did take one, in his own way. Not in the way of the intellectuals—he scorned them too much to imitate them—not by letting his imagination gallop unbridled. (Did he not claim to lack imagination?) Instead, he resuscitated the world of his own childhood and youth, not with his brain, but with his "vitals." Every time the brain predominated, Kazantzakis tore up what he wrote. He accepted only what sprang directly out of his own "vitals"—or, as the rest of us would say, out of his "blood"—in the manner of the old godfathers of humanity: Homer, Tolstoy, Rabbi Nachmann.

Foremost among the rare Greek writers who loved Kazantzakis' work was I. M. Panayiotopoulos, an acolyte of the *demotiki*, a great traveler, a professor and director of a high school, who also found time to draw up impartial literary columns; small in build, with black eyes and hair and a contagious laugh, hospitable in every possible situation. He loved his elder and was not afraid to give voice to his love. Kazantzakis

treated him in the same way and was moved to see him at the head of
the bodyguards of his Odyssey.

Aegina, March 3, 1940

*. . . Thank you for your good letter, and please understand my
delay in thanking you. I'm drowning in ink!*

*I also got the two pieces of criticism by Panayiotopoulos and was
glad he has understood many things. I was especially impressed by how
correctly he commented on the number 33,333. By now, The Odyssey
lives its own independent life. The umbilical cord has been cut; it is a
free organism now and neither needs me nor is needed by me. Let it
wrestle alone with the fearsome Kronos, eater-of-his-own-children; and if
it is able, let it be saved. I no longer interfere. . . .**

England had just been completed. *My Father* was still tantalizing.
It was all there—unsuspected, accumulated riches. But the "click" did
not take place. Perhaps the French language was to blame. Kazantzakis,
who had decided to write this book in French, knew this language well
enough to write in it on any subject at all, except on Crete. For Crete,
he needed the ancestral tool—that broad-breathing language with the
guttural sounds in the cradling rhythm of the African waves; the
language of this strange people who felt constrained in the tongue of
their own race, impelled by the need to expand it and add resonant
vowels to certain words or change their gender to make them more
"virile."

Nikos had a burning desire to go back to Crete "to refresh" his
memory, as he put it—as though he had to seek an excuse. "Not so far
as the people are concerned—them I recall down to the last detail—but
to see the places again. I must ransack the earth of my ancestors."

As I couldn't come along with him, with a heavy knapsack on my
back, Marika Papaioannou took my place—and they were joined by Tea
Anemoyanni. In his notebooks, Nikos added to the list of happy trips
this 1940 trip to Crete.

Canea, April 9, 1940

My beloved Lenotschka!

. . . Canea in an uproar at the news of the Germans' occupying

---

* Letter to Stamos Diamantaras.

Denmark. Everyone is saying, "Serves them right, since they [the Danes, the Swedes and the Norwegians] acted cowardly and didn't help Finland." Here, one is delighted by the Cretan bon sens [good sense]. I'm worried about your leaving* at such a critical moment, for I believe a new period of the War is beginning, and from now on it will be intense and dangerous. . . .

Canea is charming—narrow lanes, Turkish shops, date trees, seashore, rocks, intelligent people, mosques, oranges, anxiety and interest in international problems, extremely acute bon sens; provincial humdrum, fat ladies, amanédes and the smell of fried oil in the restaurants intolerable. . . .†

And to Marika Papaioannou on April 14, 1940, from Kandanos Selinou:

. . . The rains have imprisoned me here at Kandanos, just as I was getting ready to go up to Omalos and from there to Sphakia. A terrible downpour all night long, and this morning it's raining torrentially. I'm lying on a primitive bed in a wretched inn, listening to the wind blowing and welcoming the rain through the cracks of the dangling window. A great deal of patience is needed, because only the sky knows when the sun will come out again and the roads will open.

I arrived here yesterday from Panayià Hryssoskalítissa at the southwest tip of Crete. I spent some marvelous hours there with the old abbot Grigorios and his four nuns (the one very beautiful, young, sad chants with pathos the "Kyrie ton Dynameon").

A long march with a heavy rucksack on my shoulder, alone, and I lost my way and the shepherds came down from the mountains out of breath and asked me in alarm, "What's become of Norway?" And now the rains have immobilized me, and I no longer know when I'll be able to leave. . . . I should be in Amari, where I'll stay for several days in hopes that you'll come and that we'll set off from here for Phaistos to spend Easter in my friend's house.

Yesterday—Saturday, Eleni must have gone.‡ Please write me about the state she left in. Crete stirs me deeply—the stones, the grass, the

---

* I was leaving once again for France.
† Letter to E. Samios.
‡ I was on my way to Paris and Salis de Béarn.

people. But since I am alone, all these things oppress my heart and I often feel unendurable bitterness. It seems that laughter is the only safety valve for me, and unless I laugh I grow wild and feel like dying.

I'm impatient to finish with Crete and come back to Aegina. I don't yet know what I shall write about Crete or how. This too is a great agony and increases the sadness the rain has given me today.

I have with me only Dante and Shakespeare's Sonnets. All day long today, I shall read these to exorcise the storm. But my heart is unconsolable, unwilling to satiate itself on the "shadow of flesh." . . .

And a few days later, once again to Marika, from the Toplou Monastery in Crete:

. . . I shall never forget the nine days we spent together. Everything was superb, joyful, sweet, strong. Before you came, my trek had been harsh, inhuman, devoid of any sweetness. When we parted at Lasithi, I was very moved; but I controlled myself and tried to laugh and drive away the futile "superabundance of the heart."

I'd like to ask you to write me a word . . . to tell me about your return to Kasteli with Tea and if everything went smoothly. Because that same evening, I had many disagreeable adventures, though they ended well. I shall stay in the village of my ancestors at Varvari three days, and then I'll resume my march, and about the middle of May I hope to see you in Athens.

Toplou is a renowned monastery at the tip of eastern Crete in the midst of fierce mountains. It has splendid ikons. I am sorry that you won't see them, perhaps ever. But life is so unexpectedly good that, who knows, perhaps we shall once again walk across these Cretan planks together.

Write me whether you've gotten a letter from Eleni. . . . I'm in great agony that I may not see her again. The political sky is heavy and who knows if Eleni will be able to come back. All Crete grows dim when I think of this frail, beloved body. . . .

Before the Second World War, the good Greek writers earned nothing, or next to nothing, from their writing. Isolated on Aegina, Kazantzakis used to give his books to the publishers rather than sell them. And when he did sell them, he was embarrassed at having to claim his rightful due.

Aegina, October 2, 1940

My dear Stamos,

. . . Yesterday, I finished my novel on Crete, about 500 pages, but written in French. This is where I've ended up: I, the fanatic lover of our language, am forced to write in a foreign tongue. In Greece, I have not a single publisher, and elsewhere I have three. . . .

This morning I wrote a little poem in terza rima for Dragoumis. I'm thinking of beginning, tomorrow morning, a Chinese tragedy I have in mind.* If I remain idle a single moment, I feel suffocated and as though I'm going to die. . . .†

Aegina, October 7, 1940

. . . As for Japan, Th. himself told me that as soon as Pyrsos‡ has covered its own expenses, it will be sure to give me the rest. But if he's forgotten this, please don't remind him. . . .§

Are we to explain this tendency to let himself be duped as a latent wish for sainthood and martyrdom? I hardly think so. In order to safeguard one's own rights among human beings, one must learn to fight— that is, to lose one's time and soul. "Time is soul," he loved to say. So it was worth more to lose all the rest, so long as one saved time and soul.

Still possessed of the somber humor of his father and the firm piety of his mother—"my right hand clamors for war," he used to say, "while in my left palm I feel the warm breast of a sparrow flying over my head"—how could this man find a balance enabling him to breathe in the rhythm of his own verses—to harmonize them with the serene cycle of the stars; the capricious rhythm of the sea, the breezes and the north winds, the solar fires and the shadows; the aquamarine, bluish alternation of the dawns and twilights, beginnings and ends without end or beginning?

---

* *Yang-Tse*, a tragedy later published with the title *Buddha*.
† Letter to Stamos Diamantaras.
‡ Pyrsos, the publishing house.
§ Letter to Stamos Diamantaras.

As I evoke Aegina and our promontory, I myself am amazed by the quiet peace that reigned there, high tide or low tide. A man who was simple in his extreme complexity, who worked by day and slept as soon as he lay his head upon the pillow, pouncing upon his manuscript the moment after opening his round, mischievous little eyes.

Sleep avoided me. As a soporific, each evening my Scheherazade used to invent some new tale, drawn always from his own childhood, with Crete as his background, the way he loved to bring it to life. "The Neighbors" whose adventures abounded every evening was my favorite:

". . . As you came out of our house and went off to the right, in the first house—the house with the banana tree and the green window blinds—there lived a little hunchback, Kyrios. . . ."

On tiptoe like two thieves, we used to break into the houses of the famous neighbors, one by one, surprising them at their prayers, kneeling before the ikon of the Madonna, or thrashing their only daughter or counting their pennies or busily writing to the Tsar or the Queen of England, addressing pathetic pleas to them to come flying to the rescue of Christian Crete!

Droll stories, tragic stories, tragicomic stories, caught in the act, e-x-t-r-a-o-r-d-i-n-a-r-y stories.

"Well, Lenotschka, as we were saying?"

"We were saying that the staircase was creaking . . . and the poor girl's father had leaped out of bed. . . ."

"And, lunging down the worm-eaten staircase four steps at a time, he caught hold of his daughter by her heavy braids. . . ," Nikos resumed, and the story continued for a long moment.

When I began rambling, Nikos lowered his voice and went on stroking my outstretched palm, stopping only when the even rhythm of my breathing indicated that I had sunk into a sound sleep.

Autumn came. Mussolini attacked Greece. No weapons, no ammunition, no military administration. Our infantry fighting in the mountains of northern Epirus had frozen legs and feet. Instead of the doctors' trying to heal them, panic broke loose and the limbs were amputated.* Our entire air force consisted of sixteen new fighter planes and twenty-six bombers! In his memoirs, General Papagos decries this lamentable state of our army. Most of our airplanes were an antiquated

---

* My elder sister, a volunteer nurse, literally lost her mind from witnessing the spectacle of dozens of our soldiers having both legs amputated.

model flying no more than 100 miles per hour! And the weapons and ammunition supplied by our allies were of such poor quality that they exploded in the hands of the soldiers trying to use them. In spite of all these drawbacks and the flagrant Germanophilia in our Dictator's headquarters, the Greek army succeeded in carrying the front 60 kilometers beyond the Albanian border—from Pogradetz to Himera. Why then did Headquarters prevent our army from taking the port of Valona? No one will ever know. . . .

There were no longer any boats shuttling back and forth between Piraeus and Aegina. We had to cram ourselves into bad vessels with worn-out, vile-smelling motors that broke down, especially when the sea was rough.

I had to be away in Athens, and Nikos, who stayed behind on Aegina alone, was anxious.

Aegina, late November 1940 [postcard]

Dear Toulpitsa!*

Right after you left, Koritsa fell.† I was overjoyed. . . . This morning, I saw Kalmouko, who had climbed up to his terrace and hoisted a beautiful Greek flag. . . . I hope you arrived in good condition in the "benzína"‡ and I'm already beginning to count the days and later the hours. Please go by Pyrsos and reach some conclusion, on whatsoever terms you accept, so that the book can be published before Christmas; it's a must. . . .§

Aegina, December 7, 1940

Dear Toulpitsa,

Thanks to Mr. P., the house is suddenly full of bounties. It was night; he knocked, came in, and opened his valises. . . . I felt happy and remembered when I was a little boy . . .

About the corrections of England, you're right. Attend to them while you're there. I had written to Ganiaris, asking to have the following phrase inserted above the dedication: "Let this book be con-

---

* See Alexandr David-Neela, *Toulpas*: the creatures whom the people of Tibet contrive to create out of their own thought and who act as their servants.
† Koritsa fell on November 25, 1940, landmark of the Albanian campaign.
‡ *Benzína* is the Greek word for a motorboat.
§ Postcard to E. Samios.

sidered as an outcry for the new Great Idea: that Greece unite with England!" Please tell him to write me whether censorship will permit it.

The other day, I had a dream about Elsa and I'm afraid something may have happened to her. The following day, I saw that Düsseldorf had been savagely bombed. . . .*

Paradoxically, Nikos Kazantzakis had had the same idea for Greece as Churchill had for France: that Greece should unite with Great Britain, so as not to remain isolated in her struggle against the barbarians. Greek censorship intervened, and no one caught wind of this idea—and Nikos was not discountenanced later on, at the time of the British armed intervention in Greece.

Inasmuch as England had once unhesitatingly mobilized her fleet and blockaded us in order to protect the interests of a single individual under her jurisdiction,† would she not hasten to the rescue of any ally that became a member of her Commonwealth now? This was probably Nikos' line of reasoning, for—incorrigible idealist that he was—he often forgot the sordid motive behind certain "noble" deeds.

Many long years had gone by without Sikelianos and Kazantzakis seeing one another. They were both working incessantly; each of them, I believe, longed to see the other. And yet, neither one would take the first step.

And then the day came when I ran into Sikelianos on a mountain in the Peloponnesus, among the laburnum and the wild thyme, hand in hand with Anna (whom I had known at school), both of them radiantly happy.

---

* Letter to E. Samios.
† On Easter 1849, Don Pacifico—a native of Gibraltar, who after committing a certain indelicacy had been dismissed from his position as Portuguese consul in Athens—was the victim of a misunderstanding between the Athens police and the crowd pillaging his house. Taking advantage of his recently acquired British citizenship and, above all, of the hostility shown by Lord Palmerston, the British Foreign Secretary, against the supposedly "Francophile" Greek government of the day, Pacifico demanded the exorbitant sum of 886,736.67 drachmas in gold as damages! Great Britain blockaded Greece and as a guarantee the latter spewed out the sum of 430,000 gold drachmas. Only after two years of palavers and according to the estimate of a joint Anglo-French commission (the first arbitration between nations!), Greece paid Pacifico 3,700 gold drachmas. And so this dreary incident was closed.

"Do you think Nikos would like to come with me to Epirus?" he asked me.

And Nikos leaped at the invitation.

Aegina, December 12, 1940

My dear Brother,

> *I go with you wherever you want.*
> *Ready. A grand delight for*
> *Our laughter to be heard again*
> *Together!**

For reasons unknown, Sikelianos did not answer his friend.

Several months later, Vássanos, the carriage driver of Aegina, told us about Sikelianos:

"Kyr Nikos, yesterday evening Mr. Sikelianos told me to take him to your house. But once he reached your door, he didn't want to dismount and we turned back. . . ." (This is the unfulfilled nocturnal visit referred to by Nikos in his December 24, 1941, letter to Sikelianos.)

After a deceptive calm, the seas and winds used to rouse themselves abruptly, seized by a sudden rage one would never have imagined possible several minutes before. Nikos, unconstrained in good and bad weather alike, floated like a cork on the crest of the waves. I went all stiff and lost my foothold, obstinately striving to resist the aggressive element, my nostrils seared by the sea salt. I glued my nose to the dingy windowpanes, dreaming of a light air I knew so well, exhaling honey and resin. My companion guessed my thoughts. With the first cloudbursts in March, we left our cliff for a brief stay in Attica.

Bitter cold lay in store for us in Kifisia. It was out of the question to retrace our first excursion—the betrothal trip. Hugging the stove, we spent long hours with friends who were happy to revel in Kazantzakis without having to cross the sea. There were our friends of always and the ones who came for the first time to have a slight taste of the "monster."

Sometimes the spark flared up; the laughter fused, the hearts opened. Sometimes the penumbra remained penumbra. This was the

---

* Letter to Angelos Sikelianos.

case with the French Professor Roger Milliex and his young wife, Tatiana Gritsi—a superb, sapphire-eyed ephebus accompanied by a woman of Tanagra as brown as an olive—good writers, good husband and wife, marvelous allies, admirers of Péguy, Kavaphis and Sikelianos. What does it matter that Kazantzakis hadn't touched their innermost chords? What was important is that they had touched Kazantzakis'. For he found himself in the presence of two "authentic" young people, the way he liked them to be—lovers of human dignity.

When he went back to Aegina, Kazantzakis was no longer satisfied with *My Father* and he relegated it to a drawer. To free himself for a while from pecuniary worries, he hastened to finish two new novels to appear in serial form. He also added notes to his *Akritas*, translated *Othello* in verse from English, made the definitive revision of his translation of Dante's *Divine Comedy*, and wrote a new tragedy in verse, the *Yang-Tse*, singing its praises to me:

"Read it, my love! It's the most significant and inaccessible of all. Ah, if only I too had a Barrault! I'm sure that it is beautiful. It unfolds on two levels, like the Byzantine ikons we love. Down below, the earth and the terrestrial story. Above, the sky and the supraterrestrial story. . . . I'm waiting for your opinion to know if it's worth anything."

"Tragedies, very beautiful tragedies," I murmured, slightly exasperated. "You know very well I love them. But can't you—even if it were only to please me—write one tenth, one hundredth part of our 'Neighbors'? One hundredth of this thundering Zorba?"

"Novels demand a pulse beat different from my own, Lenotschka. I don't have the necessary patience."

"You have more than enough. All you have to do is set yourself the task."

"I advance in abrupt leaps; I'm a born playwright. I shall never know how to write an *Anna Karenina*."

Nikos Kazantzakis was dubious of his abilities as a novelist. The future would prove to him that he did know how to handle this genre too.

Throughout the night of April 26–27, 1941, from behind closed Persian blinds, Ketty, Marika and I watched the departure of our allies, and then the German motorcycles following closely on their heels. To save the Allied fighting men who had managed to hide in friends' houses, we made the rounds of the embassies with Iannis Manglis. No one was willing to give them papers with which we could ship them off to Turkey, Lebanon or Egypt.

The first day of the Germans' arrival—April 27, a Sunday blazing with sunlight—the Athenians stayed shut up inside their own homes. There were no spectacular suicides like the suicide of the renowned surgeon Martel in Paris. The next day, the crowd poured out into the streets, full of curiosity—to see. . . . And they did see—the Germans ensconced in the city's pastry shops, gorging themselves on cakes and milk.

"Three chocolate cakes and three strichnines!" the waiter at Zonar's blared out to the kitchen. "Five *baklavas*, five milks and five strichnines! . . ."

Luckily the game ended before reprisals occurred.

On May 15, I received an alarming letter from Nikos on Aegina:

Beloved Lenotschka,

. . . Please don't worry at all about the future.* There may be no future at all! Here, during these recent days of the war, the vicinity of our house has been a "danger zone." Bombs near Marini's [taverna]— Marini himself was almost killed; machine-gun shots a few meters from the house. I saw the airplanes passing over my head and sensed how much everything is hanging by a single thread. I have the notion that I will soon be taking leave of this earth and I am waiting calmly, absolutely ready. And so, dismiss things "future." Without becoming nerve-racked, we must strive to live the present terrifying moments the world is undergoing, for we too are bound to experience them. Much patience and love are needed to endure with dignity this critical era it has been our lot to live in. I am certain that I have both these qualities needed. I beg you to have them too. Now, at moments such as these, the mettle of a human being is revealed. . . .

I miss you very much. I can no longer feel you far away from me. I get very tired. . . . Come. . . .

The house is full of white lilies. I bought a lot and I've been given some, and they're waiting for you. . . .

---

* In company with Iannis Manglis, we had been hoping to be able to set off in the direction of Mani and Crete, for we thought this island would be impregnable.

396

I hastened back to Nikos. The sinister shadows cast by the German bombers racing flat on their bellies over our fields like beasts of the Apocalypse struck my eyes, and I could hear the rumble of their lethal motors.

"The earth exalts the love of life," murmured Nikos, "while human beings go about cheerfully sowing death. . . . What can we do? What can we do to halt this abominable carnage!"

And the same tragedy that had taken place in northern Greece repeated itself in the last bastion of Europe that was still free.

By May 10, 1941, the New Zealander, General Fryberg, British military commander of Crete, had no more than 36 airplanes. Dreading the mass bombings of the Luftwaffe, and the loss of these irreplaceable aircraft, he had them evacuated to Egypt. And so on May 20—the day the first German parachutists landed—there were in all but eight airplanes left in Crete and a single antiaircraft battery!

As for the men, both British and Greek, who had no appropriate weapons or ammunition, they had to defend themselves, each one as best he could. The local populace came to their rescue, entering the war with cutlasses and heavy gourds. Of the 16,000 men of the German parachute force, 7,000 died.

"What beauty will be eaten by the ground!" lamented the old Cretan women, they too taking part in the struggle. "How many mothers of Fritz shall weep!" At a later point, a man who escaped miraculously from a concentration camp in Crete could not conceal his amazement and admiration. All trace of hatred had vanished.

"We had been given orders to bury them there, near the sea. The trenches we had dug were far too small. We had measured them according to our own measurements. And then we had to transport them. O la-la-la-la! Like stone—impossible to lift them."

And after this, he told us about the horrendous reprisals made in this same poor Crete.

Exactly one day after the cease-fire in Crete, the German flag disappeared from the Acropolis, to the consternation of the Quisling government and the fury of the occupying forces. On the morning of May 31, the Athenians read a proclamation posted on their walls by the Nazi commandant:*

---

* See D. Gatopoulos, *The People Begin the Resistance.*

1. During the night of the 30th to the 31st of May, the German war flag floating over the Acropolis was torn down by persons unknown. The guilty parties and their accomplices will be punished with capital punishment.

2. The newspapers and public opinion . . . are still expressing themselves with open sympathy for the English people expelled from Greece.

3. The events in Crete and the atrocities committed against German prisoners [!] not only fail to arouse any indignation; quite the contrary, they are observed with satisfaction.

4. In spite of explicit prohibitions, manifestations of sympathy for the English prisoners have occurred on several occasions (offers of gifts, flowers, fruits, cigarettes, etc.). . . .

5. The behavior of wide circles in the city of Athens toward the German armed forces has become increasingly hostile. . . .

And the curfew was decreed from 10:00 P.M.

Not until March 25, 1945—our national holiday—did we learn the names of the two students—Manolis Glezos and Apostolos Santas—who had carried off this dangerous exploit, the first act of resistance against the occupying army.

Germans, Italians, Bulgarians—it was too much for the poverty-stricken country. Within a few days there was nothing left to eat. More than 350,000 Greeks died of malnutrition. When the Liberation came, we learned that other peoples had suffered the same.

Along with Hagios Evstratios, Aegina was the most sorely tried island. The dead could no longer be buried; they were tossed over the cemetery enclosure. The children crept about with the help of crutches. Swollen bellies, faces covered with sores and thick fuzz, bald heads full of wounds and vermin. The following scene comes to my mind:

Near the port, a skeleton-thin little boy rummaging through a German garbage can. A young soldier approached and kicked him. Child and garbage can went sprawling, rolling over the ground.

"Why all this cruelty?" I asked the German. "If this child belonged to you, would you have acted like this?"

"In your place, I would poison them all!"

I asked the name of this new Herod. He was called Koenig.

Nevertheless, on Aegina we were relatively fortunate. First of all, the German archaeologist Gabriel Welter had played at being a Nazi only a few months. The day he learned that Hitler was attacking the U.S.S.R. he rushed over to us to predict the end of the Third Reich.

The commandant of our island was also a peaceful man, native of the Rhineland and pipe merchant, we were told. He smoked all day long and drank at night, closed up in his *Kommandantur*, visiting no one. When our last mayor—a mustachioed old man of eighty—summoned the SS a few days before the Liberation to arrest Kazantzakis and our friends, this German saved our lives, by offering the SS his best wines and (it was rumored) some of the finest pieces from the Aegina Museum.

The days grew shorter. Our food supplies were running out. To keep from wasting our strength, we tried staying in bed. In these blackest days, Kazantzakis wrote his most swashbuckling novel: *Zorba the Greek*.

"Kyria Lenítsa, open up!"

If the voice came from one of our beloved old people, I begged Nikos not to open. If the voice was a child's, we hastily crammed a spoonful of our oil into its mouth.

We too would certainly have died if our friends on Aegina had not joined forces to come to our rescue, especially Thrassývoulos Androulidakis, a lawyer and the director of prisons on Aegina, with his wife, Despina; Iannis Manglis, writer and sponge merchant, with his wife, Nota; and Elly Ghiolman, with whom we became acquainted rather late in the occupation period.

As often as they could, the Androulidakises used to share their mess tin with us. Iannis Manglis used to invite us for pancakes, and in the spring of 1942 he organized a contraband expedition. Accompanied by several of his sturdy sponge divers, he set off in a tiny sailboat toward the southern Peloponnesus, pushed on as far as Crete and came back laden with potatoes and oil. (To fully appreciate our friend's daring, one should add that he had only half a kidney and even that was in a poor state.)

If I dwell so long upon the famine, it is because I hold it responsible for all our future troubles. The rest of us had a certain reserve margin. But Nikos was subjecting his marvelous organism to the regime of sacrifice and abnegation carried to the utter extreme. He was wearing himself out. During Christmastime 1948, when he fell ill for the first time, the doctors asked me whether he had escaped from a Nazi camp. He bore the stigmata thereof.

I must admit that we too considered him immortal, I first and foremost. Never complaining and having a physical endurance that could pass any test, he managed to deceive us superbly well.

"My wife claims I'm ill!" he used to say, during the last years of his life. "There's nothing wrong with me! I sleep well, eat well, work well, lack nothing!"

I'm no longer sure in which year we met Elly. Considering our situation alarming, she began playing the role of the lady who doesn't like to stay alone. Hereafter, any excuse was good enough for her to come over and "chat." At sunset she used to appear along the rocky path, with her nonchalant gait and her little parasol twirling over her head and a white bundle balanced on her left arm. As she walked past, the peasants raised their heads to greet her, their noses tickled by the garlic sauce and fried fish we were about to relish. To these improvised picnics, she added a new game: she pretended to be afraid of sleeping alone in her own home. Sartre, Bergson and Pirandello were her gods at the time. Long discussions ensued around the table, and the evenings ended—with the cries of the prison sentinels and the crunch of heavy Nazi boots—on a rather surrealistic note.

"Can you explain to us, Elly, why you always set these bowls full of pistachios by our bed? Do you really think we can eat them during the night?"

And Elly used to blush. "N-n-no, not plecisely"—Elly couldn't pronounce her r's—"but I'm vely ashamed at having so many. . . . Eat; eat as many as you can; you'll be doing me a favor. . . ."

Why hadn't the Germans requisitioned the pistachio trees and fig trees and vineyards on our island? Their haste to get a taste of them had saved us from total disaster. For ahead of season, they had cut the bunches of grapes with their bayonets and grabbed at the figs and pistachios. And their lips had gotten so bloated and their tongues so chafed that they thought these fruits were inedible.

In our neighborhood, there was also an American lady, who was married to a Greek—Giorghos Lephas. Mr. Lephas had a radio set. Every evening Nikos used to go over to his house to listen to "The French Speak to the French"—Churchill and de Gaulle filling us with hope.

At twilight Nikos abandoned work. Over the cup of that brew euphemistically called "tea," we were discussing the future of the world when Androulidakis knocked on our windowpane. Livid, he sank down on a chair.

"I've just spent a vile quarter of an hour," he sighed, wiping off his forehead. "Noon had struck. The big cauldron had just been set down in the prison grounds. The captives had formed a circle around it. And just at that point, a man went mad and jumped into the soup! We fished him out, but half of his flesh was left in the sauce. 'No one touch the beans!' I shouted in a loud voice. 'I give you my word that in twenty minutes you'll have some rice.' A few of the prisoners did muck about in the beans, and I had to call out the convict guards."

"And the man who was scalded?"

"He died—a few hours later. If you don't mind, I'll light a cigarette. My heart's wrong side up."

The Germans were not the only people who assailed the solitary man of Aegina. Since the National Theater had refused any of his original plays or translations, Nikos suggested to Prevelakis that they try to arrange another theater for their *Calandria* (the adaptation of Cardinal Bibbiena)—for example, Katerina's. Katerina accepted. But censorship intervened and vetoed it.

"I very much doubt whether even next year anything of mine will be performed at the National Theater," Nikos wrote to his "brother" Prevelakis on August 12, 1941. "As you know, I find myself perpetually persecuted. . . . Apparently, there is no regime that can tolerate me— and very rightly so, since there is no regime that I can tolerate."

Like Prevelakis, Stamos Diamantaras was also seeking an outlet for Kazantzakis. He had been working for a while now for a rich Athens publisher who specialized in law-book publications. This publisher wanted to extend his activities to literature, but what were his conditions! Nikos' letters from this period indicate the state of affairs. On August 22, 1941, he wrote to Diamantaras:

. . . I received the basket, etc. We were very sorry you couldn't come. I returned the books immediately, because the payment offered seemed to me shamefully humiliating. I believe it was not right for me to accept. . . .

I'm waiting for you to write me whether it's absolutely necessary for me to come. . . . Otherwise, let me finish the Synaxary of Zorba, which I've begun and am writing feverishly. I've already reached 150 pages. . . .

Here, my life is the same as you were familiar with: Before day breaks, I begin work. When night falls, I stop. I plunge into the sea, eat many figs and grapes and in the evening glue my ears to the radio.

Agony, but I am trying to tame it by working. . . .

And about Othello, he wrote to Prevelakis:

Aegina, September 1, 1941

Dear Brother,

Thank you for intervening on behalf of Othello. I would very much like this translation of mine to be performed, because I'd like to show how I translate Shakespeare. But I'm afraid that on the "starvation" terms they propose, nothing can be done. . . . If I weren't in a difficult economic position, I'd tolerate their exploiting me; but now, under no condition . . .

One must survive. But this is not enough. Of what value will our life be if it is robbed of the genuine power whose substance is no longer words but men? I've had enough! . . .

Yes, Kazantzakis had had enough! To go on working away at his desk, sheltered from the common enemy, became a torment for him. Once again, he rebelled against what he called his "inactivity." He had a burning desire to go down into the fray.

Thrassývoulos Androulidakis was about to set off for the mountains. Kazantzakis bade him tell the Partisans that he was ready to join them. In order to receive the answer as soon as possible, we agreed on a personal code.

Kazantzakis was aware of how much the right wing distrusted him, viewing him as a Communist. He also knew that his mysticism repelled the left wing. But he never suspected that the Resistance leaders would reject his offer, heaping calumny upon him and treating him as a secret agent of the Intelligence Service.

Meanwhile, Angelos Sikelianos had sent Nikos one of his poems, copied in his own hand. And Nikos, without hesitation, thanked him:

Aegina, December 24, 1941

Beloved Brother!

I received the precious manuscript of your poem, and in Nea Estia I read and reveled in your other poem. More than ever during these critical moments, Saint Dimitris rides alongside Saint George.* When you gave Eleni the message for me, asking whether I wanted us to go to Epirus, I wrote you at once to tell you how joyfully I accepted. I also wrote to Prevelakis, but received no answer. In January I passed by your house in Athens to see you and didn't find you. And once you came to Aegina, approached my house and did not enter.† But now, I think, it is time we meet. Perhaps at this fatal hour of Greece, it must be so. But how? And where? Decide.

"God" willing, our 1942 shall be full of action, the two horses (the white and the iron-gray) fighting side by side. . . .

1942.   At the beginning of this year, Prevelakis invited Nikos to his home in Athens, having a marvelous surprise in store for him: A meeting with Sikelianos—a bit of balm to soothe the Cretan's soul, wounded by the distrust shown him by the left wing of the Resistance.

And on February 25, 1942, he wrote to Prevelakis:

The days I spent in your home will surely never fade from my mind. Warm, full, all essence. And the great bliss for me is that I could feel their intensity and sweetness at the very moment I was living them. . . .

And that same day, he wrote to Sikelianos refound:

Dear Brother Angelos!

I arrived home with Anna's flowers, bearing the good tidings:‡ that for a surety all this ambience is going to glow with your presence. In about ten days, I'll come back to Athens and I'll see you again. God is with us, because we are with Him. Work, laughter, evening talks in front of the sea, the sky above, the earth at our feet. The eternal moment will assume its genuine essence—eternity.

---

* Some time after their first meeting, Sikelianos had written a most beautiful poem, wherein the two friends were depicted as Saint George and Saint Dimitris, mounted on their iron-gray and white horses.
† See p. 394.
‡ A play on the name Angelos and the word Angelía—"tidings."

Having finished a new canto, Nikos sent it straight off to Prevelakis:

Aegina, March 28, 1942

. . . I strongly doubt that the canto Toda Raba* I sent you will pass the censorship. . . . I reread the prologue of Pandérmi Kríti,† with the same unhesitating admiration. . . . I'm getting ready to welcome Angelos. . . . I have great hope in this invisible collaboration: The Daedalos‡ will be written and perhaps the Yang-Tse will assume its final form. Springtime is beginning and has already filled me with anxieties and hopes.

In the springtime, there were more lilies on our little island than fish in the sea. At that season, the port looked like a royal court all decked out for some princely wedding. The little sailing vessels heeled over under the weight of the flowers. The air was laden with their haunting scent. Angelos and Anna Sikelianos, radiant in the springtime of their love, landed among the mounds of lilies. Kalmouko lent them his house. Until the end of October, Anna and I, privileged women, and our cousin, Zizi (who was our hostess) were to quench our thirst in a fountain of youth.

Whoever visited Sikelianos in his handsome apartment in Athens confronted a caged lion. In the country, in the presence of the sea, his psychological and physical power, his laughter and his voice found the space they needed to develop themselves at ease. Excessive in all things, this man who was strong and sure of himself suffered like a weakling (as I have witnessed) the moment his consort moved even a hand's breadth away from him.

Sikelianos and Kazantzakis, so different in appearance; so identical in their longing for the absolute and, at the same time, so refreshing; loving laughter and jokes, detesting the coarse phrases and untrammeled behavior rampant in Athens. The Ionian bard, sweet, stentorian, bland as a prince of the Church (or, rather, as a votary of some Asiatic deity), in his long white silk, wide-sleeved robe with his rounded gestures and voluminous voice. The Cretan, son of peasants, with his delicate joints and slightly abrupt gestures, sober and solid, dressed from daybreak on

---

* The canto of *Toda Raba* was dedicated to Iannis Manglis.
† A novel by Prevelakis. A rough English equivalent of the title would be *All-Barren Crete*.
‡ Sikelianos wrote his tragedy *Daedalos* while on Aegina.

in his orange calico vest and his dark-blue trousers. Both of them at ease in the presence of the powerful or the disinherited of this earth.

In order to face the famine (the winter of 1941 to 1942), the Greek Communist Party organized the Ethniki Allilenghii (National Solidarity) in Athens. The members of this organization were university professors, instructors, bourgeois of every class and inclination. Their principal aim was to help the families of the political prisoners and deported persons—for the most part, Communists, whom the former Metaxas dictatorship had handed over to the Germans and the Italians. On September 27, 1941, after many fruitless discussions with the center and the extreme right wing, the Communists announced the founding of E.A.M., the Greek Army of the Resistance.

News reached Aegina drop by drop and after an exasperating delay; moreover, it was interlarded with lies. Occasionally, Nikos would come back from Mr. Lephas' house with a smile on his lips. The B.B.C. had been lauding the gallantry of our Partisans. Later on, the most spectacular acts of the Greek people were passed over in silence by the B.B.C. The first discords had become evident within the British camp, among the people who still believed in the rights of man and the others.

During the spring of 1942, Nikos Kazantzakis met the Homeric scholar Iannis Kakridis.* From this unforeseen meeting a fervent friendship was born and, after thirteen years of harmonious collaboration, a masterpiece: the translation of the *Iliad* into modern Greek in 17-syllable verse—without omitting a single one of those adjectives compounded of several words, so relished by our ancestors and their descendants.

The Kazantzakis-Kakridis correspondence is a stirring one: "Let us forget our own personal projects. What comes first is Homer! So that the young people may come to know him at close range, without the intermediary of dictionaries. . . . So that the *demotiki* may be enriched by a masterpiece. . . ."

"Be hard; demand of me the impossible," Kazantzakis asked Kakridis. "We shall need the patience of a donkey, and we shall have it! One by one, we shall surmount the difficulties. Homer is worth this labor. . . ."

---

* Professor and rector of the University of Thessaloniki, author of works on Homer.

The two friends often elaborated in writing the almost insurmountable difficulties they had to overcome. I still remember the qualifying adjective of the goddess "with-the-ankles-as-white-as-snow." Unable to find anything, they had asked for help from other Greeks, addressing them through the newspapers. No one did help them. They were about to despair when Nikos stumbled across some popular Cypriot poems. And miraculously, there he found it. At such moments, his joy knew no bounds.

During this summer of the famine, after a great deal of trouble, Androulidakis had managed to change our stony yard into a vegetable garden, thereby saving our lives a second time. For even fish had become impossible to find. And now I had to go off to Athens in hopes of finding some bread on the black market. Censorship became increasingly strict and Nikos' letters lost their interest, speaking only of everyday problems—books, bread, work:

Aegina, autumn 1942, Sunday

Beloved Lenotschka! I've just now received the sacred bread and I'll get the permit and send it to you with Miss Elly. . . .

The neighbors are feeding me well . . . but I feel extremely exhausted, because I find myself on the eve of birth. . . . Prometheus is kicking my vitals, longing to come out. I am suffering very much. . . .

We have worked very well with Mr. Kakridis on Homer. . . .*

Sikelianos too had worked well. He had finished the *Daedalos*, a powerful tragedy in verse that spoke directly to the hearts of the subjugated Greeks. He recited us his poem on Solon, who had feigned madness in order to have the right to kindle the Athenians to go and fight at Salamis. We wept, applauded, demanded encores exhausting for the poet. Our friends came to enjoy it too. The schoolmaster, who was not admitted to our meetings, got the idea that there were Communist conspiracies going on. And a bit earlier in the war, he had warned the police one night that we were sending light signals to the German submarines. In his panic, the poor man had mistaken the lights of the Laoussa Islands lighthouse for the flickering signs of our own satanic activities.

---

* Letter to E. Samios.

Along with the *Iliad* and the *Prometheus*, which kept him from sleeping now, Nikos once again began chasing a very old bluebird—Christ. This time, it was the *Memoirs of Jesus* he envisaged writing. And to do so, he immersed himself in the Scriptures and the Apocryphal Gospels.

Four years later, in Paris, while working at UNESCO, he was still thinking about his Christ. But at that point, he wanted to cure Christ of His Messianic spirit through psychoanalysis. A young Greek psychoanalyst, M.G., used to come to our home to lead Kazantzakis through the mysteries of this science.

With Sikelianos' departure, our environs turned destitute. The madcap wave, the salty cliffs, the inlets of tawny sand, the starred sky or the full moon, even the little owl that used to come and join our evenings, rivaling our two poets in eloquence—everything became alien and insipid.

A marvelous presence, this visionary poet who strolled at ease among his visions, taking himself for a god and never hesitating one bit to say so; whose "arrogance" was but disguised nobility and kindness, love of the next man, thirst for the high summits.

How quickly one's mockery turned to affection as soon as one followed this born lord at close range! He was as capable of finding perfect happiness among the silks and luxury of palaces as in the huts of mountain shepherds—where he jubilantly spent a large part of his life.

Aegina, October 28, 1942

Beloved Brother,

Impossible to tell you how much this place is clamoring for you, living in the hope of your returning with the swallows. . . . On the 23rd of October, I finished the Iliad and was sorry to lose a day-to-day companion such as this. Now I find myself confronting two or three paths, and I don't know which one to choose—or, to put it more precisely, which one will choose me. We have sun again—an extremely tender, moist light—and the heart is mollified, filling with shoots like the earth. I remember all the eternal moments we have spent together, and I feel no difference between recollection and actual life. All things are present, i.e., immortal. The fact that you have lived here has given a new essence to my desolate shore. . . . *

---

* Letter to Angelos Sikelianos.

The Sikelianos promises could not become a reality. The Germans stubbornly refused us the necessary residence permit. But we never stopped seeing each other again.

The more the Germans and the Fascists raged against our people, the more united the Greeks became at the fundamental level—in spite of the frequent discords at the summit. We shall never again experience so perfect a union, I believe.

On November 24, 1942, the Greek Partisans, with the help of several British secret agents (headed by Eddie Myers, Chris Woodhouse and Denis Hamson),* exploded the viaduct at Gorgopotamos, on Mt. Oitis. This was the first large-scale act of sabotage and the B.B.C. exulted. Reprisals were swift to follow.

On December 22 of this same year, Athens was in an upheaval. Forty thousand workers went on strike. On their posters could be read: "Down with Terrorism!" "Liberate the Captives!" "Long Live E.A.M."

The throng, disciplined and unarmed, moved in the direction of the Ministry of Labor. In front of the Ministry, an Italian officer in a car charged the young people advancing hand in hand. Brandishing his revolver, he aimed right at the chest of a young man. Mitsos Kostantinidis was the first student to fall on the battleground of Athens. That same evening, another student died of wounds. Many people were wounded. Italians and Germans, aided by reserve troops, proceeded to make arrests.

Aegina, January 1943
Monday

1943.

My dear L.!

I got your anxious, sad letter and I got the bread too. Iannis Manglis is thinking of setting off for Crete on Wednesday, and I'll give him everything we have . . . so he can bring us some soap. . . . I too am terribly worried about Diamantaras. Please go by Z.'s and ask about him. I saw a horrid dream the other day. . . .†

---

* See C. M. Woodhouse, *The Apple of Discord* (London, 1948); Churchill's *Memoirs* and *The Second World War* (in French); Francis Noel-Baker, *Greece: The Whole Story*; Sir Francis de Guingaud, *Operation Victory*; Lord Wilson of Libya, *Eight Years Overseas*.
† Letter to E. Samios.

My beloved L.!

Impossible to communicate by post. Your card reached me after 15 days! . . . Here, I'm getting along comfortably. Friends invite me to dinner, for fear I may be suffering from malnutrition. I eat regularly at Mr. Manglis' and every Sunday the Justice of the Peace treats me to a fish and fish-soup dinner at Marini's. . . . Sminthitsa is growing and eating. I've trained her. She's become almost perfect. In the evening when I lie down to sleep, she's learned to withdraw to her own private quarters (the little box) and all the doors are left open. All night long, she sleeps peacefully. But as soon as day begins to break, she rushes up to knock for me, i.e., scratch at my door. If it's too early, I call to her: "Not yet!" At first, she didn't know what "Not yet!" meant, and she persisted. But now she's beginning to understand. I call out "Not yet!" very loudly and she withdraws. After half an hour, she comes back and I open up for her. First, she fondles my feet. Then in one youthful bound she jumps up on the bed and sits on my chest, purring away in my ear. I write and read in bed. She finds a position, generally on my shoulder or knees, and waits for me to finish this mysterious, futile work (so she considers it and so it is) that I am doing. Then I get up and she rushes behind me, her tail sticking up like a cypress. So much for things Smintheic! . . .

Yesterday, I got a letter from Westpfahl's cousin, the Berlin publisher, . . . asking me to publish the Rock Garden. . . .

I've worked on the first 4 books of the Iliad, and Kakridis has sent the corrections for them. A great improvement. I think this work will be significant.*

. . . I've just come back. Elly didn't arrive, but the new package you've sent me moves me deeply. I opened it with all the bounties—bread, splendid olives, delicious halva, white pheta cheese. . . .

This solicitude of yours stirs me and I'm impatient for the day when I'll be seriously ill or in danger so that I can have the delight of your taking care of me. What I've always lacked in order to be

---

* Letter to E. Samios.

sympathetic even to the people nearest me is sickness—the fear of the people who love me that they might lose me suddenly, their knowledge that I too am a human being, that my heart is not of stone, and that the earth may open up for me too and swallow me. . . .*

On February 23, 1943, the day the order to mobilize was issued in the Führer's name, I was in Athens. Within a few minutes, the news had spread to the four corners of Athens. The rage of the people could no longer be restrained. Minor demonstrations took place that very day. The next day there was a general uprising. From eight o'clock in the morning on, the crowds advanced on the Ministry of Labor. This time, every person had a stone in his pocket and a stick or an iron bar hidden under his vest. Already before noon the Labor Ministry had been set on fire; and with the workers' help the students had burned the files. There were many victims, but the mobilization order was lifted. And this is how the first battle of Athens was won—a very great victory gained by the people, who were well aware of it and celebrated it in their own manner.

Aegina, March 4, 1943

. . . During Carnival the other day, some girls came home, masquerading in splendid costumes. They danced in the courtyard and sang. . . . Shortly afterward, the proletarian masked figures arrived, with their [faces] smeared with black; they were dressed in fez, baggy trousers and rags and had bare feet. They sang in high spirits, grabbed some carob fruit and dashed off. . . .

Sminthitsa is making progress. If she stays a few more months with me, either I will learn to meow perfectly or she will learn to speak pigeon Greek. . . .†

Aegina, March 11, 1943

. . . Don't worry about me at all. I'm getting along regular [regularly] insofar as possible, eating and cooking the lower-grade foods so that when you come you can have the gruel cakes, trahanà, rice, macaroni, etc. . . .‡

---

* Letter to E. Samios.
† Letter to E. Samios.
‡ Letter to E. Samios.

. . . It's very cold, but I'm not lighting the fire, because the coal's finished. . . .

I'm writing you again about the "Society of Newspaper Editors," because it's a very serious matter. They say they'll give every member a loan of 600,000 drachmas.* And this would save us. That's why I'm asking you to make an agreement with Hourmouzios. . . .

These last days, I've been a little upset or tired. I have nightmares. But it's nothing; only natural. . . .†

If the Greek "Editors" refrained from admitting Nikos Kazantzakis to their ranks, Giorghos Papandreou did his utmost to come to our rescue. When he learned that the "famous" millionaire publisher had offered but two tins of olive oil to acquire the translation of the *Iliad*, he saw red. Within a few hours, both Kakridis and Kazantzakis had received the assistance of two Greeks well known for their generosity— M. Benákis, the son of the Mayor of Athens and founder of the musem named after him; and Trikorfos-Sbaroúnis, the celebrated surgeon and bibliophile. To the money, the latter also added a little chest of provisions.

A bit of money also came in from a third source: the *Protomástoras*, Kazantzakis' tragedy, which Manolis Kalomoiris had made into an opera many long years ago.

. . . I was glad about the 180,000 drachmas from the poor Protomástoras. After all these years (I wrote it when I was a student), it's now beginning to bear fruit. God knows when the tragedies will begin bearing fruit too, Melissa, etc. Let's hope before I die. . . .

How can I thank Sbaroúnis? What can I write to him? What can I do to show him how touched I am by this generous help of a person I don't even know, in these difficult hours? . . .‡

---

* In inflated wartime currency, needless to say.
† Letter to E. Samios.
‡ Letter to E. Samios.

As I narrate our life, I perceive one immutable law acting through-out our entire existence: As soon as one hand gave us something, before we had time to enjoy it, another hand snatched it away, taking even a bit more, from what had been stored off to the side. The delights owing to Dr. Sbaroúnis lasted only several days. Our cleaning woman, Sophia, found a way of robbing us. And there we were, once again confronting empty cupboards.

"How could you do this, Sophia?"

"The devil pushed me to it, Kyra Lenítsa. Don't turn me over to the police. Take my house, but don't turn me in. I didn't eat those things I took all by myself alone. I shared them with the neighbor ladies!"

And she promised to move mountains to prove to us her remorse and gratitude. Later on, whenever Sophia made trips across the way to the Peloponnesus, she never forgot to bring us back some oranges and figs. But the handsomest gift of all she was to offer us the day the Germans left our island.

No longer knowing which saint to make our vows to, we tightened our belts and contented ourselves with wild salad greens and dandelion leaves from our own yard. But just at that point Nikos' favorite saint, Francis, came to our rescue.

"If you agree to translate Jörgensen's *Life of St. Francis* for us, we'll be glad to remunerate you in provisions," some Greek Catholic monks wrote to Kazantzakis. The proposition included also the writing of a long Prologue. Kazantzakis immediately and joyfully set about the work.

Our little alley cat, Sminthitsa of the Homeric name,* also inter-vened just in time:

Nikos had been working near the lighted stove, with the little cat sitting on his shoulder. Suddenly, the "Goddess-of-Mice" flopped to the ground, unconscious. Nikos got up, picked her up in his arms and opened the door. . . . Next morning he himself woke up sprawled out on the corridor flagstones, frozen and with a horrible headache. Sminthitsa took several days to recover from this coal-gas poisoning.

Aegina, March 25, 1943

. . . These past nights, I've been seeing a cauchemar [nightmare] about Manolis Georgiadis. Incredible delight at his being alive, and in

---

* Smintheus in Homer, the god of mice.

412

the morning I wake up exhausted. If Sminthitsa didn't come at dawn to wake me up, by knocking on my door, I wouldn't wake up at all. She comes purring away and takes her last little nap in my bed. Páli kalà!* I tell you, she really has wound up having a human expression. And as far as I go, she's aroused everything catlike I have in me. Ever since the day before yesterday, I've begun imitating her meowing—angry or tender, accordingly. I imagine that if a person lives for years in the desert with an animal, little by little the identification will become clear. The human being will fall; the animal will rise; and after some years the difference will be imperceptible. And now I am watching this Sminthitsa's interest as she scrambles up to my shoulder and observes what I am writing. She doesn't yet understand what it's all about—but she will. . . .

You shouldn't have learned about the poisoning, since I escaped. . . . As a favor to you, I'm thinking of being careful now. But my God, how difficult and annoying it is to cook for yourself! I imagine that if I were cooking for you, I'd do so with pleasure. And then, how wretchedly I cook! Sminthitsa looks at me when I set her food out for her. She bends down, sniffs the food, looks back at me again with a plaintive, dumbfounded air, as much as to say: "By your own God, what's this stuff? Is this food? Not fit even for a dog!" What can I do? Sometimes there's too much oil, sometimes too little, and I haven't yet managed human (or even cattish) pancakes. Sometimes they dissolve and other times they're soggy slop.

Reading your feelings about the poisoning and my weak state touched me—did me good like a liter of milk. . . .†

Kazantzakis had completed his sixtieth year. His thought was mature and his temples were slightly graying. His heart remained as tender and teasing as a child's.

Aegina, March 28, 1943

What are these precious delectables-of-the-throat you keep sending me? . . . I'll burst! Already, I've begun changing. Today, I've been cooking ever since morning. . . . I'll become like Epicurus' pig and I'll

---

* Roughly equivalent to "Well, it might be worse!"
† Letter to E. Samios.

lose the most precious thing I have—my reputation as an ascetic. I beg of you, stop now! The mailmen are getting out of breath bringing it all to me—"For the love of God, Mr. Nikos," they say to me, "tell her to stop! We can't stand it any more!". . .*

Nikos Kazantzakis still had his strong inclination to play the matchmaker. Every time a young girl and a young man were under our roof, unfailingly, it was a "must" to make them happy—with or without the Pope. . . .

Aegina, April 1943

. . . Elly will be coming tomorrow and the belly will be entering Paradise. She's coming, so she says, with a permanent, because she's expecting to take her examinations with K. She speaks cynically, but I tremble. If this attempt fails, I'll be heartily sorry. May God (i.e., Zeus in the comedy I meant to write—the opening of the Matrimonial Agency) lay his hand to it and drive both of them—but in the same direction—to join up.

I'm saving the honey . . . for you and the two guests we're expecting.

Summer; all the gillyflowers have opened up and in the evening the house is dizzyingly fragrant with them. And the cactus, with its leaves like herrings (or old mustaches on a policeman)—blossoming every four years—has sprouted a splendid tall flower like a little tree. . . . I hope you'll be in time for it. I'm doing my best to delay its blooming, by keeping it inside in the shade. Sminthitsa's out in the courtyard all day long, chasing butterflies. She leaps up into the air, waves her front paws and grabs at them. I save as many of them as I can. But her whiskers are often smeared with the gold dust from the butterflies' wings. . . .†

Ever since the end of April 1943, the Partisans had been in control of one third of Greek territory. The Italians and the Germans went on making their bloodthirsty incursions into free Greece, but they could no longer hold out there. For a short time now, Eddie Myers and his

---

* Letter to E. Samios.
† Letter to E. Samios.

compatriots had been going around in their jeep, dressed in uniform. From Andreas Kedros' *The Greek Resistance from the Years 1940– 1944** I quote the following German report dated April 9, 1943:

. . . Every day, large-scale sabotage activities are observed as well as assassinations of Italian soldiers. Ever since November 1942, more and more numerous *Andartes†* organizations are penetrating the regions occupied by the Germans and attacking the police stations, for the purpose of seizing weapons and ammunition. In the area of the military *Kommandantur* of Thessaloniki alone, from December to the present day, some thirty attacks of this kind have been recorded. Elsewhere, the sabotage activities and assassinations are taking place every day. . . .

The fact that the *Andartes*, men and women alike, were performing miracles and that the Italians were virtually incapacitated in northern Greece, where they took atrocious revenge on the local populace, we learned through Iannis Manglis, who, thanks to his Italian passport, could circulate more easily. He could even discuss politics with the Italian officers he met in the course of his contraband expeditions to the Peloponnesus (where the Resistance was beginning to inflict heavy losses on the enemy). Shortly afterward, the Germans intervened in the Italian-occupied zones that had been successfully liberated by the Partisans. Within a few days, several dozen villages had been reduced to ashes.

The news reached us in Aegina, colored according to the hopes and fears of the people bearing the news. And Nikos champed at the bit, condemned to isolation by those he had thought to be his brothers in arms.

In his letters, he occasionally did let his bitterness peek through. But he carefully refrained from letting the slightest shadow flit over his work, for he wanted that to be detached from all personal concern— faultless—the quintessence or the pivotal point of the present-day whirlwind.

On August 10, 1943, he informed Prevelakis that he had just begun a new tragedy, *The Trilogy of Prometheus*. He so loved the month of August that he returned to one of his favorite notions—to have it

---

* Page 254.
† The Greek word for "Partisans."

proclaimed a saint. And he thought of asking our finest painter of ikons, Fotis Kondoglou, to make him a "Saint August," whose hands would be filled with figs and grapes.

. . . I work the verse till noon [he wrote to Prevelakis on August 10, 1943] and then I rush down to the sea and plunge in. This is, I believe, the happiest moment of the day. I eat—and now that Eleni's here, even food has become a joy—I smoke my pipe and begin work again. Before the sun sets, I go back into the sea. And in the evening, I sit for a long time on the terrace, looking at the stars.

This is my day. I want nothing. I let no concern upset me. I have absolute need of keeping body and soul solid. I have no time to lose. I know that the world is decomposing and later on, insofar as I am able, I would like to help its recomposition. But, for the present, I believe the only way for me to work in harmony with the universe is to execute well, incessantly, the creative work left me before I die. Every other activity of mine now seems to me superficial or treacherous. . . .

The body is very strong and the soul totally liberated from human beings, i.e., all forms of illness. I've remained alone with my own self now, and I like its company, because I know now how good it is, how honest, hard-working, proud. Human beings I can stand less and less. Time has weighed them and found them lacking. With you I still feel a deep bond—a bond of blood—and some day I hope we may be linked in some joint work. But life is harsh. I don't know if I'll still be alive by the time you've become completely liberated of necessity. . . .

One month later, he plunged into the translation of Homer's Odyssey and asked his colleague Kakridis to hasten as well.

Aegina, September 16, 1943

Dear Friend!

. . . I've finished the Prometheus Trilogy and begun the Odyssey. It's a great joy, and every evening I wait impatiently for the next day to dawn and work to resume. I don't know what may happen to me, and I'm in a hurry to leave you this manuscript, even if it's only the first version, so that you can work on it at your ease.* For the same reason, I'm also in a hurry to start the second version of the Iliad. I've completed all the manuscripts you've sent me and I've changed all the verses again. We are now very close to the original. I've also found how to say " 'Οβριμοπάτρη" in a single word. I thought it impossible, and all of a sudden I found it. But I won't tell you. Suffer a little; perhaps you'll find a better one. Make our friends suffer too. . . .

The sea is still marvelous, the grapes still abundant. Eleni is up to her ears in grape juice—syrup cakes and jams. But she says she gives you both her hands, jam-smeared though they be, and sends you affectionate warm wishes. And I the same, with my ink-black hand. . . .

Early in the autumn of 1943 two lyric poets died in Athens: Malakassis and Palamas. At Palamas' funeral, Sikelianos and S. Skipis, another lyric poet, delivered orations and recited incendiary poems. Several days later, Sikelianos informed Nikos that the *Daedalos* (the tragedy he had written on Aegina and dedicated to Nikos) would be appearing in Athens. Nikos wrote in reply:

Aegina, October 1, 1943

Brother Angelos!

I'm eager to read Daedalos in printed form as well. Your child by Aegina, and you've given me the great joy of offering it to me! I'm impatient for the seas to open so that we may meet. Last year I came to Athens for your name day. Will I be able to this year too? The summer was magnificent. Swimming in the sea, figs, grapes; unending, jubilating work. But you were missing.

I'm making progress on the Odyssey translation too, and it will soon be finished. I want to free myself of all my manuscripts, so that whenever Freedom does return to Greece I shall be ready for a new life.

I read your oration on Palamas and was moved by it. You know how foreign this poet is to me, except for a few of his lyrical things. A

---

* This premonition proved justified. Iannis Kakridis did indeed have to finish the translation of the Odyssey by himself, his friend having completed only the first version.

small poeta major—whereas Malakassis, in his very few exquisite poems, is a great poeta minor. However opposed the rhythm of my own blood is to Malakassis' rhythm, I still feel that the best poem of Malakassis is better than the best poem of Palamas.

And yet you—thanks to your own great breath of life—were able to laud him to the sky. And everyone who heard you says your oration was a real, sublime initiation rite.

I kiss your wife's hand. Her beauty, her tone of voice, her sweetness are greatly missed on this desolate waste of a shore. . . .

During the Occupation, the Athenians carried on their literary and philosophical discourses; and at the nadir of their affliction a savage battle broke out between the conservative men of letters and the Renovators, on the occasion of Iannis Kakridis' daring to publish a book without accent marks! The war of accents! And so this Homeric scholar was banned by the University and dragged to face Justice! "Eternal Greeks, enemies of their own race!" murmured Nikos in disappointment.

But the young people sided with the Renovators. And, as many impassioned, perspicacious letters received by Kazantzakis indicate, the provinces were also awaking in their own turn, rearing their heads. . . . Among Nikos' papers I found the rough draft of a letter addressed to a young girl at the start of her literary career:

Aegina, January 1, 1944

Dear unknown friend,

. . . I was amazed to see the understanding and fire of a young girl who has been able to discern and judge the fundamental endeavors of my life and follow them as the model of her own life. And I was also happy to find myself once again among the only people I love in this world—the young people and the still younger ones. For in this way my message contains much future, and the "Cretan glance"* I live and love so much illumines—illumines and burns—other eyes as well.

Any person who has this glance, as you have, needs no help. . . . Life is a game you know, ensanguined, ephemeral, exquisite, with thousands of tiny hopes, unworthy and at the same time worthy of

---

* For the "Cretan glance," see Report to Greco.

418

man. Happy is he who can revel in them without being blinded; happy is he who can see far off the "black helmet," as a Persian poet I love says—"I shall wear the black helmet and my friends shall no longer see me." I often repeat these [words] at the happiest moments of my life, aware of some militant cry within me—as though I were already engaged in battle and charging against the abyss. Here on the island where I am staying I have found not the tranquillity—thank God, I'm still alive; how could I be tranquil?—but the rock where I can sit and wait for the seas to open till I can leave. Meanwhile, I am working intensely and joyfully . . . so as to be in time, before going back into this beloved earth, to utter what are for me the great elements—Fire, Sea, Silence, Pride, Spirit. . . .*

Four years of war had left Aegina covered with a thick mold. Throughout those four years, underneath that Nazi stratum, the earth was teeming, making ready for the springtime. And in the sky a bird foretold its undeniable arrival, every evening at the same hour, in good and bad weather alike. At times, the thunder disturbed its voice. We cursed, but the bird went on singing all the same. From one evening to the next, the neighbors used to set their clocks when they saw Kazantzakis set off for Lephas' house—"The French speaking to the French!" What modesty! The French were speaking to all free peoples.

Airplanes were flying more and more frequently over our island, not dropping bombs, but flooding us with pamphlets, better worded than the Nazi ones—"Greeks, exterminate the enemy! Even if a whole village burns for a single German killed, do not hesitate! We shall build other villages! . . ."

British encouragement was not needed. The Greeks were fighting in the mountains, organizing assaults in the plains. And if the B.B.C. had ceased talking about it, it was not the fault of our Partisans. People in the cities and the villages, men and women alike, were dying with their backs against the wall, hanging on the trees, shut up alive inside prison cells.

Whole villages were reduced to a heap of cinders. Helpless old men, women, children were murdered in cold blood. In their memoirs, English secret agents have described the affliction of the Greek people and at the same time their determination to achieve their own liberation

---

* Letter to Ephi Elianou.

in every possible way—till the day when these same people were subjected to the English bombs and mortars come to kill them in their own capital.

Nikos was beginning to foresee the dangerous turn our history was about to take and the new misfortunes our new friends were to cause us. "The fishermen of Aegina have begun throwing the fish back into the sea to keep the price from going down! And you say you want the English to land among us!" he wrote to me one day in exasperation. And on January 27, 1944, again from Aegina:

. . . I've tried to formulate the answer to Vasiliou. . . . All my conclusions are subversive. However much we need money, it's impossible for me to give a vague, unintelligible answer to such questions, for the express purpose of getting some money. Maybe the others can do so, because their conclusions are more painless. You who are always so glad to see me steer clear of compromises—you must not insist. . . .*

Aegina, July 1944
Friday

My beloved Lenotschka,

I got the two loaves of bread and the 10 million [drachmas] and could see how overwhelmingly expensive and sick the Hell of Athens is. Here in this house, life has another rhythm—the one we give it, not the one it gives us. The day you left (perhaps because I was upset), I began Kapodistrias at once. . . .

Today, I wrote the Prologue to St. Francis and I like it. . . .†

There were still several months between us and the Liberation. Even if the breadshops were still closed in Aegina and the children still starving, at least their little faces were no longer covered with sores. Gabriel Welter had already organized soup rations for them. And both German commandants of the island, the civil and the military, had a respect for human life.

One day as we came out of the sea, we caught a young German soldier in the flagrant act of theft. Instead of keeping silent, I threatened to go and bring charges against him. We were certain of having

---

* Letter to E. Samios.
† Letter to E. Samios.

seen him loitering around our house. And it was he who had robbed our poor Kalmouko's house.

The military commandant helped me recognize the guilty party. But since I had warned the thief of my intentions, he had had time to hide his loot in a dry well—as I learned several months after this confrontation.

Some days later, at twilight, we were resting in our courtyard when certain strange hissing sounds attracted our attention.

"Can it be the snakes' mating-season?" I asked Nikos, unaware of the imminent danger.

"Very likely so, my love. Shall we go in? No, no, don't turn on the light! Let's stay in the dark a little."

He had just sat down on the couch facing me when a dry, thudding sound exploded.

"As though a shutter's clacked against the window. And yet there's no shutter and no wind," murmured Nikos pensively.

What was our astonishment the next morning when Sophia and I found a broken jar, its jam spilled all over the cupboard and, buried in the jam, a German bullet! For a few seconds, we thought it was a bad joke. On the kitchen side, the cupboard was intact. But in the studio there was a little round hole in the wall of the cupboard and another hole in the windowpane on the east side. Nikos shrugged his shoulders. The only thing he did was to set himself in the place where he had been sitting the evening before. The couch still bore his imprint! The bullet had passed within a hair of his head!

The civilian commandant refused to accept it. No, no, no! They hadn't meant to assassinate us! And as he couldn't have the window-pane changed, he sent his carpenter to patch it up with two scraps of plywood.

The Germans were about to depart when we were notified from Athens that the SS was going to visit our island and that Nikos had better disappear as quickly as possible. It was a Saturday afternoon. The Kommandantur had closed its doors. I caught sight of the commandant seated at his typewriter, behind the window.

"Herr Kommandant," I called to him, "my companion is seriously ill. He must leave for Athens. Would you please give me a permit for one week?"

The commandant looked me over with a certain good-natured familiarity. His glance showed plainly that he was by no means duped.

Without uttering a word, he looked for an application form and filled it in: "I advise Mr. Kazantzakis to stay for more than a week in Athens. Fifteen to twenty days would do him a great deal of good."

And the SS came and went. In Aegina, no one suffered at their hands. When the Liberation came, there were even one or two Germans who preferred to surrender to the English rather than go back to the Third Reich.

In March 1943 the deporting of the Jews from Thessaloniki had begun. In the *Archives of the National Resistance,** Isaac Arouch describes how out of the 100,000 Jews in Greece only 20,000 could be saved—through the efforts of the EAM and the Greek people as a whole. The government's Security Department squads, armed by the Germans, had helped to exterminate them. These same squads were later to commit outrages against their own brothers.

The Nazis and the Greek reserve forces ravaged the country. H. Neubacher, whom Hitler had appointed responsible for political activity in Greece, sent a telegram to German Headquarters, stating among other things: "It is madness to kill infants, children, women and old men. . . . The brilliant result of such an *Aktion* is that the infants are dead, but the Partisans survive. . . . It is obviously more *convenient* to shoot defenseless women, children and old people than to pursue an armed band in a spirit of manly vengeance and exterminate it down to the last man."

This did not prevent Nazi troops from enclosing hostages in "cages" and making them walk in front of their convoys. And in Crete they used to put young girls on their trucks to force the Partisans to hesitate before attacking.

Roger Milliex, who was an eyewitness, describes the Athenians as the finest Partisans in occupied Europe. Which of them must be rescued from oblivion? Electra Apostolou? Lela Karayanni? The young student who clambered up on the German vehicle that was about to crush her and struck the Nazi driver's head with her heel? The young girls in their white smocks killed side by side with our war-cripples and invalids, who had been cast out on the streets by the Quisling government? The three boys who fought all alone against more than 200 Germans? How often have we dipped our handkerchiefs in their blood "to keep from forgetting"? And if we did not forget, how could we live after all that has happened in Greece?

---

* See Volumes 31 and 32 of these *Archives.*

Ever since the beginning of the Occupation, there had been six prelates of the Orthodox Greek Church who had sided resolutely with the Partisans: Gregorios, Bishop of Chalcidice; Andonios, Bishop of Ilia; Iakovos, Bishop of Attica; Ioachim, Bishop of Chios; Ioachim, Bishop of Kozane; Irininaios, Bishop of Samos. History was repeating itself. At the time of the Greek people's struggle for liberation from the Ottoman yoke, there had also been good and bad prelates, good and bad political leaders, good and bad friends. Woodhouse, who doesn't lose a single chance to show his antipathy toward EAM, was nevertheless impelled to write:

> The initiative of EAM-ELAS justified their predominance. . . . Having acquired control of almost the whole country, except the principal communications used by the Germans, they had given it things that it had never known before. Communications in the mountains, by wireless, courier, and telephone, have never been so good before or since; even motor roads were mended and used by ELAS-EAM. Their communications, including wireless, extended as far as Crete and Samos, where guerillas were already in the field. The benefits of civilisation and culture trickled into courts, and public utilities, which the war had ended, worked again. Theaters, factories, parliamentary assemblies began for the first time. Communal life was organised in place of the traditional individualism of the Greek peasant. Followed at a distance by the minor organisations, EAM-ELAS set the pace in the creation of something the governments of Greece had neglected: an organised state in the Greek mountains. . . .*

However, it was precisely this progress that was feared and reviled by the extreme right wing, with Churchill at its head.† And so, EAM, which included among its members thirty university professors, six bishops, a large number of priests, two members of the Academy, was made out to be an extremist left-wing organization rife with Trotskyists!

---

* From C. M. Woodhouse, *The Apple of Discord*, as quoted by Todd Gitlin, "Counter-Insurgency: Myth and Reality in Greece," in *Containment and Revolution* (London: Anthony Blond Ltd., 1967). Colonel Woodhouse was Chief of the British Military Mission to Occupied Greece; his book, cited above, was published in 1948.
† In the *Memoirs* of Winston Churchill, see his telegrams to Roosevelt.

423

On October 14, 1944, Athens was liberated. But not Aegina. The English, who had already arrived in the neighboring islands, were taking their own good time. A curious thing: When they did arrive, they shared their table with the rare Collaborators, who had served the Nazis before their arrival! And Kazantzakis witnessed still worse in Crete.

Before leaving Aegina, the civilian commandant decided not to burn the provisions and medical supplies of the Occupation Army. He had only the uniforms burned. When the Greeks learned the good news, they fell upon the coveted treasures. In their glee, they forgot that the school benches, windowpanes, chairs and doors were their own property, and they carried them off along with the German loot.

"Quick! Quick! Give me two empty sacks!" our Sophia begged me, her eyes flashing rapaciously. "Just let me get there in time, and you'll see whether I'm ungrateful!"

What was Sophia going to stuff into her sacks while the others grabbed the canned goods, ham and wheat—or dishes and kitchen utensils?

"Here you are! Here's what you love best of all!" she shouted to me, addressing me by turns in the second person singular and the second person plural. "Just take a little look at what's inside this sack! All for you; all for you, *Kyrámou!* [My lady!]"

Quivering with impatience, Sophia awaited my reaction. From out of her cornucopia, one hundred rolls of toilet paper fell at my feet! And from her pocket, Sophia took out a miniature English-German dictionary—"For the master," as she said. And she completed her gifts with a big can of wax "so that our tiles could get back their prewar sheen."

We were getting ready to leave Aegina just when the International Red Cross came to distribute some gifts from America. (Ah, why was Bunuel not there among us at the port of Aegina!) On donkey-back, the public herald had summoned the populace down to the port at five o'clock in the afternoon. The gifts were to be drawn by lot.

As more and more bundles were opened, the mute consternation of the first moments turned to roars of laughter. All at once—and no one knew who had given the signal—young and old alike, lackadaisical loafers and respectable paterfamilias, had all decked themselves out—some in lace ball gowns with multiple flounces, others in Chinese sheaths, others in plumed felt hats and hunting breeches and shoes that were by all means either too large or too small. Our lot was a pair of cabbage-green trousers and an eggplant-colored, terribly vampish sheath with a pair of gold sandals sized to fit the Statue of Liberty in Manhattan!

No sooner had the Germans left our island than the police knocked on our door:

"Follow us down to the station!"

"To do what?"

"To have a good laugh, by God! Come on there, *hep-hep!*" And they pointed their bayonets straight at me when I hesitated to let them go up to Nikos.

Nikos took a while to understand what they were asking of him, and one of the two policemen raised his voice.

"Try to be polite, Panayoti!" I shouted, beside myself. "Show him the respect you owe him; otherwise I'll give you a good slap!"

Nikos burst out laughing. "You'd better bring them some coffee, Lenotschka. After all, they're our guests. *Noblesse oblige!*"

Framed by Panayoti and his friend, we set off down the path for the port of Aegina, Nikos in the clouds, holding his miniature Dante, I dreadfully embarrassed by the absurdity of this forced march between two bayonets.

"Are you afraid we'll fly off? Speak up, for the love of God! What's got into you?"

"Orders are orders; you're Communists!"

"How's that—Communists?"

"Don't play around with us, Kéra Lenítsa! You see the fires over there on the crest of that mountain? Those are Communists. And wherever they are, they're killing the police. Just yesterday, they killed my brother. And I swore then that I'd kill all the Communists too."

"Panayoti, have you ever killed a man?"

"No!"

"Not even a German?"

"N-n-n-n-no!"

"And you want to start on us?"

They left us imprisoned in the station for many long hours—till the moment I began kicking at the door furiously and shouting the worst curses. At such moments, I lost all control of myself and resented Nikos, who would just stare at me with an astonished, almost compassionate gaze.

In this same year, 1944, Nikos pronounced himself ready to begin

Akritas, the Byzantine epic that was to be the companion piece to his *Odyssey*. But since it "didn't come from his vitals," as he wanted it to do, he let it go. After *Kapodistrias* and his translation of Machiavelli's *Prince*, he wrote a new Byzantine tragedy, whose hero was the last Emperor of Byzantium—Constantine Palaeologus—who died fighting on the day Constantinople was captured by the Turks: May 29, 1453.

Immediately after the Liberation, Kazantzakis set off for Athens, still extremely optimistic. One of the projects cherished by Papandreou at that time was to free Sikelianos and Kazantzakis of their financial worries. The first part of his plan—to pass a law providing remuneration for the members of the Academy—became a reality without any difficulty. The second part—to obtain membership in the Academy for Sikelianos and Kazantzakis—broke down.

In Constitution Square, we witnessed the murder of the unarmed masses. Thereafter, all hope of reconciliation was lost. The Grande Bretagne Hotel, where the Anglo-Greek high command was lodged, was also located in this square. And two steps across the way, on "Philhellenes" Street (where we were staying temporarily), the "Philhellenes" were showering us with their machine guns and their shells.

To look for a piece of bread, we used to risk our lives at every step. When we asked the young Englishmen driving the tanks why they were firing on their own Allies, they themselves were at a loss. Their only answer was that they had their orders! (In spite of all this, we loved these "tourists," these "lords"—and, what's more, we admired them.)

To catch the "Communists," who could escape them by fleeing from house to house, they mobilized their vehicles. The people living in the house that was being fired on would step out on their balcony or doorstep and beg to have the bombardment stopped. "There weren't any Partisans in *their* home, and if there were any, they'd have already escaped through the adjoining walls." "Sorry!" the well-bred soldiers would rejoin. "Sorry!" as they pointed their cannons on the house next door.

After they had gone, I went to visit my childhood school—Constantinidis-Aïdonópoulo. Everything there had been ransacked. In the Athens Conservatory, the pianos had been used as ashtrays or sinks in which they vomited their bad whiskey. There were many profanations of churches, etc., etc. Why complain of it? Who had called the English here to our homes?

In the course of these difficult days, the ladies of our "aristocracy" had begun distributing bread. One of the nieces of Segredakis, Maria, knew Madame Melas. So we went (Maria and I) to join the queue. When our turn came, Madame Melas refused Kazantzakis the right to eat!

We were also carted off to the police station—in company with Soula, our charming young servant girl. Here, I remained with mouth tightly sealed. On our own island, everybody knew us. Here in Athens, I knew that people were killed in the twinkling of an eye. I had witnessed one such arbitrary execution* in the middle of the street, before a throng of terrified mothers with families, men and children. No one— my God, what cowards we can be!—not a single person stepped forward to snatch the victim from his executioner. The only thing I could do was to go off to one side and vomit.

Disheartened by all this blind stupidity, we crossed the barricades.

Ever since the publication of The Odyssey, Tea Anemoyanni had been holding "Odyssiads" every Saturday. More and more friends met there. Giorghos Loulakakis read passages from the epic out loud. Mihali Anastassiou, Dimis Apostolopoulos and the Despotopoulos brothers commented on them; discussions were held. During the breaks, Tea used to serve cakes made of figs and Cretan grapes, sprinkled with sesame seeds.

And this time it was the home of Tea and Iannis Anemoyanni where we found refuge. For more than a year, friends—young and old, long-time friends and new ones—came to visit their cherished poet. Occasionally someone got up and went out in the middle of the meeting—generally some modern poet, by no means mediocre. Nikos respected the repugnance felt by Eliot's disciples for his epic, which was so antimodern. Adoring young people, he loved to see them rear their heads against him.

And soon afterward, another sort of meeting began at Tea's house: meetings of political "reconciliation." Young and old alike came there to discuss the future of Greece. From these meetings, the "Socialist Workers' League" was born in May 1945, Kazantzakis acting as its president.

---

* A reserve-army man had executed a hostage, shouting that he was a— Bulgar!

In Crete, the English and the Germans were still at large, the former grabbing as spoils of war everything the Germans hadn't had time to take, the latter still roaming about, fully armed. The government assigned two professors from the University of Athens—Iannis Kakridis and Iannis Kalitsounakis—to go to the sites, in company with Nikos Kazantzakis and the photographer Koutoulakis, and draft a report on the sufferings of this island, martyred several times over.

Canea, July 11, 1945

Beloved Lenotschka!

Still in Canea! Our car broke down; we're trying to find tires or have the English give us another car. . . . Yesterday, we borrowed the Archbishop's car and toured several villages. Crete is in great pain. In one village, we were welcomed only by women, all wearing black, because their husbands had been shot by the Germans. Whole villages burned, in ruins. The people have no fork or glass or piece of clothing or wine; and they weep at not having anything to offer us. One's heart cracks. . . .

They still haven't given us a car. We're suffering. Perhaps tomorrow, we'll go off to Rethymnon. . . .*

Heraklion, July 19, 1945

. . . I'm in Heraklion. The car's broken down; they're repairing it and so today we won't make any tour. . . .

Kastro† unrecognizable. Ruins, old houses, new people. My acquaintances are dead or ruined. I come and go amid bitter recollections, feeling no joy. Very difficult for me to write a book about Crete, because I am suffocating. I saw Lefteris; he's holding out well, the same as ever. You'll be seeing him soon too. I see relatives and feel no joy. This trip has been tragic, extremely heavy. . . .‡

These few lines convey but a thousandth part of what Nikos Kazantzakis had seen in Crete. The full report, written in collaboration with Professors Kakridis and Kalitsounakis, is several pages long. The photographs are hard to bear. Above each door, in the villages visited by

---

* Postcard to E. Samios.
† Kastro ("fortress") is the old Greek name for Heraklion.
‡ Letter to E. Samios.

the Germans, there were one or several black crosses, sometimes four and even more—one for each male executed by the Germans.

"I had five sons," said one woman, no longer of any determinable age. "I have none left."

"Why were they killed?"

"Because I hid some Englishmen."

"And why did you hide them?"

"Because I was thinking of their mothers."

A little farther on, in the place where a village had once stood, there was nothing but ashes, razed by a bulldozer . . . and a wooden cross—"Here lay Kandanos, razed to the ground to serve as an example."

How many Kandanoses had Crete known? And why did the English try to keep their friends from reporting the true situation? For they did everything to hinder them. Cars? There were cars, but they were being horded. In the big cities, the three men were angered and disgusted to observe the arrogance of the Germans and the English, who flaunted polite greetings to one another in the face of the ragged, hungry populace.

The kidnaping of a German officer, General Kreipe—conceived and executed by two English agents with the help of a few Cretan Partisans—did not help the Liberation struggle one bit. On the contrary, it merely provided the Germans with an excuse to sack all the villages along the kidnapers' itinerary. Xan Fielding* boasted of it in vain. He may well have been brave (no one would think of contesting that), but he often behaved with the careless air of a spoiled child on the rampage—in a stranger's house!

In company with one of the Partisans who had been involved in this kidnaping, Kazantzakis toured the villages struck by the Nazi fury. In his book, written in 1946 in Cambridge, Nikos describes his trip to Crete, just as he often used to tell me in actual conversation.

. . . *The shadows had begun to grow. Manolios, Kosmas and Noemia had reached the first village. Two or three houses were still standing. From out of the ruins, ragged women emerged. A girl threw us a sprig of basil. "Welcome!" she called.*

"Here's the first village we'd passed," said Manolios. "We have it on our conscience now, God forgive us!" Several days later, the Germans

---

* Xan Fielding, *Hide and Seek: The Story of a Wartime Agent* (London, 1954).

came. They herded the women together and locked them in the church. They herded the men into the threshing mills. "Did the Partisans pass this way with the General?" "They did." "Which way were they going?" "We don't know." "We'll kill you; speak up!" "We don't know." And they chose 40, the finest lads in the village. They took them to the cemetery and lined them up against the wall. . . . A little hunchback, withered and miserable, passed by. He felt ashamed. He called to the Germans: "I'm ashamed to be alive—me the hunchback—and all these gallant lads being killed. Kill me and let one of them go free." The Germans laughed, grabbed the little hunchback, and lined him up against the wall too along with the other forty. . . .

They'd reached the village square. The coffee places all around and the church and the school—ruins. The villagers gathered—all old men. A few women came too. They stood in back. A tall bony old man—the village elder—took off his cap and stepped forward. "We don't have a chair to give you to sit down," said he. "We don't have a glass of water to give you to drink if you're thirsty. We don't have any bread if you're hungry. We don't have anything, anything, anything!"

"We don't even have a man to talk with you," added one old woman. "Here, we're all old men and old women."

"Only these males are left us," said another old woman, pointing to a few babies suckling at their mothers' breasts. "If they die too, the village is finished!"

"Haven't they brought you boards and pieces of iron and bricks so you can rebuild your houses after three whole years now?" asked Kosmas.

The village elder shook his head. "Who's there to bring them to us?" he asked. "Who's there to build? We sleep in the caves in the winter, in the summer, among the ruins of our houses. The devil take it all!"

He turned to Manolios. "May you find the same from God, Kapetan Manolios!"

"I've done my duty to the fatherland," Manolios answered calmly. "That's war for you!"

"May you find the same from God," repeated the village elder.

"War is from God too," said Manolios.

"And the home and children and women are from God too, Manolios. They killed my two sons that day, you know. And they burned my wife that day. Forgive me if I've said more than I should have said. . . ."

430

Now they'd entered a small, fenced-in, desolate field. A few crops had begun turning yellow. Some poppies were still hanging on, wasted, gone to seed. Two or three huts underneath the olive trees; women lighting fires to cook; the air smelling of burning wood. . . . An old woman went past, barefoot, laden with wood.

"A good day to ye, masters," she said, stopping short to gaze ecstatically at the spectacle of two or three human beings going by.

"How are things with you, Kyrà?" asked Kosmas. "Are you getting along well?"

"Do dogs get along well, my child?" she answered. "May God keep from giving a person all that he is able to bear."

"Are you a Cretan?" "Yes." "Then my blessings on you! Beget children. Crete is drained. Make children and keep the Cretans from vanishing from this earth. They too are needed. . . ."

"It's a good thing she didn't throw stones at us," said Manolios. "We got off easy. That's old lady Konstandína by name. Whenever she sees a man, the poor thing goes off her head. She grabs stones and chases after him. She thinks he's a German and wants to kill him."

He took his tobacco pouch from his belt and rolled himself a cigarette.

"She had four sons, poor thing—fine lads, all four of them Partisans. One Holy Saturday, they came down to the village at night and went to their mother to celebrate Easter with her. At daybreak, the Germans swept down, entered the house and seized all four of them. . . . The mother fell at the feet of the German officer. And he just laughed. 'Choose one of the four,' said he, 'and I won't kill him.' The mother looked at all four, trembling. Which one should she choose? 'Mother,' said the three unmarried lads. 'Choose Nikolì; he's the married one. He has a family.' But Nikolì got angry. 'I've begot my children,' he said. 'The seed has not been lost. Let one of you three live; get married and beget children too.' And once again, the other three began quarreling. Each one wanted to save the other one. Till the German got fed up. He grabbed the old woman and threw her into a pit. He raised his arm and gave the command. And all four were shot. The courtyard filled. . . ."

"How can a human being endure so much?" cried Noemia, clapping her palms over her ears to keep from hearing.

"Human beings do endure, Kyrá mou," said Manolios. "They do endure. Iron, stone, diamonds do not endure; human beings do. . . ."

431

They moved on without speaking. . . . They had crossed the field now. The mountain opened before them. They went on.

"There's the village!" said Manolios, stretching out his hand. Kosmas looked, unable to discern a thing. Only stones piled on stones all up the mountainside.

"Where?" he asked. "I can't see."

"There, in front of you; those stones," answered Manolios. "The people will come into sight now. There—the dogs have already caught wind of us."

Two or three dogs had jumped up out of the ruins, barking away, their ribs sticking out from hunger.

It was already dark. "I don't see any light!" said Kosmas.

"Where could they get oil; where could they find kerosene?" answered Manolios. "Here, as soon as the sun sets, the people burrow into the ruins and they eat and sleep without any light—like birds of prey."

Five or six cheerful faces emerged from behind the boulders.

"Welcome!" Voices could be heard. "Welcome! Which way are you going?"

"To old Sourmelina," answered Manolios. "She's going to give us lodging."

"Do you have anything to eat?" a mocking voice asked.

"We do."

"Ah well then, old Sourmelina's going to eat too. Do you have any covers to put over yourselves?"

"We do."

"Well then, old Sourmelina's going to cover herself too!" repeated the voice, and from behind the stones guffaws of laughter could be heard.

"Here, they laugh," said Noemia. "Aren't they in pain? Or perhaps they've overcome their pain?"

"In the beginning, they used to weep," explained Manolios. "Later, they saw that nothing comes of weeping and they let themselves go in laughter. . . ."

When Sophoulis became Prime Minister, he proposed that Kazantzakis work in his Cabinet as Minister without portfolio. At the back of his mind, he wanted to send Nikos to the United States, Mexico and England to plead the cause of Reconstruction. He gave him free rein to choose his own colleagues. Nikos thought immediately of Angelos Sikelianos, the man most capable of galvanizing his audience. Anna would also be involved. To enable me to follow Nikos to the United States and work in the common cause without any unnecessary complications, we decided (after eighteen years of unwedded life) to get married.

On November 11, 1945, the ceremony took place in the church of Ayios Giorghos Karytsis in Athens. The priest officiating was a cousin of Marika. He knew us and abbreviated the ceremony. However, even for atheists like ourselves, he found stirring words to conclude the mystery. The church was like a beehive, fragrant with incense and honey. The saints of Orthodoxy, Anna and Angelos Sikelianos attended, acting as witnesses, along with Soula, our charming little maid from Aegina. Instead of the orange-blossom crown required by the Orthodox rite, Sikelianos set on his friend's head a delicate branch of laurel. I looked amusedly at Nikos and was pleased to sense that he was a little moved.

Once he had become Minister, Nikos began relentless work again.

Athens, November 1945
Tuesday

Beloved Lenotschka!

Impossible to describe how tired I get and how much I suffer. Everyone is pouncing on me to get a position. . . . And I address the President and rush about and struggle. . . . At the same time, I'm collecting material for America—essays, articles, photographs, films of the famine, etc. I leave home at 7:30 A.M. (often without eating anything because Eleni* happens to be late) and I get back at midnight sometimes. All our friends are hanging on me and I'm doing my best. . . .

Thousands of mondains [worldly people] are asking to go. I'm afraid the combination [of people] will be miserable unless the President steps in. I see him often, but only for a few minutes; he keeps promising to grant me an hour. . . .

Many people want to become members of the Academy. . . . They want medals, awards, positions, missions, and they rush about burdening me with their hopes and desires. And I get worn out,

---

* N.K.'s sister.

because, as is my habit, I make their desires my own and when I don't succeed I consider it a personal misfortune.

I have many things to write you, but I'm tired. Angelos . . . is exhausted too. It's a heavy thing to have to live with human beings. . . .*

During the black days of the Civil War, the friendship of the two poets became still firmer. The Sikelianoses lived through a horrendous tragedy: Anna's sister was killed on an Athens street.

Brother Angelos,

Impossible to write about what is happening. I shall come to see you and one of these days we shall talk. I too am living the grief of our race in its entirety. But I am hoping that in a few days the tragedy will come to an end—its first act.

You be well and I shall not fear.†

At a later point when Nikos was working at the Ministry, Sikelianos often used to ask him to intervene to save innocent people from the vendetta ravaging Greece.

Brother Angelos!

I will do all I can. I'll try to see the President and if that's impossible, I'll write him a fervent letter, because I know how unjust and vile calumny is.

We are passing black days. At present, I too am trying all the time to save innocent people, but I don't yet know what results my intervention will have.

May God keep you well. I have you in mind every moment. We must work very hard. The race is in danger.

I kiss your wife's hand.

Always,

N.‡

The beginning of the year 1946, fraught with such bad omens for Greece, did bring us one piece of good news: Rahel was alive! She had

---

* Letter to E. Samios-Kazantzakis.
† Letter to Angelos Sikelianos.
‡ Letter to Angelos Sikelianos.

434

managed to escape the Nazis in France. In spite of living like a hunted animal, she had been able to work, write a fine book and perform the task of rescuing children from criminal hands.

Athens, January 10, 1946

Dear, dearest Rahel,

I've just received your letter and your Dionysos. I read both of them avidly. We are still alive, Rahel. We are still capable of suffering. Gott sei dank! [Thank God!] What I have seen, heard and suffered—I too—these last red and black years is inexpressible. Only action, violent and voracious, can express it.

Dear, dearest Rahel—when I think of you, life appears to me a mystery with great black eyes. Till the very last flash of light in my life, you shall always be with me—an ardent flame, violent and mute. Blessed be the substance that has enveloped and imprisoned this spirit and given it the tangible form called Rahel!

As soon as I get back to my solitude, I'll translate your Dionysos. It moved me very deeply, and I shall try to render it incandescently in the modern Greek language.

Dear, dearest Rahel, I don't know whether this letter will ever reach you. Perhaps my outcry is being cast into the void. That does not matter. Either concretely or mystically, this cry is sure to come to find you. I have wept much for you, Rahel, in the time of the persecution, when you had to shrink like a hunted beast into the little hut.

I kiss your great black eyes, Rahel.

N.

Elsa gave a sign of life only six years later. We had given up hoping. For us, the "silent little woman" had been forever lost in the savage bombings of Düsseldorf or in some Nazi camp. But one day, the good news reached us: She was alive and promised to come and see us some day. From the hospital, Nikos wrote to her at once:

Utrecht [Holland], December 2, 1952

Dear, dear, dear Elsa,

Why have you left me in despair all these long, black years? I was no longer able to think of you; the grief was unbearable.

Fortunately, you are still on this earth—you and your husband and Dorothea! I too am still here. And I work and feel absolutely young, and every morning the universe renews itself before my insatiable, black eyes! And Eleni is there, still by my side, good and true. Much, much suffering; but it is all over and the heart remains immortal.

Today, I can't write you any more. The joy is too great. Dear, dear, dear Elsa. Welcome!

Nikos

If left to his own devices, Nikos would have refused to see any woman he had once loved. Giving way to friendly pressures, he did his utmost to keep from marring in himself the original image.

In Paris, Rahel had been saved by her laugh. In Madame Puaux's huge drawing room, a dynamic Rahel, round as a cannonball, exploded with laughter, telling anecdote after anecdote from her recent life—the Jewish street tramps, who rebelled against being offered food in a beggar's bowl; the young boys who set up a tribunal to judge one of their own people—we might as well have wept. But we laughed. Rahel's eyes flashed, casting a bridge over the abyss.

With Elsa, it was absolutely different: when she arrived in Antibes with her husband and her daughter, "Gift-of-the-Gods," she could barely see Nikos. For as the devil would have it, just exactly at the time of her stay Nikos' lip was once again deformed by allergy.

And then the "silent little woman," as slender as in the past, sat down in the Voltaire armchair. And her host shrank back as far as possible into a corner of his couch, in the dark, and began asking questions, waiting for the answers. Almost nothing could be discerned. The two voices advanced in hurried flashes, searching for some great change, some precious, lowliest detail—for such a long time counted on, from such a long way away desired.

The hours passed. The mysterious antennae of the blind were at work. The heart became fortified. No regret prevented the building of a future full of promise.

There are some years which are like torpedoes touching the frail vessels of human beings. A skillful stroke of the steering wheel might have saved the ship. But the Captain, unaware or greedy, rather brings the shipwreck down upon himself, asking for his own destruction, blinded by the shiny reflection of some short-term gain.

436

1946 had taken the form of just such a torpedo. It was invisible to the great mass of the people; only the leaders could see it coming. Some of the leaders were powerless and cowardly; the others organized for the looting that comes after the sinking of the ship.

Kazantzakis observed and rebelled against the powerlessness of himself and his Socialist friends, whose honorary president he was. Decidedly, there was nothing of the political man about him. But why, then, didn't he set himself up as a leader of the spirit?

Because inside himself he had not found the new myth he had been seeking for so many years. He did not know what to suggest to this people whom he loved and who were once again about to be shamelessly exploited by a corrupt, rapacious class. Was he entitled to reveal the result of his own ascetic practice? "He who leaps into the fire has only his own cry for a shelter."* Or (as he had commented in his notebooks on Saint Francis) should he propagate an ideal that is always far superior to man's potentialities and so arouse the mystical force, the painful, fertile tension of the spirit striving toward the impossible. Kazantzakis was genuinely strong only in the presence of his own God. He was also strong in the face of Death, because for his own self he hoped for nothing and feared for nothing. On the other hand, for his race he did hope for a great deal. And perhaps this was the hidden cause of his powerlessness. He was hesitant to lead his race to its own death, in the hope of some future resurrection.

Feeling that he was useless, he had been thinking of resigning. An English general with a blow of his whip on the table furnished him the occasion sooner than he had expected. The Sophoulis Cabinet, with all members present, had convened to pass a law about the most capable officers—the Venizelists—who had been removed from the army during the years of the dictatorship and the foreign occupation. The forty Greek Ministers were unanimously agreed. The English general, Scobee, was not, and he imposed his veto.

On March 25—the occasion of our national holiday—the National Theater performed *Kapodistrias*. Many people in the auditorium wept. The Director of the Theater was a man of letters, Giorghos Theotokas.

But as was so often the case with us, this joy too was spoiled this time by a campaign waged by Sikelianos' friends against Nikos. . . . Nikos Kazantzakis' friends had insisted that he too should become a

---

* René Char.

candidate for the Nobel Prize. But in this case as well, Kazantzakis was an exception to the rule. As President of the Greek Society of Men of Letters, several weeks previously, he had applauded this Society's decision to propose Sikelianos for the Nobel Prize. And so he didn't wish to undertake anything that might jeopardize his friend's success. To study the question thoroughly, he asked Tea Anemoyanni to procure for him the statutes of the Swedish Academy concerning the Nobel Prize. Greek literature was not well known abroad. Other countries had far more chance of succeeding. If the two names were united, Kazantzakis thought, Greece would perhaps have more chance of obtaining the prize. But before doing anything at all, he went to ask the opinion of Sikelianos himself. And the latter seemed extremely enthusiastic. "I shall set the crown upon your head with my own hands," he said, laughing, "and you shall crown me in turn!" Kazantzakis was happy. This was how brothers in arms should advance in life! A fine example for future generations.

And so the Society of Men of Letters got ready to propose Kazantzakis' candidacy for the Nobel Prize. The latter, however, demanded that an explicit condition be attached: "That Kazantzakis would accept the prize if and only if it was shared between himself and the great poet, Angelos Sikelianos."

His conscience at ease, he was about to set off for London, where he sang the praises of Sikelianos on the B.B.C. in words all the more enthusiastic because he believed in Sikelianos' greatness. But the "friends" of his friend (probably without the latter's knowledge) began a campaign of slander against Kazantzakis, a campaign rekindled even after the death of both great poets.

Before setting off for England,* Nikos went back to his "paradise," Aegina, to meditate on what he had seen and learned during his stay in Athens. Political men are limited and cynical, rarely thinking of humanity, occasionally of their own respective countries, never of the weaker man's right. They would therefore be incapable of rallying new forces to construct a new world that might give fresh content to the badly worn-out words *liberty, equality, fraternity.* Perhaps this task would be up to the intellectuals of the entire world. As far as the petty cares of everyday life were concerned—such as the withdrawal of *Kapodistrias* from the stage at the very moment when it was beginning to play to a full house—Nikos responded with his usual indifference.

---

* As a guest of the British Council.

. . . Don't worry about a thing. Kapodistrias' turn will come soon, and our turn too. So long as we are well and our hearts are always pure and upright and our love does not crumble—all the rest is smoke and air.

Here, I am at peace. I see no one and haven't gone out of the house. I'm working on Constantine Palaeologos; I've begun it over and over again. It's very difficult, but it will turn out well—don't worry. . . .*

The British Council suddenly informed Kazantzakis that he must leave with twenty-four hours' notice. And he refused.

Aegina, May 1946
Sunday

. . . I prefer to lose England rather than leave in such a state, like a madman. I'm not at all sorry. I was only sorry for fear you might be sorry. . . . If they let me leave in mid-June with Prevelakis, perhaps my stay in London may have some practical result. . . .†

But on June 2 he did leave, for good:

June 9, 1946
London Hotel, St. James's Court,
Buckingham Gate, Minster House

. . . I arrived last night. It was raining, no one at the station; millions of visitors in London for the holidays. Impossible to find a hotel. I was carrying my luggage in the dark, cursing the hour I left Aegina. Finally I approached a policeman and explained my situation to him. He took me with him and the telephone calls began. He was drunk but dignified. His hand trembled, and he made mistakes with the numbers. Then we went to the Post Office and found a high-level employee. But he was drunk too, because today was the great victory celebration. He pounded on the telephones and kept changing them, cursing away because he was sure they were to blame. Then other people came along in a less "high" state, and finally we managed to get in touch with the British Council. . . .

Regal apartment, 5 rooms to myself. . . . A marvel of luxury, silk

---

* Letter to E. Samios-Kazantzakis.
† Letter to E. Samios-Kazantzakis.

everywhere, gold, extremely lavish sets; this morning, two breackfast [sic!] in my room, etc. But no exhilaration. I went out into the streets and wandered about for hours. Today, it's Sunday and everything's closed. I didn't find anyone . . . I got The Times, spread it out on my knees and recalled the days we spent in Stratford by the fireside. The weather dark, cold, gloomy. I'm impatient to see whether at long last I shall feel any joy. From human beings I expect nothing to be said capable of making my heart bound.

This afternoon, I went out for a walk. It was sprinkling. Crowds in the streets, military tunes and flags and medals (the Victory celebration is still on), pretty flowers (mainly begonias on the balconies). I went to the National Gallery and felt happy to be seeing well-loved paintings again. But these joys are no longer enough, and I came back to my most luxurious appartement full of sadness. At noon, they brought me various foods on a huge silver tray. They're about to do the same now; and I'm thinking to myself how delightful it would be if you were here with me and we were sharing all this vain luxury. Then it would acquire a purpose and a delicious relish. I'm thinking of writing a book, Postwar Conversations. . . . From Tuesday on, I'll begin making contacts. . . .

Today, Monday, sky bedeckt; no pleasant perspective. We shall see.

At eleven o'clock a lady came from the British Council . . . and we set off to collect a Chinaman, a Chilean and a Belgian, guests, and another Englishwoman from the British Council. We went far out into the countryside to a medieval inn, drank cider and departed. Cheerful, superficial company—no elation. Only the English countryside was damp, tender, utterly feminine. It was raining softly, the air dim, smelling of a freshly opened grave. Once again I recalled Eleni S.* and my heart felt cramped.

Tomorrow, Tuesday, I shall begin work. . . . Perhaps I'll exorcise the boredom. And when will I have a letter from you? . . . Perhaps then England would seem less morne [mournful] to me. . . .

Evening has fallen now. I've come back to my appartement and lit the chandeliers. They've come and drawn the drapes for me and I'm writing to you. Where can you be? How must you be? Have you gone back to Aegina? Courage, beloved Mitkämpferin [Comrade-in-Arms].

---

* A beautiful and intelligent young woman who had died suddenly in Greece.

As long as we are together, the world is bearable and often marvelous. A thousand times I would have died if you had not been there, because I am weary of human beings. . . .*

London, June 13, 1946
. . . In a few days I'm going to talk on the B.B.C. Here the English are taking very good care of me. They escort me to and fro by car and send me theater tickets. Tonight, I'm going to see one of Wilde's plays; tomorrow, some Javanese dances; on Monday, an English ballet. . . . I'll also be seeing Morgan and I'll tell him about your translation.† I'll see them all and sate my curiosity at last, and I'll have lots to tell you when we meet. . . .

I won't leave here without getting you everything you need. A dreadful lack of butter, bacon, sugar. Even the bread they hand out with [ration] points. The English red cheeks are turning pink; and perhaps later on they'll turn white. . . .

L. comes by every day, very devoted. She's brought me sugar, butter, soap, bread. . . . She's extremely unhappy; she'll return to Greece. . . .

. Midnight. I've just come back from a party at the home of Salisbury [a very high official in the British Council], where I met Rosa's famous friend—Doña Victoria from Argentina.‡ We talked at length about past stories. Beautiful, rich, putting on a pose when you first meet her, clever. . . . I've written the questions I'm going to submit to the English intellectuals. . . .

June 14 . . . It's raining again. Muddy sky, one feels suffocated. . . . This afternoon, I'm going to the Javanese dances. . . .

Evening. Very beautiful the Javanese dances. Not overwhelming; just beautiful, full of grace, silence and self-control. . . . It's raining again and cold. . . . I've decided to make an appeal for an Internationale de l'Esprit. Perhaps this might justify my coming here. . . .§

On June 14, 1946, he also wrote to Tea Anemoyanni:

---

* Letter to E. Samios-Kazantzakis.
† I was in the process of translating into Greek Charles Morgan's The Fountain.
‡ Directress of the periodical Sur, in Argentina.
§ Letter to E. Samios-Kazantzakis.

. . . So far, London has given me no joy. . . . Only a few grand spectacles—Africa, the rivers, the ants in the jungles, the flocks, the fish in Iceland, Benares, Baghdad—could still give me joy. But Frankland* can no longer trick my heart. . . .

Every instant, I think of you with emotion and indissoluble love. How can I ever forget your loving, brave, faithful stand at my right-hand side, where you fight with invisible helmet and double spear, like Athena Promachos† descending in the Homeric verses to take her stand all of a sudden alongside the endangered hero. And the hero becomes aware of her presence from the bounding of his heart, which is no longer afraid of decay or death. . . .

Here the intellectuels can offer nothing to any person who has felt pain or who has thought and struggled a great deal. They seem extremely naïve, placid and happy even in their fits of despair. Their eyes, their mouths, their hearts have not caught fire. And if they have caught fire, they burn gently, always with the simple-minded certainty of compensation. . . .

The idea that had been maturing in his head for some time was given life shortly afterward. The periodical *Life and Letters*, in its September issue,‡ published the questionnaire which Nikos Kazantzakis had intended for British writers and men of science, preceded by the appeal he had made on the B.B.C. on July 18, 1946:

The immortal free human spirit.

This cry is addressed to pure and honorable men throughout the world. For at present, Humanity is undergoing a critical moment, and nowadays the world constitutes so unified an organism that one nation cannot be saved unless all are saved. And if one people is lost, it may well drag all the others to their destruction. The time is forever gone when one people could isolate itself and be saved or destroyed by itself alone. That is why, when you speak to people of your own race today, you have the sense of addressing all human races together. I want to express the anxiety and hopes of a man of the spirit born in Greece, who,

---

* Kazantzakis' word for Western Europe.
† Epithet of Athena in battle.
‡ Volume No. 109.

because of being Greek, feels all the more responsible vis-à-vis the whole world.

We are all vaguely aware that some great danger is threatening contemporary civilization. Let us look this danger straight in the eyes, without fear. This is the only way for us to conquer it. The most awesome enemies of the forces of evil are courage and light.

What, then, is the great danger threatening our postwar world? The following: The mind of man has developed far more quickly and intensely than his soul. The mind has acquired cosmic forces and has put them at the disposal of modern man, who has not yet attained sufficient moral maturity to use these forces only for the peace and prosperity of the world. There is a lack of balance, a disharmony between the intellectual and the moral development of man. And this, it seems to me, is the great danger. At other periods in the Orient, the opposite was true: The soul had progressed, but the investigating mind—Science—had been left behind. A dangerous lack of harmony, and it was heavily paid for by the peoples of the Orient, who were morally superior but backward as far as power was concerned. The barbarians descended and exterminated them. Nowadays in Europe, the opposite is happening.

However, in order for a civilization to remain standing at a high level, it must succeed in attaining a harmony of mind and soul. This synthesis must be set as the supreme aim of our contemporary human struggle. A difficult feat, but we shall achieve it. It suffices that we know clearly what we want and where we are going.

But until we do achieve this, it is natural that anarchy and chaos intervene for some time. Moral and spiritual chaos. Whoever comes into contact with the representatives of the spirit in the world today finds in them too the fatal consequences of the war, the misery and hunger: weariness, anxiety, uncertainty. And, above all, lack of a steady, universally recognized moral principle on which to base the internal reconstruction of postwar man. For we must not deceive ourselves: The genuine reconstruction is not to rebuild the houses, factories, ships, schools and churches devastated by the war. The genuine, the only certain, reconstruction is the internal reconstruction of man. Only on psychological foundations can a civilization be solidified. The economic and political life are always regulated by the progress of man's soul. How can this internal reconstruction of man come about in the midst of so much weariness, anxiety, uncertainty? Only one way exists: to rally all the powers of light that exist within every man and every people. The

443

renowned Abbot Mugnier told me that he had once asked his friend, the great philosopher Bergson, how he would concentrate his entire philosophy into a single word. Bergson reflected for a moment. "Mobilization!" he declared. At every critical moment, we must mobilize all our moral resources.

At the present critical moment, there is no other salvation. We must mobilize all our resources and fight against deceit, hatred, poverty, injustice. We must bring Virtue back to this world.

Who are the human beings who will advance the moral resources of the universe? We cannot hope that this rallying cry—the most vital one of all—will come from temporal leaders—politicians, technical experts, economists. Only the spiritual chieftains of the world can and must accomplish this noble mission that is beyond all personal passions. In our own day, the responsibility of the man of the spirit is enormous, because passions are blind. Desires clash. The material forces placed in man's hands by the mind are tremendous. And the way they are used will determine the salvation or destruction of the human race. Let all of us who believe in the spirit unite. Let us clearly face the dangerous moment we are passing. And let us see what is the duty of the man of the spirit today. Beauty is no longer enough. Theoretical truth is not enough; nor is passive kindness. Nowadays, the duty of the man of the spirit is greater and more difficult. In the midst of the postwar chaos, he must forge a path and create order, discover and formulate the new international slogan that will give unity—i.e., harmony—to the human mind and heart. He must find the simple word that will once again reveal to human beings this simplest of facts: that we are all brothers.

As in all creative periods, the poet is again becoming identified with the prophet. Let us have confidence in the spirit. At the most difficult hours when the fate of the world is at stake, it is the spirit that assumes responsibility. Of a surety, a great Idea is being born at present in the ensanguined vitals of the earth. And that is why it is so painful and why the forces of evil have been unleashed so furiously these past years, striving once more to stifle the newborn babe.

Precisely for this reason, the forces of good must be organized and the people who serve the spirit must acknowledge each other without egoism. They must ask themselves the anguishing questions of our era and they must try to provide answers for them. Their work must no longer be done individually, within each isolated nation. Today it is urgent and necessary not only to work but to work in unison.

444

Therefore, I address this appeal to all intellectuals of good faith throughout the whole world. And I ask the following questions, confident that the answers will facilitate a broad international cooperation of the spirit:

1. *Do you believe we are living at the end of an historical epoch or at the beginning of a new one? And in either case, what do you think are the characteristic traits?*
2. *Can literature, art or theoretical thought influence the present movement of history? Or do they merely mirror existing conditions?*
3. *If you believe that thought and art do influence reality, in what direction do you think they should lead the development of the spirit in your own country?*
4. *What do you think is the positive contribution that British thought and art can offer the world?*
5. *What is the level of contact between the British intellectuals and the large mass of the people? And what could be done to broaden this basis of contact?*
6. *What is the foremost duty of the intellectual and the artist today? How can they contribute to the peaceful cooperation of all peoples?*
7. *Would it be practical to establish an "International of the Spirit"? And if it is practical, are you willing to collaborate in it?*

The B.B.C. broadcast this appeal and questionnaire in mid-July. One month earlier, Kazantzakis had already foreseen that his efforts would bear no fruit. And nostalgia for the earth overcame him.

London, St. James's Court,
June 20, 1946

. . . The rain, mud, cold indescribably miserable. And I keep thinking of Aegina. The grapes will be turning shiny; the figs will be swelling; the sea will be refreshing, transparent—not like this Thames. I no longer like Europe at all. Paris will be good, because we shall be together.

June 25. Yesterday evening, I went to a poetic evening, where three Harpylike magpies with huge jawbones made in England shook themselves from their lethargy and began reciting verses with pathos. And then they fell back into their lethargy. I believe there is nothing more ridiculous than mediocre poetry. . . .*

After the grayness and hubbub of London, Nikos reveled in the green serenity of Cambridge. On Aegina, I was still hoping for some miracle—for example, a chair of modern Greek literature at Oxford or Cambridge—to take us far away from Aegina. I considered that absolutely necessary.

> Cambridge, June 23, 1946
> Garden House Hotel
> . . . Ineffable tranquility, peace, greenness. I wish we could spend two years here to recover from the nervousness, haste, vagueness and misery of Athens. The hotel where I am staying is on the riverbank, and punts with young men and girls are constantly passing, noiselessly, mutely gliding by. . . . Heavenly streets; tall, tall trees; and the great charm of England—the green grass enveloping the old colleges and cathédrales.
> I've met several splendid professors.
> June 24. Today, I came back to London. I'll stay here a week and then go back to Oxford and Stratford. About the end of July, it seems, I'll be with you. . . .†

In his notebooks, Nikos Kazantzakis commented:

> Cambridge, June 21. . . . The earth elastic, damp, feminine. Here the flowers find nourishment; they don't have to struggle heroically as they do in Greece. They have broad petals but lack the Greek fragrance. This afternoon, with the Provost of King's College: Sheppard. An old man full of vigor, humor, strength; slightly theatrical and narcissistic. He talks a great deal, laughs a great deal and insists that the important thing is for a person to become cultivated and not a specialist. He scorns

---

* Letter to E. Samios-Kazantzakis.
† Letter to E. Samios-Kazantzakis.

the intelligentsia, but respects the Servants of Spirit. He considers Trevelyan the finest person in the world. Sheppard: brightheartened [sic!] lion.

June 22. Sun, greenness, a stroll among the colleges; what a miracle the grass—placid, at rest, like paradise among the old Gothic colleges. At noon, I saw the Master of the Trinity, the celebrated historian Trevelyan. A splendid human being, the opposite of Sheppard—austere, ascetic, taciturn, laughterless. As soon as I showed him the questions and he had seen the first one, he sprang up in anger. "I will not answer!" he said. "These aren't questions! What do you want me to say? That the world is absurd. I cannot!" He crumpled the paper furiously and handed it back to me. Then he got up politely and showed me around the college; the room where . . . Newton had lived and worked, his books in the library, and then the room of Byron.

June 23. This afternoon, tea at Professor Lucas' in King's College. Charming, clever, full of laughter, daring, a genuine human being, as Provost Sheppard would say. We talked about Greece. He has toured the Peloponnesus on foot. . . . He said to me: "Je ne lis plus; je relis [I no longer read; I reread]. He scorns his contemporaries, has no feeling for the moderns and scoffs at them. . . .

And "in order not to forget," he set down a comment a little further on:

Remember (just before I found the professor's house) the girl with the sensuous red lips and big blue eyes. I told her as much.* We parted with a shake hand [sic!] like old friends—she to the left and I to the right, through the green English grass.

In telegraphic style, further on, Kazantzakis mentioned his meetings with David Garnett—"Charming, civilized, sympathetic old man"—who did answer his questions. With Laurie Lee, in the course of a dinner in a Cypriot restaurant in Chelsea—"Full of high spirits and

---

* N.K. had most likely complimented the young girl on her beautiful red lips.

poetic power; very left-wing; he sings Flamenco and knows Spain. I felt exhilarated . . ." With John Lehman—"Very pleasant, handsome in stature, intelligent, able. We talked about Kapetanákis.* Next year, he will go to Greece. . . ."

Lunch with Stephen Spender: Young, large, intelligent, speaks French. We spoke much and well. . . . At Dawkins' home. What vitality! He climbed the steps two at a time. He told me about the father of Hadzidákis at Myrtò—102 years old—flanked by his ox and his donkey, chattering away in his courtyard with an octogenarian he had rocked in his arms as a baby [at the time of his marriage]! A blind old priest had come to visit him, accompanied by his deacon, who wove baskets. "What are you doing there, deacon?" the old man had asked. "I'm weaving baskets." "It's better to weave baskets than scandals!" Dawkins showed me several books and we had dinner together that evening. . . .

Yesterday, I saw John Masefield, a magnificent scholar and a pleasant person. We discussed English poetry. He said that Swinburne used to write such perfect verses that afterward he had to make an effort to achieve some imperfection—to keep them from being monotonous. . . .

I went to Wadham College, to the home of Bowra, the poetry professor. A baronial house, lawn, Chinese statues (Bowra was born in China) . . . vigorous, intelligent . . . cultivated spirit. He understands poetry, hates Morgan. We read some verses. He considers Lewis and Edith Sitwell the best poets.

Dinner at Mortimer's. I was sad and talked brusquely about what the English are doing in Greece. Such an intelligent man and he hasn't understood a thing! I told him how anti-British England's policy in Greece is. . . .

I had lunch with the art critic Ironside. He speaks French superbly, is intelligent and refined and knows art perfectly—painting, sculpture. We talked extensively and I'll go to the Tate Gallery again to see him. . . . Lunch with Rosamond Lehmann and C. Day Lewis. Rosamond beautiful, charming, gray hair, pink complexion, exquisite mouth and eyes, a perfect Louis XV Marquise. Intelligent, kind. . . . Lewis a dry body, long withered face, the best young poet today. We spoke at length and well. . . .

---

* Kapetanákis was a young Greek poet who died in England.

At the home of Salisbury (Director of the "Visitor's" Department of the British Council), Doña Victoria de Campo had told an anecdote about Saint Teresa of Ávila that made a great impression on Kazantzakis:

"One day, Saint Teresa was eating some partridge with relish. A nun kept casting reproving glances at her. And Saint Teresa had retorted then: '*Cuando penitencia, penitencia; cuando perdices, perdices!* [Penance when it's time for penance; partridge when it's time for partridge!]' " And Kazantzakis added in his notebook the words of Montaigne: " 'When I dance, I dance; when I sleep, I sleep.' "

When he got back to London, he thought of Tea Anemoyanni and wrote to her on June 25, 1946:

. . . *I just got back from Cambridge yesterday. I met three splendid scholars there.* And at long last there was some sun and for the first time in England I felt joy. . . . I am seeing many erudite people, poets and scholars, and am waiting for our friend, Charles Morgan,† to get back from Switzerland. I'll go to see him at once. I'm also waiting for Eliot from America. I'm sending you the questionnaire I am going to submit to them. And I think very few of them will answer me. They find it difficult and "bold." I don't believe that thought here has reached the high point we would wish, and it will be of very little benefit to us. Our own anxiety is of another quality—another impulse— and our own spirits are far more insatiable, far closer to the abyss than the English. Here one finds a certain weariness and much control— control that is not the outcome of some great force controlling itself but of weakness that is easily controlled. Here they have no grand abominable demons to bridle, and it is easy for them to keep their peace. Every single thing that touches the abyss disturbs them. And they would like everything to preserve the serene façade of a civilization that is afraid to kindle under the crystallized crust of custom the flame that explodes and longs to shatter the crust and burn the world. They hope that everything will settle itself, that the present anxiety will become increasingly distilled until it too becomes a crust, covering with a still thicker, surer stratum the flame raging fierce in the vitals of man.*

---

* The Provost of King's College, Sheppard; the historian Trevelyan; and Myres, old and feeble, struggling to decipher the Mycenaean script.
† Our "friend," because we liked his books so much.

You understand how contrary all this is to my own nature and how I suffocate when I converse with the intellectuals here. . . .

I'm hoping that soon some of my writings will be published in certain English periodicals—though my way of thinking and writing discombobulates them—just as they would be upset by a bull all of a sudden barging into a staid, respectable English club. . . .

And from Oxford on July 4, he wrote to Tea again:

. . . Their scholars are very interesting: archaeologists, linguists, physicists, mathematicians; very eminent in their own special fields. I saw old Myres—crippled, tottering about on two crutches, an old man 80 years old, who can no longer talk clearly and who is striving day and night to read the Minoan script. He showed me his manuscripts. What a vast, difficult, complicated work! He has collected all the alphabets of that era. What combinations he has conjured up, what hopes; and when I expressed the wish that God help him and give him time to discover the key, he banged his crutch. "I shan't die! I shall find it!"

That same day, Nikos wrote to me.

. . . I was at Stratford yesterday and attended the performance of Macbeth. Unworthy, academic, pompier [bombastic]. But I was delighted to revisit the places we used to love. Everything the same—river, swans, roses in bloom, old houses with Dickensian old men coming out of them and even the wooden plate we used to like. . . . Our house* shut, smothered in ivy; a cat sunning itself outside. I passed by three times, walking very slowly. . . .

July 5. Yesterday, I went by the renowned Oxford Press and proposed that they publish the Iliad, text and translation. They gave me hopes. . . . If I do succeed, it's vital, because thereafter the publication assumes world-wide significance. When I get back to London day after tomorrow, I'll make efforts to find a publisher for the Spiritual Exercises. I saw Waterlow's daughter and she promised me a translation of the Spiritual Exercises. . . .

---

* The house of Shakespeare's daughter Susan, where we stayed in 1939.

The turn of the English intellectuals and scholars soon came to an end. Kazantzakis now returned to London to take leave of his sumptuous apartment in St. James's Court. He asked the British Council to help him find a tranquil refuge, where he could concentrate and write [he was dreaming of a novel] his recent postwar experiences.

We had not yet received from the French government the invitation promised us by the Director of the French Institute in Athens; and I was worried. Too long-drawn-out a solitude seemed to me a double-edged weapon. Even for a man like Kazantzakis, I would have wanted some university town where, in the evenings by the fireside, we could be present at enriching conversations. If we could not become acquainted with distant lands, we might at least try to become acquainted with unfamiliar, distant spirits. And these journeys could bring us as many riches as the other kind. . . . Nikos wanted very much to please me, but he was incapable of demanding anything for himself.

London, July 8, 1946
St. James's Court

. . . . If the opportunity does present itself, I shall stay and try to have you come too. . . . I wrote to [Bertrand] Russell, and his wife answered me that in a few days he'll be back from Belgium and we'll meet. . . .*

Write me at regular intervals; it's a great consolation. . . . Your letters give me a bitter sense and strength, taking me far from wintry Aegina. . . .†

Cambridge, July 30, 1946
c.o. Mrs. Laurie, Castle Bray, Chesterton Lane

. . . Since I didn't want to stay at a hotel, the British Council managed to find me two rooms in an amazing house on a peaceful lane all green with gardens. The house is full of staircases and rooms and strange young and old people and old-lady tenants. My study's on the first floor. . . . The bedroom on the third floor; it's small and inconvenient too. Gone are the grandeurs of St. James's Court! It's impossible for me to find my way from one room to the next, and I keep asking

---

* N.K. wanted to speak to Russell about the projected Internationale de l'Esprit.
† Letter to E. Samios-Kazantzakis.

451

certain suspicious-looking shadows circulating through the corridors, and they answer me extremely politely. The bathroom's on another floor— also impossible for me to find, because I have to make my way through mirrors and old furniture and climb up and down staircases and there isn't any "scent" to lead the way. And Mrs. Laurie herself is an old woman right out of the depths of Dostoyevski—thin, with boned collars around her neck and smelling of wine or beer (I haven't been able to make out which yet). And two of the ground-floor rooms have big capital Greek letters over the lintel. The one inscription says: Haire Hutra!* (That's the kitchen.) The other: Haire i Filia.† (I haven't ventured to go in and see what that one is.) . . . Yesterday evening I went to the theater and saw Sartre's work: Huis Clos. . . .‡

A brief description follows of Sartre's play, though Kazantzakis does not even for a moment recall that he himself had also published a No Exit in 1909. . . . The letter continues:

. . . I'm trying to rally my forces here to keep from being panic-struck. For I must stay here . . . and write the book. If it weren't for my pipe, I'd burst out crying. Because I keep thinking of Aegina, the ripened figs, the grapes grown all shiny, and a woman whom I love as I love no one else in this world—who's sitting in the courtyard, watching the sea, waiting for a letter. . . .

I've got the plan of the book. It will be a novel, because the intellectuals here haven't given me any material. Three parts: Crete, England, Solitude. And I myself will answer the questions I asked. I don't know whether here in this house I will find the climate I want. Fortunately, the little window of my study looks out on a beautiful garden—and there's an enormous apple tree in front of me.

It's rainy and cold. Evening has fallen and the sky is all clouds. They've brought me my food . . . a piece of salted meat, raw cabbage and stewed plums. Maigre [meager], but I wasn't hungry. . . .

On Saturday, I'll have to go up to London for a day. The Minister Noel-Baker has invited me to have dinner and tell him my opinion on

---

* Haire Hutra, "Hail Saucepan."
† Haire i Filia, "Hail Friendship."
‡ Huis Clos, translated as No Exit.

Greece. I know my opinion won't influence them at all. Nevertheless, I shall express it and, as is my habit at critical moments, abruptly and without mincing words. . . .*

Cambridge, August 19, 1946

. . . The days go by, all the same, and all of them together are like one single day: I wake up in the morning at 5:30 A.M. and go down to the study—a table full of books and manuscripts, a Louis XV sofa, an old . . . radio! And two chairs. . . .

By now I'm two thirds of the way through. By the end of August, I'll have finished. In the third part, I'll include the whole of the Spiritual Exercises. . . .

Let's wait to see what will happen with the plebiscite. I'm very upset and in great pain for Greece. . . .

I've written to Russell again. He was away in Belgium. One of these days I'll have an answer. Everyone here loathes Morgan, as a Narcissus, fatuous and insipid. When he comes to Greece, he'll be sure to come to Aegina. I've promised him a box of halva, which he's mad about. . . .†

Cambridge, August 29, 1946

. . . I'm very worried about the plebiscite. What's going to happen afterward? Where are we going? From here, I see only darkness. But let's not talk politics. It's alarming! . . .

Today's newspapers mention the death of Kaphandaris.‡ I was sorry, because he was an honest, gallant man. . . .§

The plebiscite turned out to be a huge farce. The British Council gentlemen were peeved to learn that their guest had cabled his vote in support of the Republic. "You promised us not to get involved in politics during your stay in England," they muttered between their teeth. And Kazantzakis was forced to explain to them that he had not

---

* Letter to E. Samios-Kazantzakis.
† Letter to E. Samios-Kazantzakis.
‡ Giorghos Kaphandaris, a liberal Greek politician.
§ Letter to E. Samios-Kazantzakis.

given up his civil rights when he accepted their amiable invitation. "To take part in a plebiscite on which the future of one's country depends," he answered, "is, it seems to me, the foremost duty of any responsible person!"

His discussion with Noel-Baker had left him without the slightest illusion about British policy in Greece. With a heavy heart, he was preparing to leave England. And just at that point, the invitation from the French government arrived. Octave Merlier* had kept his word. However, the amount offered for visiting France was so infinitesimal that we no longer knew whether it was worth my coming to join Nikos in Paris. And Nikos left the choice up to me. Neither he nor I could have imagined that he would never see Greece again—and that France was to become our adopted country.

Cambridge, September 12, 1946

. . . Whatever you decide is what I want too . . . The international situation is very agonizing for me. . . . There are many alarming symptoms visible here, though invisible in Greece. . . . Greece alarms me and I can no longer be at peace. There can be no solution now. I have done my utmost. I have spoken wherever it was possible. Greece is but a detail for them, a cog in their enormous international machine, which they will use (even if it is destroyed) for their own temporary, terrifyingly urgent needs. The two big blocks are now standing opposite each other, menacingly, Greece in between them like a grain of wheat between two millstones. Let's hope that once again some miracle will save Greece now. . . .

I also wrote to Herbert, about whether he can find a position in some university. We shall see. Something may turn up. At the most critical moments of our life, the miracle comes. We shall not be lost. . . . As soon as I reach Paris, I'll write to you.†

In his letter of July 30, 1946, Nikos had not hidden his turmoil. He believed he was obligated to write a book on postwar England. But his mind, riveted on Greece, refused to get drunk with creation. His book, written without joy, was condemned by himself to the asphyxiation of the poet's drawer.

---

* Merlier was the Director of the French Institute in Athens.
† Letter to E. Samios-Kazantzakis.

Before leaving Cambridge, Kazantzakis wrote to his new Nordic friend, Börje Knös,* who, like himself, was enamored of freedom and justice:

Cambridge, September 17, 1946

Dear Mr. Knös,

. . . I am increasingly alarmed about the moral crisis our era is undergoing. . . . The book I have just finished . . . treats this alarming situation in the form of a novel. . . . With genuine anguish, I sense that human destiny is passing a critical moment. It is as though the gorilla—before becoming a human being—has gone and invented fire. . . .

The day of departure was approaching. In London, Kazantzakis had met a young Cypriot Greek who was studying to become a film and stage director, while also acting in the theater and directing the B.B.C. broadcasts dedicated to Cyprus. He knew who Kazantzakis was and gave him the opportunity to talk on the radio. The first broadcast was the already-mentioned S.O.S. to intellectuals. The second and third were dedicated to Angelos Sikelianos and Bernard Shaw. There were ten programs in all. The little nest egg collected thanks to Michael Cacoyannis made it possible for us to stay in Paris while waiting for the miracle. At the time of the Zorba scenario, I reminded Cacoyannis of his kindness; and his slight smile seemed to conceal a certain feeling. Without his help, perhaps, we could not have settled in France. In this way our fate always was suspended by a thread.

On September 15, 1946, Nikos wrote to Tea Anemoyanni from Cambridge:

. . . What plunder am I taking with me as I leave Cambridge? A book, the vision of the colleges and, above all, the heavenly greenness— the grass in the college courtyards—a miracle so simple and so profound that no word can ever contain it. I've never looked at this grass without wishing that you were with me to see it too. It would give you an

---

* Knös, a Hellenist scholar from Sweden, was to become a close friend during the last years of N.K.'s life, as well as one of his main translators.

extraordinarily sweet, calm, speechless and, at the same time, violent joy—the way you love joys to be. . . . A voracious spirit such as yours must not leave this earth without seizing whatever good there is in the world. One of the most secret reasons I'd like to become rich is so that I could take you (two or three months are enough) and show you the world. . . .

And among Nikos' papers I find a letter written on September 22, 1946, from London, intended for Iannis Kakridis, but never sent:

. . . I have much to tell you that cannot be written. When I think of you, my heart feels a little appeased. The spectacle of human beings has become repulsive to me now.

These past months, a great anguish has overcome me for the fate of humanity as a whole. . . . Yesterday, the Americans proudly announced the discovery of a poison so horrendous that with 9 grams of it they can in one fell swoop kill all the inhabitants of the United States and Canada (i.e., Russia). The gorilla, you see, without taking the time to become a human being, has discovered fire and is going to burn the world. . . .

For more than fifty years now, Nikos Kazantzakis had been in the habit of dedicating his birthday to an examination of conscience, to making a report to his own God on his long solitary march.

On February 18 of this year 1947, he became sixty-four years old. What were the milestones marking this ascent? And who was this man who advanced, never deigning to turn around and look at the abyss, though never forgetting even for a second that this abyss does exist?

A first period of groping—1906–1918—with a few small red flags stuck here and there: a novella and a play published (*The Serpent and the Lily* and *Daybreak*); a tragedy made into an opera (*The Master Builder*); and a one-act play (*Comedy*—the *No Exit* which in 1909 already posed the great question that no man could answer).

A second period—1918–1924—when the poet succeeded in expressing himself with the brilliance and clarity characteristic of him, both in acts and in words: a mission to the Caucasus successfully accomplished; three tragedies of great scope (*Nicephoros Phocas, Odys-*

seus, Christ); and *The Spiritual Exercises*—his own credo concentrated into a few Biblical chapters.

A third period that of *The Odyssey*: fourteen years of a life dedicated to an epic. More than 42,000 verses molded and remolded to the point of perfection. Here, the artisan might have laid down his tools. "*The Odyssey*," he liked to say, "is the *Obra*. All the rest I write in order to amuse myself." In anyone else, this way of amusing oneself would have made one catch one's breath and excite envy. Also from this same period three tragedies and a play; three novels written directly in French; twenty-one cantos, between 150 and 180 verses, each one in *terza rima*, a challenge for modern Greek with its very few rich rhymes; the quintessence of long or very short trips in four volumes; two schoolbooks; one reader. Translation, always from the original and in verse, of Dante's *Divine Comedy*, Goethe's *Faust*, Shakespeare's *Othello*, and most of the modern Spanish poets. Other minor translations such as Cocteau, Pirandello, Hauptmann. More than forty books for children, including most of Jules Verne. Translation of the first half of the *Larousse* dictionary, 40,000 words translated into *demotiki* and *katharévousa*. . . .

If Nikos Kazantzakis had disappeared in 1938 or a bit later—in 1941–1942 during the great Famine—his friends and enemies would have had their consciences at rest, certain that the creator had thoroughly used up his gray matter. But right in the midst of the Famine, to keep death from coming aforetime, Kazantzakis had reacted by writing *The Golden Legend of Alexis Zorba*—to "appease his hunger," as he used to say with a smile—or, as I was going to say, to *rouse* it.

And so the gate was opened to the fourth period of his life—1942–1957—the final period of the greal novels. And as always, "to amuse himself," in one overwhelming surge, the two monumental translations of Homer's *Iliad* and *Odyssey*, the former happily completed in close collaboration with Professor Kakridis.

Along with all this, some timeless essays aimed at taking an active part in the political life of the nation—this beloved nation which ignores so many of the poets and free spirits it has engendered.

And now we found ourselves in Paris—February 18, 1947—celebrating the poet's sixty-fourth birthday. Like a lighthouse beam, Kazantzakis' gaze swept over the past. "No!" he said. "No; it's not enough. I've squandered my powers. I could have done better. Luckily, I still have twenty years to live."

He believed this and was comforted by it. I came to expect these moments of periodic prostration, violent and brief. And I knew that after the despair would come a period of regeneration. A pencil, a piece of virgin paper, time, solitude and laughter with a person he loved. And once again masterpieces would see the light of day, one after the other.

Externally, nothing changed in his youthful air; his gaze, piercing and indulgent at the same time; his mind, open to all the winds. Only the temples, mustache and bristly eyebrows began to be touched with ashes. In the shadows—the deficit left by the great Famine—certain hints of bodily fatigue, normal in any other man.

We were living in the Place de la Madeleine, in the home of Madame Suzanne Puaux, daughter of the composer Alfred Bruneau and widow of the Hellenophile writer and journalist René Puaux. For the first time since his university days, Nikos was comfortably settled in the heart of Paris and this fact alone made Paris enchanting to him.

For some time now, he and Prevelakis had been pondering the problem of the emigrants in the United States. Mainly illiterate villagers driven from home by endemic famine, they were catapulted onto the high tide of superproduction and superconvenience once they reached America. To teach their children the language of their Fathers, to recall their villages or talk about their own origins—what good would it do? They were almost ashamed of them. Their only thought was to gain time and assimilate themselves as quickly as possible to their environment.

Prevelakis and Kazantzakis drew up detailed plans for an Institute of Greek Culture in the United States. The Athens government, always blind wherever the future of the race was at stake, refused to renew Kazantzakis' passport. And Prevelakis, who was about to set off for New York, also became the victim of base intrigues. In this period which witnessed the nascent glory of Kazantzakis abroad, it became dangerous to utter Kazantzakis' name in Greece. Petros Haris, director and editor of the literary periodical *Nea Estia*, was summoned to the Security Office because he had published *Sodom and Gomorrah*,* a biblical tragedy by Kazantzakis. Andreas Karandonis, a literary critic well known for his anti-Communism, was threatened with having his position taken from him (and he did in fact lose ten years' promotion) because he declared on the radio that Nikos Kazantzakis' *Constantine Palaeologos* was a "tragedy worthy of the nation."

Men grow old, change camps, die. Ideas remain. After a twenty-

* The play known in America under the title *Burn Me to Ashes*.

year delay, at the present moment, Greece is clamoring for the foundation of this Institute so ardently dreamed of by the two Cretans.

All the while he went on looking for an emergency exit, Kazantzakis let his "viscera" work in silence. Perhaps, without his knowing it, they had impelled him to turn his back on the *Akritas* and dedicate himself to ripening a new fruit on a more human scale, the *Third Faust*, the novel about a gorilla that thought it was a man. . . . What Valéry had failed to achieve (according to Nikos) Nikos was hoping to carry off successfully. Several pages of his notebooks were already filled with hasty notes.

Paris, October 4, 1946

Dear Mr. Knös,

I find myself in Paris—a City of Light indeed—recalling my days as a young student when, awe-struck, I used to attend the courses of my revered master, Henri Bergson. Here again, I shall continue the endeavor begun in England: To group the "Servants of the Spirit"— writers, artists, scholars—into an "International of the Spirit" (beyond any form of politics) with the sole purpose of saving the imperiled spirit.

The intellectuals understand the danger well, but most of them have become too passive, too skeptical, and they no longer resist, letting themselves be carried away by events. But there are also people who are ready to participate in this supreme crusade. These past days, I had a profound discussion with the distinguished scholar Gaston Dupouis, Dean of the Science Faculty at Toulouse. He has a tragic vision of our era and is ready to react with all his might. Also, the great scholar the Duke de Broglie clearly sees the precipice that is suddenly gaping open in front of humanity. The forces that have been revealed to man, he says, are so terrifying that they might cause the explosion of our planet. . . .

I'm expecting to stay here till the end of November. Then, I think, at long last I shall reenter my solitude on Aegina and resume my own solitary work. I have no time to lose. The "god with the black helmet" is approaching, and I am in haste to save my whole soul, by expressing it and leaving as prey only my inanimate body. . . .*

Paris, October 17, 1946

. . . You are absolutely right: The surest and most practical means

---

* Letter to Börje Knös.

459

of making this "International of the Spirit" a reality is to address ourselves to internationally renowned personalities and to persuade them to sign the appeal.

The English intellectuals are passive, skeptical, worn out by everyday life, extremely hard. In Paris, the intellectuals are more active, more agitated, more penetrated by their responsibility toward the imperiled Spirit. A victory like the one achieved by England is very similar to a defeat, one might say. And a defeat like the one suffered by France briskly rouses the humiliated forces of the race. . . .*

Paris, November 14, 1946

. . . Here too, people are turning more and more skeptical, and confusion reigns everywhere, especially these last days since the elections. Greece, on the other hand, is groaning under the fascist yoke. Whatever is most unimpeachable and most remarkable from the intellectual and moral point of view is violently persecuted. The purest flame in present-day Greece is in jeopardy. How can it be saved? I've elaborated a plan . . . the foundation of an Institute for Modern Greek Culture outside Greece: a hearthplace to safeguard the flame. Not only the political and economic situation but also the intellectual and moral situation in Greece is extremely serious. Every beneficent activity is threatening to become submerged. This Institute would become the battleground for a few exceptionally pure Greeks—writers, artists, scholars—who might kindle on foreign soil the intellectual flame of Greece today. . . .†

---

* Letter to Börje Knös.
† Letter to Börje Knös.

PART FOUR

TOWARD THE HORIZON

1946–1957

1947.   As he had told his friend Börje Knös, Kazantzakis did make several visits to plead on behalf of the "International of the Spirit."And though he was in a very precarious financial condition, he turned down a contract that would have obliged him to write in French.

Paris, January 24, 1947

Dear Mr. Knös,

   . . . *I love the modern Greek language with such a passion that I didn't want to sign a contract for a series of books with a large Paris publishing house, which proposed that I write directly in French five books like my novel Toda Raba. My post is in Greek literature. The evolution of our language is passing a decisive, creative moment and I do not want at any cost to desert my post. The Greek language is as beautiful as Homeric Helen—*Οὐ νέμεδις τοιῇδε γυναικί πολὺν χρόνον ἄλγεα πάσχειν.*

Nikos could now rediscover his old friends: Rahel, Pierre and Mady Sauvageot, Renaud de Jouvenel, Yvonne—one of the two young Frenchwomen Nikos had met during his tour of the Peloponnesus in 1939, now married to J. Pierre Métral—Prevelakis, the Greek painter Hadjikyriakos-Ghika, Manolis Segredakis. . . . There were also new friends who gathered around a cup of cocoa in our hostess' handsome drawing room, where Kazantzakis was entitled to the "poet's armchair."†

---

* Translated roughly, "For such a woman as this, there is no Nemesis in suffering long."
† Mme. Puaux had reserved an armchair for Nikos; no one else was permitted to use it.

Among others, the young French writer Henri Duquaire, the brilliant Madame de Rivals and Segredakis' nephew Nikolas, who soon took his place in the Art Gallery on the Rue de l'Echelle. . . . And from time to time, fleeing the mists of his own country, the distinguished Hellenist, Börje Knös, Secretary of State in Sweden's Ministry of National Education, who was gradually translating the major part of Kazantzakis' novels, thereby introducing them to the Scandinavian world.

While the witch hunt was being conducted in Greece, our friend Jean Herbert was trying to find a lifeboat for Nikos Kazantzakis. Julian Huxley, who was at the time Director General of UNESCO in Paris and a personal friend of Herbert, had offered the latter the position of Director of the Department of Translations of the Classics. Exactly why had Jean Herbert been chosen? Because he had worked with Charles Malik (Ambassador from Lebanon at the time and author of the translation project) in New York, in order to test the plan. And also, most likely, because the work done by Herbert since 1935 (in his collections *Hinduism, Living Spiritual Systems*, etc.) ran parallel to the Malik plan. However, Herbert was unable to accept, because of his UN obligations, and Herbert proposed Nikos Kazantzakis to the UNESCO director, though Nikos was a total stranger to the latter.

Nikos hesitated a great deal at the prospect of becoming a "stuffed shirt." As one last argument, Herbert offered to let his younger daughter, Mme. Yvette Renoux, act as Nikos' secretary. Nikos loved and admired her for her efficiency and sweetness. And on May 1, 1947, he was officially appointed to the post of Director of the Department of Translations of the Classics.

I must not close this chapter on UNESCO without mentioning the efforts of several of our friends—such as Tea Anemoyanni, the Despotopoulos brothers and Prevelakis—to obtain a word in favor of Nikos Kazantzakis from the three Greek political leaders: Sophocles Venizelos, Papandreou, and Kanelopoulos. For, even though the post offered Kazantzakis did not depend on Greece, it was preferable to avoid the hue and cry the Greek government would inevitably raise. The three Greek politicians supported Nikos Kazantzakis. Nevertheless, the Greek Ministry of Foreign Affairs considered itself duty bound to openly admonish the Greek Embassy in Paris for having condoned such a scandal!

In Greece it has also been written that UNESCO served Nikos

Kazantzakis as a kind of springboard for establishing his world-wide reputation. Nothing could be more false. Except for J. J. Mailloux and a charming Spanish scholar long since dead, no one at UNESCO even guessed of the existence of this slender Greek who rolled his r's and, once his work was finished, resigned "so as not to touch money too easily earned."

People are also "amazed" that Kazantzakis, who claimed to be a free being, could have desired the Nobel Prize over a period of several years. And they resented his desiring it not for the glory but for the purpose of being free to travel and touch the great marvels of the earth at close range and lose himself in his own "inner riches" without having to scatter himself in works that only half interested him.

But Kazantzakis was aware of the cross that Greek writers bear, and he never bore them any grudge. To the contrary, he knew that the purer and richer their language was, the harder it was to translate, and whenever I gave free rein to my bitterness, in the face of the malice of certain of his colleagues or the difficulty of making oneself known abroad, he would lay his hand on my shoulder and smile like a good-natured child. "Our country is small, Lenotschka," he would say; "it isn't really known. Put yourself in the place of the people who write— who write well—and have so few chances of seeing their work go beyond the Greek borders. Learn to be kind."

To conclude on a gayer note: Here is what a friend we had never met says with English humor—a young English writer, who is himself well known: Colin Wilson—in his book *The Strength to Dream*, published in London in 1962:

Five of Kazantzakis' major works have been published in translation in this country, and yet his name remains almost totally unknown. This is a curious situation, which may be due in part to the fact that Kazantzakis wrote in Greek and that modern readers do not expect to come upon an important Greek writer. Even his name has a discouraging sound: if he had written in Russian and been called Kazantzovsky, his works would no doubt be as universally known and admired as Sholokhov's. There is something of tragedy in this. Readers who are familiar with his life and works have no doubt that here is a writer who can stand with the nineteenth-century giants, with Tolstoy, Dostoyevsky, Nietzsche (with all of whom he has affinities). Yet he made very little money from his writing, and

465

the Columbia Dictionary of Modern European Literature does not even mention him.

But let us return to the beginning of the year, before the "miracle." On January 19, 1947, Nikos' thoughts turned to Tea, and he wrote to her from Paris:

Dear Comrade,
This life is brief and we have no time to enjoy it as we should and as much as we should. Virtue, composed of terrified little human beings, prevents us. Sin, also composed of terrified little human beings, cannot enchant. And at the very moment we are beginning to create our Decalogue, we die.

Do you remember the dream I had last year at your house, on New Year's Eve? A tree with very straight branches like a fir tree—24 branches. And at the tip of every branch, it was as though a capital letter of the alphabet had blossomed: A, B, C. . . . And above each letter sat a little bird, warbling away with its neck outstretched. And the little birds kept flying from letter to letter, uniting, separating, reuniting, like syllables. . . .

Once in a cemetery in Constantinople I saw a superb, strong laurel springing out of a dervish's tomb, springing right out of his bosom. In the same way, I feel this tree of the 24 branches springing out of my own entrails. And at the very instant I begin to combine the syllables and compose the song, I die. God willing, you shall pass my tomb one day and hear what I am saying.

Beloved Comrade, this letter is growing bitter and I shall stop. Perhaps tomorrow my soul will be more peaceful. . . .

And on March 23, 1947, he wrote to Iannis Kakridis:

. . . I was longing very much for your letter. I've received it now and am happy that you've escaped from the bloodstained, well-loved trap of Greece. Now I'm eager to learn that you've gotten settled in the North and that you are working. . . .

God has sent you to Sweden this year. There, you'll be able to tell them about my struggle for the spirit and my life. . . . I consider it right (since it is possible) that two people, who are still creatively mature and productive, should be honored together from Greece. Which of the two will survive longer and how each one will find his own place, no one knows. But they have both worked much and risen as high as they were able. And they represent two aspects of Greece. Do your best to enlighten the people there, who are surely honest and wise—but do not know.

You too are observing what is happening in Greece with anguish. How is it possible for such a magnificent people to have such idiotic, criminal, dishonorable leaders? The destiny of Greece is tragic; and the last adventure may sink her into a deep pit, whereas it might save her. . . .

On the subject of UNESCO, he wrote to Tea Anemoyanni:

Paris, May 5, 1947

. . . It's done—I've accepted a huge preparatory task: the translation into various languages of all the exceptional works of all ages in literature, philosophy, physical sciences, sociology, etc. In November this work will be submitted to the Conférence Générale [General Assembly] to be held in Mexico. If it is approved, they will begin putting it into effect at once. Enormous work and constant conferences with comités of excellent people, but trop bureaucrates. A great effort to be able to make a little order, concentrate the cloud and give it a definitive form. People lose themselves in grand projects and fat words and are not aware of the godlike rhythm of the sure tread upon the earth. . . .

I know I'm much indebted to you too for my opportunity to enter and become familiar with the vast international organization of UNESCO. And the fact that I owe this to you also delights and stirs me. May God be with you and you with Him always! . . .

Nikos stayed on in Paris alone and wrote to me in the Pyrenees, where I had gone for a cure.

My little, musk-anointed crocodile!

. . . Here, the grève [strike] is spreading, and I'm afraid letters won't be leaving. Perhaps there'll be a general strike. Perhaps we'll have civil war? In any case, the situation is a bit tendue [tense] and interesting. Something is going to happen. Perhaps the coming course of Europe will depend upon it. . . .

Don't worry about anything, my love. . . . However much you grumble, your destiny is privilégiée. You have a solid human being who loves you; so rare, so difficult in this miserable, dishonorable epoch when everyone's confused and unable to find any solid ground to tread upon. . . .

My beloved little crocodile, stretch out in the sun, open your mouth, and let the birds fly in and out. You know that birds are useful to crocodiles as cure dents [toothpicks].

With much love,

The Big Crocodile
N.

On June 14, 1947, Nikos answered in French Börje Knös's eulogies of him.

. . . I feel elated at the idea of your being bravely plunged into the blue sea of The Odyssey.* From the point of view of poetic form and philosophical content, The Odyssey represents the highest peak I've been able to attain, the efforts of an entire lifetime in the service of the spirit.

The seventeen-syllable verse has startled our poets, who were accustomed to the classical, modern-Greek verse of fifteen syllables. But that venerable verse seemed to me too worn-out; it lacks the breath of life and is no longer capable of containing the fiery contemporary spirit which is suffering and struggling and longing to break the limits stifling it; longing to create a broader, deeper rhythm. These two additional syllables give the epic an unexpected amplitude, majesty and, at the same time, disciplined violence. . . . That is why Kakridis and I have adopted the 17-syllable verse for our translation of Homer.

When can I "see again the smoke" of my Ithaca? Greece is sinking

---

* N.K.'s Odyssey.

more and more into obscurity. The Americans, by confounding the soul and the dollar, will make big mistakes in Greece as well. The Greek people clearly see the way to salvation. They want to follow it, but are prevented from doing so. Her destiny has always been a tragic one. Let us hope that this time the sufferings will strengthen her soul. . . .

And on June 16, 1947, from Paris, he wrote once again to Tea Anemoyanni:

. . . Here, much work. I feel suffocated. A huge projet. I don't have a moment to breathe. . . . Only Sunday is left me to rush violently through a heap of books that keep piling up on my desk. The seeds inside me that were ready to blossom and become works are left buried still. How I hope this forced rest will make them strong. How I long for the blessed hour when I shall enter the incandescent Paradise of Solitude. When? When? I have no more time. . . .

Paris marvelous. When will we be able to bring you here? It's one of my favorite projects and it will happen. . . .

Paris, June 24, 1947
Beloved little Crocodile, all cured and much traveled!
. . . I'll be at the station to welcome you. Herbert is leaving tonight; we've worked well at UNESCO. . . .*

Albert Camus had read the *Melissa* thanks to the director Jacquemont. A generous man, Camus did not hesitate to write his elder and offer his services to help him find a theater in Paris:

Tuesday
Dear Sir,
Melissa is a very beautiful play and I read it with a kind of gratitude. Nothing can be added to it or cut. And it must be performed without delay. May I see you this week? . . . At this point, I want to express my gratitude to you for having let me read this superb tragedy.

Yours devotedly,
Albert Camus

---

* Letter to E. Samios-Kazantzakis.

Happy but too timid, we did not dare invite Camus home. And so, Nikos only saw him briefly at his N.R.F. office.

Of the three Paris publishers who had asked for *Zorba*, as though intentionally, we chose the least solid, the one that would go bankrupt the very same day the book appeared. The few extremely laudatory criticisms appearing in the newspapers were of no avail to us. And the book remained sequestered in the publisher's basement. At a later point, when Plon wanted to buy up this first edition, we discovered that it had been sold clandestinely, without the author's knowledge.

As I reread the twenty or so letters from Paris sent by Nikos to his friend Prevelakis during the years 1946 to 1948, I find the already familiar major concerns, as well as the personal problems Kazantzakis was trying to solve with his wonted impetuosity. At critical moments, Nikos still sought the help of his two friends—P. Prevelakis and Tea Anemoyanni—knowing that he would always find them ready for action.

[October 15, 1946]   . . . *I'm burdening you too much with my own affairs; but I am indeed at a critical moment. To return to Greece is terrifying. I won't be able to do anything and they'll stifle me. To stay abroad, I don't have enough to live on. . . . How I long for Aegina. But how can I live there? A shame, a great shame to write these things. Shameful, but not for me. . . .*

And again, concerning the Nobel Prize:

[February 15, 1947]   *By no means do I want to be proposed alone for the Nobel. Either both of us will be proposed again, or else I refuse to accept by myself alone. It is not just. . . .*

I think of you every moment. My life is passing, going to waste. What do I want? Ample time to save as much soul as possible. . . .

[August 7, 1947]   . . . *I'm in such agony for Greece that I cannot talk. Only a miracle can save us. And woe betide any man who has no other hope except the miracle! I am suffocating, and sometimes when I am alone I burst out sobbing. . . .*

And concerning a new novel by Prevelakis, *The Cretan*, he wrote:

[*April 30, 1948*]   . . . *This book is a genuine struggle, and you emerge from it more courageous. Or else, if you're a coward, you are crushed by it. It is a brave deed. I have never read a book that is so like an action.*

And I can never express the joy and the honor you have done me by dedicating The Cretan *to me. I've struggled, that's true, throughout my life. And I'm still struggling to keep my soul from dying. I know how the mortal becomes immortal. And this is precisely the great torment of my life. For it is not enough that you know. You must also become. . . .*

On October 21, 1947, Nikos Kazantzakis resumed his dialogue with his old friend Börje Knös, who even amid the northern snows never lost sight of Greece and kept on struggling for a little more justice on this earth.

. . . *There is no longer any faith capable of subjecting the "hated ego" to some higher principle beyond the individual. They're all individualists, materialists, worshiping matter and quantity, scorning quality and spirit. The delicate crust that once covered the primeval beast— morality, love, beauty—has cracked. The human volcano is smoldering and the explosion is certain. At a swift pace we are moving toward a terrifying clash, out of which we shall all emerge vanquished. . . . Hunger, nakedness, wretchedness will overwhelm the human race—and later it will try once more painfully to compose itself, become organized, and begin its trek all over again. . . . "What is the right path?" an Indian proverb asks. "The path of God." "And what is the path of God?" "The uphill path!" Humanity will once again take the uphill path, like Sisyphus.*

One joy—and one duty—is left us now: that we desire, that we make ourselves ready, that we believe in the new uphill path, in the new humanity, which will emerge out of the ruins. We know that the future does not depend on us. Nevertheless, we must act as though the future did depend on us. This is the only way that great deeds have always been done. Only in this way can the future be influenced by us. Therefore, optimisme tragique and not pessimisme. Faith again, love, respect for the upright worm we call man—these can save us.

These are my thoughts, dear friend, during these days that are so critical for France and the world. Here the two camps are organizing themselves, extreme right and extreme left. The middle road, the correct one, has been lost. Here, too, they are getting ready for a clash. A demon, the demon of the 20th century, is driving human beings to disaster—and this has always been the first, the preliminary stage of creation. . . .

It has often been claimed that Nikos Kazantzakis was a nihilist. From his entire work, life and correspondence, however, the opposite emerges.

How did he describe himself? A "tragic optimist." A person who has confidence in man, who looks straight at the demon of destruction, hates it, but is not afraid of it, because he knows that all destruction is but the preparatory stage to new creation.

Paris, November 19, 1947

. . . I was delighted by the audacity of the Swedish Academy in giving Gide the Award. Gide is a great writer and, as an intellectual, has great elasticity, delicacy and refinement of thought, as well as an anguished upward path. However, he has proclaimed and supported (theoretically and practically) several "moral theories" that have done much harm to French youth and young people throughout the world, who read him and consider him one of the gurus of the spirit, one of the leaders of our epoch. . . .*

Paris, December 12, 1947

. . . The other day, I saw the Prince de Broglie, and he too is anxious (but also hopeful for human destiny), and he is hoping that humanity will not use the atom bomb for its own suicide. He used one

---

* Letter to Börje Knös.

phrase that impressed me, because for so many years now I've been saying and writing it, and everyone misinterprets it: "Ni peur ni espoir. [Neither fear nor hope.]" I think that could be a fine motto for any man of science nowadays, and for every man who wants to be both useful and lucid. "I fear nothing; I hope for nothing; I am a free man." That is the phrase I have ordered to be engraved on my tomb. To conquer illusion and hope, without being overcome by terror: this has been the whole endeavor of my life these past twenty years; to look straight into the abyss without bursting into tears, without begging or threatening, calmly, serenely preserving the dignity of man; to see the abyss and work as though I were immortal. . . .

I was very happy to meet the great scholar de Broglie, because he has confirmed many thoughts inside me. . . .*

1948.   Immediately following the New Year's festivities, a blow came that cut us to the quick: Our good Segredakis, while visiting his native village, had suffered a peritonitis infection and, because of improper care, died of it.

"The Cretans sense when their death is near," murmured Nikos forlornly, "and they go back to the cradle."

He had now handed in his resignation to UNESCO and was preparing the speech he had to deliver on modern Greek literature before the International Congress of Literature. As always, he weighed each word, writing and rewriting his text, seeking to be as objective as possible.

"If only he would agree to stay at UNESCO another six months," I kept thinking to myself. "With the money laid aside, we could buy two apartments in Paris—live in one and rent the other—and our financial problems would be forever solved."

But Nikos envisaged our future in a different way:

"How can you give me advice to accept money for doing nothing?" he complained. "There's no longer any point in my presence at UNESCO. If I had to take the path to the office once more," he concluded with a sigh, "I'd burst out crying on the street."

I left him in peace, recovered my confidence, and on an entirely new canvas we began embroidering together our future castles in America. . . .

---

* Letter to Börje Knös.

Very dear Friend,

I haven't written you in a long while to thank you for the translation of Grandfather.* . . . But I've been very upset. One of my dearest
friends died suddenly, and for many days I was disconsolate. And the
other day the murder of Gandhi came to poison my heart and mind.
Ever since the day before yesterday, the world has contracted. Four
bullets have deeply wounded the world-wide Conscience. . . . In such
a materialistic, greedy, amoral world as the present one, it was only
natural that the hero of nonviolence be killed by violence. . . . The
doctrine of peace and love in such a miserable era arouses and organizes
hatred, so it seems. The dark forces have been unleashed—the blind
Titans—and every noble endeavor increases their fury tenfold. . . .†

At long last—on March 25, the anniversary of Greek Liberation
from the Ottoman yoke—Nikos, having resigned from UNESCO, could
write in his notebook:
"Day of Liberation—March 25, 1821–March 25, 1948!"

Paris, April 23, 1948
. . . I'm once again a free man, and I've plunged back into work of
the spirit, pure and disinterested. I had asked Greece for a passport to
America, where the translator of The Odyssey [Rhea Dalvin] is expecting me. The present fascist government in Greece refused me the visa,
because they're afraid (so they say) that I might make some political
conférences. Well, when will God stretch His hand over the head of
Greece to protect her? For we are losing ourselves. The Greek race is in
peril. Every day, brothers are killing one another, and passion is
becoming increasingly blind and inhuman.

Discord has always been one of the curses of our race. It has often
brought us to the brink of the abyss. So far, [our nation] has always
been saved. And more than saved: passion has stirred the blood; danger
has mobilized all our forces; the brain has grown more acute. The spirit,
because it has momentarily lost them, has yearned and hankered after
the grand, simple happinesses: peace, love, the state of ease needed for

* Freedom or Death.
† Letter to Börje Knös.

474

creation. And that is why after every bloodstained carnage, our race has hurled itself fervently into creation of the spirit. And today this is my great hidden hope: that out of this blood and out of these ashes and tears great works of the spirit will spring forth. And the flames shall be transmitted from the hands of destruction to the hands of God. They say that God is a Hellenophile and wears the fustanella.* Now, we shall see! . . .†

Since we could not leave for America or go back to Greece, I was hoping to persuade Nikos to stay in Paris. But he was tired of the big cities. Thrasso Kastanakis‡ described Antibes to him in such glowing terms—the ancient Antipolis, her sea, her pine forests, her ramparts, her inland regions, these maritime Alps reminiscent of Greece at every step—that Nikos packed up and was eager to set off on the spot. But before taking leave of UNESCO, he had to read his essay on Greek literature at the International Congress of Literature. UNESCO gave a banquet in his honor. And after eleven months of servitude, Odysseus took to the open spaces again.

Several weeks before he left his post, a tiny swelling had appeared on his upper lip, along with a slight fever. The UNESCO doctor had scoffed at it, calling it an "infant's fever." Nikos, who never drank tea at his office like everyone else, would come home parched and drink several glasses of tea. Then, to my astonishment, he collapsed in the "poet's armchair." At this point, neither he nor I attached any importance to these portents.

Once he had reached Antibes, Nikos searched for our new lodgings as in the past, patiently and arduously. And he found them; and they were magnificent from every point of view.

Antibes, June 3, 1948
Villa Rose

Beloved Lenotschka!
May good luck attend Villa Rose! The way this villa was found is miraculous. Once again, it was the ladies who came to my rescue. . . .

---

* The short pleated kilt, the national costume of Greek men.
† Letter to Börje Knös.
‡ Professor of Modern Greek at the School of Oriental Languages in Paris and a well-known writer; he had made his home in Antibes for 6 months a year.

I'd been wandering around by autobus, train, on foot. Not a thing anywhere. . . . I'd rushed outside Antibes, and after several adventures I fell into the hands of an agente—plump, round, blond, eunuchlike. "Let's go!" she said to me. "I have something for you!" We turned down a green-green lane and arrived at the Villa Rose—a garden with a medlar tree all laden with ripe medlars, olive trees, fig trees, apricot trees, a big cpyress in the entrance; a superb terrace, view onto the sea and the snow-covered Alps; 10 minutes' walk from the sea. . . .

I'm happy that I've found, and you'll be reveling in, a comfortable home. . . .*

Before leaving Paris, Nikos had given permission to a talented young actor-director—Georges Carmier—to stage *Julian the Apostate* and perform it at the Young People's Competition. He had even watched the preparations. . . . Some old pieces of cloth given us for the occasion by Segredakis' nephew Nikolas (Greek cottonwear dyed by Madame Carmier) served as costumes for the Warrior-Emperor, the Bishop and the Greek soldiers. In a little hall behind St. Julien-le-Pauvre, we attended the dress rehearsal.

But Nikos set off without waiting for the actual opening; and I arrived in Evian immediately thereafter.

Antibes, June 23, 1948
Wednesday

Beloved little Crocodile Glove!

. . . I was glad about the Gandhi Conférence† . . . I got letters from Duquaire, S. and Mme. Puaux about the performance of Julien. Apparently, it was a great success and much applause. . . .

Sodom and Gomorrah was finished on June 19; and so, it was written in 13 days. Now I'm copying it, for you to read. . . .

The other day a strong wind blew and knocked down all the apricots. Magnificent, ripe, etc. But I was sorry, because I'd been saving them for you. . . .‡

---

* Letter to E. Samios-Kazantzakis.
† I had spoken on Gandhi before a small committee in Grenoble.
‡ Letter to E. Samios-Kazantzakis.

While I was recuperating in Evian, Nikos hid himself away in Villa Rose, in a fit of inspiration. I found him resplendently young as in the days of Aegina, immersed in the present moment, with no regrets for our botched plans.

"Read this, Lenotschka. Tell me if it's worth anything!" And he laid on my knees two newborn works: *Sodom and Gomorrah*, the 3-act tragedy he had gotten down on paper in thirteen days; and the first spurt of a large novel that was to make him famous, *The Greek Passion*.

I read in stupefaction. Where and when had this world of the refugees been born? And this new language—tender, patient, impassioned—which I hadn't known was in him?

"But you were getting ready to write about the therapy of Christ through psychoanalysis!"

"I—maybe. But that other person, the unknown 'I' inside me, was getting ready to write what you're holding there in your hands. Come now, my love, read it and tell me if it's worth anything."

Rahel had raised a few objections to *Sodom and Gomorrah* and Nikos answered her several months later:

Dear Rahel,

Oh how I've toppled and buffeted and abused Abraham and his beard! And how I've raised and sanctified Judas Iscariot right alongside Jesus in this book I'm writing now.* For anyone who creates, all these saintly or diabolical Gestalten [forms] are but pawns for the supreme game. I needed an "Abraham-Bleating-Ewe." I found a different Abraham in the Bible. So just the way astute photographers do, I retouched him to make him serve my purposes. It's simple; and so good and just to topple tradition a bit—that old Megaira! Everything you write is correct, but the opposite is also correct. For the creator, just and unjust—good and evil—god and devil—no longer exist. There is only a hungry flame devouring all these succulent foods. And the devil's flesh is always more nourishing than God's. And I love it, provided that it is consumed, digested and assimilated. . . .

In the course of writing *The Greek Passion*, Nikos became aware of a swelling on his lip. It was no longer a knob as in Paris, but a small

---

* *The Last Temptation.*

protrusion—a sort of allergenic phenomenon—accompanied by a slight fever. On July 27, Nikos observed in his notebook: "My lip began swelling just at the moment in my novel where I describe the swelling on the face of the hero, who enacts the role of Christ."

The illness departed as it had come. And, again, we attached no importance to it, other than Nikos' interpretation: the influence of the soul upon the body.

Prevelakis had just paid us a visit in Antibes and we were overjoyed. Nikos hadn't yet entered the phase of total renunciation. He had the sense of being in exile, and he felt exultant at the thought of seeing his friend and fellow countryman again. The new book Prevelakis read to us was remarkable. And Nikos did not hesitate to congratulate him for it.

Immediately after Prevelakis, Pierre and Yvonne Métral came to our home, filling the house with sun. And then Börje Knös and Bruno Lavanini—a Hellenist of Sicilian descent. The North and the South, two spirits enamored of Greece, working with the same fervor to make our literature known in their respective countries. And Börje Knös went still further: He raised a hue and cry against the cruel outrages the Greek people were suffering in these blackest of all years. And Nikos thanked him gratefully:

Antibes, November 27, 1948

. . . Thank you very much on behalf of Greece for the brave, just cry you have made in Sweden, in defense of the truth. May God grant that this honest cry will be heard and enlighten all men who are pure and just. . . . You have offered great moral support, dearest friend, to the land you have loved so much—which is worthy of being loved by all enlightened, honorable spirits. . . .

The schools and universities had opened their gates again, and the summer people had left the Coast. We could now walk for hours on end along the deserted shore, in the Garoupe Forest, or along the heights over Antibes and Cannes, through these Maritime Alps reminding us of the light soil of Attica. The "dawn" that Nikos had been invoking for so many years had come. The doors were opening all by themselves, even the doors that should have remained forever closed.

Several days before Christmas, right out of the blue, we were offered a magnificent villa, situated in a huge park. And, as the young real-estate agent specified, staring Nikos right in the eyes, it had a belvedere ideal for isolating and working. He [that is, the agent] also proposed a three-year lease, certain of pleasing us.

"God forbid!" exclaimed Nikos in horror. "Three more years away from Greece! That means—"

I had a very hard time bringing him to sign the three-year lease.

And so, all was going well at home. And then, as always, on one of the most radiant of days, the storm broke. All of a sudden, Nikos' poor face became swollen. It was Christmas Eve. The doctors thought it was some sort of skin infection. But it wasn't that, for six months later there was a new alarm. Some unknown illness, perhaps an allergy, was to come and go twice a year in a more or less violent form, plunging us into deep despair: a sort of mask, like the one that had tortured him in Vienna in 1922.

Excessively optimistic, Nikos thought no more about it—until the day of the relapse.

Antibes, January 29, 1949

. . . I've been ill. I thought of you all the time and wanted to write you, but could not. Now, I'm well. Today, I got your tragic study on modern Greece, and I was deeply moved as I leafed through it. . . .

Even during my illness, I kept working. The new novel is progressing well. . . . Have you seen Permanence de la Grèce,* published by the Cahiers du Sud? In general, it's good and useful, but very unjust, not even mentioning our best prose writers: Prevelakis, Myrivilis, Kastanakis—and the poets Varnalis, Nikos Papas, Rita Boumi-Papa, etc. . . . Levesque is a passionate Frenchman who is the victim of a horrid clique in Athens. . . . I am very sad about it. I hope that some day you yourself will set about this honorable task. . . .†

1949.   Now we were living at Villa Manolita in the Saramartel Park. The spring was like silk. Once every week, we set off early through the fortressed villages of the Maritime Alps. Pine trees, wild thyme, laburnum, forests of mimosa in bloom, the air fragrant, the bees and the

---

* The periodical Permanence of Greece, published by Journals of the South.
† Letter to Börje Knös.

wasps bumbling, the sea scintillating at our feet. Antibes became "our Antipolis"; Greece came to us because we could not go to her.

The sun no longer left us. The figs grew ripe in our yard; the medlars and the lemons and the tangerines and the almonds and walnuts.

Nikos was working marvelously well. From each Greek friend who came to visit him, he demanded details on the Civil War ravaging Greece. He took notes and finished the first draft of his novel, *The Fratricides*, bearing the subtitle: *He Wanted to Be Free, He Said; Kill Him!*

In April of this same year, he wrote the *Kouros* (Theseus), one of his most beautiful tragedies, in verse and rhythmic prose. Between May and July, he wrote *Christopher Columbus*, subtitling it *The Golden Apple*. Between these two works, he rewrote *Constantine Palaeologos*.

Antibes, April 3, 1949

. . . I'm well now and working hard. The new novel, The Fratricides, is finished, as I wrote you. It will be printed only in French. . . . Now, I'm beginning a tragedy with four characters: Minos, Theseus, the Minotaur, Ariadne. Minos, the last fruit of a great civilization. Theseus, the first flower of a new civilization. The Minotaur, the dark subconscious, wherein the three great branches (Animal, Man, God) have not yet become separated; this is the primitive, dark Essence containing everything. Ariadne is Love. . . .

By hard work, I am striving momentarily to forget the pain of Greece. The heart breaks when I recall the Mother, the Alma Mater. When will this martyrdom be over? This year, I hope. . . . But how? I fear many things. . . .*

Nikos' face became swollen again and we still couldn't find out the causes of the ailment.

Antibes, August 26, 1949

. . . I haven't spoken with you for a long time, because all these months I've been working very much and also I've been ill. The day

---

* Letter to Börje Knös.

after tomorrow, I'm leaving for Vichy, where I'll stay for 21 days. . . . When I am ill, I work doubly hard, as though I wanted to conquer the illness by the intensity of the creative drive. . . . In this way, I finished the Christopher Columbus and the final version of Constantine Palae-ologos, in thirteen-syllable verse. And all these days, a new theme is besieging me insistently, imperatively: Baldwin IV, the leper King of Jerusalem. What an extraordinary physiognomy! A heroic, indomitable spirit in a body rotting away and stinking, day by day. What a terrifying symbol of humanity as a whole! I cannot calm myself. I must crystallize it in words in order to liberate myself of it. How suddenly and unexpectedly people dead for thousands of years come out of their tombs and besiege the living—longing to drink a little of their blood, so as to be resurrected and look on the light of the sun again. I suffered the same thing with Odysseus, Eleni, Julian the Apostate, Nicephoros Phocas and, recently, with Alexis Zorba. . . .*

From Vichy, where he had finally consented to go for a cure, he wrote to me:

Vichy, September 2, 1949
Friday

Beloved Veuve d'un vivant [Widow of a Living Man], *I'm writing you immediately after seeing the doctor. . . .*

To do any work of the spirit, I consider difficult. The whole day is saccadée [chopped up]. *Every few minutes, you have to interrupt and rush off to the various springs. Of necessity, I will be wasting my time. But let's hope the body will improve. . . . I'm in a hurry to send you this letter, so you can see what's become of the Exiled One. . . .*

Vichy, September 5, 1949

. . . I've been so happy at not knowing anyone and no one's knowing me. And I've been ambling about like an idiot, staring as though it were the first time I were seeing trees and water and women and window displays. Vichy is very aristocratic; full of parks and a charming little river—the Allier. I loaf about, trying not to be sorry about wasting my time vegetatively. I'm reading a bit and I miss the

---

* Letter to Börje Knös.

radio very much. But I have Le Monde here, at 6:00 in the morning, when I go to the Grande Grille spring. . . .*

Vichy, September 1949
Monday (after the Doctor)

. . . I've just come back from the beast. It was tamer today. . . . I asked him: "Quel est le nom de ma maladie? [What's the name of my illness?]" "Mais vous n'êtes pas malade! Ce n'est rien. [But you're not ill! It's nothing at all.]"

I insisted. And then, in exasperation, he grabbed a piece of paper and wrote: "Gastro-enteroptose avec insuffisance hépatique, sans infection [Gastro-enteroptosis with liver deficiency, noninfectious]! . . .†

And on September 8, 1949, to Börje Knös:

. . . For the first time in my life, I've experienced what laziness means. For the first time, I've noticed that there is such a thing as the body and that we have to take care of it—not for its own sake, but for the sake of the soul it bears on its shoulders. I take the baths, drink lukewarm waters, walk beneath the green plane trees and watch the throngs of melancholy people. And occasionally, as the priests do with the Bible, I open my little Dante—my Fellow Traveler—read two or three verses and am carried off to Hell or Purgatory or Paradise. . . .

Vichy, September 9, 1949

. . . Today, the Doctor found an amélioration extraordinaire in me. . . . In a week, the liver will be presque parfait [almost perfect]. . . .‡

Vichy, September 1949

Veuve d'un vivant, Haire! [Widow of a Living Man, Hail!]

I write you every day. . . . The days are like lead and do not move forward. But, meanwhile, a new work has been born inside me . . . in the Kouros series—and I shall write it as soon as I get back home. . . . I hope you'll like it. . . .

I miss hearing the radio. It seems that Russia has left the poor

---

* Letter to E. Samios-Kazantzakis.
† Letter to E. Samios-Kazantzakis.
‡ Letter to E. Samios-Kazantzakis.

Andartes [Partisans] stranded. Of course, the Communists will find excuses. But perhaps it's not like this at all; I read only Le Monde.

Wednesday morning. Today it's raining. The crowd has moved back into the pavilion where the spring is, each person clutching his own little glass and drinking with a medicine dropper. I'm sitting in a chair in the midst of greeny-yellowish women who sit knitting and melancholy men who read the newspapers. I am watching the rain falling outside on the green trees, peaceful, cool, long desired. I hold my book, light my pipe, and think of Manolita and all that it contains. I feel calm and a little tired, as one does after a hot bath. I am letting myself vegetate like a tree, as though I did not have so much left to do if I want to keep from leaving this half-finished. (For who will finish them?) However, as long as I stay here in Vichy, I'll play the fool; I won't work, so as to strengthen the body a little and hold out a few months longer. The doctor admires my organism; he was amazed that I've never had any pains or migraines or vertiges [dizzy spells!]. I explained to him in a few words (he's always in a hurry and a huff) about who my father was and he's beginning to understand. . . .*

We spent a week together at Vichy, and then Nikos went back to Antibes alone:

Aegina [sic!], September 24, 1949
Saturday

Beloved Collaboratrice!

I think I shall never forget the week we spent together at Vichy. There was a strange sweetness and tenderness about it—like a betrothal, as though we were together for the first time. I tasted each moment calmly, mutely, intensely. Even if I did not say anything, I was profoundly happy. . . .

Today on the radio, Truman announced detection of an atomic-bomb explosion in Siberia; and the speaker was all upset at Russia's having the atomic bomb! . . .†

And on October 16, 1949, to Börje Knös:

---

* Letter to E. Samios-Kazantzakis.
† Letter to E. Samios-Kazantzakis.

. . . I've returned to the Paradise of Antibes. The weather's like spring, sunny and heavenly sweet. A few trees, like the mimosas, have been deceived and are in bloom. I can't shut myself into my study. All day long, I sit half nude in the sun, writing. The ancient Romans were right—the sun is the certus deus [the sure god]. . . .

I've given the definitive form to two tragedies I wrote, and now I'm beginning a new one, Eleni.* . . . Baudouin IV [Baldwin IV] of Jerusalem I shall write this winter. . . .

At Lake Success, they say, there's an optimisme modéré. There will be some solution to the Greek problem one of these days. This solution is sure to be a paltry one, and for some years life will be unbearable in Greece. For even if the Civil War ends, the vendetta collective will begin. The destiny of the Greek race is terrifying and mysterious, as though upon this parcel of earth the spirit can be watered only with tears and blood. . . . And therefore, every Greek, in order to justify his own existence, is duty bound to struggle to transubstantiate this blood and these tears into Spirit. . . .

Once more the autumn came slowly, richly, the last white figs reminding us of how the August figs had tasted—violet outside, honey-colored inside, sweet and refreshing. Nikos was radiant. Every morning, he climbed the fig trees and brought me big bowls of this beloved fruit. Were it not for the tragic fate of Greece, we would have been happy, having adapted ourselves to this new Paradise, which duped Nikos into calling it "Aegina."

Antibes, December 12, 1949

. . . When shall I go back to Greece? So I can send you honey, raisins, figs—the eternal Greek gifts. . . .

When? Everything there is absolutely black. Slavery has oppressed us once again—scientific slavery this time, well organized, well camouflaged. And in order to free ourselves, we have need of a new 1821. This too will come, of a surety. But in the meantime, thousands of other spirits are being killed; others are withering; others are selling themselves. . . .

---

* N.K. must have destroyed this work, because no trace of it has been found in his papers.

And so I sit here, exiled in this Paradise of Antipolis, laboring on the modern Greek language and spirit to the best of my ability. For forty years now, I've been doing nothing else—with no other reward except tremendous persecution by the official Greeks. However, I'm of good earth—made in Crete—and I resist. I hope to fight in this way unto death.

The new novel on Crete progresses every day, and it will soon be ready. I am trying my utmost to resurrect my father. To pay back my debt in this way: by giving birth to him who gave me birth. . . .*

1950. Nothing was altered in the political affairs of Greece or in our own private life. As in Aegina, the almond trees were in blossom by the beginning of the year. On February 18 we celebrated Nikos' birthday by taking a long excursion in the Maritime Alps, beneath the flowering mimosas. And we spoke much of Prevelakis, who was born on this same day. During our walks Nikos once again took inventory of his life. For the first time I heard no regrets uttered about his incapacity to set himself at the head of a great political movement. He was in perfect form. To pry him loose from his worktable, I used to call him out to pick olives. Three of us, including our eighty-year-old gardener, picked some 700 kilos. Nikos also helped in the beating of the trees, and he was never the first one to tire of these rustic pleasures.

Antibes, March 3, 1950

Very dear friend,

The day after tomorrow, Sunday, elections are to be held under conditions of terror. I'm afraid they may augment the complications in our country. Thank you once again for the trouble you have taken in commenting on my work. The other day it was my birthday. For 65 years now, I've been in circulation, coming and going inside this prison called "man," looking through the two little windows at the world, never getting my fill of seeing it. What a miracle this world is! What harmonious correspondence it bears to our hunger and thirst, and our longing for God! And for 45 years, I've been struggling to transubstantiate all this spectacle, all this hunger and thirst, to garb it in the 24 letters of our Greek alphabet before I die. Turning as much of the

---

* Letter to Börje Knös.

substance as I can into "spirit." And if I were to be born again, I would not take another path. Difficult and steep the upward path I have chosen, but I do not repent. . . .*

From Stockholm the news was very good. Zorba the Greek was continuing to create a great stir. Börje Knös had completed the translation of the Theseus, which was to be performed over the Swedish radio. He had also finished the translation of The Greek Passion, a work for which he predicted a brilliant future. Nikos was moved and thanked him, but talked to him mostly about Greece, where fascism was rampant.

Antibes, March 15, 1950

. . .What happened the other day in Greece was really a miracle and showed the nobility and proud and gallant stand of the Greek people. In the midst of incredible terrorism, the people went and voted by the thousands against fascism! . . .

You are 67 years young. And I a 65-year-old lad. In both of us the heart is 20—at the very most, 21. We shall not surrender our arms easily.

One of the supreme delights I still have ahead of me is to bring you to Greece. But let me be there as well, so that the two of us together can roam the soil and climb the mountains of thrice-sacred Crete.†

Antibes, May 9, 1950

. . . Bravo for having finished The Greek Passion, and I'm glad you liked it all the way to the end. This is a real novel; Zorba was mainly a dialogue between a scribbler and a great man of the people, a dialogue between the advocate of mind and the great popular spirit. I've also finished Freedom or Death—a very tragic book about the struggle for freedom, the soul's sempiternal longing for liberation, for substance to be freed and become transformed into spirit, for God to be freed from all the human virtues that weigh Him down so that He too may become Spirit. The myth of Kapetan Mihalis is most dramatic, and I lived it in a sanguinary way when I was four years old, and later on all the time I was

---

* Letter to Börje Knös.
† Letter to Börje Knös.

486

growing up in the tragic atmosphere of Crete. The human beings in this book, the episodes, and the speech are all true, even if they appear incredible to people who were born in the light or half-light of Western civilization.

I'll let it rest a bit now on my desk, and I'll begin a tragedy which has been harassing me for some time—The Third Faust, entirely different from Goethe's Faust, the roles turned quite upside down; a very difficult work, because I have to contend with awe-inspiring prototypes. But I'll try not to be put to shame. I have a great liking for the age-old familiar themes, the familiar legends. Didn't the ancients do likewise? There were certain cycles from which they took their themes, and they tried simply to renew them, to give them greater depth and an expanded meaning. I shall try to do the same now for Faust, if I can. God help me! . . .*

The allergies recurred. The blood test showed a lack of balance between the polynuclear and the mononuclear cells. The doctor at Antibes advised Nikos to go to Paris to consult a great blood specialist. Nikos put his foot down. "There's nothing wrong with me," he said. "And I've got other irons in the fire!"

Fortunately, he agreed to mail the most recent tests to me in Vichy, never suspecting that I would go on to Paris in his place to ask the specialist's opinion.

Antibes, Wednesday, June 1950

Beloved,

On Friday the doctor will give me a letter for the sommité [head man] in Paris, as well as the X rays. Send them to Sterianos.† . . . Don't worry at all about me. I'm eating well, not getting tired. Tomorrow Sodom and Gomorrah‡ will be finished and we're waiting for you to copy it.§

This morning a young Krishnamurti arrived all out of breath to

---

* Letter to Börje Knös.
† A Greek doctor friend, practicing in Paris.
‡ Burn Me to Ashes.
§ The original version.

make your acquaintance. Everyone in Antibes had told him that you are a sommité in Indian and Chinese philosophy. . . . He couldn't understand why you hadn't tried to cure your liver by psychic methods. . . .*

Dear, dear Nikos! Always teasing, always gay, rarely thinking of his own personal troubles.

> Antibes, Monday, June 1950
> Beloved brave Akritaina,† who hast pitched a battle with Charon to save me! I've just now received your letter from Paris. It's a pity not to stay a few days after so much trouble. I'll wait for you to come, so we can make a decision. . . . But you must not worry. I feel profoundly that there's nothing seriously wrong with me; some irregularity in the blood, nothing else. My whole body feels sturdy, bien agencé [well set up]—and I still haven't reached the fatal age of eighty-three. At that point you will worry, but only for a few days. Everything will end very simply and quickly.
> I'm writing to you, listening to the morning Mozart. I'll go out to [Juan-les-Pins] right afterward to mail this letter and let you know that everything here is going like clockwork. . . . I have The Third Faust on my mind day and night, and I'm thinking of beginning a new novel. . . .
> Banine is in seventh heaven. Tomorrow Jünger is coming. Saturday evening I'll have dinner with them. I'll be glad to meet him. . . .
> Mozart's coming to an end. I'm leaving. My beloved Charon-battler, my Akritopoula, health and joy!‡

It was during my absence from Antibes that Banine, infatuated with the German writer Jünger, arranged a meeting with Kazantzakis. From this meeting she hoped to see the birth of a friendship that might be useful to Nikos. Just one more disillusionment.

---

* Letter to E. Samios-Kazantzakis.
† Sentinel of the frontiers, the name being taken from the legendary Greek hero Diogenes Akritas.
‡ Letter to E. Samios-Kazantzakis.

Antibes, Sunday, June 1950

. . . Jünger very interesting. A good physique, slender, lively, gray. Cynique and ironique, very harsh, German. Egotistical and agreeable. He laughs easily, but his laugh is thin, from the lips, ironical and teasing. How naïve, good, kind-hearted and "pure" Banine is alongside of him! . . . No important conversation took place. . . .*

Friday evening

The other day at Thrasso's [Kastanakis'] I met Chagall. Very pleasant. I was pleased.†

The writing of The Third Faust, expressing the destiny of present-day man, must have preoccupied him a great deal, for he spoke of it often in his letters.

Antibes, June 17, 1950

. . . I'm thinking of writing The Third Faust. I'm not doing so out of arrogance or megalomania, with the intention of making a continuation of Goethe. But it's a great psychological and spiritual need of mine to write about the third, the present-day, Faust: a tragedy of the fate of contemporary man, who, after having reached the peak of his intellectual perception, has now arrived face to face with the abyss. There will be four main characters: Faust, Akritas, Mephistopheles, and Helen. (You know that the word Mephistopheles is a corruption of the Greek Mi Photophilos ["He-who does-not-love-the-light"].‡

Finally, after all, Nikos decided to set off for Paris alone.

Wednesday evening, June 1950

Fourth Medical Bulletin
Beloved Comrade in Life and in Death!

All morning I spent in the Hôpital Saint-Louis, where Dr. Tsanck holds court. Much special attention. In three hours I was through with the consultations and tests. . . .

---

* Letter to E. Samios-Kazantzakis.
† Letter to E. Samios-Kazantzakis.
‡ Letter to Börje Knös.

Tsanck treats me like an old friend. I never saw a more lively and interesting old man. . . . I don't have leucémie [leukemia] at all, he says, just simple lymphotome [lymphatic irregularity]. . . . In any case, he assures me that the trouble isn't remotely serious . . . and he laughs when I tell him what I saw and suffered in Antibes. . . . Entre temps we talked about Pascal, Valéry, Claudel, Bergson, on a high niveau; he was impressed at my knowing them. . . . Thanks to that, he treats me like an old friend. Bless Sterianos for putting me in touch with him. . . . *

Paris, July 7, 1950

Fifth Bulletin, Friday morning
    . . . This evening I'll see the friend of the Métrals,† who will give the tragedies to Giono.‡ Yesterday I also saw Sophianopoulos,§ who's leaving for Athens in five or six days. . . . He's tired and not very optimistic. . . .||

Friday, midnight

Sixth Bulletin
    . . . I dined with Nicolas. . . . He gave me two big and superb mauresques [Moorish] dishes. . . . Miss Bataille very warm and devoted. . . . I think something will come of it. . . . Yvonne invited a very attractive poet to dinner. . . . Very emballé [enthused] about the Theseus.
    Leah telephoned me. I'll be seeing her tomorrow. . . . But all this fades, because over everything there is always hovering my concern about how you are getting along. I think only of you, and I'm in a hurry to come back. . . .
    The Métrals are angels, real friends. They are doing everything they can to be of help to me. . . . I get very tired. The metro wears me out. . . .¶ .

---

* Letter to E. Samios-Kazantzakis.
† Yvonne and Pierre Métral, faithful friends, in whose house at L'Hay-les-Roses N.K. sometimes stayed.
‡ The friend of the Métrals in question did not succeed in arousing the French writer's curiosity about his Greek fellow writer.
§ Iannis Sophianopoulos, an enlightened political figure in Greece, who favored Greek neutrality and was a great friend of N.K.
|| Letter to E. Samios-Kazantzakis.
¶ Letter to E. Samios-Kazantzakis.

Seventh Bulletin

Beloved,

Today the mission you assigned me when you sent me to Paris has come to an end. And so let me tell you the results:

Dr. Tsanck and Jean Bernard held a consultation and came to the following conclusions: 1) The irregularity I have is called lymphôme [lymphoma]. 2) It is very rare. 3) It is insignificant. I can eat whatever I like and don't have to take any medicine . . . I must avoid strong sunlight, take a blood test every three months and send it to Tsanck. There's no longer any need for my staying in Paris. If I swell up again, X-ray treatments. . . .*

From Peira Cava (altitude 1,450 meters), where we had gone for a few days, Nikos wrote his friend Börje Knös:

August 21, 1950

. . . I've been here since August 1 in the fresh air. My wife is resting at last. I came for the same purpose, but how can I rest? The new novel is working in my vitals and, like the embryo, consuming my flesh, drinking my blood, wanting to grow and emerge free into the sun. I hope that soon the great pangs and great joys of birth will begin. At the same time I have The Third Faust on my mind. That is to be a major work in my life, a long-drawn-out work, a companion piece to The Odyssey. It will be the last work to mark my transitory passage over the crust of the earth.

. . . It is our duty to stare at the abyss . . . with dignity and faith. To be sure, the present moment and the one immediately ahead are horrifying and will become increasingly so. . . . But the moment further on in the distance will be utterly brilliant. I'm certain that the human species has not yet revealed all its rich potentialities. The belly of the earth is still full of eggs. . . .

We now had everything we needed to be happy. So we thought at least. Health, peace, the reputation I so desired for Nikos, and his joy in

---

* Letter to E. Samios-Kazantzakis.

seeing me full of joy. To celebrate the "good news" from Paris, the Métrals offered us a trip in Spain.*

Acting with vigilance, Nikos went down to Nice and Antibes as often as necessary for the formalities of our passports. The Greek government renewed our passport for a single month and for only one trip.

From September 5 to 22 we played at being tourists. Entering Spain by way of Narbonne and Perpignan, we followed a route leading us through Barcelona, Tarragona, Valencia, Alicante, Cordova, Toledo, Illescas, Madrid, Vitoria, San Sebastian, Bayonne, and thence back to Antibes. Nikos added this to his list of "happy trips." He enjoyed the opportunity to introduce me to El Greco. The company of the Métrals was invaluable.

And to cap the events of this year, the *Theseus* was performed over the radio in Stockholm. We listened to it in Antibes, with our little cat, a ball of down and feathers, sitting on our knees. Every time I sneezed or raised my voice, she got annoyed and grumbled. . . .

But the destiny of our planet gave Nikos no rest.

Antibes, December 20, 1950

. . . *The new year descends upon us in fury. These days humanity finds itself on the brink of the abyss. As I write you, my heart is full of agony, bitterness, rage. Well then, what is this Destiny that governs human beings? Does it have eyes or none at all? Does it have a brain? Does it obey some mind superior to its own? Is it imbecility, injustice; the blood indispensable for man to progress on the earth? I've been feeling overwhelming bitterness—and, yet, all day long I sit and write, because I must. Man must act as though he were immortal. . . .†*

And to his dear friend Iannis Kakridis:

At this very moment we got your letter. Eleni danced for joy. (As for myself, I say nothing.) She's filled our house with banners and

---

* Accompanying us on the trip was Lucienne Fleury, sister of Yvonne Métral.
† Letter to Börje Knös.

awaits you. Arrange, if you can, to stay more than three days . . . a week at least. The torments of man are unending, but so are his joys. Therefore, more days!

I'm so overjoyed to be seeing you that I can't write anything to you. Why write anyhow? We'll talk about it.

We've exchanged two letters with Sophia Antoniades* this year; she says she's put together an anthology of modern Greek literature, and from all my work she's chosen only a few lines from my translation of Dante. So she presents me as a translator. . . . Eternal Greeks!

January 1, 1951. Seated on our sunlit veranda, we were really expecting nothing, when the postman brought the good news. The Greek Passion, appearing in the wake of Zorba the Greek, was enjoying a grand success in Sweden. I could not have hoped for a more precious gift. I danced and sang. Nikos looked at me, his eyes slightly misty. "Too late, my love," he murmured, "too late. And, yet, I'm happy because you are." And he went on smoking his pipe, lost in his reveries.

But that same day he wrote his friend, Börje Knös:

Villa Manolita, January 1, 1951

We could not have had a better New Year's gift than the two pieces of criticism you sent us. My wife read them and wept for joy and blessed your name, because all these joys we owe to you, dear friend. I was happy that this book too has been so well liked, and more than Zorba. But I have great hopes for Freedom or Death. This I have lived deeply . . . and I would like foreigners to know what we endured, what sanguinary ascents we have made and are still making, and how heavy is the fate lying on Greece. . . .

Alas, the inhabitants of the earth are still ape men. Out of megalomania, they call themselves "human beings." Perhaps one day we will become human beings. . . . Woe betide those who have become human beings aforetimes! . . .

Every time P. Prevelakis wrote a new book, his older friend celebrated it as though it had just sprung from his own pen.

---

* Professor of Modern Greek in Holland.

So far, I have read The Cretan three times, and I admire how you have been able to overcome the extraordinary difficulties involved in the writing of this volume [the first]. . . . There are scenes that made me quiver with emotion. When Manassis goes to the Bishop; when, in Chapter IX, Costantis comes back home. Manassis has ascended to a mythological level, and my heart leaps fiercely, because I remember what you once wrote me.* I still have a little of my life left. I will do all I can, as long as I live, but I shall never become fit to touch Manassis. Only one thing consoles me: When I do die, I shan't have to suffer any remorse for not having toiled.

And to his young friend the bookseller Stamos Diamantaras, he wrote on February 9, 1951:

. . . I am working intensely, writing novels—Hazáïn pirouit,† as you once said to me, and that will be the general title of the whole series of novels I'm going to write. So far there are five (only Zorba is published in Greek).

The body is still solid, the mind still clear. The soul is still pure and hot as a flame. These three horses are carrying me relentlessly toward the tomb without visiting any indignity upon me. May God grant that they won't be in too great a hurry so that there will be a long time for the "landlord to enjoy himself" on this earth.

. . . The Chinese have an amazing curse: "May you be born in an interesting epoch." This curse hangs over us. And it is our duty to transform this curse into a blessing, insofar as we can, by our own endeavor, by the power of our brain and by the pride of our spirit. We are living at a cosmic rate—not years—weeks, days, hours. Truly every moment nowadays has the value of a century. Whoever lives ten years now becomes a very old, old man. Time has acquired an unanticipated worth beyond calculation. So my blessings on you, and may you be born in an interesting epoch!

---

* Prevelakis had written N.K.: "When I finished [The Cretan], I understood that you are Manassis! You will see this for yourself when you read the third volume."

† For an explanation of this allusion, see p. 385.

I am happy to be talking with you again after so many years. You know how deep has always been my regard for you as a beloved friend.

And to Börje Knös:

Antibes, March 3, 1951
. . . I am working well. The new work [The Last Temptation] is progressing. Spring is coming. Everything is in bloom. The sea smells like ripe fruit. Apollo is sparkling away behind the mask of the sun. The blood circulates more quickly, and food becomes spirit faster and better.

I read Barabbas.* It's well written, the theme is very interesting. But no lofty creative invention. A "tidy" work, as we say in Greek, that is, one produced by a tidy person. The work of a good artisan, full of good sense, devoid of madness. . . .

Antibes, March 20, 1951
. . . Gide is no more. As a styliste [stylist] he was great. He was a maître écrivain [master writer], but not a grand écrivain [great writer]. His influence on French youth, morally speaking, was destructive. The form of his work is flawless. But the content I want none of. Now France is left only with the grand old man, Claudel. When he dies, all the rest will be epigoni.

On March 23, 1951, Nikos wrote to Leah Dunkelblum:

. . . Thank you for not having forgotten us. I too think of you very often, dear Leah, and I still hope to see you again one day—not in Paris, that accursed, seductive Babylon, but in Jerusalem, Tel Aviv, in the Promised Land, which I love so much! There's a very large drop of Hebrew blood† in my veins and this drop produces an effervescence and commotion in all my Hellenic and Cretan blood. I am obsessed and possessed by the Hebraic destiny. When I was ten years old, I begged my father to let me go to the home of the Rabbi of Canea to learn

---

* By Pär Lagerkvist.
† Nikos is playing with words. Actually, he had no Hebrew blood in his veins.

Hebrew. I went three times, and took three lessons. But my uncles, and more especially my aunts, were afraid and revolted against it. They were fearful that the Jews might drink my blood, and my father withdrew me from the rabbinical school.

Here in solitude, I am working hard and well. I am writing a book on a Hebrew subject now (The Last Temptation).* It takes place in Palestine, and you can understand how interesting it would be for me to see the Holy Land again. But that seems impossible. Nichevo!

. . . At home [in Greece] everything is going badly. One must be or become a hero in order to stand this base and rotten world. But at the bottom of this rottenness, there is a virgin spirit pushing up, raising its head, nourishing itself on the rot; and one day, a few centuries beyond our time, it will triumph. A Messiah is always on the march. . . .†

And once again to Börje Knös:

Antibes, June 1, 1951

. . . I am so deeply immersed in the joy and agony of The Last Temptation that I can't lift my head. And time passes. The moons get bright and fade away like lightning. My wife is away at the baths in Vichy, and now that I'm all alone I've had nothing to prevent my withdrawing once again into my wild solitude, my own real climate. My wife keeps me still within human society, not permitting me to run wild. Once when I had gone to Mount Sinai the monks wanted to furnish me a desert skiti [hermitage], consisting of a little chapel, three cells, and a courtyard with two olive trees, an orange tree, and a tiny well of water. The Monastery of St. Catherine has a number of manuscripts, which I would have read, and the most significant ones would have been published. . . . And ever since that time, this skiti has loomed in mid-air in front of me, and if it weren't for my wife, I should long since have gone back there. Nothing in my whole life has seemed so fascinant to me as the Arabian desert.

But luckily you'll be coming in three weeks, and you will reconcile me with human beings. . . .

---

* Published in the United States as The Last Temptation of Christ (New York: Simon and Schuster, 1962).
† N.K. wrote this letter in French.

One by one the great novels were falling into the fathomless cask of Time—drops of honey from some beehive perched high and out of sight among the foliage. Nikos cursed himself for not being able to stretch the length of the day at will, though he preserved the appearance of a sage. His hand could no longer keep pace with his thought. I began familiarizing myself with this new personal stenography.

Serene and amenable, he laughed, ate, slept, as before. Everything about his day-to-day life seemed to him good and propitious.

"Nikos," exclaimed a young American writer who was visiting us, "how can you work in such a furnace?"

"Oh, my friend," Nikos answered, "there's nothing like it. This heat is so invigorating."

A few months later our young American returned to find Nikos working away in his belvedere, this time in the freezing cold.

"But, Nikos, how can you work in this horrible cold?"

"Oh, my friend, believe me, there's nothing like this invigorating cold."

The cards he sent me at Vichy still had the familiar optimism and gaiety of tone.

May 26, 1951

Beloved Inhabitant-of-the-Watering-Cities: Today I'm going to go to the market to buy some fish for the cat—a bit extra so that I can eat some too. Yesterday I went to buy some pork, but as I was feeling absent-minded, instead of saying "pork chop [côtelette]," I went into the butcher shop and asked, "Do you have a pork pants [culotte]?" They burst out laughing, and the butcher answered with an absolutely straight face, "No, sir, I only have a man's pants!" And I went off to another shop—a pants shop.

May 30, 1951

. . . All last night the cat slept with me. I buy fish expressly for her—for her tail which puffs up when she sees me coming with the basket and stands as straight as a rod.

A slender tongue of earth in the sea, luxuriant vegetation, laburnums, myrtle, masticha trees, olive trees, cypress, pines, eucalyptus, oaks and holm oaks—such was Cap d'Antibes where the gods had cast us these past four years. Up in his belvedere, beaten by the east wind, tossed by the mistral, his nostrils tickled by ancestral scents, Kazantzakis looked like some old sea dog standing by the rudder, his gaze fixed always on the open spaces.

"Do you want me to see to your passport?" Iannis Sophianopoulos asked him when he came for a few days' visit.

"I would like to get it in time to see northern Italy again," said Nikos. "Greece I carry inside me. I have no desire to see it again. If I could, I'd go off to Mexico or India."

Iannis Sophianopoulos' heart was already in an exhausted state. When we would go to fetch him, we took all the precautions we could to help him climb the few yards of gentle slope separating us from his hotel. We were genuinely uneasy. But his vitality, the gift he had of holding the curiosity of his audience, his pertinent comments on international politics, his vision of a role to be played by Greece as intermediary between East and West, and our hope of seeing him some day once again at the head of a government that could drag our country out of the abyss—all this made us hope for a better future. In Athens the same thing happened with Angelos Sikelianos. We were aware that he had had new trouble with his health. But as long as the oak is left standing, no one thinks of peering closely at its roots. Sikelianos rose above the common stature. We thought he was immortal.

Iannis Sophianopoulos had just left Antibes when the bad news burst in our hands like a grenade.

"I cannot accept it, I cannot accept it," murmured Nikos, gritting his teeth. "No, it's really too unjust." Hurling away the letter he had just received, he got up and went over to glue his forehead against the windowpane. I picked up the abominable message. Angelos Sikelianos was dead.

"It's unjust," Nikos grumbled again. "Every day thousands of human wrecks are begging God to cut their suffering short. Thousands of desperate people, empty of substance, are seeking death, believing in a better life. And just at this point, the elect of the elect, the 'complete' man, is struck by lightning at the zenith of his creative powers."

It was only with difficulty that I managed to tear Nikos away from the contemplation of this freshly opened tomb. The only balm I knew was work, perhaps also a trip, so that his eyes could look upon new beauties.

In Greece, Tea Anemoyanni had at last succeeded in partially arranging the matter of our passports. And so, after the mountains, we could take a trip in Italy—Italy about which Nikos had always spoken to me so nostalgically.

On July 14, 1951, he wrote Tea Anemoyanni:

Antibes

My dear special Comrade,

Bless you! You've fought and won, and thanks to you we'll be going to Italy in early August. But the Ministry renewed the passport for only two months. Unprecedented, as though I were a criminal! I feel stifled with rage . . . And all this at a moment when a dead man is resting day and night upon my knees and I cannot close my eyes. I'll spend two weeks on a French mountain. Perhaps I'll calm down a bit. Only if my body gets overwhelmingly tired will my soul be able to find an ounce of serenity. . . .

Tomorrow we're setting off for the Alps. From there I'll write you again, as will Eleni, who is incredibly tired and sad. Death has knocked upon our door, Tea. . . .

I had to undergo some minor surgery, and decided to say nothing to Nikos beforehand. Using the problem of the cat as a pretext, I begged him to go on ahead of me to the mountains. And to keep him from thinking of death too much, I asked him a special favor.

"I don't like your second version of the *Constantine Palaeologus*," I said. "Would you like to make a third one, worthy of the *Theseus*—worthy of the new Nikos Kazantzakis?"

Nikos took note of my observations without saying anything. At Sigale, where I joined him a few days later, he read to me the first act of a *Palaeologus* in the same vein as the *Theseus*.

Sigale, so sweet in name, is an almost abandoned village, a few kilometers away from Nice, in the Maritime Alps. Every ruined house launched us upon builders' dreams. "Here is where we might settle down for the future. In this corner the desk, over there in front of that abandoned fireplace the living room . . ." There was a brook twining through the depths of the valley, and vineyards sweeping down the slope. A crucifix rose over some cone-shaped gingerbread at the entrance to the village. There was even a very old priest who looked after the church with its hidden treasures. And at nighttime, up over the vineyards, myriads of green will-o'-the-wisps: it was the fireflies celebrating their betrothals. "A good omen!" Nikos opened his eyes wide. "I never, never imagined such marriage ceremonies as these."

Sigale, Esteron, Hotel Gorda
July 22, 1951

. . . We find ourselves in a little village high in the Alps, where we'll be staying until August 3, and then we'll be leaving for Florence. . . .

Here in the solitude of the mountain, I'm trying to find peace after the terrible blow. Forty years of indissoluble friendship united me with Sikelianos. He was the only person with whom I could breathe, talk, laugh, be silent. Now Greece has become barren for me.

His last days were very bitter and unjust. By mistake they gave him poison—lysol—instead of medicine, and his vitals were seared. He struggled gallantly. The moment he drank the poison, they took him by car from Kifisia to Athens, to the big Evangelismos Hospital. There they refused to accept him, because he couldn't pay two weeks in advance. They took him back to Kifisia; then they took him to a Catholic clinic, the "Pammakaristos," but it was too late. Up to the very last moment, his mind was clear. You'll find many details in the Nea Estia. . . . It was proposed to hold the funeral at state expense, but at first the government refused, because, so they said, Sikelianos was antinationalistic, Communistic, an enemy of the Fatherland. This is where we've ended up. This shows what kind of people, what Androulises* are governing Greece today. The most Greek of the poets, the one who most worshiped eternal Greece, one of the spirits that designed this miracle called "Greece"—is considered by our present-day politicians as a traitor!

As I write you, I cannot hold back my tears—tears of pain and rage and disgust. I wish I could die, so as not to feel the shame that rests on

---

* The Greek ambassador in Stockholm who had slandered Sikelianos and Kazantzakis.

my native land. On the nineteenth of June (the day was Tuesday) around twilight, my friend died, and from that day on I have been holding his corpse in my embrace, and I walk and sleep and wake and cannot find peace. And only when I am alone do I bend over him and weep. The age-old, unanswerable questions return to rend my mind, and I cannot endure the injustice of life. A throng of intellectual apes lives and lives well, infesting Greece—and Sikelianos is dead. If God exists, he must one day account to us for this.*

We had hardly arrived at the Villa Fabricotti in Florence when we received another crushing blow.

Florence, August 4, 1951
. . . Still another national disaster has fallen upon Greece. The most honest, enlightened, and able of her politicians died suddenly the day before yesterday: Iannis Sophianopoulos. No one can take his place. I cannot see anyone capable of governing Greece. I have lost a precious friend and I am inconsolable. Charon knows well how to choose the best people. The dishonorable people do not die easily, because they are perfectly adaptés [adapted] to the contemporary world. Nowadays everything is convenient for them, collaborating with them, whereas the honorable man has to struggle against everything and gets drenched with all kinds of poison, by enemies and friends. He is not adapted to the present-day world, and the world hates him and rejects him. And Sophianopoulos was drenched with all the poisons not only by his enemies but by his friends. Because today even the friends of the honorable man are cowardly, play safe, and at any moment are prepared to go over to the other side, to the omnipotent camp of the dishonorable. And so Florence is not giving me the joy I'd anticipated. I'm carrying two dead men along with me, and I see everything through misted eyes. I've decided to write a book about Sikelianos and our forty years of friendship. . . . Perhaps in writing it I shall find a bit of consolation. We lived a great life together, Sikelianos and I, traveling through Greece. And perhaps what we saw and thought and did together may interest other people. . . .†

---

* Letter to Börje Knös.
† Letter to Börje Knös.

501

Dearest Tea,

Bless you. Without you, I wouldn't have seen Florence again. I think of you every moment as I walk here. I'm seeing Florence with emotion but not joy. In my heart I feel all kinds of grief and pain. I'm thinking of writing a book about Sikelianos. Perhaps I'll find a bit of solace for myself.

How many long years we had been waiting for this pilgrimage in Italy, when, with Nikos as my guide, I would be introduced to all its accumulated treasures! And there we were, our eyes clouded, like two mourners, two pallbearers. . . . When we went to view some statue of Michelangelo, we saw Angelos Sikelianos in a spasm of pain. When we looked at Benozzo Gozzoli's "Last of the Palaeologi," we thought we could recognize the slightly blurred features of our own Sophianopoulos. Even the little angels of Fra Angelico seemed to us to be attending some mass for the dead.

I did not dare to hasten the return trip, knowing Nikos' method of exhausting his body to the utmost in order to make it suffer and so allow him to forget the suffering of the soul. And so we carried out our plan, visiting Venice, Siena, San Geminiano, Padua, Pisa, and Genoa, Nikos refusing to eat hot meals and nourishing himself solely on fruit, cheese and bread.

The Greek Passion, after its appearance in Stockholm, won two new friends for Nikos: the German Jewish writer Max Tau and Den Doolaard, a dynamic young writer who, without wasting a moment or even waiting for Nikos' permission, had sent The Greek Passion to his own American publisher—Max Lincoln Schuster—accompanying it with a glowing letter.

When he got back to Antibes, Nikos put the finishing touches on The Last Temptation. And he resumed his conversation with his distant friend, Börje Knös:

Villa Manolita, September 12, 1951

. . . Yesterday we returned from our pélerinage to Italy. Our eyes and hearts are full of the exquisite works men have created. Three or four times in my life I've seen them before, and yet each time they seem to me different, as though I were seeing them for the first time. This time I felt deeply agitated because around each work of art I detected a halo of night in place of the erstwhile luminous halo, knowing as I did that the wing of death hovered over it. Because when I entered the Eremitani Church in Padua, where formerly I had seen Mantegna's sublime frescoes, I now saw broken fragments. A falling bomb had reduced all the paintings to dust. The same in Pisa: in the Camposanto the walls where the splendid frescoes of Orcagna and of Benozzo Gozzoli used to be are now bare, all those miracles of color in ashes. Humanity is committing suicide. I come and go, gazing in an insatiable, tender, bitter way, taking my leave of everything.

You will do the same, now that you are going to Greece. Act quickly so as to be in time to see the "Greek miracle" while it still stands. The Parthenon may turn to dust. . . .

Max Tau, called Magino ("the Magician") by his friends, is a German Jew and over a long period of years was the main collaborator of Bruno Cassirer, the famous art publisher who died in exile in Oxford. At the last moment Max Tau had managed to escape the Hitlerian inferno. He settled in Oslo, married there, and began working tirelessly with his wife to save as many persecuted refugees as possible. Although he did not succeed in saving his own family, he was not blinded by hate. As a reprisal for all this criminal stupidity, he swore to dedicate himself to the rebirth of confidence and friendship between the German people and other peoples with his writing and his actions.

Having a passion for literature, Max Tau loved to discover talented writers and set himself the task of making them better known. The poets and prose writers, both Scandinavian and German, who owe their reputations to him can no longer be counted on the fingers of two hands.

An intimate friend of Albert Schweitzer and of Thomas Mann, it was he who gave them The Greek Passion to read. He loved this book, and he made up his mind that he would get to know the recluse of Antibes and if necessary help him. Nikos' first expression of gratitude was awkward, because he was not yet acquainted with the man he was addressing. And Nikos could never plunge into a warm conversation with a shadow. But since Nikos could not go to Norway, Max Tau was to come to Antibes. Later on, the two men were to live through tragic

503

hours together. They would laugh and even try to outdo each other in framing optimistic plans. Right down to the final days, when Max Tau was to come to the clinic in Freiburg to give his friend unsuspectingly the last farewell embrace.

Antibes, September 15, 1951

Dear Master and Friend,

Your letter has done me much good in my solitude; . . . I am no longer alone—you are there and, in Holland, once again thanks to you, Den Doolaard. . . . How will I ever be able to prove my gratitude to you some day?

. . . Heretofore I have cared little about communicating my troubles and my hopes; but now that I have felt your voice responding to mine, my one aspiration is to discover other friendly voices. Ah, [how wonderful it would be] to found an order, like the religious orders of old, for the purpose of resisting the rottenness and defeatism of our dreadful, splendid epoch! . . .

*If you pass through Antibes, I would be happy to welcome you at my home. Reality aims at nothing else but complying with the fervent desires of the soul. So I hope to see you one day in Antibes. . . .**

The 40,000 words that had been translated from French into the demotic and *katharevousa†* languages and were still shut up in a chest in Prevelakis' house in Athens were on my mind day and night. Not to have a complete French-Greek or Greek-French demotic dictionary and to let this work go for naught seemed monstrous to me. I mentioned it to Nikos so often that he agreed to finish the task if he could find the proper collaborator. We both believed the time had come to see it done.

Villa Manolita, November 6, 1951

. . . The Professor of Modern Greek at the Sorbonne, M. Mirambel,‡ came to Antibes the other day on his way back from Greece,

---

* Letter to Max Tau.
† The technical term for the purist, scholarly form of the Greek language.
‡ Mirambel changed his mind at a later point and made a dictionary by himself.

504

where he'd been spending six months studying the linguistic idiom of Naxos. He stayed here three days, and we laid the foundations for the French-Greek dictionary—katharevousa and demotiki. . . . We're thinking of finishing it in two years. A tremendous job and a very difficult one. But Mirambel is so sagacious, and I love the demotiki so much, that I hope we will create a good and very useful work. . . .

I'm working a great deal. I no longer have time even to sleep. Like an avalanche, the creative storm falls upon us. . . . You must have an iron body to resist. I'd like to rest a bit, but how? I'm in a hurry. Some force within me is in a hurry, merciless. . . .*

When *The Last Temptation* was typed, we sent it off to Börje Knös:

Villa Manolita, November 13, 1951

I'm sending you this work with a great sense of emotional involvement. You have the patience to read it, and little by little you will be caught up, I'm sure, by the same emotion I felt . . . when I wrote it. I wanted to renew and supplement the sacred Myth that underlies the great Christian civilization of the West. It isn't a simple "Life of Christ." It's a laborious, sacred, creative endeavor to reincarnate the essence of Christ, setting aside the dross—falsehoods and pettinesses which all the churches and all the cassocked representatives of Christianity have heaped upon His figure, thereby distorting it.

The pages of my manuscript were often smudged because I could not hold back my tears. Parables which Christ could not possibly have left as the Gospels relate them I have supplemented, and I have given them the noble and compassionate ending befitting Christ's heart. Words which we do not know that He said I have put into His mouth, because He would have said them if His Disciples had had His spiritual force and purity. And everywhere poetry, love of animals and plant life and men, confidence in the soul, certainty that the light will prevail.

For a year now I've been taking out of the library at Cannes all the books written about Christ and Judea, the Chronicles of that time, the Talmud, etc. And so all the details are historically correct, even though I recognize the right of the poet not to follow history in a slavish

---

* Letter to Börje Knös.

way. . . . "ποίησις φιλοσοφώτερον ἱστορίας. [Poetry is more philosophical than history.]"

Writing to Max Tau, who was then in the process of reading *Freedom or Death*, Nikos reverted to the motives that had impelled him to write the Cretan saga:

Antibes, November 16, 1951

. . . *Everything that is in this book is true.* . . . *What I wanted to show above all was the sacred fury that had seized a whole people struggling for its freedom. The most insignificant men became heroes, carried away by this terrifying surge that is so human and so inhuman.* . . .

I lived so intensely through this Cretan insurrection of 1889 that even today, whenever I want to write something that has real depth and a bleeding edge, I dredge it out of these memories of mine as a child. . . . *The sky, the sea, woman, the flower, the idea of death, the brutal beauty of life, I know only through the inflamed heart of a child. It was then that I first made all these mysteries my own, and I still keep them burning and shudder at their contact. If I should lose this shuddering sense and these childhood memories, whatever remained would have no value. There would be only occidental shadows and poor little rational rationalities.*

1952.   The year began badly. After influenza and a high fever, Nikos' lip became swollen again. He was coughing. That worried me. In those good, mischievous eyes, there was only sadness. I chased away a visage that insisted on becoming incrusted like a mask over my own: that of Covarrubias in the Louvre. I said whatever came into my mind to distract the man from his suffering. He remained indifferent to the attentions of my young nephew who prepared him dishes that were works of art. He asked only one thing of us.

"Don't pay any attention to me," he told us. "It's my soul imposing its own laws on my body; it's exasperated at not being able to express itself in *The Third Faust*."

"The devil take *The Third Faust* and the fourth one too," I said.

506

"There are so many themes seething in your brain. You remind me of the old maids at home: 'I want a husband; I want him now; and if I have to wait, I don't want him at all.' "

The good news that for once had come from Greece—one swallow does not make a summer—failed to relieve the situation. P. Prevelakis had prepared the *Spiritual Exercises* for a de luxe edition. One of the best wood carvers in Greece, Iannis Kephalinos, had decorated it with very beautiful discreet vignettes. Prevelakis, aided by Emmanuel Casdagli, was already absorbed in an infinitely meticulous edition of his older friend's complete works. Kazantzakis was delighted about this too. The fact that his friend did not like *The Greek Passion* and did not share the joy and intense emotion with which the succession of great novels had been written could not alter the affectionate faith the aging writer harbored for the younger man. "I've progressed as far as I've been able to," Kazantzakis would say. "It's up to Prevelakis to go beyond me. This is the only way a son has to honor his father."

But with the other Greeks, Kazantzakis was more severe. Here is what he wrote to Börje Knös, who was preparing to go to Greece:

Villa Manolita, Antibes
January 4, 1952

The Greek people in the mountains and in the islands are superb. They have great virtues and human depth. But their leaders today are a disgrace to them. And among the intellectuals you will find a few young people full of aspiration, intellectual curiosity, and disinterested love. The older ones are all lost.

In Greece these books of mine will have no reverberation, because they deal with psychological problems that do not interest the Greeks of the present day. The major and almost the only theme of all my work is the struggle of man with "God": the unyielding, inextinguishable struggle of the naked worm called "man" against the terrifying power and darkness of the forces within him and around him. The stubbornness of the struggle, the tenacity of the little spark in its fight to penetrate the age-old, boundless night and conquer it. The anguished battle to transmute darkness into light, slavery into freedom—all these struggles, alas, are foreign and incomprehensible to the present-day Greek intellectuals. And that is why I am so much of a stranger and so solitary in Greece. . . .

Spring arrived ahead of time, every creature longing for happiness. The spirit loathed the weary body and demanded wings. The swelling disappeared from Nikos' lip gradually. But the sadness persisted. Could this be the first rift discovered by the master of the castle in his castle's cornerstone?

"When I am laid low by a liver attack and you stay by my bedside in the dark for hours on end, holding the basin, changing the compresses, what do you keep saying to me? 'Patience, patience, Lenotschka. Life is beautiful. We are privileged people.' And what do you do to conjure the sickness away? You tell me beautiful Cretan stories. Alas, I don't know any Cretan stories. But just say the word, and I'll read you the most beautiful story ever printed in the books of man."

The eyes I loved came back from very far away. For a second they looked at me with amusement, then plunged once again into an indescribable sadness.

And then—I no longer know by what association of ideas—the snows, the marvelous snows of Gottesgab, came into my mind. The universe of silence and crystal, the light air, the warm breathing of the cows.

"Do you want to go off to a high mountain, alone, and lose yourself in the snows?"

Just before his departure for the Austrian Alps, Nikos received some stirring news from Oslo. If the Greek writers were intriguing against him, the men of letters in Norway had proposed him unanimously for a Nobel prize. And if Greece was reluctant to renew his passport, keeping him a prisoner in France, Norway had agreed to grant him one. "A few hours suffice," Max Tau wrote, "for you to obtain Norwegian citizenship. And if I made an appeal on the radio, you would have enough to take care of yourself in any country you chose." But Kazantzakis, whatever he might say, did not want to change his nationality, nor would he ever ask for help from anyone.

Antibes, January 20, 1952

Dear Master and Friend,

What a miracle! You have arranged and prepared everything, and succeeded admirably. How can I find words to thank you? What guardian angel has guided you into my solitude? And you have taken me

508

by the hand and told me: "Follow me; I know the way; have confidence." And I am following you.

Your letter found me with a fever of 104 degrees. These past two months I've been making a gigantic effort to begin a new book,* and I'm experiencing enormous difficulties. My exasperated soul keeps forming, deforming, reforming my body, mistreating it, casting it onto the bed in a state of feverish inanition. This always happens to me every time that war breaks out within me between the mind and the substance resisting it. It's lucky that your letter has come. I'm sure that it has already done me good.†

On January 30, 1952, he wrote Börje Knös:

. . . In a few days, I'm thinking of leaving for the Austrian Tirol. . . . I'm very tired and must be careful. The effort to begin my new book has tired me very much. . . I've been thinking of many things these past two months. . . . I am no longer, as I was heretofore, entirely free of accountability to anyone. Now, after what has happened to The Greek Passion, I am obliged to see to it that each book of mine will be one step further ahead and higher. The Last Temptation took such a step. The new book must advance yet another stride. And this responsibility is a very heavy one, and my body has grown weary of following the spirit. . . .

And from Kitzbühel, Gasthaus Stang, he wrote to me in Antibes:

February 13, 1952
. . . Today I went down to Kitzbühel. . . . Around noon I came back home. Inexpressible the beauty of the trees, laden with snow, motionless, all in bloom. And the mountains all around white-white and very high. And it's always snowing, snowing. The snow piles up many meters high. The deer find nothing in the forests to eat and come down to the city. . . . I've been remembering Gottesgab; only here the landscape is most magnificent, one of the most beautiful in Europe. . . .

---

* The Third Faust.
† Letter to Max Tau.

I'm well, relaxed, not coughing. The last traces of the herpès [skin eruption] have vanished. From tomorrow on I'll be busy at the Ader-phophades [Fratricides], to produce the nouvelle that Vieweg is asking me for. . . .

I imagine that all goes well at Manolita, and that you've gotten used to my absence. When I go away, I'm all pangs of conscience for having tyrannized over you. Let's hope that the mountains will give me peace and that I'll behave better. . . .

What crowds, what women, what old hags set out every morning through the snows to ski. . . . What high spirits and vitality, and they come back at noon hungry as beasts. . . . White, white forests, all fir trees. No bird, no animal; the stillness of the age before birds and animals were created. Only once in a while the icicles hanging from the rooftops break off from the weight and fall. The snow-laden roofs craquent [crackle]; and all the while people keep climbing up with shovels to clear away the snow.

That's my life. All my letters will say the same thing. . . .

God be with you, my love! No one else exists in the world. . . .

From Kitzbühel Nikos soon moved to a quieter place: Lofer. The innkeeper, who had taken a liking to him, offered to tell his fortune, as he had done, so he said, for Hitler in person. . . . "Do not exhaust yourself by searching for your themes," he told Nikos, after reading the lines in his hand. "They will come to you; be patient; give them time to come. Besides you are going to live a very long time. Only you will undergo a very serious illness."

Nikos is no longer at my side to halt my regrets. And I do have regrets. I regret having lightly undertaken such and such a trip. . . . I regret having been carried away by the exaggerated optimism of my fellow wayfarer. . . . I regret not having obeyed my own instincts, which sometimes tried to warn us. . . . Above all, I regret having opened our door one day, for our Destiny had borrowed the form of a strange woman with red hair.

Through the pane in the door, I had seen sparse red hair standing up on end like matchsticks, a face marred by some serious accident, an expression as of troubled water. The stranger spoke to me in barbarous French. I was in a great hurry, about to miss the bus, and Nikos was waiting for me at Sigale. In spite of all this, I stayed and listened to the stranger. She had come, so she said, to ask for a room to lodge a friend. She had been our neighbor for a short time, and she had noticed us on our walks. She was an "artist," and she knew all the great men of our time.

In the most circumspect fashion possible, I brought the interview to an end. She wasn't at all put off; she promised to come again to make our further acquaintance as soon as we returned.

Today, after so many years of painful reflection, I still believe that behind the features of this redheaded woman our Destiny was hidden.

After Sigale and Italy, we had resumed our life in Antibes when the redheaded woman rang our doorbell once more. We accepted her invitation. In the course of reading the newspapers from her own country, she had been the first to learn about the amazing success of *The Greek Passion* in the Netherlands. From that point on, she kept at us incessantly to take a trip in her company, and to go and take care of Nikos' herpes in Holland.

And that is how, in December 1952, we found ourselves in Utrecht —in a palatial hospital.

The Dutch publisher was more than kind, night and day by our side—a marvel of a man. The Blijstras, our friends from Aegina, were charming; Den Doolaard and his young wife extremely interesting; as well as the missionary, J. von G., who used to come to discuss all kinds of metaphysical and social subjects with Nikos. Only our doctor was too young and too obstinate.

The tests had not shown any formidable illness, and we were supposed to leave the hospital on December 5. On the sixth, St. Nicholas' feast day, Kazantzakis' admirers had organized a reception in his honor in Amsterdam. But on the fourth of December, Nikos' lip became a bit swollen.

"Since my husband's lip is swollen, we shan't leave the hospital," I said to the doctor. "In any case, he won't be able to appear in public."

"I promised you that you would leave the hospital on December fifth," retorted the doctor, "and you will leave. Mr. Kazantzakis will take his streptomycin in his pocket."

"It's horribly cold, and we're not accustomed to it. Influenza is raging in Amsterdam. And you have advised me on many occasions, doctor, to take care that my husband doesn't catch cold."

"Mr. Kazantzakis will not catch cold. He's very robust."

Kazantzakis did catch cold. Worse still, he caught the flu. We had hardly had time to admire the Rembrandts, Frans Halses, Vermeers, and van Goghs in the museums scattered throughout Holland when Nikos had to go to bed with a high fever.

Impossible to describe in detail what followed. After several desperate days in Amsterdam, we went back to Utrecht. Once again the young doctor proved headstrong. In vain, I begged him to bring the hospital's ophthalmologist to examine Nikos' eye, which had gotten red and was hurting him. "It's nothing," the doctor insisted. "It's part of the general condition."

The tests showed no change in the blood. But as Nikos' face had become very swollen, the doctor did administer Cortisone to him for the first time.

Ah, Nikosmou, Nikos, how rebellious you grew then, sick man that you were! How you kicked your feet in bed, ordering me to take you back to Antibes right there and then.

"There's nothing wrong with me. As soon as we're back home, I'll be cured."

My pleas were in vain. Instead of trying to impose fortitude on his patient, the young doctor whom our Destiny had recommended to us (I learned this later) was spending his evenings in the churches, praying for him. And he begged the publisher to procure for us the return ticket that I was pretending not to be able to obtain.

Perspicacious Cassandra, I foresaw our future misfortunes. Being inexperienced as a nurse, I allowed myself to be affected by my companion's extreme nervousness. I had never seen him in that kind of state.

Once we were back in Antibes, the condition of the eye grew worse. Finally, the day when I saw the eye covered with mold, I took matters into "my own" hands.

"Doctor," I said to the oculist, "this evening my husband will leave for Paris. Another day here, and he will lose his eye."

"God gave us two eyes, Madame. If we lose the one, we still have the other one left!"

Fortunately, in Paris, our friend Dr. Sterianos and the faithful Métrals were waiting for Nikos at the station. And for the first time his eye was saved.

512

(But I am anticipating. It is difficult to recount the searing episodes of one's own life in chronological order. Quickly, quickly, one rolls head over heels through the inferno in order to come out into the light as soon as possible.

From that point on, I never left Nikos. And so I have only a series of postcards, "health bulletins," which he sent me at a later point from Freiburg, when he went there to be treated by Dr. Heilmeyer.)

Now I must move backward again—to the summer of 1952.

After Vichy and Kitzbühel, Nikos wanted to take me once again to Italy. This time we visited Bologna, Ravenna, Rimini, San Marino, Perugia, Assisi, Arezzo, Siena . . .

Unforgettable hours. The delight of discovering and rediscovering Giotto, Piero della Francesca, the Poverello. The Etruscans in Perugia. But above all Assisi, where Nikos' reminiscences brought both Jörgensen and the Countess Erichetta Pucci to life for me; where we were once again seized by the mad impulse to fix up an old house; where we wandered in shady lanes singing the *Fioretti* while eating figs and peaches, two kinds of fruit we had never before seen coupled.

"Are you capable of kissing a leper on the mouth?" I asked him abruptly one day when we had just come out of the Portiuncula.

"Never that!" Nikos replied with a shudder.

"Well then, what good have Saint Francis and Schweitzer done you? Would you be capable of living among lepers and sacrificing to them all the other resources of your being, if you had as many resources as Albert Schweitzer or the Poverello?"

"N-n-no. I am no longer like that. I never was."

"Well then?"

"Well then, I've learned one thing: that man can still make the miracle descend upon the earth. It's enough if he avoids the highway leading to easy happiness and chooses the uphill path leading to the impossible. . . ."

"Do you still regret not having taken the path of action?"

"I've tried on many occasions, as you know, to change my nature. Now I only desire one thing: to reach the end of the path that I've chosen. Who knows, Lenotschka? Perhaps there was no other for me. Perhaps, if one reaches the end, all the paths meet."

"In the miracle?"

"In the miracle we call life, which is eternal."

Once back in Antibes, he wrote Börje Knös on September 9, 1952:

Once again, I'm seated before the desk of my martyrdom and my joy, holding my pen, writing. I saw very beautiful things in Italy and was very happy. I did a great deal of thinking, and in Assisi I lived once more with the great martyr and hero whom I love so much, Saint Francis. And now I'm gripped by a desire to write a book about him. Will I write it? I don't know yet. I'm waiting for a sign, and then I'll begin. Always, as you know, the struggle within me between man and God, between substance and spirit, is the stable leitmotif of my life and work.

On returning home, I found the manuscript of the translation of the Iliad that Kakridis and I did. A great temptation, and I plunged at once into the Homeric verses, as I might into the cool sea on a very hot day. I am looking at the translation freshly, correcting it, and I am overjoyed at seeing the wealth, harmony and plasticity of our demotic language. I don't think that I've ever felt a greater sensual pleasure. What a language, what sweetness and power! . . .

Yesterday in Cannes, I made the acquaintance of my American publisher, Max Lincoln Schuster. We had a long talk. I gave him the English translation of Zorba. . . . Today I received an enthusiastic telegram from him, agreeing to publish Zorba as well. I was happy because, as you know, I love this book very much, because the human being Zorba I loved very much.

Once again the game of cat and mouse. On the one side the cake, on the other the poison. In September we were in a state of perfect euphoria, in December submerged in grief.

We had been getting ready to go to Cannes to meet the American publisher Max Schuster and his wife, Ray, when the mailman brought us a copy of Zorba the Greek in the English edition of John Lehman. Carrying this book under his arm, Nikos presented himself at the Hotel Carlton.

"Excuse me for a moment," Mr. Schuster said. "I must go upstairs to look for something." He took a very long time to come back. When he did come down, he was grinning from ear to ear. At the table, he hardly noticed what he was putting into his mouth. When he wasn't reading himself, he asked his wife to read some passage from Zorba, or to annotate some page of the book.

During the whole walk back to the hotel, he insisted that I tell him about *The Last Temptation*. Ever since this initial meeting, Kazantzakis' work kept on appearing in America, book after book. On each new visit to Europe the Schusters used to come to see their friends. We had never hoped for such understanding.

"Max, take *The Odyssey* in your arms. I want to take a photograph. Because you're going to publish it, I foresee it," said Ray, taking a photo of her husband with the great folio of *The Odyssey* in his arms.

Before we set off for Utrecht, Nikos wrote the following note to Börje Knös:

Antibes, Villa Manolita
November 7, 1952

. . . I'm sorry about having to leave Saint Francis for a month. Every morning when I go up to my desk, I find him sitting there like a model in front of the painter, waiting for me. And I feel moved as I begin to narrate his life and portray his city and visage.

In Holland the success of *The Greek Passion* kept growing. The newspapers had much to say about the Greek writer who had come to Utrecht for treatment. Once again the tests reassured us there was nothing seriously amiss. With an easy conscience, we made our plans. This country's numerous museums attracted us the way mirrors attract larks.

Utrecht, November 27, 1952

Dearest Comrade,

I read your last letter with great emotion, and I'm glad you liked The Last Temptation. *. . . Here in Holland, I have had some interesting conversations with pastors about the theological side of the work. Some were shocked that Christ had temptations. But while I was writing this book, I felt what Christ felt. I became Christ. And I knew*

515

definitely that great temptations, extremely enchanting and often legitimate ones, came to hinder him on his road to Golgotha. But how could the theologians know all this?

We'll stay three days longer in Utrecht, and then our tour of the cities and museums will begin. The doctor will tell Eleni tomorrow what diet she must follow. Yesterday they gave her a transfusion—of Dutch blood.

I'm looking forward joyfully to seeing so many canvases, and what canvases! This will be sure to benefit Saint Francis, whom I left half finished on my desk at the Villa Manolita. All the arts have the same root, and sometimes a piece of music or a painting does me more good and influences me more than a literary work. That's why I'm so impatient to see Rembrandt and Hals and Brueghel and van Gogh.

At this moment, as I'm writing you, it's snowing. The trees look crystalline. A flock of seagulls is flying outside the window. I'd been longing very much for the northern landscape and the northern silence. . . .

The photograph I sent you is now in a lot of Dutch newspapers and in the window displays of the bookshops. Eleni is pleased about it. Unfortunately I can't feel happy—I yearn now only for Saint Francis. . . .*

Utrecht, December 23, 1952

. . . The tour of Holland is over. Day after tomorrow, we're leaving by airplane for Manolita. The medical results were very good. There's nothing seriously wrong with Eleni or with me. But we know now what regimen we must follow.

Merry Christmas, dear friend, much joy, health, and happiness to your home. May all the angels who sang Hosanna in Excelsis Deo that night in Bethlehem come to sing upon the rooftop of your home too!

Pax et bonum!
Nikos†

1953.   The casual reader will never guess that between these last two letters much water had flowed under the bridge. About his own

---

* Letter to Tea Anemoyanni.
† Letter to Börje Knös.

516

personal sufferings Nikos never breathed a word to his friends. Later on, at the Bichat Hospital or in the little clinic at Buttes-Chaumont, he amazed everyone. Tove and Max Tau, who had come from Oslo;* George Hill, the English publisher from Oxford; A. Bloemsma from Utrecht; our Paris friends; our everlasting friends—how often we were to relive these painful moments at the Métrals' or at the Puaux', who had taken turns in giving us lodging. And what a lesson Nikos had given us on how to behave in the presence of suffering!

"He's a lion! I've seen a lion!" exclaimed Marie-Louise Bataille after seeing Nikos for the first time bedridden, with a bandaged eye, unshaven, and ferocious. "Fear nothing, Eleni, my dear; he's right to be optimistic. It's not he but his instinct that dictates his words to him. . . ."

Three months later, one foot in the grave, with an enormous pus-filled abscess, barely conscious of the outside world, he was to ask me for cherries and to dictate Franciscan haikai to me.† And these poems are perfect, stark, transparent, just as was his body, which was already allowing his soul to reach the surface. And he dictated them to me without crossing anything out: an exception to the rule, because this man had never been capable of dictating. This is what I called "the second miracle of Saint Francis," the first one having saved us from the famine in Aegina.

Between the first and the second catastrophes we had several weeks of calm spent by Nikos in the company of his "beggarman of Assisi."

Antibes, March 19, 1953

. . . I was glad to get your letter. The eye improves all the time, but I still can't settle down to writing because it gets tired easily. And so Saint Francis is waiting at my desk. All the same my mind is working away. The whole book is finished inside me and I now have only to copy it. As you've seen, the foreign critics are unexpectedly enthusiastic and talk in exaggerated terms, so that if I didn't have a tough Cretan brain, I would be happy. But now I know that what I want I have not attained, and time is passing, and I don't know whether I shall ever attain it. When will I get down to The Third Faust? That's where my power will show itself. I keep postponing it, because I feel that I'm not

---

* They came first to Antibes, where I was supposed to be waiting for them.
† See Report to Greco and Saint Francis.

yet worthy of it. But in the clinic at Paris, at long last, I found the myth. And so the first, the most difficult, step has been taken. God help me! . . .

But just at that point, one fine morning the eye began to get red. Panic-struck, I begged Nikos to return to Paris. He refused. The old eye doctor at Antibes was an alcoholic, but we did not know this. Intending to cauterize the eyelashes, which had grown and gotten shaggy, he burned Nikos' eye.

"Ah," he exclaimed with irritation, "I've burned you!"

And once again Nikos had to go to Paris. Just before he boarded the train, the eye doctor punctured him with a milk injection, ordering him to take two more in Paris—without explaining to him that his purpose was to stimulate a solidified abscess.

This time Nikos Kazantzakis would not have escaped death if Professor Jean Bernard had not taken him in hand.

I pass over the details of this new episode, caused once again by the doctor's lack of experience and our own destiny, covetous at all costs of removing Nikos. I cannot pass over in silence Kazantzakis' attitude. When I arrived at the home of our friends the Métrals, I found him in a state of absolute rapture, and he exclaimed as he opened his eyes to see me: "Be we-e-e-elcome! Why do you get upset over such a trifle?" And later in the clinic in Montmartre: "Read me this *Freedom or Death*, my love—no, take some paper instead and write."

Atrocious, noble hours! He dictated to me a letter to his friend, Börje Knös:

Paris, June 8, 1953

. . . During this illness, I've written several Franciscan haïkaï, and I think they are good. Brief, full of feeling and meaning and full of Franciscan familiarity with God. My life is dark and despairing: so many months inside the walls of the clinic and the hospital. If it weren't for Eleni and Francis, I believe I could not have endured it. I should have opened the door and left. But I think of you too and of the few, very few, other friends I have in the world, and I would never want to dishearten them. I resist, fight, rally all the forces of light in me to

---

* Letter to Tea Anemoyanni.

conquer the darkness. And I believe I've already begun to conquer it. I'm entirely better. Only the wound still has to heal. So don't worry, very dear friend; I'll soon be on my feet and fighting at your side. Because we're both brave fighters and have dedicated life and happiness to the great goal: the conquest of matter by Spirit. . . .

Paris, June 12, 1953

. . . Don't worry at all about my health. Everything is going well now, and I hope by the end of the month to return to Antibes. There I'll await Kakridis, so that we can harness ourselves to the great work. I persist in thinking that this work is a philosophical and literary monument that will give glory to our demotic tongue. . . .

As for Saint Francis, we must not be in a hurry. Now, in the course of my illness, this work has been growing steadily richer inside me. I took notes, wrote Franciscan songs, created scenes, and the work kept constantly expanding with the great wealth [of new material]. I shall rewrite it from the beginning with new impetus. . . . As much as I could, I've tried to take advantage of the illness to rewrite it inside of me; and so I hope that I transformed the illness into spirit.*

Nikos' fervor for Saint Francis I explained to myself by his predilection for the hero in the guise of a saint. But how would he manage to devote a book to him? At this late stage in his life, was he going to plunge into Catholic hagiology? From our long discussions on this theme, scattered remarks come back to my mind:

In the delirium of the fever (you remember the clinic at Buttes-Chaumont?) I had thought I saw the Poverello bending over me. During my nights of insomnia, he came and sat by my bedside and told me his life, like some old nurse.

In my book, I will record the words of the Poverello, but also other words that he might have spoken, as I did for the parables in the Gospels. For I am sure that Christ did not stop at a halfway point. His goodness transcended what His Disciples admitted.

I'll not be writing literature or making a psychological analysis either. What interests me are the unsuspected forces existing in the

---

* Letter to Börje Knös.

human soul which, either out of cowardice or for lack of an ideal, we allow to sleep and perish.

Saint Francis becomes contemporary both because in his own heart he had realized the perfect union with the cosmos—to which present-day science is leading us along other roads—and also because his heart had found the solution of the problems that are still insoluble: poverty, injustice, violence. Only the love preached by him could bring us to a solution of these problems.

Who was the woman saint who ran through the corridors of his monastery, uttering a piercing cry, "There is no love for love"? In our own epoch there is no love for love. And this is the only key which can unlock happiness on the earth.

The old hagiologists emphasized the Poverello's state of beatitude, neglecting the arduous path that leads to this beatitude. It must have been a hard struggle; and it's precisely this struggle that moves me. The moments when man surges toward his salvation seem to me the most sublime ones in the whole human journey. The greater the difficulty a mortal has in liberating himself, the more we derive courage from his example and find consolation in his victory.

Saint Francis tortured his body very much. But toward the end of his life he took pity on it. "My brother donkey," he said to it, "my brother donkey, forgive me, I've mistreated you overmuch."

Through his tears Saint Francis saw the face of God smiling at him. Thanks to this presence of God in all things, everything became pure for Saint Francis. Pure were the ashes he cast into his soup, pure the wolf who ravaged the flocks of Gubbio, pure Death, which was on its way and which he greeted as a sister.

On my companion's grave face was I able to detect the same tender feeling for the death that was going to carry him away? I cannot say. Perhaps, in keeping with his dignity as a human being, he could envisage it without hatred, but also without any joy.

That summer Nikos was no longer able to climb the fig trees at daybreak; nor could he help us pick the olives now. The wound was long in closing.

Nevertheless, in spite of this still-open wound and the new allergenic symptoms caused by an overdose of arsenic, Nikos preserved his even temper and creative ardor. Indeed he took joy in two events: a brief visit by P. Prevelakis and the arrival of Iannis Kakridis. The latter was to stay with us almost a month. And during this period the two men revised their translation of the *Iliad* for the last time. All that remained was to find the money to publish it.

The proposition made by a university in East Germany to publish both the ancient Greek text and the modern Greek translation in a single volume delighted Kazantzakis. But Kakridis was opposed to it. Nikos did not insist. Unconsciously, he was little by little entering the final phase of his life—that of renunciation. Everything gave him pleasure. He rejoiced in a flower, a smile, the flight of a bird with a falling feather. Nothing was indispensable to him now except music and his unquenchable thirst for justice and liberty.

And so we reach the year 1954.

> Antibes, January 8, 1954
>
> . . . My wife sends you her greetings. . . . All day long she's busy with the little new house.* The carpenters are working away. My desk is being gotten ready. We're hoping to move in in April. It's a pity you're not with us so we could celebrate. At times, as I look at the new little house that is being built, I think of the words of a tenth-century Moslem ascetic, who was asked, "Why don't you build a house too?" "Because," he answered, "a soothsayer told me that I was going to live only seven hundred years. Well, is it worth the trouble to build a house for so short a space of time?"
>
> And I was told by a soothsayer that I would live 83 years. And yet I have the naïveté and arrogance to build a house! . . .†

> January 20, 1954
>
> These days I'm looking over all my works and putting them into definitive shape, in hopes . . . that my Complete Works . . . will be published.
>
> Here it's springtime. A brilliant Cretan sun. Heat. I'm thinking of you in the cold and fog. But hyperborean Apollo has his own charm too.

---

* A tiny little house in ruins on the ramparts of old Antibes.
† Letter to Börje Knös.

The soul is compelled to become concentrated in itself, whereas in warm climates it gets diffused, goes sauntering in the sun, feeling that higher than thought is the joy of life.

. . . The little house is progressing, very small but charming. We've called it "Koukouli"—a silk-worm cocoon. You enter as a worm and emerge a soul (butterfly) . . .*

This February 18, 1954, Nikos was to celebrate one of his most stirring birthdays. Max Tau, the "magician," had many surprises up his sleeve. His pigeons arrived from the four corners of the earth, carrying in their beaks messages of friendship and gratitude.

Already on the evening before, like a still snow-covered Father Christmas, he began dazzling us with the gifts he kept laying in front of Nikos. Tangible gifts and others kept appearing, each one more pleasant than the last. The success of the play taken from *The Greek Passion* at Norske Teatret in Oslo; new publications just about everywhere; new glowing reviews; translations in preparation in more than twenty languages—a body of work that was beginning to find new hearts and ears to listen to it.

We clinked glasses full of Samos wine in Norwegian crystal. Tau broke into eulogies of Norway, his adopted land: this people that was solid because profound and faithful to its principles: these men of letters who, at their own expense, persisted unanimously in proposing a Greek, Nikos Kazantzakis, for the Nobel prize. "If you want to obtain Norwegian nationality, there is nothing easier," he said.

Kazantzakis, however, wanted to remain what he was—a Cretan with an African heart—in spite of the strange behavior of his own Crete, which had refused to react to the slander showered on him because of *Freedom or Death*, that Cretan saga.†

But this February 18, 1954, Manolita, whitewashed and all lit up, with the flag of friendship hoisted on her roof, was celebrating.

From dawn on, Max Tau in person ran to open the door and applaud the young cyclists from the post office, who were shuttling back and forth between the city and Manolita, weaving an invisible but sturdy web of friendship and confidence.

---

* Letter to Börje Knös.
† Only Mil. Hourmouzios raised his voice in the *Kathimerini* to defend the truth when the tempest was at its peak.

522

I had called our cat, Poupouli,* to give her the cream she adored, but she had disappeared. We vainly plodded through the whole of Park Saramartel, as well as the most remote streets of Antibes and Juan-les-Pins. Like thieves, we invaded all the enclosures where we could hear a miaow. She was light as a feather, all downy and tufted, and we prayed she had not been eaten by Mangia-Gatta, the Italian woman who shut cats up in boxes and fattened them like rabbits.

At first Nikos endured my laments. But I had to stop them abruptly one day when he woke up with a start, crying "Poupouli! Poupouli!" and, trembling, jumped out of bed and ran over to the window.

Poupouli did not come back, and Nikos swore never to allow another cat to cross our threshold.

In May 1954 Nikos wrote two letters to Börje Knös:

Antibes, May 1, 1954
. . . Yesterday I received a telegram from the publisher in Germany: Letzte Versuchung auf päpstlichen Index [The Last Temptation on the Papal Index]. I've always been amazed at the narrow-mindedness and narrow-heartedness of human beings. Here is a book that I wrote in a state of deep religious exaltation, with fervent love for Christ; and now the representative of Christ, the Pope, has no understanding of it at all, he cannot sense the Christian love with which it was written, and he condemns it! And yet it is in keeping with the wretchedness and slavery of the contemporary world that I should be condemned.

Antibes, May 14, 1954
. . . My New York publisher . . . was at our home yesterday with his wife. We had a long talk, and he wants The Odyssey to be translated. He will pay the translator (Mr. Kimon Friar) to come to stay in Antibes for six months, to collaborate with me. A gigantic and very difficult task, demanding superhuman patience and love.

Freedom or Death is still enraging the Greeks. The Bishop of Chios accused it of being shameful, treasonable, antireligious, and a slander against—Crete! So you can imagine in what a barbarous state my native land is wallowing; i.e., the official Greeks, politicians and church-

---

* "Downy feather" in Greek.

men. And the Orthodox Church of America convened and damned *The Last Temptation* as extremely indecent, atheistic, and treasonable, after admitting that they hadn't read it and had based their case on the articles in *Estia*. . . .

And I sit here in my solitude, calm, dedicated to my duty, to the best of my ability shaping the Greek language and the Greek spirit! "Ad tuum, domine, tribunal appello [*To thy court I appeal, O Lord*]," as Tertullian wrote.

This was the phrase from Tertullian that Nikos Kazantzakis telegraphed to the Commission on the Index. In his response to the Orthodox Greek Church, he added: "You have execrated me, Holy Fathers; I bless you. I pray that your conscience may be as clean as mine and that you may be as moral and as religious as I am."

The time was drawing near for us to be taking leave of Manolita. Five years of "joy and suffering, such as befits a human being," five years during which I was never bored—the two solemn promises that Nikos had made me in one of his very first letters—had just come to an end.

But if he was overjoyed each time he discovered a new white hair on my head—"What a joy! You're beginning to grow old in my hands"—I could not be the same as I observed his body gradually becoming desiccated and his face withering, although his mind was still as youthful as in the days of our first meeting.

We had left our cliff in Aegina with one pair of shoes and one extra shirt. It was decreed that we would never see Aegina again and that quite a few things we loved would disappear forever. Feeling himself in exile, Nikos had been horror-stricken in Antibes at the thought of having to sign a lease for three years. We were to live there for nine years, and five of those years—the best ones—at Manolita.

And then the hour of farewell tolled. Our gardener, Camous, paralyzed with rheumatism, offered us a trembling hand.

"So you're leaving us," he mumbled through his Gallic mustache. "And we'll never see each other any more."

"We'll come to visit you often, grandfather!" Nikos promised him. "We'll even come to help you eat the medlars," I added with feigned gaiety. "Pick the olives, pick the figs and grapes—and eat your kakis, grandfather."

Camous departed first. In his jacket a tiny scrap of paper was found, scribbled in pencil:

"Dear Madame Eleni Kazantzaki, I am going off to Paradise. Up there I will forgive the harm my enemies have done me. I hope we'll meet again in Paradise."

We left behind us a verdant hill, a big garden and a vast villa, to burrow into a tiny fisherman's abode, a mere basement, but a basement perched high on a cliff overlooking an old village square. From our trellis-shaded balcony we plunged headlong into the world of Utrillo, the impregnable sea in the background.

The first evening, when we had drawn the curtains and lit our lamp, we thought we were dreaming.

"Are you happy, Nikosmou? Are you going to be able to work here?"

"I think so. It's not a house; it's a downy garment that will keep us warm in winter. . . ."

"With stone walls so thick it'll keep us cool in summer," I put in.

"We'll call it 'Koukouli.' We've entered it as worms; we'll go out as butterflies," said Nikos, pursuing his dreams among the smoke rings from his pipe.

In the meantime, his books and his manuscripts had arrived from Aegina. With feverish haste, he began sorting them out. I could hear the crackle and rattling of paper being torn up.

"Is it a good thing to tear up so much?"

"Yes, I think so." And the papers kept going out to the trash by the basketful.

Antibes, June 21, 1954

. . . And so our friend Zorba has won the prize for the best foreign novel published in France. I can imagine how he must be laughing away in Paradise, where he'll be . . .

From my sun-drenched balcony here, I observe with amazement and pitié the passions of human beings. And I can't go on with my work, because of my daydreaming about a better humanity and struggling to formulate it. By formulating it, I facilitate its coming, I think.

Day after tomorrow . . . the American poet Mr. Friar is arriving. He's being sent by my publisher in New York, who is paying him for six months to stay with me so that we can translate The Odyssey. . . . I think that my whole soul, all the flame and light I've been able to extract from the substance of which I am constituted, is crystallized in The Odyssey. All the other works are parergons. That is why I have agreed to make the sacrifice of giving up six months.

Day after tomorrow, we'll be moving at last into the Cocoon. I've arranged my books; Eleni is jubilant, like a bird that has built its nest and is now entering to warm its eggs. What eggs? The books that I shall write and she will copy. They're all the children we have. . . .*

The Cocoon, tiny but comfortable, had its acolytes. Often the doorbell would ring at daybreak.

"Greetings, my midwife," Nikos would exclaim, as his young friend the painter Ladislas Kijno appeared. "What are we going to bring forth this morning?"

"I've thought of . . ." Kijno used to begin, with a loving look at the aged man, still unshaven, already bent over his manuscripts, never out of temper, if one had something to tell him.

"I've thought of . . ." And his Chaliapin bass voice used to swell.

I would hear them laughing and chattering for a few minutes. Kijno would go off, and the house plunged once again into silence.

In the afternoon, Dor de la Souchère, curator of the Antibes Museum and admirer and friend of Picasso, used to come with his notebook. For these past years he had been thinking of writing a book about Kazantzakis. And the latter answered his questions willingly.

During the years at the Cocoon, a fine-looking young man with a bronzed complexion had made his appearance. An Egyptian by birth, he lived in Aix-en-Provence and was the owner and editor of an excellent French-language periodical, Les Quatre Dauphins [The Four Dolphins]. Aziz Izzet knew how to captivate Kazantzakis. Fluent in German, English, French, and Italian; of Arabian descent; a revolutionary and at the same time a mystic—he moved with ease over a terrain that Nikos had trodden thousands of times. And so from the very beginning, Nikos had entrusted the Spiritual Exercises to him. I sincerely believe that the little book devoted to Nikos by this Oriental is perfect in its way.

In 1955, Jules Dassin came to the Cocoon too. A smiling, good-hearted child and a delightful storyteller. He read us the English text of his scenario taken from The Greek Passion. Nikos was enthralled by the

---

* Letter to Börje Knös.

monosyllabic dialogue. "Ah, ah," he kept exclaiming, "if I weren't a Greek, there's the language I would have liked to wield!" Many of the anecdotes which Dassin brought back from Crete amused the exile of Antibes, producing a sigh of incurable nostalgia in him.

Another well-loved figure, a modest but great man, also came to the Cocoon for the first time. His name was Bohuslav Martinu. Dressed utterly unpretentiously, carrying his raincoat over his arm, he presented himself to two creatures who had never heard a bar of his music. Modest to the depths of his soul, he concealed his surprise. He remained openhearted, and in a few minutes the two men knew each other like brothers.

Bohuslav Martinu wrote the libretto for his opera *The Greek Passion* by himself, with practically no help from Nikos. The composer submitted his ideas, and the writer, not finding anything to change in them, accepted them immediately. The two creators did not have the good fortune to be present at the world premiere of the opera, performed in Zurich in 1962 and conducted by Martinu's intimate friend, Paul Sacher.

Whenever distinguished travelers, Greeks or foreigners whom we already knew or who wanted to meet Nikos, visited the Castanakises (they were our neighbors now), they never failed to give us a sign.

Nikos was also working a great deal with Pierre Sipriot, well known in France for his radio program entitled *Conversations*; and this was during the same period when he had to help finish the English version of *The Odyssey*. Doing these two jobs simultaneously exhausted him beyond measure.

Some of the replies he made to Pierre Sipriot I shall summarize as well as I can. The answer to the question on the relationship of the writer's work to his own time was most explicit:

I used to believe that there must be a great difference between vital literary work and action. A genuine novelist can live only in his own time, and by living this reality he acquires consciousness of his own responsibility and assumes the duty of helping his fellow men to envisage and solve, as far as possible, the crucial problems of his era. If he acquires consciousness of his mission, the novelist endeavors to compel the reality that is flowing formlessly to take on the form he regards as most worthy of man. . . .

Concerning the history of Greece after the fall of Constantinople in 1453, the Turkish Occupation, the liberation of a part of Greece after the Insurrection of 1821, and Nikos Kazantzakis' novel, *Freedom or Death*, dealing only with the liberation of Crete, Nikos answered:

Greece was always the plaything of the Great Powers. We suffered very much beneath the yoke of the Turks; we have suffered very much and are still suffering beneath the hypocritical yoke of the Great Powers. The Greek people are a martyred people, all the more so because their need for liberty is as compelling as their need for bread. At the time Hitler was threatening to invade Norway, I was traveling in Crete. I was crossing a ravine when I heard a stentorian voice calling down to me from the mountain top: "Stop, my child, stop!" I stopped, lifted my eyes, and saw an old shepherd jumping from rock to rock. At last, standing out of breath on a boulder above me, he shouted: "How is Norway getting along, my child?" "It's doing better, grandfather," I answered; "it's doing better." "God be praised," he said, making the sign of the cross. His old face was shining with relief. "Do you want a cigarette, grandfather?" I asked. "I don't need anything, since Norway's doing better," he replied; "I don't need anything." And he raised his staff and began climbing the mountain again.

There's the Greek for you. This old shepherd certainly did not know where Norway is. Perhaps he didn't even know if it was a country or a woman. But he did know what liberty is. . . .

And now you can understand how tragic the destiny of Greece is. She, the mother of liberty, has been suffering brutal or masked enslavement throughout centuries. So how could you expect a Greek writer not to enlist all his powers in the service of liberty?

With reference to Nikos Kazantzakis' novels, Pierre Sipriot asked whether they were an extension of his political activity or whether on the contrary the human problem had come to overshadow social, political, and moral questions. The writer answered:

Everything that I experienced in the course of a brief immersion in political life was disillusioning. Every effort on the side of the Good encountered the forces of Evil arrayed against it. . . . The struggle is still going on in Greece, as everywhere else. Liberty has not yet borne fruit, but it will do so. For ·a mysterious law exists, regulating human destiny; even when it is seriously wounded, bleeding, sometimes even spattered with mud, the Good triumphs.

Having seen that I was not capable of using all my resources in political action, I returned to my literary activity. There lay the battle-field suited to my temperament. I wanted to make my novels the extension of my own father's struggle for liberty. But gradually, as I kept deepening my responsibility as a writer, the human problem came to overshadow political and social questions. All the political, social, and economic improvements, all the technical progress cannot have any regenerating significance, so long as our inner life remains as it is at present. The more the intelligence unveils and violates the secrets of Nature, the more the danger increases and the heart shrinks.

To go backward is utopian. But the machine must be harnessed to serve the mind. . . . We have arrived at a crucial crossroads in human destiny. We have entered the Apocalypse. Consequently we cannot be clearly conscious of the horror engulfing us. We must either re-create the world or perish.

Commenting on a quotation from Henry Miller, who had defined modern Greece as a holy land, because her only needs are spiritual and poverty does not make people unhappy there, Kazantzakis answered:

Poverty, when it is not excessive and does not reach the point of hunger and misery, is really well suited to any people or any individual averse to weighting the spirit down with the flesh. But when poverty is excessive, it becomes a blight that degrades man. In Greece the poverty is excessive. According to official statistics, 2,300,000 Greeks—that is, one third of the population—do not eat when they are hungry.

It is shameful to remain unperturbed by so tragic a situation. The writer, who is by nature more sensitive, cannot repress his indignation or shirk his responsibility. He is duty bound not to sleep; he must keep his people on the alert. Furthermore, I think that this role of the writer as agitator is indispensable in all countries ruled by injustice. I mean to say, throughout virtually the whole earth.

Haunted by this danger, driven by this duty as an agitator, I compel myself in my work to set heroic models before the people, not fictitious heroes who never existed, but those who have emerged from the vitals of my race. They alone incarnate the claims and the hopes of the famished and the persecuted and are capable of showing the people the way toward salvation.

In June 1954, we took refuge in Sauze (above Barcelonnette) on a peak 1,400 meters high, so that Nikos could work with Kimon Friar on the English translation of *The Odyssey.*

The exhausting work at Sauze had not benefited Nikos. Seeing how unwell he looked, we decided to follow the advice of my younger sister and go to consult Professor Heilmeyer in Freiburg after the premiere of *Sodom and Gomorrah* in Mannheim.

We arrived at the University Clinic one morning. "Come back at three o'clock to learn the results of the tests," we were told at the laboratory. "You will see Professor Heilmeyer then."

Three hours later, after drinking a good lot of brown beer, one of Nikos' lovable peccadilloes, we went back, feeling sure there was nothing seriously amiss.

"Mr. Kazantzakis, I cannot allow you to go away. I must keep you here for a cure," said the German professor.

"Impossible!" retorted Nikos. "Tell me what I must do and I'll do it in Antibes."

"Unfortunately, dear sir, you must stay in the Clinic. Madame Kazantzakis will go and get your belongings and I will put you in the hospital from this evening on."

"But I don't have the necessary funds."

"Have I asked you for anything?"

Nikos was suffering from lymphoid leukemia. And this was the first time since the abscess mishap that the white corpuscles had gone beyond the prescribed limit.

After a week of treatment Professor Heilmeyer became as optimistic as Professor Jean Bernard.

"It's not serious," he said. "Your white corpuscles are mature. There's nothing to be afraid of. You'll come back once a year and we're going to keep you in good shape."

Antibes, January 21, 1955

Today I've returned to the Cocoon at last. I'd been at the renowned clinic of the great German blood specialist, Heilmeyer. I stayed there for a 40-day cure. Everything went well. My blood has gone back to normal, and now I'm on my Caucasus rock, waiting for Zeus's eagle to devour my liver. . . .

Yes, at present I am writing The Fratricides,* but I still haven't finished it. And from this point on, three other books are crowding each other inside me, in haste to emerge into the light. I can't manage it. I don't have the time. I will die, and a heap of books will be left inside me.†

The novels of Nikos Kazantzakis were appearing in various countries at an accelerated pace. In Dublin, Professor W. B. Stanford, in his book about the Ulysses theme, had devoted a whole chapter to the modern Odyssey. But what made the writer happiest of all was the edition of his complete works that had begun appearing under the supervision of P. Prevelakis, with the help of E. Casdagli. The painter, G.. Varlamos, was in charge of the book jackets, and Galanis, the celebrated Greek engraver, at the high point of his career, was anxious to design the cover of one of the three volumes of theatrical works. But once again a shadow intervened, eating its way into the light.

For quite some time, it had been whispered that Prevelakis was ill. Nikos did not like to break into his friend's reserve, but on January 30, 1955, overjoyed at having received the first good news, he did write to him:

. . . At last, today I was capable of reading Lazarus. It is difficult for me to judge any work of yours, so strongly do I feel identified with you. It's as though whatever you write had come out of my own vitals. Lazarus moved me very much. A high peak of excellence and thought and beauty. May God give you the power to stand always and breathe always upon this peak!

In Mannheim they didn't understand a thing about Sodom and

---

* N.K. had begun The Fratricides in 1949.
† Letter to Börje Knös.

Gomorrah. *It was performed three times. Many people came, but I couldn't look at it, and I asked the director to discontinue it. They didn't consult me at all . . . as to what I meant to say, and they just went their own way. . . .*

On February 18, 1955, we celebrated Nikos' seventieth birthday—at least, so we thought. In reality he was already seventy-two years old. After his death, we discovered by chance the exact date of his birth, inscribed in his own hand, in a schoolbook. "I was born on February 18, 1883, on a Friday."

A great joy, for me at least. We had won two years from Death.

And so Kazantzakis entered his seventy-third year. He still stood straight as a cypress tree, but he no longer had the vertiginous brilliance of youth, except when he allowed himself to be carried away by some great idea and when he developed it before a small gathering of friends, especially when these friends were young.

Increasingly he was absorbed in his own work, and I had trouble making him go out for a walk.

"All right, all right, don't get angry. I'll go and walk my cane!" he used to say on the days when I had gotten overtired and suggested that he go out alone. And he would go out halfheartedly and walk his cane—the cane which had belonged to René Puaux and was given to Nikos by Madame Suzanne Puaux when he came out of the clinic. But whenever we went out together, wandering around the ramparts, he used to abandon himself to our new game in the highest of spirits: "Where will we be this time next year?"

Antibes, February 20, 1955

Thank you very much for your good wishes. I've entered upon my 71st year, but only in my body. My heart and brain have not grown old. I'll try to keep them from ever growing old. Old age is a défaitisme that overcomes cowardly and idle people. We do not belong to them. . . .*

Antibes, March 24, 1955

I have ended up by becoming famous in Greece. All the newspapers, except two, have declared themselves on my side, and from all parts of Greece telegrams are being sent in protest over the priests'

---

* Letter to Börje Knös.

*wanting to seize my books.** . . . And so my name has become well known to everyone! And the books are sold out the moment they are printed, and certain booksellers buy up a number of copies and sell them at very high black-market rates! What a disgrace! How medieval!*

As for me, I go on calmly working, bothering no one, struggling to give my fellow human beings whatever is best in me, to help them endure life and have confidence in excellence. Surely, evil, as you say, will be conquered, has already been conquered. All Greece, except for a few priests and Melases, is with me. And in a few days I hope that all will end with the triumph of the Good. This is how it always happens. . . .†

It is almost embarrassing to have to relate how the Greek Church was forced to halt its anti-Kazantzakis campaign. Exasperated at this obscurantism, a Greek cabinet official signaled an alarm to Princess Marie Bonaparte.

She read the "scandalous" books, loved them, approved of them, and recommended them to the Queen. And the Queen of Greece (a German) kept the Greek Orthodox Church from making itself ridiculous.

Marie Bonaparte was a writer. The disciple and friend of Freud,‡ she had an appreciable quantity of work to her credit. Born of French and Corsican parents, she did not allow the title of "Princess" to stifle her or keep her in shackles. She might have deemed it appropriate to invite her fellow writer to come to her home. She preferred to take the first step by asking his permission to come to him.

She came alone, with a bag full of books. Then she came with her daughter Eugénie. The third time, Marie Bonaparte came in company with her husband, Prince George of Greece. The arrival in Crete of this "young Greek prince" had coincided with the abolition of the Turkish yoke, and that is the event that Nikos had described in *Freedom or Death* as the happiest of his existence. The years had passed. Both men, in spite of belonging to opposite parties, still considered that extraordinary day as the happiest they had ever known—Kazantzakis because of his love for liberty; the Prince because, in spite of everything and in

---

* They wanted to perform an auto-da-fé.
† Letter to Börje Knös.
‡ She had ransomed Freud from the Nazis.

his own fashion, he did love Crete, "having loved it" as the dearest of mistresses.

For our holiday that year we chose Cademario, 2,000 feet above the Lake of Lugano. So as not to "waste his time," in the morning Nikos scribbled in his notebook. The afternoon belonged to me, and we used to walk through the surrounding forests.

"Where will we be this time next year?"

I proposed the most fantastic places. Nikos without hesitation tried to outdo me. "Why not? If we earn enough money, we'll go around the world three times. We'll begin with Mexico. . . ."

Friends came to visit us, and Nikos' laughter, reinvigorated and fresh, blended with theirs. Among them were Helmut von den Steinen, who was translating the *Saint Francis*; the Italian publisher from Milan, Aldo Martello, with his wife, Anna; the publisher from Buenos Aires, Carlos Lohlé; Jean Pierre and Yvonne Métral . . . At Cademario there was also a charming young German poetess with French blood in her veins. Her name was Mila Bouver. Nikos liked her poems and her conversation, teeming with unexpected things. In her company, it was as though youth returned to his own time-worn face.

> Kurhaus Cademario, Lugano
> July 10, 1955
>
> *Eleni and I are finally at peace. . . . Here I'm thinking of beginning the new work, Letters to Greco. A kind of autobiography—I shall make a confession to my grandfather, El Greco. Yesterday a wise friend came to see me, von den Steinen, and he told me that Petrarch had written Letters to Cicero, whom he loved very much. I was pleased. So my idea is not a personal one, but an ancient need of the creator to converse with a beloved dead person in whom he has confidence and to whom he can tell his grief. At present you too are resting in the country. What does rest mean for us? It means working at what we want, and not what external necessity demands. . . .**

And we were already feeling the great joy of our anticipated visit to Albert Schweitzer.

---

* Letter to Börje Knös.

534

Nikos Kazantzakis' view of this apostle of goodness and poverty is given in an epilogue to J. Pierhal's *Albert Schweitzer: das Leben eines guten Menschen*,* and was reproduced in *Report to Greco*:

In my heart I have never been able to separate the two profoundly intriguing personalities that are so widely separated in ephemeral time, so united in eternal time, that is, in the bosom of God. They are like two brothers, Saint Francis of Assisi and Albert Schweitzer.

The same fervent, tender love of Nature. In their hearts day and night resounds the hymn to our brother the Sun, to our sisters the Moon, the Sea and the Fire. They both hold the leaf of a tree on their fingertips and see in it the miracle of all creation.

The same tender emotion full of respect for every living and breathing thing: man, the serpent, the ant. For both of them, life is sacred. . . .

The same pity and kindness actively directed toward everything that suffers. One of them chose the white lepers, the other the black lepers of Africa—the most unfathomable chasm of misery and suffering. . . .

The same divine madness: renouncing the joys of life, sacrificing the small pearls in order to acquire the Great Pearl, taking the steep uphill path between two precipices that rises toward the divine madness. Of their own free will, choosing the impossible. . . .

The same good humor. . . . The laughter bubbling up from the depths of a buoyant heart. . . .

The same passionate love of music. What Thomas of Celano said of the one is also perfectly applicable to the other: "A very thin wall separated him from immortality. That is why he heard the divine melody through the wall." The delight felt by each of them in listening to this melody borders on ecstasy. . . .

And both possess the philosopher's stone which transmutes the basest metals into gold, and gold into spirit. . . .

Two years ago I spent a profoundly Franciscan autumn in Assisi. I was walking all alone along the path above the sacred plain of Umbria, gazing silently at the earth stretched out exultant beneath the rays of a gentle sun. She had done her duty, given wheat to men, and barley and hay to the donkeys and cattle. She had hung honey-steeped fruit on the

---

* Published in Munich, 1955.

grapevines and the fig trees. Subjected to the eternal laws, she had traversed the stages of childbirth and pain with patience and certainty, and had finally reached this rich autumnal harvest of her virtue.

It was there, in Assisi, in the splendor of this autumn crowned with grace, that I saw for the first time (saw with my own eyes) these two brothers walking hand in hand beneath the Umbrian olive trees laden with little green olives. . . .

This is why, after I left Assisi and began writing Pax et Bonum, my book about Saint Francis, I could feel Albert Schweitzer leaning over my shoulder, guiding my mind and my hand. If I were to write a book about Albert Schweitzer, then certainly it would be Saint Francis who would lean over my shoulder and dictate the life of his brother to me. In this way Albert Schweitzer helped me to write this book of mine that is laden with joy and pain and with that which is the supreme fruit— with certainty. . . .

Saint Francis was the last medieval soul and the first of the Renaissance. In this contemporary world in which we live, saturated with ugliness, negation and injustice, would that Albert Schweitzer may be the first soul of a new Renaissance! If this earth is to endure, this man will prefigure the model of future humanity. Albert Schweitzer in our midst is a great consolation. Blessings on him. He gives us confidence in this God-permeated mud called man.

In Paris two years later, when asked by the journalist Pierre Descargues why he had written so "terrifying" a Saint Francis, Nikos made the following reply:

The books I write are at their worst disquieting and at their best terrifying, because it is necessary to shout the warning to human beings that they are headed for catastrophe, that our world is on the brink of the great void that will swallow it up. There are almost no writers who are concerned about this. They toy with little stories of sexuality and psychoanalysis. The painters and musicians, who are more sensitive, divine how near the denouement is, but the writers amuse themselves with decadent pleasures. We have to tell them that we are approaching the end. And then, too, my books are written with the object of postponing the day of reckoning. If I have written this life of Saint

Francis, it is because our world needs heroes who are also saints. And Saint Francis is particularly dear to me. I've lived in Assisi a good deal. And he saved my life twice: the first time when we were about to die of hunger in Greece, during the occupation; the second time when I almost died from an infected eye. . . .

Speaking again about Saint Francis and Saint Francis' "contemporary brother," Albert Schweitzer, Nikos Kazantzakis described the visit we paid to the latter in August 1955:

I was overcome with emotion on that August afternoon when I took the narrow road leading to the minuscule village of Gunsbach in the Alsatian forests. The Saint Francis of our day opened the door personally when I knocked, and offered me his hand. His voice was deep and peaceful; he looked at me, smiling from beneath his thick gray mustache. I had seen old Cretan warriors just like him—full of kindness and indomitable will.

The moment was well favored by destiny. Our hearts opened to each other. We stayed together until nightfall, talking about Christ, Homer, Africa, lepers, and Bach. In the late afternoon we set out for the village's tiny church.

"Let us remain silent," he said to me along the way, deep emotion having suffused his rough face.

He was going to the organ, to play Bach. He sat down. . . . That moment, I believe, was one of the happiest of my life.

On our way back, seeing a wildflower at the edge of the road, I stopped to pick it.

"Don't!" he said, restraining my hand. "That flower is alive; you must have reverence for life."

A tiny ant was parading on the lapel of his jacket. He took hold of it with untold tenderness and placed it on the ground, off to one side, so that no one would trample it. Though he said nothing, the words "Brother Ant" were on the tip of his tongue, the tender words of his great-grandfather from Assisi.

When night came, we finally parted. I returned to my solitude, but

---

* Tribune of Lausanne, May 26, 1957.

that August day never sank below my mind's horizon. I was no longer alone. With unshakable assurance, this striver measured out his road in firm, youthful paces at my side. Though his road was not mine, I found it a great comfort and severe lesson to see him mounting his ascent with so much conviction and obstinacy. From that day onward I was convinced that Saint Francis' life had not been a fairy tale; I felt certain thereafter that man could still bring miracles down to earth. I had seen the miracle, touched it, spoken with it; we had laughed and kept silence together.*

A fine rich year, that of 1955. Albert Schweitzer; Marie Bonaparte; the appearance of the *Iliad* signed "Kakridis-Kazantzakis," as well as the first two volumes of Nikos' *Complete Works*, published in Greece; the opera and the film in the course of preparation—and the affection of the young Greeks. Some of these unknown young Greeks whom Nikos loved above all else had been frightened by newspaper clippings that had spread fears of an imminent end, so they had mimeographed and circulated a letter written by Nikos to his sister, wherein he declared that he was well, working constantly and mocking the persecutions of Popes and other shadow worshipers. When some friends mentioned it to us, Nikos was amazed and amused. "Where the devil did they get hold of that letter?" he said. "I can't imagine that my sister . . ."

In order to convey an idea of the passion with which Nikos Kazantzakis worked on his translations, I shall quote a few passages from his letters to Iannis Kakridis:

Antibes, April 29, 1955
. . . When the Iliad has been published, we shall find more things to correct. And when I have donned the "Black Helmet," you will be obliged to publish a new improved version yourself. Because let's not forget this: Sometimes an original work may not need any revision, but a translation always needs it. I found this out with largo sudore [abundant sweat], as Dante said, when I translated the Divine Comedy. . . .

---

* From *Report to Greco* (New York: Simon and Schuster, 1965), pp. 383–84.

Even during his sleep Kazantzakis used to torment himself about an adjective on which he did not agree with Kakridis.

Antibes, September 12, 1955

Very dear Fellow Combatant!

How wonderful to see the Iliad published . . . bless you! The other day I had a dream. I was laughing (so it went) and saying to you, "Ah, when will the second edition come out, so that we can correct that 'kalognomos'?" (You see, this word won't leave me in peace.) In the morning I looked it up in the big Dimitrakos dictionary and I found— Enough of that! I shan't say a word until the second edition. . . .

In the Prologue it should be made apparent that if the reader stumbles over a word, that is because he doesn't know it . . . and does not know the richness of the demotic language. The way you've put it, it sounds as though we're asking forgiveness for having used a strange word. . . .

When will we move on into the Odyssey?* I have a great longing to plunge deep into the immortal verses. . . .

Antibes, September 29, 1955

. . . I should have wished that we might translate Pindar and Thucydides together, but life is short, alas, and man sinks into his grave still filled with possibilities and desires. . . .

I'm working and in haste; a whole pile of things that ought to upset me don't upset me, for my sensitivity is coated with a protective layer of insensitivity, so that no one can disturb my inner serenity. Larvatus prodeo [I show myself in a mask], as Descartes said. It's necessary for everyone to wear a hard mask, and indispensable in the dishonest age we're living in. . . .

And the day came when we received the *Iliad*, in a marvelous edition, the way Nikos had yearned for it. He wrote Iannis Kakridis:

Antibes, November 9, 1955

Well-beloved, victorious Fellow Combatant:

I believe that this day has been one of the happiest in my life. Eleni

---

* Homer's *Odyssey*, which the two friends wanted to translate together.

came up to my desk, leaping up the steps four at a time, hiding her hands behind her. "Close your eyes!" she called to me. And I understood at once. The Iliad!

I closed my eyes, took it into my hands, kissed it, and opened my eyes. Well, how marvelous it is to struggle for years and years while the fruit of your struggle is slowly taking shape, and for you to hold it in your hands! God keep you well, my dear comrade. Without you, nothing could have been done. The honor belongs wholly to you. Now, let's roll up our sleeves. It's the Odyssey's turn! How I wish that I could attempt a third one as well, but I won't have time. You will remain alone. . . .

Antibes, December 1, 1955

. . . For some time I've been wanting to write you that I've begun preparing the second edition of the Iliad. This text refuses to leave me in peace. Every morning, as soon as I wake up, I run and open it and read it out loud, as the early Christians used to do with the Bible. Fortunately I've found very little to correct. And the very first thing of all, of course, the famous "Kalógnomos"—I'll look it all over again, two or three times. . . . As I write you, our epic August in the Villa Manolita comes back to me. What happiness that was, what a flame! . . .

Who could ever guess that this "epic" month, whose flaming happiness Kazantzakis recalled, was merely a month of suffering? Barely resuscitated, having a wound still gaping, covered with blisters caused by the arsenic medication, and despite his exhausted eye, he had worked from the crack of dawn with Iannis Kakridis on the definitive revision of their beloved translation.

He wrote "epic," thinking no doubt of the Homeric epic. But it was the power of this man's mind and spirit that were epic, for he knew how to forget all the evil, wherever it came from, and to remember only the pleasant side of life. Loathing illness and death, ashamed of every infirmity, when illness did settle upon us he could accept it with a certain impatience—incredulity at first, and then a deeper and deeper serenity. He mocked my ill-concealed anxieties and the sword which he knew was dangling over his own head.

"I know that my life is suspended by a hair; but that hair is Eleni's and it will not break!" he loved to say, looking at me with his small laughing eyes.

540

Once in Osaka I attended a puppet show.* On the right side of the stage the musicians arrived one by one and took their places with hieratical gestures. On the left, in his ceremonial kimono, the puppet master appeared. He climbed onto a small platform, invisible and low, to govern the unified whole of the spectacle. Then his two assistants entered in black hoods: one to move the legs and the other to move the left hand of the puppet.† The right hand and the head belonged to the master.

At first the spectacle irritated me. Too many human beings among the puppets one wanted to take seriously. The animator, resplendent in gold and embroideries, and his acolytes in their black hoods were still too visible on the stage.

But at that point, gradually, the incredible took place. The more animated the dolls became, the more they loved or hated or hummed or lamented, the more their animator was drained. Toward the end of the spectacle, there stood before us an empty, transparent sheath, a sort of serpent's shirt emptied of all life, upright, rigid, translucent, almost invisible, while the little men and women endowed with flesh and blood were living their adventures with unsurpassable vehemence and charm.

Petrified and enchanted at the same time, I only then understood what was happening to us. I had pushed Nikos toward this most dangerous of all games: the creation of human beings requiring his intervention not only in an intellectual and moral way but in a physical way as well. And I saw him gradually growing transparent, without realizing the obscure reasons for this total exhaustion.

How could anyone realize it in the presence of this man who, like the puppet master, once his feat was over, returned to his own flesh, ate and laughed and royally mocked those of us who entertained any anxiety about him?

1956.   This year's first letter was addressed to a poet, an incredibly youthful eighty-year-old poet, who had the same mania as Nikos for the demotic language: Spyro Theodoropoulo:

---

* The Bunraku.
† They study twenty years at the master's side to learn the movements of a single leg.

Antibes, January 3, 1956

. . . I thank you too for your new songs. I'm beginning to suspect that you are one of Swedenborg's angels—the closer they come to God, you know, the younger they grow. I revel in your youthfulness, your self-renewing heart, and your unsuppressible spirit. Truly, "μέγας ἥλιος ἐφίλησεν αὐτὴτ [a great sun has kissed it]"

And two months later to the same person:

Antibes, March 4, 1956

. . . I too love the Iliad very much. I cannot read enough of it. What a miracle this demotic is! Please, note down whatever linguistic comments you may have. I too have made several changes for the second edition. . . .

Nikos asked all his friends to send him linguistic comments, so that he could improve his translation of the Iliad—asking without any false shame, always in his characteristically modest way. As for the Odyssey (Homer's), he had already begun the translation in a state of feverish exaltation. On May 15, after thanking his collaborator for the corrections he had made in the first 150 lines, he continued:

. . . I think we must plunge into the Odyssey without wasting time. And the necessary sweetness will come of itself. I feel certain that we'll manage to render the tenderness of it, just as we achieved the ruggedness in the Iliad. So in the name of God!

I'd gone to Freiburg for 20 days for a general checkup. All is well and I came back in fine fettle. We'll do this every year.

I don't know where we will go this summer. Many plans: Vienna, Yugoslavia, China, India . . . I don't know. In any case in June I'm obliged to go to Vienna for the conferment of the peace award.

Demosthenes Daniilidis, by chance in Stockholm, had been assigned by the International Peace Committee to sound out Nikos Kazantzakis. Nikos read the communication and passed through some long moments of perplexity.

"It's not right for me to accept," he said. "This award must go to a Communist, to someone who has suffered for peace." And, taking his pen, he drafted a telegram proposing that the prize be awarded instead to the Greek poet Varnalis or to the writer Cornaros, who had actually been imprisoned by the fascist police.

At this late hour the Antibes post office had already closed. Not wanting to leave his answer till the next day, Nikos made us look for a telephone in the neighborhood. And I still remember how cheerful he was on the way home, murmuring all the while: "What a relief, what joy to have done my duty!" But the Peace Committee insisted.

"The prize has already been awarded you," Daniilidis explained. "Your refusal might be regarded as an affront to the Committee, which awarded it to you unanimously. Last year it was given to Édouard Herriot, president of the French Radical Socialist party, mayor of Lyons, writer, etc., etc. Before him, to Charlie Chaplin, Shostakovich, and Laxness; to an English pastor and to several other writers and artists. . . . This year, along with the award to you, they will give one to the ninety-year-old Chinese painter Chi Pai-shih . . ."

Another invitation as unexpected as this prize was tempting Nikos this year: Nehru invited him to India. To this I was absolutely opposed, fearing the numerous shots we would have to have.

Antibes, June 24, 1956

. . . Day after tomorrow, we're leaving for Vienna, and from there for the mountains of Yugoslavia. I'm very hesitant about going down to Greece. The Cretans will drown me with their raki and eating fests and love. Very dangerous, and I think I will forgo this joy. I must live a little while longer. . . .

Thank you for the article you wrote in Nea Estia. It's a good thing for the "honeymoon" of our collaboration to become known. It ought to become a model for present and future Greeks. And may this moon, this full moon, never set! . . .

The peace prize was very sudden. Eleni was pleased, and so I had no regrets. It's unbelievable: My indifference to all these things has become pathological. My heart is on fire for other things. But who can believe it? Only you.*

---

* Letter to Iannis Kakridis.

543

Only those who have suffered under a foreign yoke can understand the love of liberty emanating from every act, from every written or spoken word of Nikos Kazantzakis. What other subject could he speak on, addressing the International Peace Committee in Vienna, except the liberty and peace to which every people and every individual has a right?

. . . I accept the high reward, . . . like an old workman accepting his wages at the end of the day. I am left profoundly moved by it, but also profoundly confused and perplexed. Do I deserve these wages?

During the first moments I hesitated, and it was finally only in the name of Crete, the island of my birth, that I allowed myself to accept this honor. She alone . . . having won peace so dearly, deserves a reward like this.

For centuries, Crete longed for peace. But she could attain it only through rivers of blood and tears. . . . Stirred by the inspiration of Crete, I have forced myself, as a man and as a writer, to struggle for liberty, peace, human dignity.

But for me this ceremony also wears another meaning that lies close to my heart, because the jury for international peace prizes is offering the olive branch to a Greek poet. May this gesture be a precursor of peace throughout the entire Hellenic world.

In the midst of this festival of peace, the ensanguined specter of Cyprus rises before me. At this very moment the powers of darkness are raging against freedom there. . . .

Never has the ideal of peace been more indispensable than in our own day. For the first time humanity finds itself consciously confronting the abyss; whence the disorder, defeatism, and acts of betrayal among so many of the souls around us.

If we want to keep the world from sinking into the void, we must liberate the love hidden in the human heart, just as we have liberated the forces hidden in matter. Atomic power must be made to serve the atomic heart. Freedom and peace, let us not forget, lie beyond the framework of Nature. They are both daughters of man, engendered with sweat and tears. As long as man breathes on this earth, they will be there as trail blazers, faithful companions. And yet at every moment they are threatened. At every moment we must mobilize all our forces to defend them. We must remain by their side, always alert. . . .

The anguish which at present grips every man worthy of the name *is lined with a great hope, more precisely, with a great assurance: Evil always ends up by succumbing to the slow but sure omnipotence of the Good. Unless this mysterious law governed human destiny, the spirit would long since have been felled by matter. Freedom and peace would have been stifled by the Great Fear. . . .*

The greatest pleasure Nikos found at Vienna was undoubtedly his encounter with a great Colombian poet, Jorge Zalamea, as well as with an Argentinian writer, Alfredo Varela, both members of the International Committee for Peace. Kazantzakis loved Zalamea's work so much that he immediately translated "The Death of Burundun Burunda" and several other poems.

Excursions; fiery discussions; visits to the museums; seeing Greek friends who had come from afar to regale the older man; the arrival of Theodoropoulo, fresh and fit after three days in a second-class coach. Everything gave Nikos pleasure, but his laugh, his deep, resonant laugh, never erupted in Vienna, or later in Yugoslavia. Without ever becoming morose, he had ceased to be the incorrigible mischief-maker. His features, thin from illness, had assumed a grave expression.

After Vienna, our program included Ljubljana and Zagreb, where we were expected by some Slovene and Croatian writers. Then Rogaska Slatina, a tiny spa; and then Bohijn, near a turquoise-green lake.

"We should always live in the mountains," murmured Nikos, all the while eagerly breathing the fragrant air of the fir trees and the larches. "The Cretan mountain people are right to wonder if the dwellers on the plain have souls."

Unfortunately, once again Nikos was not able to rest. For once again he had to work with Kimon Friar on the English translation of his *Odyssey.*

Seated on the banks of this picture-postcard lake teeming with trout, with a waterfall in the background, Nikos wrote our Cretan friend, the former prison director of Aegina, Thrassývoulos Androuli-dakis:

Bohijn, Hotel Zlatorog
August 18, 1956

Ah for things that are gone, ah for things past,
Ah, if they could but return a single day each year!

545

My dear Thrassý, this mandinada* was winging through my mind like a butterfly all the while I was reading your marvelous letter. . . . You brought back to life for me the heroic epoch when you produced delicious vegetables from the stones, and listened to the radio, and knocked on the window, and I was standing there waiting for you, and you would bring me the news.† A black era full of splendor. You used to share your canteen food with me to keep me from dying of hunger. How often in our exile we also recall the courage of your wife and companion, Despina, and our eyes mist with feeling! Blessed be the hunger and the horror that caused your bravery and your love to shine so much.

Beloved, unforgettable friend. The days we spent with you will never fade from my memory. Those days of horror are among the most beautiful of my life, God bless you!

I was struggling then; I am struggling; and I shall go on struggling until death. That is my duty. My whole life has been reduced to ashes for the sake of man, for man's freedom. Only a person who, like you, has observed my life from close at hand can know my struggle. And surely, if Eleni were not there, I should not endure so long-drawn-out a crucifixion. But blessings on her, many times she has saved me from death and despair.

Now she's gone down to Crete for ten days to watch the film [of Dassin] being shot. She had a great desire to go. I have no curiosity at all. My own struggle cannot admit even these small human joys. "Don't stop, don't look behind you, keep climbing upward": that inhuman (and yet so human) voice keeps me from feeling any joy.

And yet I can say that I am happy, although my happiness is fierce, unsmiling, insatiable, not allowing me to take pleasure even for a moment. Joy, it tells me, is rest, and rest is sin. . . .

Next May (I hope I'll still be alive; I behave and reckon as though I were immortal)—well, next May, we're thinking of going to China. . . .

I'm bidding farewell, farewell. . . . Soon I shall go around the world to take leave of all the countries that I have loved. Farewell! I shall also bid farewell to the people that I have loved. And so, dear Thrassývoulos, we shall see each other again. . . .

---

* A genre of Cretan popular poetry.
† During the German occupation and the time of the great famine.

546

And on September 15, 1956, to Iannis Kakridis:

We've just come back from the summer trip, which lasted two and one half months: Vienna, Yugoslavia, Geneva. This year's cycle has come to an end. I was joyful to find my cell again—papers, books, manuscripts. And I am waiting longingly for the translation of the Odyssey. Act quickly. I'm still alive, but don't forget, I won't always be alive. And where will you find another collaborator and worker who is so easygoing? I have much work, but I'll drop everything else for the Odyssey. . . .

Geographical Greece is vanishing more and more from my horizon. The other Greece remains. And so I have no homesick yearning to tread her soil. . . .

Mr. and Mrs. Kakridis were worried about the fate of the translation of the *Iliad* and the *Odyssey* if anything should happen to Nikos and me. I mentioned this to Nikos, who unhesitatingly offered his author's rights to the two children of Iannis Kakridis:

Antibes, October 12, 1956

. . . I am happy that our joint labors and joys will remain united above two beloved heads. . . .

And on October 15, again to Iannis Kakridis, to thank him for having given a public address about his work:

I have just this moment received the text of the speech you made about me at the theater. I was deeply moved by it. Well, are you right? I hope so, because in that case my life has not been wasted.

I'm waiting impatiently for the Odyssey. This interests me more than the "Greco" I'm writing. The latter I've had finished for some time, but I'm rewriting it. It's a confession and needs attention. All my works are confessions, but this one even more so. I shall confess the four major stages in the uphill path of my life, passing over many ephemeral things. . . .

Success, instead of blunting Kazantzakis, aroused in him all his qualities as a thinking being and, consequently, as a responsible being. How he loved to write novels and why he wrote them he had himself explained already to his old friend, Börje Knös. I shall add some relevant extracts from his correspondence with P. Prevelakis:

Antibes, December 3, 1949

. . . I am deep in Freedom or Death. I'm struggling to resurrect the Heraklion of my childhood years. What emotion, what joy, and at the same time what a responsibility! Because thousands of dead persons rise up in my memory, demanding a small place in the sun, two or three lines, a good word. They know they have no other salvation or hope for resurrection. Who will write about them now? Even their children and their grandchildren have forgotten them. . . . Never have I felt such intensity and endurance. Before I finish one work, two or three others well up inside me, demanding to be given a body, to assume solid shape and walk upon the earth. . . . I'm struggling to finish in time. . . .

Antibes, February 28, 1950

. . . All the time I am swimming in the new novel, Freedom or Death, and I feel joy and great relief—I'm reliving old moments of mine, mythological by now, an antediluvian humanity—dinosaurs and mammoths—that have vanished. . . . The first time that writing has given me so much joy.

Antibes, July 24, 1950

. . . I'm continuing to work calmly . . . and I'm happy that I've embarked upon a new genre—the novel—because with this "my time passes," and I believe I'm becoming rejuvenated. I'm writing it in high spirits and in a virgin manner, like a newcomer who has just now begun writing. . . .

The following letter, while he was writing The Last Temptation:

Antibes, November 11, 1950

. . . I am now in the birth pangs of the new book, which requires much effort because it falls outside my usual pattern. . . .

548

The old antinomies are beginning to become organized into an organic synthesis. It seems to me that, as the Byzantine mystics used to say, I am attaining the peak of endeavor, which is called lack of endeavor. In the book I'm writing, perhaps I shall be able to formulate this organic resolution of contradictions. I'm beginning not to be bothered by any "problem" now, by any "agony." I've found the solution I have outside the realm of intellect and analysis—i.e., beyond the purlieus of "Satan." . . .

We have already seen how the hotel owner who told his fortune in Lofer had advised Nikos not to seek for his subjects, but to let them come to him freely.

Lofer, Salzburg, March 6, 1952

. . . For months my soul had been struggling with a difficult theme, The Third Faust, and it exhausted my body. . . . Eleni, who was suffering more than I, prodded me to take a trip, to go to the mountains, to breathe fresh air. . . . And so I've come to inhale these godlike, snow-laden mountains, and in three days I'm going back to Manolita absolutely rested. But I'm avoiding tackling the terrifying theme again and I'm writing a piece of prose. And in writing it, I am resting. The Third Faust I shall no longer go out to find, unless it comes to find me. That's the only sure sign that "the time has come." . . .

Amsterdam, December 18, 1952

. . . Now I'm writing Saint Francis and I think it will be good. The struggle of man and God, this is what interests me. . . .

Antibes, December 6, 1953

. . . [Saint Francis] is one of the works you won't like, and I'm puzzled as to how I wrote it. Well, is there a religious mystique inside me? Because I felt great emotion when I wrote it. . . .

Antibes, August 18, 1954

Now that I'm giving all my time to translating The Odyssey (with Friar), I am sad, because I have stopped the book I was in the process of writing [The Fratricides] . . .

At Easter time 1955 he tried to console his bedridden friend:

> . . . *This immobility may prove fruitful. Whatever is best in* The Beggar of God, *I dictated to Eleni at the time of the fever. . . .*

> Antibes, March 22, 1956
> . . . *In a few days, I'll be finishing* Report to Greco. . . . *Eleni did not want to copy it. She burst into tears, because I talk about my death. But she must get used to it. I too will become used to it.*
>
> *I work many hours, and I don't get tired. This power of endurance alarms me; it isn't natural. I have various works in my mind. The days seem short to me. The years I pass have never been shorter. I don't have enough time. The flame inside me keeps spurting up, as though it's had enough of me and wants to burn me up. . . .*

1957.   It was already apparent that it was going to be a very crowded spring. The festivities organized by the Plon publishing house in Paris for the appearance of *Saint Francis*; the two hundredth volume in the *Feux Croisés* series; the film of Dassin at the Cannes Festival; the final supervision of the translation of *The Odyssey* into English. And, we should add, various lectures and preparations for the great trip to China . . . with an interlude of several days at the Freiburg Clinic to obtain the assistance and blessings of Heilmeyer, necessary for our bold plans. . . .

On January 9, 1957, Nikos wrote Iannis Kakridis:

> . . . *I've finished the two books, V and VI. . . . I'm like the beast in Dante's Hell, who "when he has eaten is hungrier than before . . ."
> I feel so intoxicated when I enter Homer that I am almost overcome by exhaustion. . . . And Eleni had to force me to go out for a walk, to breathe a bit of air and get some sun. What a pity one cannot live for five hundred years, so that I could have time to translate all the ancients! . . .*

And a bit later, to Börje Knös:

Antibes, January 25, 1957

. . . I am struggling bravely here with work and illness, and I have no other consolation except work. At present I'm translating Homer's Odyssey, and I can forget this miserable, dishonorable world in which we are living. Like the Charioteer of Delphi, I am holding the reins as firmly as I can, struggling to guide my body where my soul wants it to go, and not where it wants to go itself.

. . . For the first time, one month ago the official Greek government acknowledged me and gave me the first prize for theater. . . . I divided the prize between Voutyrà, who is ill and poor, and the orphan child of Kotzióula. When are we going to meet? So that the heart can feel a little lighter. I no longer have anyone to talk to. Only my wife. . . .

Early in the month of February 1957 Dimitri Fotiadi sent Nikos his book on one of the most extraordinary heroes of our independence struggles, the nun's son, Karaïskakis. Fotiadi is a writer who is still young and has devoted all his power and talent to our history: our real history, not our history as it is taught in school. He writes a pure demotic and is not afraid to call a spade a spade. The Greeks love him very much; abroad he is not known at all. None of his books has ever been translated into a foreign language—in the first place, because Fotiadi does not try to be translated, and secondly because publishers are not at all interested in the real history of Greece.

As always, Nikos asked me to cut the pages for him. And he began reading. And I realized that he was crying, blowing his nose not because he had caught cold but in order to hide his tears from me. To Dimitri Fotiadi, he wrote the following letter:

Antibes, February 27, 1957

My dear Fotiadi,

May the God of Greece keep you well and bless your writing hand! I am reading Karaïskakis, and often my eyes get misty. What dishonorable acts, what gallant acts, what betrayals, what sacrifices in the

551

name of freedom! What was this 1821 then, what sort of dung, and how did the blue flower take root and blossom up above it? And furthermore, what lies they've taught us in the schools and how late—bless you—the real people have come to tell the truth!

I can't put your book down, and how sorry I am that we are so far apart and that I cannot come and squeeze your hand. Your Karaïskakis has given me great joy and left me with great bitterness. I have it on my desk in front of me and I am reading it slowly so as not to reach the end, for hereafter what other scribbler's work will be able to move me to this extent?

My dear Fotiadi, accept my gratitude. You have written a beautiful book and done a brave deed. Rarely are these two things combined. . . .

And on April 28, 1957, to Börje Knös:

. . . I have long delayed writing you, because I was away in Germany. . . . Everything went well. The blood has gone back to normal again, and I've returned to Antibes in marvelous health, and I've begun a terrible amount of work. . . . France has begun to recognize me and extend great honors to me. A bit too late but it doesn't matter. All these glories leave me indifferent. I think that I've transcended all ambition and from now on am breathing the bitter scent of the abyss. . . .

I've just come back from the premiere of the film at Cannes, presented to a few spectators. I couldn't hold my tears back. It is extraordinarily moving. . . .

In health I'm very well, but I get very tired. I hope the trip will rest me. The English translation of The Odyssey is excellent. . . . The translator is here now and we're revising together the whole translation. A horrible strain. . . .

This complaint is found in several of Kazantzakis' letters. "If I have to go on with it a few minutes more, I shall die of it!" he exclaimed, calling me to help him. "This reading out loud is very exhausting for me."

Slightly before we left for China, and forty years after her divorce, Galatea sent Nikos a queer gift: a book she had just written, a libel in the form of a novel, wherein she described him in the blackest of colors. Nikos refused to read it. In my opinion this kind of slander ought to be answered; but Nikos shook his head. "No. Poor Galatea," he murmured; "she didn't deserve such an end." And he wouldn't let anyone speak ill of her.

With Lefteris he did even better. The former had also written a novel against his ex-brother-in-law. He offered it as a gift to Nikos on Nikos' name day one year before he died. Nikos read it and complimented Lefteris on his style and language, as he had been requested to do. Several days later, Lefteris returned with a wildly enthusiastic letter. "Oh, Nikos, you're wonderful, you're the best [etc., etc.]. Please let me use your eulogies to help the sale of my book during the Christmas holidays." Nikos acquiesced. And the malicious book did sell, thanks to the laudatory blurb written by its victim! To my angry protests, Nikos answered: "Who can believe so many malicious things, my child?"

On June 1, 1957, just before our departure, Nikos wrote to Börje Knös:

. . . Day after tomorrow, I'm leaving for China with Eleni. I'll stay ten days in Moscow, one month in China, and on the return trip one month in Yugoslavia. I hope to be back in Antibes in September. I'm happy to be taking a long trip and seeing once again the Alma Mater, Asia. Here, tranquillity has lasted too long.

Day before yesterday, I came back from Paris, where I stayed ten days. Various festivities took place, and I spoke a number of times on the radio and on Télévision. And all this tired me out, because it's contrary to my nature. Now, during this strenuous trip, I hope I'll rest.

I'll write you from China, and I'll keep you always in my mind. . . .

And we did set out for China.

Seeing Nikos' exhausted appearance, our friends had the worst premonitions. But Nikos refused to listen to a word about it.

"Mr. Kazantzakis, I see an open grave in the bottom of your cup," a friend of ours, Madame Poirier, told him on the eve of our departure. "Don't leave, for the love of God."

"Bah!" Nikos guffawed. "When you see a grave, it means a marriage, just the way it does in dreams."

The day we left, Madame Poirier came back again. "Don't go, I beg of you. I've had bad dreams."

And Nikos burst out laughing again.

"Nikosmou," I begged him in my turn, "you say we're free. 'I enter, or I do not enter, just as I wish!'—as your famous Cretan used to say before the gates of Heraklion. Well, if we wish, we can leave; but if we don't wish to, we won't leave!"

"Come now, Comrade in arms, are you going to surrender your weapons? Just when I was so delighted with the prospect of acting as your guide in Peking."

When Nikos was in a teasing mood, when he laughed, fatigue, old age, wrinkles all vanished from him like footprints in the sand after the waves.

In Prague and Moscow, we avoided all fatigue. The two Greek friends accompanying us on this trip had a surprise in store for us: an invitation to Japan.

"We'll go," exclaimed Nikos, enchanted.

"You promised me not to go down to the south, not to leave Peking. You've read the newspapers. You know that influenza is on the rampage in Tokyo. And the doctor said, 'No germs.' "

"Bah! Influenza can't do anything to people like us. And so Lenotschka will see Japan too." Nikos hummed and began to list the marvels I was about to witness.

In Peking our hosts showed extraordinary sensitivity. It was enough for me to say just once: "No salt, no visits to factories, an hour of rest every day"—and it was religiously respected. To please Kazantzakis, they avoided the organized travel tours passing through Shanghai and the industrial cities. The "poet's route" was the one they chose for their guest—that is, the gorges of the Yangtze River sung by Li Po and so many other celebrated poets. Even Chungking with its extreme heat did not tire us. Nevertheless the Peace Committee, solicitous about our health, offered us several days to rest in the land of eternal spring—in Kunming—not far from the borders of Tibet, at an altitude of 6,400 feet. So Nikos did not get fatigued at all in China. And he was overjoyed at every step to observe the progress.

"Here," he would tell me, "there used to be open communal ditches, a mortal danger for the little children playing all around. . . . There, I remember, there were long lines of beggars, bleary-eyed, all covered with flies. Now even the rickshaw men wear white gloves!"

"Which are cleaner than our own!" I added in admiration of Chinese cleanliness.

Kuo-mo-jo, Chou En-lai, Mao Dun, with whom we were able to exchange a few words; the white jade Buddha; the Temple of the Sky; the universities, laboratories, public parks; the little shops; the great, the extraordinary actor Mei Lan-fang—so many unforgettable joys. And always the Chinese courtesy, inconceivable in any other country in the world.

Can you imagine the ceremonial of a visit to the University of Peking, when the guests included an aging and well-loved man whose health left something to be desired? The Director, who was waiting for us on the front steps, dispatched a young girl student to help Nikos get out of the car and climb the few steps. "I'm neither impotent nor an old man!" he exclaimed. "But I like it!" And he let himself be politely supported beneath his right arm by the adorable young girl.

Once they were settled in front of the tea table, the young student began busying her fingers, light as butterfly's wings, in unknotting the ribbons holding the big straw hat Nikos was wearing on his head. And then with all the veneration due to a distinguished guest and without saying a word, she began unbuttoning Nikos' shirt. Holding one side of the shirt with her left hand, she gently fanned his damp chest with her little fan for a long time, all the while smiling at him, as at some kind old grandfather.

We were profoundly moved by this scene, thinking how far we were from knowing the secrets of Chinese hospitality.

In the boat taking us from Hankow to Chungking, I caught Nikos sighing many times and murmuring the refrain of the Greek popular song: "If I had water from my fountain . . ." At that point I attributed his sadness to the fact that we would not let him come along to the little Chinese villages the rest of us explored at every stage.

After an excursion on the Lake of Kunming, which was alive with hundreds of fishing boats, we began climbing the steps leading through gates, temples and pagodas up to the "Temple Touching the Sky."

Nikos took the ascent at the same pace as the rest of us, and he was never the one who lagged behind. After the Dragon's Gate and the Sleeping Beauty, there was the Temple of the Dragon Lon-Men, encountered in ancient poetry. Higher up, the Temple of the Three Purities. At the summit, the pavilion of the Master of Scholars. A young man covered in gold, in the image of Buddha. In one hand he held an inkwell and in the other a pen. But the tip of the pen was broken. It had broken while the sculptor, Tchou Kiang-kouo, was still engaged in modeling the work; and in despair the young artist had killed himself.

Unfortunately in Freiburg they had forgotten to warn Nikos against all vaccinations. And in Canton he got vaccinated against cholera and smallpox.

We were in Tokyo when his arm began swelling up. Without saying a word to me, he began wearing shirts with long sleeves and taking extremely hot baths. To my astonished questions he answered, with a vague smile, "I like to imitate the Japanese." Only later did I discover the reason.

Thanks to Mrs. Evelpidi, our well-organized excursions in Japan also spared Nikos from fatigue. But his arm continued to swell. And it was only in the airplane on the way back that I became aware of it.

Twenty days criminally lost in Copenhagen almost precipitated the end. But finally Jean Bernard arrived and once again saved the situation.

"Take him to Heilmeyer at once!" he said.

"I've wanted to do so ever since the first day," I responded. "But they wouldn't let me leave."

"Now they will let you."

"Perhaps it's too late."

"I'm sure it's not. Only you must give me your word that whatever happens, you won't stop along the way. You must reach Freiburg as soon as possible."

We reached Freiburg still alive. Nikos had refused to use a stretcher. He reached the airplane walking. He sat up in the plane and at the station in Frankfurt, and he continued to sit up in the train taking us to Freiburg. But once on the steps of the Freiburg station, he crumpled up like a dying flower.

"Why did you wait until he got into this condition before bringing him to me?" said Dr. Hörder, scolding me.

"Try to save him, Doctor. Jean Bernard swore to me that you would be able to."

And the miracle happened—for the last time.

"Have you noticed, Doctor, that the streets of Freiburg are soaking wet? 'It's been raining,' one might say. . . . No, it hasn't rained. Those are Mrs. Kazantzakis' tears," said Nikos, teasing, once the trouble had been conjured away.

"They wanted to amputate your arm," I admitted to him one day several weeks later when he had been getting steadily better. . . . "If at least it had been the leg!"

"Whew! The leg would be horrible too!" murmured Nikos pensively. And after a few minutes:

"My love, please bring me a scrap of paper and a pencil."

And he began writing with his left hand.

Gradually the news began spreading that Nikos Kazantzakis was ill in Freiburg. Max Tau was the first to hasten to the scene, accompanied by the daughter and secretary of Albert Schweitzer. Ladislas Kijno began sending us splendid postcards, reproductions of masterpieces of modern painting, thus reminding us of our dear friend, Segredakis. The political prisoners condemned to death on Corfu sent a magnificent little blue-and-white sailboat that became Nikos' delight. D. Daniilidis, friend of the Berlin era of 1922–23 and friend of all time, made a very long detour to come to the older man and embrace him.

Rahel had a strange dream: my mother appeared to her, begging her to come and look for me among the dead. Nikos was so well and the doctors were so certain he would recover that I had mentioned it to him.

"Poor Rahelina," he murmured. "She worries herself for nothing."

I told him also about one of my own dreams. Once again my mother appeared, more substantial than flesh as she confronted me, and said to me: "Tomorrow you will die!" "I? I will die?" "Yes, you—you will die!"

"A very good dream," said Nikos with amusement. "We'll have some good news."

Settled comfortably in his armchair, he read an amazing number of books. The young librarian in the French Library in Freiburg couldn't believe his eyes. Among other books, Nikos had asked me for Montaigne, Racine and Molière. And at intervals he emitted sighs of impatience. "Oh, how long it takes, great gods! When will I ever be able to get back to work?"

"Patience, patience, patience on earth," I retorted, repeating his own favorite motto.

"Three new subjects jostling against each other in my head. Which will come out first? I must also rewrite the *Greco*. In an absolutely different way. If only I could dictate."

"Let's try."

The attempt wasn't very successful.

"I can work only with my pencil in my hand. At least, read me your translation of the Chinese and Japanese poems. Perhaps there will be corrections to be made."

He made some useful corrections in them, then resumed his reading. Having read at one go the little book of Roger Martin du Gard about Gide's death, he handed it to me. "I'd like you to read it, Lenotschka. That's how I'd like to die."

Every Saturday a pastor used to come to visit the patients. Nikos would greet him politely and leave me to bear the burden of conversation. When the good man had left us, Nikos would utter a sigh of relief:

"To think that he's sincere!" he would murmur. "To think that he's sincere!"

We were not rich. The long sojourns in clinics and mountain hotels exhausted our finances. Nikos didn't seem to be aware of this. The only time he seemed to worry was when I would be a little late getting back from my daily round of picking up books and French newspapers. And then from far off I would see his dear face glued to the windowpane and his little eyes scanning the paths in the park.

"Why are you standing up by the window, Nikosmou?" I would complain, hiding my emotion. "You know very well that nothing can happen to me, that I'll always come back."

"Yes, yes, I know that, but it's stronger than I am." And when I used to scold because he walked too rapidly in the room, "I feel like an entirely new man," he would say, marveling at his new-found strength. "I assure you, I feel as though I'm being borne along on wings!"

That evening I found him virtuously seated in his armchair. "Come, come quickly!" he said to me. "I've got a piece of good news."

"A very good one?"

"Yes. A very, very good one!"

"The Nobel!" I cried, very excited. Max Tau had received a telephone call from Stockholm, promising it to him, and I had the right to expect it. "The Nobel! Hurrah!"

"Still better, Lenotschka! Still better!" said Nikos, laughing. And he handed me the telegram he was holding in his hand. A telegram longer than any I had ever seen.

"Read!" he said.

It was the Committee for International Peace in Peking which, having learned of our misfortunes, conveyed its sorrow to us, sent us at the same time a sizable sum to cover the expenses at the clinic, and promised to assume responsibility for all future expenses as long as necessary—all expressed exquisitely, in the Asiatic manner.

"Hm! What do you think of it? Are you satisfied?" And without leaving me time to take my coat off and savor the telegram, Nikos went on: "Friendship is dearer to me than all the prizes in the world, Lenotschka. And now help draft a good telegram to thank our friends. All the same, we can't accept their offer. We're not going to eat a grain of rice belonging to the Chinese people."

Once the telegram was drafted, Nikos consulted his watch. "You'll have time to go to the bank to have the money sent back to Peking," he said. "Take care; pay whatever you have to so that nothing will be missing from the amount they sent. They must not lose anything on the exchange."

And that was done.

On the way I recalled the happy surprise of Mao Dun and other Chinese writers when Nikos had offered them all his novels without any conditions. "When anyone comes to China," Wang Chen-chi had whispered in my ear, "he takes paper and pencil and begins figuring: how much will this book bring in, how much will that one bring in? This is the first time that the entire work of a writer has been offered to us like this."

"But don't forget, my friend," I had whispered in turn into an interpreter's ear, "that for the first time you're seeing a man like Kazantzakis. There must be a few of them, but you haven't seen them yet."

Kazantzakis was the only person in the whole University Clinic at Freiburg who failed to feel disappointed when the Nobel prize was awarded to Albert Camus.

"Lenotschka, come quickly to help me draft a good telegram. Juan Ramón Jiménez, Albert Camus—there are two men who well deserved the Nobel. Let's go and draft a good telegram!"

Those were the last words that Nikos Kazantzakis dictated to me to be sent to a friend.*

The next day, without any apparent cause, a high fever made its appearance. Our Destiny this time sent us the Asian flu to finish off the gallant man at the very moment when he was beginning to climb back up the hill.

One after the other, three Greeks, neighbors of ours, had just died, although of mortal illnesses. This had left a powerful impression upon me.

"Dear Professor Heilmeyer, couldn't you have saved them?" I asked.

"They came at the last minute. They waited too long."

"I'm afraid—I'm afraid for my husband."

"What are you imagining, dear madam? Your husband doesn't have cancer. Your husband will live a long time yet; you can take my word for it."

And he advised me to go to Antibes to get some winter clothes that we would need for our stay in the mountains. "In a few days, you'll be able to leave the clinic," he told me. "The mountains will do both of you good."

I was about to leave, when the fever shot up. The first day they had thought he might have intestinal poisoning. He had been ordered to fast, and sulphamins were administered. The following morning the fever had come down, but in the evening it soared again like an arrow.

Throughout three days, it was the same thing. Nikos' breathing had gotten shorter and more rapid. The doctors didn't seem to be worried about it. He was also coughing and spitting. Albert Schweitzer arrived on October 25. Nikos found the strength to lift himself up in bed. He

---

* On March 16, 1959, Albert Camus wrote me the following letter:

Madame, I was very sorry not to be able to take advantage of your invitation. I have always nurtured much admiration and, if you permit me, a sort of affection for your husband's work. I had the pleasure of being able to give public testimony of my admiration in Athens, at a period when official Greece was frowning upon her greatest writer. The welcome given my testimony by my student audience constituted the finest homage your husband's work and acts could have been granted. I also do not forget that the very day when I was regretfully receiving a distinction that Kazantzakis deserved a hundred times more, I got the most generous of telegrams from him. Later on, I discovered with consternation that this message had been drafted a few days before his death. With him, one of our last great artists vanished. I am one of those who feel and will go on feeling the void that he has left. . . .

560

put his arms around his friend and spoke to him so zestfully that the good doctor went off feeling assured that when he returned in a few days he would find Nikos convalescing. No one in Freiburg was yet talking of the Asian flu, which was, however, devastating Frankfurt.*

I have forgotten to mention one significant incident.

When Dr. Hörder had come to give him his Cortisone injection on October 23, which was the first day Nikos had had this high fever, Nikos had said to the doctor as he held out his arm, "*Und jetzt Schluss!* [And now the end!]"

Was he expressing his real thought? Or was this the voice of his subconscious, to which he attributed no importance? During the four days still left him to live, he never uttered a pessimistic word.

Quite the contrary. Up to the very last moment, propped up on his pillows, he held out his arm to have the dressings changed, ate his yoghurt, and complained of nothing but an atrocious, unquenchable thirst. "I'm thirsty! . . . I'm thirsty!"

On Saturday morning, October 26, the doctor said to me, "Do you understand that today your husband is in a serious condition?"

"I've already seen him in such a condition twice. I hope you will help him to come through again."

He promised me. And he left the clinic, not to return until after ten o'clock in the evening, when everything was over.

Remaining alone at the bedside of my sick man, I summoned all the saints to my assistance.

"Nikosmou, Nikosmou," I said to him. "It's a *tri-imeros* [fever lasting three days]. Courage, my love. This evening the fever will go down. Tomorrow the dawn will shine again, a marvelous dawn."

"Yes, yes." Nikos nodded his head and asked for a drink.

"Remember Bergson: *mobilisation.* Mobilize your forces, I beg of you!"

That Saturday, two pastors came into our room. The regular one, the Protestant pastor, and then the Catholic priest. Nikos turned his face to the wall.

Full of hope, I had not thought of the end. "Nikosmou," I scolded.

---

* Several friends, including Charles Orengo, at that time literary director of the Plon publications, and Aldo Martello, the Milan publisher, had severe attacks of Asian flu, which was rampant at Frankfurt at that season, during the big book fair.

"What you've just done isn't polite. It's Saint Dimitri's Day; the poor men wanted to please us."

He didn't say a word. He only turned his face toward me and asked for a drink.

"Do you feel better, my little one?"

"Yes . . . yes."

"Are you suffering anywhere?"

"No . . . no. I'm thirsty."

At a certain point, and on two occasions afterward, I saw him putting his finger to his lip. I thought he wanted to scratch himself, for with the fever the lip was becoming once again irritated.

"Is it itching you?"

"Yes." Nikos nodded.

He was lying to me, and I understood it only too late. He was trying to find out how far the dimming of his sight had gone. For at the end of a few hours—I couldn't say how many—his eyes had become glassy.

"Nikosmou, Nikosmou!" I cried. "Can you hear me, my love?" He didn't stir. His heart was still beating. His breathing had become still more rapid and short. I took his left hand, which was silky and never damp, and I put it on my head.

"Bless me, my love. . . . Act that I may follow the path you have carved."

The hand remained on my head a long time—hot, silky, still dry, the way I loved it. And then I put it back delicately on the sheets.

Nikos Kazantzakis was no more. The second hook had closed upon my thirty-three years of happiness. The second night was waiting for me.

I went back near him, looked at him for a long time, closed his eyes—those good and mischievous little olive-colored eyes which were never again going to see the sun.

Confronting death as he had lived, he had just given up his soul. "Like a king who had taken part in the festivity, then risen opened the door and, without turning back, crossed the threshold."

APPENDIX

KAZANTZAKIS' "APOLOGY" *

To answer the charges, I must formulate in a few simple words my way of viewing the contemporary social problem.

There are three consecutive circles I must shed light on if I want this Apology of mine to be logical, coherent and a valuable diagnosis:

I The international historical moment we are living in today.

II The position of Greece and her duty vis-à-vis this historical moment.

III What I consider to be my own personal duty.

I

I believe the bourgeois system is no longer capable of regulating the present-day needs and anxieties of the social entity.

Economically, it is based on the predatory individualistic organization of production and the unequal distribution of wealth.

Socially, there is no longer any morality to support human relations.

Politically, the ruling class manages the political authority for its own benefit, to the detriment of the great majority of the people; and every change of persons or institutions proves futile.

There is no longer any loftier ideal in the bourgeois system to enhance the actions of individuals and states with nobility and coherence. There is no faith—i.e., a rhythm transcending the individual—to regulate the thoughts and feelings and acts of individuals.

We are confronting a spectacle, the likes of which can be observed at the end of every civilization. A single class—in the very beginning, it was the priests and the magicians, then the kings, then the feudal lords, then the bourgeois—assumes power, after shattering the preceding class. Then after a time, when it too has passed all the phases of the high point and the decline,

---

* After N.K.'s return to Heraklion in 1924, he was arrested by the local authorities for his allegedly subversive views. The original version of this "Apology" was an immediate response to this arrest; at a later point, the text was most likely retouched slightly.

another class comes (fated to follow the same curve) and takes its place. Such is the undulating pattern of history.

The bourgeois class shattered the feudal rule, transmitting (in magnificent quantity and quality) whatever it was capable of to thought, art, science and action. And now it is tracing the fatal curve downward.

We are living this decline, and as a consequence it is very difficult for us to be aware of it. And yet, the decomposition is so rapid that even the most thick-skinned persons are beginning to be anxious.

And two sorts of endeavors are becoming clearly delineated:

1. Some people are struggling to hold the bourgeois system together, by struggling against every opposing form of action and thought.

2. Others are struggling to knock it down and replace it with a new system, which, they are convinced, is more just and honorable.

The former—the conservative ones—are in power and, of course, have the right and duty to defend their own ideology and interests. Ignoring the intractable laws of birth, high point, decline and decay, they are hoping that now, for the first time in history, the miracle will happen and their own class will be preserved in power for all eternity.

But there is not a single example in history to show that the endeavors of the conservatives have ever borne fruit up to the very end.

If this were to happen, life would never stir from its first secure and extremely imperfect forms. Recall the famous quotation of Courier: "When God wanted to create the world, the conservative angels surrounding him cried out, 'Lord, do not destroy the Chaos!'" But God did not listen to the conservatives—he never listens to them.

What class is going to succeed the bourgeois system? I have the adamantine conviction that it will be the working class: workers, farmers, people productive in the spirit. This class has passed the first stage—Charity. It no longer, as a century ago, kowtows to the charity of the rich people, no longer begs for alms. And then it passed the second stage—Justice; no longer is it demanding to seize the ruling power because that is right. And now it has reached the third and final stage; it is convinced that it will assume the ruling power, because such is the historical necessity.

And so at present, we find ourselves at the critical point when one class, in spite of its strong outward appearance, is stumbling. Its foundations are shaking. It has lost its psychological coherence and it is decomposing—decomposing because it has no belief.

Another class is becoming crystallized and organized. It does believe, but has not yet been completely organized, has not yet been enlightened as a whole, has not yet assumed perfect consciousness of its own power and is still functioning as a slave of the rotten colossos.

The old values have lost the belief that had once sustained them and given them meaning and prestige. The new values are in the process of constant creation; they have not yet assumed a stable form. And this is precisely the point wherein lies the tragic quality of the terrifying transitional period we are experiencing.

Three facts render the danger incurred by the bourgeois system still more alarming:

1. For the first time in history, we find the following amazing fact: All the continents—all five—are now taking part in a group action. For the first time in history, the earth is acquiring a unified consciousness. All races—white, black, yellow—are becoming organized around the same purpose. The destruction of the Greco-Roman civilization is but a provincial phenomenon compared with the destruction of the bourgeois system delineated at present.

2. The second fact intensifying the danger is the awe-inspiring awakening of the peoples of Asia and Africa. In order to use them in the World War, the Europeans kindled their national consciousness, promising them that they would become free states after the victory. The Europeans armed them, taught them to fight and to kill Europeans and then went back to their own countries. Their promises were not kept. And now, all the colonial areas are seething dangerously, demanding freedom.

3. The third fact intensifying to the utter extreme the peril of the bourgeois system is this: Throughout the two fronts of this international movement, there is a leader—a leader for the international proletariat demanding its economic emancipation and, at the same time, a leader for the Oriental peoples demanding emancipation as nations. This leader is an enormous state, one sixth of the earth, possessing a very strong army, inexhaustible raw materials, great scientists, implacable political leaders and, above all, a tremendous something that does not exist in the opposing world: a new faith—Russia.

Russia is striving to provide the model for the proletarian state. And so, among the proletarian masses of the world, she arouses emulation and delineates the pattern for salvation. With propaganda worthy of a genius, she tells the Oriental peoples the simplest of things, utterly comprehensible and palatable to Oriental brains: "Drive out the Europeans! Deliver yourselves from foreign capital! Become masters of your own home!"

Russia is no longer the avant-garde of Europe in Asia; she is the avant-garde of Asia in Europe.

In the boundless Russian expanses, a difficult, ensanguined, critical experiment is taking place. All peoples—enemies and friends alike, whether in hatred or in love—have their gazes riveted on Russia. Nowadays, whether we like it or not, she is the center of the earth.

This postwar psychological anguish; this extremely acute awareness of the need of finding a deliverance from the present-day economic, social and political misery; and the organization of the two camps crystal-clearly delineated—these three factors constitute the contemporary great international reality.

II

Vis-à-vis this great international reality, we find the small local reality of Greece. What is the relationship of this small reality to the great?

Many people say: "In Greece, the class struggle is not yet clearly outlined in such sharp relief as in other more advanced, industrial nations. We have just emerged out of the feudal rule of the Turks and the village elders. The bourgeois class has still not had time to develop its full potentialities. Our proletarian workers and farmers are few and, for the most part, unenlightened and unorganized. Class struggle cannot exist among us. We are by nature conservative. We will not let the storm infiltrate past our own frontiers." So they say.

I am convinced that overthrow of the regime in Greece—if it were possible for Greece to be absolutely isolated from the rest of the world— would occur only after centuries. Nevertheless, we must not forget these three incontrovertible facts:

1. Nowadays, it is impossible for any country to be isolated. No power can localize the Idea within geographical limits.

2. Day by day, the advanced capitalistic countries are misleading us, in their own economic interests. And the virtually colonial exploitation they are imposing on us is becoming increasingly burdensome. Whether we like it or not, we are harnessed to the capitalistic chariot of Europe and America, and all their economic problems have immediate, heavy repercussions upon us.

3. We must also not forget the following: Things that before the World War required whole generations to be formulated and mature nowadays become perceptible in a very brief period of time and strive to be transformed into action extremely rapidly. This is why the class struggle has already begun in Greece and every day (we can all see it) is growing increasingly acute.

I am aware that in absolute and certain terms we in Greece should also have gone through all the forms of the evolution in a natural way. Patiently, by virtue of our own struggle, we too should have brought each stage to its normal conclusion.

But in this world, not everything can take place so consistently and logically. Many species of plants and animals have disappeared. Many histories of peoples have been left in midstream, because the peoples have not been able to adapt themselves and follow the rhythm of oncoming life, implacable for anyone who is backward. Of course, it would be reasonable and charitable for them to be given a deadline. But in physics and in history deadlines are never given. Let him who is able be saved!

Throughout the whole earth, the moment is a critical one. In Greece, it is even more critical, because for historical and racial reasons we have remained extraordinarily backward. There is probably very little time left us to adapt ourselves to an international rhythm quicker than the rhythm of Greek necessity.

The storm will come, whether we like it or not, whether we are ready for it or not. It will not do us the favor of waiting for us to mature first. The small Greek reality will be swept away by the great reality.

What is our duty? To prepare ourselves. How? By articulating a clear idea of the historical moment we are passing through, by enlightening the people and giving a new loftier content to the conceptions of work, justice, virtue.

Only in this way can the masses be prepared to make the transition from being aware of their rights to realizing their obligations. Only in this way, when the fateful moment does come, will they be able to assume responsibility.

The struggle, as I conceive it, is not merely an economic one. Economic emancipation is but a means for the psychological and spiritual emancipation of man. We must aim at achieving the material happiness of as many people as possible, so that by the time we have achieved this aim the contents of this happiness can then be shifted to a higher level.

Needless to say, the bourgeois regime is striving to stifle this endeavor. New ideas have always been characterized as immoral and criminal by the defenders of the established authority. Very naturally so, because the new idea is nothing but the seed of a new reality, longing to seize the earth and uproot all the old ideas cherished by many persons—ideas that have now become fruitless and are an impediment to life. Recall what happened in the earliest Christian era—how the chauvinistic defenders of the old regime abused, slandered, persecuted, attempted to stifle the new idea.

Viewing the international circle in this way, I have pinpointed the small arc of the circle—Greece—and, within this arc, the minimal point of individual action.

III

I have felt strongly obligated to formulate a clear, impartial idea about the greatest contemporary problem regulating our whole era—the Russian problem.

Everything I had read was contradictory, full of superficial, biased views. Russia was depicted by some as paradise, by others as hell. I had to see for myself and crystallize my own opinion. At this critical moment we are experiencing, I knew that man is duty bound to take a definite position—consciously and decisively—to the right or the left, in the international struggle. During other calm and balanced eras, the individual is entitled to withdraw into solitude or attend only to his own comfortable communication with other human beings. But in our own present-day era, any such egotistical isolation or convenient compromise would be abominable cowardice.

These are the pyschological and spiritual necessities that impelled me to go to Russia. I went there and stayed there for months. Then I went back again. I studied it with careful attention and agony, finding myself in the presence of an amazing experiment that filled me with agitation, feeling, hope. In Russia, I found neither paradise—as the simple-minded Communists proclaimed—nor hell—as the malicious, frightened bourgeoisie asserted. But I found this earth, where man is striving, seeking, testing, experimenting to find a way out—to open a path between an old world his soul can no longer tolerate and the new ideal that is struggling in vain to arrive.

This awesome endeavor, which is still not over, filled me with respect and anguish. The main thing I carried away with me from Russia is this: confidence in humanity—a confidence I had lost in the course of living with the bourgeoisie.

I came back to Greece to find the two camps confronting the great Russian problem with gross ignorance. I wanted, as was my duty, to enlighten as many people as possible—Communists and bourgeoisie alike. I wrote a series of articles, published books and spoke, always with vigilant and often cruel impartiality. For this reason, I did not please either the Communists or the bourgeois. That does not matter. My aim was not to please anyone, but to tell the truth.

I am neither a narrow-minded disavower nor a superficial eulogizer. And that is because I am not a person of practical action but a person whose aim in life is the endeavor to think and formulate his thought. And that is why I have the power and, at the same time, the right to see an idea as a whole, with all its brilliance and all its shadows. If I were a "man of action," I would overnourish whatever benefited my action and undernourish (consciously or unconsciously) whatever impeded my action. And then I would proclaim roughhewn dogmas that would be easy to comprehend.

I am not so naïve as to believe that once an idea has been formulated, it can be transformed immediately into reality. My aim has been to make as many people as possible contemplate more profoundly the historical moment we are experiencing and prepare themselves for a rebirth of their individual and social life: a psychological rebirth first of all, of course; and then a spiritual and social one; and finally (in time) an economic and political one.

In this way, with my own minimal forces as an individual, I too have helped to pave the only way for Greece as well, the most logical and the shortest path to salvation: the gradual adaptation of the small Greek reality to the great reality.

This I believe and have proclaimed. To be sure, you have the right and the duty to strike the idea as hard as you can. Nevertheless, the dilemma facing you is a terrifying one, I think: If you do strike, you easily create heroes and martyrs. And thereby, as has always been the case, you help the new faith to triumph. If you do not strike, you leave the idea unhindered to undermine the old foundations and overturn them.

Whatever you do and however much time passes, Your Honors, I am convinced that the few will always multiply; the victims of injustice will always come out stronger; and the class perpetrating the injustice will always fall.

This is what I believe. I considered it my duty to state it with absolute sincerity—and your duty, if you find my thought worthy of punishment, to punish me.

570

INDEX

310, 312, 327; war on Soviets (1919), 72fn.; repatriation of Greeks from Caucasus and Asia Minor, 72–75, 89

NK's frequent tours of, 57, 122, 125; NK's dissatisfaction with, 131, 151, 163, 166, 214, 264, 498; NK's fear of government reprisals, 171, 174–75; government prosecution of NK and Glynos, 177, 179, 180, 240; lack of recognition for NK in, 273, 390, 458–60, 464, 507; NK's hope for renaissance in, 335; NK's proposal of union with England, 393; NK wins recognition in, 532–33, 538; NK's analysis of in his "Apology," 565–70

reactionary government of, 327, 337–38, 392, 425, 426, 464, 466, 467, 470, 471, 474–75, 486, 496, 500–1, 523; Italian attack on (1940), 391–92; German invasion and occupation of, 395–99, 402, 406, 408, 409, 414–15, 420–26; liberation from Germans, 425, 426; English intervention, 426, 437, 448, 452–54; postliberation civil war, 434, 480, 484–86; plebiscite and elections in, 452–54, 485, 486; American intervention in, 469

Greece: The Whole Story (Noel-Baker), 408fn.
Greek army, 89, 338, 391, 392, 437
Greek language, modern, 18, 390, 405, 418, 435, 457, 463, 485, 504–5, 514, 521, 524, 536, 541
Greek literature, 41, 357, 438, 446, 463, 465, 468, 473, 475, 493, 500–1, 533, 544
Greek Orthodox Church, 76, 412, 423, 519, 523, 524, 533
Greek Passion, The (Kazantzakis), novel, 24, 76, 417, 486, 493, 502, 503, 507, 509, 515, 522, 526, 527
Greek Resistance, The (Kedros), 415
Greek Society of Men of Letters, 438
Gregorios, Bishop of Chalcidice, 423
Grehtlein publishing house, 224
Grigorios, Abbot, 388
Grindelwald, 65
Gritsi, Tatiana, 395
Guehenno, author, 209
Guernica (Picasso painting), 76, 351–52
Guingaud, Sir Francis de, 408fn.
Gunalakis, Edvige, 127, 128, 148, 149, 225, 257
Gunalakis, Mihalis, 68, 69, 128
Gunsbach Forest, Alsace, 537

Hadjikyriakos-Ghika, Nikos, 360, 463
Hadzidákis, centenarian, 448
Hagios Evstrátios island, 398
Hailie Selassie, Emperor of Ethiopia, 338
Halifax, Lord, 381
Hall's Croft, Stratford, England, 378, 380, 382
Hals, Frans, 512, 516
Hamlet (Shakespeare), 326
Hamson, Denis, 408
Hankow, China, 555
Hapsburgs, 358
Harassova, Lilian Georgievna, 170, 171
Haris, Petros, 458
Haritákis, D., 283
Hasidim and Hasidism, 91, 97, 333
Hatzopoulos, Konstantinos, 336
Haumont, publisher, 246
Hauptmann, Gerhart, 457
Hawaii, 288
Hearn, Lafcadio, 356
Heilmeyer, Dr., 513, 530, 531, 550, 556, 560
Hejaz, 137
Hellespont, the, 167
Herakles, 53, 60, 260
Herakles (Kazantzakis), verse tragedy, 60fn., 76, 77
Heraklion, Crete, 36, 43fn., 78, 218fn., 271, 428, 554; NK's letters from (1924–25), 24–33, 114–21; NK and Galatea married in, 50; NK arrested in (1924), 565
Herbert, Jean, 289, 302, 320, 321, 334, 352, 353, 454, 464, 469
Hermitage, the, Leningrad, 192
Herriot, Édouard, 255, 543
Hide and Seek: The Story of a Wartime Agent (Fielding), 429fn.
Hideyoshi, Toyotomi, 333, 334
Hilker, educational reformer, 90
Hill, George, 517
Himera, Albania, 392
History of Russian Literature (Kazantzakis), 229
Hitchingbrooke, Huntingdon, England, 368
Hitler, Adolf, 225, 287, 368, 381, 399, 410, 422, 503, 510, 528
Hlemoutsi Castle, Kyllene, 348, 349
Holitscher, Arthur, 171, 215, 286
Holland, see Netherlands; Utrecht
Homer, 88, 97, 405, 442, 457, 468, 537, 542, 550, 551; NK likened to, 76, 386
Homo Bolshevicus (projected work by NK), 203, 217

Aegina, 163–66, 181, 239–40, 278–302, 323–39, 344–48, 350–61, 365–66, 389–426; his prescience about Africa, Egypt and British Empire, 217; and post of library director, 284, 289; and proposed directorship of National Theater, 350–51, 365; his literary appraisals, 209, 223, 225, 296, 495; and the Partisans, 402, 403; and Nobel Prize, 438, 465, 470, 508, 522, 559; his UNESCO post, 464–65: 467, 469, 473, 475; International Peace Committee prize, 542–45; illnesses, 81–83, 354, 399, 436, 475, 478–83, 487–91, 508–21 passim, 530–31, 540, 556–62; death, 562

His Travels:
postgraduate days in Paris (1907–9), 41–47; tours of Italy (1909–26), 45, 47–48, 106, 109–13, 146–51; tours of Greece (1914–37), 53–59, 122–28, 345, 347–51; to Switzerland (1917–18), 65–70; in Austria and Germany (1922–29), 79–91, 96–99, 103–6, 215; sojourns in Crete (1924, 1930, 1940), 24–33, 113–21, 239, 387–89; tours of Russia (1925–28), 128–34, 165–77, 182–215, 218–21; to Palestine and Cyprus (1926), 135–37, 139; in Spain (1926–36), 137–39, 143–47, 251–77, 340–43, 379–80; tour of Egypt, Sudan and Arabia (1927), 156–63; sojourns at Gottesgab (1929–32), 216–17, 222–30, 241–49; sojourns in Paris (1930–39), 230–32, 249–51, 277–79, 283, 367; at Periwinkle Villa, Nice (1930), 232–38; to Japan and China (1935), 303–21; to England (1939, 1946), 366–82, 438–55; sojourn in France (1946–47), 454–60, 463ff.; at Villa Rose, Antibes (1948), 475–79; at Villa Manolita, Antibes (1949–54), 479, 483, 493, 502–10 passim, 515, 516, 522, 524, 540, 549; at Koukouli, Antibes (1954–57), 521–22, 525–27, 531; to Spain (1951), 492; to Italy (1951–52), 499, 501–3, 511, 513; to Vichy (1949), 481–83; to the Tirol (1952), 509–10; to the Netherlands (1952), 511–12, 515–16; to Freiburg (1954–57), 513, 530–31; to Switzerland (1955), 534–35; to Vienna (1956), 542–45; to Yugoslavia (1956), 545–47; to China and Japan (1957), 553–56

His Works:
earliest literary work, 36–37, 40–41; contracts for school textbooks, 51, 52, 79; his newspaper assignments, 135, 137, 138, 157, 167, 192, 340–43, 345; prosecuted for lecture and book, 177, 179, 180, 240; his scenario writing, 179, 182, 184, 185, 189–90, 191, 247, 249, 259; translation and adaptation of children's books, 235; his suit over broken contract for dictionary, 255–56, 259, 264, 296; doubts his skill as novelist, 395; recognition slow to be granted, 390, 458, 507, 532–33; his life work reviewed, 456–57; his Complete Works published, 521, 531, 538

Keats, John, 284, 356
Kedros, Andreas, 415
Kemal Ataturk, 89
Kephalinos, Iannis, 507
Keyserling, Count Hermann Alexander, 299
Khabarovsk, 202, 203, 205
Kharkov, 173
Khartoum, Sudan, 157
Kiev, 168, 174, 175, 182–89
Kifisia, 77, 156, 312, 394, 500
Kijno, Ladislas, 526, 557
Kindzios, Justice of the Peace, 335
King Lear (Shakespeare—translated by Rotas), 385
King's College, Cambridge, 446–47
Kisch, Egon, 215, 286
Kitzbühel, Austria, 509, 510, 513
Klabund (Alfred Henschke), 91
Klio, niece of NK, 262
Kliouev, Nikolai, 192fn., 222, 246
Knös, Börje, 464, 486, 548; NK's letters to (1946–49), 455, 459–60, 463, 468–69, 471–75, 478–85; —(1950–52), 485–87, 489, 491–93, 495, 496, 500–3, 505–7, 509, 514–16; —(1953–57), 518–19, 521–23, 526, 531–34, 551–53
Knossos, Crete, 43, 45, 79, 121, 146
Kobe, Japan, 313, 314
Koenig, German soldier on Aegina, 398
Kondoglou, Fotis, 385, 416
Kondylis, Giorghos, 140, 327
Konstantarakis, Iannis, 75
Koran, the, 160
Koritsa, Albania, 392
Kösen, Germany, 97
Koshima Maru, S.S., 305
Kosmas, 429–32
Kostantinidis, Mitsos, 408
Kotopouli, 346fn.

580

584

Prastova, 65, 67
Pravda, 191
Prayer to Russia (Benavente), 252, 254
Prevelakis, Pandelis, 38fn., 55fn., 165fn., 258, 260, 269, 270, 273, 322, 326, 403, 458, 464, 485; start of friendship with NK (1927), 162; with NK on Aegina, 181, 278–79, 286; NK's letters to, 190–91, 242–43, 248, 255–56, 268, 276, 368, 404, 415, 416, 470–71, 494, 548–50; collaboration with NK on dictionary, 231, 235, 239, 504; in Paris to complete studies, 235, 239, 240, 249, 259; visits NK at Gottesgab and Antibes, 245–46, 478, 521; his literary work, 271, 275, 289, 404, 471, 479, 493–94; his efforts in NK's behalf in theater, 351, 401; supervises publication of NK's Complete Works, 507, 531
Primo de Rivera, Miguel, 144
Prince, The (Machiavelli—translated by NK), 426
Proïa, 167
Prokopi, Aegina, 326
Prometheus (Kazantzakis), trilogy, 415, 416
Prometheus Bound (Kazantzakis), verse tragedy, 23, 406, 407
Protomástoras, see Overseer, The
Provence, 232
Puaux, René, 458, 517, 532
Puaux, Suzanne, 436, 458, 463fn., 476, 517, 532
Pucci, Countess Erichetta, 112fn., 262, 513
Putschow, village on Black Sea, 98
Pyrenees, 143, 344, 467
Pyrsos publishing house, 365, 390,392

Quatre Dauphins, Les, 526

Racine, Jean Baptiste, 557
Radiodiffusion Française, 225
Rafina, beach at, 20
Rahel, 83, 84–89, 91, 96, 110, 111, 120fn., 132, 134, 146, 164, 258, 463, 477; stormy scene with NK, 97; survivor of the holocaust in Paris, 434–36; her dream about ESK, 557
Ralli, Maritsa, 299, 322
Ravenna, Italy, 96, 113, 513
Red Sea, 161, 306
Reed, John, 279fn.
Reger, Max, 65
Reinhardt, Max, 243
Rembrandt, 192, 202, 512, 516
Renaissance, 167, 177

Renaud, see Jouvenel, Renaud de
Renoux, Yvette, 464
Renovators, 418
Report to Greco (Kazantzakis), 24, 33fn., 38, 39, 40fn., 112fn., 267fn., 268, 295–96, 350fn., 351fn., 418fn., 517fn., 535, 538fn., 547, 550
Resistance, the, see Partisans
Rethymnon, Crete, 428
Rieder, publisher, 222, 225, 246, 255, 258, 261
Rilke, Rainer Maria, 96, 203 250, 334
Rimbaud, Arthur, 225
Rimini, Italy, 513
Rivals, Madame de, 464
Rivera, Miguel Primo de, 144
Robertfrance, M., 224, 227, 246, 254, 258
Robin Hood, 376
Rock Cloister, The [Felsenkloster] (Kazantzakis), 332
Rock Garden, The [Felsengarten] (Kazantzakis), 330–34, 345, 409
Rodin, François Auguste René, 56, 58
Rogaska Slatina, Yugoslavia, 545
Rolland, Romain, 120, 249
Roman Catholic Church, 76, 274, 343, 519, 523
Rome, 45, 47, 140, 148–51, 251, 383
Romeo and Juliet (Shakespeare—translated by Karthaios), 385
Rosa, 91, 111, 134, 441
Rossignol, Madame, 231–32
Rostov, U.S.S.R., 206, 208
Rotas, author, 385
Roth, J., 209
Rousseau, Jean-Jacques, 129–30
Rousseau the Douanier, Henri, 29
Royalists, 95, 279, 280, 283
Rubio, Rosa Chacel, 252fn., 357
Rubio, Timoteo Perez, 252, 255, 259, 266, 270, 357
Rumania, 137, 138, 272
Russell, Bertrand, 451, 453
Russell Square, London, 368, 379, 382
Russia, see U.S.S.R.
Russia (Kazantzakis), 207, 216
Russia, Holy Russia (Benavente), 252, 254
Russian Revolution, 74, 165, 171, 221
Russland, 286
Russo-German Pact (1939), 371

Sacher, Paul, 527
Sadoul, writer, 172
St. Catherine, Monastery of, 496
Saint Francis (Kazantzakis), see Pax et Bonum

Society of Social and Political Sciences, 64

Sodom and Gomorrah (Kazantzakis), tragedy, 458, 476, 477, 487, 530, 531–32

Sohum, 74

Solomon, King, 71

Solon, 406

Sophia, servant on Aegina, 344, 412, 421

Sophianopoulos, Iannis, 490, 498, 501, 502

Sophoulis, Prime Minister, 432, 437

Sorbonne, the, 42fn., 504

Souchère, Dor de la, 526

Soula, servant girl, 427, 433

Sounion, Cape, 182, 291

Sourmelina, old woman of Crete, 432

Spain, 192, 367; NK's 1926 tour of, 137–39, 143–47; NK's articles on, 153, 278; NK's 1932–33 sojourn in, 251–61, 263–71, 273–77; civil war in, 338–43, 366; NK's 1936 tour of, 340–343; NK, ESK and Métrals visit (1950), 492

Spain (Kazantzakis), 343fn.

Sparta, 57

Spender, Stephen, 448

Spengler, Oswald, 155

Spetsai, 141

Sphakia, Greece, 388

Sphakianakis, Kosta, 66, 77, 116, 157

Sphinx, the, 158, 159

Spinoza, Baruch, 87

Spiritual Exercises (Kazantzakis), 90, 99, 125, 165, 166, 167, 171, 177, 179, 240, 261, 330, 365, 450, 453, 457, 507, 526

SS (Schutzstaffel), 399, 421, 422

Stalin, Joseph, 170, 221, 381

Stalingrad, 383

Stamatis, Kapetan, 335

Stanford, Professor W. B., 531

Stanislavsky, Konstantin, 173

Stavridakis, Iannis, 40fn., 66fn., 68, 75, 173fn.

Stavronikita Monastery, 55

Steinen, Helmut von den, 334, 336, 534

Stekel, Dr. Wilhelm, 81, 83

Stephanidis, Harilaos, 35fn., 51, 52, 53, 273, 282

Sterianos, Dr., 487, 490, 512

Stevenson, Robert Louis, 225

Stockholm, 486, 492, 500fn., 502, 542, 558

Stoeker, Helene, 215, 224

Stoupa, 65

Stowe, Harriet Beecher, 235

Stratford, England, 378, 380–81, 385, 440, 446, 450

Strauss, Richard, 65

Strength to Dream, The (Wilson), 465

Sudan, the, 156–58 passim

Suez Canal, 305, 306

Sumatra, 310

Sunion, see Sounion

Sur, 441fn.

Sverdlovsk, U.S.S.R., 206

Sweden, 464, 466, 486, 493

Swedenborg, Emanuel, 542

Swedish Academy, 438, 472

Swift, Jonathan, 235

Swinburne, Algernon Charles, 448

Switzerland, 65–71 passim, 121

Sykia, suburb of Athens, 59, 60, 79, 108

Symposium (Plato), 70, 86

Symposium (Kazantzakis), 61, 62, 70, 86

Synaxary of Zorba (Kazantzakis), 401

Syra, island of, 122

Syria, 134

Tagore, Rabindranath, 125, 297

Tagus River, 146

Tahiti, 230, 288

Tamerlane, 210, 211

Tanagra, 395

Tantine, see MacLeod, Josephine

Tarragona, Spain, 492

Tashkent, U.S.S.R., 210, 213

Tatoi, 156

Tau, Max, 502, 503, 504, 506, 508, 509fn., 517, 522, 557, 558

Taygetus, 57, 226

Tchaikovsky, Pyotr Ilich, 134

Tchou Kiang-kouo, 556

Tel Aviv, 136, 495

Temps, Le, 237

Tennyson, Alfred Lord, 284

Teresa of Avila, Saint, 138, 152, 294fn., 449

Tertullian, 524

Theanthropists, The (projected novel by NK), 45

Thebes, 57

Theodoropoulo, Spyro, 541–42, 545

Theodoros, laborer on Aegina, 329, 330, 355

Theodossiadis, Eleni, sister of NK, 35, 42–47 passim, 134, 183, 236, 290, 299, 326, 433

Theory of Emotion, The (James—translated by NK), 50

Theotokas, Giorghos, 206fn., 437

Therisso, Greece, 41